# ECHOES FROM OLD CALCUTTA

Conjectural View of the Black Hole, with Part of Barracks, as seen from interior of Verandah.

*Frontispiece.*

# ECHOES FROM OLD CALCUTTA

BEING CHIEFLY

## REMINISCENCES OF THE DAYS OF WARREN HASTINGS, FRANCIS, AND IMPEY

*By*

**H. E. BUSTEED, C.I.E.**

FOURTH EDITION

MUCH ENLARGED AND WITH ADDITIONAL ILLUSTRATIONS

GYAN

*Published by*

Gyan Publishing House
5, Ansari Road
Daryaganj, New Delhi-110002
Phone: 011-47034999, 9811692060
E-mail: books@gyanbooks.com

*Distribution Network*
gyanbooks.com
India, USA, Canada, UK, Australia, France



ISBN: 978-81-212-3343-9 (PB)
First Published, 1908

2nd Impression 2020

*Printed at:* Gyan Press, Delhi.



**Echoes from Old Calcutta**
Author: H. E. Busteed

# INTRODUCTORY LETTER

Hackwood, Basingstoke.
April 16, 1908.

DEAR DR. BUSTEED,

It is with very sincere pleasure that I learn that yet another and a greatly enlarged edition of your fascinating "Echoes from Old Calcutta" is about to see the light; and, as the advanced copy which I have been privileged to see assures me, that it bears, in so striking a manner, the evidence of your inexhaustible knowledge and untiring erudition. Since first I read this book on my way out to India, I have never failed to find in its pages both a romance and an inspiration: a romance, because with the early days of British dominion in Bengal were interwoven the fortunes of famous men and women as remarkable for the vicissitudes of their lives as for their talents—an inspiration, because your stimulating narrative must have tempted scores of others, as it tempted me, to explore those obscure but prolific strata of the past from which you have extracted so rich a spoil.

Calcutta, frequently designated one of the most commonplace, is, in reality, one of the most interesting cities in the world; and it is not the less interesting because so many of those Europeans who have sojourned there have been only temporary residents whose local footprints have soon been covered up, but who trod the Asiatic stage in the heyday of their youth or ambitions, and then retired, perhaps to make greater reputation or to figure on a wider stage elsewhere. When we recall that, at the period which you have specially illumined, there were living in Calcutta within a space of twenty years characters so diverse or so conspicuous in different ways as Warren Hastings, Sir Philip Francis, Sir Elijah Impey, Rose Aylmer, the painter Zoffany, and the future Princess Talleyrand, one cannot but admit that the period and the place were equally worthy of commemoration.

As we draw further away from the past and manners and customs change, until an almost impassable chasm appears to separate us from an age which our great-grandfathers might have seen, as great (if not a greater) interest attaches to the personal incidents and characters of those days as to their more familiar historical landmarks; and it is not the least attraction of your delightful book that it recovers from oblivion and breathes new life into a crowd of images that seem almost to belong to another world. In your company we picture again the mortal agony of the Black Hole; we trace the tender passion of Warren Hastings, the intrigues and jealousies of Junius, the career of the beautiful adventuress who, born on the Coromandel coast, became the mistress and the wife of the most consummate diplomatist in Europe.

But perhaps your greatest service is to have taught the modern generation in India that business or administration, however absorbing, may yet leave leisure for scholarly research, and that they owe a duty of reverence to a past which was the unconscious seed-time of our present Imperial harvest.

In the hope that your new edition may rival, and even excel, its predecessors in spreading this valuable lesson, I subscribe myself, dear Dr. Busteed,

Yours very faithfully,

CURZON OF KEDLESTON.

# PREFACE

THE fact of a fourth edition of this book being called for suggests that it retains the gratifying opinion formed of it, mainly by readers in India.

To make it more deserving of the favour continued to it, matter has been added to this Edition not appearing in its predecessor, and the book has been generally amplified during revision by new material collected from time to time. It has also been more liberally illustrated, and furnished with an index and chronology. It may be explained, perhaps, though scarcely necessary even for readers out of India, that the first article deals with an historical event long anterior in point of time to the period mainly contemplated in the title page. Still the subject is one which of necessity finds a place in a volume, such as this, purporting to look back on Old Calcutta.

Mr. S. C. Hill's valuable work has of course been referred to by me when revising this article.

His exhaustive labours facilitate the work of chroniclers who may now or henceforth have occasion to treat of Bengal or Calcutta in 1756–7.

It is satisfactory to recognise that much more interest is now shown in the events and historical characters of the period first named, and of that which followed it, than was the case not many years back.

The recent starting of the much-needed Calcutta Historical Society, and its establishment under very favourable auspices, are promising signs that the growing interest in old times is not to be ephemeral, but is to be fostered into sturdy growth. All well-wishers to Calcutta (indeed to India) must hope for the successful progress of a society which will find much useful work for its kindly hand.

It remains but to express my acknowledgments and thanks to those who have generously enabled me to add some portraits of Anglo-Indian and other celebrities to the illustrations in this edition. I gratefully thank first Dowager The Lady Napier and Ettrick, who not only permitted me to have photographed the portrait of Sir John Clavering in her possession, but graciously gave me from herself a photograph of a miniature of his eldest daughter (afterwards Lady Napier) which she sets much store by.

Lord Monson, to my regret, does not possess a portrait of Colonel the Hon. George Monson, the very distinguished colleague of General Clavering in Old Calcutta, but he very kindly sent me a photograph of the nearest approach to it that he has—namely a silhouette, which I have had reproduced. To the authorities of University College, Oxford, I am indebted for leave to have photographed the portrait of Sir Robert Chambers which they possess; and very specially so to the master, Dr. Macan, for his courtesy in furthering my request, and for letting me also have a photograph of an excellent mezzotint engraving of the same portrait in his private collection.

My friend Colonel Lewin, of Parkhurst, Surrey, added to my obligation to him by furnishing me with the best photographs that he had of family portraits of his grandfather.

In conclusion, it is but fair to express my appreciation of the pains taken by Messrs. W. Thacker & Co., to make the most of the illustrative material supplied to them; and of their efforts to insure that this issue of a book long associated with their firm's name, should be worthy in its general out-turn of their established reputation as Publishers.

H. E. B.

1908.

# TABLE OF CONTENTS

## THE BLACK HOLE, 1756.



## PHILIP FRANCIS AND HIS TIMES.



## APPENDICES

# LIST OF ILLUSTRATIONS

* There appeared, about eighteen years ago, in a London magazine entitled *The Woman's World*, under the actual editorship of Oscar Wilde, an article on "The Princesse De Talleyrand (Madame Grand)." It was more or less accurate as to her Indian and subsequent career, and the writer had apparently read "Echoes from old Calcutta." The article was embellished by a wood-cut under which was printed, "Madame Grand—Princess De Talleyrand (from a portrait by Gérard at Versailles)." The portrait—a half-length—represented a beautiful woman, apparently a brunette, in Oriental costume, but was so unlike presentments hitherto associated with the exquisite blonde of old Calcutta, that I could not believe in its being a portrait of her. To solve my doubts, I took the wood-cut over to Versailles, but I searched in vain for the original. I showed the magazine-portrait to several of the experienced attendants

in the galleries of the Musée, but all assured me that no such portrait by Gérard was there. I came away concluding that some strange mistake had been made by the writer of the interesting article in *The Woman's World*. So matters remained until two or three years ago, when my friend Mr. Julian Cotton, of the Madras Civil Service, a very enthusiastic and enterprising antiquarian, in discussing with me portraits (veritable and alleged) of Madame Grand, brought to my notice a correspondence that he had had regarding them with a courteous and well-informed French gentleman, M. André Hallaye, who had written on the subject in the *Journal des Debats*, a notice of which had appeared in the well-known Bombay paper, *The Times of India*. From M. Hallaye's letter to Mr. Cotton, an extract from which I here give, it would appear that the writer in *The Woman's World* was wrong only as to the ownership of the painting by Gérard; it is (or was) in a private, not in a public collection: viz. "Le portrait de Gérard qui appartient à Madame la Comtesse de Castellane represent Madame De Talleyrand vetue à l'antique et coiffée d'un turban d'ou s'echappent les lourdes boucles d'un admirable chevelure, c'est un portrait d'apparat qui m'a semblé assez inexpressif: mais je n'ai jamais eu sous les yeux qu'une reproduction photigraphique." M. Hallaye is more captivated by the portrait by Vigée Le Brun, which he thinks amply explains the seductive allurements of the original. The wood-cut of Gérard's portrait is now before me. The head is surmounted by a neatly folded turban, embroidered. Thick clusters of curls appear beneath it, covering each temple—they seem to be dark; the centre of the forehead only is bare; the eyes, glad and well open under delicately pencilled brows, look to the right; the mouth and rich lips show the Cupid's bow; the nose is straight and shapely, very unlike the *nez retroussé* which suggested the curious likeness between Talleyrand and his wife; the bust and shoulders are draped with a fringed shawl which covers the left shoulder fully, leaving the finely curved neck and the upper part of the chest to be seen; the shawl is fastened at the point of the comely right shoulder with a brooch having an ornamental rim and showing the head and bust of a female painted on it; the left hand holds between two of its well-shaped fingers what seem to be a link or two of the metal cincture which adorns the waist. The original must be a most beautiful picture, but, as I have already said, as unlike as it possibly could be of any conception formed of the type of beauty of Madame Grand.

# CHRONOLOGY

1655. Job Charnock goes to India.
1688. Job Charnock withdraws to Madras.
1690. Charnock returns to Bengal.
1693. Charnock died.
1696. Fort at Calcutta Factory commenced.
1711. J. Z. Holwell born.
1717. Trading privileges obtained by East India Company from the Mogul.
1725. Lord Clive born.
1732. Elijah Impey born.
1732. Warren Hastings born.
1737. Robert Chambers born.
1740. Ali Verdi Khan viceroy of Bengal.
1740. Philip Francis born.
1741. Mrs. Carey (survivor of the Black Hole) born.
1742. Maharrata ditch constructed.
1750. Warren Hastings goes to India.
1754. Talleyrand born.
1756. Death of Ali Verdi Khan; succeeded by Murza Muhammed (Siraj úd Dawla).
,, Capture of Calcutta by Murza Muhammed.
,, (June 20). Prisoners done to death in the Black Hole.
,, Warren Hastings temporarily imprisoned by Nawab of Bengal.
1757. January 2. Calcutta retaken by Clive; he defeats the Soubadar at Plassey, 23rd June.
,, Present Fort William commenced.
1761. Warren Hastings member of Calcutta Council.
,, November 21. Madame Grand born.
1764. Warren Hastings returns to England.
1768. Publication of letters of Junius begun; ends in 1772.
1769. Warren Hastings returns to India.
1772. Elijah Impey counsel for East India Company.
,, Hastings governor of Bengal.
1772-3. Parliamentary inquiry on Clive.
1773. India Bill; (Regulating Act) Supreme Court established.
1774. Lord Clive's death.
1774. Sir Elijah Impey goes to India; knighted; Chief Justice of Bengal till 1787.

1774. Robert Chambers, Judge of Supreme Court, Bengal.
,, October 19. Philip Francis arrives in India.
,, Philip Francis, Indian Councillor.
1775. Warren Hastings accused by Nuncomar of corruption, &c.
,, Nuncomar tried, sentenced to death by Impey, and hanged for forgery (August 5).
1777. August 8. Warren Hastings marries Mrs. Imhoff (*née* Chapusettin) at Calcutta.
1778. Sir Robert Chambers knighted.
1779. February 8. Madame Grand suit begun; damages against Philip Francis 50,000 sicca rupees.
,, December 3. Hon. Rose Whitworth Aylmer born.
1780. December 29. *Bengal Gazette* started; ends 1782.
,, August 17. Duel between Warren Hastings and Philip Francis.
,, Philip Francis leaves India.
,, November. *India Gazette* started.
,, December. Madame Grand leaves India.
1784. February. *Calcutta Gazette* started.
1785. Warren Hastings leaves India.
,, February. *Bengal Journal* started.
,, April 6. *Oriental Magazine or Calcutta Amusement* started.
1786. January. *Calcutta Chronicle* started.
,, September. Lord Cornwallis arrives in India.
1788. Motion in the House of Commons for impeachment of Sir Elijah Impey, who had been recalled to answer for his conduct as Chief Justice, Bengal. The motion was lost by a narrow majority of 18 in a house of 128 members.
,, Warren Hastings impeached for High Crimes and misdemeanours while Governor-General of Bengal; concluded 1795.
1791. Sir Robert Chambers, Chief Justice, Bengal.
1798. J. Z. Holwell died.
1799. Sir Robert Chambers leaves India.
1800. Hon. Rose Whitworth Aylmer died.
1801. Mrs. Carey (survivor of the Black Hole) died.
1802. September 10. Madame Grand married to Talleyrand at Paris.
1803. Sir Robert Chambers died.
1808. Sir John Day died.
1809. Sir Elijah Impey died.
1811. May. Lady Day died.
1818. Warren Hastings died.
,, Sir Philip Francis died.
1835. Princess Talleyrand died.
1838. Talleyrand died.

# ECHOES FROM OLD CALCUTTA

## CHAPTER I

### THE BLACK HOLE, 1756

#### 1.—The Capture of Calcutta

THERE has been a marked impetus given within recent years to the issue of literature about India. It is still going on. We have the inevitable tourist's India—the real India, a vision of India, etc., etc.

Of guide-books and handbooks, memoirs and letters, there is no stint. And last, not least, the solid material brought to the surface by capable and laborious burrowers in the official records of the past. All these books, light or heavy, provide information, for those who would seek and appreciate it, of a very useful and very attractive kind, and must have cost their writers much care and thought. And the upshot of it all? Has it brought India and its lovable people, and the exotics zealously toiling there for their welfare, any nearer to the knowledge and to the interest of the stay-at-home English man or woman? Candidly, I do not think so. The home press, no doubt, when it has to tell of some grand pageant in India, destined to be historic, attended by many gorgeous Princes and Rajahs and by some members, perhaps, of our Royal Family, and illuminated by splendid military display, evokes from time to time some temporary enthusiasm. Much complacent gratification is felt when the public reads its newspaper and becomes expansive about "our great dependency," or "the brightest jewel in the crown." But there the matter ends, so far as the so-called man in the street is concerned. Not that this want of more lasting interest is confined to him. It pervades every stratum of society, and all ranks—low, high, middle. Ask almost any member of what are recognised as the learned professions about the great Eastern trust confided to Great Britain, and, unless he be either officially or domestically, directly or indirectly connected therewith, it will soon be apparent that he feels little or no interest in what he practically knows nothing about.

In the present writer's experience it is nearly as true to-day as when Macaulay wrote his essay on Clive, that to most English readers in this fast-living age it would be uninteresting, even distasteful, to learn the "insipid" story, how "a handful of our countrymen, separated from their home by an immense ocean, subjugated in a few years one of the greatest empires in the world."

Macaulay seems inclined to attribute much of this ignorance (source of the strange indifference) to most histories on Indian subjects, though admirable in many ways, being in his opinion deterrent, owing to what Johnson long ago deprecated, as the most fatal of faults—tediousness. He exemplifies Orme. How is it he asks (as Mr. Morrison recalls in his biography) that art, eloquence, and diligence, may all be employed—in making a book dull? It is obvious that to write what people like to read, as he said of Walpole; to engage attention, to allure curiosity, are gifts as desirable in the historian, or the essayist, as in the writer of fiction. Giving due weight to all this, there remains the paradox that India, apart from special reasons, is in this twentieth century a wearisome subject to the average reader or familiar talker in England. It must be allowed, too, I fear, that our countrymen, dwelling in temporary but prolonged exile in India, manifest less interest than might perhaps be expected of them, regarding the country in which their lot is thrown, in some portions, that is, of its not remote history, especially of the British India of old days. If this be so, it applies mainly to the large centres of commercial and official activity. Engrossed in the ever-increasing demands of the busy present, the toilers there have scarcely time to unseal the past; and so the generation of to-day hurries on, knowing little, and therefore caring little, about those which went before and dragged a lengthening chain over the same ground.

Still, to those who are tired of the anxieties and routine of business, and take but a languid interest in the warfare and controversies of modern politics and literature, one may suggest that it would be a relief to seek refuge in a bygone world, and in its records to learn something of the official and everyday life of their predecessors in Indian exile. Such a retrospect, far from being profitless or dull, would afford fresh and instructive entertainment even to those who are restricted to the occupations of social life, and must grow weary of "the constant revolution, stale and tasteless of the same repeated joys." Confining the looking back to the capital of

British India alone, it would at least enable many to take an intelligent interest in those sites and scenes in their midst which are intimately associated with memorable doings, and with the historic names of their own people, which are now daily passed by without even curiosity being awakened, because so little is known of those who flourished or who faded in Calcutta of the olden time.

The twentieth of June (destined to become a very auspicious date in the Victorian era) is associated with a tragedy which occurred in the infancy of the chief city in India, for which it will be for ever notorious. So universal is this notoriety, that perhaps it is no exaggeration to say that the words "The Black Hole of Calcutta" have grown into a proverbial expression of comparison, peculiarly suggestive, among all English-speaking and European nations.

The facts about the taking of Calcutta in 1756, and the calamity in which it culminated, are of course known in a general way to most readers, and familiarly to the students of history; still it may be worth while to retell, in the interest of the busy and the curious, a few of the leading events which led up to, attended on, and followed the capture of the settlement, when struggling into growth; to enter into one or two topographical details connecting old with modern sites, which may seem necessary for illustration, and while bringing into prominence some personal doings, to unbury a few of the half-forgotten names of those actors who played their parts in the scenes, which chiefly conspired to stamp the main incidents with the notoriety attaching to them.

At the outset it may be useful to trace very briefly what the settlement on the Eastern bank of the Hooghly had grown into as regards territorial extent, population, and commercial importance. English trading in Bengal had been in existence for nearly fifty years when the many quarrels and conflicts between the Company and the Mogul authorities issued in the withdrawal to Madras, in the end of 1688, of the Company's head Agent, the Rt. Worshipful Job Charnock, and his entire establishment, involving a suspension of all commercial relations for close on two years. Aurangzēb, who recognised the advantage to his treasury of European traders in his country, directed his Bengal Viceroy, Ibrahim Khan, to invite the English to come back. The Agent, after some consideration, accepted the invitation, and set sail for "The Bay," accompanied by his factors and writers and a few soldiers. The river-side village of Sutanutti had been the latest site of English enterprise in Bengal, and it was to this that Charnock now returned in August, 1690, and where he and his people literally set up their tents, and sheltered themselves, as best they could, in those and in huts and boats, as the houses of their previous occupation had disappeared during their absence.

Under the matured guidance of the old chief, trading was resumed, and building operations of the simplest kind at first, were gradually taken in hand. As the result of conciliating the local powers, and of winning general confidence, Armenians and other wealthy merchants were attracted to the English, and as success followed industry, the settlement extended itself southward along the river's bank, bringing into the sphere of occupation the contiguous villages of Calcutta and Govindpur. The former, the intermediate one of the three, was probably the first to be supplied with buildings of a more substantial kind to serve as magazines for the Company's increasing wares and investments, and so the middle territory came to give its name to the whole.

When in course of a little time further a factory grew into existence, the Company's servants, who learned the necessity of possessing some central stronghold, sought permission to surround it with defensive fortification. Circumstances exceptional and opportune (connected with what is historically known as Subha Sing's rebellion, which indirectly benefited the English from many points of view) happened to favour the obtaining of this concession, which the policy of the native powers had hitherto wisely forbidden to European traders in the country. The walls of a future fort accordingly soon began to arise. This was in the end of 1696.

A year or two later certain territorial privileges were judiciously secured, which added greatly to the assurance of the English position; so much so, that in December, 1699, the Court of Directors were able to write out (rather grandiloquently considering what a mere shell their "fort" was yet): "Being now possessed of a strong ffortification and a large tract of land, hath inclined us to declare Bengall a Presidency, and we have constituted our Agent (Sir Chas. Eyre) to be our President there and Governor of our ffort, etc., which we call ffort William." So cautiously and gradually was the fort constructed, that it took nearly twenty years before it could be called a fortification.

Job Charnock, indeed, saw but the dawning of these better days. He did not live to welcome prosperity coming, through difficulties and interruptions, to abide with the settlement that he had thrice selected. But he planted the foundation on which his countrymen were destined to build a mighty edifice, and thus he crowned a long life and faithful service of much warfare and many hardships and vicissitudes, ere he was laid to his rest (January, 1693) under the mausoleum which still recalls his name in Calcutta. In the Diary of Sir Wm. Hedges, published by the Hakluyt Society, there is (in Vol. I.) a quotation from Bruce's Annals, which tends to show the high estimation in which the services of rugged Job Charnock were held many years before his death by his Honourable Masters, viz. the Court of Directors wrote to the Government of Fort St. George that "they would rather dismiss the whole of their other agents than that Mr. Charnock should not be the Chief of Cassimbuzar."

The fifty years which followed brought with them rapidly extending and lucrative trade. The Company's agents were enabled to send handsome remittances to their masters in England, and to trade profitably on their own account; also to divert many goodly sums into the yawning coffers of the never sated native rulers. Each succeeding Bengal Viceroy was more extortionate than his predecessors, and his ministers more rapacious. When money was needed by the Court at Murshidábád or at Delhi, the remedy was to vex the stranger sojourning in their land. The expedient was always ready of finding a pretext for hindering the Company's trade and imperilling their investments, until the Viceroy's favour and forbearance had to be purchased. A feeble show of resistance was sometimes offered to this shameless bullying, but it was found on the whole safer and cheaper to truckle to it. Once, indeed, the worm turned, and had the temerity to appeal—greatly to his chagrin—over the head of the Viceroy to the Emperor at Delhi. The Company sent an embassy (well laden with presents) to the Great Mogul, as he was called, to pour out their grievances and seek redress. This, after two years of tedious intriguing and lavish bribery, returned (1717) fairly successful, bringing the Imperial firman for the craved territorial and commercial privileges.* The latter comprised some valuable concessions in the way of facilities for freer trade, which, amongst other results, brought an increased inflow of the inhabitants around to live under the protection and liberty of the favoured settlers. From this onward the career of the "United Company of Merchants trading to the East Indies" may be said to have steered a progressive and profitable course (always tempered by the necessity of "soothing the Nabob," as the irregular tribute to him was euphemistically described) until the epoch which immediately concerns us.

By 1756 Calcutta had reached such a stage of industrial progress,

* See Appendix—The Hamilton Tradition.

that its trade is stated to have exceeded one million sterling yearly, and that some fifty vessels or more annually visited its port. Its territory extended in a crescent along the bank of the river from north to south for about three miles (say from modern Chitpur Bridge to site of present fort). Standing nearly midway between these limits was the little fort. The houses of the English inhabitants were scattered in large enclosures for about half a mile to the north and to the south of the fort, and for about a quarter of a mile to the east of it. Beyond the English houses were closely clustered the habitations and huts of the natives: the better classes of them, including the "Black Merchants," dwelt to the north; the lower sort in the bazaars to the east and south.

The circumference of the black town, as it was called, was alleged to be about four miles. The European Collector of Calcutta officially recorded in 1752 that he computed the native population lying within the Company's bounds to be considerably over 400,000 "without reckoning the multitudes that daily come in and return, but yet who add to the consumption of the place." *

About a mile, or a little further, east of the river was a wide fosse dug in 1742 as an obstacle to apprehended Maharatta raids. It was intended to go all round the Company's bounds from north to south, but when the panic which suggested it died away, the work was discontinued, only three miles or so having been dug: the southern portion was never executed. It was known as the Maharatta Ditch.

To these insanitary surroundings were added the near vicinity of a dense jungle, of unsavoury marshes to windward, and of an inundating river. We shall see, later on, what the European population, with its terrible death-rate, was. Modern Calcutta can scarcely realise the appalling insalubrity amidst which those poor forgotten pioneers had to maintain a perilous struggle for existence, and what a tale the glutted graveyard close by their factory could tell.

The year 1756 brings us to the close of the reign of the Nawab Ali Verdi Khan, a Tartar adventurer who in 1740 had acquired the Subaship, or Viceroyalty, of Bengal, Behar, and Orissa, by usurpation, accompanied with the not unusual formalities of perfidy and ingratitude to his predecessor and to his family, and aided, it was said, by bribery of irresistible magnitude to the Mogul Court at Delhi.† The dignity

* The earlier attempts at estimating the population of Calcutta gave very conflicting results. Mr. C. R. Wilson has shown that that of 1752 must be very far too high, and arrived at also by including some outlying villages, beyond the Maharatta Ditch, not then belonging to the Company.

† There is a conflict of evidence about this; Holwell, in his "Interesting

to which he had intrigued his way did not bring Ali Verdi repose. His restless life was mainly passed in the tented field (where he was known by his title, Mahabat Jung (terror of war)), clearing his dominions of the marauding and hungry Maharattas, from whom at last he purchased a sort of peace by cession of territory in Orissa and by yearly tribute. To the English in Bengal his treatment was not on the whole oppressive: he applied to them of course for money occasionally, on the rather plausible pretext that he was protecting them from other and less considerate robbers. He wished them to be in his dominions, but simply as traders, and showed marked jealousy of any dominant power, save his own, arising in the country. He had the sagacity to recognise the sea-power of England, and was wont to tell his courtiers of the respectful apprehension in which it would be prudent to hold it. Though this old warrior's career had been passed amidst scenes of bloodshed, he was in private life mild and amiable, much given to domestic virtues. Orme tells that he was that phenomenon amongst Oriental potentates, a disapprover of the seraglio, and the husband of one wife. Hence his descendants were few, and he had none in the direct male line. Accordingly, when three years before his death he saw the necessity, owing to age and infirmities, of nominating his successor to the Subaship, his choice fell on his favourite grandson, who was also his grand-nephew. To him he at once delegated the practical government of the provinces in supercession of his two uncles, and to the consternation of many influential subjects. For in truth the object of the old man's dotage was badly equipped for ruling. He had been a spoiled child from infancy, brought up in his grandfather's palace as an over-indulged little despot, surrounded by profligate favourites. He grew up in ignorance, seeing nothing and hearing nothing except through the eyes and ears of his barbarous and corrupt environment. It would have been strange if his early manhood had not been marked by evil temper and by a disposition at once cruel and revengeful. His name was Murza Muhammad, but he is better known to history by his title of Siraj úd Dawla (lamp of the state).

On the death of the old Nawab at the age of eighty-two, in April, 1756, this youth, then about twenty-five years old, ascended the

Historical Events," denies that there was ever any "farmān" from Delhi confirming the usurper in his Government: Marshman, in his history, says there was, and that Ali Verdi kept his promise to Delhi, and sent there one crore of rupees and seventy lacs in jewels obtained from the estate of the late Nawab. Marshman gives no definite authority for this.

musnud. After his three years' *de facto* introduction to rule, his actual elevation was sullenly acquiesced in by the nobles at Murshidábád, more readily perhaps as a series of deaths and some murders had within the last few years put out of the way most of his possible rivals, and as his provident grandfather had left him an army, which might prove useful in case of his accession being disputed, and had gained over in his support its paymaster and Commander-in-Chief Meer Jaffar, and also the Seths the Court Bankers.

Immediately after being proclaimed, the new Nawab was not slow to find reasons for quarrelling with the English settled in Bengal; in furtherance, probably, of a long-formed design founded on the anticipation of getting possession of the vast wealth which rumour credited them with having accumulated.

Varying degrees of importance are attached in the official controversies of the time to the alleged pretexts. Of the two or three most prominently assigned, one was that the Calcutta authorities were harbouring a subject of the Nawab's, one Kissendas, whom he accused of absconding with certain treasures that had not been accounted for. Another, that they had persistently abused the privileges of trade secured to them by the Emperor's farmān. A third, that they were extensively increasing their fortifications without acquainting, or getting permission from, the Nawab, who peremptorily ordered them to desist and to destroy those recently added. The Governor wrote to the Nawab that they were merely repairing their fortifications in expectation of another war between France and England, and that they apprehended the French might sack the English settlement at Calcutta as in the last war they had that at Madras. Siraj úd Dawla was at this time at Rajmehal, having just arrived with a large force destined for Purneah, the Rajah of which, his own cousin, he proposed to chastise for withholding submission to him. The Governor's letter reached him there. The explanations in it had the very opposite effect to that intended; they increased his ill-feeling. The prospect represented of two European nations introducing their quarrels into his country, and conducting them with fire and sword, added, probably, some apprehension to his wrath. He at once countermanded the Purneah expedition, and resolved on another against a foe more worthy of his resentment. Directing the march of his army on Murshidábád, he sent forward a large detachment to invest the Company's out-factory at Kásimbázár close to it. By the 1st of June the Nawab himself was back at Murshidábád. What immediately followed is an interesting

Nawab Siraj-ud-Dawla, Viceroy of Bengal, etc.

*See p. 9.*

and painful story in itself which must not detain us now. Suffice it to say that partly by threats, partly by treachery, the Nawab's people managed to seize the chief (Mr. W. Watts) and other officials at Kásimbázár, and to gain unopposed possession of the fortified factory with its guns, ammunition, stores, etc. This was completed by 4th of June, under circumstances of such contumely that Ensign Elliot, commanding the small garrison, became so unhinged as to take his own life.

The easy and ample success of this the first act of hostility put the Nawab in heart for following it up; he had encountered no resistance; he was now well provided with artillery; what was to prevent him from driving the foreigners out of Calcutta also, and capturing and plundering their settlement, if he only acted with promptitude and vigour before they could proceed further with their defences, and before the season of the south-west monsoon was advanced enough to bring them assistance by sea? He immediately set out for Calcutta by forced marches so as to get over the ground before the daily-expected rains should delay his progress. The number of the forces constituting his army have been variously estimated; adopting those given by the Adjutant-General of the time, he had with him 30,000 foot, 20,000 horse, 400 trained elephants, and 80 pieces of cannon, most of them light guns taken at Kásimbázár. About 20,000 of his troops were armed with muskets, matchlocks, and wall pieces, the rest with lances, swords, bows and arrows, etc. Fully 40,000 followers and banditti of all sorts are said to have attended the army to take part in the plunder of Calcutta, so strong was the confidence of the rabble in the success of the expedition. Messrs. Watts and Collet accompanied the march as prisoners in the Nawab's camp. In about ten days the host covered the distance between Murshidábád and Hughli, whence and from Chandarnagar the immediate crossing of the river was effected in an immense fleet of boats assembled there for the purpose.

From the French and Dutch factories at Chandarnagar and Chinsurah, Siraj úd Dawla demanded submission and aid in his enterprise against the English. But these pleaded their peaceful trading occupation and the international treaties existing between their respective governments in Europe. They appeased him, however (for the time), with promises of substantial donations of money. The Nawab thought it politic to dissemble, and while insisting on the fulfilment of the promises, to reserve any overt act of hostility till he could dispose of the English.

In the meantime, how was Calcutta prepared, from a military

point of view, for the approaching visitation? We have seen what was the origin of the fortification there. It was a protective work enclosing the blocks of buildings where valuable and bulky merchandise was stored, and where a large export and import business was conducted by the Company's servants, some of whom, as well as of the garrison, being provided with resident accommodation—of a sort. The fortress (which was of brick-work strongly cemented) was designed as a defence, and a possible refuge, against "a country enemy" mainly. It had been added to and strengthened from time to time as occasion seemed to suggest, or as opportunity offered for doing so without arousing the watchful jealousy of the Nawab's people. The entire enclosure is often spoken of by contemporaries as the factory or the fort indifferently.

Regard being had to the fact that the river reclamations of the intervening years have thrown the bank some 250 yards outwards, or to the west, it may be said that old Fort William, standing on the river's bank, occupied nearly the site now comprised between Coelah Ghât Street and Fairlie Place. It was irregular in shape, the east and west curtains being longer than the other two, and the southern being again longer than the northern. The enclosed area roughly measured 210 yards by 120. It had four bastions; the two to the land side mounted ten guns each, those to the river eight each. The outer walls, or curtains, were not 4 feet thick, and were about 18 feet high. The terraces which these helped to support, formed the flat roofs of ground chambers inside. A little less than half the east side was opposite what was then called "the Park and Great Tank," still such a notable feature in "Tank Square." The main gateway projected from the eastern wall and carried five guns. Those standing in it could look up the road then known as "the avenue leading to the eastward," now recognised as Dalhousie Square North. Under the west face, on the river's bank, was a line of cannon mounted in embrasures of masonry.

The weakest part of the fort was to the south, where the erection of a most ill-placed building (called "the new go-downs") had been allowed.* Its terraced roof carried a battery of very light guns.

* The nature and position of this unmilitary excrescence will be understood from this description of it by a contemporary, viz. :—"About fifteen years ago, the Company being in want of warehouses, Governor Braddyl built a very large one against the south end of the fort; it was nearly square, for it extended from the S.E. to the S.W. bastion, and projected 60 or 80 feet beyond them. By these means these two bastions were rendered of very little use for defending the

This so-called fort was unprotected by any ditch or outwork, and was quite commanded on the land faces by the houses nearest to it. Poor as the defensive arrangements were at the best, their insufficiency was intensified by the state of disrepair into which they had been allowed to fall. The terraces had become so shaky as to preclude the use of the lightest guns on them, and their parapets were too low for the effective employment of musketry. Heavy fire, therefore, was restricted to the bastions and main gate, but even there the embrasures were dangerously wide. To ventilate the chambers against the east curtain several "windows" had been struck out, "so many breaches made for the enemy."

The records from the year 1754 show that this state of things was the subject of much anxious correspondence between the Court of Directors and the local government. The letters from the latter are fruitful in promises and nothing more. "We shall pay due regard to your orders in regard to the fortification." "The death of Colonel Scott put a check to our pursuing his plan for securing the settlement from any attack of the country forces." "We were cautious about laying out much money until," etc., etc., and so on. Amidst many pages marked by this sort of procrastination, one is gratified to come on a few which can be commended for their vigorous call to action. They present a refreshing little oasis where all around is barren through irresolution and feebleness.

In August, 1755, one of their military officers pointed out officially to the Bengal Government, how unfairly they were treating their employers' interests, in not even mounting the new guns they had sent out, "while not a gun mounted is fit for service," "so that

south end of the fort. For the curtain between them was now become the inner wall of a warehouse, and a large passage broke through it into the fort by way of a door to this new warehouse. The outer or south wall of this warehouse being now in place of the curtain, was not stronger than a common house wall. It was also full of very large windows, and by projecting beyond the bastions could not be flanked by their guns. It is true there was a terrace and a parapet with embrasures upon this warehouse, but the terrace would only bear a 2-pounder, and there was nothing after this to prevent them from scaling the warehouse wall, which was equal in height to the curtain, and joined both to it and the bastions." There are still in existence at the site of the southern limits of the old fort the remains of an arcaded structure pronounced to be contemporary with it, which have exercised archæologists and given rise from time to time to some friendly controversy. Hence I have given the above details verbatim, written by one who knew the locality well and was there in the siege. They may prove locally interesting and useful. They occur in a letter written in 1756 to Orme, the historian, then at Madras, headed "Reflections on the Loss of Calcutta," by Captain David Rennie, a mariner.

we seem to look more like a ruined and deserted Moor's fort than any place in possession of Europeans." He exhorted them to set their house in order, "this the sooner we set about the better whether we have to do with an enemy or not, as it at present shows a sloth and idleness which make us in some measure the ridicule of our neighbours." He told them that he thus addressed them "in vindication of myself," adding with prophetic pessimism "for fear it may be asked who was your Captain of Artillery after the loss of your Settlement?" *

As a matter of fact, the only defensive preparations attempted, in obedience to the latest and most earnest warnings from home, were the repairing and strengthening the line of guns towards the river, the erection of some trifling works, the chief of which was a redoubt near the river and ditch at Perrin's garden (Chitpur); but even these were suspended in deprecation of the Nawab's anger.

It was known in Calcutta on 1st of June that Kásimbázár was threatened, but not till the 7th did authentic information arrive that it had fallen without striking a blow, and that an immediate descent on the Chief Settlement was proposed. "When the Nawab's intention of marching on Calcutta was known" (reports the officer, Captain Grant, who was appointed Adjutant-General of the garrison), "it was felt time to inquire into the state of defence of a garrison neglected for so many years, and the managers of it lulled in so infatuate a security that every rupee expended in military service was esteemed so much loss to the Company." Preparations thus deferred till

* The only tribute that I can pay to the memory of this honest gentleman is to recall here his homely name; it was Jasper Jones. His warnings received the attention and recognition accorded not unusually then, as now, to the provident man vainly preaching to his drowsy, self-satisfied countrymen on the text, "Be ready." This captain of artillery, who showed too much zeal and too little observance of red tape, got from the Council Board a curt acknowledgment of what they called "his sentiments on the fortifications of the place," and an intimation that his letter was "irregular, improper, and unnecessary." Having thus asserted their claim to superior wisdom, they resumed their attitude of intending—to do something. Poor Jones, after this experience of the *vox clamantis in deserto*, said no more. He did not live to see the Nemesis in the crowning proof of the accuracy of his military foresight, for, as the Board recorded, he "demised of a violent fever" in less than four months after he had so plainly reminded them of their duty. Well may the experienced cynic, knowing how history repeats itself, quote the refrain—

"Still spoke the oracle just as before,
Would'st thou have peace, leave the world to its mulishness,
Things to their natures and fools to their foolishness,
Beetles were blind in the ages of yore."

invasion was imminent could result only in disaster. Urgent calls for help were sent by small native vessels to Madras, and an appeal was made to the Chinsurah and Chandarnagar Factories to stand by the English in the common cause. The Dutchmen begged to be excused. The French offered a defensive and offensive alliance, provided the English would quit their settlement for that of the French, which, they said, was much better adapted for resistance. "We wrote them a very genteel letter" (says a contemporary youthful member of the Civil Service), "thanking them for their offer of assistance, and as we were in very great want of ammunition, requested they would spare us a quantity of powder and shot. To this we had no reply till the Nabob was near Calcutta, when the Frenchmen put off their grimace, assuring us of the impossibility of complying with our demands, as they might provoke the Nabob by it. That we should expect the French would assist us and be dupes of that fantastical nation is intolerable. However, when the Nabob demanded supplies of powder from them soon after, they could then find sufficient to give him 150 barrels, and could connive also at the desertion of near 30 men which joined the Nabob's army." The Adjutant-General also mentions that the enemy had with them "25 Europeans and 80 Chittygong Fringeys under the command of one who styled himself Le Marquis de St. Jaque, a French renegard (*sic*), for the management of their artillery." * The English also had a French officer fighting on their side, a Monsieur Le Beaume, who behaved very gallantly before he escaped.

Thus left to fight for themselves, the English mustered their force.

The garrison proper at this time consisted of about 250 men, including Eurasians and native "Portuguese." The European element barely amounted to 80 soldiers and gunners. None had any active military training. Their experience was limited to guard and sentry duty and to the escorting the Company's merchandise to and fro, by land or by river, between headquarters and the out factories. All the inhabitants, therefore (including the sea-faring people who could be spared from the vessels in port), capable of bearing arms were enrolled as Militia and formed into two companies. "About 50 persons," says a resident, "detached themselves

* Efforts were secretly made to try and get the Europeans and Faringis, etc., to withdraw from the Nawab. Letters from the Priests in Calcutta were conveyed to them, representing how contrary to Christianity it was for them to be fighting with the Moors against their co-religionists. The letters reached, but the recipients said there was no chance for them to escape.

from the Militia and entered volunteers among the military to remain during the troubles, 34 of these were Company's Servants." Counting these, the Militia numbered about 260, largely made up, however, of Armenians, Portuguese, and Slaves. "The Black Militia" were found to be "entirely useless," many of them "not capable of even holding a musket." Mr. C. S. Hill, in his "Bengal in 1756," Indian Record Series, says, on Friday, June 11, 1756, a general review of the whole force was arranged for next morning. There mustered—Military (of these not above 45 Europeans), 180; Volunteers, European, 50; Militia, European, 60; Artillery, European, 35; other volunteers, *i.e.* sea-officers and Portuguese Helmsmen, Militia, Armenians, and Portuguese, 150; making 515 in all. We get a tolerably close idea of what the small European population of Calcutta was at this time when told that between the military proper and the Militia not more than about 200 Europeans could be mustered. Peons were also enlisted in large numbers for quasi-military duty, but took the earliest opportunity for deserting.

The military were under five principal officers, of whom Captain Minchin was the senior, and who to general military incapacity and inexperience added an indolence which from the first filled the Civil Authorities with misgivings. Captain Clayton, the next, was also without experience. Captain Buchannan was the only one of the seniors who had seen active service. The Artillery officer, or "Captain of the Train," was named Witherington. The Governor and President of the Council was Roger Drake. He was son of a Director, and held the post of President by seniority since 1752: not yet formally confirmed from home. He was only thirty-four years old.

Ill adapted as the fort was for defence, still the best hope of a protracted holding out, till relief or withdrawal offered by the river, lay in trusting to it, and in concentrating the garrison and European inhabitants within it, having first demolished as many as possible of the adjacent houses overlooking it, or occupied them in force. The fort was, however, pronounced incapable of defence, and it was arranged by the too many counsellors who were suffered to have a voice in the matter, to meet the enemy in the principal streets and avenues, and at improvised outposts. No better scheme for spreading out and wasting the untrained and insufficient defending force could have been devised. It is very evident, from the contemporary records, how little Calcutta realised, even at the eleventh hour, what an avalanche was about to burst on it. One writer says, "The military were very urgent for demolishing all the houses, knowing

Fort William at Bengal.

Reduced from an old engraving by Vandergucht.

that if once the enemy got possession of the white houses there would be no standing on the factory walls. However, the pulling down the houses was a thing they would not think of, not knowing whether the Company would reimburse them the money they cost." Captain Grant says, on the same head:—

"It may be justly asked, why we did not propose the only method, that as I thought then, and do now, could give us the least chance of defending the place in case of a vigorous attack—the demolition of all the houses adjacent to the fort, and surrounding it with a ditch and glacé? But so little credit was then given, and even to the very last day, that the Nawab would venture to attack us or offer to force our lines, that it occasioned a general grumbling and discontent to leave any of the European houses without them. . . . And should it be proposed by any person to demolish as many houses as should be necessary to make the fort defensible, his opinion would have been thought pusillanimous and ridiculous." Further on, however, this authority gives another reason, viz. that both time and gunpowder were wanting for the necessary destruction of buildings. Trenches and breastworks were therefore made, and all the narrow passes leading to the town were obstructed by ditches. "Intrenchments were begun to be thrown up across the park, and a ravelin to defend the front gate of the factory, but had no time to finish them."

Three principal outlying batteries were also constructed and mounted. One about 300 yards in front of the main gate (about where now stands the Scotch church). Another to the south of the fort, at the edge of a creek leading to the Salt-water Lake (*i.e.* at the corner of the old burial ground, about where Hastings Street, Council House Street, and Government Place now meet). The third was to the north on the bank of the river (about at the foot of Clive Ghât street). A large number of peons and burkundauzes occupied posts at the Maharatta Ditch, but they went over to the enemy. In fact, with their small force, no serious attempt was made to defend this work.

Early on the 16th June the approach of the enemy was announced. A large proportion of the native inhabitants now fled in all directions into the country. The military and Militia were called to their posts, and the "white houses" were only then, on an arranged signal (*i.e.* "three guns fired, at a minute's distance, from the N.E. bastion"), deserted for the very poor shelter of the fort by the European women. Amongst these, it must be borne in mind, were delicately nurtured ladies with their little children, to share in the humiliations and sufferings of 1756, as their countrywomen a hundred years later shared with patient heroism, in those of the great military revolt in India. And the work which devolved on these poor souls throws an additional ray of light on the general unreadiness. "Our women," writes Governor Drake, "diligently employed themselves in making cannon cartridges." By noon the van of the Nawab's army was at the northern bounds, and tried to force an entrance across a deep rivulet there connected with the Maharatta Ditch and river. Here stood a redoubt and drawbridge. Three ships—the *Prince George*, *Fortune*, and *Chance* (so named by some)—were sent up to assist and cover this redoubt.

This attack was successfully resisted, a small party having been detached to strengthen the post under Ensign Piccard, who, when the enemy desisted at night, crossed over, beat up their quarters, and spiked their guns. On the 17th the enemy did not renew the attack at the north, but the whole force turned eastwards towards Dum Dum, and from that direction entered the Company's bounds.* In the afternoon they set fire to the great bazaar within half a mile of the fort on the north-east, and generally gave themselves up to plundering. On the same day the English also set fire to as many bazaars as they could to their front and to the south as far as Govindpur, "where many of our people being detected plundering were instantly punished with decapitation." The Portuguese women and children and such-like unfortunate creatures who, being country born, went by the name of "black Christians," now thronged into the fort. "In the evening," writes the Governor, "the general attack being now soon to be expected, a confused noise of the shrieks and cries and entrance into our factory of the several women and children and their attendants was heard who had before situated themselves in the houses within our lines." He computes the number of them to be 2500; and the discipline prevailing may be inferred when he adds, "about 500 of them took immediately with our shipping." †

* It was alleged that the enemy were guided to the undefended eastern entrance by the head Jemadar of Omichund's peons and retainers, incensed at the dishonour put on his master by his arrest and imprisonment in the fort. Huzzoormull, Omichund's brother-in-law, was also apprehended concealed amongst the latter's women. The same Jemadar (Jaggernaut by name) wiped out this stain by (according to Drake), "killing thirteen women and three children with his 'catary,' and afterwards set his house on fire, where it was believed were deposited several letters." Omichund (Amin Chaund) was a wealthy and influential merchant who lived in Calcutta. He was confined, with Kissendas, as he was suspected of communicating with the Nawab. He is best known to fame as the victim of Clive's forged treaty afterwards.

† In the following January the Bengal Government told the Court of Directors,

This night was anxiously spent under arms by all; but the enemy made no nearer approach. The next morning (18th) he advanced against the outposts, attacking them chiefly with matchlock fire from the unoccupied houses near.

The most resolute assault was made in very strong force on the battery to the eastward and its outposts in the jail close to it. This post was partly held by a detachment of Militia, commanded by Mr. J. Z. Holwell, one of the junior members of Council. It was in a very exposed position, and was very resolutely defended. So heavy was the fire brought to bear on it that only the men necessary to work the guns were at last allowed to remain in it; the rest got under cover within the Mayor's Court close by, ready to take the places from time to time of those who were shot down. At length, Clayton, the military officer in charge, despairing of being able to hold his ground, directed Holwell to go to the fort, report the state of things, and get orders. On Holwell's return with orders to withdraw "and to spike up the cannon which we could not bring off," he found the post in the utmost confusion and already in the course of being hurriedly abandoned, the principal guns, two 18-pounders, being spiked, but so ineffectually that they were drilled before long and turned most damagingly against the fort. Only one field-piece was brought away. The loss of this post led to the somewhat precipitate recall of the other batteries the same evening. Thus, after a few hours' fighting, the ill-selected outside defences—on which reliance had been foolishly placed—crumbled away, and the garrison found themselves driven to their citadel, having in the mean time lost many brave men in vain. Small parties were now thrown into the buildings which most closely commanded the ramparts, such as the church facing the east curtain (present western end of Bengal Government Offices), a Mr. Cruttenden's house (afterwards site of the Bonded Warehouse) on the north, and the Company's or Governor's House on the south, these being some thirty or forty yards from the fort.

Following on these disasters, the utmost consternation prevailed within the fort itself. The Militia drawn from the dusky inhabitants became quite demoralised from fear. The gun lascars disappeared. The English soldiers and inhabitants alone stood firm, but they were

"The inconvenience we experienced at the siege of Calcutta from the prodigious number of Portuguese women who were admitted into the fort, and the very little service which that race of people are to the settlement, induced us upon our return to interdict the public exercise of the Roman Catholic religion, and to forbid the residence of their priests in our bounds."

nearly jaded to death from constant work, no attempt at regular tours of duty having been organised. "Provisions," writes the Adjutant-General, "had been laid in, but proper persons had not been appointed to look after them, and the general desertion of the black fellows, amongst whom were all the cooks, left us to starve in the midst of plenty." All the men at the outposts had no refreshment for twenty-four hours, which occasioned constant complaint and grumbling all this night. We were so abandoned by all sorts of labourers that we could not get carried up on the "ramparts cotton bales and sand-bags for the parapets of the bastions, which were very low." Before eight p.m. the small party occupying the Governor's house were driven out by a stronger fire from a house further south, where the enemy had effected a lodgment. This exposed "the new go-downs," which the enemy made a half-hearted attempt to carry by escalade. By a merciful dispensation the Moors on this night also suspended their operations when it became dark. This gave the opportunity for getting the European ladies and women and children on board the shipping, as decided at a council summoned for the purpose. The embarkation was so hurriedly done, and with so little order, that several women, the Governor's wife amongst them, were left behind and were obliged to remain till next day for want of boats. Two members of council, Messrs. Manningham and Frankland, embarked with the ladies, "having tendered themselves" for this duty. "Our Colonel and Lieutenant-Colonel of Militia," writes a very bitter eye-witness, "preferred entering the list among the number of women rather than defend the Company's and their own property. Accordingly they went off with them, and though several messages were sent them to attend council if they did not choose to fight, still no persuasion could avail."

A second council, or rather public confabulation, since it was open to almost any one, took place during the night. As the possibility of holding the fort against a triumphant enemy now drawing closer to it in every direction, was more remote than ever, the main question was how best to withdraw the garrison and effects, and the families of the fighting men, leaving to the enemy the least possible *matériel* of any service. And the crisis was one where a decision must be made and a course of action taken promptly. Two conditions were essential to any hope of success, should retreat by the river be decided on, namely secrecy to the moment of execution, so as to obviate further panic amongst so disorganised a crowd, and some orderly plan of embarkation, under rigorous discipline, adapted to the means available. The public nature of the so-called council of war quite defeated the first condition, and no senior in civil or military authority, had the inspiring force and masterful capacity demanded by the second. It is alleged by Mr. Holwell (and by others) that he strenuously advocated their setting to the work of withdrawal at once before the demoralisation spread, or before their necessary means were further crippled. But he and those who agreed with him were out-voted. When a choice between evils has to be made it is easy enough to urge the difficulties of this or that course as being insurmountable; so "every one," we are told, on this occasion "was officious in advising, yet no one was properly qualified to give advice."

Amidst such clamour within and the deafening uproar amongst the miscellaneous wailing throng huddled without, a calm survey of the situation was impossible, and the attempt at consultation was, of course, unproductive. The bitter thought that must have been uppermost in the mind of every member in that so-called council was *nox ruit nos flendo ducimus horas.* All knew that darkness and the ebbing tide favoured instant action, yet the precious night hours flew by, and 4 o'clock in the morning found the prostrated council still talking, still undelivered of any feasible scheme of providing for the common safety. By this time the flood tide was setting up strongly, so the distracted meeting broke up, agreed upon nothing definite save that retreat was inevitable. "In this state of irresolution, attended with great confusion," writes Captain Grant, "did we remain without fixing on any settled scheme till near daylight, then adjourned to wait what the morning might produce in hopes of making our retreat next night."

What the morning did produce was this:—"19th June, by daybreak the enemy began playing upon the church and factory from two 18-pounders; they fired with wall-pieces and small arms from every hole and corner, and all our efforts to dispossess them of the houses proved ineffectual. Appearing in prodigious swarms all round the factory, they struck a panic in many, expecting every moment the place would be stormed, and as no quarter was given none could be expected." The artillery from the fort during the early morning did "terrible execution" amongst the crowded enemy, but did not at all keep down the attacking fire.

By nine o'clock the small parties occupying the church, and the house on the north being nearly cut off, were ordered to come in, first setting fire to the house. The defenders were thus strictly cooped up in their fortress, which was now becoming surrounded by burning buildings.

"Now," writes the Governor, "appeared the utmost horror among the women in the factory running to and fro with their children (many sucking at the breast) to escape the shot flying about us." Meanwhile, as it was found that many boats had deserted during the night, the pressing need of embarking the remainder of the European women was seen to. These, with some of the wounded, were put on board a vessel. This vessel, without the Governor's orders, it is said, moved three miles down to avoid the fire-arrows, and other missiles from the bank now open to the enemy. Several other vessels followed this lead, and as the means of escape were disappearing, the terror and confusion amongst the black Christians became quite uncontrollable. The orders of those attempting to conduct the embarkation were unheeded, or, indeed, unheard in the uproar. A stampede set in, resulting in the overcrowding of the boats and the swamping of several, so that but a small proportion of the frantic multitude who rushed to them succeeded in getting away.

So far so bad, but worse remains. Matters had reached this unpromising stage early in the forenoon of the 19th, when the situation was intensified by the withdrawal from the fort of the Governor and the chief civil and military officers, who joined the fugitives in the river.

Desertion in the presence of the enemy on the part of those to whose lot had especially fallen the duty of seeing the struggle, however hopeless, to the end, is a charge not to be lightly made. Any reference, therefore, to an occurrence which carries with it so deep a stigma, should in fairness be accompanied by what has been alleged in exculpation of their conduct by those chiefly concerned. Both the Governor and the Adjutant-General have liberated their consciences on this subject. Their personal narration, though it may not quite fulfil the object of the writers, will perhaps help us to realise more vividly the scenes in which they were prominent actors. Drake gave this contrite account of his action. "To justify my quitting the garrison I shall not attempt contradiction thereto. I, with as much fervency as any one can do, blame myself for that inconsiderate action, whereby I acknowledge that charge against me to carry a truth I can in no way vindicate. Fatigued in body by continual harassment for two days and nights, without any proper refreshment or sleep I still kept up, and with Messrs. Holwell and Baillie and others went through the factory in ye morning of 19th June to encourage the soldiers and Militia, who were in the fort resting themselves, to take up their arms and go to the relief of those who had not been off duty all night. This I think Mr. Holwell can attest, and that I was myself acting in filling bags of cotton as soon as day appeared, without his or any other persons surmising by any of my actions, words, or show of diffidence then or before, that the lot would fall on me to make answer for quitting the factory, which I solemnly declare never entered my thoughts until the moment my confused ideas hurried me off shore. Impatient to know and be an eye-witness of every event that might happen, I refused the solicitation of Mr. Holwell and many others to go to rest, for he plainly saw I could scarce support my own weight for want of sleep, nor indeed could I any longer keep active. Hence about 8 a.m., when I took my seat on a chest below stairs and slumbered for about an hour, when, walking to and fro, a man astonished me, who had charge of the delivery of the powder, by whispering in my ear that the whole that was good was delivered upon the several curtains and bastions. This knowledge caused my first perplexity. . . . I stayed on shore till 10.30 a.m., when, perceiving the ships and vessels dropping down the river without orders, and several persons had quitted the factory, my imagination suggested it would be impossible to make a general retreat, the method proposed being frustrated by the desertion of the boats, and therefore it appeared to me justifiable and necessary to provide for my own safety, as I then thought my longer stay could be of no service, which I did by going on board a small pawnsay, the only boat remaining at the wharf, except a large budgerow full of people." *

Captain Grant says that between ten and eleven a.m. he saw the Governor standing on the stair-head of the ghaut leading from the back gate, and asked him if he had any commands, but found that he was only beckoning to his servant, who stood in a pawnsay a little above the ghaut. Several boats were at the time setting off from different places with Europeans in them, amongst them a budgerow, aboard of which were getting Mr. Macket (member of council) and Captain Minchin. The Governor just remarked the bad consequences of the ships dropping down, and that every one was providing for his own security, and then ran up along the shore to the pawnsay. Seeing him step in hurriedly, Grant followed, and

* The smallness of the boat in which he escaped, being mentioned apparently in deprecation of censure, has a touch of unconscious humour in it. This long letter of Drake's was elicited by certain communications which he received in answer to a notification which he posted "at every mast and every public place on shore." It was dated from "Ship *Fort William* off Fulta, 31st October, 1757," and it requested, with a mixture of assurance and humility, "the gentlemen of council that they will be pleased jointly and separately to acquaint me publicly of the censure that in their judgment I merit by the late misfortune that has befell our Settlement of Calcutta."

called out to know what he was about. On learning that he was going on board the ships, Grant earnestly entreated that he would first acquaint the garrison of his design. Drake pointed out "the impossibility of making a regular retreat," and that when the others saw him going, such as could possibly find boats would follow. Grant then "considered the retreat to be general, and that every one who could lay hold of a conveyance would choose to escape falling into the hands of a merciless enemy; so thought it justifiable to follow the Governor in a state of such apparent confusion and disorder, though greatly grieved to see how many of my friends and countrymen were likely to fall a sacrifice for want of boats." They got on board the *Dodalay* (of which Drake was part-owner), and there found Frankland and Manningham with most of the women. Grant alleges that he then in vain "represented to the Governor the cruelty of abandoning so many gentlemen to the mercy of such an enemy; and requested that he would order the ships and sloops to move up before the fort, by which means we should be able to send the boats under their cover to bring off our distressed friends."*

* Minchin and Grant were subsequently sentenced to be dismissed the service for desertion of their posts. Grant successfully pleaded the circumstances stated above—his urging the return of the Governor's ship—as he was afterwards reinstated. "It does not appear," says Colonel Broome ("History Bengal Army"), "that they were tried by court-martial, but that they received their sentence of dismissal from the Governor and council, most of whom must have blushed to record their decision." Minchin was even summoned home immediately, but a higher summons intervened, he died in Calcutta (January, 1758). Grant's career was a curious one, he was with Clive at Plassey and voted for immediate action. He resigned owing to Clive's promotion of a junior, he returned to India as a Free Merchant, and died in 1765, a contractor for Military Stores (Hill). He is said also to have fought under Charles Edward at Culloden (1746), and when the Jacobite cause was lost to have made his way to Bengal. Incredible as it may seem to-day, the official civilian deserters do not appear to have been called to account by the Home Government; Manningham, Frankland, and Macket were even promoted in council. Drake was practically not deposed until a despatch arrived in Calcutta, June, 1758, revoking the Governor's commission, and constituting a Committee of Clive and two others to have the powers of the President and council ("List of Bengal Chiefs and Governors," by Mr. F. Danvers). It is vexatious to think that in the mean time he had the opportunity by virtue of his position of sharing to the extent of £28,000 in the vast sum "presented" by the new Nawab, Meer Jaffar, on his accession after the battle of Plassey. Grose, in his "Voyage to the East Indies," is the authority for the very improbable story that Drake pleaded his being a Quaker as a reason for a man of peace hurrying away from a scene of bloodshed, etc. Voltaire got hold of this excuse, and thus cynically observes on it: "Le Gouverneur de Calcutta nommé Drak etait bien different du fameux amiral Drak. On a dit, on a ecrit qu'il etait

All that can be said for the Governor is that under the stress of mental and physical exhaustion he lost his head and yielded to evil example and the impulse of terror. "What weak heart," as Thackeray wisely says, "confident before trial may not succumb under temptation invincible." His subsequent conduct, however, and that of his fellow-deserters in continuation of their flight, admits of no palliation, as we shall see. The indignation aroused by this latest and most prominent addition to the fugitives, is indicated by this scrap of information from one of the witnesses to it, *i.e.* Tooke: "Upon the Governor going off several muskets were fired at him, but none were lucky enough to take place!"

The remnant of the defenders now with one accord insisted on that being done which should have been done a week before, namely, that seniority and all ideas of responsible control founded merely on stereotyped official procedure, should be disregarded, and that the man who seemed best adapted for action in the crisis now reached should be given absolute command. "The general voice of the garrison," says Cooke, the Secretary to Government, "called for Mr. Holwell to take charge of their defence upon him, who thereupon acted in all respects as commander-in-chief, and did his utmost to encourage every one." He was not the senior of the members of council left behind, but Mr. Pearkes, who was, waived any claim at a council hastily summoned for the occasion.

The gate towards the river was immediately secured to prevent further desertion. During all this day the enemy pressed on their attack with great vigour. Having now got possession of the church, they opened a heavy fusilade from it and galled the defenders severely, killing and wounding many. To get some sort of shelter from this commanding fire, bales of broad cloth were dragged up and placed as traverses along the curtain and on the bastions, also cotton bales were fixed against the thin parapets to resist the cannon balls.

de cette religion nazaréene primitive professée par ces respectables Pensylvaniens que nous connaissons sous le nom de *quakers*. Ces primitifs dont la patrie est Philadelphie dans le Nouveau-Monde, et qui doivent faire rougir le notre, ont la même horreur du sang que les brames. Ils regardent la guerre comme un crime. Drak etait un marchant tres habile et un honnête homme : il avait jusque-la caché sa religion, il se declara et le conseil le fit embarquer sur le Gange pour le mettre à couvert." In Mr. Hill's work it is told that a M. Durand, in the French Company's Service at Chandernagore, in writing an account of the capture of Calcutta to a friend (July 2, 1756), says, "Drake thought no further of defending the place, disclosing himself to be a Quaker (who never fight)." A translation of this appeared in the *London Chronicle* for June 18, 1757, and is probably the foundation of Grose's story and Voltaire's sarcasm.

The possibility of making good the defence with their diminished number, exhausted strength, and failing ammunition seemed now beyond reach. The utmost, therefore, they hoped to do was to hold out until a country vessel, which about noon hove in sight above the fort, could drop down low enough to give them an opportunity of getting on board.

The vessel was the *Prince George*, which on the 16th had been sent up stream to assist the redoubt at Chitpur, and her delay in returning thence to her station left her now a welcome sight to the isolated defenders.

Two of them were immediately deputed to board her and to explain to the captain (Tom Hague) "our situation and distress" and to give him instructions to bring his vessel as near the fort and as speedily as he could. But the hopes thus aroused were cruelly shattered, for the anxious watchers had soon the bitter disappointment of seeing the approaching vessel suddenly go aground. The pilot, "a Dutchman named Francis Morris," in his hurry to press on had become flurried, and let his charge get irretrievably on to a shoal,* in sight of all those to whom she was "the only glimmering hope left to escape falling into the hands of the Moors." Signals were in the mean time thrown out from every part of the fort for the ships to come up again; but they were unheeded. So the defenders had in desperation to maintain their position as best they could; their strength ever decreasing. When darkness came it brought the usual and welcome suspension of attack, but the night was a dreadful one. All the houses nearest to the ramparts and the marine yard were now in flames, and, says a witness, "exhibited a spectacle of unspeakable terror." The enemy hemmed them in closely all round. Holwell, who was in the best position to gauge the situation, gave his deliberate opinion afterwards, that if on this night the boats and vessels had moved up, as they might easily have done, and anchoring safely under the guns of the fort inspirited the defenders by giving them the aid of fresh men and ammunition, there might still have been safety for all. There was nothing to prevent in such a case the embarkation of their effects and the orderly withdrawal of the garrison.

At early dawn on the 20th the enemy renewed their cannonade, and generally pushed their attack during the morning "with more

* There were twenty-one vessels of all sorts lying at Calcutta in June, 1756; of these sixteen were lost, says Drake, "by various accidents." A strong testimony to the confusion and incompetence that prevailed afloat as well as ashore.

warmth and vigour than ever they had done." But in spite of the heavy loss caused thereby, and the general demoralisation of the worn-out soldiery, superior numbers did not yet prevail. The defence replied indeed with sullen resolution, but it was clear that "the Moors," flushed with success and enabled hour by hour to bring a heavier fire to bear, could not be much longer denied admittance.

Even now at the eleventh hour, if the fleet had only come up on the flood the embarkation might have been carried out securely in the face of day, without the enemy being able to efficiently obstruct it. "We had it in our power," writes Holwell, "to leave the Suba the bare walls of your fort." The despairing hopes of all could turn in this extremity only to some help from their late companions in arms. They were in sight, in full view of the signals of distress. They had heard the fight raging during all the previous day, and had seen their brethren and countrymen in a circle of conflagration all that night. Now they could hear how furiously the cannonading on each side went on, and could see the English colours still fluttering at the flagstaff. "But we deceived ourselves," writes an indignant comrade, "and there never was a single effort made in the two days the fort held out after their desertion to send a boat or vessel to bring off any part of the garrison." Drake had the hardihood to plead, that by bribes and threats he had tried to induce some boats which he passed on his way down to go back, but the native crews were afraid. As a survivor bitterly retorted, if he as President had hoisted his flag upon his vessel and *led* the way back, all would have followed him. But he showed no stomach for this, especially when the commander of his vessel * did the reverse of advocating it by using, in Captain Grant's hearing, the matchless argument that the attempt would indeed be attended with danger!!

It is not pleasant to have to recall this portion of the story of Calcutta, but the episode just dwelt on—full of humiliation as it is for Englishmen—could not be slurred over, if only in fairness to the memory of the few whose fidelity was the more conspicuous and was followed by so much suffering. Nothing, I fear, can be urged in arrest of judgment for the cravens skulking in their ships,—for the Governor who forsook his trust, for the officers who deserted their men, for the sailors and soldiers who abandoned their comrades,

* This poltroon, named Young, Captain of the *Dodalay*, would not, according to one of the manuscript accounts, give a cable and anchor to aid in the attempt to get off the stranded *Prince George*, supporting his refusal on the ground that as bad weather was at hand all the gear would be needed for his own vessel.

and, worst of all, callously withheld from them the means of retreat, leaving them to their fate, with a perfect consciousness of what that fate must be.*

By noon of the 20th, of the one hundred and seventy people (about) left after the desertion, twenty-five had been killed and some fifty wounded, at the lowest of varying estimates. These losses were largely due to an attempt of the enemy to carry the northern curtain by escalade, under the support of a heavy musketry fire from what remained of the house facing it, and from the church and other buildings near. All were worn out, and it is not to be wondered at that several in the lower ranks ("the Dutch soldiers, the military and garrison mostly consisting of that country," as one witness records) had been seeking support and courage from the proverbial source in the liquor store.

Great pressure had been put on Holwell to make overtures to the enemy for a cessation of hostilities, pending the ascertaining of the pleasure of the Suba. He strongly opposed this as futile; however, to quiet his own people, he caused letters to be thrown over addressed to two of the Suba's generals, explaining that the defence of the fort was maintained in preservation of life and honour. By this, too, he hoped to gain time to put in execution a desperate scheme of forcing a retreat that night through the southern barrier by the river side, and of marching to the cover of the ships lying at "Surman's" (modern Hastings). This, he says, they meditated, "having no dependence on the clemency of the enemy we had to deal with."

For more than two hours after the repulse of the northern attack, the enemy disappeared, but about four p.m. word was brought Holwell that a man was advancing with a flag, and calling out to cease firing, and offering quarter in case of surrender. It was hastily agreed that this should be answered by the showing of a flag of truce, with which Holwell repaired to the S.E. bastion. Soon afterwards "multitudes of the enemy came out of their hiding-places round us, and flocked under the walls." While there they succeeded in setting fire to some of the cotton bales blocking up the openings in the east curtain, thereby adding much to the confusion. In

* It would be very unfair not to quote in connection with this what Mr. Hill has extracted from manuscript record. It may justly be pleaded *quantum valeat*, viz. "Some of the gentlemen on board tried to get ashore, but even Mr. Macket's offer of 1000 Rs. for a boat met with no response." . . . "Thus many gallant men who had gone on board with full leave from their superiors, who had no intention of deserting their comrades and who had stayed on board under the impression that a general retreat was being made, were involved in the shameful action of their commanders."

answer to Holwell, one of the enemy's officers called out that the Suba was there, and his pleasure was that we should strike our colours and surrender. Before Holwell could reply, Mr. Baillie, who was standing by him, was wounded, and an attempt was simultaneously made to force the S.W. barrier and eastern gate. A gun was brought to bear on the latter, and the enemy ordered to withdraw, which they did, the flag of truce was taken down, and Holwell "hastened to the parade to issue orders for a general discharge of our cannon and small arms." "The moment I arrived there, Captain Dickson, who now commands the *Lively* (grabb), at present in our service, and just after him Ensign Walcot, came running to me and told me the western gate was forced by our own people and betrayed." Several of the defenders escaped by that means, as during the brief parley the enemy stormed the S.W. bastion "under cover of a prodigious thick smoke." When Holwell rushed from the parade to the S.E. bastion, where Captain Buchannan was in charge, he found some of the enemy's colours planted even there. "I asked him how he could suffer it; he replied he found further resistance was in vain." The sight that met Holwell's look round convinced him that it was so, as "the Moors," with the aid of bamboos and ladders were swarming in by the S.W. barriers and by the new go-downs. This was the end. The stormèrs, "the enraged and merciless enemy," were more humane, in the moment of victory, to the defenders, than their former comrades had been, for they spared their lives. It is right to remember this unexpected forbearance. Some records which Mr. Hill consulted authorise him to differ from Holwell and others on this point, or rather to quote what was written on the other side, viz. "Immediately after the natives scaled the walls on all sides by means of bamboos, which they used as ladders, with precipitation scarce credible to Europeans, and cut to pieces all who resisted, especially all who wore red-coats, amongst them Lieut. Blagg, who refused to lay down his sword." I confess I find it very difficult to understand this. Why should the officer in command of this post resist? Quarter was apparently offered to him, but he refused it; and though it must have been obvious to him and to all of them, that the game was played out and lost, he chose to sacrifice his own chance of life, and, what was harder still, that of his men and comrades! They refrained from bloodshed, according to most eye-witnesses, and took to the more congenial relaxation of looting instead, depriving the gentlemen of their watches, buckles, and such personal valuables. The lust of plunder is often greater than the lust of blood among Orientals. They also busied themselves in appropriating the portable belongings in the apartments of those who resided in the factory, an engrossing occupation which gave an opportunity of escape by the river to a few more of the captured who were sharp. To the first native officer whom he saw coming towards him from the S.W. bastion, Holwell delivered his pistols, and was told to order instantly the British colours to be cut down. This he refused to do, saying that, as masters of the fort, they might order it themselves. His sword was demanded then, but this he declined to give unless in the presence of the Suba. With this object he was conducted round the ramparts till they came opposite to where Siraj úd Dawla was outside. Holwell salaamed to him from the rampart, and then delivered his sword to the Jemadar. The Suba returned the salaam from his litter, and then moved round by the northern curtain and entered the fort by the small river gate. His younger brother was with him. Holwell "had three interviews with him that evening, one in durbar," which Cooke says he held in the open area of the fort, sitting in his litter. At first he "expressed much resentment at our presumption in defending the fort against his army with so few men, asked why I did not run away with my Governor, etc., etc., and seemed much disappointed and dissatisfied at the sum found in the treasury; asked me many questions on this subject, and on the conclusion he assured me on the word of a soldier that no harm should come to me, which he repeated more than once." The Armenians and Portuguese, who so embarrassed the defence, were now immediately set at liberty and "suffered to go to their own homes." Grant, the Adjutant-General, acknowledges the stubborn defence offered by those who stood by their trust and their colours to the last, and who determined that the captors should have to pay dearly for their prize. To say, as Macaulay does, that "the fort was taken after a feeble resistance," is to ignore the latter stages of the struggle maintained chiefly by the civilians. The enemy's list of killed and wounded warrants the belief that the resistance on the whole was the reverse of feeble. Holwell, in his first report of the loss of Calcutta written to the Bombay Government in July from Murshidábád, to which the Nawab and most of his officers had returned, says, "Of the enemy we killed first and last, by their own confession, 5000 of their troops and 80 Jemadars and officers of consequence, exclusive of their wounded." *

* Within a month of his success at Calcutta the young Nawab wrote a letter to the Governor of Madras, which, though it anticipates matters a little, may be given here, as it will fittingly enable us to dispense with any further mention of

Governor Drake. The letter reads quaintly in its English dress, and suggests that the sender began, thus early, to have qualms, as to whether he had quite done the best thing for himself and his country in expelling the English from their settlement. "To the Principal or Head of all Merchants, Mr. Pigott, who has always in remembrance the favour of God,—It never entered into my heart or thoughts to deprive the English Company of trading in Bengal, but Mr. Roger Drake, your gomastah, is a very bad man, and gave harbour and protection to those that had accounts with the King. I did all that lay in my power to make him sensible that he was wrong, but he, without shame, persisted in his resolution. Those who come here for the service of the Company, why do they act in this manner? He, Mr. Roger Drake, being a very bad man and without shame, is punished accordingly, and is gone from the subaship. Mr. Watts, being a good man and without fault, we have despatched to you, who we esteem to be greatly in the Company's favour, for which reason we have wrote you the news of this bad man. Year the third of the King's reign and the first of the Shawant Moon, (Signed) SEIR RAJA DOWLETT" (*sic*). (From the Orme MSS. in the India Office. It is headed "a literal translation of a letter sent to Mr. George Pigott, Governor of Madras, by Surajud Dowlett, Nabob of Muxadabad, after the taking of Calcutta, July, 1756").

# CHAPTER II

## THE BLACK HOLE

### 2.—The Imprisonment

THE captors were in possession of the fort about six o'clock in the evening of the 20th of June; at that time of year in Calcutta there is still an hour or so of daylight remaining. For the due understanding of what occurred next, a little explanation as to the arrangement of certain rooms in a portion of the fort will be necessary.

The main entrance tô the fort was through a fortified gate in the eastern curtain wall. At each side of this gate extended a range of chambers adjoining the curtain; in other words, the whole length of space inside of, or backed by, the curtain was divided into sections of the needed dimensions by light cross walls; the roofs of the rooms so obtained was the parapeted terrace above. We are now concerned only with the chambers on the left of the gate, *i.e.* between the gate and the south-east bastion. The first room on the left of any one entering the fort by the east gate was called "the court of guard;" it was simply the room occupied by the soldiers who were on duty at the main gate. The next room on the left, and led into from the guardroom, was a larger one called the barracks. Further still to the left, beyond the barracks, and separated from it by a partition wall, was the last room, adapted for and used as a cell. Along the back of the barracks and of the last room ran a platform, raised from the ground, and wide enough for men to lie on. The chambers were about fifteen feet deep from east to west, where they ended in arches; at their west entrance, running along the ground between the arches, was a low so-called parapet wall. These arched entrances to the chambers opened into a verandah; the latter was probably about twelve feet deep from east to west, where it also ended in arches, which led into the open area and parade ground of the fort. Any one looking east from the body of the fort into the chambers thus described, must therefore see them through a double row of arches, between which longitudinally intervened a passage some twelve feet wide, sometimes referred to as a "piazza." The outer and the inner arches were practically opposite each other. Those who may not be familiar with the ordinary Indian verandah, with its arches and columns, will now, perhaps, understand what Holwell wishes to convey when he says the barracks "were open to the west by arches and a small parapet wall, corresponding to the arches of the verandah without." "Before the chamber," writes Orme, "was a verandah or open gallery of arched masonry, and intended to shelter the soldiers from the sun and rain; but being low, it almost totally obstructed the chambers behind from the light and air." In fact, the low arched masonry opening (outside) was found probably to be the most economical and durable expedient for keeping out the driving rain, to which, during the long south-west monsoon, chambers opening to the west were exposed.

Dark, dismal, and stifling as this accommodation for the well-behaved soldier was, it must have been paradise when compared with that provided for the refractory one, when, maddened to insubordination by arrack, mosquitoes, and heat, he was "run in" to the punishment cell at the further or southernmost end of the barracks. The dimensions of this prison room are roughly given by Orme as "not twenty feet square." Holwell calls it a cube of about eighteen feet; but Cooke particularises a little more, and says it was about eighteen feet long and fourteen feet wide. It was obtained by cutting off some feet from the length of the barracks by a dividing wall reaching to the roof; in this interposed wall was a door which opened inwards. The custody of any occupant, and intensified heat, gloom, and isolation, were secured by building up the two inner arches of it, which looked on the verandah, leaving in each of these a barred opening called by courtesy a window. It was bounded on the east and south by dead walls, on the north by the partition wall and door, and on the west by the bricked-up arches, the windows in which, strongly barred with iron, afforded the only inlets for light and air from the dark verandah. No wonder that in barrack parlance this chamber, a vile and stupid importation of western barbarity, went by the name, which through an awful calamity has become historic—the Black Hole.

The number of people who became prisoners, on the fort falling into the enemy's hands, was one hundred and forty-six; they consisted of those who had borne arms, and were of all sorts and conditions, black, brown, and white. Most accounts agree that there was only one woman amongst them. Many of this shattered remnant were wounded; all were in a state of exhaustion. When it was dark they were directed to collect, all, without distinction, under the arched verandah described, and to sit down quietly in one body. This they did, their backs being turned to the barracks and its prison, and their faces looking out west towards the parade ground of the fort, where "were drawn up about four or five hundred gun-men with lighted torches." Besides the guard immediately over them, "another was placed at the foot of the stairs at the south end of this verandah leading up to the S.E. bastion, to prevent any of us escaping that way." At this time the factory buildings were on fire to the right and left of the collected prisoners, and as the flames advanced towards them they apprehended that their death by suffocation and fire was designed. This fear was strengthened by their seeing, about half-past seven, some officers with torches going into the chambers at their right and at their backs, as though they intended to set those on fire also. A hasty determination was come to "of rushing on their guards, seizing their scymitars, and attacking the troops on the parade, rather than be thus tamely roasted alive." Before attempting this, Holwell went back to the torch-bearers, and found that they were merely looking for a place to secure the prisoners in for the night, "the last apartment they examined being the barracks of the court of guard behind us." One account (possibly more) has it that the confinement was an afterthought and was due to a few drunken Europeans, some say Dutch, assaulting the natives who complained to the Nawab. It was then thought prudent to lock up all the prisoners for the night (Hill).

What occurred immediately after this had better be given in Holwell's own words:—

"We observed part of the guard drawn up on the parade advance to us with the officers who had been viewing the rooms. They ordered us all to rise and go into the barracks to the left of the court of guard. In we went most readily, and were pleasing ourselves with the prospect of passing a comfortable night on the platform, little dreaming of the infernal apartment in reserve for us. For we were no sooner all within the barracks, than the guard advanced to the inner arches and parapet wall, and, with their muskets presented, ordered us to go into the room at the southernmost end of the barracks, commonly called the Black Hole prison; whilst others from the court of guard, with clubs and drawn scymitars, pressed upon those of us next to them. This stroke was so sudden, so unexpected, and the throng and pressure so great upon us next the door of the Black Hole prison, there was no resisting it, but, like one agitated wave impelling another, we were obliged to give way and enter; the rest followed like a torrent, few amongst us, the soldiers excepted, having the least idea of the dimensions or nature of a place we had never seen; for if we had, we should at all events have rushed upon the guard, and been, as the lesser evil, by our own choice cut to pieces."

The following incident occurred just before they were locked up:—

"Here I must detain you a little to do honour to the memory of a man to whom I had in many instances been a friend, and who on this occasion demonstrated his sensibility of it in a degree worthy of a much higher rank. His name was Leech, the Company's smith, as well as clerk of the parish; this man had made his escape when the Moors entered the fort, and returned just as it was dark to tell me he had provided a boat, and would ensure my escape if I would follow him through a passage few were acquainted with, and by which he had then entered. (This might easily have been accomplished, as the guard put over us took but very slight notice of us.) I thanked him in the best terms I was able, but told him it was a step I could not prevail on myself to take, as I should thereby very ill repay the attachment the gentlemen and the garrison had shown to me; and that I resolved to share their fate, be it what it would; but pressed him to secure his own escape without loss of time, to which he gallantly replied that then he was resolved to share mine and would not leave me." *

Holwell, having been amongst the first thrust into the prison, gained one of the windows (that nearest to the door), into which he took two of the youngest wounded officers, who soon died either from suffocation, or under the awful pressure occasioned by all trying to get near the opening. It was now about eight o'clock.

The night was the hottest and sultriest of the whole year, that immediately before the first fall of the monsoon rains; these did not begin till the night of the 21st, when it rained in torrents. When the heat and smoke proceeding from the buildings on fire all around are taken into account besides, no estimate coming up to reality can be formed of what the stifling temperature must have been.

It would serve no useful end to recall in any detail the sufferings of the victims in the Black Hole. Those curious about such matters can find in Holwell's narrative a minute account of the ten hours'

* This noble fellow's gratitude and fidelity cost him his life; he died in the Black Hole.

incarceration :—"Nothing in history or fiction approaches the horrors which were recounted by the few survivors of that night."

What Holwell's experience was may be summarised thus: On realising the trap they were in, he still acted as their chief, and besought them to try and keep calm, as the only chance of escape from death. At first they listened to his entreaty, and nothing was heard save the cries and groans wrung from the many wounded. He next promised money to an old Jemadar of the guard to try and get the door opened or the prisoners divided ; this could not be done. In a few minutes all were streaming with perspiration, giving rise to intolerable thirst. Many expedients were proposed as a possible means of getting more room, or some movement of air. All, save Holwell and two or three next him, got out of their clothes. An attempt was made to sit and rise alternately at word of command, but this proved fatal to the weaker captives who, so tightly were they wedged, had not strength to struggle to their feet again, and were trampled to death by their stronger neighbours. From time to time fruitless efforts were made to force the door. In about an hour all except those at the windows were becoming outrageous from thirst, and cried for water. The old native officer, through mistaken pity, had some brought in skins. Then came the wild raving and the agony of struggle; all control was lost. Holwell and the two wounded lads took in the water as fast as they could, in hats squeezed through the bars, but the little that reached the lips of those clutching at it merely intensified their terrible thirst. More agonising to Holwell even than his own thirst, was the feeling that he could not reach those at the back of the prison, who implored him with parched throats for one drop, "calling on me by the tender consideration of friendship and affection, and who knew they were really dear to me." So eagerly was the water raged for, that those who had posts of vantage at the other window, left them and the life-saving air, to fight to that at which it was; not till later was it brought to the further window also. This awful scene went on for two hours, to the devilish enjoyment of the guards without, who kept the supply of water going, and held up lanterns to the bars to enable them to see the frenzied struggles for it in the crowd within. Entreaty and abuse were alternately resorted to, for inducing or provoking the guards to shoot their tortured victims, who now longed for any death that would close their sufferings. By about half-past eleven the greater number of those still living, the occupants of the windows excepted, were delirious. It was at length realised by all that the insufficient water merely added fuel to the fire, and shrieks were raised for "air, air." To get to this as a last effort several who were behind leaped and scrambled on the backs and heads of those in the front rows, and grasping the bars so held their position while life or strength lasted. By degrees, as death mercifully released the greater number, the air admitted sufficed to keep alive those whose endurance, or place near the openings, was favourable for survival. Only twenty-three (not one-sixth of the whole) were taken out alive when the door was opened at dawn on the 21st of June. Holwell's personal remembrance of the night ceased at two a.m., as he then (for the second time) gave up the struggle of life, and sunk into what he believed and hoped was the shadow of death. Wonderfully touching it is, to read of the obedience and affection which this man inspired, and which the sufferers preserved for him in that den of horrors, while reason lasted, or until all distinctions were lost in the common agony. A few brief extracts may fittingly exemplify this, as well as the nobility which our poor countrymen manifested in the hour of extreme trial.

When the struggle for water at the window had been going on long, and Holwell's immediate companions were dead at his feet, he thought it useless to prolong his pain and misery while being slowly and surely pressed to death.

> "Determined now to give up everything, I called to them and begged, as the last instance of their regard, they would remove the pressure upon me and permit me to retire out of the window to die in quiet. They gave way, and with much difficulty I forced a passage into the centre where the throng was less by the many dead. I travelled over the dead to the further end of the platform. Death I expected as unavoidable, and only lamented its slow approach, though the moment I quitted the window my breathing grew short and painful. Here my poor friend, Mr. Edward Eyre (member of the Council), came staggering over the dead to me, and, with his usual coolness and good nature, asked me how I did ; but fell and expired before I had time to make a reply."

Soon, however, the deprivation of air caused torturing pains in the chest, and the instinct to seek it was so overpowering, that in a very few minutes he was pushing his way to the opposite (further) window, and, by "an effort of double the strength I ever before possessed," gained the second rank and grasped a bar.

> "In a few moments my pain, palpitation, and difficulty of breathing ceased, but my thirst continued intolerable. I called aloud for water for God's sake. I had been concluded dead, but as soon as they heard me amongst them, they had still the respect and tenderness for me to

cry out, 'give him water, give him water'; nor would one of them at the window attempt to touch it until I had drunk."

A vivid idea of what the throng and pressure were, even when the floor was strewn with dead, will be got from his statement that while at his second post he was thus burdened, viz. a heavy man was on his back and head, a Dutch sergeant on his left shoulder, and a Topaz (native soldier) bearing on his right. He could only have supported these from being himself propped and sustained by pressure all round.

"In the rank close behind me was an officer of one of the ships whose name was Carey, who had behaved with much bravery during the siege (his wife, a fine woman, though country born, would not quit him, but accompanied him into the prison, and was one who survived). This poor wretch had been long raving for water and air; I told him I was determined to give up life, and recommended his gaining my station. On my quitting he made a fruitless attempt to get my place, but the Dutch sergeant who sat on my shoulder supplanted him. Poor Carey expressed his thankfulness, and said he would give up life, too; but it was with the utmost labour we forced our way from the window (several in the inner ranks appearing to me dead standing). He laid himself down to die, and his death, I believe, was very sudden, for he was a short, full, sanguine man. His strength was great, and I imagine had he not retired with me I should never have been able to have forced my way. I found a stupor coming on apace, and laid myself down by that gallant old man the Revd. Mr. Jervas Bellamy, who lay dead with his son, the lieutenant, hand in hand, near the southernmost wall of the prison." *

. . . . . . .

"When the day broke and the gentlemen found that no entreaties could prevail to get the door opened, it occurred to one of them (I think to Mr. Secretary Cooke) to make search for me in hopes I might have influence enough to gain a release from the scene of misery. Accordingly Messrs. Lushington and Walcot undertook the search, and, by my shirt, discovered me under the dead upon the platform. They took me from thence and, imagining I had some signs of life, brought me towards the window I had first possession of; but as life was equally dear to every man, and the stench arising from the dead bodies was grown intolerable,

* When the City Imperial Volunteers returned from the war in South Africa and were given a public welcome in London (October, 1900), much disgraceful rowdyism went on in the streets through which the procession passed. Amongst those injured by the violence of the mob and taken to St. Bartholomew's Hospital, as reported in the daily papers (30 Oct.), I noticed the name "Gervase Bellamy, aged 60, suffering from injuries to the abdomen." The Christian name suggests his descent from, or kinship with, the clergyman who died in the Black Hole.

no one would give up his station in or near the window. So they were obliged to carry me back again. But soon after, Captain Mills (now captain of the Company's yacht), who was in possession of a seat in the window, had the humanity to offer to resign it. I was again brought by the same gentlemen, and placed in the window."

One of those who searched for him had good reason to remember the garment, the identification of which saved the life of its wearer. Holwell, it has been said already, was one of the very few who did not strip. He went into the cell without coat or waistcoat (a covetous "Moor" had relieved him of the latter while sitting in the verandah), but he retained the rest of his clothing.

"Whilst I was at the second window, I was observed by one of my miserable companions on the right of me in the expedient of allaying my thirst by sucking my shirt-sleeve. He took the hint, and robbed me from time to time of a considerable part of my store; though, after I detected him, I had ever the address to begin on that sleeve first, when I thought my reservoirs were sufficiently replenished, and our mouths and noses often met in the contest. This plunderer, I found afterwards, was a worthy young gentleman in the service, Mr. Lushington, one of the few who escaped from death, and since paid me the compliment of assuring me he believed he owed his life to the many comfortable draughts he had from my sleeve."

The "young gentleman" referred to here was Henry Lushington, who was then but eighteen years of age.

When Holwell was taken to the window he slowly revived, and just then, he says, "the Suba, who had received an account of the havoc death had made, sent to inquire if the chief survived"; on the Suba being informed that he was alive, "an order came immediately for our release, it being then near six o'clock." This and another passage in Holwell's narrative would go to show that the young Nawab spent the night at the fort, but the early hour at which he proceeded to business does not bear out Macaulay's amplification that he "slept off his debauch." It is strange that Mr. Secretary Cooke says distinctly, "between six and seven (*i.e.* p.m.) Siraj úd Dawla left the fort, the charge whereof was given to Manick Chund as governor,"

However this may be, it is, I think, beyond dispute that the Nawab had nothing to do with the measures adopted for securing those who fell into his power. He very probably gave orders that they should be confined for the night; this order was delegated, as usual in the East, to several gradations of ignorant subordinates. When it came to be ascertained that such a thing as a military prison existed in the fort, the question as to the best place of confinement must have appeared solved; the guard were careless as to the dimensions—indeed, they probably were as ignorant of what these really were, as the throng were whom they were driving in. Callous brutality and fear of responsibility on the part of the bandits who had charge over the prison for the night must account for the door not being opened again, when the insufficiency of space was so horribly demonstrated. But where the Nawab deserves execration is, that he showed no concern whatever, on learning the next morning the terrible sufferings of his prisoners during the previous night. His narrow mind was occupied in appraising the plunder that had fallen into his clutches, and giving vent to his vexation and disappointment at its being so much below the exaggerated amount that his greedy imagination had expected. He sent for Holwell, who was lying exhausted on the grass outside the verandah, and when supported to his presence unable to speak, he directed some one to give him water and to place "a large folio volume" for him to sit on, and then questioned him about money. Next, according to the civilian's manuscript, "he issued orders for every European * to quit the place

* Four of the survivors were handed over to Meer Muddun, one of the generals, under the conviction that there was buried treasure, whose discovery might be extorted from them. These were Messrs. Holwell, Court, Burdett, and Ensign Walcot. Meer Muddun sent them to Murshidábád. This journey lasted over a fortnight: the prisoners were conveyed in a leaky boat, with no shelter over them by day or night. They lay on bamboos, and were often half immersed in water. Their food was rice and the water alongside, "which you know," writes Holwell, "is neither very clear nor very palatable in the rains, but there was enough of it without scrambling." Their bodies were covered with large painful boils, as was the case with all those who survived the Black Hole; in this condition they were heavily ironed. Holwell, though in extreme pain himself, was obliged to tend and feed his still more helpless companions. On arrival at Murshidábád, they were led in chains through the crowded city. On their way up, and afterwards, they received every mark of active sympathy and kindness that they were allowed to avail themselves of, from the gentlemen of the Dutch and French factories. It is only fair to say that of the extreme brutality of the treatment suffered by those four gentlemen on their agonising journey to his capital, the Nawab knew nothing till afterwards; and when he himself reached Hughli, where he released Watts and Collett, on his return from Calcutta, he inquired for Holwell and his fellow prisoners, and expressed anger at their having been sent to Murshidábád. Soon after his arrival there, when the prisoners managed to attract his notice as he passed by in his palankin, he seems to have but just recalled their existence, and he at once ordered them their liberty, directing at the same time that, when their irons were cut off, they were to be conducted wherever they chose to go, and that care was to be taken that they suffered no trouble or insult. And even when pressure had been put on him by his courtiers to detain Holwell, and hand him over to Manick Chund to

before sunset under the penalty of cutting off their nose and ears," and "orders were given out by beat of tom-tom that the town should not any longer be called Calcutta, but Allinagore." Most of the survivors made their way to the ships. The greatest kindness was shown by the Dutch at Chinsura and Fulta to all the British refugees down the river. Stores and comforts of all kinds were liberally sent to them by Adrian Bisdam, the Dutch Governor. Nevertheless, disease ran riot amongst them, and so pitiable was the condition they were reduced to before the cool dry season came, that many must have wished they had died on their walls at Calcutta.

The fact of a woman surviving the Black Hole is a most extraordinary one; her husband, poor Carey, probably exerted his strength as long as he could in helping her to withstand the pressure and struggling near the window where she must have been, and it may perhaps be to this that her escape was mainly due.

I am much indebted to Mrs. Henry Beveridge, formerly in Calcutta, for having let me see the book to which she refers in the following letter written by her some few years ago, to the Calcutta *Englishman*, which was copied into some London papers, and transcribed thence by me into the first edition of this book as a record of historical interest, though I had not then the pleasure of knowing whom the writer's initials stood for. The gentleman who chronicles his visit to Mrs. Carey was, I think, an attorney in the Supreme Court, as one of that name was practising in Calcutta from 1780, and died there early in this century.

"I am able to quote the following interesting notes from a flyleaf at the end of our copy of Holwell's 'Tracts.' They are presumably in the handwriting of the former owners of the book:—

"Note 1.—August 13th, 1799.—This forenoon, between the hours of ten and eleven o'clock, visited by appointment, in company with Mr. Charles Child, at her house in Calcutta, situate in an angle

be "squeezed" on the plea that he *must* be able to procure money, the young Nawab replied, "It may be; if he has anything left, let him keep it; his sufferings have been great; he shall have his liberty." Siraj úd Dowla was brought up in a bad school for the development of generosity, or any other laudable quality. The pampered and ungrateful favourite of the old Nawab never, probably, had a wish thwarted, or never had a mentor who would venture to tell him the difference between right and wrong. His short life is said to have been fruitful in vice and crime. Very probably it was. But writers (amongst recent ones let me notably except Colonel Malleson) have dwelt on these, and have kept out of sight the few good acts which might fairly be shown, not in exculpation, but in mitigation of damages. So true is it that "men's evil manners live in brass; their virtues we write in water."

at the head of the Portuguese Church Street, and east of the church, Mrs. Carey, the last survivor of those unfortunate persons who were imprisoned in the Black Hole at Calcutta, on the capture of that place in 1756 by Suraj ud Dowla. This lady, now fifty-eight (58) years of age, as she herself told me, is of a size rather above the common stature, and very well proportioned; of a fair Mesticia colour, with correct regular features, which give evident marks of beauty which must once have attracted admiration. She confirmed all which Mr. Holwell has said on the subject of the Black Hole in the foregoing letter, and added that, besides her husband, her mother, Mrs. Eleanor Weston (her name by second marriage), and her sister, aged about ten years, had also perished therein, and that other women, the wives of soldiers, and children, had shared a like fate there.

"(Signed) THOMAS BOILEAU.

"Note 2.—Mrs. Carey died Saturday, March 28, 1801.

"Note 3.—(Written by another hand.)—Mrs. Carey was made the subject of somevery pleasing Latin verses by Dr. Bishop, Head Master of Merchant Taylor's (where Clive was educated). See 'Neniæ Poeticæ' (p. 230), A.D. 1766:—

"'Quum jussu Eoi, Calcotticâ in arce, tyranni
Captiva heu! subiit tristia fata manus,
Et passim furibunda siti, moribunda calore,
Corpora robustis succubuere viris,
Fœmina languori, horrorique superfuit, omnes,
Tam varie miseras fœmina passa vices.
Scilicet ante pedes, spirantem extrema maritum,
Viderat illa, pari membra datura neci;
Nec mora; prosiliunt oculis quasi fontibus undæ.
Et subita humectant ora gementis aquâ;
Hinc vita, unde dolor; nescit sitiendo perire,
Cui sic dat lacrymas quas bibat ipsa fides.'

"(See H. B. Wilson's 'History of Merchant Taylor's School,' p. 1098)."

The above may be thus translated:—"When, by the command of an Eastern tyrant, a captive band suffered, alas! a cruel fate in the Fort in Calcutta, and on all sides strong men fell, maddened by thirst and dying with heat, a woman outlived the weakness and the horror, a woman endured all the turns of such varied misery. She saw her husband breathe his last at her feet, and was about to yield herself to a like death, when lo! the waters leap from her eyes as from springs, and bedew her lips with sudden moisture. Grief gives her life. She

cannot die of thirst, to whom fidelity itself thus gives tears for drink."
—A. S. B.

If this survivor's statement is given correctly by her interviewer, there can be no doubt that others of her own sex were amongst those shut up. Mrs. Carey could not have been mistaken as to her mother and sister. Holwell certainly does not say in so many words that only one woman went into the prison, but his phrase, "one hundred and forty-six wretches exhausted by continual fatigue and action," seems to allude to men only. Cooke *does* say that there was only one woman; still, the probability seems to me to be in favour of the evidence attributed to Mrs. Carey. It is confirmed, moreover, by Captain Mills, who, writing immediately after the events, gives the number shut up as "144 men, women, and children, of whom upwards of 120 were miserably smothered." But, strange to say, Mills omits Mrs. Carey's name from his list of survivors. The retreat by the boats was such a hurried and disorganised one that it is very unlikely that every woman and child but one were got off. Holwell and Cooke might easily have been mistaken, considering that the thrusting into the prison occurred in the dark, and that in the morning they were very unfit for any observation, even were time or opportunity for it afforded, which was not the case, as the dead were immediately thrown promiscuously into the ditch of the unfinished ravelin and covered with earth.

It is suggestive of uncertainty as to the number that went into the Black Hole that Holwell, in his letter to the Bombay Government from Murshidábád on the day after his being set at liberty (July 17), gives it at "about one hundred and sixty-five or one hundred and seventy," and says that "about sixteen" came out. So that it is evident that the numbers accepted by historians were only adopted by Holwell for his narrative, after he had had an opportunity of comparing notes with other survivors.

The relegation to a harem, which tradition assigns as the fate of Mrs. Carey, rests on no substantial basis. Holwell says vaguely, "the rest who survived the fatal night gained their liberty, except Mrs. Carey, who was too young and handsome." No poor creature emerging from the ordeal that she did, could then look either young or handsome, and the probabilities would be that she tottered on along with the rest towards Cooly Bazar, where the ships were still in sight. Orme (who accepts the belief of her being the only woman) consigns her to Meer Jaffar; while Macaulay gives her to the Prince at Murshidábád (Siraj úd Dowla), a discrepancy suggestive of the untrustworthy evidence on which the story is founded, at all events in its ordinarily accepted significance. Asiaticus, writing within thirty years of the event, gives the story thus :—"An English lady who saw her husband perish at her feet survived that miserable catastrophe, and the tyrant was so captivated with her beauty that he promoted her to the honour of his bed, and she remained seven years in his seraglio, when she was released at the request of Governor Vansittart, and is now alive at Calcutta." It is unfortunate for this author's gossip that "the tyrant" himself only survived the catastrophe for one year.*

Within recent years I had the pleasure of making the acquaintance in India of a near connection by marriage of a direct lineal descendant of Mrs. Carey, who was in a position to give much interesting information about her, as he had often intimately conversed with one who had been brought up by her. My informant, a European gentleman of the highest respectability and intelligence (since dead), gave me to understand that the few direct descendants of Mrs. Carey now in India, would be unwilling, as many retiring people are, to have any reference made to them by name in print, so that in deference to this feeling I am not able to mention a good deal of what the gentleman I allude to told me in conversations which I had with him. I may, however, authoritatively say this much: Mrs. Carey was not carried off by "the Moors" † at all. On the contrary, she remained in or near Calcutta, and before very long married again, her second husband being a military officer of field rank. By this marriage she had two sons and, I believe, one daughter. During her later life she reverted to the name of her first husband. She was

* M. Jean Law, Chief of the French factory at Cassimbuzar, seems to have written a memoir about 1763, and, speaking of the survivors of the Black Hole, writes, "The woman was amongst the latter, also M. Holwell, and four or five officers and Company's servants. The woman was placed in the Nawab's harem. She was, I believe, the wife of one of the Ganges pilots" (Hill). Law's account is not in accordance with that of Holwell and others, and seems quite untrustworthy gossip.

† The Mahommedan historian relates a circumstance about which, however, all other contemporaries are silent, viz. that soon after Drake's flight some women of the English fell into the hands of Mirza-Emir-Beg, an officer attached to one of the Nawab's generals. This man, he alleges, behaved most chivalrously, giving them decent shelter, and conducting them secretly the same night by boat to Drake's vessel, on board which he put them, refusing all reward. "Such," adds the historian, "ought to be the actions of a gentleman. As to those men who style themselves Mussulmans, and have laid their hands upon the properties and honour of other people, their actions are no better than so many suggestions of the demon of concupiscence, and so many allusions of the devil, their prototype and master." (Siyar-ul-Mutakherin—Monsieur Raymond's translation.)

buried in the Moorgchatta (Catholic Cathedral) churchyard, Calcutta; the site of the grave was afterwards, I think, absorbed by some enlargement of a portion of the church. There is in existence still a well-executed miniature of her painted on the inside of the lid of a trinket box; it certainly testifies to the truth of what Holwell records about her personal appearance, for the artist has shown her in her comely youth.

While these pages are going through the press I have received, from a correspondent in Calcutta, a copy of *The Englishman*, in which appears this letter referring to the death and burial of Mrs. Carey—

"Readers of 'Echoes from Old Calcutta' will remember that, according to Dr. Busteed's informant, Mrs. Carey, the country-born wife of Peter Carey, Mariner, was 'buried in the Murgihatta (Catholic Cathedral) churchyard' (1801). In confirmation of this statement it may interest some of your readers to know that both the announcement of her death and the entry of her burial have now been traced.

"The following, from the *Calcutta Gazette* of April 2, 1801, is not included in Seton-Karr's 'Selections':—'Deaths. On Saturday last (March 28) Mrs. Carey.' In the Cathedral burial-register the entry, which is in Portuguese, runs as follows:—'28 Marco de 1801. Faliceo Maria Carry (*sic*) foy sep. no adro de Igreja com accompanhamto: de 1 Padre.' The foregoing may be freely translated thus:—'28th March, 1801. Died Mary Carey; was buried in the churchyard, with the accompaniment of one priest.' This does not give her age at the time of her death. It was 60 years, for she was but 16 when she entered the Black Hole. There is no inscription over her grave.

"I am greatly indebted to the courtesy of the Cathedral authorities who kindly permitted me to search their registers, favouring me with a copy of the entry. They even indicated the place where Mrs. Carey is believed to have been buried, to Mr. Dunbar, the energetic Secretary to the new Calcutta Historical Society, and myself. About the exact spot there may be some difference of opinion, but in any case a tablet should be placed in the adjacent wall.

"Calcutta, May 2, 1907."

This letter is signed "FitzWalter."

Of Secretary Cooke I have been able only to trace that he became member of Council, and afterwards in England gave evidence before the Parliamentary Committee of 1772. His name is not mentioned in the despatch from the Directors (November, 1757), in which two years' service are allowed to his fellow-civilians, Lushington and Burdett, "for their sufferings and good behaviour." Holwell complains that he also was not a participator in this indulgence. Richard Court, who held the rank of Senior Merchant in the Service, was nominated to Council for "behaving very well," but he can scarcely have enjoyed this promotion, as he was drowned in Ganges in May, 1758. His house was bought by Government "for holding of Council."

Lushington's short life was an eventful one. He eluded death at Calcutta merely to meet it at "a massacre surpassing in atrocity that of the Black Hole," for only seven years later he was among the first of Sumroo's slaughtered victims at Patna. His knowledge of Persian got him attached to Clive as interpreter and secretary; after the battle of Plassey he played a subordinate part in an incident destined to become historical—the forging of Admiral Watson's name to the fictitious treaty devised for the deception of that badly treated man, Omichund. By Clive's order it was Lushington's hand that signed the name which the Admiral himself declined to write. A monument and bust were erected to young Lushington's memory in Eastbourne church by his father, the vicar of the parish. In the lengthy inscription on the monument it was told how bravely he confronted his murderers. "While the sepoys were performing their savage office on Mr. Ellis, fired with a generous indignation at the distress of his friend,* he (Lushington) dashed upon his assassins unarmed, and, seizing one of their scymitars, killed three of them and wounded two others, until at length oppressed by numbers he greatly fell," etc. His parents were afterwards buried in the same church by their own desire.

> "In humble hope that they by *his* renown,
> To distant ages will be handed down."

William Lindsay, a civilian who was in the siege, and being disabled was allowed to go on board the ships and remain, said that Cooke and Lushington simply walked out of the fort after their release, got on board a boat and went to Fulta.

But length of days was given to (at least) three of those who came out of this great tribulation. James Mills, the humane ship captain who gave up his place at the window to Holwell, wrote a few rough notes of his doings immediately on being released. From these it appears that he, though covered with boils, walked with extreme difficulty, accompanied by his brother sailors Dickson and Moran, and one other whose name is illegible. They got to "Surman's" by evening, only to find that the ships had just sailed. The natives

* Ellis was at this time crippled, having lost a leg while fighting under Clive outside Calcutta in February, 1757. He had been through the siege and escaped when the fort was taken.

MRS. MILLS.

FROM A MEZZOTINT BY J. R. SMITH OF A PORTRAIT BY G. ENGLEHEART.

*See p.* 45.

whom they came across were kindly disposed to them. They then toiled back to Govindpur, and stayed three days in a hut, protected and fed by natives. The Nawab then passed an order that the English might return to their Calcutta houses. "The wounded man"—*i.e.* the third companion—being dead, they with several others collected in Mr. Knox's house, where they were fed by Omichund. The Nawab left about June 25, and on the 30th a drunken European sergeant killed a moorman, whereon the Governor (Manick Chund) ordered all Europeans out. Then Mills and his friends sought the hospitality of the French at Chandarnagar, and remained there till August, when they took a boat and joined the refugees at Fulta. When on leave in England a few years later, he married a bewitching widow who loved him for the dangers he had passed. The lady who became Mrs. Mills, and returned with him to India, was a celebrity on the English stage, much admired both as Miss Birchell and as Mrs. Vincent for her melodious voice and amiable, simple disposition. She was the "Polly Peachum" in the "Beggar's Opera," thus praised by Churchill in the "Rosciad" (ed. 1765)—

"Lo! Vincent comes, with simple grace array'd;
She laughs at paltry arts and scorns parade;
Nature through her is by reflection shown,
Whilst Gay once more owns Polly for his own."

It is recorded that for this part she was instructed by Kitty Clive. In Geneste's account of the English Stage the cast of the "Beggar's Opera" at Drury Lane in September, 1760, shows Yates as "Peachum," Mrs. Clive as "Lucy," Mrs. Vincent as "Polly," who was put forward as a rival to Miss Brent at Covent Garden. She must not be confounded with another Mrs. Vincent who was acting "Celia" in "As You Like It," when Pegg Woffington was seized with paralysis while speaking the Epilogue as "Rosalind" (May, 1757).

Mrs. Mills died in June, 1802, at Hampstead, London,* aged 67. Her husband long outlived her, retaining his mental faculties well

* I happened to come across her epitaph in a collection (Cansick's) of those rescued from old St. Pancras Churchyard. It begins:

"And art thou then in awful silence here,
Whose voice so oft has charmed the public ear,
Who with thy simple notes could strike the heart
Beyond the utmost skill of laboured art," etc., etc.

The epitaph is "in memory of Mrs. Isabella Mills, wife of James Mills, Esq., of this parish."

preserved till shortly before his death. His pecuniary resources must have fallen short in advanced life, as the East India Company then generously assisted him with an annuity, on some friends of his making, without his knowledge, a representation in his favour to his old employers. He died at Camden Town, London, in September, 1811, aged 89. But though Captain Mills survived the Black Hole for over fifty years, he was not the last survivor. *The Gentleman's Magazine*, in noticing his death, says that his fellow-prisoner Burdett, "late of Eling, now a resident at (Totton, near) Southampton, is still in existence." For how long further this patriarch continued to defy the Old Man with the hour-glass and the sickle, my searchings have failed to discover. John Burdett, a young gentleman volunteer, as Holwell calls him in one report, had seen the British driven to their ships in Bengal, and as a captive of its Nawab had been led in fetters through its capital; yet he lived into the Regency of Queen Victoria's uncle. What a creation of yesterday does our Indian Empire seem, when we reflect that there are persons still alive in England who may have seen, or conversed with, survivors of the terrible Black Hole! *

Mr. Hill says John Burdett (or Bourdett) was one of Clive's opponents in Council in 1765, and was dismissed and sent home. A despatch from Fort William, September 30, 1765, signed by Clive and four others, alludes to the (recent) "resignation" of Messrs. Johnstone and Burdett.

Holwell, too, lived to a fine old age in England, where he died in 1798, aged 87. I cannot, however, take leave of this remarkable man with a bare record of his death. Though this sketch already far exceeds its proposed limit, still I must not grudge something in conclusion regarding the career and the memory of one to whom Indian history owes so much; of a man whom Orme (writing just after the loss of Calcutta) calls "the gallant defender of the fort, and the asserter of the reputation of the nation." As suggestive of the trust which Holwell's capacity inspired, it may be mentioned that when in November, 1759, Clive denuded Calcutta of fighting men to strengthen his Lieutenants Forde and Knox, he assigned the charge of Fort William to Holwell with the Militia, about 250 Europeans, and some Portuguese.

* In the *London Standard*, January 21, 1889, there appeared a letter from one who said that he heard from an elderly relative that he had been living in Hastings about 1840, and that there was then "living in the neighbourhood a man of about one hundred years old who had been one of those thrust into the Black Hole of Calcutta!"

John Zephaniah Holwell * was the son of a London merchant, and the grandson of John Holwell, well known as a learned mathematician and astronomer, who wrote towards the close of the seventeenth century, who was Royal astronomer and surveyor of Crown lands, and mathematical preceptor to the Duke of Monmouth, and who was deputed to lay down a plan of New York. The father and grandfather of this gentleman gave their lives in support of the Stuart cause, which involved the loss to their descendants of an ample patrimony in Devonshire which had been in the family for generations. J. Z. Holwell was born in Dublin, and baptised at St. Werburgh's Parish Church; the certificate, in which he is described as the son of Zephaniah and Sarah Holwell, is dated September 23, 1711. The officiating clergyman was the Rev. Edward Synge. At an early age he was sent to a school at Richmond (in Surrey), where he greatly distinguished himself in classics. His father having determined to bring him up to mercantile pursuits, he was removed to an academy in Holland, where he acquired a knowledge of French and Dutch, and of bookkeeping. He was next settled as a clerk in the counting-house of a banker and "husband of ships" at Rotterdam, a friend of his father's, who agreed to take him into partnership after a stipulated time. After some time here, his health broke down under hard work, and he went for a trip to Ireland, and he returned from that country with a fixed aversion to the life of a merchant. The profession of medicine was next adopted for him by his father, who had him articled to a surgeon in Southwark, on whose death he was placed under the care and instruction of Mr. Andrew Cooper, the senior surgeon of Guy's Hospital. On his quitting the hospital, he was engaged as surgeon's mate on board an Indiaman, which arrived in Calcutta in 1732. From Bengal he made two or three voyages in the Company's ships as surgeon. While so engaged, he studied Arabic, which after a prolonged stay at Mocha and Jeddah he spoke fluently. After he had received an appointment on shore, he went twice in medical charge of "the Patna party," about four hundred fighting men, which annually left Calcutta with the Company's trade for the Patna Factory. On these occasions he bore a rank which seems to

* I have laid under contribution for this notice some letters which Major W. A. Holwell (who died at Toronto in October, 1890) was kind enough to write to me, giving items relating to his great-grandfather's domestic history. To this gentleman there descended many family papers and relics of great historical interest. Some of these were, he told me, destroyed, to his never-ceasing regret, by a great fire in Quebec in 1881; on a date, too, of ominous significance in his family history, viz. June 20.

have been revived of late years, viz. that of "surgeon-major." After having served for a short time as surgeon to the Factory at Dakha, he returned to Calcutta at the end of 1736, where he was elected an alderman in the Mayor's Court. In or about 1740 he was appointed assistant surgeon to the Hospital, and having been brought on the fixed medical establishment under orders from home,* he soon became principal surgeon to the Presidency. He tells us himself that for two years successively he was elected mayor.

In 1748 ill-health obliged him to return to England; during the voyage he drew up a plan he had formed for correcting abuses in the Zemindar's Court at Calcutta, and proposed it to the Court of Directors, who, adopting it, appointing him perpetual zemindar (a post carrying with it fiscal and magisterial duties) and twelfth in Council. He accepted this office, though when he arrived in England he had no idea of returning to India. The reason of his going back was one that has been a powerful motive in the same direction with his countrymen ever since, viz. he "found that money does not go as far in England as he fondly imagined."

On his arrival in Calcutta as a covenanted civilian in 1751, he began his system of reform, which eventually gave such satisfaction at home, that his annual salary was raised from two to six thousand rupees; and a prohibition against his rising in Council, which was at first stipulated, was conditionally removed. By the time that the war broke out he had risen to the position of seventh in Council. On his release from Murshidábád he made his way to the ships at Fulta.

Being shattered in health he was sent home with despatches in February, 1757, in the *Syren*,† a sloop of only eighty tons, and had a perilous, but rather quick voyage of five months, during which he wrote his narrative of the Black Hole. In consideration of his distinguished and meritorious services, he was nominated by a large majority in the Court of Directors to return to Bengal as successor to Clive, but this he seems to have modestly declined in favour of Mr. Manningham; he was then named second in Council. But a fresh election of Directors having occurred before he started, the

* "In obedience to your commands of March, 1742, we appointed Mr. John Zephaniah Holwell one of your surgeons in this establishment in the room of Dr. W. Lindsay, who departed this life of a fever."—(Extract from Bengal despatch to Court of Directors.)

† The *Syren* took home despatches announcing the recovery of Calcutta. She reached Plymouth on July 19, 1757. It was only in the previous month that the news of the loss of Calcutta had come to England.

J. Z. HOLWELL.

FROM A PORTRAIT NOW IN POSSESSION OF GOVERNMENT OF INDIA.

*See p.* 48.

above arrangements were reversed by a majority of the new-comers, who were not friendly to him, and he was relegated to the position of ninth in Council. However, on his arrival at Calcutta, he found himself fourth, owing to the departure of seniors; and in 1759 he became second. By virtue of this position he succeeded Clive as temporary Governor on the latter's proceeding to Europe in February, 1760. He held the governorship but for a few months.*

The Court of Directors of those days was broken up into factions. Holwell did not pull well with them, nor did Clive, and acrimonious letters passed between the Bengal and Home Governments. In a well-known despatch from Fort William, December, 1759, the Governor (Clive) and Council wrote—

"Permit us to say that the diction of your letter is most unworthy (of) yourselves and us, in whatever relation considered, either as master to servants or gentlemen to gentlemen. Mere inadvertences and casual neglects have been treated in such language and sentiments, as nothing but the most glaring and premeditated frauds could warrant. . . . Faithful to little purpose if the breath of scandal has power to blow away in one hour the merits of many years' service."

The original of this despatch in Holwell's writing was at one time in the possession of his great grandson. Manningham, Frankland, and Mackett were amongst the members of Council whose names appear signed to it in the Blue Book. John Cooke, Richard Becher and C. S. Playdell (Holwell's son-in-law) also signed it. Both the latter returned to Calcutta again—R. Becher seems to have been restored to the service. His return to "fill a vacancy in the Board of Trade" is chronicled in the local newspaper, October, 1781, where it is announced that "the circle of beauty has been greatly added to by the arrival of Mrs. Becher" (second wife), who in the following year had to put on his tomb one of the saddest of the many sad epitaphs to be seen in South Park Street Cemetery. Playdell returned in 1771 to collect what was due to him, and to try for employment in the gift of local patronage. He too brought a young wife with him, and died in Calcutta. We shall meet with his name again.

The answer to this, written a year afterwards, was,—

"We do positively order and direct that immediately upon the

* Amongst the Orme MSS. there is a gossipy letter written to Drake from Calcutta, in which a personal trait of Holwell is incidently mentioned, viz.—"As soon as he heard of Mr. Vansittart's appointment, he seemed greatly shocked, but with his usual gaiety, and taking a pinch of snuff, said he was glad of it, for the fatigue of the chair was too much for him to be able to hold it three months longer."

receipt of this letter, all those persons still remaining in the Company's service who signed the said letter of the December 29, viz. Messrs. J. Holwell, etc., etc., be dismissed from the Company's service; and you are to take care that they be not permitted on any consideration to continue in India, but they are to be sent to England by the first ships that return home the same season you receive this letter."

This was what the oft expressed commendation and gratitude all came to. One is glad to think, however, that long before this despatch reached India,—indeed, before it was penned,—Holwell had the self-respect to write to Mr. Vansittart, the Governor, for permission to resign the service, pointing out that—

"The many unmerited, and consequently unjust marks of resentment which I have lately received from the present Court of Directors, will not suffer me longer to hold a service, in the course of which my steady and unwearied zeal for the honour and interest of the Company might have expected a more equitable return."

The permission was given, and concern expressed at the loss of so valuable a colleague. He retired in September, 1760.

On returning to England, Governor Holwell, as he was generally known, devoted much of his leisure to literary pursuits, writing on historical, philosophical, and social science subjects. He was always ready to enter the lists where matters relating to India were in controversy. His best-known works are his "Narrative" and "Interesting Historical events relative to the Province of Bengal," etc. He was a deep student of the religion and customs of the Hindoos, and published a work on their "Mythology, Cosmogony, Fasts, and Festivities"; many valuable and curious materials towards which, in the shape of ancient manuscripts which he had collected, were lost at the capture of Calcutta. Like many another Englishman, Holwell was "not without honour, save in his own country." It was left to an illustrious foreigner to appreciate and eulogise what he had done for Oriental literature. Voltaire pays him this ungrudging tribute:—

"C'est ce meme Holwell qui avait appris non seulement la langue des brames modernes, mais encore celle des anciens brachmanes. C'est lui qui a écrit depuis, des memoires si precieux sur l'Inde, et qui a traduit des morceaux sublimes des premiers livres écrits dans la langue sacrée. . . . Nous saisissons avec reconnaissance cette occasion de rendre ce que nous devons à un homme, qui n'a voyagé que pour s'instruire. Il nous a devoilé ce qui etait caché depuis tant de siècles. Nous exhortons quiconque veut s'instruire comme lui, à lire attentivement les anciennes fables alligoriques, sources primitives de toutes les fables qui ont depuis tenu lieu de verités en Perse, en Chaldée, en Egypte, en Gréce, et chez les plus petites et les plus miserables hordes, comme chez le plus grandes et les plus florissantes nations."

"These things," continues Voltaire, "are more worthy of the study of the wise man than the quarrels of some dealers about muslin and dyed stuffs, of which we shall be obliged in spite of ourselves to say a word in the course of this work." *

Holwell died at Pinner, near Harrow, on November 5, 1798.†

In noticing his death the *Gentleman's Magazine* says that he was one "in whom brilliancy of talents, benignity of spirit, social vivacity,

* Fragmens historiques sur l'Inde.

† Though Holwell attained the great age of (at least) 87, he was far outstripped in longevity by his mother, who lived to be 102, and even then did not die of old age, but was accidentally burned in her bed on January 21, 1763, having on the same evening, according to the family tradition, "danced a minuet with her grandson on the occasion of the anniversary of his birthday." Holwell was twice married; three of his children survived him, viz. Lt.-Colonel James Holwell, of Southborough, Kent; Mrs. Birch, wife of W. Birch, Esq.; and Mrs. Swinney, widow of Rev. Sidney Swinney, D.D. It would appear from the copy of his will amongst the family papers that he died wealthy. Still it is stated on Mr. Weston's tombstone, in Calcutta, "he manifested a grateful mind by cherishing in his old age his former employer and benefactor, the late Governor Holwell" —*quod mirum.* Possibly after devising his money, as shown in the copy of the will which his descendants have, he may have dropped it into one of the many pits always yawning for simple and benevolent old Indians. At all events if what is alleged on the Calcutta tombstone be not a mistake, Holwell had not cast his bread on the waters in vain. Charles Weston had served his time as surgeon's apprentice to Holwell, and had once accompanied him to Europe. On Holwell's getting into the Civil Service, Weston also changed his pursuits. "What could I expect," said he, "from following the medical profession, when I saw a regular-bred surgeon and so clever a man as Mr. Holwell charge no more than 50 rupees for three months' attendance and medicine." Weston served as a militiaman at the defence of Calcutta, and escaped by having been sent on the river to look after his patron's baggage boats the day before the fort was taken. He took refuge in Chinsurah. He was often heard to say that Siraj-úd-Dawla's forbearance to Holwell, and the latter's release from fetters, were due to the intercession of the Nawab's wives instigated by the natives of Calcutta, who loved Holwell. When Holwell left India he gave Weston 2000 rupees, and lent him 5000 more. With this capital he made a large fortune, chiefly by safe agency business, and became well known for his charities during his lifetime. In 1791 Weston won as the chief prize in a lottery, the "Tiretta Bazaar," which was to fall to the drawer of the last ticket; it was valued at 196,000 sicca rupees, and its rents gave a large monthly return. These Weston applied to his own use. The rest of his fortune was invested in Government security, and the whole interest of this he monthly distributed to the poor of all nations, classes, and religions, without distinction. The lac of rupees which he left at his death to the poor was the smallest of his charities. He died on Christmas Day, 1809, aged 78, and is buried in South Park Street Cemetery.

and suavity of manners were so eminently united as to render him the most amiable of men." But the best proof of the high estimation in which he was held by his fellow-men has been already shown in the general call for him to take the lead, when matters looked most critical and alarming; and in the unselfish veneration and gentleness evinced for him by his panting fellow-captives in the moment of their own great extremity. Let us now see what "respect and tenderness," to use his own simple words, succeeding generations of Englishmen in Calcutta have shown for his memory.

Holwell erected at his own expense a monument to the memory of those who died in the Black Hole; he had it placed over their rude grave, and had inscribed on a stone tablet on its front, the names of forty-eight of our countrymen, an act so natural, so kindly, and so deserving of all sympathy, that one would have thought that every Englishman in Calcutta would have regarded the monument's preservation as a personal trust. Yet it was allowed to go to ruin, and its demolition was so effectually completed, that no knowledge survives of what became even of its inscription marble. The generation sojourning in Calcutta in 1821 substituted no memorial for that which was suffered to disappear in their time. Since then, for 66 years (so written in 1888) Calcutta has been allowed to be without any commemorative structure, or sculptured tablet of any kind sacred to those few "faithful found among the faithless," whose memory their fellow-sufferer, who best knew their deservings, wished and tried to honour. This is all the more strange when it is borne in mind that for more than half this long period, the province of Bengal, including the metropolis of India, has been under the continuous rule of successive members of the Covenanted Civil Service of India, the order to which Holwell himself belonged, and in behalf of which he spoke up to the Court of Directors in these words: "From the militia, about 65, chiefly Europeans, entered as volunteers in the battalion (*most of them your own covenanted servants*) in whose just praise I can hardly say enough. They sustained every hardship of duty greatly beyond the military themselves; and though their bravery may have been equalled, I am sure it has not been exceeded by any set of men whatsoever."

Several of those over whose remains Holwell's Monument stood, were Bengal civilians, from members of Council down to junior writers. One of the youngest of them all was Robert Byng, and it is a coincidence worth recalling that in the very month of June, 1756, in which an order went from England to Gibraltar, to arrest and send home Admiral John Byng to his trial and execution at

Portsmouth, his young nephew gave up his life in defending Calcutta. Every section of an Anglo-Indian community as it exists to-day was represented amongst the gallant few whose names Holwell wrote on his monument, in memory of that Sunday night in June, just 132 years ago;* nor did he omit to enumerate the lowlier victims, though he could not name them. There was the clergyman, the civilian, the merchant, the sailor, and the soldier. To the reproach of Calcutta, their neglected dust has for so long been silently crying out (*dum tacet, clamat*) against the carelessness and thoughtless indifference which have consigned it to oblivion and disrespect. "Doubtless," as the Indian historian says, when advocating the claims of other neglected men,† "doubtless, they are the representatives of a gigantic disaster, not of a glorious victory. But the heroism of failure is often greater than the heroism of success."

I have allowed the preceding page to stand as the simplest means of making plain the contrast between the present and the condition there deplored. Happily Calcutta need no longer blush for the neglect of, and ingratitude to the memories of, those who fought and suffered and died for her in 1756. This is due to the large-hearted sympathy of Lord Curzon, who turned away her reproach by re-erecting in marble the all but forgotten Holwell monument, and inscribing on it the carefully gathered names of those who perished during the short siege. This, with much other work, having for its object the recalling and preserving the memory of Old Calcutta, was undertaken as a labour of love, and completed under his own personal direction and supervision. Surely Calcutta will ever "remember with advantages" this graceful and kindly tribute to the days of its struggle and suffering.

The motives which actuated the Viceroy in his wise and gentle policy regarding the relics and memorials of the past, and the sacred and impartial duty of the present towards them, are briefly set out in the public address which he gave in December, 1902,‡ when presenting from himself to the citizens of Calcutta a beautiful marble replica of the old monument. The present writer may be permitted to add that it is a source of pride and gratification to him to recall

* Now (1907) 151 years.

† *I.e.* Kaye, when speaking of the then unrewarded pluck and good service of the survivors of the Cawnpore Massacre (1857); Colonel Delafosse was afterwards decorated; but the only other officer (my old friend Mowbray Thomson) received no similar recognition. The two escaped privates died early.

‡ Since published in the volume of Collected Speeches delivered in India (London, 1906).

that on the same occasion, Lord Curzon had the kindness and generosity to associate this book with the inception of his valuable memorial work.*

## SUPPLEMENT

The old Fort of Calcutta was nearly all taken down about 1818 to make way for the present Custom-house, built on a great portion of its site. Its demolition must have been a work of great labour, owing to the solidity and closeness of its masonry, in the cement of which, tradition says, molasses and chopped hemp had been mixed. Lord Valentia, writing of his visit to Calcutta in 1803, says: "The Black Hole is now part of a go-down or warehouse; it was filled with goods, and I could not see it. The little fort is now used as a custom-house." A resident of Calcutta also, who visited the cell itself in 1812, has left a very brief record of the appearance it presented.

It is likely that the disappearance of the fort led by degrees to the losing memory of the site of the tragedy of Sunday, June 20, 1756, a result easily intelligible in such a changing and fleeting community as that of (European) Calcutta; indeed, even before the levelling of the first Fort William, erroneous ideas seem to have been locally current, not only as to the scene, but as to the circumstances of the Black Hole catastrophe.

Much that had come to be only conjectural regarding the topography of the old fort, was either confirmed or disproved in 1883, when Mr. R. Roskell Bayne, C.E., of the East Indian Railway, read a paper on the subject before the Asiatic Society, Calcutta. This gentleman, in preparing for the foundation of the new East Indian Railway Office in Clive Street, came down on what he saw must be the northern curtain and bastions of the levelled old fort, and he at once took careful notes of what he then and subsequently uncovered, with the view of being able from these fixed data, and by the aid of old outline plans with scales and measurements, to plot out and verify the recorded descriptions of the fort to be found in the evidence of contemporary writers.

"The measurements taken by me," writes Mr. Bayne, "comprised the whole of the north-east bastion, a portion of the north-west sufficient to determine its junction with the curtains, all

* See Appendix 2—Inscriptions on the new Monument, etc.

the north curtain with about 150 feet of each of the east and west curtains. All these dimensions I have accurately taken, and with these and Orme's figures I have laid out the east, the west, and also the south sides." Mr. Bayne found Orme's figures to be exact on the north face. Particular attention was directed to estimating what should be the position of the Black Hole, a question which had been recently under some little public discussion. Hitherto all that was known with certainty regarding it was, that it was at the southernmost end of the chambers used as barracks, which were backed by the east curtain, and that it was approximately of certain dimensions. As there was no opportunity then of further exposing or tracing the eastern curtain, its southernmost limit was determined by scaling from Orme's map, and accepting his figures as to the length of the east face, viz. 210 yards. The result of this plotting out was to disclose the curious fact that the computed site of the Black Hole chamber had remained, until then, almost quite unbuilt over, and was simply buried under a passage or roadway in the General Post Office enclosure, not many feet from the place which conjecture and, it is believed, tradition had assigned to it. Mr. Bayne's work in the precincts of the old fort began in 1880; he gave a full and interesting account afterwards to the Asiatic Society (accompanied with plans and sketches) of his findings and investigations and conclusions, etc. The result of his final excavation, made with a view to confirming or otherwise his opinion as to the site of the Black Hole, he never added, I believe, to the record of his previous work.

A much better chance for inquiring into the topography of the Fort presented itself ten years later (1891–92), when all the buildings between the General Post Office and the Custom House were taken down preparatory to laying the foundations of new public offices, etc. etc. The extensive excavations necessitated by this exposed some of the most interesting remains of Old Fort William, which promised to throw light on points where it was much desired. This very favourable opportunity was fortunately seized on by Professor C. R. Wilson, of the Education Department, who went to work with unflagging industry, pursuing systematically the timely excavations available, also making and exploring others. He was thus enabled to identify several sites of importance. That of the Black Hole came in, of course, for much careful consideration and investigation at Mr. Wilson's hands, so that after patiently encountering some baffling difficulties here and there which he has recorded, he felt himself able to determine it confidently. The valuable results of this gentleman's labours also were contributed in great detail to the *Asiatic Society Journal.*

Later on, when the useful and most desirable work, already mentioned, in connection with Old Calcutta and the perpetuating of some of its memories, was taken in hand by the Viceroy, the site of the prison cell of world-wide notoriety got his special attention. The securing of its identification and commemoration was arranged for by His Excellency in 1901. It was paved with black polished marble, and protected by a neat and appropriate surrounding railing; an unsightly obstruction was removed so that the memorial might be visible to all Calcutta residents and visitors, who may read on a marble tablet fixed above it this inscription:—

THE MARBLE PAVEMENT BELOW THIS SPOT
WAS PLACED HERE
BY
LORD CURZON, VICEROY AND GOVERNOR-GENERAL OF INDIA,
IN 1901
TO MARK THE SITE OF THE PRISON IN OLD FORT WILLIAM
KNOWN AS THE BLACK HOLE
IN WHICH 146 BRITISH INHABITANTS OF CALCUTTA
WERE CONFINED ON THE NIGHT OF THE 20th JUNE, 1756,
AND FROM WHICH ONLY 23 CAME OUT ALIVE.

Thus the spot which has "a thousand claims to reverence" from all our people was at length paid it, one hundred and forty-five years after the tragedy of which it was the scene. Its memorial and the restored "Holwell Monument" are a very prized possession to the Calcutta of to-day, a sacred trust to be guarded and handed down to the Calcutta of the future.

And so with other recovered sites in the old fort—such as bastions, curtains, gates, arcade, etc.;* the positions they held have been marked, or indicated on the adjacent ground by brass lines let into stone pavement; their identity is explained by several inscribed marble tablets fixed in various places to the walls of the modern adjoining buildings now occupying the site. One is thus enabled to realize the outlines and general structural features of Old Fort William, thanks to the provident thoroughness of Lord Curzon when dealing with a site which is incomparably the most interesting historical relic in India in connection with the rise of British rule.

* All that is still to be seen of the old fortress above ground are two lines of twelve arches, portion of the shapely piazza that was within the south curtain.

# CHAPTER III

## PHILIP FRANCIS AND HIS TIMES

### 1.—FRANCIS AS JUNIUS

IT is a very striking coincidence, that there should have been living in Calcutta at the same time, the two men whose lives have since been the subject of more extraordinary investigation than has been directed towards any statesmen of modern or probably ancient times.

The whole public life of Hastings, we are told, "was subjected to a scrutiny unparalleled in the history of mankind." Perhaps the only life of which something similar can justly be said is that of his colleague and bitter opponent, Philip Francis. It is true that only a portion of Francis's early career has come in for this exhaustive scrutiny, but that portion has been retrospectively ransacked, not only in its public, but in its private details as well. It has occupied the attention of the ablest writers and politicians, and taxed the ingenuity of the subtlest controversialists and critics; their object being to trace his identity with that of the invisible political censor, whose writings to the public press under various pseudonyms, but especially that of Junius, created so profound a sensation in England in the early years of George the Third.

Happily, it is now almost universally conceded, that the calm of solution has settled on the once fiercely disputed question of the authorship of the "Letters of Junius."

The claims of three dozen or more candidates to the honour, which were advocated from time to time, were hopelessly abandoned one after another. The case made out for the claim raised for Philip Francis, however, stands forth only the more convincingly the ampler the investigation, the wider the range and nature of the scrutiny applied to it; till at length a vast array of independent arguments and circumstances have been brought together, with ever-accumulating force, which all tend to furnish the same conclusion, to lead to the one ultimate inference. To this accumulation of circumstantial evidence has been added the material evidence afforded by the professional examination of the handwriting of Junius, minutely compared with that of Francis, and of some other candidates, by the late M. Chabot, the expert (published by the Hon. Mr. Twistleton some years ago), which annihilates all other claimants, and leaves no room for doubt that the hand which wrote the "Letters of Junius" was the hand of Philip Francis. The marvellous fact thus becomes demonstrated, that the caustic writer, the audacious State satirist, whose accurate information and envenomed shafts perplexed and wounded even the highest, proved to be a clerk in the War Office, whose craft and subtlety in guarding the secret of his newspaper writings were such, that he was almost wholly unsuspected by his contemporaries, and that his name was scarcely mentioned in connection with the famous Letters till forty years after the appearance of the last one.

In a former edition much more was said in connection with the identity of Francis with the dreaded Junius which is now omitted. The subject, though a fascinating one to many, and very much so to myself, cannot be held to be of general interest, and had better be left to the burrower amongst the curiosities of literary and political history. "Never," said Disraeli (Lord Beaconsfield) in paternally advising a youthful Tory, "Never in Society ask who wrote the 'Letters of Junius,' or on any account inquire on which side of the Banquetting Hall Charles 1st was beheaded, or if you do you will be voted a bore, and that is—well, something dreadful." Let me nevertheless quote in support of the opinion of those most familiar with the Junian controversy, what an acute reasoner and one who knew Francis well, thought on the question. Lord Chancellor Erskine wrote as follows two years before Taylor published in 1813 his "Junius identified with a distinguished living character." "DEAR LAUDERDALE,—I have read the book regarding Junius's letters, so far at least as was necessary to prove that they were all written by Francis. Indeed, I have no difficulty in saying that, though he has been for many years a very kind acquaintance, I should be obliged, if the publication were the capital offence, and I were upon his jury, to find him guilty without going out of the box. The utmost I could do would be to recommend him to mercy, and that only upon the Divine principle of compassion, and not from any doubt of the fact. No man but Francis, when all the inferior and collateral writings are considered, could have gone on with such unvaried, unrelenting perseverance to carry the point he had in view.—July 13th, 1811."

But the crowning proof of the identity of Junius with Philip Francis was supplied by the last surviving grandson, the late Mr. H. R. Francis, in his book "Junius Revealed" (1894). A short but wonderful piece of work (82 pages only) for an octogenarian to have produced, marked as it is by vigorous, incisive English, and by the logical reasoning of a well-trained, judicial mind, which had thoroughly mastered its subject. The author elaborates briefly and supplements the evidence of Francis having control of the unmistakable Junian hand, in which he wrote a note to a young lady at Bath (Miss Giles), at Christmas, 1770, accompanied by some complimentary verses copied by his friend and companion Tilghman. These verses Francis presented to his second wife, at her request, as a specimen of his youthful versifying, and in his own handwriting, which Tilghman had copied. It remained but to identify the paper. This, too, was done, as explained in the following letter from Mr. Francis, dated November, 1897 :—

"Soon after the publication of my little book, 'Junius Revealed,' an interesting meeting between descendants of 'Belinda' and of her admirer took place at my house, at which Mr. Giles Puller, of the Treasury, directly descended from the fair Belinda, and several members of my own family were present, with the valuable support of Mr. George Inglis, the well-known expert in handwriting. Mr. Puller brought with him the verses to Belinda in Tilghman's handwriting, with the complimentary note in the feigned hand of Junius, which furnished the envelope in which they were enclosed to Miss Giles. I produced the Belinda verses in my grandsire's own handwriting, of which a copy was made by Tilghman, and by him forwarded to Miss Giles. This original manuscript was found by me in the possession of Lady Francis, to whom my grandfather gave it in his old age, as a specimen of his youthful muse. It was found on comparison that all these three remarkable writings were on portions of the same paper—identical in size, texture, and colour, and bearing the same watermark."

All the other proofs of identity, great though the sum of them is, are small compared to this one, brought forward by the grandson of the great mysterious writer who was, no doubt, proud of the polished work which he could not openly avow.

Professor Goldwin Smith, in reviewing "Junius Revealed," wrote : "England has hitherto had her mystery in Junius, but she will enjoy it no more, for there can be no longer any shadow of doubt that the Letters were written by Sir Philip Francis." I confess I cannot appreciate, or understand, the type of mind which, after a study of the facts, is not driven to the same conclusion. Let me here mention with respect another recent source of information on the Junian controversy. I refer to the admirable statement of it up-to-date by Mr. C. F. Keary, in his introduction to "the Francis Papers," 1901. It is a most moderate summing up by a clear-headed restrained writer who could probably have said much more. To judge from their silence it seems to have satisfied the few hitherto unconvinced.

The interest accordingly concentrated on the pre-Indian career of this remarkable man has been so absorbing, that the years passed in India have been comparatively overlooked. For the student of Indian history, however, he should have an interest quite independent of his European celebrity.

If (to give but a single instance) to be in advance of one's time is an indication of greatness, Sir Philip Francis must be ranked as a great Indian statesman. It is claimed for him in his biography that, within a short time after his arrival in Calcutta, he sketched out in a letter to the Prime Minister of England a plan for the government of India, which was not appreciated for many years, and was only adopted in its main features nearly a century later. It is also beyond doubt that he sent home a land-revenue scheme for the "permanent settlement" of Bengal, which, though carried out by Lord Cornwallis and associated with his name, was first officially planned and advocated by Francis, as claimed by him in the House of Commons in 1806. Yet, unfortunately, this is the period of his career of which his biographers have least to say.

When Francis, at the age of thirty-three, was nominated by Lord North for a seat in the newly-formed council to the Governor-General of India, his good fortune puzzled not only his acquaintances, but his most intimate friends. It was only in later years, when his name came to be associated with Junius, that some people (notably Lord Campbell, C.J.) fancied they had solved the puzzle, that the appointment was hush-money to ensure the silence of Junius, and to transport him to the unhealthy climate of Bengal.

Such a device would at least have had the merit of cheapness from the minister's point of view, as somebody else (India) had to find the money—a financial arrangement not quite obsolete even to-day. His grandson says that he finds it difficult to disconnect the Indian appointment from his success as Junius. This was the opinion of his son and of the daughter who most resembled Sir

Philip in intelligence, *i.e.* Mrs. Johnson. He adds, "But who were the parties to this arrangement besides Junius himself? A close conspiracy of silence was the natural policy of all concerned, and if it is difficult to learn what each of them did, it may well be deemed hopeless to ascertain what each of them knew. All the parties to the arrangement, as far as they are known to us, or indicated by strong probabilities, had the gravest reasons for keeping it dark. Secrecy being thus the common interest and object of all parties, we are less surprised at finding how little can be known about the manner of Francis's promotion or the persons who arranged it." Mr. Francis names four or five persons who most probably knew the secret, and he gives very plausible reasons for his selection. Lord North, who sanctioned and carried out the arrangement, was certainly one. But the evidence on the point has hitherto been so unsatisfying that Mr. Merivale, the biographer of Francis, can only see in his appointment a "provoking mystery—an extraordinary promotion from the position of a young and obscure retired clerk in the War Office," thus re-echoing an objection of the Court of Directors when his nomination by Parliament was brought to them.

It is unfair thus to sum up his qualification for a high office by a reference to the comparatively humble one recently held. Having left St. Paul's School (London) with the reputation of being its cleverest scholar, he had been from the age of eighteen undergoing severe and varied official training under several diplomatists and statesmen. While thus engaged in the public service at home and abroad, he had been a deep student of political science, and finally occupied the responsible and confidential position of First Clerk in the War Office for nine years. Many a man without a fourth of such promising qualification has since been appointed to the Supreme Council in India, and, it may be safely predicted, will be in the future, without his nomination being considered a mystery.

It will be seen later on how small the prize seemed to Francis on realisation, and how little it satisfied his tastes or his legitimate ambition.

Though Philip Francis may in his early life have schemed as a political adventurer, and may have been disparagingly sneered at as "a mere War Office clerk" when selected for high preferment, it must not be forgotten that he justified the selection by the exhibition of a virtue which enabled him to look down on all his predecessors and most of his contemporaries, and which, standing supreme as a qualification for exalted position and influence in India, earned this florid, but truthful tribute to his memory from an ex-Lord Chancellor, Brougham :—

"He had been an Indian satrap in the most corrupt times, and retired from the barbaric land, the land of pearls and gold, with hands so clean and a fortune so moderate, that in the fiercest storms of faction no man ever for an instant dreamt of questioning the absolute purity of his administration."

It is also necessary for a further elucidation of the "mystery" to bear in mind who his fellow-councillors from England were to be—two military officers of distinguished professional service, General Clavering and Colonel Monson, with powerful connections, to whose share these Indian loaves and fishes fell, mainly to satisfy Court and Parliamentary influence. The presumption was never sanguinely entertained that, either by ability or previous training, were they well fitted for the duties of the high and novel position assigned to them ; and this was amply verified in the days, few and evil, allotted to them in Calcutta. Some make-weight therefore was essential; and where could this have more suitably been found than in the hard-working, well-trained official of such varied experience as the ex-First Clerk in the War Office, who was then in the enjoyment of the full ripeness of his cultivated talents? Francis might be relied on for the brains and the work ; his colleagues for the more stately and less onerous duties of the position. That Francis himself complacently fell in with this apportioning of their respective functions is tolerably clear. In one of his earliest letters from India, written to the brother of Edmund Burke, he says, " When I see this glorious Empire, which I was sent to save and govern, tottering upon the verge of ruin," etc.

To Lord Clive he wrote, " Look sharp after the fate of your jaghire . . . I will not scruple to say to you what I have never suggested to any other person, that if I am recalled, or if an arrangement should take place under which I cannot exert myself with effect, you may as well take leave of Bengal for ever."

To another correspondent in England he confided this opinion of himself: "The situation of the country demands instant arrangements for its recovery, and by all that is just I see only one which can save it." When we mark this portentous egotism we are not surprised to learn that his nickname in Calcutta was " King Francis the First."

Any modern Indian administrators who may perhaps be dreaming of fame, or even flattering themselves that their memory will outlive their generation, may derive some prospective consolation from the reflection, that this brilliantly-gifted man sojourned for six years of the prime of his life in Calcutta, waging with venomous zeal a constant war against unscrupulous government, and endeavouring to maintain, what he believed to be, the cause of right against wrong, and yet that he has left behind him scarcely the shadow of a name. Were Philip Francis to be mentioned in ordinary conversation in Calcutta to-day, his name would be unknown to many as that of an Indian statesman, or would be dimly recognised in connection with something relating rather to social than official life. It would be associated probably with some passages in one of Macaulay's essays, and the question would be asked, if he were not the man who was angry because he did not land under royal honours from Fort William; or the remark would be hazarded that he was the profligate who ran away with somebody's wife, and then fought a duel about her with the Governor-General under a big tree on the maidan, or under two trees "so well known as the trees of destruction," as the story sometimes goes.

Let me, therefore, as my object is chiefly to gossip about old times, make a starting-point of the vaguely remembered circumstances just alluded to, and endeavour to get rid of some of the inaccuracies with which time has embellished them. We may as well see in the first place what are the actual facts in connection with the landing at Calcutta of Francis and his fellow-councillors, and what was the etiquette observed as placed on official record.

Before recalling the incidents of the duel between the Governor-General and the senior member of the Council, a still more memorable duel which followed hard upon the landing of the new arrivals must be detailed.

It may then be of interest to turn our attention more to the social doings of Francis and his contemporaries; to take a look at their everyday life, and to see what some of them thought of an Indian career. A survey, too, may be taken at the press and other institutions of Calcutta a hundred years ago.

# CHAPTER IV

## 2.—The Arrival of Francis in Calcutta

THERE is no anecdote more frequently repeated regarding Calcutta and its passed-away celebrities, than the one which tells of the chagrin and disappointment, said to have been evinced by the newly arrived members of Council, because they were not received with a "royal salute" on their landing at Chandpal Ghat on October 19, 1774. The story, too, is paraded whenever it is desired to quote an apt illustration of mighty events springing from little causes. Thus Macaulay says:—

> "The members of Council expected a salute of twenty-one guns from the batteries of Fort William. Hastings allowed them only seventeen. They landed in ill-humour. The first civilities were exchanged with cold reserve. On the morrow commenced that long quarrel which, after distracting British India, was renewed in England, and in which all the most eminent statesmen and orators of the age took active part on one or the other side."

Two other well-known writers on India (Marshman and Kay) allude to the circumstance as though Philip Francis were the head and front of the vexation at the breach of etiquette, and therefore alone responsible for the subsequent embroilment; and tradition as it exists to-day adopts this view, and Francis (possibly because he alone is of historical importance) is gibbeted by common consent when there is no evidence whatever to show that he was more to blame than his fellow-passengers in the new Council.

A few extracts from a musty blue-book, to be seen presently, will perhaps give a juster idea on the merits of this question than seems to be generally held. Whatever the new members of Council may have said in society about the want of ceremony attending their landing, or whatever society may have said for them (which is just as likely), it is certain that they made no official complaint or representation about the slight, and there seems no ground whatever for attributing early action in the matter to Francis more than to any one else. That some reflections on the inferred or apparent want of courtesy were freely indulged in socially is more than probable, and the fact of Hastings taking notice of them before they had assumed a tangible official form was a blunder, as it laid him open to the retort of "qui s'excuse s'accuse," which the opposition in their rejoinder were not slow to avail themselves of.

Before referring to official documents for information on this subject, we may see what can be gathered from contemporary private sources. It may be premised that the four Judges, appointed by the New Regulating Act for India, started from England at the same time (in the spring of 1774) as the new members of Council. The former sailed in the *Anson*, the latter with their party in the *Ashburnham*. Francis was accompanied by his brother-in-law, Alexander Mackrabie. Between the two a warm friendship of old standing existed. Amongst the many sins attributed to Francis, closeness in money matters was one; but his treatment of his brother-in-law, a young man of about his own age, showed the utmost kindness and generosity. A few years before Francis resigned his War Office appointment, Mackrabie had left England for Philadelphia, where he had obtained the managing clerkship in some British mercantile house, but the place did not seem to suit him, and Francis, who was not over well off himself, wrote to him: "We have long since agreed how easy it is to find fault, but whoever fails you, be always assured that my heart will ever be open; in short, if you cannot determine on any plan where you are, you have nothing to do but to return to my house and stay in it until something else can be thought of." A month later he wrote again: "I need not repeat what I hope you are convinced of, that though all fail, my house is your sure retreat, so be not unhappy about a disappointment more or less." When the Indian appointment came to Francis he provided for his brother-in-law with the post of private secretary. Mackrabie repaid all this kindness with an affection amounting to devotion.

On the voyage, and in India afterwards, this brother-in-law kept a diary, extracts from which find a place in the Memoirs of Francis, who preserved it among his own papers.*

* I am indebted to the courtesy of Miss Francis, the great-granddaughter of Sir Philip, for letting me see Mackrabie's journal and Francis's own diary (Calcutta) in original; they are beautifully legible. These, like all the documents, volumes

Several of the entries relating to the voyage are spiced with humour, and must have afforded much amusement to the relatives and friends at home, for whose general information the journal would seem to have been written. One of his ship reflections is, "It is not in the power of fair weather to make a long voyage pleasant. We are in hysterics at the bare apprehension of a calm: people who pray for long life have it in their power to live as long as they think proper, they need only go to sea to turn seconds into centuries."

The following observations of the secretary very probably reflect the feelings of his chief and of the other councillors, and give the earliest indication of the jealousy as to official authority and position, between them and the judges, which was before long to bear abundant fruit. While the ships anchored for ten days in Funchal Road, the diary notes:—

"We observe that the commission with the great seal constantly attends the Judges. The Chief Justice has stolen a march on the gentlemen of the Council in point of precedence, a mark of distinction which takes from the dignity of the latter without doing any credit, in my opinion, to the other honourable gentlemen."

At Madras the pestilent judges are in the way again, but the secretary seems to have been comforted.

"Supreme Court always take the lead of us. They sail better than we do, and their charter gives them precedence.* Their worships landed two days before us. What marks of honour and respect they may have been distinguished by, I know not; but nothing could exceed those shown to our party. Scarce had we cast anchor when a letter and message arrived from the Governor inviting us on shore."

They landed while "the sun flamed in the zenith," and were honoured with much military parade and firing of salutes, etc. "We were received like fallen angels into a little hell of our own." Mr. Wynch, the Governor, and the small social world showed them

of correspondence, etc., etc., which are numerous and in good preservation, would well repay further gleaning from. It is a pity that the papers left behind by so prominent a public character have not, like those of Warren Hastings, become the property of the nation.

* Francis thus remarks on this precedence: "The Chief Justice of the Supreme Court of Judicature, who is not a member of the Council, immediately takes place of all those persons (except the Governor) to whom the regency of the country is committed; and the same pre-eminence is secured to the present puisne judges over those who shall succeed us in Council. The natural conclusion in the mind of the native must be that the judicial is the first power, and the judges the first persons in the State."

profuse hospitality, having ready for them on the very first evening a concert, assembly, and supper, where the newly arrived ladies, "by exciting different passions in the two sexes, did all the mischief they could desire." All the attention showered on them during the days passed at Madras must have whetted their expectancy as to the much greater ceremonial awaiting them at the seat of their future Government, Fort William. On October 12 their vessels arrived at Higili, where they were met by well-provided budgerows for the voyage to Calcutta; six days later they anchored three miles below the city.

Next morning, Wednesday, October 19, at ten o'clock, the plan of landing being settled, the three new Councillors, attended by members of their staff, were conveyed on the Commodore's barge to the *Swallow* sloop, where they were joined by the Supreme Court. "Exactly at noon, a comfortable season for establishing the etiquette of precedency, the whole party are disposed in three boats, and both courts safely landed at the capital of their jurisdiction. The procession to the Governor's house beggars all description; the heat, the confusion, not an attempt at regularity. No guards, no person to receive or to show the way, no state. But surely Mr. Hastings might have put on a ruffled shirt."

"The ceremony of introduction gone through, the audience broke up, and we changed the scene though not the climate. At two the whole party, increased by this time to one hundred and fifty, met again at the Governor's house to dine. In such a company little order can be expected. We eat and drank and endeavoured at Society, but even wine in ale glasses cannot remove suspicion. At four everybody retired to sleep or meditation. At six rose to tea, dress, and go visiting. We welcome all our fair companions to Calcutta."

Chandpal Ghât, as Calcutta tradition has handed down, was presumably the scene of the historic landing, as it has been that of the arrival and departure of many official personages since. All the details recorded by the diarist suggest a procession on foot to the Governor's house, not far away, *i.e.* on the Esplanade. That at Madras must have been on foot also through the soldier-lined streets, as Mackrabie says "the rabble trampled us." Hastings refers to this official residence (see Gleig's Memoirs, vol. iii. p. 240, for one instance) as "*his* house on the Esplanade." Here occurred the ceremony of introduction, and here, it may be inferred, were entertained the very large number at dinner. The matter possesses some little interest as it is sometimes said that Belvedere was the scene of the official reception, but the accommodation there would have been insufficient; nor would distant Alipore in any way fit in with the facts recorded above.

Francis himself, writing to a cousin in America a few days afterwards, says simply: "We landed here October 19, upon which occasion the acclamations were as loud and the congratulations as sincere as we expected." Not a word about the insufficiency of the guns in all the private writings.

Only once does Francis refer to the reception at the landing, and then no doubt with displeasure, but he seems rather to be reflecting General Clavering's opinion than his own. The allusion occurs in a private memorandum reviewing public transactions since their arrival.

"The mean and dishonourable reception we met with at our landing gave Clavering the second shock."

Francis's biographer did not attach much importance to his connection with the suggested cause of the terrible six years' war that followed, for he says in a footnote: "The common story that the three new members of the Conncil took offence at being greeted with a salute of nineteen guns only, instead of a royal salute, finds no confirmation that I can discover in the Francis papers." The biographer had probably never seen the despatches from which the following extracts are made.

Extracted from Governor-General's letter to the Court of Directors, dated December 3, 1774:—

"I am ashamed to call the public attention to a subject so exceedingly frivolous as that which I am now compelled to enter upon in my own further justification. They accuse me of having failed in paying them the honours due to them. Their accusation against me on this head is confined to the following particulars: Only seventeen guns were fired on their arrival; troops were not drawn out to receive them; they were met at my own house, and not at the Council-house; there was a delay from Friday till Monday, three days, in the order for issuing the new commissions in Public Orders; and, lastly, the proclamation of the new Government was not made with sufficient parade.

"To these five articles I must reply separately—

"*1st.*—The orders given for salutes were, that seventeen guns should be fired for the Chief Justice and the judges; the like number for General Clavering; fifteen, as ordered by the Court of Directors, for Sir Edward Hughes; and thirteen for each of the members of the Board, if they come separately; if they should all arrive at the same time, the highest salute directed to be fired for the whole; and this was agreeable to the practice which hitherto had been observed—I had no other rule to go by. They did arrive together, and were accordingly saluted with seventeen guns.

"*2nd.*—If they had landed at the fort, the garrison should have been under arms to receive them. It appeared to me unmilitary to draw troops out of garrison to compliment their landing at a distance from it.

"*3rd.*—If I could have defined their expectations of being received, not at my house, but at the Council-house, or if I could have imagined that this was considered a matter of any sort of significance, I certainly should have answered their wishes; but the circumstance neither occurred to myself, nor was it suggested to any other person. I thought then, and truly I think still, that the deputing the senior member of the Board to wait on them in the river, and attend them to town, and the assembling of all the other gentlemen of the old Council at my house for their reception, were ample marks of attention and respect to them.

"*4th.*—The delay of three days in issuing the commissions was occasioned by a request of mine, dictated by my feelings on first perusing them. I had before received private intimation of their purport, but my information was not complete, and I was hurt at the extraordinary reduction of my authority which was to take place, and the apparent inconsistency of investing the second person in the administration with greater ostensible powers than the first. While I was agitated by these considerations, I requested this time to determine within myself whether I would accept of this new Government, or conclude the period of my services to the Company with the close of the late administration, before they were published; and when my request was acquiesced in, I did not expect to have found it stated as an exceptionable part of my conduct.

"*5th.*—With respect to the want of parade in proclaiming the new Government, the members of the Board have themselves been to blame for any deficiency in this particular. They formed a majority, and might have ordered what pomp and ostentation they pleased, but it is extraordinary that they should agree to measures and then throw the blame of them upon me. I am averse to parade myself, and have never used it.* I proposed a written advertisement as the usual mode of proclamation here; they thought a military attendance necessary, which was accordingly ordered to attend upon the Sheriff, whom I thought the proper officer to publish a Civil Government. But it may be necessary to remark that if there was any deficiency of respect in my conduct on the above occasion, it could not be personally intended against them, since the new Government was its object, and I myself

* Surely this avowal of Hastings' own sentiment about "parade" should dispose of the love of pomp, "the more than regal splendour which he sometimes displayed," which are attributed to him to this day.

had the highest interest in the honours paid to it, being the head of the Government.

"Upon the whole, I must remark that I paid them higher honours than had ever been paid to persons of their rank in this country; as high even as had been paid to Mr. Vansittart and Lord Clive, when they came in the first station as Governors, men whose names will ever stand foremost in the memoirs of the people of this country, and who merited as much from their employers as any who have filled, or are likely to fill, that station. I wrote letters severally to the three gentlemen at Madras, bespeaking their confidence as a measure necessary to the safety of the Company. The Board sent their senior member down the river to meet them; and, as a mark of personal respect from me, one of the gentlemen of my staff attended them; the whole Council assembled at my house to receive them on their landing. What more could I do without derogating from my own rank? But they seem to have considered themselves as the Government, and to have required the honours done to it entire to be paid to their own persons, forgetting that they were only a part, and that it was from the head they expected such concessions."

In a minute from the new Councillors, sent home about the same time, occur these observations in reference to the above. We would not be far wrong in assigning the authorship to Francis.

"21. Some inattention to the ceremonies on the part of the Governor in the mode of our reception is supposed to have had a share in creating or confirming in us those hostile resolutions which we are accused of having formed against him. The first objection we make to all that the Governor has said on this article is, that it is a defence without a charge. We leave it to our superiors to judge what sort of consciousness is implied in so hasty an anticipation of charges not advanced against him.

"22. Our second objection would be to his statement of the facts, if we thought it worthy of ourselves or consistent with the prosecution of business of a far heavier nature, to descend to such a detail. As for the rest, we hope it will be thought too much to be believed, on no better evidence than Mr. Hastings' bare affirmation, that we are capable of engaging in measures which, if they are such as he describes them, may subvert an empire, merely to revenge an omission of ceremony, for which the slightest concession from Mr. Hastings ought to have been so sufficient an excuse, that we could not have declined accepting it without betraying an injudicious appearance of hostility to him and disgracing ourselves.

"23. If the charges of a personal failure in the respects due to Mr. Hastings had had any foundation whatsoever, we think it ought not to have been described by so gross a term as that of a 'warfare of scurrility.' The expressions to which he himself applies and confines that description are on record, and referred to by himself. Our superiors will judge whether they have a reference to the public measures of the late administration, or personally to Mr. Hastings; and whether, supposing them to be directed against measures only, they were, or could be, too strong for the occasion."

Francis's overweening belief in his own powers, great though they were, led him to under-estimate strangely those of others. When but little more than officially acquainted with Hastings, and with scarcely any experience of the manifold difficulties of his administration, he wrote this to the Prime Minister of England:—"If in this or any other instance the Governor-General's conduct, or the motives I attribute to him, should appear upon examination to imply a weakness and want of judgment in him that exceed probability, I can only say, with an appeal to your Lordship's future observation, that without denying him some little talents of the third or fourth order, we were as much deceived with regard to his abilities and judgment as to his other qualifications." Macaulay's sagacity—wise after the event, no doubt—gave him a deeper insight into Hastings:—"Quick and vigorous as his intellect was, the patience with which he endured the most cruel vexations till a remedy could be found resembled the patience of stupidity.*

"Of the numerous servants of the Company who have distinguished themselves as framers of minutes and dispatches, Hastings stands at the head. He was, indeed, the person who gave the official writing of the Indian Government the character which it still retains. He was matched against no common antagonist. But even Francis was forced to acknowledge, with sullen and remorseful candour, that there was no contending against the pen of Hastings." From the glimpse or two that we shall get in the following pages, we shall see that it was not only against his pen that Francis came off second best. He made an injudicious use of his abilities and opportunities by rashly and prematurely provoking (possibly with good intentions) a prolonged official contest, with so wary and resolute a combatant as Hastings—fighting on his own ground, too. The result was much mischief (the extent of which might have been incalculable), a very little good, perhaps, and, as regards Francis's Indian career, bitter discomfiture and failure.

* In about five months after landing, Francis's private secretary wrote this to his cousin in America. "Your whole line of rulers from the first Penn, with the broad brim, down to the present day cannot furnish out such a Governor as H. The debates of your Colony Councils are the squabbles of boys about tops and marbles compared with the dissension which prevails here." He then glances at daily "fraud, oppression, and peculation," and adds, "it has hitherto been held meanness in Bengal to examine an account, and economy has become infamous."

# CHAPTER V

## PHILIP FRANCIS AND HIS TIMES

### 3.—NUNCOMAR (1775)

"AN Indian Government has only to let it be understood that it wishes a particular man to be ruined, and in twenty-four hours it will be furnished with grave charges, supported by depositions so full and circumstantial, that any person unaccustomed to Asiatic mendacity would regard them as decisive. . . . Hastings was now regarded as helpless. The power to make or mar the fortune of every man in Bengal had passed, as it seemed, into the hands of the new Councillors. . . . It would have been strange indeed if, at such a juncture, Nuncomar had remained quiet. That bad man was stimulated at once by malignity, by avarice, and by ambition. Now was the time to be avenged on his old enemy, to wreak a grudge of seventeen years, to establish himself in the favour of the majority of the Council, to become the greatest native in Bengal. From the time of the arrival of the new Councillors, he had paid the most marked court to them, and had in consequence been excluded, with all indignity, from the Government House. He now put into the hands of Francis, with great ceremony, a paper containing several charges of the most serious description. By this document Hastings was accused of putting offices up for sale, and of receiving bribes for suffering offenders to escape. . . . The triumph of Nuncomar seemed to be complete. He held a daily *levée*, to which his countrymen resorted in crowds, and to which, on one occasion, the majority of the Council condescended to repair. His house was an office for the purpose of receiving charges against the Governor-General. . . . On a sudden, Calcutta was astounded by the news that Nuncomar had been taken up on a charge of felony, committed, and thrown into the common gaol. The crime imputed to him was that six years before he had forged a bond. The ostensible prosecutor was a native. But it was then, and still is, the opinion of everybody, idiots and biographers excepted, that Hastings was the real mover in the business.

"The rage of the majority" rose to the highest point. They protested against the proceedings of the Supreme Court, and sent several urgent messages to the judges, demanding that Nuncomar should be admitted to bail. The judges returned haughty and resolute answers. All that the Council could do was to heap honours and emoluments on the family of Nuncomar; and this they did. In the mean time the assizes commenced; a true bill was found; and Nuncomar was brought before Sir Elijah Impey and a jury composed of Englishmen. A great quantity of contradictory swearing, and the necessity of having every word of the evidence interpreted, protracted the trial of a most unusual length. At last a verdict of guilty was returned, and the Chief Justice pronounced sentence of death on the prisoner."

The foregoing passages from Macaulay's essay on Warren Hastings give the pith of the historical incident, to some account of which it is proposed to devote this chapter.

On looking to the record of the train of occurrences which conspired to give importance and political signifiance, to the first great criminal trial before the new Supreme Court at Calcutta, and to the circumstances attending it, we trace the active brain and busy pen of Philip Francis, and see that he was a vigorous promoter of those events. He had colleagues who acted with him, it is true, but so greatly did this aggressive man tower over them, and over all his Calcutta contemporaries—but one—in ability, energy, and subtlety, that the eye is idly bent on those, their prattle is comparatively of no account. Indeed, it may reasonably be said, that had Philip Francis never been to India, the trial or the execution of even so prominent a native as Nuncomar, would have been but a nine days' wonder; history would have had no cognisance of it.

Again, when Francis's fellow-actors had long passed away, the course of events led to the half-forgotten forgery drama being brought into stronger light than ever on another stage; even there while the story of Nuncomar, and of the alleged political and judicial atrocities of which he had been the victim, is being passionately told in all its harrowing details to an English audience, behind the scenes we see Philip Francis—the voice is Jacob's voice, but the hands are the hands of Esau.

Therefore, as the period of Calcutta life with which these sketches deal, is that indicated in the title of "Philip Francis and his Times," the trial of Nuncomar claims early notice.

It is not proposed just now to follow at any length in the well-trodden steps of those who have discussed the political or technical features of the prosecution and its result. The object rather is to look back for a little across the intervening century, and while bringing into light from mouldy volumes, a few of the dimly remembered facts and circumstances attending a celebrated trial and execution, to recall the names of some of the more prominent actors in a scene which brought Calcutta into such unenviable notice one hundred and thirty-two years ago. Which profoundly moved public feeling in England, engaging the scrutiny of her Parliament, and exercising the keenest attention of some of her greatest orators and statesmen, one of whom, Edmund Burke, is described as having had "as lively an idea of the execution of Nuncomar* as of the execution of Dr. Dodd."

From his earliest days Nuncomar was employed in various official capacities under the (Native) Government of Bengal. In the time of Siraj úd Dowla he was Governor of Hooghly. From then, during the several changes of government in Bengal, he led an intriguing, aspiring, and unprincipled career. Though his life had not been free from some adverse vicissitudes, his talents and experience gained him wealth, and his services to the Government at Murshidábád, and to that of the Company at Calcutta, raised him to the position of a very influential and conspicuous personage in Bengal. The title of Maharajah was conferred upon him by the Emperor Shah Alam about 1764. In appearance he has been described as tall and majestic in person, robust, yet graceful. When the misfortune which has immortalised his name befell him he was nearly seventy years of age.

When the charge of forgery was laid against Nuncomar on May 6, 1775, Mr. Justice Lemaistre happened to be the sitting magistrate; for the judges of the Supreme Court were then also justices of the peace for Calcutta, an objectionable arrangement, which involved the eventual trial of a prisoner at the assizes by a judge who had already come to a conclusion as to his guilt. Lemaistre requested the assistance of Mr. Justice Hyde, who attended with him the whole day till ten o'clock at night, "when, no doubt remaining in the breast of either of us upon the evidence on the part of the Crown," a commitment was made.

The following copy of their warrant will explain matters, and will show that two of the judges who afterwards took a most prominent part in the trial, thus early applied the statute law which made forgery

* I have retained this faulty spelling because the adoption and use of it by the great ones of the past have made it classic :—

Nand (a) Kúmar would be more correct ; the word means the son of Nanda—a name of Krishna.—(Beveridge.)

in Calcutta not a misdemeanour, but felony, and so far committed themselves to an opinion upon what afterwards appeared to be a doubtful, or at all events very arguable, point of law.

"*To the Sheriff of the Town of Calcutta and Factory of Fort William in Bengal, and to the Keeper of His Majesty's prison at Calcutta.*

"Receive into your custody the body of Maharajah Nuncoomar herewith sent you, charged before us upon the oaths of Mohund Persaud, Cumal-uil-Dien Khan and others, with feloniously uttering as true a false and counterfeit writing obligatory, knowing the same to be false and counterfeit, in order to defraud the executors of Bolaukee Doss, deceased; and him safely keep until he shall be discharged by due course of law.

"S. C. LEMAISTRE,
"JOHN HYDE.

"Given under our hands and seals this sixth day of May in the year of our Lord, 1775."

It may be here explained that the bond or deed which the accused was charged with uttering, knowing it to be forged, purported to be the acknowledgment of a debt to him from a native shroff, or banker, incurred several years before. The banker died in June, 1769, and when his affairs were being wound up some few months afterwards, Nuncomar's bond was, with the other claims, settled by the executors; on its being paid, Nuncomar cancelled it (by tearing it downwards at the top for a couple of inches), and gave a receipt in satisfaction of his claim. These documents, with others relating to the banker's estate, found their way afterwards into the Mayor's Court, presumably in its capacity as a court of probate. Other money also of the deceased banker came into Nuncomar's possession, but the amount of that in this bond alone was nearly 70,000 Rs.; if this was obtained by fraud, the crime was one of great enormity, for it deprived the shroff's family of half their substance. It was the betrayal of a trust, too, which in all countries, even the most wicked men have been found reluctant to violate; for the dead man had been his friend, and said to Nuncomar, who came to see him in his last illness: "Here are my wife and daughter: I recommend them to your care, and I wish you to behave to them as you have behaved to me." *

When the two justices were about to go away, Mr. Jarrett, an attorney, came in and requested to be heard on the part of the

* Mr. Beveridge, "Nanda Kumar," p. 31.

prisoner. He represented that Nuncomar "was a person of very high rank, of the caste of Brahmins," and that he would be defiled if placed in the common gaol. But it appeared there was no other place to confine him in, and the judges considered it improper that he should be sent to a private house.

Under pressure they agreed to consult the Chief Justice, which they proceeded to do at once at the Chief Justice's house.

The result of the conference was the following note to Mr. Tolfrey, the Under-Sheriff:—

"Upon consultation with the Lord Chief Justice, we are all clearly of opinion that the Sheriff ought to confine his prisoner in the common gaol on this occasion.

"S. C. LEMAISTRE."

The prisoner was committed on Saturday; on the Monday following he sent a verbal message to the Chief Justice through the latter's moonshee, saying that he could not eat, drink, or bathe in the place where he was confined without losing his caste. The Chief Justice sent back the messenger to learn from him how he might be accommodated, to which Nuncomar made answer, "That the only accommodation consistent with his caste was, that he should live in a house in which no Christian or Mussulman had ever been, or should be admitted, and that he might be at liberty to wash once a day in the Ganges."

On being told that such indulgences were impossible, he continued to abstain from food, and sent a petition to Government setting forth the danger he was in of losing his caste, owing to his close confinement, although the jailer had given up two good rooms in his own quarters to him and his attendants, which were detached from the rest of the prison.

At a meeting of the Council on May 9, 1775, General Clavering says:—"I acquaint the Board that I received a letter from Mr. Joseph Fouke, who is just come from visiting Maharajah Nuncomar, acquainting me that it is the opinion of the people who are about him that they do not think he can live another day without drink. He says his tongue is much parched, but that his spirit is firm. In the conversation that he had with the Rajah, the Rajah told him, "Don't trouble yourself about me; the will of Heaven must be complied with. I am innocent."

Government directed the Sheriff to wait on the Chief Justice, and represent to him the situation of the prisoner.

In answering this, Sir Elijah sent the opinions * of some pundits on this subject, who, having visited Nuncomar in confinement, declared that he could not perform his ablutions, nor eat where Christians or Mahommedans inhabited; but that, if he did so, he might be absolved by penance (prauschit). Against these opinions Nuncomar protested, and desired that other pundits might be consulted at Nuddea, who were of a higher caste and better informed. This favour having been denied him, he persisted in his resolution of dying rather than defile himself.

On Wednesday, May 10, the Chief Justice sent Dr. Murchison (father of the late Sir Roderick) to see him, who doubted that he had been entirely without food since Saturday, but reported that if he had been without sustenance for the time above mentioned, it was necessary he should take some before the next morning. It was after this report apparently, that, according to the evidence of Matthew Yeandle, the jailer, the Chief Justice, on the night of the 10th, tried to get Lemaistre to consent to let the prisoner go outside

* *Translations of the opinions of the four Pundits, Kissen Jewan Surmah, Banisser Surmah, Kissen Gopal Surmah, and Gouree Caunt Surmah, when questioned by Impey, Chambers, and Lemaistre at Impey's house.*

If a Brahmin is confined, washes, eats, and drinks in a house where a Mussulman or others live, he must do the penance known by the name chundraeen, but as that species of penance lasts for one month [1] and as the men of this age have not strength for so long a penance, it has been altered, and instead of performing chundraeen the Brahmin must forfeit eight milch cows and their calves; but if it should so happen that the Brahmin is poor and unable to do this, he must pay thirty-eight cawns and seven puns of cowries; [2] having paid the Brahmins for the trouble they will have in this affair, [3] and having paid for the serraud, or cleansing cake, [4] and fed a cow, the Brahmin is purified.

The above penance is for one day, and the same penance must be performed for every day he remains in confinement.

A Brahmin who is confined within four walls of a prison in which Mussulmans and others live, and is permitted to inhabit a house not under the same roof with them, though within the walls, to perform his ablutions with water of the Ganges, and to eat and drink of things mixed with the water of that river, and who washes with and drinks of the water of the Ganges, when he is set at liberty will not lose his caste.

*Explanation of the Pundits.*

[1] In ancient times, when men lived to the age of one thousand years, then strength was proportionately greater, and they could fast a month or more without endangering their lives, or without considering it a very severe punishment.

[2] The price of a milch cow, with its calf, is from three to four rupees, and the value of the cowries is about eight rupees.

[3] Seldom amounts to above two rupees.

[4] The cake is not valued at more than six annas.

the prison gate, but Lemaistre would not give his sanction. However, Yeandle was empowered by Impey (and by Hyde, it is presumed, as he, too, was present when the jailer came to the Chief Justice's house) to grant the permission. It may be inferred, I think, from the jailer's deposition on this subject, that this indulgence was only to be for once, and for the purpose of taking the sustenance suggested by Dr. Murchison. On Yeandle's hastening back with the permission about ten o'clock at night, the prisoner did not then avail himself of it, but waited till between ten and twelve o'clock next forenoon, when "he walked to the outside of the said prison without any assistance, and did not appear anyways exhausted, and had recovered his speech and talked in the same tone of voice he usually did."

Eventually a tent was pitched for him on the top of an outhouse within the prison walls. His counsel often visited him in prison, and believed "his mind was perfectly at ease on that subject" (accommodation). All his friends, too, had free access to him, amongst whom were the witnesses who afterwards appeared in his defence. He was also visited by the aide-de-camp and by the secretary to General Clavering, and by other Europeans (friends of "the majority"),* and messages of condolence were sent him by the ladies of General Clavering's household and by Lady Anne Monson. At no period of his incarceration was he ironed. His food consisted of sweetmeats for the most part.

The Criminal Sessions following the commitment of Nuncomar were opened on June 3, before the Chief Justice and the three puisne judges.

Pending the erection of a new court-house on the Esplanade where its successor stands now, the sittings of the Supreme Court were at first held in the old Mayor's Court, on the site of the present St. Andrew's Church. This was a somewhat spacious building, but consisting only of a ground floor and one story; a long room in the latter was used for the conducting of trials, and also for the purposes usually served by the public assembly rooms. This structure was pulled down in 1792.

There is no record of the cases which may have occupied the earlier days of the term; they were probably unimportant. *The King* v. *Nuncomar* was called on June 8.

* In the preceding month, when Nuncomar and Mr. Fouke were charged by Hastings with conspiracy, and the judges had seen cause sufficient for holding him to bail, the three new members of Council paid Nuncomar the compliment of a visit at his house.

STREET VIEW IN CALCUTTA.

SHOWING THE OLD COURTHOUSE, ETC.

*See p.* 78.

The following gentlemen composed the jury :—

| | |
|---|---|
| John Robinson (*foreman*). | John Ferguson. |
| Edward Scott. | Arther Adie. |
| Robert Macfarlin. | John Collis. |
| Thomas Smith. | Samuel Touchet. |
| Edward Ellerington. | Edward Sutterthwaite. |
| Joseph Bernard Smith. | Charles Weston. |

From an observation which the Chief Justice made in his charge, viz. "You have been resident long in the country, some I see who were born here," it may be inferred that at least two of the jury were Eurasians. It is unlikely that there were more, because a Native, owing perhaps to prejudice, would, as a rule, much prefer to entrust his interests to the pure European than to the Eurasian, and would have weeded out the latter element in his challenge. Mr. Weston was probably one of the gentlemen born in the country, but his well-known character for benevolence the most catholic, would have overcome such prejudice. The foreman was in the Company's service. Joseph Smith was at the time a "junior merchant" in the Civil Service. The prisoner had the privilege of challenging twenty on the panel; he exerted it in the cases of eighteen, reading their names out from a paper in his hand. Amongst those directed to stand aside were Richard Johnson (also in the Civil Service), Bernard Messink—who afterwards was connected with the *Indian Gazette*—and Tilly Kettle, the artist, who soon after took the Chief Justice's portrait. So far as intelligence goes there ought to have been no lack of it in the class whence the petty jury was drawn.

The name of the counsel for the Crown was Mr. H. Durham, for the defence Mr. Farrer (with him Mr. Brix). Farrer was the first advocate admitted by the Supreme Court: he had only arrived in India in the previous October. He was on very friendly terms with General Clavering and Colonel Monson, which helped his professional progress much. He had made such good use of his time that he retired in less than four years with £60,000.

His purse would have been still fuller perhaps but for his gambling experience. Francis alludes to Barwell as "sitting up all night winning Farrer's money." He afterwards sat in Parliament for Wareham. The *aliquid amari* in his lot was that his health never recovered the fatigue and anxiety of the Nuncomar trial. He was a close ally of Francis; this should be kept in mind should any bias appear in his evidence at the impeachment of Impey. Francis writes in his diary, "March, 1778, Farrer going to England; understands my cause there heartily."

After the jury had been sworn, an objection was made by Farrer, at the instigation of his client, to the gentlemen who it was proposed should interpret during the trial "as being connected with persons whom the prisoner considered as his enemies."

This was Mr. Alexander Elliot, "eminently skilled in the Persian and Hindustani languages," an intimate friend both of the Governor-General and of the Chief Justice, and, strange to say, brother of Sir Gilbert Elliot, who took so leading a part in the House of Commons on the motion for the impeachment of Impey thirteen years afterwards.* He was twenty-one years of age at this time.

*Chief Justice.*—The principal interpreter of the Court is absent. The gentlemen of the jury have heard the interpretation of the assistant interpreters on other occasions. Do you, gentlemen, think we shall be able to go through this cause with the assistance of those interpreters only?

*Jury.*—We are sure we shall not be able.

*Chief Justice.*—It is a cruel insinuation against the character of Mr. Elliot.

[Here Mr. Elliot begged he might decline interpreting.]

*Chief Justice.*—We must insist upon it that you interpret. You should be above giving way to the imputation. Your skill in the languages and your candour will show how little ground there is for it.

*Counsel.*—I hope Mr. Elliot doesn't think the objection came from me; it was suggested to me.

*Chief Justice.*—Who suggested it?

*Counsel.*—I am not authorised to name the person.

The jury then, as well as the prisoner's counsel, begged that Mr. Elliot would act as interpreter.

When the prisoner was ordered to the bar to be arraigned, Farrer asked that he should not be put into the dock, but be allowed a place near his counsel; nor that he should be obliged to hold up his

* Young Elliot died early in India (1778). Hastings was much attached to him. Sir Gilbert, in writing to his wife (February, 1788) of Hastings at his impeachment, says, "I never saw Hastings till to-day, and had not formed anything like a just idea of him. I never saw a more miserable-looking creature, but indeed he has so much the appearance of bad health, that I do not suppose he resembles even himself. He looks as if he could not live a week. I always feel uncomfortable in the reflection of his connections with Alick, and I cannot say I was insensible to the idea of seeing him to-day." Hastings on his last voyage home wrote some verses (dedicated to Sir J. Shore) in imitation of the *Otium Divos rogat* of Horace. His old friend is lovingly referred to—

> "An early death was Elliot's doom,
> I saw his opening virtues bloom."

hand, but be allowed to identify himself by declaring that he was the person arraigned. Both requests were refused.

He was arraigned and the indictment read. Then followed a deal of technical skirmishing where various legal points were raised and disposed of. The most important of these was a plea to the jurisdiction of the court which was read. The Chief Justice gave a decided opinion against it, and was concurred with by Hyde and Lemaistre. Whether Justice Chambers said anything or not, Mr. Farrer (whose evidence before the impeachment committee is the authority) could not remember. This plea, however, was withdrawn for technical reasons, "more especially as the Court had so strongly intimated an opinion that if not withdrawn, but left to be formally decided against as upon a record, that in that case the defendant would be precluded from pleading over not guilty to the indictment."

Mr. Justice Chambers then called for the indictment; and after reading it said he had great doubts whether or not it was well laid being for a capital felony on the 2nd George II.; that he conceived *that* Act was particularly adapted to the local policy of England for commercial and other reasons; "that he thought the same reasons did not apply to the then state of Bengal" (*sic* Calcutta?); "that it would be sufficient, and as far as the Court ought to go, to consider Bengal in its then state, as upon the same footing that England had been between the statute of 5th Elizabeth and that of 2nd George II." *

"He therefore proposed from the Bench that that indictment should be quashed and that the prosecutor might be at liberty to prefer a new one." The Chief Justice and the other two judges were, however, of a contrary opinion, and considered that the trial ought to proceed. †

* The last culprit who forfeited his life in England for forgery was Thomas Maynard, hanged at Newgate, December 31, 1829.

† Impey at the bar of the House of Commons said that Chambers made this proposition more *in favorem vitæ* than from any sound reason in law; and added that he then understood that Chambers was convinced he was wrong by Impey's arguments; "he most certainly acquiesced; I never understood him to have been overruled, and his subsequent conduct, if any doubt could be entertained, proves most manifestly that he was not." Nevertheless, Chambers' open expression of opinion about the indictment made this strong impression on the prisoner's counsel: "I thought at the time, and even until within a few days of the prisoner's execution, that this was a certain presage of his life being safe, let the event of the verdict be what it might, and such my opinion I repeatedly communicated both to the prisoner and to his friends, as well as to Mr. Monson, General Clavering, etc., etc." He also advised Nuncomar to arrange for sending a person to England "in case the verdict should be against him."

This interposition of one of the judges anticipated a similar objection to the indictment which the defendant's advocates were prepared to make, and they thought it prudent to let it rest on the grounds which had been stated.

After some further sparring the prisoner was called on peremptorily to plead—" Mr. Justice Lemaistre adding, to the best of my recollection, under the pain of being considered as standing mute,"—*i.e.* under the pain of being convicted.* He accordingly pleaded not guilty in due form. On the plea of not guilty being recorded, the prisoner was asked by whom he would be tried, to which he answered, " by God and his peers."

The Court asked whom the Rajah considered as his peers? His counsel said he must leave that to the Court.

*Chief Justice.*—" A peer of Ireland tried in England would be tried by a common jury. The Charter directs that in all criminal prosecutions the prisoner should be tried by the inhabitants of the town of Calcutta, being British subjects." The issue which the Court had to try was whether the jewels-bond † was genuine or not:

* This savagery was the law until 1827, when an Act was passed directing the Court to enter a plea of " not guilty " when a prisoner refuses to plead.

† Some readers may be curious to see the wording of this document; it was written in Persian; the following translation may perhaps make more clear what has already been said about it, viz.:—

" I who am Bolaukee Doss.

" As a pearl necklace, a twisted kulgah, a twisted serpache (*i.e.* turban ornaments) and four rings, two of which were of rubies and two of diamonds, were deposited by Rogonaut-Roy Geoo on account of Maharajah Nundocomar Bahadur, in the month of Assar in the Bengal year 1165 (1758) with me in my house at Moorshedabad, that the same might be sold; at the time of the defeat of the army of the Nabob Meer Mahomed Cossim Cawn, the money and effects of the house, together with the aforesaid jewels, were plundered and carried away. In the year 1172, Bengal style (1765), when I arrived in Calcutta, the aforesaid Maharajah demanded the before-mentioned deposit of jewels. I could not produce the deposit when demanded, and on account of the bad state of my affairs was unable to pay the value thereof. I therefore promise and give it in writing that when I shall receive back the sum of two lakhs of rupees and a little above, which is in the Company's cash at Dacca, according to the method of reckoning of the Company, I have agreed and settled that the sum of forty-eight thousand and twenty-one sicca rupees is the principal of the amount of the said deposit of jewels which is justly due by me, and over and above that a premium of four annas upon every rupee. Upon the payment of the aforesaid sum from the Company's cash I will pay that sum without excuse and evasion to the said Maharajah. I have for the above reasons given these words in the form of a bond under my signature, that when it is necessary it may be carried into execution.

its publication was not denied: if forged there could be no doubt that the prisoner knew it to be so.

The evidence on the part of the Crown purported to show that Bolaukee Doss not only did not execute the bond, but never owed the money, that its statements were all false and its attestations all forgeries, etc., etc.

The evidence for the defence, on the other hand, maintained that the whole business was genuine, and witnesses were produced who saw the deed executed, and who gave a detailed account of the transaction from their own personal knowledge, etc., etc. All these allegations involved a display of contradictory swearing which must have been startling to those whose experience had hitherto been limited to Western Courts of Law.

Were the Nuncomar case to be committed for trial before the High Court of Calcutta to-day, with all its facilities for inquiry, derived from the accumulated experience of an additional century of native litigation, the investigation would probably be considered an intricate one. It is no disparagement therefore to the Supreme Court to surmise what up-hill work it must have proved to the judges of 1775, who had been but a few months in the country and were unfamiliar with the customs and habits of thought and dealing of the people. To instance the accounts alone, which formed so prominent a feature in the case, how complicated and perplexing these must have seemed, as well as the strange documentary "exhibits" which, like the accounts, were in divers languages, and which, with every word of the evidence, had to be filtered to the understanding drop by drop through an interpreter.

An unusual disadvantage, too, at which the first judges of the Supreme Court were placed was this, that *all* were new;* there was

"Written on the seventh day of the month Bhadoon in the Bengal year 1172 (August 20, 1765)—

| | |
|---|---|
| "It is witnessed— | ALABD (this word, literally slave, |
| "MAHAB ROY. | denotes that the bond was |
| "SCILAUBUT, the Vakeel of Seat. | sealed by Bolaukee). |
| Bolaukee Doss. | BOLAUKEE DOSS. |
| "ABDEHOO-COMMAUL MAHOMED." | |

(Copied from Mr. Beveridge's "Nanda Kumar.")

* Indeed, the members of the Court were not only new to India, but to their functions as judges. Their only practical experience as such, with a jury, was in the cases that may have come before them during this or possibly a preceding session. There was a formal assize opened at the end of the previous year, but Farrer said no business was done. It would probably be correct to say that Nuncomar's case was the first important criminal one which came before this Bench or any member of it for decision.

no member of the tribunal of longer or of local experience, who could show a friendly light to his brother; each had to cautiously grope his way. And this difficulty was intensified when it became manifest to them, as it soon did, that the counsel for the Crown was a broken reed to lean on, for Mr. Durham (in spite of his prenomen being Hercules) was unequal to the labour of the prosecution, especially that of cross-examination. Accordingly, the judges (Chambers excepted) took this duty on themselves, and carried it out in prodigious detail, recalling witnesses over and over again. Added to all this, there must have been very present to them the consciousness that they were conducting this capital trial under the eyes, it may be said, of a critical and hostile audience, in the shape of the prisoner's influential supporters in the Government, and that all the patience and temper which they could command were needed.

Readers in India will be able to appreciate the remark that the physical surroundings were not over favourable to a command of the judicial virtues which it was so desirable to have in hand.

The trial commenced on Thursday, June 8, and went on for eight days, the intervening Sunday included. The Court, as was then the rule, made no adjournment, but one of the judges, at least, always remained in the Court, or in a room adjoining and open to it. The jury retired to another adjoining room (under charge of the Sheriff's officers) to take refreshment or sleep.

The Court sat each day from eight in the morning till late at night. The verdict was not given till four o'clock in the morning of the 16th.

On each of those days the temperature at that season of the year, in that crowded room, must have stood for several hours between 92° and 98° Fahr. The thirst produced by such heat had (while on the bench, at all events) to be endured; or, as a perilous alternative, to be assuaged by a bumper of tepid water from the common tank in "Lall Diggee," whose reputation was by no means unstained. Ice there was none; in those heroic times people had to pant through the hot days and hotter nights without it; or, worse still, without the swinging punkas of a later date. Possibly standing behind the judges' chairs were a bearer or two, lazily waving fans of peacock's feathers, partly with the object of contributing to an imposing ceremonial; but the comfort derivable from this must have been very equivocal. In fact, the judges arrayed in their red robes and heavy wigs (rather than abandon which, in those brave old days, they would have undergone dissolution) must have been in a most distressing condition, from their heads to their trickling fingers.

None but those who have had the privilege of living inside the Calcutta ditch during the month of June, can feelingly understand what an awful experience this prolonged trial must have been to all engaged in it at such a time, *i.e.* the heavy sultry week just before the rains. It is suggestive that the one memory of the Nuncomar trial, which Calcutta tradition has not let die, is that of the four judges solemnly retiring "three or four times daily to change their linen." Still in spite of the ferocious heat many Europeans in society attended the trial. Thus a lady, a relative to Chas. Grant, writes to his brother, "All the world has gone to the Court-house to hear the trial of Nuncomar."

On the second day, counsel for the prisoner informed the Court that the Maharajah had been taken ill in the night, which rendered him incapable of taking his trial. The Court desired Drs. Anderson and Williams to examine the prisoner, which they did, and reported that he had now "neither flux nor fever, and was very capable of taking his trial."

When the case for the defence had been going on for some time a curious circumstance occurred, owing to the severe cross-examination to which the prisoner's witnesses were submitted by the judges.

Nuncomar begged permission to be allowed to leave the dock and speak in private with his counsel. Accordingly he and Farrer retired to the end of the Court-room. Neither could understand the language of the other, so an interpreter had to be made use of. The old man warmly thanked his advocate for the pains he had taken to save him, and said he was convinced that his exertions would be fruitless, as the Court were decidedly his enemies. He grounded his belief of this on the difference between the treatment shown by them to his witnesses and to those for the prosecution. He concluded with an expression of his intention to give no further trouble, but submit at once to his fate. Farrer strongly dissuaded him from those ideas, and assured him that the Court would do him justice; but as the treatment he spoke of made such an impression on him, that he (Farrer) would seek a means of communicating his apprehension to the judges, and would tell him with what result later on.

Immediately after his own dinner that day, Farrer, with much reluctance, sought an interview with the judges in the room where they were dining, and with their permission told them what had passed between him and his client. The judges explained why they thought this examination necessary (*i.e.* the inefficiency of the Crown prosecutor to cross-examine the witnesses for the defence, as sufficiently as Farrer had cross-examined those for the prosecution).

Mr. Justice Chambers said nothing before the other judges, but when he and Farrer were alone, he told him that his communication gave him great uneasiness; and he particularly desired the advocate to tell the prisoner from him, that every question he should put to his witnesses would be as much in support of them as against them, and that he would put as few as possible. Farrer conveyed this message, and tried to relieve his client's mind as well as he could. Sir Fitz-James Stephen takes strong exception to this half-and-half attitude of Chambers on this occasion. Elliot (the interpreter) spoke of him as "a man of mild and flexible character, though of great knowledge and integrity."

So the wearisome trial plodded on for four or five days more. The cross-examination by the judges was longer and more rigid than ever—Lemaistre and Hyde taking a more conspicuous part in it than the Chief Justice.

At length, about midnight of Thursday, the 15th, the counsel for the defence closed his evidence. Then an incident occurred pregnant with warning to all prisoners and captives who may venture to take in hand such a double-edged tool as "evidence." The Court were informed that Nuncomar had something to say. He desired that one of his own witnesses, one Juan Dass, should be re-called and questioned as to a "karar-nama" (a written statement of account); with what result we shall see.

When he had closed his case, Farrer, utterly exhausted, quitted the Court and went home to bed, and the Chief Justice began his summing up in the early morning of the 16th.

One can fancy the scene now arrived at in that muggy, oil-lighted Court-room. The motley standing crowd, the outside portion of it, unable to hear let alone to follow the drama going on, many of them no doubt more than half asleep, till roused by some vague intelligence that the *denouement* was coming; but asleep or awake determined to await, with the patience of the Hindoo, the fall of the curtain.

By an exceedingly hard rule then in force, counsel for a prisoner charged with felony could not address the jury.* The Court,

* Sir J. Stephen, in his "Story of Nuncomar, etc.," condemns the essential badness of this rule, and says it was a pity the Court did not hold that it did not apply to India. Allowance must be made, however, he adds, for the influence of technical rules over professional men. Even the small relaxation allowed was a point strained in the prisoner's favour. This detestable rule lasted long enough into the present century (1837) to be denounced by Sydney Smith in these scathing words: "When the prisoner says to the judge that 'he leaves his

however, allowed the prisoner's counsel to hand up any points or observations which they desired to make, and undertook to read them to the jury. This concession, such as it was, the counsel availed themselves of. They were also told by the Bench that if Nuncomar desired to urge anything in his own defence it would be interpreted. But he said nothing.

Very different opinions have been expressed about the Chief Justice's summing up. In the article of impeachment against Impey, drawn up thirteen years afterwards, it is described as characterised by "gross and scandalous partiality." It seems to have displeased some, by what is not in it, as much as by what is in it. It would be inconsistent with the object of this sketch of the trial to give the charge here, but readers may form some idea of the impression likely to be made on the jury by this the concluding portion of it :—

"There is certainly a great improbability that a man of Maharajah Nuncomar's rank and fortune should be guilty of so mean an offence for so small a sum of money. It is more improbable, as he is proved to have patronised and behaved with great kindness to Ballakey Doss in his lifetime, that he should immediately after his decease plunder

defence to his counsel ;' we have often blushed for English humanity to hear the reply, 'Your counsel cannot speak for you ; you must speak for yourself.' And this is the reply given to a poor girl of eighteen, to a foreigner, to a deaf man, to a stammerer, to the sick, to the feeble, to the old, to the most abject and ignorant of human beings. It is a reply, we must say, at which common sense and common feeling revolt, for it is full of brutal cruelty, of base inattention of those who make laws, to the happiness of those for whom laws were made. We wonder that any juryman can convict under such a shocking violation of all natural justice." How hardly this legacy from savage times died, may be inferred from the fact, that the great and enlightened statesman, Sir Robert Peel, argued in 1826, against the motion to bring in a bill enabling persons accused of felony to make their defence by counsel ! ! I took the following statements from a gossiping paper about law and lawyers. I have had no opportunity of verifying them, or of consulting Lord Campbell's "diary," so cannot fully vouch for their accuracy, though I believe them true, viz. when the Prisoners' Counsel Bill was being discussed in the House of Commons, Park, J., found himself so disgusted with its provisions that he wrote to Sir John Campbell, A.-G., threatening that if the measure were passed he would forthwith resign his seat on the Bench. This stern resolution, however, he subsequently amended, for he died in harness in 1838. The Bill permitted counsel appearing for prisoners charged with felony "to make full answer and defence"—that is to say, to make a speech. Till then they had only been allowed to discuss points of law. Lord Campbell, in his diary, expresses the view that bills for abolishing the Star Chamber, for prohibiting torture, or for allowing the prisoner's witnesses to be examined on oath, would all have been strenuously opposed by Lord Eldon, Lord Redesdale, and Lord Tenterden. He adds that twelve of the fifteen judges who reigned in 1837 were against the Prisoners' Counsel Bill.

the widow and relations of his friend. There does likewise appear to have been a suit in the Adalat, which must have been a civil suit; but it does not indeed appear that Mohun Persaud was a party; and, indeed, for what reason I know not, neither side thought fit to produce the proceedings.

"I have made such observations on the evidence as the bulk of it, and the few minutes I had to recollect myself, would allow me to make. You will consider the whole with that candour, impartiality, and attention which have been so visible in every one of you during the many days you have sat on this cause. You will consider on which side the weight of evidence lies; always remembering that, in criminal, and more especially in capital cases, you must not weigh the evidence in golden scales; there ought to be a great difference of weight in the opposite scale before you find the prisoner guilty. In cases of property the stake on each side is equal, and the least preponderance of evidence ought to turn the scale; but in a capital case, as there can be nothing of equal value to life, you should be thoroughly convinced that there does not remain a possibility of innocence before you give your verdict against the prisoner.

"The nature of the defence is such that if it is not believed it must prove fatal to the party, for if you do not believe it you determine that it is supported by perjury, and that of an aggravated kind, as it attempts to fix perjury and subornation of perjury on the prosecutor and his witnesses.

"You will again and again consider the character of the prosecutor and his witnesses—the distance of the prosecution from the time the offence is supposed to be committed—the proof and nature of the confessions said to be made by the prisoner—his rank and fortune. These are all reasons to prevent you giving a hasty and precipitate belief to the charge brought against him; but if you believe the facts sworn against him to be true, they cannot alter the nature of the facts themselves. Your sense of justice and your own feelings will not allow you to convict the prisoner unless your consciences are fully satisfied beyond all doubt of his guilt. If they are not, you will bring in that verdict which, from the dictates of humanity, you will be inclined to give. But, should your consciences be thoroughly convinced of his being guilty, no consideration, I am sure, will prevail on you not to give a verdict according to your oaths."

At four o'clock the same morning Jarrett, the prisoner's attorney, went to Farrer's bedside and woke him up, to tell him that the jury had just brought in a verdict of guilty. And when the beaten advocate dragged himself out of bed some hours later in the morning, he found on his table this note from his junior:—

"DEAR SIR,

"It is with infinite concern I communicate to you what you may probably have already heard from Messrs. Jarrett and Foxcroft, that the Rajah hath not only been found guilty, but Mr. Durham, on behalf of the prosecutor, hath undertaken to prosecute Mir Asad Ali, Sheikh Yar Mahomed, and Kissen Juan Dass for perjury at the instance of the Court. How unlucky is the Rajah to have brought this misfortune upon himself by desiring the last examination of Juan Dass, which hath overset all the weight of his former evidence. Sir Elijah, in summing up the evidence, observed that having proved from the first moment of his examination till the time the evidence was closed a fair and candid witness, he would have directed the jury to find him not guilty, as he looked upon the existence of the corornama clearly proved by him till the moment he prevaricated in his examination after the evidence was closed. I enclose the notes you gave Sir Elijah, of which, as well as of mine, he made use; after having taken some rest, which I am much in want of, not having slept more than two hours since three o'clock yesterday morning, I will wait on you to consult what steps are necessary to be taken, in which I will with pleasure afford you every assistance in my power, as I really pity the old man's case.

"I am, dear Sir, very truly yours,

"Friday morning. "C. F. BRIX."

The advocates in the next few days devised every scheme they could think of, which offered a chance of saving the prisoner's life. These, in the first instance, took the form of applications to the Court on technical grounds.

A week after the verdict a motion in arrest of judgment was made by Farrer, "though still being very ill," before the full Bench. Each judge gave his opinion against the arguments put forward. Chambers spoke last; the conclusion of the note of what he said, taken down by Farrer, reading thus: "That was he alone to pass sentence, doubts would still remain in his mind as to the indictments (?) capital." * Farrer's next note on this day's proceeding is,

* Copied from Farrer's evidence in Beveridge's "Nanda Kumar": the hiatus is provoking. It is but fair to mention that Farrer's memory is not supported by what Impey himself said in Farrer's presence at the bar of the Commons. "He (Chambers) not only sat through the whole trial, but concurred in overruling every objection in arrest of judgment, assented to the summing-up of the evidence, was present and concurred in the sentence." Then he read a letter which all the judges had signed asserting their unanimity, "Whatever representation may be made to the contrary." On the day of the execution Justice Chambers officiously wrote to Impey, advising that the "malefactor's" goods should be seized by the sheriff; this "ought not, I think, be delayed a minute." Some years afterwards he judicially held that the statute under which Nuncomar was convicted did not apply to Calcutta. If he was believed to have really concurred in the sentence on Nuncomar, the hardihood and indecency of Francis in writing as follows to him, twelve years after, were astounding: "Impey's going to Lucknow to take those depositions is the blackest and

"Sentence per Chief Justice—a definite sentence—must not expect mercy—death."

In those days the warrant for execution was a copy of the Calendar (or list of cases tried at the assize) signed by the judges and handed to the sheriff. The Calendar, in this instance, does not appear to have been signed before July 24. The Court appointed no time for the execution; this was left to the discretion of the sheriff. Saturday, August 5, was the date fixed on.* Then various petitions for respite to admit of an appeal to the clemency of the King in England were proposed; these were to be from several sources. Some, though prepared, fell to the ground; amongst these was one which was to have reached the judges through the Council; this died at its birth, owing to Clavering and Monson declining to have anything to do with it, though Francis approved of the measure. Some did reach the judges, and included one from the condemned man himself; one from some of the native inhabitants; and one from the Nawab of Bengal. All were unsuccessful. No movement in the prisoner's favour was made by the European community.

An incident connected with the getting up of one petition is worth recalling.

On a former occasion, in 1765, a native named Radachurn Mittre had been tried in Calcutta for forgery under the statute made applicable to Nuncomar's case, and sentenced to death, and "ordered into the condemned hole." A petition was sent in to Governor Spencer from the native community of Calcutta, asking either a

basest transaction, except one, that has yet dishonoured the British administration in India." The "*except one*" can only refer to the Nuncomar trial—and this up to the face of the judge who wrote that he concurred in it all!! "Limber" and "Sir Viner Pliant" were the appropriate nicknames under which this weak-kneed judge went in vulgar Calcutta. Some very indifferent lines by Mrs. Thrale on Chambers' portrait (by Reynolds) at Streatham have this suggestive beginning:—

> "In this luminous portrait requiring no shade
> See Chambers' soft character sweetly displayed," etc.

* In a note on the trial with which M. Belchambers courteously favoured me some years ago, he says, "There is at page 1 of one of the earliest vols. of Hyde's notes this memorandum, 1775, July 24: 'Signed the Calendar containing the order for the execution of Nundo-Comar. He was hanged, I think the day was Saturday, Augt. 12, but I am not sure.' The fate of this fellow-creature did not seem to have made much impression on the memory of this one of his judges—who evidently did not write up his notes until a good while after events.

reversal of the sentence, or a respite pending an application to the throne.

The petition pointed out, amongst other reasons for this, that the jury had recommended the prisoner to mercy. The prayer was granted, and Radachurn Mittre got a free pardon from the King.

Farrer now prepared a petition to the judges for the signature of the jury, praying for a stay of execution and a recommendation to the sovereign for mercy, pleading "the very advanced age of the unfortunate criminal," etc., etc. This he sent to the foreman of the jury on the last day of July.* That individual returned a pompous platitude about "a British juryman's oath," which had no connection whatever with what he was asked to do. Farrer explained the position to him in a clear, manly note, adding "suffice it for me, in compliance with the earnest solicitation of an unhappy victim, to have acquitted myself to my own feelings in having made the application; you will judge and act for yourself." The rejoinder that the juryman (his name was John Robinson—it is difficult to allude to him with becoming forbearance) made to this, was an hysterical whine about his "conscience" and his "tender feelings," which were "very much hurt," etc., etc. Into his note he drags "the veneration I have for the Bench of judges." and then sends the correspondence up to the Chief Justice. This he effected through a Mr. Belli, who, in a covering note, remarks that "the word victim in Mr. Farrer's address is very remarkable. This business gives Mr. Robinson much uneasiness, and he hopes Sir Elijah will permit him to make a complaint to him if Mr. Farrer persists in his solicitations."

When Farrer next appeared in Court, the Chief Justice administered to him a severe reprimand, and told him his conduct was derogatory to his professional character; that no advocate in England, who had a proper regard for the dignity of the Court, would have so acted. Juries must be protected from improper application to them. What did he mean by "unhappy victim"?

* On this same day, July 31, Nuncomar wrote a letter to Francis imploring his interposition in his behalf. It is signed "Nundcoomar," and is marked in Francis's letter-book "a translate from the Bengal original." The ungrammatical English of the translation seems to make the appeal all the more piteous. One sentence, which has a Scriptural tone, is, "I am now thinking that I have but a short time to live, for among the English gentry, Armenians, Moores, and Gentoos, few there is who is not against me, but those that are not for me is continually devising all the mischief they can imagine against me."

Farrer gave the respectful explanation, which it is to be hoped would have satisfied most judges, "but the Chief Justice still seemed to dwell on the expression 'unhappy victim'; but Mr. Justice Chambers, I think, interposing, the matter ended there."

Eventually this frustrated petition found its way back to the hands that drew it up. One man alone out of the twelve "drew near the nature of the gods in being merciful," and came to Farrer's house, though he did not know him, and signed it there. Amongst the Parliamentary papers connected with the Nuncomar case the petition may be seen in print; at the foot of it is the name "Edward Ellerington." To my regret I could find no local record showing who this gentleman was; he wore "nobility's true badge."

While these petitions were getting but few signatures, and no success, there was a canvass made for signatures to representations of another kind, which was highly successful, viz. addresses expressive of confidence and satisfaction were tendered to the Chief Justice and to the Supreme Court by various sections of the community. One of these (presented to the Chief Justice himself) is from "the free merchants, free mariners, and other inhabitants." The little adjective is singularly inappropriate in this respect, that the address is remarkable for its servility. It can find no more suitable ground for praise and thanksgiving, than the pains he "bestowed, during the late tedious and important trial, in patiently investigating the evidence." It extols him, too, for "repressing the spirit of litigiousness, and the chicanery and quirks of practitioners." It also introduces the set-phrase "our reputation, our fortunes, and perhaps our lives" might have been at the mercy of every profligate informer (*i.e.* but for the establishment of the Supreme Court), and does not fail to notice "the candour, wisdom, and moderation of the Chief Justice." At the head of the names of the eighty-four inflated persons who signed this imprudent panegyric, stand those of Playdell, the Superintendent of Police, and Robinson, the foreman of the jury. In reference to these addresses the majority say in a minute, January 25, 1776: "The second appears under the auspices of Mr. Playdell and Mr. Robinson, who have both been turned out of the Company's Service. As to the dismission of Mr. Playdell we have assigned our reasons, and we disclaim any right in Mr. Hastings to attribute our conduct to other motives." Playdell would appear to have been afterwards restored along with other Company's servants, friends of Hastings, by the Home Government (see Gleig, vol. 2). Robinson's name does not appear amongst those restored. The Grand Jury also paid homage and sent, July 14, 1775, a complimentary and grateful address to the Chief Justice, thanking him and the Court for the great "attention they have been pleased to show us," and expressing the satisfaction we feel in possessing in your Lordship a Chief Justice from whose "abilities, candour, and moderation," and so on. There is a strong family likeness in both addresses.*

Forty-three Armenians also made haste to bow down to the rising sun. Nor were the mixed native inhabitants of Calcutta (amongst them, be it noted, were Hindoos of good respectable position) behindhand with their meed of honeyed praise; in an address with a hundred signatures they asked the Court, with exuberant adulation, to believe, that "confidence and joy sprang up in our hearts, and we are thoroughly convinced that the country will prosper, the bad be punished and the good be cherished." It would have been more decent if these representative bodies had repressed their overflowing gratitude, if only for a few days. The Chief Justice, however, complacently received and replied to all, modestly disclaiming any special merit, and gratified the "free" admirers by consenting ("with the greatest alacrity," he said) to sit for his portrait for the town hall.

While these *dramatis personæ* were thus bandying compliments the aged Hamlet of the play was lying in jail awaiting his execution.

Where was Nuncomar hanged? If there were an indisputable foundation of fact for Macaulay's account of the profound veneration manifested for the prisoner's hereditary and religious dignities (apart from that attaching to his great wealth and former influential position), one might suppose that, among a people so eminently conservative as the Hindoos, some trustworthy information would be forthcoming as to the exact locality where so deplorable a shock to their religious feelings was inflicted. One might reasonably fancy that the terrible story would have been handed down between the three or four intervening generations so faithfully, that even the very spot could be pointed out where the life of him who was "the head of their race and religion," who "had inherited the purest and highest caste, had

* We get an interesting glance at old Calcutta names, some of which we shall see again, on reading the signatures to these addresses. Amongst those to the Grand Jury one, are George Hurst, Wm. Pawson, Page Keble, Joseph Price, Cudbert-Thornhill, and Charles Grant (*clarum et venerabile*). Amongst the "Free" signatures are several of the petty jury (such as C. Weston); E. Tiretta, the irrepressible Joe Price, John Belli, Wm. Swallow (is it his name that is preserved in Swallow Lane?), Tysoe S. Hancock, James Augustus Hicky; this gentleman, we shall find later on, must have often regretted his haste in giving such a gushing welcome and testimonial to Impey and his brethren. We cannot fail to remark also the namesake of one who to this hour continues to carry fun and mirth into thousands of English homes—the immortal Sam Weller!

been so degradingly taken. Yet it is far otherwise. Frequent inquiries in Calcutta, amongst natives of every creed and condition, reluctantly led me to the conclusion that there does not exist in native Calcutta to-day any tangible tradition as to the identity of the place where this 'Brahmin of the Brahmins' was put to death."

Certain circumstances, however, which are beyond dispute, render it all but certain that the place assigned to the execution by the Rev. J. Long in an old number of the *Calcutta Review* is correct—viz. in "Cooly Bazaar, close to Hastings' Bridge—a platform being erected for the purpose." In a Calcutta newspaper of 1793 it is incidentally mentioned that "near the Cooly Bazaar" was the usual place of execution. It is in evidence, too, that the execution of Nuncomar was visible from the ramparts of the New Fort. Captain Price,* who was in Calcutta at the time, and had served on the Grand Jury at the previous assize, says that it was to the *County* jail that Nuncomar was committed, so referred to, I suppose, as being outside the ditch. The jail in question would be that on the site of the late Calcutta jail, and so in the direction of Cooly Bazaar.

The following is the account of the execution written by Alexander Mackrabie, the sheriff, whose distasteful duty it was to see it carried out:—

"Hearing that some persons had supposed Maharajah Nuncomar would make an address to the people at his execution, I have committed to writing the following minutes of what passed both on that occasion, and also upon my paying him a visit in prison the preceding evening, while both are fresh in my remembrance.

"Friday evening, August 4. Upon my entering his apartments in the jail, he arose and saluted me in his usual manner. After we were both seated, he spoke with great ease and such seeming unconcern that I really doubted whether he was sensible of his approaching fate. I therefore bid the interpreter inform him that I was come to show him this last mark of respect, and to assure him that every attention should be given the next morning which could afford him comfort on so melancholy an occasion; that I was deeply concerned that the duties of my office made me of necessity a party in it, but that I would attend to the last to see that every desire that he had should be gratified; that his own palanquin and his own servants should attend him; and that such of his friends who, I understood, were to be present should be protected.

"He replied that he was obliged to me for this visit; that he thanked me for all my favours, and entreated me to continue it to his family; that fate was not to be resisted; and put his finger to his forehead—

* Price commanded an Indiaman which traded to Calcutta. He was a strong partisan of Hastings and a voluminous pamphleteer.

'God's will' must be done. He desired that I would present his respects and compliments to the General, Colonel Monson, and Mr. Francis, and pray for their protection of Rajah Gourdass; that they would please to look upon him now as the head of the Brahmins. His composure was wonderful; not a sigh escaped him; nor the smallest alteration of voice or countenance, though I understood he had not many hours before taken a solemn leave of his son-in-law, Roy Radicum. I found myself so much second to him in firmness, that I could stay no longer. Going downstairs, the jailer informed me that, since the departure of his friends, he had been writing notes and looking at accounts in his usual way. I began now to apprehend that he had taken his resolution and fully expected that he would be found dead in the morning; but on Saturday, the 5th, at seven, I was informed that everything was in readiness at the jail for the execution. I came here about half an hour past seven. The howlings and lamentations of the poor wretched people who were taking their last leave of him are not to be described. I have hardly recovered the first shock while I write this about three hours afterwards. As soon as he heard I was arrived he came down into the yard and joined me in the jailer's apartment.

"There was no lingering about him, no affected delay. He came cheerfully into the room, made the usual salaam, but would not sit till I took a chair near him. Seeing somebody look at a watch, he got up and said he was ready, and immediately turning to three Brahmins who were to attend and take care of his body, he embraced them all closely, but without the least mark of melancholy or depression on his part, while they were in agonies of grief and despair. I then looked at my own watch, told him the hour I had mentioned was not arrived, that it wanted above a quarter to eight, but that I should wait his own time, and that I would not rise from my seat without a motion from him. Upon its being recommended to him that at the place of execution he would give some signal when he had done with the world, he said he would speak. We sat about an hour longer, during which he addressed himself more than once to me; mentioned Rajah Gourdass, the General, Colonel Monson, Mr. Francis, but without any seeming anxiety; the rest of the time, I believe, he passed in prayer, his lips and tongue moving, and his beads hanging upon his hand. He then looked to me and arose, spoke to some of the servants of the jail, telling them that anything he might have omitted Rajah Gourdass would take care of, then walked cheerfully to the gate and seated himself in his palanquin, looking around him with perfect unconcern. As the Deputy Sheriff and I followed, we could make no observation upon his deportment till we all arrived at the place of execution. The crowd there was very great, but not the least appearance of a riot. The Rajah sat in his palanquin upon the bearers' shoulders and looked around at first with some attention. I did not observe the smallest discomposure in his countenance or manner at the sight of the gallows or any of the ceremonies passing about it. He asked for the Brahmins who were not come, and showed some earnestness, as if he apprehended the execution might take place before their arrival. I took that opportunity of assuring him I would wait his own time; it was early in the day, and there was no hurry. The Brahmins soon after appearing, I offered to remove the officers, thinking that he might have something to say in private: but he made a motion not to do it, and said he had only a few words to remind them of what he had said concerning Rajah Gourdass and the care of his zenana. He spoke to me and desired that the men might be taken care of, as they were to take charge of his body, which he desired repeatedly might not be touched by any of the bystanders; but he seemed not in the least alarmed or discomposed at the crowd around him. There was some delay in the necessary preparations and from the awkwardness of the people. He was no way desirous of protracting the business, but repeatedly told me he was ready. Upon my asking him if he had any more friends he wished to see, he answered he had many, but this was not a place, nor an occasion, to look for them. Did he apprehend there might be any present who could not get up for the crowd? He mentioned one, whose name was called, but he immediately said, 'It was of no consequence! probably he had not come.' He then desired me to remember him to General Clavering, Colonel Monson, Mr. Francis, and looked with the greatest composure. When he was not engaged in conversation he lay back in the palanquin, moving his lips and tongue as before.

"I then caused him to be asked about the signal he was to make, which could not be done by speaking, on account of the noise of the crowd. He said he would make a motion with his hand; and when it was represented to him that it would be necessary for his hands to be tied, in order to prevent any involuntary motion, and I recommended him making a motion with his foot, he said he would. Nothing now remained except the last painful ceremony. I ordered his palanquin to be brought close under the gallows, but he chose to walk, which he did more erect than I have generally seen him. At the foot of the steps which led to the stage he put his hands behind him to be tied with a handkerchief, looking round at the same time with the utmost unconcern. Some difficulties arising about the cloth which should be tied over his face, he told the people that it must not be done by one of us. I presented to him a subaltern sepoy officer, who is a Brahmin, and came forward with a handkerchief in his hand! but the Rajah pointed to a servant of his own, who was lying prostrate at his feet, and beckoned him to do it. He had some weakness in his feet, which, added to the confinement of his hands, made him mount the steps with difficulty; but he showed not the least reluctance, scrambling rather forward to get up. He then stood erect on the stage, while I examined his countenance as steadfastly as I could till the cloth covered it, to see if I could observe the smallest symptom of fear or alarm, but there was not a trace of it. My own spirits sank, and I stept into my palanquin; but before I was seated he had given the signal, and the stage was removed. I could observe, when I was a little recovered, that his arms lay back in the same position in which I saw them first tied; nor could I see any contortion on that side of his mouth and face which was visible. In a word, his steadiness, composure, and resolution throughout the whole of this melancholy transaction were equal to any examples of fortitude I have ever read or heard of. The body was taken down after hanging the usual time, and delivered to the Brahmins for burning."

This account was read thirteen years afterwards by Sir Gilbert Elliot in the House of Commons (when he moved for the impeachment of Impey).

In a former edition of this book I quoted from Mr. Impey's memoir of his father what he there says about the foregoing account by Mackrabie, viz.:—

"Yet Mr. Macaulay is not without a ground-work, such as it is, for his picture. That ground-work exists in a letter *which was never seen or heard of until twelve or thirteen years after the execution*, when it was produced by the enemies of Sir Elijah Impey, to strike the Parliament and people of England with horror."

Again—

"This letter, which was made to pass as the production of Francis's brother-in-law, was now produced for the *first time*, and read to the excited House by Sir Gilbert Elliot."

He adds, it bears internal evidence of having been composed or retouched by Junius. I then remark that Mr. Impey must have been mistaken, as it would appear that the sheriff's account was in the hands of the English public at least seven years (if not more) before the motion for the impeachment of Impey, and I quoted an extract from Hicky's *Bengal Gazette*, October, 1781, *i.e.* some ten months after Francis left India, and while Elijah Impey was still in Calcutta. Sir FitzJames Stephen ("Story of Nuncomar") discounts this contention of mine as deficient in proof as to the identity of two accounts—this cannot be gainsay'd. He writes—

"Mr. Busteed has discovered a statement made in a Calcutta paper, published in October, 1781, referring to the late Mr. Mackrabie's minutes about Nuncomar having been published in England, but it certainly does not appear that the minutes referred to in 1781 in Hicky's *Gazette* were the same as those published in the *Annual Register* in 1788; and, if they were, Francis may have retouched them between Mackrabie's death, in 1776, and the publication referred to in 1781. There is, however, no evidence that he did so."

The extract is, however, sufficiently curious and suggestive perhaps, to be quoted again. It recalls a regrettable step which Clive unfortunately thought necessary. Omichund, who was not a Bengalee, but a bearded Sikh, survived the deception and died very wealthy in December, 1758:—

"The following remarks are taken from an English paper, which took their rise from the appearance of the late Mr. Mackrabie's minutes being published relative to the behaviour of the Rajah Nuncomar, from the time of his being visited by Mr. Mackrabie at the jail, on the morning of his execution, until the fatal moment that he was launched into eternity. The humane and intelligent reader will not fail to recollect that in Bengal, in 1757, the East India Company's servants, with Colonel Clive at their head, were guilty of a most infamous forgery in counterfeiting the signature of Admiral Watson to a treaty by which they defrauded Omichund, a Gentoo merchant, of £250,000 promised him. Colonel Clive had even the malignity in person to inform Omichund of the deception by which he had cheated him. The Colonel's words overpowered him like a blast of sulphur, and he fell fainting on one of his attendants. . . . We first committed a successful forgery on a native of Bengal, and gloried in it, though it occasioned his death. Soon after we sent out English judges to establish English laws in that country, and with a justice peculiar to wise and innocent men, a retrospective view of past crimes is taken, and a native of the country, who knew nothing of English laws, is hanged for a crime which we had triumphed in committing. Clive was made a peer in England, though he committed in Bengal the same crime for which we hanged Nuncomar."

When Sir Gilbert had read Mackrabie's account, he added—

"While this tragedy was acting, the surrounding multitudes were agitated with grief, fear, and suspense. With a kind of superstitious incredulity, they could not believe that it was really intended to put the Rajah to death; but when they saw him tied up, and the scaffold drop from under him, they set up an universal yell, and with the most piercing cries of horror and dismay betook themselves to flight, running many of them as far as the Ganges" (which they were at already), "and plunging into the water, as if to hide themselves from such tyranny as they had witnessed, or to wash away the pollution contracted from viewing such a spectacle."

The foundation, if it deserves to be so called, for this peroration, which was skilfully followed by Macaulay, was derived from the evidence of a witness before the Parliamentary Committee, a Captain Cowe, who saw the execution "from the parapet of the New Fort, not quite half a mile away," and who said that "there were eight or ten thousand people assembled, who, the moment the Rajah was turned off, dispersed suddenly, crying, 'Ah baup-aree,'" and that "many of them even ran into the river from the terror of seeing a Brahmin executed." The Committee did not, apparently, ask this witness how he heard the words he testified to if he was half a mile off. He explained "Ah baup-aree" to be "an exclamation of the black people upon the appearance of anything very alarming and when they are in great pain." The Parliamentary orator, however, preferred to translate it into "universal yell, with the most piercing cries of horror and dismay." Macaulay, it may be remarked, converted the modest "many of them" of the eye-witnesses into "hundreds."

Captain Price, who was also examined before the same Committee, did not at all approve of the false impression likely to be conveyed by this evidence of Captain Cowe, and accordingly proceeded to demolish it in his usual downright fashion. He wrote to Edmund Burke that Captain Cowe's statement "deserves no credit at all; he had no knowledge of the customs or manners of the people, having himself been bred in the navy and came to Bengal a very little while before the majority." * He then gave his own explanation as follows :—

> "The exclamation, 'Au-baup-a-ree,' and the saying the people ran into the river on the Rajah's being turned off, convey improper notions to the mind of the reader. . . . The fact is as follows : had a calf been knocked on the head they would have done the same; the exclamation cannot be rendered into English, the idioms of the languages are so very different; but if a Hindoo was to see a house on fire, to receive a smart slap on the face, break a china basin, cut his finger, see two Europeans boxing, or a sparrow shot, he would call out, 'Au-baup-a-ree.' When the Rajah was hanged it was to them a very extraordinary sight, and it was natural for Hindoos to suppose that it in some degree defiled them. The remedy was at hand; near to the gallows where the Rajah suffered runs a branch of the River Ganges, the waters of which river, in the idea of all the Hindoo nation, cleanse them from every kind of impurity. Had a common pickpocket suffered, had a European spit by accident on the outer edge of their outer garment, had they touched any dead animal, or fifty thousand other the most trifling cases would have induced them to go and purify themselves in the Ganges. At all hours of the day and night, at all seasons of the year, thousands of them are seen, men, women, and children, mingled together indiscriminately dabbling in the river, to purge away the impurities of body, soul, and garment at the same instant and by the same means.

We all know that any large city will vomit forth its riff-raff in

* "Majority" and "minority" were expressions in common use at the time in reference to the notorious differences between the members of Government. Thus Francis's private secretary writes in January, 1776, "Mr. Barwell was at the Governor's last night, 'And pray,' says he, 'what brought you here: coming over to the minority, I suppose?' 'Without doubt, sir,' replied I; 'I breakfasted at *your* house this morning.'"

thousands to enjoy an execution; such people have no delicate sensibilities to be wounded; morbid curiosity is their motive. This observation applies to the East as well as to the West. I fancy that respectable and religious Hindoos kept away then as they do now from such debasing spectacles. "I have many more friends," answered Nuncomar to the sheriff at the foot of the scaffold, "but this is not a place, nor an occasion to look for them."

A few words may be said in personal relation to each of the four judges who conducted this historical trial, though the materials to admit of this are scanty. They certainly did not deserve the insolent query about them which Francis entrusted to a correspondent in England so early as 1776, presumably because they asserted their independence of Government. "I wish you would inquire and tell me in what dirty corner of Westminster Hall these cursed judges were picked up. I have no personal quarrel with any of them, but assuredly they are driving hard to the destruction of this country."

Stephen Cæsar Lemaistre—to begin with the one who died first—would seem to have been a *protégé* of the licentious Lord Sandwich. He was of the Inner Temple, and had been Recorder of Rochester. His wife, who did not, I believe, accompany him to India, was Mary, daughter of James Roche, of Dublin, and sister of "the celebrated Captain D. Roche" (for what he was celebrated I have not found), but she also was "celebrated for her charms and elegance of manners." So described even still in the catalogues of rare engravings.

Mackrabie writes, March 18, 1776, "Judge Lemaistre has a large party at his house to commemorate his wedding day; what a plague is that to us that we must lose our ladies and our music." Mrs. Lemaistre re-married with Baron Nolcken, Envoy from Sweden, in 1779. Impey writes of him as being "violent beyond measure," and (with Hyde) "in direct opposition to me in everything." Francis hints that Hastings was well disposed to Lemaistre. He was a convivial man and for some time joined in the high play indulged in by Francis and others. "Lemaistre," writes a fellow card player, "kept us laughing for two hours. These lawyers are always in Court—dispute, contention, cavil upon the most ordinary topics." On the voyage out, when some of the *Anson* passengers visited the *Ashburnham* in a calm, Mackrabie notes, "Judge Lemaistre kept the table on a roar for several hours yesterday; his brother Hyde maintained his dignity with a proper degree of silence." His house in Calcutta was on the site of the present school in Free-School Street. Lemaistre died in November, 1777, and was buried in South Park Street Cemetery; his tomb never had an inscription; it is one of two east of, and near to, that of General Clavering, which it resembles in shape.

The vacancy in the Supreme Court caused by Lemaistre's death was eventually filled by Sir Wm. Jones.

Hyde was called to the Bar from Lincoln's Inn, and, with Lemaistre, was mainly indebted to Impey for his Indian judgeship; but if Impey had a difficult colleague to pull with in Lemaistre, he had a still more difficult one in Hyde. "He is even abusive on the bench, which I have never been provoked to reply to," writes Impey to Dunning; and to Thurlow he complains, "For the conduct of Lemaistre I cannot account. As for Hyde, I much fear the return of the old disorder, but it is too delicate a matter to touch upon. He is absolutely under the management of Lemaistre. What you said to me concerning Hyde frequently occurs to me. He is an honest man, but is a great coxcomb. His tongue cannot be kept still, and he has more parade and pomp than I have yet seen in the East. I write this to you in confidence and beg it may not be mentioned, except to Dunning." The little weakness for parade in his brother thus remarked on by the Chief Justice is exemplified in this entry in Hyde's own note-book:—

"4th Term.

"Monday, 25th October, 1779.

"*Present:*

"MR. JUSTICE HYDE.

"I came to Court in my Scarlet Robe to-day, because it is the day of the King's accession, and is therefore treated by the Courts of Law in England as a Gala day, to appear in their finest cloaths, and I think it proper, most particularly in this place, that all manners of tokens of respect to His Majesty should be shown, and especially by those who have the honour of holding offices under His Majesty's authority on his appointment. All signs of loyalty to the King of England are too much neglected in this country. I believe they did not even fire a salute at the fort, which is a shameful neglect, if it is not worse—a designed disrespect."

Mrs. Fay, writing from Calcutta in 1780, says that "on the first day of every term the professional gentlemen all met at a public breakfast at Mr. Justice Hyde's house, and went thence in procession to the Court House." Fortunately, the procession had not far to go, as Hyde lived next to the Supreme Court, in a house on the site of the present Town Hall, for which he is said to have paid twelve hundred rupees a month. Hyde was a married man and with his wife a great favourite in social life, where their hospitality was genuine. "Mrs. Hyde after her return from the country sees company in all the forms. Lady I—— sits with her, though they hate each other like poison," is the testimony of Francis's secretary. He died in harness (aged 59) after twenty-one years' uninterrupted service, handsomely acknowledged in a Government notification which also referred to the virtues of his private character. He was buried (July, 1796) in South Park Street Cemetery. The tablet on his tomb records his "boundless benevolence," and speaks of him as "a model of unexampled, yet cautiously concealed charity." Nevertheless, the tomb of this first parent of the High Court in India has been allowed to become a model of neglect, neither unexampled nor concealed, I am sorry to say, in the cemeteries of Calcutta.

"Chambers supports me and behaves handsomely to me," is what Impey writes when giving his confidence to Dunning regarding the puisne judges.*

Chambers was the only one of the first four judges who may be said to have had an English reputation prior to coming to India. He was born at Newcastle-on-Tyne, and was educated with the future luminaries, Lords Stowell and Eldon. He was of the Middle Temple, a member of University College, Oxford, and Vinerian Professor of Law. He had the distinction, too, of being a friend of Johnson's, and, as a member of the Literary Club, of Burke, Reynolds, and Goldsmith, etc. Chambers had been introduced to the Club by one who afterwards became his colleague in India, Sir William Jones. Chambers wrote the inscription on the monument by Flaxman to Jones at Oxford. Johnson was very fond of Chambers, as may be seen in the frequent references to him in Boswell. It was in Chambers's rooms in the Temple that occurred the scene which Boswell tells with such humour, on coming out from which the great man was in such convulsions of laughter that he was obliged to lay hold of one of the posts near the foot pavement at the Temple Gate, "whence he sent forth peals so loud that in the silence of the night his voice seemed to resound from Temple Bar to Fleet Ditch." "I

* His two disloyal brothers wished to undermine this support, according to Francis's Journal, viz. "At the request of Lemaistre and Hide (sic) I write a strong letter to Justice Chambers at Chittagong to prevent his taking part with Impey, etc." Again—ten days later he writes: "Sept., 1777, Lemaistre and Hyde dine with me at the Gardens and engage body and soul with me *envers tous et contre tous*."

then accompanied him to his own door," writes his faithful satellite, "where he gave me his blessing." When Johnson was setting out to join Boswell for their journey to the Hebrides, Chambers went with him as far as Newcastle. When Chambers sailed for India the fact was communicated to Boswell in a letter which alone should confer immortality on Chambers's name, as it there happened to be linked with that of one who, as a minstrel and as a man, is familiarly loved wherever English is spoken, "whose sweet and friendly nature bloomed kindly always in the midst of a life's storm and rain and bitter weather." The passage has been often quoted as exemplifying what Thackeray refers to as "the great wise benevolence and noble mercifulness of heart" of Johnson, but let me honour this page by quoting it once again. "Chambers, you find, is gone far, and poor Goldsmith is gone much further. He died of a fever, exasperated, I believe, by the fear of distress. He raised money and squandered it by every artifice of acquisition and folly of expense—but let not his failings be remembered; he was a very great man."

Chambers was the bearer to Calcutta of a letter of introduction from Johnson to Warren Hastings, the original of which is now amongst the select manuscripts in the British Museum. Macaulay alludes to this circumstance, saying how "the old philosopher referred in the most courtly terms, though with great dignity, to their short, but agreeable intercourse" when Hastings had been last in England. Macaulay does not mention the ostensible object of Johnson's letter, though it is worth bearing in mind in connection with a certain letter written by Hastings afterwards. The letter which Chambers took with him concluded thus:—

"I am now going to take leave, perhaps a very long leave, of my dear Mr. Chambers; that he is going to live where you govern may justly alleviate the regret of parting; and the hope of seeing both you and him again, which I am not willing to mingle with doubt, must at present console as it can,

"Sir, your most humble servant,

"SAM JOHNSON.

"March 30, 1774."

Before Hastings or Chambers saw Europe again, poor Johnson's kindly heart was still.

Macaulay closes the Nuncomar episode with this passage—

"It is a remarkable circumstance that one of the letters of Hastings to Dr. Johnson bears date a very few hours after the death of Nuncomar. While the whole settlement was in commotion, while a mighty and ancient priesthood were weeping over the remains of their chief, the conqueror in that deadly grapple sat down, with characteristic self-possession, to write about the tour to the Hebrides, Jones's Persian Grammar, and the history, traditions, arts, and natural productions of India."

The letter here referred to was simply Hastings' courteous acknowledgment of the letter brought by Chambers a few months before. The multitudinous cares and worries undergone by the Governor-General since the arrival of the councillors and judges, must have left him no leisure for private correspondence. By the association of ideas, the recent trial may easily have turned Hastings' mind to the introduction brought him by one of the judges, which he had not yet acknowledged; and his far-seeing sagacity may have suggested to him that the opportunity was a suitable one for paying attention to, and reciprocating the friendliness, of so powerful an influencer of public opinion as Johnson.*

The above passage from Macaulay's brilliant essay is a notable instance of the way in which he sometimes strains the facts for the purpose of literary effect. As a matter of fact, Hastings' letter to Johnson is dated August 7, *i.e.* two days after the death of Nuncomar, forty-eight hours after the Brahmins had burned all "remains" of their chief. The words "a very few hours" keep out of sight the more literal realities, whose colour would not harmonise with the effective picture intended.

Chambers, like his colleagues Impey and Hyde, arrived in India married. His mother, in her great affection for him, also accompanied him to Calcutta, where she died in 1782. The Chambers lived for several years in a garden-house at Bowanipore, and afterwards at Cossipur. They had also a town house in, I think, Old Post-office Street. They lost several children, as may be seen by the inscriptions in the family tomb in the South Park Street ground. Their eldest boy, aged six, was lost in the wreck of the *Grosvenor* on his voyage to England in 1782. He was appointed judge of Chandernagóre and Chinsurah in 1781, and narrowly escaped having had to answer to Parliament for accepting a post of profit under the Government; Mr. Impey says that General R. Smith, who gave notice of motion about it, allowed it to drop at the instigation of Francis; and reflects on the treatment shown to his father and not to Chambers for simliar offences. Sir Robert Chambers became

* In fact, it would seem that the other side did try unsuccessfully (through Fowke) some years afterwards to get Johnson to take up the Nuncomar case. See Beveridge's "Nunda Kumar," p. 161 n.

Chief Justice in 1791; he was knighted some years before. He remained in India till 1799, a peerage was proposed for him, but he preferred a pension of £2000 a year. He died near Paris in 1803. His widow brought his body to England, and it was buried in the Temple Church, where a monument by Nollekens was placed to his memory. At the date of the Nuncomar trial Chambers (as Hyde also) was 38 years of age. Lady Chambers survived him till 1839, when she died, aged about 81. Their daughter married Colonel Macdonald, the son of Flora.

There is a very good likeness of Chambers in his robes (a half length, with the hand up to the face) in the judges' library in the High Court of Calcutta. This was taken at Calcutta. A copy of it is in the hall of University College, Oxford, having been presented by Lady Chambers.

There is scarcely anything interesting of a personal nature to be retailed about Impey himself. He was a distinguished graduate of Cambridge (Trinity), being senior optime and Chancellor's gold medallist in 1756. He was of Lincoln's Inn and went the Western Circuit, where he was second only to Dunning. He devoted much time in India to a profitable study of Oriental languages. Though older than any of the colleagues who left England with him, he survived them all. He was but little over nine years in India, having, as is well known, been recalled to answer before Parliament certain charges against his conduct as Chief Justice in India. The motion for his impeachment was lost in the House of Commons. He died at Newick Park, in Sussex, in 1809, and was buried at Hammersmith. He was 43 years of age at the time of the Nuncomar trial. I have a note that it never fell to his lot again to pass another capital sentence, but I am unable to quote any authority for this.

There are two portraits of Impey in his official costume in the Calcutta High Court—one by Kettle, which shows a very marked double chin. This is probably a faithful likeness, as it has been engraved for Impey's memoir by his son. The other* is a more pleasing one. In this his full-length figure is standing with one hand raised, as though the subject were addressing an audience. In both portraits the face wears a self-satisfied and rather benevolent

* The name of the artist printed under this painting is "Zoffany—1782." If it be by Zoffany the date is wrong, as he did not leave England till 1783; he may have arrived in Calcutta in time to paint Impey, who left in December, 1783. A sitting portrait of Impey by Zoffany is in the National Portrait Gallery; he is in the ordinary dress of the period.

expression. Sir Elijah lived in Calcutta on the site of a house now a convent, behind the Roman Catholic Church in Middleton Row. The map of 1785 shows that there was a round tank where the church now stands. The house was surrounded by an extensive deer park (enclosed by walls) lying between, but not quite up to Camac Street and Russell Street; a gate in the southern wall opened into Middleton Street. The present Middleton Row was the avenue which led up between trees through the park from "Burial Ground Road" to the dwelling-house. The name of the above road was changed to the more euphonious one of "Park Street," because it led past the Chief Justice's park. The eastern ends of the gardens attached to the houses in Russell Street (*i.e.* 12 and 13), occupied a century later by Chief Justices Peacock, Norman (who was murdered when officiating as Chief Justice), and Couch, where once a portion of the park of their earliest predecessor whose name, thanks to Nuncomar and Macaulay, will be known to fame when those of his successors will be quite forgotten.*

* See Appendix IV. Hastings and Impey in relation to the trial of Nuncomar.

Sir Robert Chambers.

Sir Elijah Impey.

FIRST CHIEF JUSTICE, CALCUTTA.

Mr. Justice Hyde.

*See p.* 106.

# CHAPTER VI

## PHILIP FRANCIS AND HIS TIMES

### 4.—DUEL BETWEEN FRANCIS AND HASTINGS, 1780

THOUGH it is stepping aside from the order of events, this historical occurrence in the Calcutta life of Francis may now be recalled. Before coming to details, it will not be superfluous, even for Indian readers, to explain the origin of this duel, which has become obscured by the dust of time. Some believers in the *cherchez la femme* doctrine have pressed this combat into their service as one more proof of its almost universal application. For instance, a Calcutta reviewer, writing about twenty-five years ago, says—

1. "Nearly opposite Alipore Bridge stood two trees, called 'The Trees of Destruction,' notorious for duels fought under their shade; here Hastings and Francis exchanged shots in the days when European women were few; jealousy often gave rise to these affairs of honour."

And M. Charles de Rémusat, discoursing on Junius and the Memoirs of Francis in the *Revue des Deux Mondes* in 1869, writes—

2. "Ce récit prouve que, *contairement à des suppositions souvent répetées*, la beauté de Madame Grande fut complètement étrangere aux démêlés de Hastings et de Francis, et que ce n'est pas elle qui leur mit les armes à la main." (The italics are mine.)

Substantially the cause of the quarrel was this (says Francis's biographer): "Francis had promised Hastings not to interfere with his conduct of the war against the Mahrattas, then carried on near the Malabar coast. Hastings wanted to carry on operations against the same enemy on the Jumna. Francis deemed himself not precluded by his promise from opposing this. Hastings maintained that he was." Some sort of informal compact had been negotiated between the two, with a view to the public service being carried on harmoniously, when Barwell was about to leave India. At this time (March, 1780) Francis wrote with characteristic egotism this despairing letter to his friend Godfrey in England : "The dreadful aspect of our affairs in this country has forced me to yield to a temporary pacific action with Mr. Hastings, on public grounds and no other. Since it has pleased the Demon who presides over England to continue and confirm Mr. Hastings and Mr. Barwell in possession of absolute power over this part of the Empire, nothing was left for me but to try if possible to save it from instant destruction, or at least to delay that ultimate ruin of which the foundation is laid. This I most solemnly avow to you is the sole motive of my conduct, unmixed with any personal interest, direct or indirect."

If Francis had not given a promise of co-operation with Hastings, Barwell would not have gone, as it was Barwell's vote in Council which at this time gave Hastings the preponderance. Francis, it may be mentioned, wrote a letter to his friend and cousin Tilghman on the night preceding the duel, denying in the most solemn manner that he had given assent to the measures which, it will be seen, Hastings with equal steadfastness said he had.

At the end of June, 1780, a minute signed by Francis and another member of the Council, Wheler, was sent in to the Secretary to Government withholding their consent from the military operations, the immediate execution of which the Governor-General considered of the utmost importance, and making propositions which would frustrate his policy. Hastings, through the personal intervention of Sir John Day, seems to have tried to prevail on Francis to come to some accommodation, but without success, and on July 3 he wrote the celebrated hostile minute which provoked the duel.

Though written and dated on July 3, it was not made use of for about six weeks. The reason of this delay was probably due to the illness of Francis, who under the above date has this entry in his journal:—"July 3. . . . Feeling the approach of a fever very strong upon me, about noon very ill and forced to go to bed." "4th. Worse. H. goes up the river with Mrs. H."

Hastings, knowing what the result of his minute must be, determined probably to wait for Francis's recovery, and meantime to take Mrs. Hastings out of the way.

Both he and Francis also expected despatches in August announcing whether or not Hastings was to be continued in the Government; this, too, may have suggested to him the desirability of waiting. In the local newspaper the Governor-General's departure from the Presidency is chronicled—Sooksagur being given as his destination, accompanied by the intelligence that, on his journey up the Hooghly, he was saluted with twenty-one guns from the Danish and Dutch Settlements of Serampore and Chinsurah. On Monday, August 14, Hastings returned to Calcutta and wrote to his wife whom he left with the Governor of Chinsurah: "I have seen nobody and heard nothing. But I have a letter from Madras which mentions the arrival of the Company's ships. The only news of consequence is that it is determined that I am to remain as long as I choose, *but with the same associate.*" The words I have underlined most probably indicated to Hastings the hopelessness of carrying on the Government harmoniously, and the conviction that the contest between him and his associate must now be *à outrance.*—The minute must no longer be withheld.

Francis's journal of this date (14th) records—"Mr. H. does not return till the evening. No Council. At night receive his minute which he says he had reserved till my return, with a private note."

Hastings' minute is long; it will be sufficient to give an extract or two from the most provocative paragraphs in it. Though called forth by a minute from two of his colleagues, he avowedly treats the latter as solely that of Francis.

"I did hope that the intimation conveyed in my last minute would have awakened in Mr. Francis's breast, if it were susceptible of such sensations, a consciousness of the faithless part which he was acting towards me. I have been disappointed, and must now assume a plainer style and louder tone. In a word, my objections do not apply to the special matter of his minutes, to which I shall separately reply, but to the spirit of opposition which dictated them." . . .

"By the sanction of this engagement and the liberal professions which accompanied it, I was seduced to part with the friend (to whose generous support steadfastly yielded in a course of six years I am indebted for the existence of the little power which I have ever possessed in that long and disgraceful period) to throw myself on the mercy of Mr. Francis, and on the desperate hazard of his integrity. My authority for the opinions I have declared concerning Mr. Francis depends on facts which have passed within my own knowledge. I judge of his public conduct by my experience of his private, which I have found to be void of truth and honour. This is a severe charge, but temperately and deliberately made, from the firm persuasion that I owe this justice to the public and myself as the only redress to both, for artifices of which I have been a victim, and which threaten to involve their interests with disgrace and ruin. The only redress for a fraud for which the law has made no provision is the exposure of it."

The Governor-General, as we have seen, sent a copy of this

minute to Francis on the evening before the Council day on which it was to be officially read, because he judged it "unbecoming to surprise him with a minute at the Council table, or to send it first to the secretary."

What happened on its being read we learn from Francis's journal. "August 15, Revenue Board. When it was over I took him into a private room and read to him the following words:—

"'Mr. Hastings,—I am preparing a formal answer to the paper you sent to me last night. As soon as it can be finished, I shall lay it before you. But you must be sensible, sir, that no answer I can give to the matter of that paper can be adequate to the dishonour done me by the terms you have made use of. You have left me no alternative but to demand personal satisfaction of you for the affronts you have offered me.' As soon as I had read the preceding words to Mr. Hastings, he said 'he expected the demand and was ready to answer it.'"

A place and time of meeting were fixed before they parted. Francis further writes in his diary on the same day that he "mentions the affair to Watson, who happens to dine with me; he agrees to provide pistols in order to prevent suspicions." Colonel Watson was the chief engineer at Fort William. Mr. Hastings engaged the services of Colonel Pearse, the Commandant of Artillery, to whom he wrote on the evening of August 15, asking him to breakfast the next morning. He then, after enjoining secrecy, asked Colonel Pearse to be his second in a hostile meeting which had been arranged for between him and Mr. Francis for Thursday morning, August 17. The entry in Francis's journal for August 16 is:—

"Employed in settling my affairs, burning papers, etc., in case of the worst—dull work."

On the same day he wrote to his colleague in Council—

"My dear Mr. Wheler,

"Mr. Tilghman will deliver to you a copy of the papers which have passed between Mr. Hastings and me. You will see that I am forced into the field by such insults as I think no degree of resentment nor any sense of injury however just will warrant among gentlemen.

"The declaration I have left behind me is true—at a moment like this I will not affirm that Mr. Hastings could not possibly have misunderstood me, because I will not risk the doing him an injustice. He knows best. You know better than any man on what principles I have acted. Defend my memory and leave this country as soon as you can, to its fate. My dear Friend, Farewell for ever.

"Yours while I still live,

"P. Francis."

16: August. 1780.

My dear Mr. Wheler.

Mr. Tilghman will deliver You a Copy of the Papers, which have past between Mr. Hastings & Me. You will see that I am forced into the Field by such Insults, as I think no degree of Resentment, nor any sense of Injury, however just, will warrant among Gentlemen. The Declaration I have left behind me is true. — At a Moment like this,

I will not affirm that Mr. Hastings could not possibly have misunderstood me; because I will not risk the doing him an Injustice. He knows best.

You know, better than any Man on what Principles I have acted. — Defend my my Memory I leave this Country, as soon as You can, to its Fate — My dear Friend, Farewell for ever. — Yours while I still live, P. Francis.

See p. 110.

That for the 17th—

"Arrived at the ground near Belvedere near an hour before Mr. H., who comes about six with Colonel Pearse. Watson marks out a distance about fourteen common paces, the same, he said, at which Mr. Fox and Mr. Adam stood.* My pistol missing fire, I changed it; we then fired together, and I was wounded and fell: I thought my backbone was broken, and of course that I could not survive it."

Sir Elijah Impey writes on the same day to a friend:—

"This morning Mr. Hastings and Mr. Francis fought with pistols: they both fired at the same time. Mr. Francis's ball missed, but that of Mr. Hastings pierced the right side of Mr. Francis, but was prevented by a rib, which turned the ball, from entering the thorax. It went obliquely upwards, passed the backbone without injuring it, and was extracted about an inch on the left side of it. The wound is of no consequence, and he is in no danger."

Colonel Pearse, who was Hastings' second, and whose detailed account of the duel has been published,† says:—

"The next morning, Thursday, August 17, I waited on Mr. Hastings in my chariot to carry him to the place of appointment. When we arrived there we found Mr. Francis and Colonel Watson walking together, and therefore, soon after we alighted, I looked at my watch and mentioned aloud that it was half-past five, and Francis looked at his and said it was near six. This induced me to tell him that my watch was set by my astronomical clock to solar time. The place they were at was very improper for the business; it was the road leading to Alipore, at the crossing of it through a double row of trees that formerly had been a walk of Belvedere Garden, on the western side of the house. Whilst Colonel Watson went, by the desire of Mr. Francis, to fetch his pistols, that gentleman proposed to go aside from the road into the walk: but Mr. Hastings disapproved of the place, because it was full of weeds and dark. The road itself was next mentioned, but was thought by everybody too public, as it was near riding time, and people might want to pass that way; it was therefore agreed to walk towards Mr. Barwell's house (the present Kidderpore Orphanage Asylum) on an old road that separated his ground from Belvedere (since the official residence of the Lieutenant-Governor of Bengal), and before he (we?) had gone far, a retired dry spot was chosen as a proper place.

"As soon as the suitable place was selected," continues Colonel Pearse, "I proceeded to load Mr. Hastings' pistols; those of Mr. Francis were already loaded. When I had delivered one to Mr. Hastings, and Colonel Watson had done the same to Mr. Francis, finding the gentlemen were

* The duel referred to occurred in England on November 29, 1779.

† It was originally furnished in a letter to England to Lawrence Sulivan, Esq., dated October, 1780.

both unacquainted with the modes usually observed on those occasions, I took the liberty to tell them that, if they would fix their distance, it was the business of the seconds to measure it. Colonel Watson immediately mentioned that Fox and Adam had taken fourteen paces, and he recommended the distance. Mr. Hastings observed it was a great distance for pistols; but as no actual objection was made to it, Watson measured and I counted. When the gentlemen had got to their ground, Mr. Hastings asked Mr. Francis if he stood before the line or behind it, and being told behind the mark, he said he would do the same, and immediately took his stand. I then told them it was a rule that neither of them were to quit the ground till they had discharged their pistols, and Colonel Watson proposed that both should fire together without taking any advantage. Mr. Hastings asked if he meant they ought to fire by word of command, and was told he only meant they should fire together as nearly as could be. These preliminaries were all agreed to, and both parties presented: but Mr. Francis raised his hand and again came down to the present; he did so a second time, when he came down to his present—which was the third time of doing so—he drew his trigger, but his powder * being damp, the pistol did not fire. Mr. Hastings came down from his present to give Mr. Francis time to rectify his priming, and this was done out of a cartridge with which I supplied him upon finding they had no spare powder. Again the gentlemen took their stands, both presented together, and Mr. Francis fired. Mr. Hastings did the same at the distance of time equal to the counting of one, two, three distinctly, but not greater. His shot took place. Mr. Francis staggered, and, in attempting to sit down, he fell and said he was a dead man. Mr. Hastings hearing this, cried out, 'Good God! I hope not,' and immediately went up to him, as did Colonel Watson, but I ran to call the servants."

Another part of Colonel Pearse's narrative says that Francis "admired the beauty of Hastings' pistols" when Pearse produced them, and then goes on—

"When the pistols were delivered by the seconds, Mr. Francis said he was quite unacquainted with these matters, and had never fired a pistol in his life, and Mr. Hastings told him he believed he had no advantage in that respect, as he could not recollect that he had ever fired a pistol above once or twice." Also—"While Mr. Francis was lying on the ground he told Mr. Hastings, in consequence of something which he said, that he best knew how it affected his affairs, and that he had better take care of himself, to which Mr. Hastings answered that he hoped and believed the wound was not mortal, but that if any unfortunate accident should happen, it was his intention immediately to surrender himself to the sheriff."

* A contemporary (G. F. Grand) says in his narrative: "The seconds baked the powder for their respective friends."

When Francis was shot, Colonel Pearse says:—"I ran to call the servants and to order a sheet to be brought to bind up the wound. I was absent about two minutes. On my return I found Mr. Hastings standing by Mr. Francis, but Colonel Watson was gone to fetch a cot or palanquin from Belvedere to carry him to town. When the sheet was brought, Mr. Hastings and myself bound it around his body, and we had the satisfaction to find it (*sic*) was not in a vital part, and Mr. Francis agreed with me in opinion as soon as it was mentioned. I offered to attend him to town in my carriage, and Mr. Hastings urged him to go, as my carriage was remarkably easy. Mr. Francis agreed to go, and therefore, when the cot came, we proceeded towards the chariot, but were stopped by a deep, broad ditch, over which we could not carry the cot; for this reason Mr. Francis was conveyed to Belvedere."

The place originally fixed for the meeting probably corresponds to the second gate (from the western side) leading into Belvedere compound. Francis proposed to turn aside into what was seemingly a disused, overgrown walk of Belvedere, close to their left; but Hastings, who, apparently, meant to do mischief that morning (note his remark about the fourteen paces and his deliberation in firing his pistol), and therefore wished to see clearly, objected on the score of the weeds and darkness caused by the overhanging trees. Somebody then proposed the main Alipore road, but he was outvoted by all the others. Colonel Pearse does not say (although there were only three of them present while Colonel Watson was fetching the pistols) who the individual was who had so little regard for appearances as to suggest the public road; possibly it was his own principal, the daylight-loving Hastings. After this proposal was rejected, they turned to their right into the cross-road leading to the west, and from which branched off, as we venture to assume, the "old road" already alluded to.

It is evident they could not have been far from where they left the carriages, as it may be presumed the servants, from the calling of whom Colonel Pearse returned in "two minutes," were syces and perhaps a chapprassi or two, and Belvedere must have been close at hand, since Colonel Watson himself went there to fetch a cot, leaving the two combatants by themselves. What occurred after the binding with the sheet is not easy to follow. The duellists, on first arriving, *drove* up to the place of appointment. Why, then, not take the cot back into the main road to the "chariot" by the way which Colonel Pearse had gone and returned so quickly? The supposition that occurs to me is this: they probably thought it prudent to carry the wounded man as little in the carriage as they could, as the cot must have been easier for him; they therefore directed the carriage to go on towards Alipore bridge, meaning to take a short and diagonal cut across country with the cot, and pick up the carriage at the Belvedere side of the bridge; so they proceeded through the low marshy ground in the direction of the present Hermitage compound and the Zoological Gardens, till they were pulled up by a deep watercourse, a very likely thing to meet in the height of the rainy season. There they had to retrace their steps, and finally emerge by the cross-road into the main road, where they had first assembled. Mr. Francis was probably in much pain and weakness by this time, and was counselled to give up the idea of going into town, but to make for the nearest port—Belvedere. Unless records or trustworthy tradition point to another locality, I am inclined to think that the compound of No. 5, Alipore Road, holds near its northern boundary the site of this memorable duel.

The account goes on to say that Hastings and Colonel Pearse went to Calcutta to the residence of the former "to send assistance to meet Francis, but he had been prevailed on to accept a room at Belvedere, and there the surgeons, Dr. Campbell, the principal, and Dr. Francis, the Governor's own surgeon, found him. When Dr. Francis returned, he informed the Governor that the wound was not mortal." "After the first confusion had subsided," writes Francis himself, "and after I had suffered great inconvenience from being carried to a wrong place, I was at last conveyed to Major Tolly's * house on a bed."

Having escaped Hastings' bullet in the morning, Francis had next to encounter the danger of being put to death during the day by a well-intentioned, but armed and meddlesome man, for he tells us that "the surgeon arrived in about an hour and a half from the time I was wounded, and cut out the ball and bled me twice in the course of the day."

The next entries in Francis's journal are—

"*August* 17.—Mr. Hastings sends to know when he may visit me."

* I have ascertained that Foley as originally printed in Francis's Memoirs was a mistake. There is no clue as to where the "wrong place" was. If, by "Major Tolly's house" Francis meant Belvedere, to which Pearse and Hastings say he was taken, then Tolly must have been occupying it, possibly as the tenant of Hastings, though it became later on part of Tolly's Estate. The words "prevailed on to accept" suggest Francis's unwillingness to go to Belvedere.

COLONEL HENRY WATSON.
CHIEF ENGINEER OF BENGAL.

*See p.* 115.

"*August* 18.—In these two days the pain I suffered was very considerable."

"*August* 19.—Desire Colonel Watson to tell Mr. Hastings as civilly as possible that I am forced to decline his visit."

"*August* 24.—Return to Calcutta."

"*September* 11.—Attend Council, great civility between H. and me."

The account concludes with a formal assurance that "both parties behaved as became gentlemen of their high rank and station. Mr. Hastings seemed to be in a state of such perfect tranquillity, that a spectator would not have supposed that he was about an action out of the common course of things, and Mr. Francis's deportment was such as did honour to his firmness and resolution."

Warren Hastings, writing a few days afterwards to his friend, Lawrence Sulivan, says:—"I hope Mr. Francis does not think of assuming any merit from this silly affair. I have been ashamed that I have been an actor in it, and I declare to you upon my honour that such was my sense of it at the time, that I was much disturbed by an old woman, whose curiosity prompted her to stand by as spectatress of a scene so little comprehended by the natives of this part of the world, and attracted others of the same stamp from the adjacent villages to partake in the entertainment." In the "Siyar ul Mutaquerin" the Mahomedan historian has an allusion to the duel translated quaintly thus:—"Meanwhile the fire of dissension which had been raging with so much violence between the Governor-General and Mr. Francis, had now risen to such a height that from bad words and disputes they had proceeded to fighting. At the end of Redjeb or the beginning of Thaban both parties according to the established custom of the nation went out by themselves and fought with pistols. The Governor being befriended by destiny came off harmless, but Mr. Francis was wounded. As he was predestined to live a great deal more, the pistol ball although it entered at his right side did neither break the bone nor even rend the curtain (*sic?*); it stopped between bone and flesh and in a few days he was cured."

I subjoin here, as being of special interest, three letters from Warren Hastings to his wife relating to this duel; they have never been published before (*i.e.* 1888) that I know of.

No. 1 is very steadily penned, though written immediately on his return from the duel. It fully bears out the state of "perfect tranquillity" vouched for by his second. Like most of his letters to his wife, it is dated merely with the day of the week.

*Calcutta, Thursday morning.*

MY DEAREST MARIAN,

I have desired Sir John Day* to inform you that I have had a meeting this morning with Mr. Francis, who has received a wound in his side, but I hope not dangerous. I shall know the state of it presently and will write to you again. He is at Belvedere, and Drs. Campbell and Francis are both gone to attend him there. I am *well* and *unhurt.* But you must be content to hear this good from me ; you cannot see me. I cannot leave Calcutta while Mr. Francis is in any danger. But I wish you to stay at Chinsura. I hope in a few days to have ye pleasure of meeting you there. Make my compts. to Mr. Ross, but do not mention what has passed. My Marian, you have occupied all my thoughts for these two days past and unremittedly.

Yours ever, my most beloved,

W. H.

*Thursday evening.*

MY BELOVED MARIAN,

I despatched a letter to you this morning at seven o'clock under cover of one to Sir John Day, whom I desired to break the subject of it to you before he delivered it, that you might not be alarmed by any sudden report of what passed between Mr. Francis and me this morning. I hope you received it before dinner, as the hurkaru had strict injunctions to be quick, and there was no other risk of the letter missing you, but that of Sir John's having left Chinsura or being out of the way. I have now the pleasure to tell you that Mr. Francis is in no manner of danger, the ball having passed through the muscular part of his back just below the shoulder, but without penetrating or injuring any of the bones. As you say, "Who knows what may happen ! who can look into the seeds of time," etc. I have sent the rice to poor Naylor, but I fear it is too late for diet or medicine to do him service. Mr. Motte † will return you your key. I have also given him in charge your hundred gold mohurs which you desired me to carry with

* The Advocate-General.

† This name often occurs in the private correspondence of Hastings. Mr. Motte was a free merchant ; in 1766 he undertook a journey to the diamond mines in Orissa by direction of Clive, and wrote an account of it. He afterwards lived at Benares, and moved thence to Hooghly, where the Hastings used to visit Mrs. Motte, who was a great friend of Mrs. Hastings. For some time Mr. Motte held a police appointment in Calcutta, where his name is still preserved in "Mott's Lane." About that time he must have got into financial difficulties, as in 1781 there is an advertisement in the newspaper calling a meeting of his creditors. Amongst the Impey manuscripts in the British Museum, there is a petition from Mr. Motte written from the Calcutta Jail in 1783, in which this friend of the Governor-General's begs that his creditors will assent to his release from prison on the score of humanity. His wife accompanied Mrs. Hastings to England in 1784.

me. I am obliged to stay in Calcutta at least until Mr. F. is known to be free from all danger, lest my absence should be called a flight, so that I cannot join you this week, but do not let this bring you to Calcutta before the time you have fixed for your return.

I am well and the remains of the influenza are scarcely perceptible about my ancles (*sic*). You do not tell me how you are. Do not presume upon your good appetite, and be abstemious at night.—Adieu,

Your ever affectionate,

WARREN HASTINGS.

Did I tell you that I had a letter from Scott, who mentions his passing young Touchet, my lion and zebra all in perfect health. Pray tell Mrs. Motte so. Calcutta is horridly damp and dismal besides.

*Calcutta, Friday morning.*

MY DEAR MARIAN,

"I have received yours. You must not be angry; perhaps it is best that what has passed has passed, and it may be productive of future good. My desire that you would not leave Chinsura proceeded only from the apprehension lest, by a precipitate departure, your spirits might be agitated and your health affected by not chusing (*sic*) proper seasons and making the fit preparation for your voyage. Do now as you please. You will find me here free from both sickness, anxiety, and trouble; and if you chuse to stay longer where you are, you may have the same satisfaction of knowing that I am so. Mr. Francis continues well and I pronounce his cure certain. Poor Naylor is dead. Will you let Sir J. Day know that there is no reason for his returning to town.

I will write to him myself. I am sorry to hear Lady Day is sick: my compts. to her, to Bibby Motte, and Mr. Ross,

Yours,

W. H.

You are much obliged to Col. Pearse.*

* Colonel Thomas Deane Pearse, of the Artillery, who died a few miles up the Hooghly, where he went for change of air, in June, 1789. His body was brought to Calcutta and buried in South Park Street Cemetery, where the tomb is still to be seen. The newspaper of the day says that eight officers came from Barrackpore to carry the body to the grave, but arrived too late. Lord Cornwallis was present at the funeral, or, as the local chronicler puts it, "His Lordship attended and drop't a tear with the crowd."

# CHAPTER VII

## PHILIP FRANCIS AND HIS TIMES

### 5.—HOME AND SOCIAL LIFE, 1774–1780

### (I)

> "'Tis pleasant through the loopholes of retreat
> To peep at such a world."

UNDER this heading it is proposed to say something about the general routine of life in Calcutta during and about the period that Philip Francis sojourned there, keeping him as the central figure, so to say, of the society whose sayings and doings and amusings, etc., may come under review.

Culled from many sources, the contents of the next chapter or two must necessarily, I fear, be of a rambling, discursive nature.

In thus gossiping upon the social life of Francis and his Calcutta contemporaries it may be interesting to see, as a preliminary, whether there are any data which would help us to say where he resided.

In his own and his brother-in-law's letters allusions are found to three houses occupied by Francis. Thus, in the December of the year of their arrival, *i.e.* in 1774, Mackrabie * writes: "The expenses of this settlement are beyond all conception. Mr. F—— pays £500 a year for a large, but rather mean house like a barn, with bare walls and not a single glass window." † A year later he says: "You can have no idea of the importance of a large cool house in this climate; ours is positively the hottest in Calcutta—a torrid zone, and we

* This oft-recurring name is spelled "Macrabie" by Francis and by old Calcutta newspapers, where it seldom occurs. His later-day kindred, however, have it "Mac*k*rabie," which must be more correct.

† A lady, writing from Calcutta in 1783, says: "Glass is a dear commodity to Calcutta, and imported solely from England; on which account the Governor's house is almost the only one that can boast that distinction." Venetians and windows of cane-work were mostly in vogue.

can't get another." I have found no clue to the whereabouts of this house; it must be the one thus referred to by Mackrabie in a letter dated March, 1775. "Mr. Francis' house is surrounded with mosques and pagodas, where they make, night and day, such a cursed clatter with drums, cymbals, horns, and pans you would think a legion of devils were keeping jubilee."

The same authority writes that, by the following February, Francis has purchased what Mackrabie calls a "Lodge" in the neighbourhood of Calcutta, which, he says, "consists of a spacious hall and four chambers, surrounded by a verandah and colonnade, and stands in the midst of twenty acres of ground, pleasant to the last degree." In another letter he says that Francis "talks already of quitting Calcutta, or of having only a small house by way of office and dressing-room. None but friends to be admitted here (the Lodge); Lady Impey yesterday, Lady Anne and Colonel Monson to-day." The Lodge so described I believe to be on the site of the house occupied for many years as the official residence of the Collector of the Twenty-four Pergunnahs.

As Mr. Francis bought the Lodge in 1775, and sold it to Mr. Livius for Rs.30,000 in April, 1780, it is not likely that he lived in any other suburban residence during his sojourn in India. In Colonel Mark Wood's map "of the country and the banks of the Hooghly from Calcutta to Ooloobareah," and in Colonel Call's map, dated 1786, the names of the residents in many of the suburban houses are given, and that of Mr. Francis is attached to the house on the site indicated. The present house is a double-storied one, therefore the "Lodge" must have been added to or rebuilt, as from Mackrabie's description it was originally a bungalow, but on an ample scale, as Messrs. Livius and Collings lived there with Francis for a time. This entry in Mackrabie's diary early in 1776 gives further evidence as to the locality. "At the Gardens, being Sunday, we wrote special hard all the morning. Colonel Monson, Mr. Farrer, and Mr. Thompson dined with us, so did Major Tolly, he is cutting a navigable canal close by."

It is evident that the Lodge stood on low marshy ground, such as the neighbourhood of Tolly's Nullah might have been expected to be, from the following letter addressed to Francis by some humorous fellow signing himself D., who had been reading Pliny's Epistles:—

*March* 31, 1779.—I was in pursuit of you last night near two hours without success. I went first to your "*villa inter paludes*," where I found not the smallest vestige of society. I then returned to town, and, quitting my chariot, I took to my litter and proceeded in it to your house near the Capitol, where, to my utter astonishment, I found the same appearance of desertion and desolation. It struck me that you might have repassed the Rubicon, and with your slaves have gone again upon some private plan of pleasures into Cis-alpine Gaul (*i.e.* Chandernagore). While I was ruminating upon these things, a Ligurian tax-gatherer, whom I remember to have seen among your followers, informed me that, having been forced by certain putrid exhalations from the marshes in which your villa stands to discontinue your weekly symposium there, and having at a late meeting at Nasidienus drank too deeply of Falernian, you had retired with two females (Contemplation and Temperance), with whom you had been very lately made acquainted, to the gardens of Rufillus near the fourth stone on the Falernian Way, to enjoy with him and his freedman, Petronius Macer, the feast of reason and the flow of soul, or to prepare yourself for the more momentous matter that may be debated in the Senate this day, etc.

It would seem, however, that Francis did not content himself with a small house in town for an office, etc., from these passages in Mackrabie's journal :—

*February* 21, 1776.—We have at last engaged a capital house, the best in town ; but such a rent ! £100 a month is enormous ; * neighbour Collings and I must contribute towards it. We are bound to do so, I swear ; we have no wives nor children. He adds a month after :— There is a drawing-room in the upper story about 50 feet long, a dining room below as large, besides two spacious halls and a suite of three rooms upon each floor to the E. and W., that is, fourteen rooms in all. 'Tis by far the largest, loftiest, and most superb house in the place. And Francis says, a month later, in a letter to John Burke :— Here I live, master of the finest house in Bengal, with a hundred servants, a country house, and spacious gardens, horses and carriages, yet so perverse is my nature, that the devil take me if I would not exchange the best dinner and the best company I ever saw in Bengal for a beefsteak and claret at the Horn, and let me choose my company.

Where was this vaunted house? It is stated by a witness at a trial in Calcutta in 1778, in which Francis was a principal, that he recognised the defendant as "Mr. Francis, who lived behind the

* Rents in Calcutta seem to have been higher in the eighteenth century than in the next. Thus in 1786 Wheler's house is advertised to be sold with 3½ begasi of ground, "present rent 900 Sicca Rs. monthly." From 450 to 850 Rs. would appear to have been the ordinary rent for a large upper-roomed house with extensive compound in a good locality. The Calcutta Exchange, on the S.W. corner of the Great Tank, let for 350 Rs. monthly. Mrs. Fay says she paid 200 Rs. for a house "in a part of the town not much esteemed," otherwise she should have to pay 300 or 400 Rs.

Playhouse." The Playhouse referred to, known as the new one, stood in the block now called "New China Bazaar," behind (north of) Writer's Buildings. A reference to old maps shows that the house (apparently a very large one) standing about this time nearest to the theatre, on the north, is one at the corner of Old Fort Ghaut Street and Clive Street; there is no house near it, and its site exactly corresponds with that occupied by the Oriental Bank afterwards.

Tradition assigns this as the site of the house lived in by Clive, whence Clive Street derives its name.

In the absence, therefore, of any direct evidence to the contrary, the probability is great that this was "the finest house in Bengal" for which Francis paid 1000 rupees a month. Here he gave his dinners and balls, and here, too, we may suppose he spent the day before his duel with Hastings, in burning papers which it is not unlikely could have thrown much light on the Junius question; and here he was brought wounded a week after the duel.

In the last century, work occupied much less of the European's time in Calcutta than now. The young civilian, for instance, went to office during the hot weather from 9 a.m. to 12, and during the cooler months from 10 to 1.30, and again from 7.30 to 9 in the evening. When a despatch had to be sent to England special attendance in the evening was enjoined. The easy-going pace * of the official rank and file was adopted by the rest of the community. The periodic arrival and departure of the Europe ships gave a temporary stimulus to all business, and then the comfortable jog-trot was resumed. The comparatively small amount of routine work to be got through admitted of a more rational allotment of time for public or other duties, and for social refreshment than prevails in these busy days.

A very good idea of how an ordinary day was disposed of can be gathered from the letters of Miss Sophia Goldborne and of Mrs. Fay, written from Calcutta in the time of Warren Hastings, and from diaries and letters preserved by Philip Francis, and from other similar and contemporary sources. If we follow a day's routine, some obsolete old customs and fashions will be brought into view.

The early morning ride or walk was taken by the generality of the men and by some of the ladies, just as now. In the cool season hunting was much indulged in. The Calcutta community maintained a "good pack of dogs, 50 couples" in the time of Francis. A light

* Chief Justice Impey writes to his brother:—"I take great care to spare myself, never sitting in Court after one at noon."

breakfast came off about 9, or earlier. "The fashionable undress, except in the article of being without stays (and stays are wholly unworn in the East) is much in the English style, with large caps or otherwise, as fancy dictates. No care or skill is left unexerted to render the appearance easy and graceful, a necessary circumstance (adds Miss Goldborne), as gentlemen in the course of their morning excursions continually drop in, who say the prettiest things imaginable with an air of truth that wins on the credulity and harmonises the heart."

Two o'clock was the usual hour for dinner; Mrs. Fay gives an ordinary day's bill of fare for this meal for herself and husband, viz. soup, a roast fowl, curry and rice, a mutton pie, a fore-quarter of lamb, a rice pudding, tarts, very good cheese, excellent Madeira. Not bad for a lady "still much of an invalid," and a rather briefless barrister given to idleness and dissolute ways. She accounts for the abundance, by her experience that the heat in Bengal does *not* "destroy the appetite." In preparation for dinner "the *friseur* formed the person anew." Those ladies who did not wear ornamented caps had artificial flowers "intermixed with their tresses." Powder was used in great quantities on the hair. Gentlemen generally sat down in white jackets.* In describing the dinner the lady last quoted says:—

> To every plate are set down two glasses; one pyramidal (like hob-nob glasses in England), for loll shrub (claret); the other a common sized wineglass for whatever beverage is most agreeable. Between every two persons is placed a decanter of water and tumbler for diluting at pleasure. Hosts of men on all occasions present themselves at dinner, but the sexes are blended (I will not say in pairs, for the men are out of all proportion to the female world) so as to aid the purposes of gallantry and good humour. . . . The attention and court paid to me was astonishing. My smile was meaning, and my articulation melody; in a word, mirrors are almost useless at Calcutta, and self-adoration idle, for your looks are reflected in the pleasure of the beholder, and your claims to first-rate distinction confirmed by all who approach you.
>
> After the circulation of a few loyal healths, etc., the ladies withdraw, the gentlemen drink their cheerful glass for some time beyond that period, insomuch that it is no infrequent thing for each man to

* It was not till Lord Wellesley's time that white clothing began to be considered too undress for public occasions, and that cloth came into general use. So writes Lord Valentia. Still, up to the middle of the nineteenth century, say up to 1860, it was not unusual for gentlemen to attend private dinner parties bringing white jackets with them to be substituted for their cloth coats at the host's invitation.

STREET VIEW IN CALCUTTA, 1786.

SHOWING EASTERN CURTAIN AND BASTIONS OF THE OLD FORT AND HOLWELL'S MONUMENT.

*See p.* 123.

despatch his three bottles of claret, or two of white wine, before they break up.

This young lady was a fresh arrival, and was a member of an official's household who saw a good deal of company; one is not, therefore, surprised at her remarking that "wine is the heaviest family article, for whether it is taken fashionably or medicinally, every lady (even to your humble servant) drinks at least a bottle per diem, and the gentlemen four times that quantity." * Nor to learn, that after such potations "the ladies at Calcutta retire (after dinner) not to enjoy their private chat, for to sleep is the object of their wishes and the occupation of their time—a refreshment that alone enables them to appear with animation in the evening. Accordingly both ladies and gentlemen entirely undress and repose on their beds in the same manner as at the midnight hour, and on awakening are a second time attended by their hair-dresser,† and thus a second time in the twenty-four hours come forth armed at all points for conquest."

At sunset Calcutta became alive again: society went out for its airing; those who could not afford vehicles walked amongst the trees and shrubs round the great tank (Lall Diggee), or on the ramparts of the Old Fort. The more prosperous went in chariots and phaetons of English build. It is mentioned incidentally in his secretary's diary that Francis, and presumably other high officials, drove four horses. Ladies of *ton*, we are told, adopted phaetons, and "always make a point of having a gentleman companion who lolls at his ease, the office of managing the reins, etc., being wholly assumed by the lady—the horses finely set out with silver nets to guard their necks from insects, and reins elegantly decorated. To finish the whole a kittesaw (a kind of umbrella) is suspended not unfrequently over the lady's head, which gives her the true Eastern grandeur of appearance." The roads in and about Calcutta were very bad; that

* "English claret" cost at this time 60 Rs. the dozen; "Danish do.," 28 Rs.; porter or beer, 150 Rs. the cask; cheese, 3 Rs. per lb.; hams, 2 Rs. per lb.; hats, plain, 36 Rs. each; silk stockings, 20 Rs. per pair.

† The hair-dresser was indispensable in those days of powder and pomatum, not only for ladies, but for gentlemen too, who twice daily passed under his hands. The lowest pay which a native hair-dresser got was two rupees monthly, but in many instances it ranged much higher; each gentleman entertained the services of a hair-dresser as well as of a "shaving-barber." There were two Frenchmen settled in Calcutta as special hair-dressers. One of them, M. Malvaist, charged two gold mohurs monthly for dressing ladies' hair; the other, M. Sivet, charged eight rupees to ladies for one hair-cutting, and four rupees for hair-dressing, and half these amounts to gentlemen.

along the river did not yet exist. The "Course" was the only drive, but the dust, for which it was remarkable, tempered the enjoyment of an airing taken there. Many resorted to the river for its cooling breezes, though its surface and its banks must have presented many unsavoury sights. Private budgerows and pinnaces, many-oared and of a size and magnificence not often seen now, were then in fashion. They may be seen advertised in the old newspapers occasionally, viz. "A pinnace budgerow fifty-six feet in length, sixteen feet in breadth, tight as a bottle, glass windows, astern lockers, and well found in everything for the longest trip on the river;" or, "A fourteen-oared pinnace consisting of a hall fifteen feet long by twelve feet broad, drawing only two feet of water—Price 900 Sicca rupees." Whole families went for their evening airing in them. Some carried bands of music. The gilded youth of the period rather affected being attended by an African slave or two from Bourbon or Mauritius (called Coffres), who to their other accomplishments, added that of being able to play on the French horn.

On return from the Course, tea or coffee was served in every house. Formal and friendly visits were paid at this sensible hour, each visit being very short, as a lady would, perhaps, have several to pay, and then to hasten home to receive her own callers. Gentlemen also were allowed to make their calls in the evening, after tea, and if asked to lay aside their hats, it was understood that they were invited to stay for supper. This was generally announced at ten o'clock, cards or music filling up the interval; the company generally broke up about midnight. In ten minutes after your return home, writes Mackrabie, the servants desert and leave you to your meditations.

These entries in the secretary's diary tell what the social evenings and suppers were like, viz.:—

*September*, 1775.—In the evening played cards at Lady Anne Monson's; three whist tables and two chess. Quadrille is little in vogue here. Lady Anne is a very superior whist-player. Mr. Francis generally fortunate.

*November* 3 (A party at the Claverings).—We have been in the heart of the enemy's camp. The whole house of Barwell, with Sir Impey and Lady. We wanted only the Governor to make it complete.

*Entre nous*, the evening was stupid enough, and the supper detestable; great joints of roasted goat, with endless dishes of cold fish. With respect to conversation, we have had three or four songs screeched to unknown tunes; the ladies regaled with cherry-brandy, and we pelted one another with bread-pills *à la mode de* Bengal.

It was probably the suppers which were accountable for this entry:—

This bile is the devil. Mr. Francis has another attack of it, and has headache and fever. I will make him dine quietly at home, though we are invited to a card and supper party. He says he cannot be sick, with any degree of comfort, unless his dear wife is at hand.* But soon after he writes, We drank enormously to-day, considering the set.

This was at one of the frequent festive visits to "Barasutt," where Barwell had what he called a hunting lodge which is praised for its freedom from mosquitoes, "while we are devoured by them at Calcutta and forced to use every art to keep them off." Weekly card parties were held regularly by the gentlemen, who sometimes met at a tavern as a club, and where much high betting was indulged in, as many entries in Mackrabie's diary show, viz.:—

*Nov.*—Being Wednesday it may not be amiss for me to look at my card account, and see how the reckoning stands between me and the world. I have been losing all this month. Let me see. Pretty even. I am not ten pounds gainer or loser upon that account since I left England. But that is not right. I want money; I begin to love money; and if I can get it fairly I will have money.

*February* 2, 1776.—At Barrasut. This day passed in much the same manner as the former; at the close of it and of our accounts we found that the house of Francis and Co. were winners several hundred pounds. Everything in this country is upon an enlarged scale, and the superior skill and attention of Mr. F. will make him successful both in business and sport.

*February* 6, 1776.—Mr. Barwell has lost again, and we have all won. I told you of his heavy losses at Barrasut. We all shared in the spoil, nor has any of this house declined giving him his revenge. Justice Lemaitre, who had before been a very considerable loser, having recovered his sufferings at the expense of Mr. Barwell, has tied up, as it is called, and plays no more. Colonel Leslie does the same. This a little vexes Mr. Barwell, who is fond of play and will play for anything. We still go on.

*March* 2.—Mr. F. was fortunate in being absent last night, as he would infallibly have lost his money had he been there; Mr. Barwell, against whom he constantly plays and bets, won every rubber he sat down to. Collings was damaged, so was I.

*March* 9.—We supped at Mr. Barwell's and lost our monies. I have lost seven rubbers running. Oh, sad, sad, sad!

* "I charge you," wrote an American cousin to Francis, when starting for India, "not to let Mackrabie play the quack with you. He is a mighty man for physic, and will be offering you doses every day; but don't you take them, if you do he will work you to death before you get to Fort William."

On the nights not devoted to the whist club Mackrabie and his party joined the ladies in their ordinary social gatherings and amusements, viz.:—

*March.*—All were at the assembly. You never hear of our dancing. No, we are past all that; besides, the ladies are generally engaged for two months. So we have no chance.

We have two sittings up in town; Mrs. Larkins, a bride, her husband is a young Compy. servant, under age but looks forty. He is sub-accountant. Mrs. Hyde is the other.

Mrs. Hyde has her concert on a Tuesday. She is an unkind fair one. I remember at Madeira when, Syren as she is, she stole away my simple heart, she promised I should have free admission to her house and parties; but those happy days are past and gone.

*Saturday, March* 9.—Why, there was a ball at Colonel Gallier's, and the French women dancing cotillions as if they had not another hour to live. Mrs. Clavering was there and the Misses and the General and Bibby Johnson, and Miss Ashe, and Miss Howe, who lives with Lady Impey and is going to marry Dr. Campbell, who has fewer hairs and more years than I have. There was he capering about and gallanting the lady and exercising her fan; she is not above sixteen—January and May! Colonel Gallier is a jolly fellow, and we who did not dance must needs drink. I have got the biles and the indigestion cruelly this morning, and there is General Clavering gone out at six and carried out those dear girls with him on horseback, though they were not in bed before two. Mrs. Walton told us so. But who is Mrs. Walton? Why, you are to know that she was house-keeper to Mrs. Clavering, and is now going to hold the same office in this family, by which Mr. F. will probably save £1000 a year. She is an excellent manager, and being absolutely on the wrong side of forty causes neither scandal nor envy. Mrs. Clavering acknowledges it is a wise measure; she has seen our new house and made all the arrangements.—"The Francis Papers," 1901.

Regarding the Calcutta Sunday in the olden time, Miss Goldborne's letters disclose a privilege allowed to gentlemen which would seem to have been highly valued. It may be premised that the church which she refers to was the space in the Old Fort set aside for the purpose. She calls it "a ground floor, with arrangement of plain pews." If so, it was near the main gateway, between it and south-east bastion, and was used (under orders of Government in 1760) as a chapel for over twenty-five years, though much too small for the increasing congregation.

"I have been at church in my new palanquin (the mode of genteel conveyance) where *all* ladies are approached by sanction of ancient custom by all gentlemen indiscriminately, known or unknown, with offers of their hands to conduct them to their seat. Accordingly, those gentlemen who wish to change their condition (which between ourselves are chiefly old fellows) on hearing of a ship's arrival make a point of repairing to this holy dome and eagerly tender their services to the fair strangers."

I believe antiquarians who have touched on the subject of this temporary chapel have not agreed as to its position. Rev. J. Long gives in his selections from the Government records, the original Government order about it, 1760, viz. "that the Surveyor examine the remains of the gateway in the Old Fort, and report what it will cost to put it in tolerable repair to make it fit for a chapel" (temporary). Mr. Long then says vaguely, "this chapel was over the gateway and next the Black Hole," which suggests a topographical contradiction. Marshman ("History of India"), speaking of the prison cell, says: "Orme calls it a dungeon, but the room immediately adjoining it was used as the Settlement church for twenty-eight years." Asiaticus, writing in 1774, says: "There is a noble playhouse, but no church, the want of which is supplied by a spacious apartment in the Old Fort adjoining to the room so well known as the Black Hole." And here we find Miss Goldborne also describing it as on a ground floor. But why then the architectural rarity of a high-pitched roof, as shown by Daniell in 1786, and which probably got it, or gave it, the name of the "holy dome"? If it were known how far south that temporary chapel extended, or whether it was (accurately) "next" the Black Hole or not, much discussion as to the site of the latter might have been spared.*

Like most new arrivals in India, Francis and his friend were much exercised at the number of servants that inexorable custom planted on them. The remarks wrung from Mackrabie on this head have lost none of their force and appropriateness after the lapse of more than a century:—

* Mackrabie writes to his father, November, 1774, "One of the first observations we made here was that they have no church. The same edifice serves upon the first day of the week for the celebration of Divine Service, and during the other six for the entering of goods and collecting of customs. The Company's servants were much amazed to see us go thither in a body the Sunday after our arrival; but we afterwards perceived, with pleasure, that the example had produced a good effect, though not sufficient to break up a sporting club who constantly go a-hunting on that day." Surely this was a serving of two masters under the one roof! To the Rev. S. Baggs he writes early in 1775, "We are upon excellent terms with the Clergy here. They are not numerous, but thoroughly orthodox. One rivals Nimrod in hunting, a second supplies bullocks for the army, another is a perfect connoisseur in Chinese gardening. I endeavour to obtain some light from them all; but the fear of God is not the kind of wisdom most in request in Bengal."

"One hundred and ten servants to wait upon a family of four people, and yet we are economists! Oh, monstrous! Tell me if this land does not want weeding! . . . The domestic cares in this country to the person who thinks it in the least degree essential to his welfare that bills should be examined before they are paid, and that servants who are born and bred rogues should cheat within some degree of moderation, will find full employment for his faculties. To superintend this tribe of devils and their several departments we have a numerous collection of banyans, chief and subordinate, with their train of clerks, who fill a large room, and are constantly employed in controlling or rather conniving at each other's accounts. We are cheated in every article both within and without doors. . . . Collings is at this moment scolding a circar who means nothing more than to cheat him of £150 by mere confusion of figures. 'Oh-ho! What, you have found it out; you admit it at last do you, Mr. Banyan? Yes, yes, very right what master say; my way bad way, master's account right.' They are the most indefatigable incorrigible thieves. My greatest comfort is to turn them all out and lock the doors. These brutes possess every bad quality except drunkenness and insolence: indeed they make full amends for the first by stupefying themselves with chewing *bang*, and their want of the other is pretty well supplied by a most provoking gravity and indifference."

The Court of Directors struggled hard against the tendency on the part of their *employés* to entertain many servants and to become luxurious. In 1757 they directed that a junior civilian without a family should be allowed only two servants and a cook, that he should not keep a horse, or have a garden house, or wear other than plain clothes.

From the earliest days of the English settlement in Bengal, servants appear to have been a fertile source of worry, and to have always been adepts at the passive resistance and the organised combination to injure and annoy, which characterise them to this day. In the old proceedings of Government it may be seen that this matter was often taken into consideration at the instance of the inhabitants complaining of the "insolence and exorbitant wages exacted by the menial servants."

A set of rules were drawn up of a very stringent nature for the mutual observance of master and servants. Rates of wages were accurately defined for each class of servants, and to avoid the market being spoiled by the wealthy or the careless, to the prejudice of his poorer neighbour, it was ordered that "if any master presume to exceed the established rate of wages on any pretence whatever, he shall be debarred all redress from the Court of Zemindary, and the protection of the Settlement shall be withdrawn from him." Servants leaving without stipulated notice were punished very severely.

To show that all the law was not on the side of the Europeans, it may be noted that a Mr. Johnson was visited with fine for striking his servant, and for non-payment and non-appearance he was cast into prison, whence he petitioned Mr. Vansittart for release, urging that he had been three months "rotting in a loathsome gaol, having not the wherewithal to pay or provide the common necessaries of life." In 1766 it was resolved that an office be established in Calcutta for keeping a register of all servants, but it was soon found that the Europeans would not take the trouble to combine for vigorous action; they neglected to send their servants for registration, or to employ only registered ones; they lazily preferred to let the old state of things go on, so that the servants became literally the masters of the situation. Between 1760 and 1787, servants' wages became doubled, and, in many instances, trebled in amount. The average rates existing to-day are pretty much the same as those of a hundred years ago. The reason for this is probably that servants look as much to their gains from picking and stealing as to their pay. Many functionaries who have a place in old lists have no representatives now, such as the wig-barber, hookaburdar, soontabardar, crutchpurdar (this person relieved his master of the trouble of making actual payments; his pay was four rupees a month; his opportunities may be fancied), "comprădor," who bought the table supplies—pay, nominal, *i.e.* three rupees; power of extortion very enviable.* The lady who wielded the broom had her native appellation tortured into the composite word "Harry-wench." Her indispensable functions were appraised (in the early days of the Settlement) at the modest sum of one rupee monthly, or in case of a whole family, two rupees.

It is worth noticing that the designation "punkah pullers" does not occur among the list of servants employed at the period with which we are concerned. The swinging punkah, as in use now, dates after Francis's time in India. By comparing various references to domestic life in Calcutta at the close of the last century, it is possible to fix within very narrow limits the date of the introduction of the hanging punkah into India. The letters of Miss Goldborne were written about 1783-4, but were published under the title "Hartly House, Calcutta," in 1789. In describing a dinner, she says, "during the whole period of dinner boys with flappers and fans surround you, procuring you, at least, a tolerably comfortable artificial

* *E.g.* Mrs. Fay's comprodore (*sic*) complained at not being able to make enough out of her, alleging that "at other houses he always made a rupee a day at least, besides his wages."

atmosphere." But M. L. de Grandpré, in his "Voyage to Bengal, undertaken in 1789–90," says:

"To chase away the flies and occasion a free circulation of the air, many houses have a large fan from the ceiling over the eating table, of a square form, and balanced on an axle fitted to the upper part of it. A servant standing at one end of the room puts it in motion by means of a cord which is fastened to it, in the same manner as he would ring a bell. Besides this, there is a servant behind the chair of each individual with another kind of fan made of a branch of the palm tree. The stalk serves for a handle, and the leaves fastened together and cut into a round or square shape give it the appearance of a flag. By these contrivances a little fresh air is procured."

These two extracts show that the hanging punkah came in between 1784 and 1790. The following paragraph, which I found in the *Calcutta Chronicle* for December, 1792 (quoted from the "Journal"), makes it evident that the institution was in full swing, viz.: "It is not generally known that the punkahs which we suspend in our rooms are machines originally introduced into this country by the Portuguese; they are used to this day in Spain." It is probable that the use of the punkah was not extended to the bedrooms for a good while after its introduction, and was reserved for meal-times only. Under the heading "Punkah" in the glossary of "Anglo-Indian Terms," by Colonel Yule and Mr. Burnell, there is some exceedingly curious and interesting information. Passages are there quoted which show that the true Anglo-Indian punkah was known to the Arabs as early as the eighth century!

The popular tradition in Calcutta is that the suspended punkah was the device of a Eurasian clerk, whose duties lay in one of the small low-roofed rooms of the present Fort William, and who one day, being driven frantic by heat and mosquitoes, slung the half of the camp table at which he was writing to a beam overhead, and attached a rope to it, which he put into the hands of a bewildered cooly, with instructions to pull it. If this be the origin of a contrivance to which succeeding generations of Anglo-Indians owe so much, it is humiliating to be obliged to record that the name of this benefactor remains unknown to fame.

Before leaving the subject of servants, a further insight under this head, into the customs of the last century, may be got by referring to the summary mode in which the police dealt with this class (and others) when brought up as offenders. This will be fairly exemplified by a few ordinary extracts from the charge sheet of the Superintendent of Police in 1778, C. S. Playdell.*

* We have already seen more than once this well-known name in Old

John Ringwell, against his cook named Runjaney, for running away from him and beating another servant who had been engaged in his place. It appears that he had one of his ears cut off for some offence. The present complaint being fully proved—ordered he receive ten rattans and be dismissed.

A slave girl of Mr. Anderson, Piggy, having again run away from her master and being apprehended by the Chowkedar—ordered her five rattans, and be sent to her master.

Mooleah, a boy, was apprehended by the Pykes of the 8th Division. The boy has been frequently punished in the cutcherry for robbery, and but a few days since received twenty rattans and was sent over the water never to return, notwithstanding which he has thought proper to come back. Ordered to receive fifteen rattans, and to be again sent over the water (*i.e.* across to the Howrah side of the Hooghly).

Captain Scott complains against Banybub for not complying with his promise to repair his carriage. Ordered ten slippers.

(It may be explained for readers not in India that blows with a slipper are considered in the East as adding insult to injury. This mode of punishment is still in vogue in China : it is there a brutally severe one. "The blows" (writes a traveller, 1887), "to the number of fifty, were given square on the upturned features." The victim was a woman.)

Colonel Watson against Ramsing, as an impostor receiving pay as a carpenter when actually nothing more than a barber. Ordered fifteen rattans, and to be drummed through the Cooly Bazaar to Colonel Watson's gates. (His garden house was at "Watgunge," called after him.)

Jacob Joseph against Tithol, cook, for robbing him of a brass pot and a pestle and mortar. Ordered him to be confined in the Hurring-Barree till he makes good the things.

Mr. Nottley against Calloo for putting a split bamboo and laying there in wait purposely to throw passengers down and apparently to rob them. Ten rattans.

Coja Janoose against Sarah, the slave girl of Coja Offean, for running away; it appears she has frequently done it. Ordered her

Calcutta. Its owner seems to have been the subject of much dismissing and restoring. He entered the Civil Service in 1744. Hastings gave him the police appointment in 1773. His grave is in South Park Street cemetery (1779). His final return to India is thus referred to by Dr. Hancock when writing to his wife in September, 1772. As a letter writer he was apt to be censorious; he posed as a moralist too.

"I will answer your queries relating to Mr. Pleydell (*sic*), I say he is either a fool or in desperate circumstances. If his abilities can support him, who need to despair? Neither his abilities, nor abilities much greater than his, can support him on the footing he is come hither. Compassion for a man who was once by succession entitled to the Chair, and who like a fool, declared himself incapable, may possibly induce the Great to assist him, or a lively, handsome young wife may promote his success; but what an infamous wretch must be he who can think of the latter without horror."

fifteen rattans, and to be kept in the thannah, 1st division, till her master returns.

Mr. Levitt against Nursing for inducing one of his slave girls named Polly to rob him of a quantity of linen of sorts, the above girl Polly giving evidence against him. Five rattans.

Mr. Wilkin's servants having undergone the rice * ordeal, Golaut, a dye (wet nurse) in his employ, appeared to be the guilty person, and on confirmation of her delinquency she gave the Mullah a silver punchu from her arm, and promised a further reward of Rs. 10. Ordered she be confined in the thannah of the 3rd division till some further lights can be obtained on suspicion.

Hulloder Gossein against Bulloram Byraggee for cutting from his neck, while he was asleep, a gold necklace, etc. On examination of the prisoner he confesses the fact, and being from appearance (having lost one of his ears) an old offender, ordered that he be sent to Mr. Justice Sir Robert Chambers, and that the jewels be likewise sent with him as further evidence.

Birnarold Pinto against his slave girl Pekeytase for running away; this being the second time of her being guilty of the like offence, to prevent her doing the same in future,—ordered she receive five rattans and be returned to her master.

Lourmerey, Bearer, against Mahomed Ally, an old offender, for robbing him of a number of turbands, all of which were recovered and produced in the office. Ordered he receive twenty rattans and be turned over the water not to return on pain of severe punishment.

Ramhurry Jugee against Ramgopal for stealing a toolsey dannah off a child's neck; he says he was running along, and his hands caught in it by accident. Ordered him twelve rattans.

Cortib, a Portuguese, against his boy, Jack, for stealing a silver

* When a theft was committed in a household, it was usual to send for some man reputed to be wise and good—*vir pietate gravis*—who assembled all the servants, and on their denying knowledge of the theft, each was sworn to this effect. The wise man then with befitting solemnity took down all their names and went home, he *said*, to pray. To discover who had made the false oath, the following procedure was adopted next morning by the religious detective: Some rice was half-soaked and then dried in the sun, and a tola weight (generally weighed against a square Akbar rupee) given into the hand of each of the assembled servants. At a signal all were directed to put the rice into their mouths and chew it, and then spit it out on a piece of plantain leaf given for that purpose. All were warned that from the mouth of whoever had lied to the holy man, the rice would come forth, not like milk, but quite dry and unaltered. The theory was that fear and excitement kept back the salivary flow necessary to mastication—an effect, however, just as likely to result in the case of those nervous and innocent as in that of the consciously guilty. When Mr. Motte had a police appointment in Calcutta, this method of detection was so successfully adopted that a set of grave men were kept for the purpose, called "Motte's Conjurers." See Fanny Parke's "Wanderings of a Pilgrim," vol. i., where an instance of successful resort to this ordeal is related.

spoon; the boy at first confessed the fact, and said he had given the spoon to a shopkeeper, who, on being summoned, declared his ignorance of the whole transaction; he then accused another person, who, on examination, proved to be as little concerned as the first; in short, Jack appears a complete little villain, and the whole of his account nothing but lies. Five rattans.

Samah Goalah, confined 5th October, is now released under a penalty of being hanged if ever apprehended by any one. (The "penalty" promised here under such wide possibilities was probably a grim professional joke on the part of the police clerk.)

Here follow four cases which I beg to commend to the notice of modern Calcutta magistrates.

Banker Mahomed against Rumjanny complaining that the wife of the latter abused his wife. It appearing, on examination, they were both equally culpable,—ordered each to be fined Rs. 5 for giving trouble to the Court by making trifling litigious complaints.

Mr. Cantwell against his Matraney for stealing empty bottles. This she has practised some time, and constantly sold them to a shopkeeper Bucktaram, which he himself confesses. To deter others from following so pernicious an example,—ordered Bucktaram twenty rattans, the Matraney ten rattans, and both to be carried in a cart round the town, and their crime published by beat of tom-tom.

Mr. Sage against Khoda Bux and Peary for receiving advances of wages, neglecting business and hiring themselves to others before their engagements to him are expired. Each ten slippers.

Mr. Dawson, against his Mosalchee, Tetoo, for stealing his wax candles and preventing other servants from engaging in his service by traducing his master's character. Ten rattans.

The publicity with which prisoners were punished was a notable feature in Old Calcutta. Miss Goldborne describes the machine in which those convicted were conveyed to prison. "The wheels of this machine are fourteen feet high, and under the axle is suspended a wooden cage (sufficiently large to contain a couple of culprits) perforated with air-holes, and in this miserable plight, guarded by Sepoys, they are exhibited to the eyes of the populace." The first judges of the Supreme Court do not seem to have done anything in the way of suppressing these public exhibitions. On the contrary, with that acquired professional belief which judges often hold in the wisdom of the laws they administer, and of the punishments prescribed, they signalised their establishment in Calcutta by invoking to their aid a detestable atrocity which they had been accustomed to in England, and which, as a punishment, was grotesquely unsuitable to India. Sheriff Mackrabie thus writes of it in January, 1776:—" The Supreme

Court of Judicature has introduced the use of the pillory among us. I have the credit of drawing the plan, but Judge Lemaistre gave me the outline. The horrors which the common people have here of this machine are not to be described. I suppose it must affect them in their caste, a consideration which never loses its weight, even with pickpockets. In a session or two they may perhaps become reconciled to it, and practise the ceremony of pelting as well as an English mob." * The following is but a typical instance of what must

* One is sorry to see recorded this instance of blunted sensibility and seared conscience, which permitted so bright and kindly a man, as Mr. Mackrabie evidently was, to write thus of the introduction to India of this Western method of torture. It was one of the most prominent of the many disgraces of the then criminal law in England, in which she wallowed up to about 70 years ago. People living in these comparatively enlightened days have no idea what barbarity this method of punishment, and shockingly evil example, fostered in the public mind. It is strange that the origin of the pillory in England, or in other countries, dates so far back as to be practically untraceable. Stranger still it is to realise that the clement England of to-day, took centuries to emerge out of the dreadful darkness testified to by its criminal law. The pelting of the mob (the reconcilement to which on the part of the poor natives this gentleman in Calcutta was betrayed into complacently looking forward to) resulted sometimes in the victim's death. Cases of this occurred in England in the years 1731, 1756, 1763, 1780. ("Bygone Punishments," by W. Andrews, 1899.) Here is an appalling instance of the use to which it was turned, which I find recorded in a book about Charing Cross and its neighbourhood by Mr. MacMichael (1905): "In 1730, or thereabouts, Thomas Hayes, commander of a merchantman, stood on the pillory at Charing Cross from the hour of twelve to one, when a surgeon, attended by the proper officer, got upon the pillory, where the victim sat in a chair, and the surgeon with an incision knife cut his left ear off, delivering it to Hayes with his own hands. Then the officer took it from him and held it up between finger and thumb to the view of the spectators. . . . He was a plain, elderly man, with grey hair, and was not pelted by the populace, which was very numerous." I do not know what discretion the judges had who administered the law in those brutal days, or whether they did so with lenity on the whole, as their successors do now; but I fear it was not then the fashion to show much consideration "for the poor devil in the dock" (as a great and humane judge on the English Bench—now in retirement—wrote of him not very long ago). The great agitator against the continuance of hanging for trumpery offences, and other horrible sentences then in vogue, was Sir Samuel Romilly (1808), but he was far in advance of his age, and his efforts met with but little success at first. And though he failed three times to have capital punishment abolished for stealing to the value of four shillings from a shop, he earned the odium of the law officers of the Crown, who sighed that he was "breaking down the bulwarks of the Constitution!" In this sentiment they but re-echoed Thurlow, A.-G. In 1777 he prosecuted the Rev. John Horne (Tooke) before Lord Mansfield for issuing a sympathetic manifesto in favour of our revolted fellow-subjects in America. The sentence was one year's imprisonment and a fine of £200; Thurlow proposed the pillory, styling it, in his admiration, "the restraint against licentiousness provided by the wisdom of past

almost daily have been also seen in the Calcutta streets. I take it from an original note kindly placed at my disposal by Mr. Belchambers, Registrar of the High Court. The culprit was a poor Hindoo woman—her crime perjury. "Let her be imprisoned in the common gaol until Friday next, on that day let her be taken to the Lall Bazaar and there placed in and upon the pillory for one hour—next day let her be taken to the police office and whipt from thence to the house of Mr. Willoughby Leigh in the Bow Bazaar and back again." This whipping was repeated in public twice more at intervals of a month, and then she was relegated to two years' hard labour! Surely all this was, as Macaulay says, "in the highest degree shocking to all the notions of Hindoos." Yet this happened in 1799, twenty-four years after the execution of Nuncomar.

How difficult it seems now to realise the state of things which we just get a glimpse of here. Slavery in full bloom; the right of ownership under it being so recognised that its mere plea was sufficient to justify (in law) an English magistrate in ordering a poor girl, who in running away had presumably acted in self-defence, to be "beaten with rods" and sent back to the fangs of her master.

Some idea may be formed of the ill-usage given to slaves in Calcutta at this time, from the fact that even ten years later, when public opinion was becoming enlightened, the *Calcutta Chronicle* calls out against "the barbarous and wanton acts of more than savage cruelty daily exercised on the slaves of both sexes, by that mongrel race of human beings called Native Portuguese." The same paper refers also to an alleged "intention" of Government to adopt measures to lessen some of the miseries endured by slaves, one of which was to be that "no slave of either sex was to be shackled with the marks of bondage which many of them are now constrained to put on."

ages!" This *laudator temporis acti* bloomed in a few months after into the Keeper of His Majesty's Conscience. Lord Ellenborough in 1812 sentenced a blasphemer to the pillory for two hours once a month for eighteen months. Two years later he sentenced the great sailor, Lord Cochrane, after noble service to his country, to a heavy fine (or imprisonment) and to be pilloried for being found guilty (a wrong verdict) for conspiring with others to spread false news. The Government, however, thought it prudent to waive the pillory in deference to public opinion—and temper. Poor Job, in his rejoinder to his rather wearisome and uncharitable friend, Bildad the Shuhite, asked where shall wisdom be found, and where is the place of understanding? What a pertinent question it would have been concerning law-givers and lawyers and judges who had to do with the penal code in England less than a century ago! The pillory was restricted to cases of perjury in 1816. The last victim in London was one Boissy, who stood in it for an hour in 1830. It was abolished by Act of Parliament in 1837.

And the wearer of these shackles would often be perhaps an intelligent little child, such as the one thus advertised for (1780): "Eloped from his master's service, and supposed to have gone up country in the service of some officer, a little slave boy about twelve years old; can speak, read, and write English very well." Most of the slaves were the children of the poor who had been sold by their own parents from their inability to support them.*

With our present knowledge it is strange to reflect that, at the time referred to in the police record, a prominent member of the Government, under the ægis of which this great iniquity flourished, was the champion of political and personal liberty, the renowned Junius. It may be, however, that the hateful aspect under which slavery presented itself to Philip Francis in Calcutta was not without its effect; for we find him afterwards in Parliament as one of the most ardent and zealous supporters of Wilberforce in his efforts for the abolition of the Slave trade. In illustration of this it gives me great pleasure to quote the following honourable action of a public man, regarding whom many hard things have been said. Mr. H. R. Francis writes this of his grandfather in his "Junius Revealed" before referred to—

"Briefly, he resigned the inheritance of a fine West Indian estate rather than withdraw a Bill which he had introduced for improving the position of West Indian slaves. The wealthy connection, who had destined the property for him, wrote to warn him that if he pressed his measure it would be otherwise disposed of. He had in the mean time learned that he would not have the support, which he had hoped for, from Mr. Pitt. But he brought the threatening letter into the House, pressed his Bill to inevitable defeat, and lost an inheritance which would

* For some allusion to slavery as it existed in former times in India, and to the barbarous punishment and mutilations executed on criminals under the orders of the British Government, see two curious and instructive appendices to Mr. H. J. Cotton's "Revenue History of Chittagong" (1880). The natives of India, however, were not the only slaves there. History and local records make frequent allusions to Africans, called there Coffrees. In the newspapers of 1781, many advertisements occur as to the disposal by sale of Coffrees. One is offered for 400 rupees who understands the business of butler and cook. Some seem to be valued for their musical skill, and dexterity in shaving and dressing and waiting at table. There is an advertisement also for "three handsome African ladies of the true sable hue, commonly called Coffreesses," between fourteen and twenty-five, for marriage with three of their own countrymen. The advertisement is long, and is too often repeated to be a mere joke, though it strains at being suggestively indecent. In all probability it means this, that there were Englishmen in Calcutta little more than a hundred years ago who not only bought and sold African slaves, but went in for the breeding of them for the slave market.

have doubled his income. When it is remembered that he had a large family, and barely sufficient to maintain his high social position, and that he was by no means careless in money matters, but attached the highest value to complete pecuniary independence, surely the pride which supported him under such a sacrifice was that of a high-minded gentleman, true to duty and honour."

(II)

His biographer tells us that Francis had no curiosity about travelling in India. In his voluminous writings he left behind no observations about scenery or places. He never moved a hundred miles out of Calcutta, where he buried himself in business and in a most extensive correspondence. "He keeps four of us in constant employment, and is sometimes dictating to all at a time," writes his private secretary. The hours not devoted to this were given up to card-playing and to the other social recreations in vogue. Though he was remarkable for a haughty and unapproachable manner, he seems to have had the good sense to cultivate the social acquaintance of the ladies, even of his official foes. "I profess to admire beauty," he writes, "on both sides of the question, and am not afraid to pay my respects to an agreeable woman even in the enemy's camp. In spite of all their politics Mrs. Hyde and Lady Impey are pleased to except me from my friends, and, as I take care to acknowledge their respective merits, allow me, in that instance at least, to be a just and generous enemy. As long as they show me the same countenance they may be sure of the same attachment." He seems to have been amused, too, by the ordinary gossip of Anglo-Indian society, and even to have cynically recorded the petty heartburnings of ladies arising out of that still vital question as to who should call on whom. Of course the problem which most immediately exercised the upper circles in Calcutta society in those days was, as to what social recognition should be extended to the lady who was to become the wife of the Governor-General, as soon as a legal divorce from her husband had been obtained.

The earliest announcement of this lady's arrival in Calcutta is to be found in some curious old letters preserved amongst the Hastings manuscripts. The writer was a Dr. Tysoe Saul Hancock, who in his later life attended more to commercial enterprise than to medicine; he was in some respects a *protégé* of Hastings, who was very liberal to his family. This gentleman died in Calcutta in 1775. The letters were written to Mrs. Hancock in England. Under the date February 17, 1772, he writes: "Mr. Hastings is arrived this day, he is thin and very grave, but in good health." Again in April he says: "I promised to give you some account of Mr. Hastings. He is well and has been in the Government six days, during which time I have seen him twice. His residence at Madras has greatly increased his former reserve, and he seems inclined to break through many Bengal customs. This is not much relished by the present inhabitants." (He then enumerated the members of his staff, including Mr. Stewart, Colonel Ironside, Captain Weller, and continues)—

"There is a lady, by name Mrs. Imhoff, who is his principal favourite among the ladies. She came to India on board the same ship with Mr. Hastings, is the wife of a gentleman who has been an officer in the German service, and came out a cadet to Madras. Finding it impossible to maintain his family by the sword, and having a turn to miniature painting, he quitted the sword and betook himself to the latter profession. After having painted all who chose to be painted at Madras, he came to Bengal the latter end of the year 1770. She remained at Madras, and lived in Mr. Hastings' house on the Mount chiefly, I believe. She is about twenty-six years old, has a good person and has been very pretty, is sensible, lively, and wants only to be a greater mistress of the English language to prove she has a great share of wit. She came to Calcutta last October. They do not make a part of Mr. Hastings' family, but are often of his private parties. The husband is truly a German. I should not have mentioned Mrs. Imhoff, but I know everything relating to Mr. Hastings is greatly interesting to you."

Again he writes in the following February (1773):

"Mr. Imhoff is going to England. I shall give him a letter of introduction to you: his Lady stays here. As—— He intends returning in the service." * Mr. Imhoff, however, never did return.

* I have copied this exactly as written and punctuated, retaining the capital letters of the old style. It is not very clear what the dash is intended for; it is a deliberate heavy line, over half an inch in length, with no full or other stop after it. It seems to me that the words "He intends, &c., were the *alleged* reasons given to society for Mrs. Imhoff's remaining in India, but the dash is meant to convey to Mrs. Hancock the writer's own, possibly erroneous and uncharitable, idea as to the real (unmentionable) reason. It should in fairness be stated that Tysoe Hancock was much given to curious dashes and full stops in his letter writing; *e.g.* he thus writes to his wife in December, 1773: "The young gentleman who will deliver this to you is the son of Mr. and Mrs. Imhoff, whom I mentioned to you in a former letter—your taking great Notice of him and doing Him any good offices will be grateful to Mr. H., who patronizes Him, on which account I so strongly recommend Him to your. Notice as we cannot do too much to oblige that gentleman who has been so great a friend to —— P.S.—I believe Mr. Anderson will carry for you a piece of Dimity —— He is a particular friend of mine." It is curious to note that when his wife retaliates by sending letters of introduction to him, he censures her in a curt note beginning not as usual, "Dear Phila," but, freezingly, "Dear Mrs. Hancock."

There can be no doubt that his attentions to Mrs. Imhoff placed her in a very equivocal position, to say the least of it, at Madras first, and at Calcutta afterwards, when his late colleague, Macpherson, could thus venture to write to him from Madras in reference to a lady: the occasion was when the condemnation of Nuncomar became known, and when it was considered prudent that Hastings should take precautions for his personal safety: "Employ from the hour you receive this no black cook: you are the most moderate of eating men; let your fair female friend or some trustworthy European, oversee everything you eat while in the cooking room." Mrs. Imhoff could only have been the "fair friend" thus disrespectfully alluded to.*

The Imhoffs were friends of the Royal robe-keeper, Mrs. Schwellenberg (the "old hag from Germany," as Macaulay was betrayed into styling her in his indignation about Fanny Burney), and through her, Queen Charlotte's influence was solicited for leave from the East India Directors for the Imhoffs to go to Madras; so Wraxall says.

Francis also writes on this subject to a friend in England, but the venom in his letter deprives it of the historical value which it would otherwise have:

"To complete the character, as it will probably conclude the history, of this extraordinary man, I must inform you that he is to be married shortly to the supposed wife of a German painter with whom he has lived for several years. The lady is turned of 40, has children grown up by her pretended husband, from whom she has obtained a divorce under the hand of some German prince. I have always been on good terms with the lady, and do not despair of being invited to the wedding. She is an agreeable woman, and has been very pretty. My Lord Chief Justice Impey, the most upright of all possible lawyers, is to act the part of father to the second Helen, though his wife has not spoken to her this twelve month."

He thinks it worth while to write the following tittle-tattle in his journal:—

"*July* 5 (1777).—Sup with Hastings at Impey's.—Long faces.

"*July* 9.—News of Imhoff's divorce, and hopes of her marriage with Hastings.

"*12th.*—The Chief Justice very low. His lady enraged at the match and distressed about the future visits.

"N.B.—The dames for a long time were bosom friends.

* See Appendix V. "Hastings and the Imhoffs."

"*24th.*—An entertainment made on purpose this night at the Governor's to effect a reconciliation between Lady Impey and Madame Chapusettin; the former sends an excuse. A mortal disappointment.

"*26th.*—Sup at Impey's. Her ladyship swears stoutly that Madame Imhoff shall pay her the first visit—an idea which I don't fail to encourage.

"*29th.*—Mrs. Imhoff sups at Lady Impey's by way of submission."

Though the marriage came off ten days afterwards, Francis's journal is silent about it, so we unfortunately lose his sententious account of the festivities with which it was said, by the native historian, to have been celebrated.

In the vestry records of St. John's Cathedral, Calcutta, it appears that the marriage was solemnised on Friday, August 8, 1777, by the Rev. William Johnson, most probably very quietly, and in a private house. The bride was married under her maiden name of "Miss Anna Maria Appolonia Chapusettin." Hastings is described in the marriage register as "The Honourable Warren Hastings, Esq., Governor-General of India."

We find nothing in Francis's memoirs of the story told in Syur ul Mutaquerin (popularised by Macaulay) of the great entertainment in honour of this celebration, given by Hastings, and to which he brought Clavering *nolens volens* a "vanquished rival in triumph," a proceeding which brought on the General's death illness. It would have been quite in keeping with Hastings' amiable character to have held out the hand of social friendship to an official foe at such a time, but the probability is that the wedding was not marked by any festivities. In some correspondence of General Clavering's which I once met with, I remember seeing a note of his to Francis, within a couple of days after the marriage, in which he discussed the question of visiting Hastings or not, saying that he was in favour of so doing as it would show that the opposition to him was not personal. But he added (showing that it was not only in official matters that he subordinated his judgment to that of Francis) that if Francis did not think as he did, he would not visit. It would seem likely, therefore, that Clavering's (and Francis's) relation to Hastings' wedding was limited to an ordinary social visit after it.

It is curious that the name "Marian," by which Mrs. Hastings is best known, was not one of her proper Christian names at all. As she was born in 1747 she was thirty years old at the time of her second marriage. Hastings was fifteen years older. Francis, in writing to his wife shortly after the marriage, says of Mrs. Hastings:—
"The lady herself is really an accomplished woman. She behaves

with perfect propriety in her new station, and deserves every mark of respect." The Governor-General's wife, however, does not seem to have forgotten the humble pie that Mrs. Imhoff had to eat in the matter of that first visit to Lady Impey, for as soon as ever her position is assured she promptly brings the Lady Chief Justice to her bearings.

Francis records—

"*September* 20 (1777).—Lady Impey sits up with Mrs. Hastings; *vulgo*—toad-eating.

"*21st.*—At the Governor's, Mrs. Hastings very handsomely acknowledges my constant attention to her.

"*22nd.*—Mrs. Hastings returns Lady Clavering's visit, attended by Lady Impey *in formâ pauperis.*

"*October* 5.—Supped at Impey's; as gracious as ever. Many symptoms convince me that Mrs. H. and Lady Impey hate one another as cordially as ever.

"*8th.*—Lady Impey *furens* against Mrs. H. worse than ever.

"*November* 4.—Sup at Impey's. Explanation with the lady, she swears that Hastings has deserted them. Complains of his ingratitude, etc. I believe their hatred is sufficiently cordial. But there are *some ties* which cannot be dissolved.

"*January* 3, 1778.—Formal supper at Impey's for Mrs. Wheler;* Mrs. Hastings sends a silly excuse, an intended slight to Lady Impey."

Francis took his share in dispensing the hospitality which was then expected not only from the head of the Government but from the members of Council also. Twice a week he gave a public breakfast to about thirty guests. But this was soon reduced to once; his secretary remarks that "it was all nonsense at any time." His household was at first under the management of a European steward, later of a stewardess who, as we have seen, had been housekeeper to Mrs. Clavering. He frequently gave dinner-parties also where often fifty sat down. The Governor gave very large public dinners on all national holidays, those on New Year's Day and the King's birthday being followed by a ball and a supper to the whole "Settlement."†

* Mrs. Wheler had arrived in the previous month. Francis writes of her to his wife: "She appeared in public for the first time at our ball in wonderful splendour. At sight of her hoop, all our beauties stared with envy and admiration. I never saw the like in all my life."—She was the first wife of Edward Wheler, member of Council, and survived the climate only seven months. Her tombstone tells that her name had been Harriet Chichely Plowden.

† These were held either at the Old Court House or at the Theatre, Government House not being large enough. Grandpré, the French traveller, comments, even in 1790, on the poor accommodation provided for the English Governor-General. "He lives," he writes, "in a house on the esplanade, opposite the citadel—many private individuals in the town have houses as good. The house of

Of the first Christmas Day he spent in India, Mackrabie thus wrote—

"The Governor gave a public breakfast, dinner, ball and supper, at all which we assisted. The ladies were unanimous in making their appearance in the evening. It is the most absurd of all possible ceremonies. Every Member of the Council, the Judges, the Board of Trade, Field Officers, Clergy, and Heads of Offices are pestered with the repetition of a 'Merry Xmas, etc.'" "New Year's Day was a second part of Christmas, public dinner, supper, ball." Overflowing loyalty was a very prominent feature of these festive celebrations: "toasts *as usual echoed from the cannon's mouth*," and "merited this distinction," says an old Calcutta newspaper, "for their loyalty and patriotism." There is a record of one of those parties (that of January 1, 1787, given by Lord Cornwallis, who no doubt merely kept up a time-honoured custom) which lasted from two o'clock one day till four the next morning, as the ladies after supper "resumed the pleasures of the dance and knit the rural braid in emulation of the poet's sister Graces (*sic*) while some disciples of the jolly god of wine testified their satisfaction in pæans of exultation." Lord Cornwallis, who led the most abstemious life himself, wrote to his young son (Lord Brome) about another festive occasion when he gave a concert and supper to all the Settlement, and tried to have illuminations which the rain put out; "the supper which could not be put out was a very good one: some of the gentlemen who stayed late, however, were nearly extinguished by the claret. Seven of the finest ladies of the place and twelve gentlemen sang the Coronation anthem, so that on the whole it was a magnificent business."

In the letters of a gentleman who visited Calcutta in 1779 is given a copy of a card of invitation in which Mr. and Mrs. Hastings "request the favour of his company to a concert and supper at Mrs. Hastings' house in town"*—a postscript requests him to bring only his "huccabadar." This introduces us to a custom happily passed away. So indispensable was the hooka that at all parties it was admitted to the supper-rooms and card-rooms—even to the boxes in the theatre, and between the pillars and walls of the assembly rooms.

the Governor of Pondicherry is much more magnificent." It was not till the time of Lord Wellesley that the Governor-General of India had a residence in which he could comfortably accommodate his public guests. The first occasion on which the State rooms in the present Government House were lit up, was in January, 1803, when Lord Wellesley gave a ball with a display of illuminations and fireworks in honour of the general peace. Eight hundred persons were supposed to be at the ball. Lord Valentia was present.

* Tradition points to No. 7, Hastings Street, as being this house.

Grandpré describes all the hookah bearers coming in together with the dessert, each carrying his master's hookah—and the consequent clamour and smoke which filled the room.

The rage for this sort of smoking was commoner with "country-born ladies," one of whom fascinated Miss Goldborne with her graceful attitude while enjoying her hookah, the long ornamental snake of which was coiled through and round the rails of her chair. The young lady was at the same time under the hands of the hair-dresser. But it extended to some English ladies too; it was considered a high compliment on their part to show a preference for a gentleman by tasting his hookah. It was a point of politeness in such a case for the gentleman, when presenting the snake of the hookah, to substitute a fresh mouthpiece for the one he was using.*

Masquerades were a very common means of amusement in the old days; dominoes were advertised for hire, also various female costumes for gentlemen; and evidently the fun raged fast and furious. They generally wound up with suppers, at which in the cold weather, fresh oysters and ices were to be had in abundance. Miss Goldborne says the ice came from "some slender inland rivulets of the Ganges," by which she probably meant to indicate the "ice fields" that were worked near Hooghly then and much later. Theatricals were in special favour amongst Calcutta pleasure-seekers, the subscription theatre (erected in 1775) being shut off from the southerly wind by Writer's Buildings, was furnished with wind-sails on the roof "to promote coolness by a free circulation of air." The auditorium consisted only of pit and boxes; the prices of admission were to the former eight rupees, and to the latter one gold mohur. The characters were all taken by gentlemen amateurs. Mrs. Fay saw *Venice Preserved* acted there in 1780, the part of Belvidera being taken by a Lieutenant Norfor. The performances were by no means confined to the cool weather, and in addition to the most ambitious musical entertainments, such as the whole of Handel's "Messiah," included anything from *Othello*, or *The Merchant of Venice*, down to the *Irish Widow* or the *Mock Doctor*.

* So late as 1822 a correspondent to the *Calcutta Journal* calls attention to the annoyance to ladies and others by the habits of the gentlemen of hookah smoking in society, and suggests that "his letter be printed once a month till the custom be banished from society." The present Sir Antony MacDonnell gave me, I remember, in Calcutta a still stranger instance of the linking of modern with old Indian days: he told me that he saw the hookah smoked at table by two old gentlemen soon after he arrived in India (in, I think, 1866).

The bill of fare for one evening included *The Busybody*, followed by the *Recruiting Sergeant*, "a musical thing," as Mackrabie called it, and the *Mayor of Garrett*—in short, Seneca could not be too heavy nor Plautus too light for them.

But dancing was the chief enjoyment to which Calcutta society in the last century devoted itself. All writers about the English Settlement in Bengal, remark with surprise the insatiable ardour with which this pursuit was followed. There was no special season for it, public and private balls went on all the year round. The cool weather merely intensified the dancing fever, and added to the number of "assemblies" which could be concentrated within the month. "I attribute," writes Lord Valentia, "consumptions amongst the ladies to their incessant dancing. . . . A small quiet party seems unknown in Calcutta." Even on the nights when no large dancing party was going on, it was not unusual, according to Miss Goldborne, to have "Nautches of six or seven black girls at private European houses after supper."

Minuets and country dances were most in fashion. At public balls it was the custom to lead the ladies out to the minuets according to the rank of their husbands. Those ladies whose husbands were not in the services, were led out in the order they came into the room, and this was the rule also in the case of unmarried ladies. Country dances, however, were more in general favour; one notice of a ball says that "the lively country dance runners were bounding and abounding." This active element in the dance appears to have enhanced its merits, because a professor of the art soon established himself in the Settlement, and undertook for one hundred Rs. to teach any lady or gentleman "the Scotch step in its application to country dancing," and a variety of other steps in addition to "the athletic and agile." When Mackrabie saw dancing first in India, he made this note about it: "If splendour accompanied heat, a ball in India ought to be uncommonly splendid. The appearance of the ladies, even before the country dances, was rather ardent than luminous. The zeal and activity with which they exert themselves in country dances is exercise enough for the spectators. By dint of motion these children of the sun in a very few minutes get as hot as their father, and then it is not safe to approach them. In this agitation they continue, literally swimming through the dance, until he comes himself and reminds them of the hour." In fact, people who had to make the best of Indian life in the times referred to, seem to have acted up to the belief that great heat, like great cold, is best defied by violent exercise.

In connection with this hasty retrospect at a few of the hospitalities and pastimes of Old Calcutta, it may be allowable now to take a cursory glance at some of the queens of society who, in the time of Philip Francis, graced those festive gatherings. In doing so we shall see whether their contemporaries have thrown any light on their personal claims to this social distinction.

To begin with Mrs. Hastings, and to answer the homely question, "What was she like?" The description left of her by Mrs. Fay will help us. The writer was the wife of a barrister who arrived in Calcutta in May, 1780; she spent a day with Mrs. Hastings, she says, at Belvedere (which she found "a perfect bijou, most superbly fitted with all that unbounded affluence can display") in the same month, and thus recorded her impressions: "Mrs. H—— herself, it is easy to perceive at the first glance, is far superior to the generality of her sex, though her appearance is rather eccentric, owing to the circumstance of her beautiful auburn hair being disposed in ringlets, throwing an air of elegant, nay, almost infantine simplicity on the countenance, most admirably adapted to heighten the effect intended to be produced. Her whole dress, too, though studiously becoming, being at variance with our present modes (which are certainly not so), perhaps for that reason she has chosen to depart from them. As a foreigner, you know, she may be excused for not strictly conforming to our fashions; besides, her rank in the Settlement sets her above the necessity of studying anything but the whim of the moment. It is easy to perceive how fully sensible she is of her own consequence: she is, indeed, raised to a giddy height, and expects to be treated with the most profound respect and deference. She received me civilly, and insisted on my staying dinner," etc.

Another extract from Mrs. Fay's letters will exemplify the deference paid to Mrs. Hastings, who attended a party where Mrs. Fay was. The latter was asked by the lady who brought her, "'If I had paid my respects to the Lady Governess?' I answered in the negative, having had no opportunity, as she had not chanced to look towards me when I was prepared to do so. 'Oh,' replied the kind old lady, 'you must fix your eyes on her and never take them off till she notices you; Miss C—— has done this, and so have I: it is absolutely necessary to avoid giving offence.' I followed her prudent advice, and was soon honoured with a complacent glance, which I returned, as became me, by a most respectful bend. Not long after she walked over to our side, and conversed very affably with me."

Miss Goldborne gives us another glance at her: "The Governor's dress gives you his character at once, unostentatious and sensible. His lady, however, is the great ornament of places of polite resort, for her figure is elegant, her manners lively and engaging, and her whole appearance a model of taste and magnificence."

Her beautiful hair must have been one of Mrs. Hastings' chief attractions, because when she first appeared at Court, on her return from India, she presented herself in her own simple hair unfrizzed up or unadorned (?) with the pyramid of gauze, powder, feathers, pomatum, etc., then so astoundingly the fashion. This (added to her splendid display of jewels) made her an object of much observation in London society. Miss Burney describes her in London Society (1792) as a "pleasing, lively, and well-bred woman with attractive manners, and attentions to those she wishes to oblige. Her dress now was like that of an Indian princess, according to our ideas of such ladies, and so much the most splendid, from its ornaments and style and fashion, though chiefly muslin, that everybody else looked under-dressed in her presence." The translator of the contemporary native chronicle qualifies his admiration for Mrs. Hastings by an allusion to this weakness of hers, viz.: "Indeed, she must have been a woman of uncommon merit to have made so lasting an impression on so sublime a genius as Hastings. At the same time it must be acknowledged that she did him some little harm by unseasonably parading in jewels after landing in England."

The first introduction that we have to the social queen, who may fittingly be mentioned next, is in a passage of a letter from Johnson to Boswell (1774): "Chambers is either married or almost married to Miss Wilton, a girl of sixteen, exquisitely beautiful, whom he has with his lawyer's tongue persuaded to take her chance with him in the East." Frances Wilton was the daughter of a well-known Royal Academician, Joseph Wilton.* We have a slight sketch of Lady Chambers, also, from the pen of Mrs. Fay, who enjoyed her hospitality for a short time in 1780. "She is the most beautiful woman I ever beheld—in the bloom of youth; and there is an agreeable frankness in her manners that enhances her loveliness and renders her truly fascinating." In "Hartly House" she is mentioned amongst the drivers of gaily caparisoned horses on the Calcutta course. "Lady C—m—rs is one of the most celebrated on this fashionable

* Mrs. Thrale, in alluding to Chambers, writes, "He married Fanny Wilton, the statuary's daughter, who stood for Hebe at the Royal Academy. She was very beautiful indeed, and but fifteen years old when Sir Robert married her." What Mrs. Piozzi referred to probably was the fact that Miss Wilton (with Miss Meyer, also an Academician's daughter) sat to Reynolds for his Hebe.

MISS BENEDETTA RAMUS
(AFTERWARDS LADY DAY).

*See p.* 147.

list, and for attendant beaux, both as to smartness and variety, yields to no one."

The wife of Sir John Day, the Advocate-General, was another lady in Calcutta society who was gifted with beauty of a high order, which the canvas of Romney and Gainsborough has not let die. Lady Day had been Miss Benedicta (or Benedetta) Ramus. Mr. Andrew Lang, when referring to this lady, says: "A proof of whose beautiful likeness by Romney came into the market at the recent Addington sale at Sotheby's. The engraving by Dickinson is one of the most beautiful things that the art of mezzotint—almost a lost art—has left to us. Horace Walpole's copy of it is in the hands of a collector, and that which I possess belonged to Sir Thomas Lawrence." There is a copy of Dickinson's engraving of Romney's portrait* in the print room of the British Museum (published 1779). Another portrait of her with her sister was taken by Gainsborough. Speaking of this, Mr. Lang says: "The portrait of Miss Ramus and her sister, by Gainsborough, has lately been sold at Christy's for ten thousand pounds.† The lady looks not nearly so bewitching in the art of Gainsborough as in that of the less eminent painter." He adds that the ladies on Gainsborough's canvas look like Jewesses—which they probably were. In Mrs. Papendiek's "Court and Private Life in the Time of Queen Charlotte" (1887), to which Mr. Lang refers, it is said that Queen Charlotte objected to the beautiful Benedicta being presented to her on her marriage, because of the position held by her father as the King's page. "But when, shortly after, Sir John Day was appointed Governor of one of our East India settlements, the right of presentation could no longer be disputed."

Mrs. Papendiek was probably inaccurate in more than the particular of Sir John Day's appointment. If the Queen ever put forward the objection mentioned, it was more likely got over by conferring knighthood on the lady's husband, to procure which she probably begged her father's intervention. This may be the origin or foundation of an anecdote I found reproduced in an old Calcutta newspaper, headed "Royal Bon-mot." "When old Ramus, the King's page, solicited in autumn the honour of knighthood for his son-in-law, Mr. Day, then about to embark for India, His Majesty observed that he had no other objection than the fear

* The original Romney belonged to the late Right Honourable W. H. Smith.

† The actual prices which the portrait of Lady Day with the Baroness de Noailles (Gainsborough, 1775) fetched were 6300 guineas in 1873—and 9500 guineas in 1887. Its present value in the open market would probably be higher.

of verifying Mr. Dunning's proposition that 'the influence of the Crown had increased, was increasing, and ought to be diminished,' for that he should thus turn Day into knight and make Lady Day at Michaelmas." At all events, the beautiful Lady Day cherished no ill will against Queen Charlotte, because it appears from a letter of Francis after his return to England, that he was the bearer of a little present from her to Her Majesty at Windsor. John Day was one of the very few mourners who followed poor Goldsmith's remains to the grave in the Temple: he accompanied a namesake, another young barrister. He died in England in 1808, and Lady Day survived him until May, 1811.

So much remains to be said that the briefest allusion to two or three others, whose claims are undeniable, must suffice. Young Mrs. Motte, the inseparable companion of Mrs. Hastings (at whose house Mrs. Fay met her) must not be omitted. Prior to her marriage in January, 1779, she was known as pretty Mary Touchet—the very name has sweetness in it—and like her namesake in French history she charmed all.*

Of the art of winning and bewitching, so gently wielded by Mrs. Barwell, we shall see evidence in another page.

Of the loveliness of Madame Grand it would be unbecoming to speak in sequence to that of others. This can only be told of with bated breath and whispering humbleness; she must get a chapter to herself.

These few have been instanced from amongst the married ladies who were at the head of society, but whose title to social sovereignty was independent of the accidental position of their husbands. The list might be extended were we to include the known favourites of nature, amongst the fair ones still in maiden meditation. Any one of those named would have been a bright particular star in any society. What must the brilliancy of the small community have been which such a constellation illuminated? Has the "City of Palaces" ever since been able to show at one time such a garden of flowers?—if she has, it is a pity that she should have been "without a bard to fix their bloom."

Perhaps the only room now remaining in Calcutta, in which all this grace and comeliness were often gathered together, is the ball-room of Richard Barwell's garden-house at Alipore.†

* Je charme tout:—"Marie Touchet, fille de noble Jean Touchet, maitresse du Roi Charles IX. portait pour devise cette anagramme composeé par ce roi."

† Now "Kidderpore House," where, in the writer's time, Mrs. Colquhoun Grant presided, and gave a kindly welcome to her many visitors.

What generations of exiled feet—the gayest and lightest—have not disported on this floor! The very lamps and wall-shades which were lighted in the consulship of Warren Hastings are sometimes lighted still. What stately minuets and cotillons and romping country-dances long obsolete, have those old lustres not looked down on! Who does not wish that they could light up the past and its faded scenes, and tell us stories of the merry "ladies and gentlemen of the Settlement"—of their frolics and their wooings—their laughter and their love?

## (III)

Allusion has been made to the card-table as one of the occupations of Francis. High play was one of the prominent fashions of the time amongst the upper society in England. The ladies followed it with almost as much ardour as the gentlemen.

When imported into Calcutta this vice flourished with tropical luxuriance. The games most in vogue seem to have been Tredille, Put, five card Loo, and Whist. Mrs. Fay found that "a rupee a fish, limited to ten," were the ordinary stakes at loo; and Miss Goldborne says of whist, "What was my astonishment when I found five gold mohurs spoke of as a very moderate sum a corner." Mrs. Fay says the ladies often found whist very nervous work, owing to the high bets made by the gentlemen over and above the stakes.

Several allusions to their card enterprise occur in the journal and letters of Francis and Mackrabie, as we have seen.

Even to gaming Francis betook himself with characteristic energy and purpose. For some time, while playing for high stakes, he seems to have made whist rather a business than a recreation.* The result of his luck, and presumably of his skill, was that his winnings at cards enabled him to leave India with a moderate fortune much earlier than he could have done if he had been dependent on his savings alone.

Very exaggerated accounts of his and his colleagues' gambling, and of his gains, found their way home, and tended to prejudice him in the eyes of the Ministry, and of the Court of Directors. Rumour credited Francis with having won thirty lakhs at whist,

* This passage occurs in a letter which Francis wrote when leaving England to the gentleman who had charge of his son's education. "There is nothing I dread or abhor so much as gaming, and I beg that if hereafter he should discover any turn that way, you may do everything in your power to check and discourage it."

and lost ten thousand pounds at backgammon. A cynical friend writes to him that people in England are astonished that men sent out to reform India should have contrived to win and lose so much in a short time, and he sagely advises him, since he has incurred the world's censure, to be sure and keep the money to console him. From his own letters, however, to friends at home and in India, a much more moderate estimate of his gains may be formed. In March, 1776, he writes—

"An extraordinary stroke of fortune has made me independent. Two years will probably raise me to affluent circumstances."

To a friend at Benares, whom he asked to buy diamonds for him, he says—

"I have actually won a fortune and must think of some means of realising it in England. Keep all this stuff to yourself."

To another in England, to whom he remits an order for the proceeds of a parcel of pearls sent home, he writes—

"You must know, my friend, that on one blessed day of the present year of our Lord, I had won about twenty thousand pounds at whist. It is reduced to about twelve, and I now never play but for trifles, and that only once a week. Keep all this to yourself."

Elsewhere he computes the losings of all at about three lakhs, of which the lion's share (possibly fifteen thousand pounds) fell to him, and the rest to Judge Lemaistre and a Colonel Leslie. It was an accidental burst, he adds, which lasted only a few weeks. We may assume that Barwell was the chief loser.

With reference to this card-encounter between Barwell, Francis, and Co., there is a curious circumstance alleged as connected with it.

There was published in Leadenhall Street, in 1780, a rather stupid and scandalous book called the "Intrigues of a Nabob,"* which professed to give certain details of Mr. Barwell's private life in India. The writer's object seems to have been revenge for the deprivation of his mistress, for whose loss he had received inadequate consideration. In this book, the production of one who represents himself as knowing Mr. Barwell intimately, or at all events, as having had ample opportunity of being familiar with Calcutta gossip, it happens to be mentioned, quite incidentally, that so perplexed was Barwell at the upsetting and overruling of the plans of the minority by their newly-arrived colleagues from England, that he, being wealthy, declared he would willingly part with twenty thousand pounds to break up the opposition, or to bring over one of them to his and the Governor-General's side.

* See Appendix VI. "The Intrigues of a Nabob."

The story goes that he fixed on Francis as the one most likely to be amenable to pecuniary influences, and challenged him to high play in the hopes of getting him in his debt, and so in his power, thereby not only mistaking Francis's character entirely, but, as we have seen, catching a Tartar. This book puts Barwell's losses to Francis at £40,000. Now, though this story comes from a tainted source, still it is suggestive that Francis himself professed to believe that even Hastings once contemplated buying off the *three* new Councillors, as the easiest way of preventing them from doing mischief. He writes thus in a private memorandum, which he drew out on the course of public affairs, "He (Hastings) had no conception of what sort of persons he had to deal with. In the first place, he concluded it would be an easy matter to gain us by corruption. His experience had not furnished him with instances of resistance; his principles excluded the possibility of it. On this ground I am assured he was prepared to meet us with an offer of a hundred thousand pounds a-piece." * In the same memorandum he had previously commented thus: "Europeans, by long residence in Bengal, contract the character of the country, and without the insignia of black faces and white turbans are as completely Banyans as the people who serve them. There are no such men in Europe, for example, as Hastings, George Vansittart, and Barwell."

Of Barwell, Francis almost uniformly writes contemptuously, and attributes to him the very qualities which might be supposed to give rise to the crafty actions alleged against the "Nabob," viz. (Diary, September, 1777): "H. and B. are certainly on bad terms, though they dare not proceed to an open rupture. I have many hints from B., through Mackenzie, of his disposition to buy Hastings out, if he could be assured that I would not distress him in the government." Again, in the private memorandum, already referred to, he says—

"Mr. Barwell, I think, has all the bad qualities common to this climate and country, of which he is in every sense a native; but I do not affirm that there is no mixture whatsoever of good in his composition. He is rapacious without industry, and ambitious without an exertion of his faculties or steady application to affairs. He would be governor-general if money could make him so; and in that station he would soon

* Francis may have heard it rumoured that a similar device was occasionally resorted to by Clive. When an influential patron foisted a needy and worthless *protégé* on the revenues of India, Clive thought it economical and salutary to get rid of him at once by purchase. Accordingly, when the new arrival presented his importunate letter of introduction, the Governor (as the story goes) asked him, with genial bluffness, "Well, chap, how much do you want?"

engross the wealth of the country. He will do whatever can be done by bribery and intrigue. He has no other resource.* His mind is strictly effeminate and unequal to any serious constant occupation except gaming, in which alone he is indefatigable."

Nor does Francis extend the smallest pity to the victim whom he had phlebotomised so freely. In April, 1776, he writes to a friend, who seems to have addressed some platitudes to him—

"With regard to gaming and all its dreadful consequences, your advice is good, and not the worse for being tolerably obvious. It is true I have won a fortune, and intend to keep it. Your tenderness for the loser is admirable. If money be his blood, I feel no kind of remorse in opening his veins; the blood-sucker should bleed and can very well afford it."

Even before the whist tournament came off, Francis conceived a rabid dislike to Barwell, which would certainly warn him against plunging into high play without seeing his way clearly.

In March of the previous year (1775), he had written to Lord North—

"It is settled that Barwell shall marry Miss Clavering. After the censures of him to which General Clavering has signed his name, and branded as he is in this country by the utter ruin of a province, by enormous peculation of every sort, and by a personal depravity of character of which he alone perhaps furnishes an example, I cannot but foresee, etc., etc."

A few weeks later to another—

"Mr. Barwell in Council supports the Governor, but abroad is endeavouring to make a bank apart in order to screen his own iniquities. He is to marry Miss Clavering, a damnable match, which can produce nothing but misery and dishonour to the lady and her family, and disappointment to himself. He is cunning, cruel, rapacious, tyrannical, and profligate beyond all European ideas of those qualities."

It may be here remarked parenthetically that Francis gives his opinion of most of his official contemporaries with an appalling frankness. This is what he writes to England of another of them to his friend D'Oyley, November, 1779—

* Francis could see pretty clearly through his colleague. In Sir James Stephen's "Story of Nuncomar" is a letter from Barwell to his sister (dated on the day of Nuncomar's execution) where this "resource" is suggested without much circumlocution. "The state of our Council remains the same as described in my former letters, and if any alteration is to be brought about by the influence of money, in that case no risk of private loss should be regarded. Nor must you regard the expense of some thousands to secure ultimately any great object to your brother."

GENERAL SIR JOHN CLAVERING, K.B.

See p. 153.

"I will not content myself with saying I never knew, but upon my soul I never heard of so abandoned a scoundrel. It is a character to which your English ideas of dirt and meanness do not reach. Nor is it to be met with even in Bengal; even here it excites execration and contempt."

Possibly it is distance that lends enchantment to the view, but we, while reverently contemplating his monument in Westminster Abbey, look back on the man thus described as the great Sir Eyre Coote.

Francis's strongly expressed disapproval of the alleged matrimonial views of Barwell is so heated that it gives rise to a suspicion that his objection was not founded merely on the apprehension of the General's being thus officially drawn away from him. Miss Clavering, with her step-mother * and two younger sisters, had been fellow-passengers of Francis's in the *Ashburnham*, and it is not impossible that the propinquity and idleness of a long voyage gave rise to a *tendresse* on his side (he was only thirty-four and she eighteen) sufficient to account for his jealousy at the idea of a girl, reputed to be very attractive, marrying one whom he cordially disliked.

Though allied in public matters, there was no love lost in private between Francis and General Clavering. Francis, however, seems always to have maintained kind feeling towards Lady Clavering and her step-daughters, and very friendly relations with them after their return to England.† When the General received the "Red Ribband," Francis wrote: "June 30, 1777.—General Clavering invests himself with the Order of the Bath, and we attend Council. A lucky star it is, and appears to us at a most seasonable juncture. The Governor orders a salute, and recommends circulars to notify the honour done to Clavering." And when he died, Francis records—

"August 30, 1777.—Sir John Clavering, after a delirium of many hours, expired at half-past two p.m., and was buried at eight, in the most private manner. The Governor ordered minute guns. I waited on the

* General Clavering had been twice married; firstly to Lady Diana West, daughter of the Earl of Delaware, by whom he had two sons and three daughters; she died in 1766. Secondly to Miss Catherine Yorke—the Lady Clavering of the text.

† Mrs. Francis writes in her journal (May, 1778), "We all drank tea by invitation at Lady Clavering's; saw only Miss Charlotte, who is very fat, and Miss Caroline, who is much grown. She seems haughty, though very agreeable. Lady C. seems very fond of us all." "Wed., 13 Dec., 1780, 'This morning your pretty friend, Miss Caroline Clavering, was married to Sir John Warren; there is supposed to be more love than money—she would have him." Francis himself writes to Wheler, November, 1781, "Lady Clavering, Miss Clavering, and Miss Charlotte, are in town. I have seen them frequently, and endeavoured to do them service."

ladies and pressed them to remove to my house, but they declined. I attended the funeral on foot to the grave."

It may be seen from Impey's letters that General Clavering died of dysentery. "He was taken ill about a fortnight ago" (writes the Chief Justice on the day after his death), "returning home from a visit to my house."

Clavering was laid in South Park Street Cemetery, where his grave may still be identified by the white marble slab on the side of the tomb, which tells that he was Colonel of H.M. 52nd Foot. The tomb should be saved from ruin. The General was a well-known man in England, and popular as a brave soldier. He was Brigadier at the attack on Guadelope in 1759, where he led the British force in person. "Clavering was the real hero of Guadelope," writes Horace Walpole, "he has come home covered with more laurels than a boar's head. Indeed, he has done exceedingly well." His house in Calcutta was in Mission Row, south of the church.

It will serve, as well as any other opportunity for gossiping about those times, to mention here whom Miss Clavering and Mr. Barwell did marry. It would seem that Francis might have spared himself his anxious apprehensions, for we learn from quite an independent source that the General had fully determined that Mr. Barwell was never to become his son-in-law. This is disclosed in a contemporary's (Grand's) narrative.

In April, 1775, the General "imprudently and hastily charged Mr. Barwell with malversation in the Salt Department. So ill-founded an accusation * drew an instantaneous bitter reply. Mr. B., conscious of the unmerited imputation, declared that the man who dared to come forward with such a charge destitute of any proof was a ——. The General put his hand to his sword, Mr. Barwell bowed and retired. The Council broke ; and in the field next morning, attended by proper seconds, the former had a shot at the latter.

* A reference to Mr. Beveridge's most interesting "History of Backerganj District" (page 138) would seem to show that the General's accusation was anything but "ill-founded." We there learn that Barwell held the lease of two salt farms, which he sublet to two Armenians, on condition of an extra consideration to himself of Rs. 1,25,000. One of these merchants afterwards complained that Barwell, having taken the money, dispossessed him and relet the farms to some one else for another lac of rupees. When first called to account about this transaction he naïvely confessed it, and seemed to imply that he was within his rights as wishing "to add to my fortune": he concludes, "I cannot recall it, and I rather choose to admit an *error*" (*risum teneatis?*) "than deny a fact." The matter, which was a complicated one, came afterwards before the Select Parliamentary Committee. Burke (in the Ninth Report) is very sarcastic about it.

"Fortunately no evil consequences resulted, and Mr. Barwell, lamenting a man otherwise of such amiable virtues could in this instance have been so injudiciously biased, would not return his fire. His antagonist, suspecting this delicacy arose from a growing attachment which he had observed to prevail between him and Miss Clavering, called out loudly for him to take his chance of hitting him, for, in whatever manner their contest might terminate, the General added, Mr. Barwell could rest impressed that he had no chance of ever being allied to his family; and in the same passionate tone expressed his resolution of firing a second pistol. Mr. Barwell, without explaining, but perfectly confident of the good grounds which dictated his mode of acting, persisted in his previous intention, and thus compelled the seconds to withdraw the hostile parties, professing to their opinion that the *point d'honneur* had been in full satisfied."

Francis also alludes to the duel, but his strong bias against Barwell manifests itself in his sarcastic version of the affair—

"The General challenged Barwell, who desired a respite of a few days to make his will. They met on the Sunday following. Barwell received one fire and asked pardon. I could easily collect from Clavering's account of the affair that Barwell behaved very indifferently in the field. This circumstance has since been confirmed to me by old Fowke. He had reason to be satisfied with his good fortune. The wonder is how the General, who is perfectly correct in all the ceremonies of fighting, happened to miss him. Clavering was highly pleased with himself on this occasion, and showed me his correspondence with Barwell with many tokens of self-approbation. It has been since printed."

Another account of this duel has come to light in recent years, viz. in a letter from the well-known Bengal civilian Charles Grant to a cousin of his. Grant was for a time Secretary to the Board of Trade, and was very intimate at first with Mr. Francis. He writes as a contemporary. The letter appears in his life by Henry Morris, published 1903, viz. Calcutta, May 26, 1775—

"About a month ago these two gentlemen were arguing at the Revenue Board about the propriety of Mr. Barwell's holding farms for his own benefit. The General (Clavering) asked, 'Well, but, Mr. Barwell, how do you hold this act to be consistent with your oath of fidelity to the Company?' Mr. Barwell, after some recollection, answered, 'Whoever says that I have done anything inconsistent with my oath to the Company is a rascal and a scoundrel.' 'These are strong terms, Mr. Barwell—very strong,' replied the General. They were going to put it to the vote whether he had not broke his oath, but this, after some discourse, was overruled. The town remained long ignorant of the altercation, and even the members were not at first in the secret of what followed. In the evening the General sent Mr. Barwell a message to meet him next morning. Mr. Barwell agreed to the meeting, but desired it might be put off two days until he should settle his affairs. It is said he afterwards asked two days more, finding the first delay not sufficient. The fifth day they met at five in the morning, on the new road to Budge-Budge, without seconds. They walked on a good way, until they found a convenient place. 'What distance do you choose, sir?' says Mr. Barwell. 'The nearer the better.' They stood within eight yards. 'Will you fire, sir?' said the General. 'No, sir, you will please to fire first.' 'Is your pistol cocked, Mr. Barwell?' 'Yes, sir.' 'You will give me leave to look, sir, I did not hear the drawing of the cock.' He advanced, satisfied himself, looked at the priming too, then retired to his stand and fired. The ball passed between Mr. Barwell's thighs, grazing the inner part of one. 'Fire, sir,' said the General. 'No, sir, you will give me leave to decline that. I came here in obedience to your summons, and think I may now, without any imputation to my character, declare that I have no enmity, and that I am sorry for what is past.' 'Sir, I must insist upon your firing, if you continue to refuse you will oblige me to fire again.' Mr. Barwell repeated his reluctance to carry the matter further, and his desire to end it by accommodation in such a manner as should be satisfactory to the General. At length the latter yielded so far, with many conditional clauses, as to consent to accept of an apology before the same persons and in the same place where the affront had been given, stipulating particularly that if the apology should not be entirely satisfactory, it should pass for nothing. Upon this they returned; the apology was made in the most ample manner, and the affair thus terminated.

"You will probably hear many accounts, but you may depend upon the substance of this to be genuine."

Here we have three accounts of the same event, written by three contemporaries on the spot; yet they differ materially. Grand distinctly says they had "proper seconds," and agrees with the other two that it was the General only who fired; but he is wrong about the combatants having met the "next morning," *i.e.* after the Council. Charles Grant's account, written while the occurrence was recent, reads very circumstantial, but he flatly contradicts Grand, and says there were no seconds. Surely this was a most extraordinary omission on the part of the military principal, who was "perfectly correct in all the ceremonies of fighting." It is very difficult to believe it. Where did Grant get all the minute details of the conversation? He is the only one who says that Barwell was slightly hit, and in a place which suggests that he was standing square, not sideways. Francis does not mention the absence of seconds. How diffident we should be about historical incidents.

In the month following the duel, Barwell writes a letter about it to his sister (given in Sir J. Stephen's "Nuncomar"):—"His daughter at one time plays with my affections, if not with her own. I deal plainly with her, expose my situation, and intimate my expectations from her. Matters are brought to a point. The father then interferes, begins suddenly to doubt my public conduct, and withdraws his daughter. But it is without effect, and having proved me not to be the dupe of passion, he begins to bluster. He threatens me with the terrors of the law—he brings forward a false charge touching the benefits I derived from salt while at Decca. I do not deny the profits I made. I avow them. I always avowed them. They were neither secret nor clandestine, but I object to the conclusions drawn and refute them. . . . The young lady I sometimes meet in public assemblies, and though I confess a pleasure in perceiving the same conduct and the same attention on her part that I ever received, yet there is something more due in my opinion, etc., etc."

The pugnacity of General Clavering would appear to have been remarkable even in an age when it was the custom to be ever ready with the pistol. He challenged the Duke of Richmond for some alleged reflections on his character in the heated debates at the India House after the passing of the Regulation Act. The "challenge," writes Francis, "produced a disavowal of the words." But he declined to gratify the bluster of a Count Donop at Chandernagore, who professed to be insulted. Clavering refused a visit from him on the ground that he had known about him when he was at Hesse Cassel, and that he considered he had acted an ungentlemanly part in accepting an unauthorised commission to make inquiries at Hamburg—in fact that he had been a spy. Donop wanted to fight Clavering for not receiving his visit, etc., and M. Chevalier (French Governor) tried to make out that Donop had done nothing dishonourable in Europe, but Hastings and the rest of the Council quite approved of Clavering's conduct in the matter ("Bengal Consultations," and Beveridge, "Story of Nuncomar").

After the lapse of nearly three generations, Sir John Clavering's blood became again represented in Calcutta.

Amongst those who had the opportunity of listening, in the crowded Council chamber, to the few dignified and sorrowful sentences addressed* to his colleagues in the Government by

* I have always looked back on this exquisite little address as the most appropriate to a sad and difficult occasion that I ever heard. But to appreciate the effect produced on the audience, one should have heard the gentle pathos in the distinct voice, and have seen the evident emotion. "Gentlemen, I have to claim your sympathy in the performance of the saddest duty of my life. The seat which I have the honour to occupy for a moment, has been opened to me by a cruel crime perpetrated against the most just and most compassionate of men.

Lord Napier, on the occasion of his being sworn in as temporary Viceroy on the murder of Lord Mayo in February, 1872, few perhaps remembered that the speaker was the great-grandson of the General Clavering who, abetted by Philip Francis, had, nearly a hundred years before, attempted to violently seize the Governor-Generalship from Warren Hastings.

Maria Margaret, the Miss Clavering, about whose matrimonial fate we have found Francis so apprehensive, married the seventh Baron Napier of Merchistoun. Though the Lord Napier who married Miss C. was eighth in the line of succession, he was the seventh Baron. The fifth in the line was a Baroness, the succession being open to heirs general whatsoever. Lady Napier died at Enfield in 1821, aged 65. She left two sons, the eldest of whom was the father of the above Lord Napier and Ettrick, then the kindly and popular Governor of Madras.

Again, having recourse to the narrative above alluded to, we are informed of the quarter in which Mr. Barwell became a successful suitor. Let the authority (who, by the way, had much experience of feminine attraction, as we shall see) speak for himself, as he throws light on some of the curious frolics indulged in by society in the days which we are discussing—

"In the enjoyment of such society, which was graced with the ladies of the first fashion and beauty of the Settlement, I fell a convert to the charms of the celebrated Miss Sanderson, but in vain with many others did I sacrifice at the shrine. This amiable woman became in 1776 the wife of Mr. Richard Barwell, who will long live in the remembrance of

It would be superfluous for me now to expatiate on the merits of the statesman and the friend whom we have lost, though no one knew those merits better than myself, and no one felt them more. Other voices more eloquent and authoritative have done justice to the dead, but during the brief period of my presence in your deliberations it will be my study to honour his memory, to follow his counsels, and to benefit by his example. Gentlemen, if I find myself surrounded here by friends and not by strangers, it is still to his goodness that I owe this consolation and advantage. You gave your cordial, zealous, and independent support to the Earl of Mayo in the labours and responsibilities of his beneficent and successful Government, I need not express my confidence that you will grant me the like assistance—assistance of which I shall stand in far greater need." It is worth noting that in little more than four years after this, Lord Lytton wrote to Sir Fitzjames Stephen, April, 1876: "It was not without great hesitation that in the last moment I decided on breaking through all precedent, by addressing to the Council as soon as I had been sworn in and while the public were present, the little speech, of which I send you the report." His Lordship, amidst all the varied duty calls of his fresh arrival, must have forgotten the above precedent of Lord Napier. The present chronicler was fortunate enough to hear both of these excellent speeches.

MARIA MARGARET, DAUGHTER OF SIR JOHN CLAVERING.
MARRIED TO THE 7TH LORD NAPIER OF MERCHISTON.

*See p.* 158.

his numerous friends who benefited from the means of serving them which his eminent station so amply afforded him, and which, to do justice to his liberal mind, he never neglected the opportunity to evince where the solicitation had with propriety been applied. To this lady's credit also may be recorded that those who had been partial to her were ever treated with esteem and gratitude. Much to their regret the splendour of her situation lasted not long; the pain of childbearing with the effects of the climate brought on a delicate constitution a decay which too soon moved this fair flower out of the world. Of all her sex I never observed one who possessed more the art of conciliating her admirers equal to herself. As a proof thereof we met sixteen in her livery one public ball evening, viz. a pea-green French frock trimmed with pink silk and chained lace with spangles, when each of us to whom the secret of her intended dress had been communicated, buoyed himself up with the hope of being the favoured happy individual.

"The innocent deception which had been practised soon appeared evident, and the man of most sense was the first to laugh at the ridicule which attached to him. I recollect the only revenge which we exacted was for each to have the honour of a dance with her; and as minuets, cotillon's reels, and country dances were then in vogue, with ease to herself she obligingly complied to all concerned, and in reward for such kind complaisance we gravely attended her home, marching by the side of her palankeen regularly marshalled in procession of two and two."

Richard Barwell's marriage with Miss Elizabeth Jane Sanderson is to be found in the local vestry records for September, 1776. Mrs. Barwell survived her marriage a little over two years, as she died in November, 1778. She is buried in South Park Street ground, where her tomb, though without an inscription (as noted by Asiaticus), is recognised by the stupendous size of the massive broad-based pyramid over it. She must have left two infant sons, as Mr. Sterndale's history of the Calcutta collectorate refers to a registered deed of trust for them, executed by Barwell about the time of his leaving India. His retirement in March, 1780, and Francis's consequent promotion in Council were, according to the newspaper chronicle of the day, each honoured with a salute of seventeen guns—a ceremony, I believe, not observed now. The last entry but one about him in Francis's journal is "February 29.—Mr. Barwell's house taken for five years by his own vote at 31,720 current rupees per annum to be paid half-yearly in advance; Mr. Wheler and I declare we shall not sign the lease." The house so called was "Writer's Buildings," now the Bengal Government Offices.

It is not surprising that a gentleman who looked so keenly after his personal interests should have accumulated a colossal fortune.

If it was a fortunate thing for Great Britain that her interests in India, in most troublous and critical times, remained in the strong hands of Warren Hastings, it must not be forgotten, in estimating the services of Barwell, that were it not for the steady support of this colleague, Hastings would have been deprived of all power, and early in the struggle must have succumbed to the rash and inexperienced majority.

There is a tendency to assume that the Barwell of Macaulay's Essay was a grave official advanced in years; yet his Indian service was closed when he was little over eight and thirty. At this age he sat down in England to enjoy the fruits he had gathered in the East. He married again, and had several children. His second wife was a sister of Sir Isaac Coffin, and is described as "a lady remarkable for beauty and accomplishments." He purchased a fine estate (Stanstead in Sussex) and a seat in Parliament (for St. Ives first, then Winchelsea), and posed as a typical Nabob for a quarter of a century longer. He had also for many years as his London residence (the present) No. 7, St. James's Square. His Indian idea of plenty has been handed down in the "bring more curricles" story, of which he was the hero. He died at Stanstead in September, 1804, aged sixty-three.

## (IV)

The speedy attainment by Francis of the position of Senior Member of Council is suggestive of a lesson taught by previous and later experience in India, viz. that it is only when young that a tree may be safely transplanted. So impressed was a former Government with the uncertainty of exotic life in Calcutta, that it pleaded this as a reason for not being able to obey orders about fortifying the Settlement properly. When asking for a reserve of qualified engineers (in 1755) their despatch to the Court urged, "Experience teaches us to verify the general observation that men's lives, advanced to or nigh the age of forty, are very precarious in such a change of climate from their native country, therefore successors should be appointed to prevent the inconvenience we now labour under." Over thirty years later, when Lord Cornwallis had some experience of the work devolving on the head of the Indian Government, and the strain that it and the climate put on the health, he wrote to Pitt, "It might therefore be advisable that you should look about for a Governor-General among your friends in the Civil line. Any person with a

RICHARD BARWELL, ESQ.

FROM A PORTRAIT BY REYNOLDS.

*See p.* 160.

good constitution, not much above thirty-five, might reasonably expect to be able to hold the office long enough to save from his salary a very ample fortune." *

Of his two fellow-councillors who sailed from England with Francis, General Clavering was fifty-two when he arrived in India for the first time, and Colonel Monson but a little younger; both succumbed to the climate, the former in less than three years, the latter in less than two. Francis had much the advantage of both in point of youth, and for this reason mainly was able to record, "I begin to fancy that I myself have a very good constitution, or I never could have resisted such a climate and such toil in the manner I have done. My two colleagues are in a woeful condition—Colonel Monson obliged to go to sea to save his life, and General Clavering on his back covered with boils. I see no reason why Barwell should be alive (he never misses an opportunity for a cut at Barwell), but that death does not think it worth while to kill him. He is a mere shadow. As for Hastings, I promise you he is much more tough than any of us, and will never die a natural death." To Sir John Day, at Madras, he writes later:—"I hate the thought for my own part, of dying of the spleen, like a rat in a hole. If I had given way to it heretofore I should now have been stretched alongside of Clavering, Monson, and Lemaistre with a damned *hic jacet* upon my heart. I have many reasons for not wishing to die in Bengal."

In Francis's diary is a melancholy record headed "Dates of Facts," in which he has methodically entered the deaths amongst his co-pilgrims to Calcutta. The list is headed by the Monsons, who were the first to go. Colonel Monson died at Hooghly, on September 25, seven months after his wife, his grief for whom is described as inexpressibly distressing; she died at Calcutta in February, 1776. Their remains were interred side by side in two

* This was in 1788, when a mail to or from England was but an occasional event. The speculation would be interesting as to the advice which Lord C. would have given to the Prime Minister could he have looked forward a century and seen the quantity and quality of the work to be got through by the Governor-General now. The reflection suggests the practical view to be taken of the hot weather migration of the Indian Governments to the hills. If the charge of the higher interests of the Indian Empire must be entrusted to men old enough to be experienced administrators, and experienced statesmen, such men must be shielded as much as possible from the climatic influences doubly hostile to those Europeans who have attained, or passed, middle life. When one is called to the post of Hercules he is expected to accomplish the labour of Hercules, and this he cannot, if, in addition to excessive mental toil and much anxiety, he has got to wrestle with the climate of the plains of India.

similar but separate graves, over which no tomb bearing an inscription was ever erected.* Mackrabie writes in his journal: "February 18. Lady Anne Monson is no more. After lying speechless through the day, she departed last night about ten. The loss of such a woman is generally felt by the whole Settlement, but we who had the honour and pleasure of her intimacy are deprived of a comfort which we shall long regret." The love and respect which this accomplished woman won from all during her brief sojourn in Calcutta, were testified to by the sincere and universal sorrow at her death. Every one attended the funeral. "Mr. Wilton was chief mourner at the Colonel's request. The pall was borne by the Governor-General, the Chief Justice, Mr. Justice Chambers, Mr. Francis, Mr. Farrer the counsellor (a particular friend of the family, at whose house Colonel Monson now is), and Mr. Thompson, who is of the Colonel's family. At the cemetery gate six ladies took the pall and bore it to the grave."

Lady Anne was a special favourite with Francis, who admired and appreciated her cleverness, and her many shining social qualities. They appear to have enjoyed much familiar intercourse from the time they started as fellow-voyagers to Calcutta. He records, for instance, that he "was repeatedly assured" by her that Warren Hastings was the natural son of a steward of her father's, who sent him to Westminster School with his own sons, and where he was called "the classical boy." This was just the sort of malicious tattle that amused Lady Anne's cynical confidant. In the memoirs of Lord Malmesbury it is told that "Sir P. Francis used to say that he had written memoirs which he meant to be published after his death, which would be the ruin of every lady in society, and have the effect of destroying all filiation, as he has clearly proved that not a single person was the son of his reputed father." Fortunately for Society this bomb-shell has not fallen—as yet. Hastings, "the greatest man who has ever borne that ancient and widely extended name," had no cause to blush for his parentage, or for his ancestry, who, once wealthy, became poor through their fidelity to

* I took some pains, with the aid of a member of the firm of Messrs. Llewellyn, the undertakers, to identify these graves some years ago. They are mentioned by Asiaticus. They are in South Park Street Cemetery, near that of General Clavering; they lie near the path west of his grave—two long graves, covered with low-arched brickwork hastening to decay. Monson served in the Carnatic Wars: he is mentioned by Orme for his great bravery; he was severely wounded at the siege of Pondicherry; he also served in the expedition against Manilla under Colonel Draper, who was the sturdy literary antagonist of Junius (1769).

COLONEL THE HONBLE. GEORGE MONSON.

FROM A SILHOUETTE IN THE POSSESSION OF THE RIGHT HONBLE. LORD MONSON.

*See p.* 163.

the Stuarts—from which stock Lady Anne was sprung.* Even if she believed what was so untrue, spiteful gossip of the kind came very badly from her. Lady Anne Vane Monson was the great-granddaughter of Charles II., her mother having been Lady Grace Fitzroy, daughter of the first Duke of Cleveland, son of Charles II. by Barbara Villiers (Lady Castlemaine). She was the eldest daughter of the first Earl of Darlington, and had been the second wife of the Honourable Charles Hope-Weir, prior to her marriage with the gallant and Honourable George Monson. She must have been at least forty-five years of age, if not more, when she left England for an unequal struggle against a tropical climate.

But the saddest entry in his journal which, perhaps, Francis ever made was that of the death which comes third on the list, viz. "1776, November 29, Mr. Alexander Mackrabie at Ganjam." This poor fellow was taken ill in August, and was sent to sea—but, getting worse, he landed at Ganjam, where he lingered till November. He had just been appointed to a writership in the Service.

"The loss," says Mr. Merivale, "of this clever, lively, unselfish, and most attached dependent evidently affected Francis very deeply. There is something very touching in Mackrabie's numerous letters to his chief during this absence, addressed to his 'dearest and best friend,' wishing him once more all happiness, and assuring him, 'sick or well, I am yours with the truest affection.' He seems not only to have loved his brother-in-law as a friend, but to have worshipped him almost as an idol." "Your own feelings," Francis writes to an old friend of both, "will give you the best idea of the affliction that has fallen upon me."

When Francis had been in Calcutta about two and a half years he wrote to a friend in England, "My health is perfectly established, my spirits high, and, with good management, I am a match for the

* Lady Anne would have avoided trenching on this or similar topics in the familiar conversation with Francis, if she had had a suspicion that he was the man who had written this about a cousin of hers, another offshoot from the same stock of the "Merry Monarch." "The character of the reputed ancestors of some men has made it possible for their descendants to be vicious in the extreme without being degenerate. Those of your Grace, for instance, left no distressing examples of virtue even to their legitimate posterity, and you may look back with pleasure to an illustrious pedigree in which heraldry has not left a single good quality upon record to insult or upbraid you. You have better proofs of your descent, my lord, than the register of a marriage or any troublesome inheritance of reputation. There are some hereditary strokes of character by which a family may be as clearly distinguished as by the blackest features of the human face." (Junius to Duke of Grafton.)

climate." A year later he wrote jubilantly in the same strain to another friend, "I am now, I think, on the road to the Government of Bengal, which, I believe, is the first situation in the world attainable by a subject. I will not baulk my future; if that hope be disappointed I shall assuredly not stay here. . . . But we shall be still young, my friend, with the means and powers of enjoyment." What room there was for congratulation in the result of Francis's good "management" as regards his health will be realised by remembering that Calcutta at this time stood in what was little better than an undrained swamp, in the immediate vicinity of a malarious jungle, that the ditch surrounding it was, as it had been for nearly forty years previously, an open cloaca, and that the river banks were strewn with the dead bodies of men and animals.

From 1780 and onwards correspondents in the newspapers make frequent complaints about the indescribably filthy condition of the streets and roads, which is fully confirmed by the account of Grandpré in 1790, who tells of the canals and cesspools reeking with putrifying animal matter—the awful stench—the myriads of flies, and the crowds and flocks of animals and birds acting as scavengers. An editor severely censures "the very indecent practice of naked Fakeers parading through the town." "We saw," he says, his indignation finding vent in bad Latin, "about fifty of them on Wednesday last nudus velut ab utero materna" (*sic*). But the sight which must have most outraged decency and modesty, in addition to every other sense, was the treatment to which the bodies of the dead were subjected. These might be seen at any hour while being carried to the river, "slung loosely across a bamboo from which they frequently fall off," or "the feet and hands tied together and when so slung carried naked through the streets." Often the police authorities are reproached in the public papers for suffering dead human bodies to lie on the roads in and near Calcutta for two or three days. The bodies alluded to were most generally those of poor creatures who had died of want and hunger—sometimes of dacoits or other malefactors who had been executed: occasionally of mutilated dacoits who had crawled into the town to beg. In the times of Hastings and Francis, and for a long time after, dacoity and highway robbery close to the seat of Government were crimes exceedingly prevalent. This, for instance, was the state of things within a mile of the Supreme Court, as described in the Calcutta papers of 1788: "The native inhabitants on the roads leading to the Boita-Khana tree are in such general alarm of dacoits that from eight or nine o'clock at night they begin to fire off matchlock guns till daybreak at intervals, to the great annoyance of the neighbouring Europeans. The dacoits parade openly on the different roads about Calcutta in parties of twenty, thirty, or forty at so early an hour as eight p.m." *

A typical instance of the neglect of sanitation at the period we are most concerned with will be found in the condition of their drinking-water supply, the chief source of which was the tank in Lall Diggee (Dalhousie Square).

A correspondent writes in April, 1780, regarding this to the newspaper of the day—

"As I was jogging along in my palanqueen yesterday, I could not avoid observing without a kind of secret concern for the health of several of my tender and delicate friends,—a string of parria dogs, without an ounce of hair on some of them, and in the last stage of the mange, plunge in and refresh themselves very comfortably in the great Tank. I don't mean to throw the least shadow of reflection upon the sentinels, as the present condition of the Palisadoes is such that it would take a Battalion at least of the most nimblefooted sepoys to prevent them. I was led insensibly to reflect upon the small attention that is paid by people in general to a point of such unspeakable importance to their health and longevity as the choice and care of their water, the great vehicle of our nourishment."

Another writes on the same subject—

"Should you believe it that, in the very centre of this opulent city, and almost under our noses, there is a spot of ground measuring not more than six hundred square yards used as a public burying ground

* The *Calcutta Chronicle* in the following year gives a terrible account of the example which was made of a gang of dacoits. Fourteen were sent by a Mr. Redfern from Kishnagur to Sulkey to take their trial at the (Native) Fouzdary Court. On being found guilty the following sentence was ordered to be carried out at Sair Bazaar, near Calcutta, on the Howrah side of the river. Each man to have his right hand and left foot cut off at the joint. The victims were taken one by one, each in the sight of the others, and pinioned to the ground: a fillet or band was then tied over the mouth to drown the cries. "The amputation was most clumsily performed with an instrument like a carving-knife by hacking to find out the joint: each limb took about three minutes. The stumps were then dipped in hot ghee, and the criminal left to his fate." None died under the operation. Four died soon after, but more (it is said) from the effects of the sun and neglect than from "the savage severity which was applied." The *Chronicle* regrets the necessity for such examples, "but we bless God they are not authorised by the laws of England." Scourging to death was another punishment frequently put in force. Sir Roland Wilson ("Introduction to the Study of Anglo-Muhammedan Law"), in commenting on this extract, points out that "the English criminal law, however, was at this period, taken, as a whole, considerably more severe than the Muhammedan. It was not till 1790 that the punishments of disembowelling, etc., for high treason, and for burning women alive for petty treason, were abolished."

by the Portuguese inhabitants, where there are annually interred, upon a medium, no less than four hundred dead bodies; that these bodies are generally buried without coffins, and in graves dug so exceedingly shallow as not to admit of their being covered with much more than a foot and a half of earth, insomuch that after a very heavy fall of rain some part of them have been known to appear above ground. . . . Moreover, the quantity of matter necessarily flowing from it assimilating with the springs of the earth can scarcely fail to impart to the water in the adjacent wells and tank any morbid and noxious quality, laying by this means the foundation of various diseases among the poorer sort of people who are obliged to drink it, nor can those in more affluent circumstances, from the natural indolence and deception of servants, promise themselves absolute exemption from it."

No wonder that the inhabitants on whom these unpleasant facts were thus obtruded, took every opportunity of converting the water into arrack punch prior to consumption; or that those who could afford to do so, gave it the go-by altogether by the substitution of mulled claret or madeira, which drinks were, we find, very much in fashion. No wonder that a most ordinary formula for accounting for the absence of such or such a one from society, was that, in the unvarnished language of the day, he was "down with a putrid fever, or a flux."

Little wonder either that as the close of each October brought round what was considered the end of the deadly season, those Europeans who were fortunate enough to find themselves above ground, all met in their respective circles and thankfully celebrated their deliverance in that truly British device, large banquets. One of them, a poet, who was grateful not only for his own respite, but for that of his lady love, composed, I find, an ode for one of those dismal festivities. It was headed, "On the introduction of the Cold Weather—in opposition to Horace's 'Solvitur acris hiems.'" It begins—

"The summer's raging rays are gone,"

And ends—

"But cease, my muse, since she is well,
And Death's destructive season's o'er,
Let's life enjoy nor loveless dwell
On summers that can kill no more."

"The unwholesome weather which ever attends the breaking-up of the rains," is a text often discoursed on by the old newspapers. One editor tells his subscribers that he has the authority of a medical correspondent for recommending them to "drink deep in rosy port" in September, to guard against the influenza. This prescription was made public probably because it was an innovation on that in favour with the faculty. In June, on the other hand, the newspapers give the public the much-needed advice not to eat too much in the hot weather, and the moral is pointed by quoting (June, 1780) the recent and awful fate of "the Surgeon of an Indiaman, who fell dead after eating a hearty dinner of beef, the thermometer being 98°."

Diseases, too, of a mysterious kind seem to have occasionally appeared and claimed their victims. The local purveyor of news records in perplexity, in August, 1780: "We learn that several people has (*sic*) been suddenly carried off within these few days by tumours in the neck, symptoms of a very unusual nature."

Possibly this is the symptom alluded to in the following methodical extract from Mr. Justice Hyde's notes. It will be seen that "the fever" was accepted as a matter of course towards the close of the rains. It is sometimes referred to as "pucca fever"—

"The Fourth Term, 1779, in the 19th and 20th year of the reign of His Majesty King George the Third. Friday, October 22nd, 1779. The first day of the Fourth Term, 1779.

"Present: Mr. Justice Hyde. There were only common motions.

"Mem.: Sir E. Impey, Chief Justice, was absent by reason of illness. He has a swelling of the double chin. It came after he had the epidemic fever, which prevailed here in September and this month, and still does prevail here; but Dr. Campbell told me he did not think the swelling any part of the disorder usually following that fever, but a nervous disorder of the nature of that Sir E. Impey had before he went to Chittagong, which then affected his arm and head.

"Sir Robert Chambers was also absent by reason of illness. Yesterday the fever began with him.

"I (John Hyde) have had the fever, and am not yet perfectly free from the consequences, for I have a slight degree of pain and weakness in my left foot, and a slight degree of dizziness still affects my head."

Impey himself, when referring to his health, tells his friends in England that, "thank God, it is better, but acknowledges that he has to put up with what he calls the 'Cholera Morbus,' once or twice a year." The strangest disease of all, however, was one (not attributable to climate, perhaps) which I find noted by Asiaticus as having caused the death of a young married lady "celebrated for her poetry and misfortunes;" "she died of pure sensibility," he says. It is gratifying to be able to record that this disease—in its aggravated form, at all events—has become extinct in Calcutta.

It must be borne in mind that in those days there were no changes to the hills for the sick; no sanitaria; no steamers to take them away in the face of the long monsoon. Sickness, the almost necessary consequence of climate, aided by the madly unsuitable style of living in fashion, had too often to be encountered where it was incurred. Nor had the poor invalid the benefit or comfort derivable from skilled professional attendance at his sick bed. Medical science was, as yet, unenlightened; any one announcing himself as a doctor was apparently allowed to prey on his fellow-men; indeed, it is hinted in the local newspaper of 1780 that the practice of medicine was occasionally adopted on no better qualification than that possessed by a midshipman, "who handles your pulse as he'd handle a rope." It is not surprising, therefore, to find it recorded that the success attending the efforts of the medical man was not so marked as to inspire the public with much confidence in him. The Poet's Corner contains much evidence of this disbelief in the old Calcutta practitioner, one or two instances of which may be given. Amid the forced fun in the following, which is called a "Jeux d'esprit," can be seen the hopeless resignation to his fate, which must have come over many a man when heavy illness overtook him in India in the last century.

"To a man who deny'd ev'ry medical aid,
When worn out by a tedious decline,
A friend and relation affectionate said,
'Surely never was conduct like thine.

"'Go to Mádras by sea, or to Chittágong Spa,
Get Hartley and Hare to prescribe;'
But still he in obstinate humour cried—'psha!
How I hate all the physical tribe.

"'What are Hartley * and Hare to grim Dr. Death
Who moves slowly, but perfects the cure?
Their prescriptions may rob me too soon of my breath,
And heighten the pains I endure.

"'Commend me to this famed physician of old
Who attends folks of ev'ry degree;
Who is staunch to his patient and ne'er quits his hold,
But kills—without bolus or fee.'" †

* This was Bartholomew Hartley, M.D., who projected a famous lottery in 1784, for raising a fund in aid of the erection of St. John's Cathedral.

† "Doctors visit in palanquins and charge a gold mohur a visit." "The extras," adds poor Miss Goldborne, "are enormous." She instances a bolus, one

It was usual to describe the practice then in vogue as being active and heroic; and of course it was thought necessary to apply it with superlative energy in a country where experience seemed to show that the crisis was rapidly reached. The maxim was *venienti occurrite morbo*. Accordingly, when summoned to the bedside, it became a race between the doctor and the disease. A certain rhyming formula addressed in the imperative mood to the apothecary, commencing "physic blister," was promptly brought into force, and the patient who had undergone these vigorous and well-meant invasions, was uncommonly lucky if he escaped being then and there "cupped and blooded" into the bargain. It is superfluous to add that the only benefit following this misdirected zeal, was that derived by the apothecary and undertaker. It should be added, in justice to the Calcutta medical men of a hundred years ago, that they naturally enough followed the system in which they had been indoctrinated in Europe—they merely energetically adopted the practice which was the orthodox one till far into the present century. The letting of blood was its panacea. Its time-honoured motto was "saignare, saignare, ensuita purgare." * Men and women, even delicate ladies, got themselves bled at regular intervals to improve their blood, as they were told. "Patty has been bled," writes Francis to his wife while absent, about a relative of hers; "her blood is so bad that Price says she must be bled once a week for two years and some months." And Mrs. Francis writes to her husband in Calcutta, January, 1777: "Whilst I was away Dr. Adair came and said it was proper to bleed Sally and Harriet, which he did; when I came home I was much frightened but hope it will be of use. Harriet after the bleeding fainted away several times and was very weak and low, but the pain in her side was much relieved. She had but a poor night and is very indifferent." ("Francis Papers.") How almost incredibly dreadful does this dangerous meddling read to us now. N.B.—Sally was scarcely fourteen and the poor little Harriet was only

rupee; an ounce of salts, ditto; an ounce of bark, three rupees. Such a lot of these commodities had to be swallowed, she ruefully came to the conclusion that, "literally speaking, you may ruin your fortune to preserve your life."

* From Molière's satire on the medical practice of his day—"Le Malade Imaginaire." In the "Marche de la faculte, au son des instruments," members of which sing a medley, with the refrain—

"——— donare
Postea seignare
Ensuita purgare

*Re*-seignare, re-purgare et re-clysterizare."

eleven! Even good, sensible Samuel Johnson, who, as Boswell tells us, strongly disapproved of all this periodical bleeding (though too frequent a victim to the professional practice himself), was unable to impress his opinion upon his own or the next generation. Who has not been amused by his want of patience with Dr. Taylor, whose nose happened to bleed, and who attributed it to his having allowed four days to pass after his quarter's bleeding was due. Johnson suggested other means of bringing about the relief supposed to be needed. "I do not like to take an emetic," pleaded Taylor, "for fear of breaking some small vessels." "Poh," retorted the downright sage, "If you have so many things that will break, you had better break your neck at once, and there's an end on't—you will break no small vessels (blowing with high derision)."

Readers of Madame D'Arblay's memoirs may recall that old Mrs. Delany, the valued friend of George the Third and his Queen, while living as their guest at Windsor, in 1785, and presumably within reach of the highest medical skill in the kingdom, was "blooded" for a little ailment, for which in these unheroic days the poor old body would probably have been advised to take a hot foot-bath and to stay in bed, as she was eighty-six years old, almost quite blind from age, and with much more than the proverbial one leg in the grave! Forty years later still, the half-starved and fever-shattered Lord Byron was bled to death at Messalonghi.* In spite

* This terrible case should be better known or remembered than it is, if only to emphasise the abyssmal darkness in which the practice of medicine was then sunk, and the mild and beneficent administration of it to-day. With this object the following may be quoted from Jeafferson's book, "The real Lord Byron." "Byron was only 36 when he died; his death, preceded by epileptic seizures and by exposure to malaria, was clinched, it was generally felt, by medical perseverance in crystallized error. Two youthful and incompetent doctors, Bruno and Millingen, did their best and their worst for him. He had been living by his own rule for five weeks on toast and tea, and at last, in response to the urgent appeal and insistence of the two doctors, he consented to be bled (April 16, 1824). Casting at the two the fiercest glance of vexation, and throwing out his arm, he said, in his angriest tone, "There you are, I see a damned set of butchers; take away as much blood as you like and have done with it." They took *twenty* ounces. The next day they repeated the bleeding twice, and put blisters above the knee because he objected to have his feet exposed to the blistering process. In spite of all he lived on, and on the 18th actually rose from bed and tottered into an adjoining room, leaning on his servant Tita's arm. There he amused himself with a book for a few minutes and then returned to bed: after they had left him he took one anodyne draught. Some time later he took another draught of a similar kind, and at six o'clock he uttered his last intelligible sentence, "Now I shall go to slee——" He slept for twenty-four hours, and at a quarter to six

of his own piteous appeal, "Have you no other remedy than bleeding?" "In these days," adds the *Lancet*, sixty years after, "we look with wonder at the medical art which in twenty-four hours could bleed three times a fasting man, then blister him, and finally supplement the so-called treatment with two strong narcotic draughts."

It has been remarked in a former page that Philip Francis, after the duel, was bled twice in one day for a slight flesh wound in his back, though this was towards the sickly season, when libations of "rosy port" were advocated as a precaution by the unorthodox newspaper. It is curious that in the following year, though not in connection with the instance just alluded to, the local newsprint has a satirical tirade against the indiscriminate use of the lancet. Much of it would be quite unquotable in modern days, but I venture to append some verses of it to show its tendency. It is the first local evidence that I have come across of an impatience of the laity under a system which outraged common sense; it is an early indication of a reaction which slowly gained strength, and culminated many years after in the do-little systems of Homœopathy and Hydropathy.

"Some doctors in India would make Plato smile;
If you fracture your skull they pronounce it the bile,
And with térrific phiz and a stare most sagacious,
Give a horse-ball of jalap and pills saponaceous.

"A sprain in your toe or an anguish shiver,
The faculty here call a touch of the liver,
And with ointment mercurii and pills calomelli,
They reduce all the bones in your skin to a jelly.

"Broke down by the climate, low, weak, 'twould surprise ye
To hear them insist that your blood is too sizey;
If a compound of ills from such treatment you boast,
The plan next advised is a trip to the coast.

p.m. on the 19th surprised his watchers by opening his eyes and instantly shutting them. He died at that instant.

"Tita" was his Italian servant, who with his valet and head man, Fletcher, was with Byron when he died. It is an interesting coincidence that Tita had been the faithful attendant of Byron's friend, "Monk" Lewis, and had prepared his body for burial at sea on the voyage home from the West Indies. Another curious coincidence, one indirectly afterwards associating Byron's death with the India Office, is that "Tita," whose name was Giovanni Batista Faleieri, became an India-Office messenger, through the sympathetic interest of Mr. Disraeli, and died as such in December, 1874, aged 76. So, as well as I can recall, it is stated by Colonel Laurie in, I think, a book of sketches of some Anglo-Indians.

"With a shrug of concern Galen shakes you off easily,
And sends you to pester the famed Doctor Paisley;
You may pine on the coast till your money's all spent,
And then you return full as well as you went.

"If your wife has a headache, let Sangrado but touch her,
And he'll job in his lancet like any hog butcher;
Tho' in putrid complaints dissolution is rapid,
He'll bleed you to render the serum more vapid.

"And for stemming the tide of all "critical fluxes,"
Doctor Phlebos demands most exorbitant "buxis;"
By such spurious systems Dame Nature they force,
And if you escape you've the strength of a horse.

"Against such a system the College may preach
Still Sangrado bleeds on like a human horse-leach (*sic*),
And as if predesigned by a regular plan set,
To the Shades we're despatched by a touch of his Launcet.

. . . . . . . . . . .

"In a very few days you're released from all cares—
If the Padre's asleep, Mr. Oldham reads prayers;*
To the grave you're let down with a sweet pleasant thump,
And there you may lie till you hear the last trump."

The writer of this doggerel looks forward, he says, to singing the delinquencies of the Calcutta bar in a future number, but I have failed to find his muse's labour in so promising a field. But the darkness in which we have seen them some pages back, was not any denser than that encompassing their medical contemporaries.

Yet, though life in Old Calcutta involved the exposure to much physical suffering, with none of the alleviation which art has since introduced, it is significant that when Francis sums up his impressions

* The obliging Mr. Oldham, whose name occurs above, was a very important local personage in the last century. He was the first undertaker proper who settled in Calcutta; he first cut stones from the ruins of Gour. Before his time Bengal indented on Madras for tombstones. It goes without saying that Mr. Oldham amassed a fortune before he himself was laid (1788) in South Park Street Cemetery, surrounded by numerous specimens of his own handicraft. His tombstone tells merely his name, age, and date of death. His epitaph might appropriately have been *si monumentum requiris—circumspice.*

I find the following in one of my notebooks (authority not quoted). This undertaker, I have read, was also a shining light amongst the masonic brethren of Calcutta. It is hinted, too, that he first intended to practise medicine in Calcutta —on what qualification?—but he seems to have thought it more profitable to bury his fellow-townsmen, than to try to, let us say, cure them.

*Qui chirurgus erat nunc est vespillo Diaulus.*

of a residence there, he does not dwell on the active miseries which may be ameliorated, but rather on the passive ones which will be always incidental to, and inseparable from, the life of a European in (the plains of) India. For instance, this is how a man of his amazing energy and his boundless mental resources is reduced to write: "The waste of spirits in this cursed country is a disease unconquerable, a misery unutterable." "I relinquish my family and friends, and I pass my life in one eternal combat with villainy, folly, and prostitution of every species. If I carry home £25,000 by the severest parsimony of five years, it will be the utmost I can accomplish. I would now gladly accept two-thirds of the money if I could be up to the neck in the Thames." Have not this experience and this aspiration of Francis, or something much akin to them, been heard often since, wide and far over the East? Listen to one who knows India and its exactions well, melodiously discoursing a century later, in sympathy with the exotics honestly and faithfully serving England there—the strangers that shall fade away.

> "Has he learned how thy honours are rated ;
> Has he cast his accounts in thy school ;
> With the sweets of authority sated,
> Would he give up his throne to be cool ? " *

After his card-winning he places his wants a little higher, as the possibility of attaining them seems open to him, but his horror of India is unabated. "Whenever I am worth a clear entire sum of forty thousand pounds secure in England, Bengal may take care of itself. No, not for that fortune would I spend the same two years again."

It is interesting to see how nearly in the same strain Macaulay writes some sixty years later, after an experience of a much improved Calcutta: "Let me assure you that banishment is no light matter. No person can judge of it who has not experienced it. A complete revolution in all the habits of life—an estrangement from almost every old friend and acquaintance—all this is, to me at least, very trying. There is no temptation of wealth or power which could induce me to go through it again." "We have our share of the miseries of life in this country. We are annually baked four months, boiled four more, and allowed the remaining four to become cool if we can. Insects and undertakers are the only living creatures which

* Sir Alfred Lyall, whose "Verses written in India," notably "The Land of Regrets"—humorous, pathetic, and sadly true—will be ever green for Anglo-Indians.

seem to enjoy the climate." Elsewhere Macaulay records his experienced conviction that "all the fruits of the tropics are not worth a pottle of Covent Garden strawberries, and that a lodging up three pairs of stairs in London is better than a palace in a compound of Chowringhee."

But to return to Francis. He thus writes to the gentleman who had declined the nomination to India which then came to him: "We shall meet again, I trust—I mean in this world—and may I be d—d in the next if ever I venture myself into such a hell as this, with my own consent at least. I certainly am obliged to you for my post, but I fancy by this time you are quite satisfied that you did not take it." To Mrs. Strachey, who had asked him to provide for her children when old enough to go to India, he writes—

"DEAR MADAM,—Be so good as to live till I return, and you shall see wonders; you shall see me, whom India has made neither rich nor saucy. I profess to have one or two qualities at least to which this infamous climate cannot reach, the rest is at the mercy of the sun, whose light the moment I can command wax candles and a coal fire I solemnly disclaim for ever. Let him ripen his cabbages and show peasants the way to their daily labour. I desire to have no further communication with him, but to vegetate in a hothouse as a gentleman should do. . . . And so you have determined that I shall stay in Bengal till I have settled your infant colony for you, and can leave it in a flourishing condition. Indeed, madam, I am not satisfied with the share you have allotted to me in this useful work. I would rather be employed as you are. Leave it to me to provide emigrants, and do you come here and settle them. Soberly and sadly, this is no market for young ladies; the same heat which ripens the fruit reduces the appetite, whereof the proofs are rather melancholy than pregnant. How long beauty will keep in this country, is too delicate a question for me to determine. You, who can read faces, would see lines in some of them which Time ought not to have written there so soon."

But if the Europeans who went to India in the old days had a hard time of it, they at all events got what they went for—money, and if they survived they returned home wealthy men. In the year following Francis's departure from Calcutta, the Government of India remonstrated against the number of covenanted servants far in excess of the wants of the country which greedy patronage had sent out, and added, "Many of them are the sons of the first families in the Kingdom of Great Britain, and every one aspiring to the rapid acquisition of lakhs and to return to pass the prime of their lives at home, as multitudes have done before them." The modern average official is lucky if, in a lifetime given to India, he can put by a fifth of the sum which Francis sneered at as attainable in five years.

Sir Elijah Impey, after he had been five years in office, wrote: "I have not been able to lay up *more* than three thousand pounds in any year."

In comparing the conditions of the two periods it must not be lost sight of that, to all the other drawbacks of an Indian life, poverty has in recent years been added. It is not an exaggeration to say that of the Anglo-Indian officials who have got families dependent on them, at least seven out of ten go through their expatriation feeling the pain and knowing the burden "of heavy, tedious penury," till their pensions (which die with them) come. Fortunate are they for whom by that time life has not lost all its salt and all its savour. Then they retire to husband their means in some country town or village in England, where they hope to find a grammar school for their children, for whom during their long servitude abroad they have been unable to make any friendly interest or any influential connection, such as they might reasonably have expected to make in any other community or walk in life.

A retrospect at the life of Francis in India, such as has been attempted, would be incomplete without some reference to the result of his sojourn there on his home domestic welfare.

Early in life, when twenty-one years of age, he had married a Miss Mackrabie, a well-educated,* attractive girl of his own age, with some of the accomplishments which embellish life. It was a love match, opposed, for prudential reasons, by the fathers of both; but Francis's ardent temperament could not brook much delay, and his self-reliant nature impelled him to disregard the parental prohibition, and to persuade the lady to marry him without the father's sanction, and when the means of supporting a wife were but slender. And, small as his resources were, he soon found that with a rapidly increasing family he had occasion to be generous, not only to his own father, but to his wife's relations as well. Glimpses at the *ménage* which the struggling couple maintained are got in the good-humoured and sometimes cynical letters which Francis wrote at the time to his brother-in-law Mackrabie, then in America, viz.: "If your sister writes to you by this pacquet you must thank me for the injunction laid upon her, for otherwise, between the delightful occupation of scolding her maids and mending her children's stockings, I doubt she would hardly have found time to think

* In referring to one of his wife's early letters to him he compliments her thus: "You really improve much in your style"—high praise this from the future Junius.

of her relations." "Domestic news is as insipid as usual; children bawling, servants fighting, my wife scolding, your father and mother weeping, and Patty raving mad." When announcing one of the annual domestic occurrences as imminent, he says: "In the mean time your sister is tormented with only the following disorders, viz. cramp, toothache, swelled legs, and heartburn, to say nothing of a perpetual cholic and slow fever; otherwise she finds herself in perfect health. I am well, and live the life of a prince." In after years, when sending from Calcutta a present of five hundred pounds to his wife to buy "diamond earrings or other jewelry you may think fit," he wrote:—"Fortune has taken extraordinary care of me, and I am much her humble servant. She was certainly in my debt, if it be considered how many years you and I lived upon little or nothing." The answer to that letter is dated November, 1777, viz.: "We are both infinitely indebted to Fortune, and I am grateful to her. As to our former difficulties in making both ends meet, I am always happy when I think of those days, for they were full of pleasure and satisfaction in acting as we should, and everything turned out well. But notwithstanding your success, our absence from each other, and in that the loss of all that is dear is in a great degree truly affecting, but I must always endeavour to bear it as well as I can." Again she writes: "How happy do your letters make me, indeed, my dearest Philip, if it was possible I love you more than ever. I shall like to wear your beautiful present of muslin if it is not too fine . . . you are too good to me." Yes, the early home days were the happiest of Philip Francis's life; so little did the narrow income cloud their sunshine that he was able to tell Mackrabie, in 1769: "I believe I lead a happier life than a prime minister." The letters of Francis to his wife before the Indian appointment testify to the strong attachment which existed between them, and to the winning and delicate thoughtfulness on his part regarding her and his children.

"My dear soul . . . enclosed you will find a bank note for ten pounds—don't talk of necessaries. I desire you will have everything you like, and so, dearest, adieu." When ill-health obliges her to go for a short change to Brighton by herself, he tries to amuse and please her with such little domestic trifles as this: "I had little Betsy in my arms this morning, which made Sarah so jealous that she roared with vexation. But I am very good to them both." "The two children and I played together this morning above half an hour on the carpet." When his little ones are away from home with her, he never forgets to ask her to "kiss my children" and to give him "all the news of them." "My sweetest Betsy, I hope you think of me, and that you really wish to be with me again, etc.—Yours for ever, P.F." Again, "Indeed I am very serious when I say I think your absence long, and the prospect of three weeks more appears almost an age. However, if you and the children are benefited by it I shall be satisfied.—Yours, my dearest love, always, and with the greatest truth, P.F." Sometimes he writes to her, "My dearest honesty." The following is one of many similar passages:—

"Words cannot express my impatience to have you in my arms. At seven on Monday I expect you. Will the machine bring you to the door, or where shall I order James to wait for you? To say the truth, my dear girl, I have been dining with honest Fitz and Co., and am not in my perfect mind, but you see that even while I forget myself I still remember you. It is true I am endowed with a most capricious humour, but I am always wise enough to know that I am possessed of the best girl in the world, and that I never could be happy without her. Adieu." *

* There is plenty of evidence, and some of an amusing kind, furnished by himself to show that during his pre-Indian career Francis was far from temperate. While the letters under the signatures of Atticus, Lucius, and a multitude of pseudonyms prior to the regular adoption of the more famous one, were attracting great notice, Francis on his own showing was leading a joval, wine-bibbing life. There is but little if any direct evidence of this during the exact period embraced by the Junian letters (November 22, 1768, to January 21, 1772), as if, when he became conscious of the tremendous influence which he exerted, and the extraordinary attention which Junius commanded, he recognised the danger involved in forgetting the *in vino veritas* maxim. The following from his letters to his intimate, Mackrabie, exemplifies what has just been said:—

"But even if I had anything of consequence to communicate, neither my hand nor head at this moment are in a condition to give it utterance; all yesterday! all last night! an Atlantick of claret! Your friend Nugent furnished the wine, and being one of the company himself took care that it should be excellent. At eleven we adjourned to the Bedford Arms by way of changing the scene, not the liquor, for there, too, this worthy gentleman assured us he could answer for the claret. In short, he answered for it so well that I left him speechless, the rest of the company stark mad; notwithstanding I exerted every possible artifice to preserve my reason I was at last obliged to surrender at discretion, or rather all discretion. But all this is innocent mirth compared to what Nugent threatens us with at his own house next Tuesday. Oh! is this the temperance, soberness, and chastity which my godfathers and godmothers answered for at my baptism?"

Again, January 4, 1769 (a fortnight before a Junius letter), he writes to the same: "I am just returned from spending a riotous fortnight at Bath. . . . While I lived in Bath, in every species of debauch, my health was unimpaired; but the moment I returned to this cursed regularity of drinking nothing and going to bed and getting up early, *me voici enrhumé comme un tigre*. I can hardly see, breathe, or speak; therefore I see no reason why I should write any more. Sick or well, drunk or sober, yours I remain." "About a month ago I had the satisfaction of losing a note for ten pounds in much the same way, and with the same success—intoxication,"

Soon after he got the Indian appointment, he tells a lady: "You already know that Mrs. Francis is not to accompany me to India; it is her own choice and resolution, and severely felt by us both. What are five little girls and a boy to do deprived both of mother and father!"

Few of Francis's letters from India to his wife have been preserved. Mrs. Francis's communications to her husband in India were mainly in the form of a journal, which was sent to him at regular intervals. It relates altogether to domestic matters, the progress of their children's studies, their gaieties, and "her own little excursions into a social world for which she was by no means made."

It is described by Mr. Merivale as the production of a tenderly attached and admiring wife, as the extracts just given and one or two others will show. "December 9, 1778.—This morning I set out for the India House to take my packet and enquire after my picture. . . . I was shown your picture, it is very like, but the original far exceeds it." A couple of weeks later she writes, "I often talk to your dear picture and kiss it, 'tis almost alive." And so she goes on in her winning affection, using words so fond and so foolish that one has not the heart to quote them, or the little wifely confidences they convey. As the time draws nigh when, as originally arranged, Francis should be leaving India, her eager anxiety becomes very marked. In October, 1780, she records, "A gentleman from India called and gave me a letter from you. He spoke of you and of what great chance you had of being in the Chair, and many such things which gave me great pain. How grieved should I be if that should happen, my joy would then be over, for I should have small hope of ever seeing you again. What would the world be to me or all its riches? I could never value or enjoy them without your company . . . but I trust you will not be tempted by such glare, and will resist its greatness for the sake of making me happy."

In his uncertainty as to what the Home Government might do regarding the prolonging of Hastings' tenure, Francis must have tried to prepare his wife for his own possible detention in India, for she writes in sadness and natural bitterness, "Your staying in India one year more is the most dreadful disappointment to me. What can detain you, my dear Philip? Indeed, I cannot say as you, it is quite indifferent to you whether you stay or come home; it is not so to me, I can assure you, for all my happiness depends upon my seeing you. I am sorry to find it is not so with you." And then, on finding, as she apprehends, that her happiness is not his first consideration, she, so absolutely confiding in her fondness all along, adds this, "but separation I was but too sure for almost seven years would make a great alteration in your affection, and I am sorry to say I fear it has —a very great one indeed." As Mr. Merivale, one of Francis's biographers, remarks, her poor journal is touching in its homely way as it teaches a sad lesson when it shows the gradual effect of distance and the evil influences engendered by long absence on domestic love which had been so deeply rooted as theirs. "She was not, however, qualified to be a sharer in her husband's plots, or a partner in his fierce ambition; nor to partake in his public or literary pursuits." She was only a noble, simple, and most lovable woman. Francis gained money by going to India—but he risked the loss of what no money can buy.

"My political connections with India since 1774," he wrote to Sir R. Chambers, "have employed the whole of my life, and embittered too much of it." When we read this, and recall what this ambitious man said of himself in the House of Commons afterwards, "I passed six years in perpetual misery and contest in Bengal at the hazard of my life, then a wretched voyage of ten months, and two and twenty years of labour in the same cause unsupported and alone, without thanks and reward, and now without hope, I have sacrificed my happiness and forfeited every prospect of personal advantage," we may incline to be wise after the event and to think that his fine appointment there was dearly purchased, and that he would have done better for his own welfare and for his domestic peace and happiness if he had remained, and with his great abilities, fought the battle of life at home.

But—

"He did list to the voice of a siren,
He was caught by the clinking of gold,
And the slow toil of Europe seemed tiring,
And the grey of his fatherland cold;
He must haste to the gardens of Circe,
What ails him the slave that he frets
In thy service? O Lady Sans Merci,
O Land of Regrets."

It is pleasant, however, to be able to record that on his return to England he resumed his old domestic habits and proved again a kind attentive husband and a fond father to his daughters, to whom he was devotedly attached. When absent his letters to his wife were affectionate and frequent and occasionally playful as of old. As regards his income, he wrote to his ally, Shee, "I have above £3000 a year to spend, and I live with rigid economy, yet it is the utmost I can do not to exceed my income." This need of care is not to be wondered at, as he had to maintain a seat in Parliament, Yarmouth in Isle of Wight, and later, Appleby, and went much into society, where as guest or host he was made welcome and thought much of by its most distinguished members, from the Prince of Wales downwards. In 1806 he lost the companion of his youth, and of his early struggles and contented poverty. Mrs. Francis had for some years fallen into very bad health before death released her.

In the same year the death of Lord Cornwallis opened to him as he hoped the Governor-Generalship of India, a position which, even at his advanced age, he ardently coveted. With his old vigour he set to work to canvass for it, and very soon he quarrelled with Fox for what he considered deserting him. But he was passed over—by his own party, too, the Whigs—and Gilbert Elliot (who, in 1772, had been a fellow-clerk and junior of his in the War Office) reigned in his stead as Lord Minto. His disappointment and indignation were extreme, though his friend, the Prince of Wales, courteously tried to mollify him in every way that he could, even to the obtaining for him the distinguished appointment, alluded to in this letter from his daughter Catherine to one of her sisters.

"You must before this have guessed that the first object of his wishes was not to be attained. He has been offered the Government of the Cape with the salary annexed to it of £10,000 a year, the Order of the Bath, and to be one of the privy council. The Government he has refused. To quit his country again for any situation but that which he has so good a right to and which would gratify all his wishes, could not be expected by his family, and *I* at least rejoice that he has refused it." And, writing himself, still bitterly, though years after, to Mr. Perry of the *Chronicle*, he says, in allusion to widow burning, child drowning, and "the horrible excesses at Juggernaut, offences against God and all religions, the causes of which should be found out and mitigated or removed." "Do you think," he adds, "that if Mr. Fox had found it to coincide with his politics or his partialities to have permitted me to return to India, in 1806, in the office that was full as much my right, as it was his to be Secretary of State, I would not have put a stop to such enormities?" Every project relating to India in which he was involved proved a failure, and the bitterest expression which he gave to his disappointed labours were perhaps those words wrung from him in the Commons, "I will never be concerned in impeaching anybody. The impeachment of Mr. Hastings has cured me of that folly. *I* was tried, and *he* was acquitted." A civil Knight-Companionship of the Bath was "the final reward of Francis's fiercely agitated life."

SIR PHILIP FRANCIS.

FROM A PORTRAIT BY HOPPNER.

See p. 281.

After remaining a widower for eight years Sir Philip married again, on losing the companionship of his daughter Catherine, who married Mr. Cholmondeley. He was then seventy-five and some forty-three years older than Miss Emma Watkins, who, nevertheless, we are told by Mr. Merivale, rejoiced in being "the most uncompromising of all possible admirers." She proved a devoted wife and companion to him; and this he needed much, as in his old age he was much of a physical sufferer. His letter to Perry was, he tells him, written (1813) "in the midst of incessant bodily pain." And in 1815 he wrote to his gifted daughter Mary (Mrs. Johnson), "They who tell you I am much better since I came to town talk at their ease, as most people do about the sufferings of others. In truth my life is a burthen to me and has been so for a long time." * But though he was not exempt from the pains and penalties foreshadowed in the everlasting question, *quid fert longa senectus?* he yet lived as cheerfully and with as much patience and in as good spirits as he could. He maintained his old courteous playfulness (which was always a feature in his dealings with women) and wrote his wife pleasant letters in half-French, half-English. He was wont to salute her as "Infanta Carissima," or "Carissima Bambina." Francis died peacefully almost in his sleep, and during the faithful watching of his wife, on December 23, 1818, aged 78, four months after his illustrious antagonist, Warren Hastings. The house in which he died had many historical associations, and had been in his occupancy for about twenty-eight years. It was then No. 14, St. James's Square; its site is now comprised in the southern portion of the East India Club.

Francis's death is thus recorded in the *European Magazine and London Review*, December 22 (*sic*), 1818. "Soon after five o'clock at his house in St. James's Square, after an illness of upper of five months, Sir Philip Francis. An express was immediately sent off to Mr. Francis, his son, who was on a visit to the Earl of Bristol at Ickworth Park, Suffolk. It is a singular coincidence that this is the fourth death within a very short period in that corner of St. James's Square, viz. Lord Beauchamp, Lord Anson, Lord Ellenborough, Sir Philip Francis." He was buried in the same grave at Mortlake as his dearly loved daughter Elizabeth, and by his own order as privately and plainly as possible, as "of all human follies, posthumous vanity seems to me the silliest."

* This extract and several previous ones from members of his family are taken from "The Francis Papers," 1901, a valuable and carefully compiled work full of interesting and historical information.

# CHAPTER VIII

## PHILIP FRANCIS AND HIS TIMES

### The Life and Death of the First Indian Newspaper, 1780—1782

THE following is a copy of a paper affixed to the door of the Council House and other public places used for advertisements at Calcutta, in September, 1768.

"To the Public.

"Mr. Bolts * takes this method of informing the public that the want of a printing press in this city being of great disadvantage in business, and making it extremely difficult to communicate such intelligence to the community as is of the utmost importance to every British subject, he is ready to give the best encouragement to any person or persons who are versed in the business of printing to manage a press, the types and utensils of which he can produce. In the mean time, he begs leave to inform the public that having in manuscript many things to communicate, which most intimately concern every individual, any person who may be induced by curiosity or other more laudable motives, will be permitted at Mr. Bolts's house to read or take copies of the same. A person will give due attendance at the hours of from ten to twelve any morning."

We look back now with surprise and amusement at this primitive method of public advertisement in a city, then so rapidly striding

* Bolts was a Company's servant who had resigned the Service and taken to commercial pursuits in Calcutta, at which he amassed a fortune in a few years. He was eventually forcibly deported as an interloper. He became the author of a valuable work, "Considerations on Indian Affairs."

into importance, that in six years it will be the seat of a Governor-General and Council and of a Supreme Court of Judicature. Yet for over eleven years more did the want, thus so publicly demonstrated by Bolts, remain unprovided for, and not till 1780 did the first city in Asia possess a medium which combined the object of conveying public intelligence in print, with that of promulgating the ordinary business or social wants of its European inhabitants.

Enumerated in chronological order the earliest newspapers published in Calcutta, so far as I can trace them, were :—1. The *Bengal Gazette*, 1780; 2. The *India Gazette*, November, 1780; 3. The *Calcutta Gazette* (under the avowed patronage of Government, and as such exempted from postage), February, 1784; 4. The *Bengal Journal*, February, 1785; 5. The *Oriental Magazine, or Calcutta Amusement*, April 6, 1785: a monthly paper, in the first number of which "is given an elegant engraving of the late Governor-General, with some account of his life and transactions"; 6. The *Calcutta Chronicle*, January, 1786. A correspondent of the latter paper says (February 8, 1787): "All these papers are now existing and are printed in folio except the *Calcutta Gazette*, which is folded in quarto." This statement is certainly not correct, so far as relates to the *Bengal Gazette*, as this came to a premature death in 1782. It is to this paper that I shall direct attention, as it was the one nearest in point of time to the period, characters, and general society with which this volume deals, and as it dates from the last year of Philip Francis's stay in India. The *Bengal Gazette* started on Saturday, January 29, 1780, and announced itself as "A weekly political and commercial paper open to all parties, but influenced by none." It consisted of two sheets about twelve inches by eight, three columns of printed matter on each side, much of which was devoted to advertisements: the greater portion of the small budget was made up of correspondence from local and distant contributors, and occasional extracts from the news last received from Europe. The paper and printing were very poor. It was the first newspaper printed or published in India.

The proprietor was a Mr. James Augustus Hicky, who was probably a printer by trade, and had come out from England, possibly under engagement from the India House, as in one of his early addresses to the public (a form of communication in which he was fond of indulging) he describes himself as "the first and late printer to the Honourable Company," and in another as "free of the Printers and Stationers Company in London." Judging from his editorial notices, which affect a high moral aim, and are variegated with lofty maxims and saucy roughness, he was a poorly educated man. At one critical period of his newspaper career he informs the public how he took such an enterprise in hand, but his explanation does not go back to his European antecedents, but starts with his being locally engaged in a trading and ship-owning venture. He then states that in the years 1775-76 he met with many very heavy losses by sea—that in the latter year his vessel returned to Calcutta with her cargo damaged, while a bond of his became due for some four thousand rupees. To meet this he offered his all, two thousand rupees, but "the black Bengal merchants proved inflexible." Finally he gave up his vessel, cargo, and all his household effects to his creditors, and in October, 1776, "delivered up his person at the jail of Calcutta to free his bail, and for the first time in all his life entered the walls of a prison." How he got out again he does not say, but he next appears "striking out a plan of industry to maintain his family and work for his creditors, instead of giving himself up to melancholy reflections and indulgence." "With his two thousand rupees he purchased a few types, set carpenters to work to make printing materials, and advertised to print for the public." At this he laboriously continued with fair encouragement from several gentlemen of the Settlement for two years, and then ventured further in the same direction, "although," he explained, "I have no particular passion for printing of newspapers, I have no propensity; I was not bred to a slavish life of hard work, yet I take a pleasure in enslaving my body in order to purchase freedom for my mind and soul." The result of this magnanimity was, that he put to sea in another vessel which he named *Hicky's Bengal Gazette*, and "formed a resolution to jog on under easy sail, and by a well-conducted helm to shape his course right between the rocks of contention." There is a copy of this newspaper in Calcutta in a tolerable state of completeness and preservation, from its commencement down to the end of 1781, and there is a still better copy, though also incomplete, in the British Museum, from March, 1780 to March, 1782. The paper is a curiosity in these days, and helps to give a glimpse at certain phases of the contemporary European social life in Calcutta, which could not, perhaps, be got elsewhere.

In returning thanks for the first list of contributors, the proprietor states that "should he be so fortunate in his endeavours as to bring so useful an undertaking as a newspaper to perfection he will think himself amply rewarded, as it may in a very little time prove an antibilious specific, from which he hopes his subscribers will receive more natural benefit than from tincture of bark, castor oil, or columba root."

During the first few months of its existence the new undertaking seems to have led a tolerably prosperous and peaceful life. It is often dull and is invariably vulgar, but on the whole it is harmless.

As a newspaper it looked for its patrons, both at the Presidency, and in the Mofussil, mainly amongst the free merchants and traders and the general non-official European classes. To these and to their commercial and domestic requirements the advertising columns are devoted. The editor makes no pretence of advocating native interests, indeed, when he ventures into the region of political discussion, he distinctly holds that these should give place on all occasions to the interests of the governing race.

His profession of faith on this head is very simple, as evinced in the following, which must surely have struck a sympathetic chord in the breast of at least one very exalted member of the European community, who had few scruples as to where money was to come from, when it was needed for state exigencies :—

"Governor Whittal (Whitehill, Madras) has acted with great judgment and spirit at this critical juncture ('Hyder Alli') by compelling the Armenians and rich dubashes to pay into the treasury at Madras a crore of pagodas at interest, a measure truly politic and justifiable, that those who derive their wealth under the liberality of the English should contribute during exigencies in return for the protection they receive. The banians here who are amassing incredible fortunes by imposition, usury, and extortion, might be made more useful instruments to Government than they are at present; they now in some degree resemble the drones, the rich abbots in England before the time of Henry VIII., that pucca Monarch."

Nor does the editor forget to provide recreation for his subscribers, so there is a little space provided for the literary man, and of course there is the indispensable "Poet's Corner" for the would-be funny or for the sentimental contributor.

A few random selections will serve as examples of some of the innocent and original productions of the Calcutta muse which *Hicky's Gazette* saved from oblivion. The sender of the following calls it a "short poem," and modestly hopes that "the singularity of the thought in the last part of it may probably please some of your readers."

"On a lady whose name was Susana" (*sic*)

"O lovely Sue,
How sweet art thou,
Than sugar thou art sweeter;
Thou dos't as far
Excel sugar
As sugar does saltpetre." *

This contributor thinks it well to explain in a foot-note that "thou" in Scotland is pronounced "thoo." A less gifted poet, who had not the advantage of being a Caledonian, would probably have satisfied the exigency of the rhyme with a "you," but then the result, perhaps, would not have been poetry.

When the aspirants for literary or poetic notoriety begin to feel that a field sufficiently wide is not reserved for them in the *Gazette*, one of them thus appeals to the proprietor—

"Shall attic wit be forced to yield
To salted beef and pork the field;
Shall Donald † come with butts and tons,
And knock down epigrams and puns,
With chairs, old cots and buggies, trick ye?
Forbid it, Phœbus, and forbid it, Hicky."

The following testifies to the many conflicting interests which the distracted editor has to provide for.

A dialogue between the driver of the Calcutta *vehicle* for news, poetry, etc., and a wit—

*Wit.* "Stop your vehicle, Hicky, one minute for me,
And take a small bundle of rhymes to Parnassus;
A draft on the Muses I'll give for your fee—
You must know I'm a wit, and my note always passes."

* The Calcutta poets were given to unusual expressions of comparison when moved to sing of their idols. I found in a later newspaper some verses on a Miss Kate Pawson, whose father is referred to in Francis's journal as Paymaster-General in 1780. Whether one of the two verses extracted, which seems to feelingly refer to a personal experience, gives any clue to the nationality of the love-sick poet is more than I can say.

"Let some talk of Devonshire's grace,
Let some recollect Nancy Dawson;
None, sure, for a shape or a face
Can compare with my dear K——y P——n.

"The itch, how it tickles the wretch,
The tooth-ache, how terribly gnaws one,
But I feel not the tooth-ache or itch,
When sooth'd by my dear K——y P——n.

† A local auctioneer.

*Driver.* "Hang your wit and your nonsense, I'm loaded enough,
I'm brimful already of dulness and stuff;
Besides, if I take your nonsensical trash in,
Where the deuce must I put all my people of fashion?
"I've no room for wit, I'm surprised you should ask it;
Must the Circle of Beauty be jammed in the basket?
And as to Parnassus, I've no more to do
With the Muses and Phœbus ('od rot 'em)—than you."

And the subjoined excerpta will show how he did dispose of his "people of fashion." Beercool, it may be explained, was at one time contemplated as the Brighton of Calcutta; a special correspondent there, in the month of May, thus extols its virtues for the panting Calcutta readers of the *Gazette*—

"We are informed that the following persons of figure and consequence are arrived at Beercool for the benefit of their health and fish:—Henry Grant, Esq., and lady, and brother-in-law, Major Camac, Captain Robinson of the Yellow, Dr. Allen (lately returned from Europe), Simeon Droze, Esq., with his lady and son and heir, Miss Burne, an extremely elegant and agreeable young lady, — Naylor, Esq., the Honourable Company's lawyer. And we have the pleasure to assure the friends of the above honourable party and the public in general that they have received the most essential benefit from the salubrious air of that admirable spot, which, we doubt not, will make it a place of fashionable resort every ensuing season, it being proposed to erect convenient apartments for the reception of the nobility and gentry whose constitutions require such refreshments. The sea beach forms, perhaps, the finest road in the universe for carriages, and is totally free from sharks and all other noxious animals except crabs."—*Selim.*

"*February* 26, 1780. Married last Saturday, at Cossimbuzzar, the Honourable David Anstruther, Lieutenant of the Yellow, to Miss Donaldson, of that place, a young lady of beauty and infinite accomplishments." This announcement gives birth to the following in the next number:—

"Thessilia late joined to a modish young fellow—
He was styled in the paper Lieutenant of Yellow,
Which in praise of the fair is much as to say
That with some 'tis the yellow boys carry the day."

Which is followed next week by—

"The Bucks of the Yellow have late borne the Bell (*sic*),
And each week's *Gazette* with their praises you swell,
Which fully evinces the force of a name,
For when green was their facing, but small was their fame:
Then your marrow-bones bend, boys, to that jolly fellow
Who has changed your sad fronts from dull green to bright yellow."

"*April*, 1780. A new Cotillon was danced at the last Harmonic to the great wonder and astonishment of many of the spectators. It is universally allowed that this exhibition was infinitely superior to anything known here of late. The merit of this performance is principally attributed to three young ladies lately arrived."

"*June*, 1780. We hear there are several treaties of marriage on foot which promise the supremest felicity, the consummation of which is postponed only till the weather is a few degrees cooler."

Had the paper only continued as it began, it might in no very long time have grown into something better, but it soon took to catering for the lowest tastes, and gradually went from bad to worse in this objectionable direction, and admitted contributions which, while hypocritically affecting to teach and uphold public and private morality, in reality pandered to the impulses of the prurient and the vicious. Thus many dreary chapters (each ending with a "to be continued")* are stuffed with the autobiography of one who is styled "a late very extraordinary man," which is simply the unsavoury details of the alleged progress in the vulgarest vices, of a typical young scoundrel who had not one redeeming feature. Later on, subjects are clumsily paraded which are utterly unfit for public discussion, the introduction of which could have had but one motive. So, running through several numbers, in each succeeding one of which the raiment of decorum and modesty is offensively raised a little higher, is a florid essay entitled, "Thoughts on the Times, but chiefly on the profligacy of our women and its causes." This is unctuously addressed "to every parent, husband, and modest woman in the three kingdoms." One part treats of "The folly and bad tendency of a fashionable life," another of the "Evils that arise from French refinement," a third denounces the employment of obstetric physicians (less technical language, however, is used) as "tending to destroy the peace of families and endanger virtue"—in this large capitals are used to emphasise the most indelicate allusions, to the violation of all decency. The dulness of these diatribes is profound; as literary compositions they are execrable.

The trail of the serpent is too visible, if only in the companionship provided for them, viz. short paragraphs and rhyming contributions reeking with jocular indecency and obscenity, that no English newspaper could now venture even to paraphrase, and when we read what has been admitted we can only guess what has been proffered

* A grateful correspondent congratulates Mr. Hicky himself, while calling him "the papa of the press," as being "the composer of the entertaining history with which you have favoured the world under the signature 'To be Continued.'"

and rejected, from a pharisaical notice like this among the answers to correspondents:—"Lothario's letter and poetry is received, but is not fit for insertion, nor will anything ever be inserted in the *Bengal Gazette* that can possibly give offence to the ladies."

But if the *Bengal Gazette* had contented itself with being characterised by dulness and want of decency, it might in that tolerant age have gradually passed away into obscurity; its proprietor, however, soon discovered that a certain section of the public always craves for items of local personal news: accordingly these are provided tentatively at first, but when the managerial troubles (to be presently described) came on, the weekly pabulum for the subscribers becomes more and more highly seasoned with personalities, all, no doubt, intended to be more or less funny.

A fresh stimulus was given in this direction by the entrance of another newspaper on the scene before the first had been a year old. The rival (a well-printed paper of four pages, each about sixteen inches long, divided into three columns) was started by a Mr. Peter Reed (a salt agent) and Mr. B. Messink, who had something to do with theatrical speculation or proprietorship. For the purpose of ridicule and abuse they are always referred to by Hicky as "Peter Nimmuck" (or Obadiah Broadbrim) and "Barnaby Grizzle," and their paper, the *India Gazette*, is by him nicknamed the "Monitorial Gazette," in allusion to a weekly contribution in it, alleged by Hicky to be from Reed, addressed, as all letters were, to "Mr. Monitor," which went on for some months. This contribution ceased, owing, it was asserted in Hicky, to Grizzle having been detected cheating Nimmuck, which led to the withdrawal of the latter from the joint undertaking. Its disappearance was hoped to prelude the collapse of the new paper, and was notified by a grimy pæan in the *Bengal Gazette*, where more than the usual raillery, vituperation, and indecency did duty for triumphant humour.

A grievance in connection with the new paper was that the type for its production were got by purchase from the venerable missionary, Kiernander. This is too suitable an opportunity for reproof for Mr. Hicky to pass over. Accordingly he appeals to the aged pastor as "that man whose eve of life is fast verging to the shadow of death, whose silver head bows down loaded with the blossoms of the grave, and whom the sepulchre is already yawning to close upon." * He attacks him with the spiritual weapons which he thinks

* The Rev. John Zachariah Kiernander provokingly survived this appeal for nineteen years, dying in Calcutta in 1799, aged 88, after a residence in India of sixty years. He was a Swede, and the first Protestant missionary sent to Bengal,

most appropriate to the circumstances, as directed against a clergyman, and bombards him with texts of Scripture, the burden of his remonstrance being that the plant and type were sent out for the propagation of the gospel in foreign parts, and not to be used for taking the bread out of the mouths of a "true-born Englishman and his little family." But the unkindest cut of all felt in regard to the rival newspaper, was that certain privileges in connection with the Post-office were, as alleged by Hicky, conceded to it. In commenting on this, he asserts that he, too, could have had similar concessions if, as he had been advised by a leading public man (his alleged "dialogue" with whom he gives verbatim), he had gone the right way about it, viz. to solicit Mrs. Hastings, who had given out that she was ready for such solicitation, but that Mr. Hicky declined to do so, as he thought "there was something so sneaking and treacherous in going clandestinely to fawn and take advantage of a good-natured woman to draw her into a promise to getting that done which I know would be highly improper to ask her husband, though his unbounded love for his wife would induce him to comply with, etc., etc." This and much more in a similar strain. Impudence directed against his wife was probably the only aggression coming from such a quarter which would have claimed the notice, or aroused the indignation of the Governor-General. Whether the liberty thus publicly taken with Mrs. Hastings' name produced, or only precipitated, the following order of Government, which came out before the next issue of the offending newspaper, it is more than likely that Hastings himself was the promoter of it.

"*Fort Wm., November* 14, 1780.—Public notice is hereby given that as a weekly newspaper called the *Bengal Gazette* or *Calcutta General Advertiser*, printed by J. A. Hicky, has lately been found to contain

where he arrived from Southern India in 1758. He had not been long in Calcutta when he "lost his lady," but, continues the precise Asiaticus, "he had the fortitude not to give himself up to vain lamentations; on the succeeding year the remembrance of all former sorrows was obliterated in the silken embraces of opulent beauty." The adjective qualifying this last word must not be understood in the physical (or Gallic) sense, but in the pecuniary, as we read that the missionary was afterwards able to live rather extravagantly and to give banquets, thereby making the judicious grieve. It is stated in Marshall's Christian Mission that Kiernander "ogled from the pulpit with two fat and rich ladies of his congregation," and married them. But it should not be forgotten that he devoted much of his wealth to the cause of Christianity, and built a church and school at his own expense. This he named Beth-Tephillah (the House of Prayer); to-day it is known as the "Old Mission Church."

This celebrated man, it is sad to think, died in straitened circumstances, mainly through the imprudence of a son, I believe.

several improper paragraphs tending to vilify private characters and to disturb the peace of the Settlement, it is no longer permitted to be circulated through the channel of the General Post Office."

To deny even a prepaid passage through the Post-office, and so deprive it of all present or prospective subscribers up country, was a measure well calculated to strangle a struggling newspaper; more especially if, as the elder paper complained, a free passage was at the same time given to its rival. When we take into consideration the jealousy and irritation natural under the circumstances, and that apparently no warning (as to the consequence which would ensue if the alleged vilification did not cease) was given to Hicky before this highly penal blow was struck, it must be allowed that he was not given very much rope.

It would be interesting to know what Francis thought of this high-handed proceeding. Under many Latin *aliases*, he had been in England the eloquent upholder of freedom of speech and liberty of the Press, "that just prerogative of the people." Did he now oppose, or did he assent to the issue of this order from a Council of which he was the senior member? He must have winced when he found the *Bengal Gazette*, in the very first protest that it had an opportunity of making, appealing to the authority of Junius thus: "Comparison between Mr. Wilkes and Mr. Hicky. The case of Mr. Hicky is exactly similar to that of Mr. Wilkes; the one standing up for the liberty of the Press, the other for that of the subject. Junius makes the following just and elegant remark on the oppression of Mr. Wilkes, 'that the rays of Royal indignation tended rather to illumine than to destroy the persecuted object of it, etc., etc.'"

But though nominally a member of the Government still, the sun of Francis's power in Calcutta had just at this time set for ever. He had virtually acknowledged that he could no longer contend against the stronger will, the calm resolution and tenacity of purpose of his great antagonist, when he confided but a few days before, the last entry but one to his Indian journal.

"*November* 2, 1780.—Governor moves that Mr. Rider (who returned with his rank some months ago, and to succeed to the first vacancy in the Board of Trade) shall be allowed the full salary of that office from his arrival till he succeeds. Agreed. Yet nothing, I believe, can be more improper: *Mais qu'importe?* When the ship is sinking, what does it signify how soon we eat up the provisions? The moment I shall have made my exit, enter desolation."

The despairing tone of these words may fitly be contrasted with that of exulting resolution in some sentences of a remarkable letter, written by Hastings to a friend in England in the following week, four days before the thunderbolt was launched against the *Bengal Gazette.*

"... Mr. Francis has announced his intention to leave us. His departure may be considered as the close of one complete period of my political life and the beginning of a new one. ... I shall have no competitor to oppose my designs, to encourage disobedience to my authority, to excite and foment popular odium against me. In a word, I shall have power, and I will employ it."

It was with reference to this time, too, that Hastings some few years afterwards wrote, with well-deserved self-congratulation, "I suffered in patience; I did my duty when I could; I waited for better and more lasting means. ... My antagonists sickened, died, and fled; I maintained my ground unchanged, neither the health of my body, nor the vigour of my mind for a moment deserted me."

There is another point in connection with Francis and this newspaper which invites conjecture. Though he was a year in Calcutta with it, neither then nor afterwards does he ever fall under its ribaldry: it cannot be said that his conduct was uniformly so immaculate as never to afford an opportunity for the moral platitudes so dear to Hicky; occasions which would fairly justify public comment are either not availed of or are employed in his favour. He almost alone amongst the official leaders of society is dealt gently with.

It is pointed out in Francis's memoirs that even he himself evinced a tenderness about putting on record a defeat of his own; and it is shown as a conspicuous instance of this that in his diary for June, 1777, where many personal and official matters are chronicled, he passes by the nineteenth, the day on which the attempt was made to oust Hastings from the Governor-Generalship, and no mention is made of so momentous an occurrence in which Clavering and Francis were so signally discomfited.

A notable instance of suppression regarding another defeat of Francis's may be found in *Hicky's Gazette.* The duel with Hastings occurred on Thursday, August 17, 1780. The next number of the *Gazette* is for the week commencing on the following Saturday, 19th. The copy of this number in the British Museum is quite perfect (that in Calcutta has been mutilated); still there is no allusion in it whatever to the duel which occurred only two days previously between the two highest personages in the Government.

Yet we may infer that Hicky's readers would have relished such a *bonne bouche* when we find him serving up in the very next number a vulgar morsel like this: "A few days ago a dispute arose between two young gentleman not many miles from Serampore about a lady of a sooty complexion. The friends of both were under some apprehension that a duel would have been the consequences, but it happily ended in a reciprocal bastinado."

Mrs. Fay, writing from Calcutta in this very year, says:—"Mr. Francis is highly respected here." Very probably his pronounced hostility to Hastings and His Majesty's Judges was in itself a strong recommendation to the *Bengal Gazette;* but there was, perhaps, a further reason for the singular immunity noticed. He himself, as proved by his pseudonymous writings in England, could be, when he liked, master of the whole gamut of vulgar abuse—he had shown himself an adept in the coarse personalities which disgraced the political controversies of the time. He knew the pain thus inflicted, and shrunk from it in his own person as the surgeon dreads the knife, and the flogger the lash—so it is not unreasonable to surmise that he, who, his biographer says, had all his life been a controller of the secret influence of the press, contrived means of securing the mute forbearance of the scurrilous Hicky.

But to return to the proprietor of the *Bengal Gazette.* He did not faint in the day of adversity; he was very wrath at the action of Government, which caused him an immediate loss of four hundred rupees monthly. Nevertheless, he was nothing daunted. Writing in the first transports of his indignation, he says: "Before he will bow, cringe, or fawn to any of his oppressors, was the whole sale of his paper stopped, he would compose ballads and sell them through the streets of Calcutta as Homer did. He has now but three things to lose: his honour in the support of his paper, his liberty, and his life; the two latter he will hazard in defence of the former, for he is determined to make it a scourge of all schemers and leading tyrants; should these illegally deprive him of his liberty and confine him in a jail, he is determined to print there with every becoming spirit suited to his case and the deserts of his oppressors." "Shall I," he asks in an address to the public, "tamely submit to the yoke of slavery and wanton oppression?—no, my case and complaints in my own newspaper shall be conveyed to the foot of the throne of Great Britain, and the breach of my privilege as Freeman of the first city in the British Empire shall also be presented in my own newspaper to the Father of the City, the *Chamberlain* * of the City of London. He

* Jack Wilkes, who after a chequered career of sturdy "patriotism" and defiance of law and order, and after passing through the phases of demagogue and martyr, had settled down into the above peaceable and lucrative post.

will soon feel for my case, bearing so strong an affinity to his own, and without doubt he will sympathise more strongly when he considers where I am and who I have got to deal with."

Henceforth, all the worst features of the *Bengal Gazette* become exaggerated; personality assumes intolerable licence; many who are conspicuous in official or social life are assailed in terms indicative of malicious hostility, while the more prominent amongst them are given up to public odium and contempt veiled under the most obvious nicknames; frequently these latter derive their significance from infirmities, either real or attributed, which are referred to with inept jocosity in the most cowardly and indelicate manner. Private individuals who incurred the displeasure of the editor or contributors are held up to derision in the poets' corner, in spite of the ethics paraded in the following rebuke:—

"Trim's poetry is received, but cannot be inserted, as it seems to abound more with rancour and private pique than with innocent mirth and jocularity."

Similarly, a portion of another correspondent's letter relating to ladies is suppressed, while the following exposition of the editor's sentiments on this interesting topic is thus set out:—

"Mr. Hicky begs leave to say that he is of opinion that the greatest blessing that his sex enjoys in this savage part of the globe, is the refined and delicate conversation of his fair countrywomen; cheered and animated by their heavenly smiles, we are made ample amends for the intemperance of the climate; was it not for them we should be unpolished and brutish; to them alone we stand indebted for all those noble refinements of our manners."

Nevertheless, ladies in society are not spared public mention in the *Bengal Gazette*, though, as a rule, they are spoken of with what is intended to be approbation.

They are generally designated by their initials, or occasionally by some peculiarity of dress. Under the heading "Bon Ton" their graces and attractions (and in some instances even their matrimonial successes or prospects) are dealt freely with. They are watched at the public balls or festive gatherings, or on "the course"; and the progress which certain gentlemen seem to make in ingratiating themselves is frankly commented on, with congratulation or disapproval, according as the gentlemen may happen to be on friendly or on hostile terms with the *Bengal Gazette.* Poetasters, also, are enlisted in their behalf, and their charms are duly complimented in limping verses, entitled "Song" or Ode," or even "Epithalamium," which, like most of the contributions, either in rhyme or prose from this out, it is easier and more becoming to allude to generally than to exemplify by selection. But though one is precluded from bringing before modern readers the most striking examples of those sins against decorum and good taste, without enfeebling them by expurgation, still a few instances of the least offensive of them must be culled to justify what has been said, and to give an idea of this old newspaper which it would be otherwise impossible to convey.

"In a few days Edward Hay, Esq., Secretary of State for the Southern Department, is to be married to Miss Wagstaffe, a most beautiful, amiable, and highly accomplished young lady—sister-in-law to Colonel Morgan—a lady endowed with every elegant requisite to render the marriage state (what it was intended to be) a scene of ecstatic joy and felicity."

"Married, at Madras, Mr. Richard Newland to Miss Cuthbert, of the same place, with a fortune of 4000 star pagodas and Mr. Cuthbert's friendship, who intends giving him the rice contract that Mr. Ferguson lately had; the lady is well accomplished."

The following "poem" (June, 1780) would suggest that the supply did not keep pace with the demand in the matrimonial market.

"To a Young Widow.

"What pity, dear widow, that bosom, those eyes,
Should be spoiled—these with weeping, the other with sighs;
For sighs, like to wind in a bladder, will swell ye,
And tears will but furrow your cheeks, I can tell ye.

"Ah, why should you grieve thus, and pleasure forego
For a husband who died a full twelvemonth ago?
Now, custom prescribes you should make no more pother;
Forget your first 'Hubby,' and choose you another."

But with the view of retaining some connection in the necessary extracts, and perhaps lending them more interest, the simplest plan will be to confine the selection at present to some of those referring to a young lady who came in for the most prominent notice from the contributors to Hicky's paper, on whom she must have made the deepest impression. To maintain continuity it may not be always practical to observe due sequence in dates. The social star referred to was a Miss Emma Wrangham, daughter of William Wrangham, Esq., a gentleman who was Member of Council in St. Helena at the time. She probably came to friends in Bengal, where her "guardians" are spoken of: one at Chinsurah, where she sometimes visited, was nicknamed "Pomposo" by the *Bengal Gazette*.

This young lady was evidently the belle of Calcutta while Hicky chronicled its social doings. Her youth and beauty, her attractive form and figure, her graceful accomplishments, her dress and her merry indifference to the wounds these arrows inflicted were a favourite theme in Hicky's columns. When not defined by her Christian name or by her initials, she is often spoken of, in allusion, apparently, to the most killing feature of her attire, as "Turban Conquest" or "Hooka Turban," sometimes as the "Chinsura Belle" or "Chinsura Beauty." Under "Racing Intelligence" the newspaper refers to her as "the famous filly, St. Helena," and, in auguring success to her starters, opportunity is afforded to note a winning qualification, which, however, commendable in the racing quadruped, is not so frankly appraised in the biped—in polite society. One of her many strong points was dancing. Under the heading "Intelligence Extraordinary" Hicky's *Gazette* announces that, at a ball at Chandernagore—

> "Many very graceful minuets were walked by the beauties of the age, amongst whom the inimitable Miss W—— excelled in every step and motion, and so minutely graceful was that young lady, and so charmingly easy in the Minuet de la cour, that the pen must inevitably fail that pretends to do her justice by description. Suffice it to say, that a band of music might have been led with the exactest time by the motion of her foot."

Amongst the satellites who most assiduously revolved round this luminary, and for whom also Hicky had nicknames, were a Mr. Livius ("Idea George," or "Titus"); he was a *protégé* and intimate friend of Francis, who had got him made military storekeeper; a barrister named Davis, or Davies, counsel to the Honourable Company ("Counsellor Feeble"). A gentleman who is not limited to one nickname, and who could not have been an associate of the Francis circle, but rather of that yielding allegiance to Hastings, as the *Bengal Gazette* is uniformly so scurrilously hostile to him; his least objectionable name there is "Jack Paradise Lost," hence he may be guessed at as a Mr. Milton, but this, I regret to say, is only a guess—once he is alluded to as "Black Jack." A fourth was an official in the Board of Trade, named Mr. John Taylor; hence he is designated "Durgee," often, more offensively, "Peegdany Durgee." Hicky held this last gentleman in abhorrence, for no better reason, apparently, than that, while ostensibly one of Miss Wrangham's "guardians," he suffered much extremity from love and aspired to a tenderer relaton. The *Bengal Gazette* twits him occasionally on his (alleged) versifying, and in "Friendly advice to J. Durgee," he appeals to him as "Dear Jack," and conjures him to let the muse alone, as Nature ne'er a lover made to charm with skin and bone—

> "Sit cross-legged on thy Board of Trade
> O'er shreds and remnants pour,
> Drive Emma W——m from thy head," etc., etc.

It is with one or more of this quartette that this young girl's name is most frequently associated, and to whom the allusions in the following extracts mainly refer.

"*March*, 1781. Public Notice: Lost on the Course, last Monday evening, Buxey Clumsey's heart, whilst he stood simpering at the footstep of Hooka Turban's carriage: as it is supposed to be in her possession, she is desired to return it immediately, or to deliver up her own as a proper acknowledgment."

Ode on the birthday of Miss W——m, by J. Durgee—

> "Celestial nine assist my lay
> With all your native fire,
> To sing fair Emma's natal day
> My humble Muse inspire.
> 'Tis now just eighteen years ago
> Since the sweet maid was born," etc., etc.

But the homage she commanded was not confined to Europeans; even the natives were anxious to signify their devotion to this young lady, for it is recorded that Rajah Nobkissen gave a *nâtch* and magnificent entertainment (in August, 1781) "in commemoration of Miss Wrangham's birthday," at which, after supper, there was a ball, which was opened by Mr. Livius and Miss Wrangham in the characters of "Apollo and Daphne," "and when the minuets were ended, country dances struck up and continued till past three in the morning." When the Rajah was conducting his fair guest to her carriage he gracefully thanked her "for having illuminated his house with her bright appearance."

The devotion of lawyer Davis to the fair one is thus noticed—

"A correspondent informs us that Counsellor Feeble now constantly drinks a sort of cordial dram which he calls W—g—m eye water, and of which he drinks so freely that he, d'ye see, retires tipsy—he, he!"

A contributor, signing himself "Trim," affects to be thus censorious about another of her attractions in a verse "on the present mode of dress—humbly inscribed to a certain fair damsel"—

> "If Eve in her innocence could not be blamed,
> Because going naked she was not ashamed,

Whoe'er views the ladies, as ladies now dress,
That again they grow innocent sure will confess.
And that artfully, too, they retaliate the evil—
By the devil once tempted, *they* now tempt the devil." *

We may fancy what a crowd of suitors must have sighed to this highly favoured beauty in the Calcutta of her day. A long-suffering society seems to become impatient at last that their favourite should so obstinately continue to remain fancy free, while triumphantly exercising her (real) "Woman's Rights" of winning and holding in safe but gentle captivity the mere man. Envy and uncharitableness are aroused, and the story of the "crooked stick" is no doubt quoted. Her obduracy is really provoking, and as she will not select a husband herself, busy-bodies, of both sexes, do so for her. One poet accordingly sends a "Recipe to soften the heart of Miss W——," while a female member of Society whom the *Bengal Gazette* calls Messalina in a very gross conversation about her with "a gentleman!" takes the opportunity of observing that "it were a thousand pities so fine a woman should be doomed to perpetual celibacy." Another, on the contrary, "A matron of great experience to Miss W——," counsels her *not* to marry but to "remain a maiden and a charm for ever," and conveys sage reflections on post-nuptial disappointment, which, in more quotable language, were sung for our great-grandmothers in the ballad commencing—

"Ye fair married dames who so often deplore
That a lover once blest is a lover no more." †

* In culling from the "Poet's Corner," I have assumed to be original whatever I may not remember to have met with elsewhere myself. I am very conscious what a fallacious plan this may be."

† This song was a great favourite in its time; it was written by Garrick for Arthur Murphy's play, *The Way to Keep Him*. It was set to music by Dr. Arne and sung by some of the most famous actresses of the day, including Mrs. Abington and Mrs. Cibber. Angelo, the Fencing-Master, in his reminiscences, tells that he attended a lecture by the notorious quack, Graham (1783), at his temple of health in Panton Street, Haymarket, which was crowded by a fashionable audience of both sexes. The "Doctor," a tall, handsome man of forty, came on in a single night garment and got into an "earth bath" in the middle of the room, and when the earth had been shovelled up to his chin, he, sitting in it on a stool, gave a long lecture on the merits of this treatment. The lecture concluded, he was called on for a song, and he sang, or rather recited, the above popular ballad. It is alleged in more gossiping histories than one, that the beautiful Emma Lyons (Nelson's Lady Hamilton) amongst the vicissitudes of her early youth was employed to illustrate as an exquisitely formed Hebe, or rather Hygeia, the lectures of this fashionable humbug.

And the counsel would seem to have had some effect, for in "Bon Ton Intelligence" the *Gazette* tells its anxious readers, "The celebrated beauty has again, we hear, refused Idea G——. It is true there is a little disparity between the parties, yet there are few ladies in her situation who would have declined the offer on that account, or would have thought it could have counter balanced a settlement of £20,000. The truth is Counsellor Feeble has capered her out of her senses."

The next allusion suggests that two of her rival lovers soon came to blows about her, viz. "Turban Conquest has been advised by her chota guardian, 'Peegdany Durgee,' to remain a few weeks longer at Chinsura in order to let the personal fracas respecting her between (here follow two unquotable aliases for Mr. Paradise Lost and Mr. Feeble) blow over. It is hoped the hue of Holland will meliorate her manners, for she has hitherto shown too much vivacity." A month later a paragraph tells that "A marriage is now much talked of between Counsellor Feeble and the Chinsura belle." And the rival aspirants are thus addressed: "Ye witlings, give o'er; the contest is vain, for Emma has chose for her partner a swain whom fancy and reason approve, who laughs to behold you," etc., etc. Two months after (February, 1782) it is mentioned as a fact that "On Thursday last" she "was united in the sacred and indissoluble tie to the elegant Jack Paradise Lost."

In the next issue, however, under "Bon Ton Intelligence," it is announced that "the report of the marriage between —— and Turban Conquest is without foundation. It seems the day of their nuptials was fixed; on the eve of the wedding, however, the lover changed his mind and decamped without beat of drum, to the astonishment of the intended bride, on whose conduct calumny itself had not attempted to fasten the smallest imputation." Durgee then is alleged to have "taken the field afresh," with the sanction of Pomposo, and "was seen that very day (*sic*) with the insolent fair one on the course."

We shall meet this lady once again in one of Mr. Hicky's fading announcements in the shape of a supposed concert-bill or programme, where a prominent place is assigned to her. When taking leave of her, then the secret will come out as to who was the fortunate man into whose keeping this favourite of nature, who strutted her hour so gaily on the old Calcutta stage, did eventually entrust her heart and her liberty. In the mean time it is interesting to note that, at the very time when local gossip and curiosity were at fever heat about her matrimonial fate, an inquiry regarding it should have been addressed to one of her suitors from a very remote and unexpected quarter. Within a couple of months or so of his landing in England Philip Francis wrote this letter (January, 1782) from London to Mr. Livius in Calcutta. His usual cynical acidity discloses itself, viz. "If you have literally married the Wrangham, or if Mackenzie should have married her or Collings or Archdekin, I must beg leave to decline your society in future, at least until the death of her father and mother, whom Heaven confound. I spent five months with them very agreeably in the middle of the Atlantic and most devoutly pray that I may never see the face of either of them again. You need not mention this affair to the daughter nor even to Mrs. Stevenson. I should be sorry to wound their delicate sensations or any of the refined sentiments they derive from St. Helena. If ever you visit that Island keep your hands on your pocket ("Francis Papers"). It may be explained that Francis, who sailed from Calcutta, as we have seen, in the *Fox*, Indiaman, was detained for some months at St. Helena waiting for convoy, owing to the war going on between England and France, Spain and Holland. He used ever after say that the patron saint of St. Helena was Ennui.

The later extracts from the *Bengal Gazette* have somewhat anticipated the order of events; it is therefore necessary to go back a little and resume briefly the consideration of the more general features of the old newspaper.

It may have been only as a means of keeping up an interest in his paper and himself that the Editor startled his subscribers with this announcement one morning in April, 1781—

"Mr. Hicky thinks it a duty incumbent on him to inform his friends in particular and the public in general that an attempt was made to assassinate him last Thursday morning, between the hours of one and two o'clock, by two armed Europeans, assisted by a Moorman."

Having thus aroused curiosity, he details the circumstances in next week's number, making rather a cock-and-bull story of it, and wishing his readers to understand that he has become so pestilent to Government as a public censor, that they resorted to assassination in order to get rid of him. Then follows what he calls—

"Reflections in consequence of the late attempt made to assassinate the printer of the Original *Bengal Gazette*.

"Mr. Hicky verily believes that fate decreed that he should come out to India to be a scourge to Tyrannical Villains, and upstart Schemers and Embezzlers of the Company's property, Stainers of the British Flag and Disgracers of the English name; and notwithstanding the repeated attempts which have been made for his destruction, Mr.

Hicky is determined to go on and persevere with redoubled confidence in his plan, unawed by the frowns of arbitrary Tyrants in Power," etc., etc.

But Hastings and Impey were, above all others, the target for Hicky's most poisoned missiles; and bitterly did they pay him out when the time came to strike. The Governor-General he aimed at and insulted through Mrs. Hastings chiefly; Impey he stung by nicknames and allusions which kept alive the Nuncomar business, and the stories as to his love of money, and the means, direct or indirect, by which he gratified it. It is noteworthy that the satirical or venomous hits at Impey in Hicky's paper, and which were presumably but the expression of vulgar contemporary belief, nearly all refer to circumstances on which charges were founded, which the recalled Chief Justice had afterwards to defend himself from. A couple of extracts will serve as instances. "A displaced civilian asking his friend the other day what were the readiest means of procuring a lucrative appointment was answered, 'Pay your constant devoirs to Marian Allypore, or sell yourself soul and body to Poolbundy.'" *

The following shows that whatever may have since been urged in explanation of the Chief Justice's part in the transaction, the allegation was locally current at the time, that in accepting the presidency of the Sudder Adawlut, Impey came in for a very substantial extra salary and large patronage. † The Chief Justice is supposed to be

* Pul-bandi, *i.e.* the keeping bridges or embankments in repair (Beveridge), in allusion to a lucrative contract given to Impey's relative, a Mr. Frazer, Sealer of the Supreme Court. Calcutta scandal alleged that the real contractor was the Chief Justice himself. Francis thus trenchantly recorded in his Diary his plain opinion of the transaction:—"February, 1778. Poolbundy of Burdwan given for two years to Mr. Frazer; one lakh and twenty thousand the first and eighty thousand the second; job, job! This is a wretch of the lowest order, a creature and distant relation of Impey, and already well provided for in the Supreme Court. The present shameless contract is a clear £15,000 in the contractor's pocket, for whose real profit I submit to the reader."

† Francis in his place in Council opposed and strongly minuted against the control of the Sudder Adawlut being vested in the Chief Justice as proposed by Hastings. It is a coincidence worth noting that one of the best known passages in the Essay on Warren Hastings, in which Macaulay sums up his denouncement of the arrangement, viz. "the Chief Justice was rich, quiet, and infamous," is an adoption of a sentiment, and almost of the language in which it was conveyed, of Philip Francis, who, writing as Junius (in the last famous letter to the Duke of Grafton, February, 1770), says of another transaction: "Your Grace is afraid to carry on the prosecution. Mr. Hine keeps quiet possession of his purchase, and Governor Burgoyne, relieved from the apprehension of refunding the money, sits down for the remainder of his life *infamous and contented.*"

triumphantly addressing the Sealer of the Supreme Court thus, on the disgust and discontent of the Company's civil servants at the recent appointment :—

"But that which to me is the pleasantest part,
No one of the servants dare point out the smart ;
Nor do I much wonder, for H——s has said
No remonstrance from them that may come shall be read,

"And should they our door with petitions assail,
We'll send all the mutinous scoundrels to jail.
However, to keep them from forging of lyes,
Mr. H——s the feeling, the just and the wise,

"Has appointed Ad—l—ts, whose payments at large,
My dear little Archey, are under my charge.
What Company's servant, tho' bred up in College,
To manage my post has competent knowledge?

"What though the ten thousand friend W——n may give,
And which condescending I monthly receive." Etc., etc.

. . . . . . . . . . . . . . . . . . . .

"By which should the Company lose a few pence,
They ne'er will perceive it a hundred years hence;
And as long as we jointly can manage the rudder,
No doubt but I'm snug in my post at the Sudder,

"When I talk to Sir R——t or dear brother H——de,
And bid them throw qualms and scruples aside,
They preach up old conscience 'till I lose all patience,
And leave the poor d——ls to their own meditations.

"As for you, my dear Sealer, I trust you're grown wise,
From my bright example and candid advice :
Do never let conscience molest or offend you,
For conscience should keep all the time we're in India."

A favourite method with the *Bengal Gazette* for pillorying those whom it desired to show up to public ridicule, was to announce a play or masquerade or concert (which were then fashionable amusements), and to assign certain suggestive parts or characters to members of society disguised under the thinnest veil. We may as well see two or three of these, as they will introduce us to several old celebrities at once, and will serve as "the abstract and brief chronicles of the time." The pasquinade of this sort which immediately follows came out in June, 1781.

A couple of characters which would not admit of a reappearance have been omitted, and the "persons represented" have been added in brackets so far as it has been possible to identify them.

## PLAYBILL EXTRAORDINARY.

At the New Theatre, near the Court-house, is now in rehearsal,
A Tragedy, called
"TYRANNY IN FULL BLOOM, OR THE DEVIL TO PAY."

With the Farce of
"ALL IN THE WRONG."

*Dramatis Personæ:*

| | |
|---|---|
| Sir F. Wronghead ... ... | By the Grand Turk. (Hastings.) |
| Judge Jeffreys ... ... ... | By Ven'ble Poolbundy. (Impey.) |
| Sir Limber ... ... ... ... | By Sir Viner Pliant. (Mr. Justice Chambers.) |
| Justice Balance ... ... ... | By Cram Turky. (Mr. Justice Hyde.) |
| Judas Iscariot touching the 40 pieces ... ... ... ... | By the Rev. Mr. Tally Ho. (Rev. Wm. Johnson.) * |
| Don Quixote fighting with Windmills . ... ... ... ... | By the Great Mogul, commonly called the Tyger of War. (Hastings.) |
| Whipper Snapper, Balance's Footman ... ... ... ... | By Rawton Guinea pig. (Mr. Wraughton.) |

* This clergyman was a notable figure in Old Calcutta. He tied the nuptial noose for several whose names have become familiar to us in the social records of the time. Not the least memorable of his doings was his own marriage (1774) to a lady whose life would supply materials for an almost incredible romance. She had been a prisoner of Siraj úd Dowla at Moorshedabad in 1756, at which time she was the wife of her third husband, Mr. Wm. Watts, through whose daughter by him she became the grandmother of a Prime Minister of England (Earl of Liverpool). She died (1812) the oldest European resident in Bengal, at her house in Calcutta (on the site of the afterwards 'bonded warehouse'). Her tomb in St. John's Churchyard is, or ought to be, well known to most Calcutta residents. The reverend gentleman to whom she gave her hand for the fourth time, apparently got tired of her, because he left India for good in February, 1788, and she remained behind for nearly a quarter of a century longer, dispensing, as the "Begum Johnson," a "dignified hospitality," and delighting society with her anecdotes of old times and with her cheerful and polished manners. The Duke of Wellington used to tell of his having known the grandmother of Lord Liverpool in Calcutta, and erroneously referred to her as a survivor of the Black Hole. There is what seems to be a very speaking likeness of the Rev. Wm. Johnson in the vestry room of St. John's Cathedral—a young-looking, healthy, round and smug-faced gentleman—with his hair short and brushed down flat over the forehead.

| | |
|---|---|
| Double-Fee Ferret ... ... | By C——r Avis from the Marshalsea. (Counsellor Davis.) |
| Idle Charley, the Bankrupt Merchant ... ... ... ... | (Mr. C. Croftes.) |
| Cato, also the True-born Englishman * ... ... ... ... | By Mr. Hicky. |
| Mammon ... ... ... ... | By a German Missionary. (Rev. J. Z. Kiernander.) |
| Irish Link-boy crying a brass farthing, your Honour ... ... | By Sir Barnaby Grizzle. (Mr. Messinck.) |
| Slaves, Train-bearers, Toad-eaters, and Sycophants ... | By the Grand Jury. |
| Liberty Boys ... ... ... | By the Honest, Independent, Disinterested Petty Jury. |

Between the Play and the Farce will be introduced

A DANCE OF DEMONS OF REVENGE BY THE CALCUTTA LAWYERS AND THEIR BANYANS.

*The Dance to conclude with the song of*

"From mortal sighs we draw the groan,
To make their sorrows like our own."

Which Sir Barnaby promises to accompany on the Bassoon, assisted by his German Missionary Brother Printer.

Two Ghosts will be introduced for the sake of variety. First Ghost by Nuncomar; second Ghost by Peter Nimmuck (Mr. P. Reed).

Chancellor Murder English from Gothland will entertain the audience with a doleful ditty on the hurdy-gurdy, about his card losses and pluckings at Lady Poolbundy's routs."

Why the first character should stand for Hastings will be understood when it is remembered that Sir Francis Wronghead is a character in Vanbrugh's and Cibber's comedy of *The Provoked Husband*, who, says a commentator on the play, "having overdrawn his estate, deems it advisable to quarter himself on the public purse, and who has ventured all for love 'to please his eye and vex

* Daniel De Foe (of Robinson Crusoe fame later) published his poem, "The True Born Englishman," in January, 1700, which helped him, it is said, to the personal regard of the Dutchman, William III. The poem ends: "For fame of families is all a cheat, 'Tis personal virtue only makes us great." It is a curious comment on the above introduction of the title that, many years after the publication of the poem, De Foe wrote, "None of our countrymen have been known to boast of being 'True-born Englishmen,' or as much as used the word as a title or appellation ever since a late satire upon that national folly was published."

his heart,' and if he has been guilty of any libertinism in his youth, he is more than atoning for it by a wedded life of penance and mortification—his wife being thoughtless and extravagant."

I have some doubt as to whether Don Quixote also is intended for Hastings. He is often alluded to as the Great Mogul elsewhere in the *Bengal Gazette*—and his fondness for war is remarked on—but it is strange that he should be under two characters in the same piece. Sir R. Chambers had been Vinerian professor at Oxford. He had a character for being weak and infirm of purpose, easily influenced. Justice Balance is a character in Farquar's play of the *Recruiting Officer*.

But evil days were now close at hand for our poor newsmonger: One day in June an armed band, consisting, he avers, of "several Europeans, some sepoys, and between three or four hundred peons," came to arrest him under an order from the Chief Justice at the suit of the Governor. His gate having been battered in with a sledge hammer, he says, he sallied out on them with his arms, and, refusing to be forcibly taken away, undertook to attend the Judge in Court on being shown a legal authority for his arrest. The Court having adjourned before he got there, that same day he was lodged in jail, and the next morning before the Supreme Court "two indictments" were read out to him on the prosecution of Warren Hastings, Esq. Bail for forty thousand rupees for his appearance to each of them was demanded; he offered all that he could muster, namely, five thousand, which was refused, and he was accordingly remanded to jail to prepare his defence as best he could. This is Hicky's own account given publicly in his paper, in a letter addressed by him to the Clerk of the Crown, pointing out that excessive bail is unconstitutional, and involves, especially in the case of a poor man, grave injustice. The *Bengal Gazette* also draws attention to the fact that the bail demanded of Woodfall, the printer of Junius' letter to the King, was not equal to 20,000 rupees.

Amongst the Impey Manuscripts there are a few letters relating to the proprietor of the *Bengal Gazette*, the earliest of which is dated three months after the incident just related. Hicky seems to have been in jail waiting sentence;* Impey was at Baughulpore (whence

* At the Assizes, late in June, 1781, the Chief Justice, his colleagues, and a Jury were occupied in trying Mr. Hicky upon three "indictments instituted at the suit of the Honble. the Governor-General" for libels published in the *Bengal Gazette*. On two of these charges he was found guilty. In the same week he was found guilty of libel at the suit of the Rev. J. Z. Kiernander. After the Assizes Impey left Calcutta (in July) to visit the Provincial Courts. At Monghyr

he was soon to set out for Lucknow, a journey which he was afterwards to hear so very much about). He writes to Hyde, to Calcutta—

"Nothing occurs to me as material in the Court except Hicky's business (and etc., etc.). . . . . With regard to the first what think you, if his paper (which I have not seen) should not have been offensive since the trial, of three months' imprisonment for the record (recent?) contempts, six months for each of the Governor's indictments and four for the Padre's, with a fine of one thousand rupees for each of the Governor's, and five hundred for the Padre's, if he lays no affidavit to prove his poverty before the Court, and if he does, to add two months' imprisonment for each of the Governor's and one for the Padre's, or shall we remit the contempts?"

The object of sending Hicky to jail, and keeping him there, was no doubt to extinguish his paper; but in this it failed, for the fact remains (and a very singular one it is in connection with the infancy of the press in India) that though the man who was proprietor, editor and printer, had been imprisoned from June, the *Bengal Gazette* still managed to struggle on for several months longer with no falling off in the punctuality of its appearance, nor with any change in the style of its matter. Nor does it mend its manners in the least; the observation of social and official doings is as watchful, and the rebuke or the approbation as prompt and as personal as ever. These are conveyed in all the favourite vehicles as of yore, the Rhymer's "squib," the "Bon Ton Intelligence," the "Contributor's Letter." Lengthy manifestoes headed "Addresses to the Public" are issued, too, which proclaim that in defence of their rights the *Bengal Gazette* and its proprietor will so bear themselves that the opposer may beware. Hicky from his dungeon seems to direct the storm, and hurls defiance at his oppressors with all the resources of his copious invective. This bold front seems to have enlisted much sympathy in the community amongst whom the *Gazette* found readers, and letters of congratulation reach it from many correspondents, one of whom (secure on the outside of a jail himself) thus, with vicarious stoicism, bids the poor captive to be of good cheer. "Do not, I conjure you, bate a jot of heart or hope, but still bear up and steer right onward in the glorious cause of the *English Nation*, even in the gloom of a prison. After a few tedious months' confinement you will look back with joy on your

he heard from Hastings of the Benares disturbance in August; he thence went on to Patna, and to Benares (at the pressing call of Hastings), and there arranged to go to Lucknow.

past sufferings, and the happy consequence of them to British subjects, and to this poor distressed and exhausted country." As if to show that when called to a martyr's crown, he can wear it *as* a crown, Hicky about this time thus chides a correspondent, and heaps coals of fire on his chief persecutor's head—.

"Your letter cannot be inserted, as it is repugnant to a plan of the Editor's previously resolved upon by him—never to lash at the fair sex; the poorest of those ladies is a very valuable woman, and the other, though highly exalted, may have faults, but the Editor is of opinion that the goodness of her heart makes a sufficient and ample atonement in the sight of God for everything laid to her charge. If so we ought to be content, and although she is nearly allied to a man that has ungenerously and unremittingly pursued the Editor to his ruin, yet he is unconscious of any part of it being owing to her influence, so he is determined never to give her an uneasy moment from anything published in this paper."

Thus the crippled newspaper battled on through the rains and cold weather of 1781. Early in the following year Hastings returned to Calcutta after some months' absence. His arrival brought stormy weather for the *Bengal Gazette*, which has soon to thus inform its supporters of a fresh disaster—

"In January, 1782, was tried before Sir E. Impey an action brought by Warren Hastings, Esq., against J. A. Hicky on the same indictment on which the said Warren Hastings had the said J. A. Hicky tried and found guilty at the Assizes last June, and for which the said J. A. Hicky was sentenced to remain one year in prison and pay a fine of 2000 rupees to the said Warren Hastings, who has on Wednesday last had damages given him by Sir E. Impey to the very heavy sum of 5000 sicca rupees, which with the fine of June amount to 7000 rupees, with a long confinement of one year in jail in this dangerous and scorching climate."

Crushing as this blow was, the contumacious Editor does not yet bend the knee. No, "he tackles the trouble that comes his way with a resolute heart and cheerful." He arms himself again for the fight and goes into action in the old fashion, his return fire being as brisk as ever. News had about this time percolated into the Calcutta Jail of the coercive measures employed by the Governor-General, after his recent Benares warfare, against certain members of the Royal Family at Oude, and of the officious zeal with which the Chief Justice came to his aid, and journeyed from Benares to Oude to take what have since become historically known as "The Lucknow Affidavits." The imprisoned Editor was not likely to neglect such an opportunity of letting his oppressors see that he had his eye on them. So a prominent place is assigned them in the *Bengal Gazette's* next satire on Society. This takes the form of a "Congress at S—k—r," and a "Vocal Concert given previous to the rising of the Congress." The characters in the latter are very numerous, but it will suffice to instance the most easily recognised ones in each. It may be explained that Sooksagur (Sukh Ságar, *i.e.* sea of delight), the scene of the Masquerade, was a pretty place up the river where the *élite* of Calcutta sometimes went excursionising in the cold season on festive pursuits.

"In the Congress at S—k—r some of the most conspicuous masks were—

| | |
|---|---|
| Dictator . . . . . | In the character of Sir Francis Wronghead (crying we are on a forlorn hope, and must drive on neck or nothing). |
| Old**** . . . . . . | A travelling justice of the peace taking affidavits gratis, with the following motto on his breast, "Datur pessimo," and "all was false and hollow." |
| Ned Silent * . . . . . | A windmill; he wore the habit in which he recanted the errors of the St. Franciscan faith: he had a label on his breast, on which was inscribed:—"Good tho' late, if sincere, but seldom sincere when so late." |
| Thane, John Macpherson, member of Council (1781), an old friend and colleague of Hastings, and his temporary successor as G.G. . . . | Appeared in a Highland dress thrumming on the bag pipe. He was overheard whispering to the Dictator, "Keep all secret, mon, and I'll help thee oot." |
| Viner † . . . . . | Having lost his own character by his acceptance of a place in May last, came into the room with his hands under his shirt in that of a Fiscal. |

* Wheler, Member of Council: this backsliding of his is curiously confirmed by Francis himself in his journal in the month following that of the duel, viz. "Visit Mr. Wheler in the evening at the Gardens. Find his house full of the Government people, and perceive plainly from his own discourse that H. and he are not in a state of mortal enmity, *nimiun familiariter exercere inimicitias videntur*. They are often closeted together, etc." Wheler was also nicknamed Ned Wheelabout by Hicky.

† Chambers; Hicky announced with disgust in the previous September that the "new office of Judge of Chinsura and Chandernagore had been bestowed

| | |
|---|---|
| Justice Balance . . . | Of No Body. |
| Jack Paradise Lost* . . | A patriot in a coat out at the elbows, which he endeavoured to patch up with a string of love-letters supplicating a celebrated beauty to undertake the shortest part in *Duke and no Duke.* |
| Behar Judge . . . . | A Courier laden with affidavits taken before the travelling Justice. Sir F. Wronghead was overheard enjoining him not to peach, and making him assurances of being highly provided for. |
| Turban Conquest . . . | Representing the parable of the foolish virgin in the Scripture carrying a lamp without oil. |
| Pomposo, Her Guardian . . | A Dutchman. |

In the concert at S—k—r the following songs were set down for the chief performers :—

| *Songs.* | |
|---|---|
| Know then war's my pleasure . | By Sir F. Wronghead. |
| How I am weather-beaten and shattered . . . . | Ditto. |
| Gold from Law can take the sting . . . . . | By Poolbundy. |
| The laws were made for the little . . . . . | Ditto. |
| There's truth and good sense in friend W——n's defence, affidavits shall answer them all, sirs . . . . . | Thane. |
| "I'm bubbled, I'm bubbled; oh, how I'm troubled, bamboozled; and hit" . . | Affidavit Courier. |
| He that weds a beauty . . | Jack Paradise Lost. |
| 'Tis impossible for me, as I hope to be saved, Madam . . | Jack Paradise Lost. |
| Our Emma is a sad slut, nor heeds not what we taught her | The Community. |

with a handsome salary on one of the Judges of the Supreme Court." This extra place of profit conferred by the Company's Government, attracted comparatively little notice, considering the uproar created by the similar patronage in Impey's favour.

* I have substituted the least objectionable of this gentleman's aliases.

| | |
|---|---|
| And when we fly them, they pursue us, and leave us when they've won us . . . | Turban Conquest. |
| The best wines if kept too long will turn to vinegar . . | Ditto. |
| That Girl runs in my head strangely . . . . | Pigdanny Durgee. |
| When those we love enrage us,<br>How soon our passion flies!<br>The sluts can re-engage us,<br>And kill us with their eyes. | Ditto. |
| Let's be gay while we may . | Lady D——y and Mrs. M——e. |
| Dear me, how I long to be married,<br>And in my own coach to be carried! | Miss C——p.* |

The Sooksagur pleasantry gave the finishing stroke to Mr. Hicky's editorial career. It was not enough to scotch the snake; it must be killed; and killed it very soon was in this unexpected fashion. Early in March, 1782, the following announcement appeared:—

"Mr. Hicky addresses his citizens and fellow-subjects with heart-felt joy, and tells them that on March 7 the king's judges inclined to admit him to plead *in formâ pauperis* in defending four fresh actions brought against him this term by Warren Hastings, Esq.; and that Mr. Counsellor Davis (for plaintiff) did make a motion and plea in bar of Mr. Hicky's types being exempted from seizure, setting forth that the said printing types did constitute and form a great part of Mr. Hicky's property, and hoped their Lordships would not protect the said types from being seized upon should judgment be obtained against him. This motion the honourable the king's judges strongly opposed as repugnant to the British Legislature and constitution, and treated it with the contempt it so very justly merited. Thus, by protecting the types, they have protected the liberty of the subject and the liberty of the press."

In the next number he makes this appeal to the public—

"A scene of continued tyranny and oppression for near two years having reduced Mr. Hicky very much in his circumstances, involved him more in debt and injured his business very considerably, though he is still immured in a Jail where he has been these nine long months separated from his family and friends, at the suit of Warren Hastings, Esq., and where he still expects to remain, as the said W. H. has brought no less than six fresh actions against him this term," etc., etc.

* If the initials here refer to a Miss Crisp, as they probably do, both her wishes were soon granted, for the Calcutta Register of Marriages records that G. Shee, Esq., and Eliza Crisp were united at Hoogly in 1783.

Then follows the rates at which advertisements, etc., etc., will continue to be inserted.

In the same number he announces the recent appearance of Lady Wronghead at a masquerade "habited like a Tartarean (*sic*) princess, almost sinking under the weight of pearls and diamonds. The brilliancy of her dress was only eclipsed by her usual urbanity and vivacity."

This was the last opportunity allowed to the Editor of taking Mrs. Grundy into his confidence. His jubilant announcement of the repugnance of the Court to the proposal regarding the seizure of his type was premature. At all events the types were seized. The bound copy of the paper in the British Museum bears this entry on the fly-leaf, "from March, 1780, to March, 1782, The Day the Types were seized by Order." The *Bengal Gazette* was strangled, and the *India Gazette*, its well-behaved rival, was left blooming alone.

Possibly if the *Bengal Gazette* had not been thus summarily done to death, and its assiduous purveyors of "Bon Ton Intelligence" deprived of their vehicle, Calcutta would have been better prepared for an announcement about two months later which must have fluttered the Volsces and robbed them of an interesting speculation which for two years had exercised their invention and their tattling tongues. "*India Gazette,* Saturday, June 1, 1782. On Monday last, at Chinsurah, John Bristowe, Esq., to Miss Wrangham." The bride's christian name not being chronicled, it became desirable to try and find if any fuller detail of this marriage existed. In the Bengal Marriage Records (outside stations) the entry of this one is as follows :—

"May 27, 1782, at Chinsurah, John Bristow, Senior Merchant in the Honble. Co.'s service, and Amelia Wrangham, by permission of the Honble. the Governor-General.

* * * * * *

"The above parties were legally married by me,

"WESTROW HULSE,

"Chaplain to the Army."

The officiating chaplain was a great friend of the Commander-in-Chief and of Lady Coote; the latter was a daughter of a former Governor of St. Helena (Hutchinson), and may possible have bespoken the services of Mr. Hulse in behalf of her fellow-islander on this happy occasion. "Emma," no doubt, was a diminutive or variant of "Amelia." *

* The marriage of another Miss Wrangham, though recorded in the Calcutta

It is curious what a "dark horse" the winner of this oft-discussed race must have been. Hicky's paper suggests the wide field of selection open to the obdurate fair one, and this is confirmed in the letter from Francis naming three additional possible suitors. John Bristow will not fit in with any of the described or named candidates. His wooing was probably short and sharp, not long-adoing, otherwise Francis's ignorance of it would have been extraordinary. He and Bristow were close friends and official allies.* It was in reality Francis who, on the formation of the New Government, used the power of the majority to supersede Middleton at the Court of Oude by Bristow, a process which was promptly reversed by Hastings as soon as he got a chance. Bristow soon after appeared in Calcutta. He went to England in 1777, and Francis wrote about him to a friend there: "Bristow is keen, intelligent, well-connected, and devoted to my interests." Accordingly he ear-wigged his influential friends, and secured an interview with Lord North mainly with a view to impressing him with the necessity of retaining Francis's services in Bengal, and especially in case Hastings' tenure of office should not be continued. In 1780 he turns up again in Calcutta, having obtained from the Court of Directors a pressing recommendation or order to the Bengal Government for his restoration to Lucknow, which Hastings sternly refused to comply with until two years later, though at one time willing to do so as a peace-offering to Francis when arranging a truce on the departure of Barwell. Bristow was not a little importunate about his reappointment, as an entry in Francis's diary, in April (1780), shows: "Plagued out of my life by Bristow, whom nothing but instant possession of his post will satisfy." Bristow must have remained some months longer in Calcutta without official employment.

In December, 1780, there is advertised in the *Bengal Gazette*,

*Gazette*, September, 1784, occurred, I find, at St. Helena in March of same year. This was that of Captain Ralph Dundass to Miss Elizabeth Wrangham, a younger sister of Emma's, the parents being William and Elizabeth Wrangham. Captain Dundass was Commander of the Indiaman *Royal Henry*, then returning to England from China and the Coromandel coast. The young lady to whose charms he succumbed on his way home was born in 1768, and thus was only sixteen, *i.e.* she began her successful captivations at an earlier age even than her elder sister, whose field was India. I am under obligation to Mr. Foster of the Record Department, India Office, for tracing these marriages for me, and to "Letters of Hastings," S. C. Grier, for remarking my omission in not noticing the Bristow one.

* Hastings used to say that Bristow, Livius, Shee, and Ducarel were "the lees of Mr. Francis."

"To be let, the house at present occupied by John Bristow, Esq., near the John Bazaar (*sic*) on a pleasant spot of ground. Apply, E. Tiretta." His next traceable appearance is at Chinsurah, getting married. It must be remembered that the old Dutch Settlement * was then in the hands of the British, and had been so since its occupation by them in July, 1781, as only then had the official news arrived that Great Britain had declared war against Holland nearly seven months before (December 20, 1780).

Possibly Mr. Bristow may have been deputed there in some official capacity and so met his fate; Hicky has told us that the Chinsura belle was there in February, 1782.

Not until October, 1782, did the Governor-General consent to Bristow's return to the Residency at Lucknow, but he withdrew from it in little more than a year, then he returned to Calcutta. His name occurs amongst those who attended the foundation meeting of the Bengal Asiatic Society in January, 1784. He probably remained for the rest of his service in Calcutta, where, in 1788, he was member of the Board of Trade. At the time of his marriage he was thirty-two years of age, his wife nineteen. The union would seem to have been a very suitable and happy one. They took a very prominent place in the social life of Old Calcutta, where the lady became as great a favourite, or even greater, as a charming woman as she had been as a merry girl. Perhaps, after all, the flippant familiarities of the *Bengal Gazette* may have chastened her into wise resolves; possibly the songs assigned to "the Community" and to "Turban Conquest" at the S—k—r Concert, though suggested in fun, may have been a little in vulgar earnest, and have helped to bring home to her that man, even at his best, is a fickle creature, easy enough to catch, but not so easy to cage, and that if he is to be held in silken bondage, it must be with the aid of attractions which custom cannot stale.

Such fetters Mrs. Bristow had the wit to weave and to cultivate. She became an accomplished actress, and by the indulgence of her admiring husband, had a private theatre of her own in her Chowringee house in the time of Lord Cornwallis, where they entertained their wide circle of friends. Her strong points were in comedy and in humorous singing. If she ever staged there, as she most probably did, a play then still much in vogue whose title expressed the principle and the motto of her wedded life, *The Way to Keep Him*,

* Of a visit which Francis paid there in 1777, he diarises thus: "Sup at Chinsura with all the Dutch Factory: plenty of victuals and civility, but as dull as Rotterdam."

we may fancy with what archness she sang Davy Garrick's words for the benefit of her frivolous sisters (some of whom may have lectured herself in the old days) when warning them that—

> "The bloom of your cheek and the glance of your eye,
> Your roses and lilies may make the men sigh,
> But roses and lilies and sighs pass away,
> And passion will die as your beauties decay."

She is credited with the honour of being the first in Calcutta who brought lady * actors into fashion—female characters having previously been taken by beardless youths.

"Polly Honeycombe," in Colman's play of that name (made popular by Miss Pope), was a favourite part of hers. Referring to another of her performances, a highly gratified critic writes, "She went through the whole of the humorous part of 'the English Slave in the Ottoman Seraglio' with a justness of conception and success of execution most admirable. Magnificently decorated by Art, and more beautifully adorned by Nature, the extravagances of the amorous Sultan seemed justified by her charms." Surely nothing more need be said of her dramatic accomplishments.

Mrs. Bristow went to England in January, 1790; her departure eclipsed the gaiety of Calcutta, but how long her absence from the scene of so many triumphs lasted I have not traced.†

* But the lady amateurs, once started, soon became more ambitious, and took a turn occasionally at some of the male characters. A Calcutta paper, in 1790, is most enthusiastic about one of these performances, and comes out with an ode "On Mrs. ——— appearing in the character of Lucius in the tragedy of Julius Cæsar at the Calcutta Theatre." This begins—

> "When with new powers to charm our partial eyes,
> Thy beauteous form appears in virile guise,
> Such tempting graces wanton o'er thy air,
> By gentle Love's enchanting wiles I swear
> Each throbbing youth would——"

and then the poet becomes so carried away by his theme as to be quotable no further.

† Though Francis did not in his letter to Livius write very enthusiastically of "the Wrangham," she won upon him after her marriage. From England he wrote not infrequently to Bristow. Thus, in 1791, he tells him, "We had not the good fortune to see Mrs. Bristow for some weeks before her departure." In 1796, in writing to "most dear and worthy Collings," in Calcutta, he says, "For three or four years past Mrs. Bristow has sworn to me by all her gods that she would take you and your affairs under her immediate patronage and protection. I saw her last night at the opera, and I think her perjuries seem to agree with her mightily: every vow she breaks creates a new charm, and there! am *I* such a fool as to tell her so? Encouraged by my success in my care of the East, I have lately

John Bristow died in Calcutta in October, 1802, aged fifty-two. He sleeps in the "Great Burial Ground," South Park Street, where so many of our old Calcutta friends were laid.

Now, to return to the *Bengal Gazette*, the ill-fated proprietor and editor can be traced a few steps further, in two or three letters and petitions of his addressed from jail to the Judges of the Supreme Court, which may still be seen in original among the Impey manuscripts. They are in respectful terms, coming from a man naturally sunk in misery on realising that his hostages to fortune have been deprived of support; their tone is humble, but is not abject. The first is dated January 17, 1783, and is addressed to the Chief Justice. In it he complains of "being surrounded by very drunken, riotous fellow-prisoners, and his peace and repose interrupted by their clamorous broils." He especially names a Lieutenant Gould for "assaulting his ears with the most gross and ungentlemanlike abuse," though he had shown him many little neighbourly attentions. After his complaint the letter goes on thus—

"I have now been confined in this jail upwards of nineteen long months, and nine long months of that time have been deprived of the means of earning one rupee for the support of my family, entirely owing to the seizure of the implements and tools of my profession; and not being able to pay the rent of a small brickhouse for my children to live in, they have been, until the Christmas holidays, immured in the jail with myself. You, Sir, who have many fine children of your own (God bless them) cannot be at a loss in forming an idea what the feelings of a tender father must be who daily beholds his little innocent children pining away under the contaminated air of a filthy jail,* *who has the inclination but*

turned my thoughts to the West, from Hindoos to negroes. And Mrs. Bristow says, 'What signify negroes? aren't they black? and don't *I* make a slave of every man I meet?'" To herself he writes in forwarding a letter for her to see and despatch, "Honoured madam, To save you trouble I have left the inclosed open for your perusal. Whether you read it or not, I pray you to seal it carefully with your own pretty fist, your arms may be better employed: when you have nothing else to do be so good as to squander some loose thoughts upon your most dutiful servant, P.F."

* In the Report of the Select Committee of the House of Commons, published in 1782, we get a glimpse of what a Calcutta jail was like. A Mr. Creassy, who had been imprisoned there, said "the gaol was an old ruin of a house, formerly the residence of some black native." A Mr. W. Hicky testified, "In the middle of the gaol enclosure was a tank about thirty yards square in which the prisoners promiscuously bathed and washed their clothes. Europeans were generally indulged by the gaoler with permission to erect and live in small bamboo and matting huts near this tank; it would be impossible for any European to exist for any length of time within the prison. The stench was dreadful. There was no infirmary or provision for the sick that he ever heard of Debtors and criminals were not

*not the power to relieve them.* Yet great and afflicting as those hardships really have been and still will continue to be, I have never complained of them, nor do I complain of them now; my only motive for this short description being to prove to your Lordship that these afflictions are full sufficient for me to bear without having them wantonly aggravated by a man to whom I never gave the least offence. Was it in my power to shift my place of abode to such a distance that my ears could not be offended, and my mind thereby inflamed, I would not have troubled your Lordship."

He winds up by saying that he will do very well if Mr. Gould is removed.

This letter is thus endorsed in Impey's writing, "Hicky's letter; gave Mr. Church, the Sheriff, an account of it, and desired him to redress any grievances he may labour under."

In the following August he petitions the Court, and dates from "Birjee Jail," thus using the native designation for the quarter where the common prison was situated then—as now. He asks for release and remission of the rest of the fines, and points out that "Mr. Hastings last June did generously forgive your petitioner his part of the fines." I am glad thus to be able to record this instance of absence of vindictiveness towards a fallen man, on the part of one who has often been referred to as implacable and unforgiving. He urges that he had been "already two years in jail, during sixteen months of which he had been deprived of the means of earning a rupee for the support of his family, twelve in number, whose only subsistence was derived from the produce of a few bills which happily he had by him."

The answer to this, he says, was, "that there was no resource but to pay the money, or lie in jail till next term."

In a week or two he petitions again, saying that though he has received his release from Mr. Hastings he apprehends detainers from

separated, nor men from women (but of this he was not positive). An old woman prisoner who begged of him said, in answer to his question, that she wanted the money to buy water." From other evidence it appeared that there was no gaol allowance, and that many died from the want of the necessaries of life. Hindoos, Mohammedans, and Europeans were all together. In addition to this, the prisoners, at the time deposed to numbering 170, there were daily there a number of women and attendants who brought provisions or came to cook them.

Creassy's account suggests the "Lal Bazāār" jail, famous in 1756, which Captain Grant located "200 yards advanced before the Eastern battery, where three roads terminate into the place." Either the old "Ambassador House" or on the site of it? (Wilson, "Fort William," vol. i.). Captain Price, as we have seen, says Noncomar was in the *county* jail in 1775, as if there were two prisons then. It is on record, no doubt, *when* "Birjee jail" was built and opened.

other creditors. He asks the Judges, "who are fathers themselves, whether they can be devoid of feeling for a man in his situation, separated from his helpless children, who are now at that age that they ought to be sent to school." His final prayer is that "as he is now stripping his family of the necessary furniture that they had got about them, which he had so long struggled to keep for them, that when they are sold at outcry, and the proceeds paid to the Clerk of the Crown, that he will no longer be detained in prison 'by any other demands upon him relative to this business.'"

The Chief Justice sent this petition on to Mr. Justice Chambers with this note :—

"DEAR SIR ROBERT,—I send you another letter from Hicky; please to send your answer, and transmit that and this letter to Brother Hyde."

Chambers wrote at foot of the Chief Justice's letter—

"The improprieties in Mr. Hicky's letter may well be pardoned on account of his distress; but I do not see how we can relieve his distress. As to his request that he may be informed of all the demands that can be made upon him relative to this business, the Clerk of the Crown will undoubtedly inform him if he applies to that officer."

When this reached Mr. Justice Hyde he seems to have made some reference back to Chambers, the purport of which may be gathered from this rather crusty note :—

"DEAR BROTHER HYDE,

"I had no intention to write more than you received, and that was not meant to be sent to Hicky, but merely to communicate to you and Sir E. Impey the idea that occurred to me. I do not believe that Sir E. Impey intended that I should compose a written answer to be signed by all the Judges, for he knows that in the present state of my health it would not be proper for me to so employ myself. I agree with you in thinking that it is not necessary to send any written answer to Mr. Hicky.

"I am, dear Brother Hyde,
"Yours affectionately,
"R. C.*

"August 19, 1783."

The answer from the Judges was unfavourable, and was verbally conveyed. This is evident from the last despairing wail of the imprisoned Editor that is traceable—

* Chambers signs his notes to Impey, "yours very affectionately." One in which he asks that his absence from court may be excused is addressed to the *Right* Honourable Sir E. Impey—a mistake which Mr. E. B. Impey notices in an endorsement.

"The only resource he has now is to implore the assistance of God to give him patience and fortitude to stand the shock which your Lordships' memorialists received last Sunday night when Mr. Forbes delivered him your Lordships' message. . . . Now every dawn of hope is fled, and nothing but a gloomy picture of horror, confinement, and distress appears before his imagination."

Ah me! how different all this from that serene evening, the "blest retirement, friend to life's decline," to which he thus told his patrons in one of his addresses his mind's eye looked forward when he embarked on his newspaper enterprise. "I hoped to pay off all my debts, and secure six thousand pounds in England, in order to support me in my old days in a land of freedom and liberty. To purchase a little house in the middle of a garden, rise with the lark, sow my own peas or beans, graft or innoculate my own trees according to the season of the year, and live in peace with all mankind."

In the year (or the next) when the journalist was thus letting his fancy roam, there may have reached Calcutta a volume of recently published poems, in one of which, he who had yet to write "The Task" and "John Gilpin," tells how universal is the aspiration of our battered old exile.

> "The statesman, lawyer, merchant, man of trade,
> Pants for the refuge of some rural shade,
> Where all his long anxieties forgot
> Amid the charms of a sequestered spot,
> He may possess the joy he thinks he sees,
> Lay his old age upon the lap of ease," etc., etc.

When Hicky's bonds were loosened is not disclosed in any record that is known to me, but he was living in freedom and in poverty in Calcutta sixten years after his fruitless appeal to the judges written in jail.

A friend in Calcutta (Mr. J. Cotton) was good enough to send me a copy of a document found amongst the records of the Accountant-General's Office, Bengal, viz. a release or acknowledgment, signed by Jas. A. Hicky, of the receipt of six thousand and odd rupees from the united Company of Merchants trading to the East Indies through the Governor-General of Fort William, "in full satisfaction and discharge" of a claim made by him in July, 1793, for money stated to be due to him for printing and publishing certain Orders and Regulations for the Government relating to the army of the Company on the Bengal establishment. Though the attorney to the Company tendered the above sum in the same month, Hicky apparently did not accept it until March, 1795. There is nothing to show when the claim arose, *i.e.* whether before or after his imprisonment; the phraseology suggests an old debt.

We get further glimpses of him in letters written by him from Calcutta to Warren Hastings in England, appealing for help. Such appeals, coming from one who had despitefully used him testify to Mr. Hicky's knowledge of, and reliance on, the benevolent nature which characterised Hastings abroad as well as at home. He was ever ready to hear the cry of the unfortunate and, when he could, to give "an arm of aid to the weak, a friendly hand to the friendless"; and, as so often happens in such cases, his secret charity and generosity to the importunate were in some instances abused.

In November, 1793,* Hicky writes that he has not had any employment for several years, and is "much distressed with a very large family, which, with repeated and severe fits of sickness, has reduced me very much."

He was often told that it was Hastings' intention to do something for him before retiring, and he hopes that he will not think Hicky less deserving now than then, as he has not done anything since to forfeit those good wishes. "Had I any place here under Government by which I could bearly (*sic*) and with frugality support my children, I would entirely give over all thoughts of leaving this country. But as I am now a very old man, should I die here my children must beg through the streets of Calcutta, as they are by their youth unable to earn their own bread." The burden of his prayer is that Hastings may exert his influence in Calcutta and obtain for him some such post.

He suggests that the Clerk of the Market, being old, very rich, and inefficient from his infirmities, should be provided with a deputy at a small salary. In this post it is considered "by several people in the Settlement that I would render great service to the public, as I am allowed to be a good judge of all kinds of provisions." A further fitness for such a berth is vouched for in the assurance that "though old, I am, thank God, one of the activest men in the Settlement." "A line or two from you, Sir, would procure me the place alluded to, or any other which might enable me to support my family with frugality."

When in jail, it may be remembered, he pleads his large family, "twelve in number," left without support, the children at an age

* I am indebted to "Letters of Warren Hastings" (Introduction), Sydney C. Grier, for the knowledge of the existence of this and of a later letter of Hicky, which had formerly escaped me in the Hastings' manuscripts.

when they ought to be sent to school. Ten years later we find him here urging again the helpless youth of his children, a fresh brood presumably that he had provided himself with in the interval.

There is a passage in this letter of Hicky's which must not be omitted, as it affords us a glance at what our predecessors in India had to encounter "in journeyings often, in perils in the sea, in perils by their own countrymen." Should he fail in obtaining the local means of supporting himself and family, he says, "I had better endeavour to get my passage home as a surgeon on board of one of the ships of the season, and by that means get liberty to carry my children along with me. I have some friends still living, and should it please God to take me from my children after my arrival in England, my friends could get them placed in the Blue Coat Hospital, as I am, by being a Freeman of the City of London, entitled to that indulgence." It is worth noting here that the writer expresses no diffidence as to being able to get employment as a surgeon, and this confirms a fact satirised, as we have already seen, many years before in his own paper, namely, that any professional training or experience was superfluous in the case of those embarking on the general practice of medicine in Calcutta. When it is borne in mind that amongst the passengers of those home-returning ships were English ladies, delicate children of tender years, officers fever-stricken, often wounded, perhaps; in short, invalids of all sexes and sorts, weary and climate-worn, it is very grievous to think that the too-needed medical man provided for their relief and comfort on a voyage of six months, was one with the qualification of old Mr. Hicky the printer. And this case is probably merely a typical one. The needs of the army often gave full occupation to the insufficient supply of military (and civil) medical officers in the Company's service. Hastings' friend, Colonel Ironside, had a very poor opinion of the assistant-surgeons, "numbers of whom are well known in this service to have deserted from Indiamen, or escaped from sweeping shops in Edinburgh, and hearing lectures (which they call going to College) for two and two pence a week." Almost any substitute could not be much worse on a voyage than one of these practitioners. Therefore any English adventurer, ne'er-do-well, or hopeless failure, who wished to return home and could speak plausibly, was deemed good enough, in an emergency, to be taken on and rated as a surgeon, and let loose on a ship's company. The incompetence of such men must have been often brought home to them; accidents, if not frequent, must at least have been occasional, and required surgical interference; how this was afforded will not bear thinking of. As regards aid in general illness, most of these men, it is to be hoped, had the merciful sagacity to do nothing beyond invoking the beneficence of kindly Dame Nature, and, as a rule, "worked out their passage" by punctual attendance at meals in the cuddy, where one of their expected and more ornate functions was, to say grace before meat daily; and to read prayers, and possibly a sermon or two on Sundays.

What a tale might the escaped survivors of such a voyage have to unfold on landing in England! If modern voyagers to or from India should occasionally incline to be regretfully effusive about "the good old times," the thoughts suggested by this not overdrawn picture may be salutary, and enable them to endure with fortitude, the luxurious discomfort of a couple of weeks on board a P. and O. steamer.

Mr. Hicky, however, did not carry out his intention of getting to England in the capacity of ship's surgeon or of any other. He seems to have remained in Calcutta, whence, at Christmas, 1799, *i.e.* six years later, he signs his last letter to Hastings, written for him by some clerkly hand. He calls to mind his former appeals—once through his old friend Captain Joe Price, to whom Hastings, he says, spoke very kindly of Hicky and praised his patient endurance under suffering and trials. Again, later on, he recalls that he wrote a letter through "Captain Manning of the Pitt," to be delivered by him personally to Hastings. This was done, and many questions were asked of Manning as to Hicky's welfare; the ex-Governor-General adding, "I cannot do anything for him until my own troubles are over." In reminding Hastings of this promise, the poor applicant gives a piteous account of his impecunious condition—the letter ending thus—

"it would be painful to you to read a long and particular account of the distress of myself and children: let it suffice that everything which I had has been sold and mortgaged for my unhappy family, and none but God and ourselves know the keenness of our distress.

"Wishing you and Mrs. Hastings, health and every other blessing,

"I remain, with due respect,

"Your obedient servant,

"JAS. A. HICKY."

I could not find what response this last melancholy application met with; the name disappears at this point from record. Many of Hicky's letters, including those written from jail, are not without some pathetic dignity. On reading them (less still on seeing them in original) one is little disposed to indulge in obvious moralities or in unqualified condemnation, but rather to feel only pity for the writer. He was not deficient in enterprise; he manifested through his varied and stormy career much of the doggedness which characterises John Bull, yet, owing to some kink in his nature, he was not wise in his generation, and his life was a dismal failure. What became of him is not revealed; that useful but melancholy book, the "Bengal Obituary," does not enshroud him; but the last sad letter of his that we have seen leaves very little ground to hope that he ever saw again the longed-for country of which it was his boast to proclaim he was a free-born son. I suppose he must be classed amongst the worthless men, but as the pioneer of the Indian Press his name and his story should have an interest for Calcutta.

# CHAPTER IX

## PHILIP FRANCIS AND HIS TIMES

### MADAME GRAND, 1777—1780

### I

THE incident in the Calcutta life of Philip Francis, which maintains a notoriety second only to that of his duel with Warren Hastings, is his appearance before the Supreme Court as defendant in a suit successfully instituted against him by G. F. Grand.

The circumstances which led to a member of the Government being forced to occupy so unenviable a position were first brought directly to the notice of Indian readers by Sir John Kaye, in a very bitter article on Francis, in the second volume of the *Calcutta Review* (1844).

Kaye derived his information altogether from the account written by the plaintiff many years after the event in the "Narrative of the Life of a Gentleman long resident in India," from which he gave an extract detailing some of the more prominent facts constituting the wrong which necessitated a recourse to law. Mr. Herman Merivale, who completed and edited the "Memoirs of Sir Philip Francis," published in 1867, when dealing with the Calcutta scenes in this domestic drama, is obliged to rely entirely on the extract quoted in the *Review*, and alluding to the "Narrative," says, "I have never seen this very scarce production." English writers and others who have in recent years touched on this subject have followed the account reproduced in the "Memoirs," and seem to have adopted the view held both by the Editor of the latter and by the Calcutta reviewer, that, however desirable it is, as a general rule, to avoid such subjects, there are occasions when they justly fall within the province of the biographer. It will not be difficult, for instance, to show that the incident in question was "not merely a domestic episode in the Life of Francis," but one, the consequences of which tended to embitter his resentment against Impey—an incentive to action on the part of so good a hater as Francis, which bore fruit a thousand-fold a few years afterwards.

As regards the lady concerned in the Calcutta proceedings, French writers naturally take an interest in the career of one who emerged from obscurity to occupy a very conspicuous position in the highest Parisian society, as the Princess of Benevento, several years afterwards. Conjecture had, of course, been long busy as to the antecedents of a lady so suddenly exalted, and stories vague and shadowy and remote from truth, were in circulation about them. However, long before her death, even curiosity about her seems to have subsided, and for the generation succeeding, her name ceased to offer a topic of commentary. But, on the publication of the "Memoirs" of Sir Philip Francis fifty years after his death, circumstances were brought into prominence which revived an interest that had long slept; and English and French reviewers, in dealing with the "Memoirs," recalled a forgotten *cause célèbre*, and confessed that, till they appeared, little was known of the Indian antecedents of a lady, who is thus alluded to by one of them (M. Amedée Pichot): "Parmi les contemporaines de Madame Récamier il en fut une qui, très-belle aussi, avait vainement eu pour premier adorateur un des hommes les plus spirituels de l'Angleterre, Sir Philip Francis, à qui sont attribuées les fameuses *Lettres de Junius;* et pour époux M. de Talleyrand, réputé les plus fin des diplomates européens."

The same writer says, that the lady arrived in Paris from India after a number of adventures—"suffisant pour rivaliser avec la fianceé du roi de Garbe." * The comparison is a harsh one, but the fragmentary form in which anything relating to Madame Grand has come before the general reader, would leave room for much misrepresentation, as would the gossip, resting often on very slender authority, which tradition has associated with her name. It is remarkable that even the author of the "Memoirs" of Sir Elijah Impey says: "I do not remember to have once heard my father relate the circumstances of the trial, nor do I find a single allusion in his papers to the cause of Le Grand (*sic*) *versus* Francis, which produced so great a sensation in Calcutta at the time."

It is proposed, therefore, to now re-tell, in a more connected form

* Readers of Boccaccio will appreciate the allusion. "Veuve de huit galants, il la prit pour pucelle, et dans son erreur par la belle apparement il fut laissé."

than has yet been attempted, the story of this celebrated cause, and to bring together the circumstances surrounding and arising out of it. With this in view recourse will be had to a source not hitherto made use of, viz. the original record of the trial itself as preserved among the archives of the Calcutta High Court.

It will be convenient, in the first place, to see who and what the plaintiff was (as after the lapse of so many years some misconception exists even on this point), and from this quarter to get a look into Anglo-Indian society in the last century, by tracing him through his career, both before and after the painful domestic episode which has rescued his name from oblivion.

Of Madame Grand herself but little can be told up to the time when she left India. After that there is a long portion of her life during which even tradition is almost, and probably ever will be, silent; but from the time when her name becomes connected with that of a great historical character, materials are not wanting to follow her career. An outline of this, gathered from French and other sources, will be given to complete the sketch before we take leave of her.

Mr. George François Grand was not "established in business at Chandernagore," as the biographer of Francis and other writers assume; but he was a member of the Indian Civil Service duly appointed in England, and had previously been in the Company's Military Service. It will be best as we go on if we let him, as a general rule, tell his own story, by placing before the reader extracts from his quaintly written "Narrative"—a source from which I shall have occasion to make copious drafts.

And first a word or two about this book. There is a copy * of it in the British Museum, on a pasted-in fly-leaf in which, written apparently in a senile hand, is this note signed Jno. Row—

"The annexed "Narrative" was the first book printed in the English

* The India Office library contained, for many years, a copy of this scarce publication, which disappeared a few years ago under accidental circumstances not necessary to be detailed. This was, most probably, the copy made use of by Kaye, but he extracted from it only enough (and this on one or two special points) to arouse a curiosity to see more, as the writer had evidently resided in India during stirring times. Kaye shows what misrepresentations as regards the after-career of Mr. Grand might have been avoided (notably by Macfarlane) if this little-known "Narrative" had been consulted. The present writer looked for it in vain many years ago in the British Museum, but lit on it there most unexpectedly in 1878, a copy having been obtained by purchase in July, 1874. There is again in the India Office library a copy of the book, which was presented to it by Archibald Constable, Esq.

language at the Cape of Good Hope, and was given to me by Mr Smith."

The book is a thin quarto of seventy-five pages, and an Appendix of xxxi. Its full title is—

"NARRATIVE OF THE LIFE

OF

A GENTLEMAN LONG RESIDENT IN INDIA,

COMPREHENDING

"A period the most eventful in the history of that country, with regard to the revolutions occasioned by European interference, and interspersed with interesting anecdotes and traits, characteristical of those eminent persons who distinguished themselves at that juncture,

'CAPE OF GOOD HOPE:

PRINTED FOR THE AUTHOR.

1814."

An "Advertisement" on the first page tells the reader that—

"I had long determined upon writing a narrative of my life. It was suggested to me by friends who felt for the vicissitudes which I had experienced. I began it therefore in 1801, and continued it from time to time, till in 1808, I have brought it to a close. The reason of the delay in its publication has been detailed by Notification inserted in the *Cape Gazette.* I thank those who have now afforded me the opportunity of giving it to the world without subjecting me to a pecuniary loss."

Where opportunities exist for comparing portions of the Narrative with contemporary or collateral authorities, it will be found to be reasonably accurate, some allowance being made for one who is stating his own case, and who is writing of events long gone by, and at an age when memory must have lost much of its tenacity. When I come to speak of the latter portion of his book, however, I shall have to notice one or two rather disingenuous suppressions.

As was not uncommon, the narrative is in the form of a letter to a friend, and thus opens in the old-fashioned stereotyped way.

"Born of a virtuous and noble family (my mother's name being Clerc de Virly, which Virly was a seignorial patrimony in Normandy, long the property and residence of her ancestors till the despotism of

Louis XIV., by the revocation of the Edict of Nantes, drove the Seigneur de Virly to take refuge with his family in England, leaving his fair possessions and wealth to the spoil of a tyrannical king). Educated at Lausanne (in the environs of which delightful city and country the Lordship of Ecublanc, situated on the banks of the Lake of Geneva, between Lausanne and Morges, had long been the seat of the Grands), in the house and under the superintendence of the best parents, assisted by a private tutor, a clergyman living in the house, and with whom I used to attend the lectures of the first professors of science in that celebrated University, I could not otherwise be formed, when I opened my career in the world, but with a disposition inclined to honour, virtue, and fraught with every social tie."

His father, having a large family, accepted the offer of an old mercantile friend in London, Mr. Robert Jones, of Clement's Lane, Lombard Street (afterwards an East India Director and M.P. for Huntingdon), to receive his son as apprentice for seven years, gratis, with the view of his succeeding at the end of that time to a regular business estimated to bring in about £5000 a year.

The next extract will show how Mr. Jones received the youth, who arrived in London "in charge of a voiturier," and how young gentlemen were taught to become British merchants a hundred years ago—

"He welcomed me most roughly; he asked me indeed how my father and mother were, and if I had brought him any Gruyère cheese, which, the voiturier answering for me in the affirmative, seemed to work a happy change. He smiled and bade me approach him; called for the footman, and, observing his spare beds were removed to the country, committed me to the care of him, who was directed to afford me half his bed to sleep on. The next morning, after breakfasting with Mr. Jones, I was introduced into the accounting house, and my first duty prescribed to see it cleaned, the fire well lighted, the desks brushed, the chairs, etc., etc., well placed, and told I should be favoured to run about with bills for acceptance, as soon as I became acquainted a little with the streets of London to be able to find my way in them, until when I was ordered to accompany the footman, who on such errands threw off his livery jacket, to assume an old brown coat cast off by his master, and he was enjoined to point out to me the principal resorts where this duty called him, after my pigtail had been changed for a cropped head of hair, in order, as Mr. Jones wittily remarked, the people might not take me for a French monkey imported on English grounds.

"And now, my friend, view the contrast which so sudden a change created; picture to yourself a youth dressed in embroidered and laced clothes, curled head and chapeau bras, solitaire and sword by his side, accompanied and introduced by his tutor into the first assemblies, both public and private, taught by the attention of those frequenting them almost to consider himself a man, and behold the transition of the same youth in a plain English frock, round hat, and hair cut close, trudging after a footman in all weathers through the streets of London !

"The disgust was natural. I seized the first moment of well-grounded discontent to absent myself."

From Mr. Jones's office he took refuge with an aunt, widow of Mr. John Payne, who seems to have had much interest at the India house. By her he was sent to the village of Thornhill in Yorkshire for the purpose, amongst others, of perfecting himself in English. From there he went to Greenwich Academy to learn gunnery (*sic*) mathematics, etc., "my friends having determined on a military life for my career, apprehending, as they expressed it, the vivacity and fire which I displayed were qualifications not suitable to the gravity and sedateness requisite to a desk and regular mercantile pursuits."

Finally, through the interest of this aunt, he got a nomination to a cadetship in Bengal, and sailed in January, 1766, in the *Lord Camden*, in which he found himself "accommodated with eleven writers, each with a standing bed in the great cabin, not one of which gentlemen, excepting Mr. John Makepeace Thackeray, of Hadley, is now (1802) living." (He refers to *William*, the grandfather of the novelist.)

They anchored in Madras in June, where he waited on Mr. Palk, who from being chaplain had succeeded Lord Pigot in the Government. In Calcutta he was well received by Clive, who regretted that he could not entrust one so young with a commission, but who sent him up to join the second brigade which stood on the roll for field service, with an injunction to its commanding officer to let him act as ensign as soon as he seemed fit. Before very long he got a commission as ensign signed by Clive.

In 1768 he became a lieutenant, in which rank he served till 1773 * (without apparently seeing any active field service), when, owing to broken health, he was "ordered by the Faculty to make a trip to Europe." To follow this prescription involved in those days resignation of the service—a step which he most reluctantly took and returned to England. He sailed, March, 1773, in the *Marquis of Rockingham*, Captain Alexander Hamilton, in which a fellow-passenger was Baron Imhoff. Prior to embarkation he remained three months at Calcutta with General Anthony Polier, when he saw a good deal of Warren Hastings, then the Governor. He gives

* In Dodwell and Miles' Army List (Indian) the dates of his commissions are, ensign, 1766 (when he could not have been more than 17 years of age) lieutenant, 1768, captain, 1773.

a curious glimpse into the social life of the Presidency during the sojourn.

Eventually he obtained a writership on the list of 1775–6, "which station was accepted, accompanied with the assurance that I should be so recommended to the Government of India as to be deemed eligible to such situations as Factors were placed in." He arrived in Calcutta in June, 1776, and having been entrusted by Mr. John Macpherson at Madras with official despatches from Colonel Macleane to the Governor-General, he "was received by Mr. Hastings with that affability and benevolence which were so characteristic in that great man, and directly was taught to consider myself an inmate of the family, and one partaking in a certain degree of his confidence, having the honour of being admitted to his bureau to transcribe his official despatches and secret papers."

But let us pass on to where the narrative introduces us to the lady whose beauty, and the strange fortune to which it conducted her, made her at one time a celebrity even amongst the highest in Europe.

"While I remained in the family of Mr. Hastings I was in the habitude, with my friends Major Palmer and Gall, to make occasional excursions at the end of the week on the river. Our rendezvous generally was either at the lamented Mr. Croft's plantation of Sooksagur, in which he had introduced the growth of the sugar-cane, or at Ghyretty house, the residence of M. Chevalier, the Governor of the French settlement of Chandernagore. At this gentleman's mansion there reigned the truest hospitality and gaiety. His admiration and personal friendship for Mr. Hastings insured the most welcome reception to those who were patronised by this excellent man. In one of these trips from the Presidency I formed an attachment to Miss Nöel Catherine Werlée, the daughter of Monsieur Werlée, Capitaine du Port and Chevalier de Saint Louis, a respectable old man whose services had deservedly merited this mark of distinction from his sovereign. We were not long in expressing to each other our reciprocal inclinations, and our engagement in matrimonial alliance took place, which we agreed should be solemnised as soon as I could obtain a situation which might enable me to commence housekeeping.

"The considerate Mr. Barwell, becoming acquainted with our mutual wishes, and pleasingly, as he said, desirous to alleviate the sufferings of a young couple ardent to be united, opened of himself the subject to me, and with that liberality of mind which he truly possessed, authorised me to impart to Mr. Hastings that whatever he could devise for my welfare should meet with his hearty concurrence. The Paymastership to the garrisons was the first office which became vacant, and to this I should have been appointed had not Mr. Hastings sacredly engaged his promise for that station to Mr. Kneller. By the removal, however, of Mr. Coates at the same period to the commercial residency of Chittagong, these worthy friends obtained from the Board of Trade for me the office of Secretary to the Salt Committee, and Head Assistant and Examiner in their Secretary's office, then the present Mr. Charles Grant, the Director.

"These situations producing an income of thirteen hundred rupees per month, I felt at full liberty to claim from the young lady and her worthy parent the performance of their promise. The 10th of July, 1777, was accordingly fixed for the auspicious day, and as Miss Werlée was of the Catholic persuasion it became necessary for us to be married both in the Romish and the Protestant church. To these we conformed. On the morning of that day, at 1 a.m. (*sic*) the Popish priest legalised our union in the church at Chandernagore, and at eight the same morning at Hughely House, where my old Benares friend, Thomas Motte, Esq., dwelt, the Revd. Dr. William Johnson, by special license * from the Governor-General, pronounced, I had fondly hoped, our indissoluble tie in this world so long as our respective career of life lasted.

"I might well have entertained a reliance of this nature, for never did an union commence with more brightening prospects; on our parts it was pure and disinterested, and blessed with the sincerest attachment. This continued, I may aver, to the cruel moment which separated us never to meet again. Those who frequented my house verified the same. When called upon for their evidence before the Tribunal of Justice in order to identify the person who had committed the irreparable injury, and who with the boldest effrontery had, as will be seen, denied in writing his trespass, it was evident how they sympathised in my unfortunate lot. To the question repeated by the Bench of Judges to each witness their answer was uniform: 'You were accustomed, sir, to visit at Mr. Grand's house; did you ever observe any mark of disunion between them?' 'On the contrary, my Lords, the happiest domestic union, and we remarked that the most minute and reciprocal attentions prevailed until this fatal event.'"

When Mademoiselle Werlée became Mrs. Grand,† she was about

* The marriage may be seen thus recorded, by the chaplain who officiated, in the register now existing at St. John's Church, Calcutta.

"*July*, 1777.

"Mr. Francis Grand, writer in the Hon'ble Company's service, and Miss Varlé, of Chandernagore.

"WILLIAM JOHNSON, *Chaplain*."

I am under obligation to the courtesy of M. de Lessard and of Monsieur l'Abbé Barthet for the knowledge that the original record of this marriage does not now exist at Chandernagore: the changeful times through which the French settlement passed since then will account for this.

† Her husband being an Englishman (by adoption), it was as "*Mrs.*" Grand that she was spoken of when in Calcutta. As such he always mentions her. The

three months short of fifteen years of age, having been born at the Danish Settlement of Tranquebar on the Coromandel coast, on November 21, 1761.

It is customary, especially amongst French writers, to speak of Mrs. Grand as an "Indian." Talleyrand himself writes of her as "Une Indienne bien belle," and Napoleon at St. Helena referred to her as "Anglaise ou Indienne;" Capefique in the "Biographie Universelle," speaks of her as "rare et nonchalante beauté Indienne." These allusions to her Indian origin seem intended to convey the impression that she was not directly sprung from unmixed European stock. But her enduring comeliness, which charmed long after middle life, is opposed to this, as indeed is the physical character of her beauty which contemporaries have handed down. In all probability it would be as inaccurate to designate her as an "East Indian" (in our acceptation of the word), in whose case, as a rule, when youth is gone all is gone, as it would be so to describe the offspring of European parents because born in Calcutta to-day.

All authorities agree in testifying to the extreme beauty of Mrs. Grand: in face, form, figure, and gracefulness of carriage she seems to have presented a combination quite unrivalled. But beyond this she was dowered with woman's crowning glory, a luxuriant head of hair; an attraction which has ever been found to exercise witchery over men, especially when associated, as in her case, with blonde colours. One enthusiastic French writer alludes to this special beauty of hers as "la plus belle chevelure blonde qui ait peut-être jamais existé." Have we it not on the high authority of Pope that "Fair tresses man's imperial race ensnare."

I shall have occasion further on to refer to the matured beauty of her later bloom, but the following is from the description of her in the morning of her life, given by Francis to his second wife. All that this lady tells on this subject, as said to come from Francis, must be taken with the greatest reservation; but on this point her testimony is in harmony with that from independent sources: "Mrs. Grand was at that time the most beautiful woman in Calcutta. She was tall, most elegantly formed, the stature of a nymph, a complexion of unequalled delicacy, and auburn hair of the most luxuriant profusion; fine blue eyes, with black eye-lashes and brows, gave her countenance a most piquant singularity." The writer in the *Calcutta Review*, before quoted, says that "her picture painted by Zoffany now (1844) adorns the walls of Mr. Marshman's residence at

French form, "*Madame*," by which she is now most generally alluded to, dates from the period of her European notoriety.

Serampore;" * and with a discrimination which perhaps is somewhat imaginary, he adds, "there is more of feminine softness than of strength of character in her fair countenance; the sensual prevails everywhere over the intellectual."

A painting of her by Gérard may still be seen in the Musée at Versailles. This I shall refer to again.

Such was the lady who was singled out in the social life of Calcutta for the marked attentions of Philip Francis.

To him also nature had been prodigal in her gifts. In addition to his rare mental endowments he was remarkable for an exterior described as "strikingly handsome." His contemporaries speak of his tall, erect, well-proportioned figure; his classical features; his small delicately-moulded ears and soft shapely hands, etc. Lady Francis (a very devoted witness, however) records that so noticeably good-looking was he as a young man, that when in Paris in 1766 he was alluded to as "le Bel Anglais."

His manner towards ladies is said to have been characterised by an air of easy politeness and attention marked with deferential admiration. A good idea of this may be gathered from the letters scattered through his memoirs, notably from those to the beautiful Duchess of Devonshire, to Lady Thanet, and others. "Many of his letters to women," says his biographer, "have that mixture of playfulness, humour, and sentiment which is said to be particularly captivating to them. He had also that peculiar attraction which they are sometimes apt to find in one who is feared by men, and reputed haughty and unyielding among them, but who shows himself tractable and submissive to the other sex and eager to obtain their favour."

It is evident, therefore, that he was well equipped with—

"the charms
With which a lover Golden Venus arms;
Soft moving speech and pleasing outward show
No wish can give them, but the gods bestow."

At the period to which the circumstances about to be related refer, Mr. Francis was eight and thirty years of age. His personal and other qualifications for ingratiating himself would not be worth

* Kaye seems to have been wrong about "her picture painted by Zoffany," no such portrait has come to light. The error arose from the portrait of another lady having for many years been traditionally accepted as that of Mrs. Grand. The question has been discussed at some length in the Author's pamphlet on "The Serampore Portrait," etc., etc. (1903).

mentioning; but that, in recalling the early incidents in Mrs. Grand's life, it would be unfair not to take into account some of those elements of success in what is called "gallantry," to which as a child-wife she was exposed; and such qualifications, it must be remembered, would have rather an ally than the reverse, in the disparity of years which existed in the special occasion for their employment with which we are concerned. For it is "a tale often told" that a girl's self-love in the first instance is flattered and gratified, at being selected in society, as the object of the preference and attention of a gifted and experienced man of the world; and such a man's getting into further favour is facilitated in India especially, by high official position, owing to the peculiar constitution of Anglo-Indian society.

In the diary which Francis kept in India, and in which official and social matters are mixed up with sententious brevity, we find, under date November 23, 1778—"Ball at my house; Hastings, etc., etc." There is evidence existing, as shall be seen further on, that young Mrs. Grand was at this very ball, and received marked attention from the host, which probably accelerated matters towards the climax, for next day, November 24, the entry is "Omnia vincit amor; job for Wood, the salt agent."

On the 8th of the next month, after a few lines about public business, the diary notes this pithy sentence: "At night the *diable à quatre* at the house of G. F. Grand, Esq."

Mr. Grand tells us that he lived with his "recent-acquired consort at a garden house,* a short distance from town." His recollection of the general course of the events of this night may, in the first place, be given in his own words, summarised in part. The details, necessary for the due understanding of what actually occurred, had better be left to unfold themselves in the evidence given at the subsequent trial by some of the principal witnesses—

"On December 8, 1778, I went out of my house, about nine o'clock, the happiest, as I thought myself, of men; and between eleven and twelve o'clock returned the same night to it as miserable as any being could well feel. I left it prepossessed with a sense that I was blessed with the most beautiful as well as the most virtuous of wives, ourselves honoured and respected, moving in the first circles, and having every prospect of speedy advancement. Scarcely had I sat down to supper at my benefactor, Mr. Barwell's society, who required of his friends to join him every fortnight at this convival meeting, than I was suddenly

* I regret that I have been unable to get any further clue to the locality or site of this house.

struck with the deepest anguish and pain. A servant, who was in the habit of attending Mrs. Grand, came and whispered to me that Mr. Francis was caught in my house, and secured by my jemadar (an upper servant exercising a certain authority over other servants). I rose up from table, ran to the terrace, where grief, by a flood of tears, relieved itself for a moment. I there sent for a friend out, who I requested to accompany me; but the rank of the party, and the known attachment which, I was well aware, he held to him, however he execrated his guilty action, pleaded his excuse with me."

He then appears to have set out for his own house alone, and called in his way on his friend Major Palmer (Hastings' secretary) with the view of borrowing his sword and securing his attendance, his intention being to release Francis, see him out of the premises, and there and then "measure" himself with him "until one of us fell." This programme having been agreed to by Palmer, they proceeded to put it in execution.

But on reaching Grand's house they were astonished to find, not Francis, but Mr. Shee * (afterwards Sir George Shee) held down on a chair in a lower apartment, begging of the servants to let him go, while Mr. Shore (afterwards Lord Teignmouth) and a Mr. Archdekin were alleged to be standing by joining in Mr. Shee's entreaty. The

* This gentleman appears to have been as much in Francis's official confidence as in his private. In another part of Grand's "Narrative" he tells, that when the dispute between Hastings and Clavering as to who was legally Governor-General was referred to the Judges, each member of the Government was represented at the conference of the Judges by deputy, Mr. Shee being present for Francis. The Judges were convened at Impey's house, and sat till four in the morning. Grand as an eye-witness gives an interesting account of this crisis, but, with a lapse of memory, he says he was married at the time (June 20, 1777). His marriage occurred three weeks later. Grand elsewhere says that Francis, on another occasion of historical interest, was represented by Messrs. Ducarel and Shore, who pledged themselves on his part that there would be no factious opposition to the Governor-General on Mr. Barwell's vacating his seat in Council. He here gives rather an incoherent account of the circumstances that led up to the duel following the alleged broken pledges of Francis; here also the narrator's memory is treacherous, because he says that Hastings had at this time (1780) been "deprived of his old colleague Sir Eyre Coote by death." Coote did not die until early in 1783. Shee became a Baronet in 1793. He must have been a friend of Edmund Burke's, who in a letter to his kinsman, John Burke (1777) (sent on to Francis), says, "You are happy that you have our friend Shee under the immediate protection of one who knows so well what power owes to friendship." And John Burke writes himself to Francis in 1776, "George Shee, that nephew of mine, must be with you before now. . . . I never knew so deserving a young man. I do not know a virtue which he wants nor a vice of which I can accuse him—he is my *albus gallus*.

jemadar's explanation was that he had secured Mr. Francis "to meet the vengeance of his master," until Mr. Shee and some other gentlemen had, in answer to a whistle from Mr. Francis, scaled the wall and rushed in; that a scuffle with the object of rescue had taken place, during which Mr. Francis managed to escape. Whereupon it would seem that the jemadar, deeming it prudent to retain some tangible proof of his prowess, for the satisfaction of his master, had substituted for the escaped prisoner the most prominent of his liberators.

Mr. Grand questioned the intruders, but got, he says, only evasive and unsatisfactory answers in their exculpation. He then ordered their release, and, without seeing his wife, returned himself to Major Palmer's house for the rest of the night, where—

"Seated on a chair, borne down with the deepest grief, I anxiously awaited the morning to require from the undoer of my happiness the satisfaction which the laws of honour prescribe as a poor relief for the injury committed. I wrote to Mr. Francis that, void of every spark of principle and honour as I deemed him, still I trusted he would not deny me the meeting which I summoned him to immediately with any friend whom he might choose to bring. His reply was laconic and easy. It was couched on these terms: That conscious of having done me no injury, and that I laboured under a complete mistake, he begged leave to decline the proposed invitation, and that he had the honour to remain my most obedient, etc., etc.

"I now returned home, sent for Mrs. Grand's sister and brother-in-law from Chandernagore, occupied the lower apartments of my house, whilst Mrs. Grand remained in the upper; and on the Sunday following everything was arranged for Mrs. Grand's returning with them to live under their mansion and protection, myself contributing what was requisite for her support independent of the monthly allowance which I chose to allot to her own disposal.

"An interview was entreated, and could not be denied. It lasted three hours, interrupted with the most poignant lamentations. I heard an unvarnished relation of the baseness of the arts employed for the seduction of a stranger, and attained only to her sixteenth year. I pitied her from my heart. I sincerely forgave her, and with a sorrow approaching to distraction we parted."

If what is here stated be true regarding the reception the challenge met with, as represented in the very slipshod sentence alleged to be the "terms" of Francis's answer, it is difficult to avoid viewing the latter's attitude not only with the strongest reprehension, but with contempt. On the other hand, it will be conceded that to refuse the satisfaction which, according to a social code then in vigorous existence, it was dishonourable and unmanly to shrink from, must have done more violence to a man's natural impulses than to give it.*

Francis, we know, was ready enough himself to seek personal satisfaction for any affront, and did so on at least two occasions afterwards.

Lady Francis, who was not, however, over-accurate in her reminiscences, heard from Francis that Sir R. Sutton, M.P., quoted one night in the House my Lord Chancellor Thurlow's alleged wish that the vessel carrying Clavering, Monson, and Francis had been lost at sea, and added some personal reflections on the latter. Francis sent a tremendous fire-eater to him, Captain Macnamara, R.N., who obtained a disavowal of insult, etc. Macnamara for this service got Francis to be his second in a duel which was interrupted after two shots had been exchanged and ended amicably. Macnamara afterwards fought a notorious duel with Colonel Montgomery.

Therefore, before charging him with the poltroonery which the above allegation would seem to justify, we are driven to look for

* Had Francis consented to accept Grand's challenge, no man out of Europe at the moment, or indeed in it, could have gone to the ground better assisted through the necessary formalities. He might have provided himself with an experienced second, who with congenial ardour would have seen the business carried through to the bitter end, according to the strictest canons of taste and fashion. The potential friend referred to was his terrible Irish cousin, Major Phil Baggs, who had just then arrived in Calcutta on a gambling speculation, and fresh from the glory of a duel with no less redoubtable a personage than Fighting FitzGerald. Francis, in recording his cousin's arrival in the river on the very day of the escapade at Grand's, adds in his diary the suggestive words "il ne me manquoit que cela." As soon as it came to the knowledge of the Court of Directors that this firebrand had turned his steps to India, they despatched orders that he was to be sent out of the country forthwith. Baggs fought eleven duels in his time. He once won £17,000 at hazard; he lived in great splendour at Paris for many years, presumably on his gambling skill. The *Gentleman's Magazine* in chronicling his death at seventy, remarks that "his countenance was terrible, though his manner and appearance were gentlemanlike." The following account of his most celebrated duel (1777) was written out to Francis by another cousin (Tilghman), "Since his (Baggs') return to France he has fought a desperate duel with bully FitzGerald, in which he behaved with his wonted gallantry. He wounded his antagonist in the thigh, and was himself wounded in the leg, the small bone of which was broken and forced into the 'tendo Achillis,' as the newspapers say. When he received the shot he fell; but having a pistol in reserve, and being at liberty to break ground, he crawled towards Fitz, who unable to endure the grimness of his countenance, broke ground the wrong way, and ran off at such a rate that he plainly discovered *his* tendo Achillis had received no injury. Upon this Baggs took a flying shot, but missed his mark, and so the matter ended."

some other possible explanation for his declining a hostile meeting in this case.

If there be even a grain of fact in the bushel of romance which Lady Francis (in her "Miscellaneous Recollections") has recorded in connection with this episode, it may very probably be found in a circumstance strongly dwelt on—namely, the prolonged implacability of young Mrs. Grand to her tempter's ardent entreaties. When the whole "wretched business," as Francis was wont to call it retrospectively, had long been past and gone, he always maintained that he had not then been a "successful lover," and he left it to be inferred that the extent of his transgression on the night in question was limited (legally, it may be supposed) to something far short of criminal trespass, and amounted but to intrusion. We shall see that one of the judges who heard the evidence found that there was not only no proof, but no strong presumption to the contrary.

His illicit object being, therefore, unattained, and being now likely to be put securely beyond his reach, he may possibly have reasoned that the best thing now to be done was, in the lady's interest, to firmly disclaim consciousness of having injured (in the meaning *he* evidently attached to the phrase), and so, as a last chance, to leave an opening for a possible hushing up, while the circumstances were confined to comparatively few, and to avoid, by any further action of his, the tarnishing of the lady's name by the wide dissemination of the midnight scandal, which would be the inevitable result of a duel about her.

If any calculation like this actuated him in holding back from Mr. Grand's morning invitation, he must have been rudely undeceived, when he found very soon after that his answer was simply looked upon as adding insult to injury, and as the justification in the husband's eyes for that recourse to law which ensured such a publicity to the whole affair as to put it beyond doubt that the nocturnal visit had fatally compromised a helpless woman.

On determining to carry his domestic grievance to a court of law, Mr. Grand seems not to have found it very easy to put his project for relief into execution, owing to a difficulty which surely was never felt before or since, viz. the want of a lawyer, "most of the complaisant Advocates of the Supreme Court having either being retained by him (Francis) or intimidated from acting." Passing by this reflection on a profession ever remarkable for its independence, I shall merely point out that the hindrance did not last long, and that his case was taken up by one of the most respectable members of the attorney profession.*

Mr. Grand, however, does not mention in his "Narrative" that he authorised his lawyer to ask for the most prodigious damages which were probably ever alleged in a similar case in a Court of Justice.

The following is an extract from the plaint, etc., copied by permission from the records of the Old Supreme Court of Calcutta :—

"*Pleas at Fort William before Sir Elijah Impey, Knight, and his companions, Justices of our Sovereign Lord the King of the Supreme Court of Judicature at Fort William in Bengal, of the Fourth Term, in the year of our Lord Christ one thousand seven hundred and seventy-eight.*

"G. F. Grand, Esq., by Ralph Uvedale, his attorney, complains against Philip Francis, Esq., that he, on the 8th day of December, 1778, with force and arms, on Nöel Catherine, the wife of the said G. F. Grand, made an assault, etc., etc.,† whereby he the said G. F. Grand was deprived of, and lost the help, solace, affection, comfort and counsel of his said wife.

"And also that he, the said Philip Francis, on divers other days and times between the said 8th day of December and the 21st day of the same month of December,‡ with force and arms, did, etc., etc., and other enormities to the said George Francis Grand, against the peace of our said Lord the King, to the damage of the said G. F. Grand of fifteen hundred thousand sicca rupees, and thereupon he brings his suit."

PLEA.—"And the said Philip Francis, by Samuel Tolfrey and North Naylor, comes and defends the force and injury when, etc., etc., and saith that he is in nowise guilty of the trespass above charged on him, and of this he puts himself upon the Court."

REPLICATION.—"And the said George Francis Grand doth so likewise.

* These assertions are hardly supported by certain documents filed with the record in the High Court. The writ directed to the Sheriff, J. H. Doyley, ordering him to summon Francis to appear in the Supreme Court is dated December 24, and refers to Grand as having filed his plaint of record on the 18th day of November. It is endorsed by the Sheriff as complied with and returned January, 1779. Another document shows that "G. F. Grand puts in his place Ralph Uvedale, his attorney against Philip Francis, in a plea of trespass this eighteenth day of December, 1778."

† I have used the pruning knife here; the old pleadings did not err on the side of want of fulness or detail.

‡ This part of the plaint would seem to be inconsistent with Mr. Grand's own account of the arrangements made on the day succeeding December 8.

"And now on this 7th day of January, 1779, to which day was given as well to plaintiff as to defendant to inform the Court of the premises, came the said parties by their said attorneys, and the said Justices then heard the respective allegations of the parties as justice required, and examined the truth thereof, and duly considered the evidence produced on both sides, but because the said Justices here are not yet advised to give their judgment of and upon the premises. Day therefore is given to the parties aforesaid before the said Justices until," etc., etc.

The laying of the damages at the enormous amount quoted is very suggestive of there being a prevalent idea that, even after Lord Clive's reforms, a member of the Government of India was not dependent on his official salary as a means of acquiring wealth—an idea which I believe to be wholly unfounded in the case of Francis, if gains in the slightest degree incompatible with official probity were contemplated. Elsewhere I have alluded to the extravagant rumours in connection with his card-winnings; possibly the plaintiff, or his legal advisers, may have had an eye on that fancied hoard. However this may be, fifteen hundred thousand sicca rupees were represented by, say, sixteen lacs of the rupees now current,* and then probably equivalent at a favourable exchange to £160,000 (pounds sterling).

From the time of his arrival in India up to date, Francis's high official salary had barely amounted to a quarter of this sum; and to pay the amount which the plaintiff asked as a salve to his lacerated feelings, would have swallowed up the whole of the defendant's legitimate allowances, even were he permitted to retain his Indian appointment for sixteen years instead of six.

Though but little delay occurred in putting the legal machinery in motion, still the final hearing of the suit was deferred owing to the absence of a principal witness "on whose evidence every hope of crimination rested," according to Mr. Grand. But we had better take the facts relating to this from an unexceptionable source, viz. from the notes of one of the Judges conducting the trial, Mr. Justice Hyde.

"*1st Term.*

"Monday, 18th January, 1779.

"*Present:*

"SIR E. IMPEY, SIR ROBERT CHAMBERS, AND MR. JUSTICE HYDE.

* The sicca was one-fifteenth ($\frac{1}{15}$th) more valuable than the current rupee.

"*George Francis Grand, Esq.*, versus *Philip Francis, Esq.*

"*Mr. Newman.*—This cause, which is of a particular nature, is for criminal conversation with the plaintiff's wife. We are obliged to apply for the indulgence of the Court to put off the trial of this cause, and save our notice of trial for a few days, as the Court may think fit, for the absence of a material witness. We have used our utmost endeavours to subpœna Mr. Shee, who is a very material witness, and has gone away to Chandernagore, as we suspect, purposely to avoid giving evidence in this cause, and secretes himself so carefully in Chandernagore that we have not been able to serve him with the subpœna. Mr. Shee being in the service of the Company, we propose making an application to the Governor-General, on which we hope he will be obliged to come down.

"*Impey, C. J.*—The Court have nothing to do with any application to the Governor-General and Council. When the Court see that a witness is kept out of the way, to be sure they will let you save the notice of trial, and perhaps, if it is necessary, they will let you put the trial off from time to time till the witness appears.

"We cannot help taking notice of the names of the parties, and that one of them, the defendant, is a member of the Council. When in such a cause we see a witness kept away, we can but suspect it is by his influence.

"When we see influence and power exerted to prevent appearance of a witness, it is but just to delay the trial to get at his testimony if possible.

"In England, if a witness, being subpœnaed, does not appear, the party for whom he is subpœnaed may proceed against him by action, or he may be punished by fine or imprisonment on an attachment for the contempt. I had a considerable share in advising on our Charter * with the Attorney-General, Mr. Thurlow, now Lord

* This allusion was evidently a favourite weakness of Impey's, as a year before this we find Justice Hyde thus unbosoming himself in his note-book, *à propos* of a difference of opinion between him and two of his brethren: "This is another effect of that doctrine of October or November, 1777, that although the charter allows six months for every party aggrieved to present his petition of appeal, yet Impey and Chambers, by this doctrine, take off several months from that time if the six months happen to expire in a vacation, for all the time from the last day of the preceding term is taken from the six months allowed by the Charter. Let Impey, who is continually talking of adhering to the Charter, and boasting in court almost every day of the great share he had in forming it, justify, if he can, his counteracting it in this instance."

Chancellor, and being aware that in this country influence and power to prevent witnesses from attending was likely to be exerted, I particularly advised that the coercion of their appearance might be greater than in England. If you have the Charter in Court, I believe you will find on reading it, that the Court is empowered to punish the absence of witnesses, not only by fine and imprisonment, but by punishment not extending to life or limb, which includes whipping, pillory, and the like corporal punishments.

"It is necessary for the dignity and power of this Court that no witness should be kept away."

The case was again before the Court on January 21 and 22, and on each occasion postponed owing to Mr. Shee's non-appearance.

Eventually this difficulty having been got over, we find in the above Judge's notes the date on which the actual trial commenced—

"*1st Sittings.*

"Monday, February 8, 1779.

"*Present:*

"SIR E. IMPEY, SIR R. CHAMBERS, AND MR. JUSTICE HYDE.

"*George Francis Grand, Esq.*, versus *Philip Francis, Esq.*

"An action for criminal conversation with the wife of the plaintiff.

"The damages alleged to be fifteen hundred thousand sicca rupees.

"The plaintiff is a writer in the Company's service.

"The defendant is the second of the four Counsellors (*sic*) of the Presidency of Fort William in Bengal."

Mr. Newman was Counsel for the plaintiff, and Mr. Tilghman for the defendant.*

* Richard Tilghman, who defended Francis, was his Philadelphian cousin, and, after the death of Mackrabie, his dearest friend. His letters show that he, too, like Mackrabie, was a most amusing, cheery, affectionate fellow. He studied law in England, and it was conjectured by Mr. Parkes that he supplied legal lore to Junius. His name is well known in the Junius controversy, as a quotation in a letter of his to Francis supplies evidence connecting Francis with a copy of certain complimentary verses in Tilghman's writing, which were sent to a young lady at Bath (about Christmas, 1770), accompanied by an anonymous note in the unmistakable Junian hand. While Junius was perplexing the British public, Francis wrote often to Makcrabie in America about his doings in London with Tilghman. "I am going to-night to sup at Tilman's (*sic*) chambers. He leads a pleasant sort of life, and studies the law like a dragon. His principles are truly patriotic, especially when in liquor,". When Tilghman was about to return to Philadelphia in

I shall now give at some length extracts from the evidence of the chief witnesses examined, which will not only show the extraordinary facts connected with the escapade at Mr. Grand's house on that December night, but will give us a glance at the manner and customs of the day.

*Meerun*, kitmutgar (or table-servant) examined.—The day of the disturbance was on the day when plaintiff went to sup with Mr. Gallan; * it was between ten and eleven o'clock at night. I was in my own house in the compound, sitting, when the iya (*sic*) came down and told me that her mistress wanted a candle, and that, on her returning, she had found the door locked. I went out of my house and saw a bamboo ladder; it was against the outside wall, on the inner side of it. I thought it a strange thing, and went to acquaint the jemadar of it.

Describe the ladder.—It is made of a whole bamboo split in two, and when it is closed it is like one bamboo; it has movable steps

the autumn of 1771, Francis wrote again of him: "He breakfasted with me for the last time on Wednesday. Our parting was no other than if we were to dine together the day following; yet I shall probably never see him again. I do not think that as to the choice of friends or companions it is an easy matter either to please my fancy or to satisfy my judgment. This villain succeeded in both completely, and now I ought to hate him heartily for giving me such cause of regret as will last as long as I live." When Francis got the Indian post Tilghman wrote, "By Heaven, I would follow you to Bengal with the greatest pleasure." He went to India at Francis's invitation, and arrived in November, 1777; he first got called to the Irish Bar. In December, 1778, a despatch from the Court of Directors shows that he was nominated to a writership in the Bengal Presidency (with John Belli and thirteen others), but he does not seem to have taken up the appointment. He returned to England with Francis in 1780, and must have been invaluable in helping to relieve the tedium of a ten months' voyage. He started for Calcutta again in January, 1785, bearing a letter to Mr. Wheler from Francis: "Poor Tilghman is to deliver you this. I pray you, my friend, to serve him if you can. I have no other object now in life very deeply at heart." Long before he arrived in Calcutta Wheler's death was known in England, and Francis wrote out to say that he would still watch over his interests. "If you keep your health I have no doubt of your success. If not, come away directly. Better live anywhere than die in Bengal." Poor Tilghman tried to act on this advice, and left Bengal, but died on the voyage home in January, 1786, aged 39. Before his death was known his father was written to by a friend in London to say that it was in contemplation to appoint his son Advocate-General at Calcutta in room of Sir John Day, Warren Hastings, to his everlasting honour, having told the Directors that this intimate friend of Francis (then intriguing against himself) was the fittest person for the office.

* This evidence, which is supported by that of other witnesses, shows that Grand's memory was at fault as to the scene of the supper. Mr. Le Gallais' house was the one testified to.

to it inside, and has iron points to it. The jemadar was also surprised to see the ladder. While we were talking, a gentleman came out of the house, whom I recognised as Mr. Francis, the Counsellor, who lived behind the play-house. He is tall. I knew him, because Mr. Grand was often at meals at Mr. Francis's, and I attended him there. When Mr. Francis came out, he said, "Give me that thing" (the ladder). "I will give you money. I'll make you great men." He spoke to the jemadar and all the servants. He also said, "Don't you know that I am Mr. Francis?"

What language did Mr. Francis speak?—The same as I do, in broken Moors. Not so well as you (to the interpreter). The jemadar took hold of Mr. Francis's hand and said, "My master is not here, what do *you* do here?" While the jemadar was carrying Mr. Francis into the house, Mrs. Grand said something to him, which I did not understand. After Mr. Francis was taken into the lower part of the house I went to acquaint Mr. Grand.

Between the time of the ayah's coming down to tell you of her having been up with a candle and had found the door locked, to the time of your seeing the gentleman coming out of the house, what time elapsed?—One or two Hindustani ghurries* it might be.

When did you see defendant come out?—Between ten and eleven o'clock (English hours).

*Cross-examined.*—You say that in passing by the wall you saw a man coming out of the door; what time was it between your first seeing the ladder and that time?—I cannot say the time.

Have you not mentioned the time before?—I told you about one ghurry or two.

Do you mean a Bengal ghurry or two?—I can't say exactly.

*By the Chief Justice.*—Was the conversation you have related at the ladder the only conversation that passed?—I was sent away. I was not there. I heard no more.

Did you know Mr. Francis before he told you who he was?—I knew defendant before he told me.

Did he go quietly with the jemadar or make resistance?—Defendant made no resistance.

Did you not swear before Mr. Justice Hyde that the time between your seeing the ladder and the gentleman coming was a quarter of a ghurry?—I had no watch that I could know the distance of time exactly.

Did you not mention a quarter of a ghurry before Mr. Justice

* A ghurry is a period of time equivalent to about twenty minutes.

Hyde to what you now say one or two ghurries?—I was not exact to the time.

Did you or did you not swear so before Mr. Justice Hyde?—It certainly took up time.

Will you swear that it was more than a quarter of a Bengal ghurry?—I did not see the gentleman go into the house, therefore I can't say; it was undoubtedly more than a quarter Bengal ghurry.

*Sheik Ruzullah* (durwan or door-keeper) examined.—Locked the door when Mr. Grand went out to sup at Le Gallais, and kept the key; only opened the door for those servants who waited on his master at meals, during the latter's absence that night; opened it to no English gentleman 'till his master came with some that night.

*To the Chief Justice.*—Knew of no gentleman coming over the wall; heard no whistling.

*Bowanny* (hurcarah or messenger) examined.—Has been in plaintiff's service two years; knew defendant by his stature and voice.

You say when they laid hold of defendant you also did so; at what place was it?—It was at the back of the house, near the steps at the back of the house leading to the hookaburdar's house.

Did defendant do or say anything at the time when you went with the other two?—Yes, he spoke to Mrs. Grand, who was standing upstairs.

What did he speak to Mrs. Grand?—Defendant spoke in his own language. I did not understand.

Did defendant say anything to you, or Meerun, or the jemadar? —Defendant said to the jemadar that he would make him a great man, and put his hand in his pocket and took out gold mohurs.

(In further answers says)—When we were leading defendant from the place where we laid hold of him, and were carrying him opposite to the front door, the jemadar sent Meerun to acquaint Mr. Grand, after this defendant again offered presents to jemadar; took defendant to the front of the door, when Mrs. Grand came down and told him to let defendant go; jemadar replied, "I will not hear you, you may go to your room." We kept defendant opposite to the door of the house; we made him sit down in the house, in the part that leads to the upper part; there is a lanthern there and a staircase.

*Rambux* (jemadar, or chief over the servants) examined.—Do you remember the disturbance that happened at plaintiff's house in December last?—Yes, I remember it.

What was the first knowledge you had of it?—Meerun asked me where I had been. I told him I was just come from abroad; I went with Meerun; he carried me and showed me a ladder.

Where was the ladder at the time?—It was fixed at the inside of the wall where Mr. Grand lives in a red house.

About what time of night was it when you first received the information from Meerun?—About ten o'clock or eleven; it will be past eleven o'clock.

Do you remember the day of the week?—A Tuesday.

What did you do on the discovery of the ladder?—I took it away.

Why did you take it away?—I did not know whose ladder it was, therefore I took it away.

Have you seen the ladder here to-day?—I have; that is the same ladder.

Was anything done by you after removing the ladder?—I was standing at the same place near the necessary house, waiting to see whether the person who brought the ladder would come there or not.

Did you see any person come?—Yes, I saw a gentleman.

Who was that gentleman?—It was Mr. Francis.

What Mr. Francis?—Mr. Francis the Counsellor (*sic*).

That was about eleven o'clock at night. How could you distinguish that it was Mr. Francis?—I knew him by his face and shape.

Was it sufficiently light to distinguish his face?—I went near his face and looked. When he was at a little distance I did not know; when I was near I knew him.

Did you know before any conversation passed between you and him?—Yes, but before the conversation I did not know him very well.

What led you particularly to know him after the conversation you had with him?—By his figure, his face, and his colour.

By anything else?—That gentleman was in black.

You say defendant came to the place where the ladder was; from whence did he come?—He came downstairs and then stood at the place where the abdar's chest was.

How do you know that he did so?—There was a great alarm at the house.

(Here followed several questions about the topography of the house, which went to elicit that on one side in the lower part was a hall or passage, off which four doors opened; the western one led into Mr. Grand's room, which again looked towards Mr. Ducarel's house. Defendant seems to have descended into Grand's lower room, and emerged thence into the hall and stood for a while at the abdar's chest on the opposite side of the hall.

When the defendant came downstairs what passed between you and him?—I went up to that gentleman and said to him, "What business have you here?" He said, "Give me my thing." He asked for the ladder, he had no other thing of his at that house but the ladder; therefore he must mean that; he came out and was looking, and as he had not found the ladder there he could not go. Then he said, "Give me my thing."

Give us an account of what passed between you when he looked about and asked for his thing.—The first words he said to me when I went up to him were, "Give me my thing." I then answered, "I have not that thing with me;" I then took hold of his hand; then he took out gold mohurs and offered to give them me; I refused them; he said, "Take that (offering both his hands to me). I will make you great men, and I will give you a hundred gold mohurs more."

Had you done anything, previous to the offer being made, to prevent his going away?—I stood on the side where the ladder was; he wanted to go that way, and I prevented him.

Why did you lay hold of defendant's hand?—Because I found that gentleman in the house. Certainly, if I had let him go my master would take my life away. After the offer of the money, he further said, "Do you not know me?" I answered, "Yes, I do; you are Mr. Francis." He said, "I am the Burra Sahib; I am Mr. Francis." When I first took hold of his hand he twisted it a little. I then said, "Is there nobody here? Seize him." Meerun and Bowanny (hurkara) * seized him and brought him down from the steps which lead from the abdar's † chest to the compound. I then sent Meerun to acquaint Mr. Grand. When I was going to take the gentleman to the lower part of the house (*i.e.* apparently across to the other side of the house), he whistled four or five times; as I led him from the east side to the western, he whistled five to seven times. When I carried him opposite to the door, some conversation passed with my mistress.

Where was your mistress?—She came and desired me to let him go: she came near me and told me so. I had then hold of Mr. Francis. I said, "I have sent people to acquaint my master: I will not attend to you."

What did you then do with the defendant?—I desired my

* *Hurkara* as used here means "messenger."

† The *abdar* is the servant in charge of wine, liquor, etc., whose chief function is to keep them cool for drinking.

mistress to go upstairs, and said to her, "I will not obey you." I then led the gentleman towards the northern door. I gave him a chair to sit down.

After the defendant was seated in the chair what was done?—I made him sit down in the chair, and then I put my hands on the arms of the chair to keep him there.

What more passed?—I heard a great noise at the outside door; they were using force; there are two gateways of the compound, one always remained locked—the northern gate; bearers were near me, and a syce; I told them to go to the doors, to let nobody in. I am not certain whether there were one or two syces there. On the side where I first seized Mr. Francis two gentlemen came, Mr. Shee and Mr. Ducarel; they scaled the wall. After I had made Mr. Francis sit in the chair, those two gentlemen came in and broke open the door of the house (room?) where my master used to write; this was in the lower part of the hall where Mr. Francis was. As soon as Mr. Francis heard this noise he got up from his seat. I then endeavoured to keep him in his seat; he was going to that part where the gentlemen came; in that room it was dark. Those gentlemen shoved me and pushed me; I am not certain whether Mr. Francis fell, but I am certain I fell on the chair. When I kept both my hands on the chair nobody was with me, the servants were at the door. When I fell on the chair I called to those servants who were at the door. When I fell Mr. Francis escaped out of my hands, and then I called to the servants. When I recovered myself I got up; it was dark; I seized a gentleman, a Mr. Shee; I did not then know whether it was Mr. Francis or not at first; afterwards I found Mr. Francis had escaped. The bearer and the syce, when they returned, came to the place where I was, and laid hold of Mr. Ducarel. I took hold of Mr. Shee and carried him up. The bearer and syce took Mr. Ducarel out. Mr. Keble was standing on his own house looking, and asked, "What is the matter?" The bearer and syce said to Mr. Keble, "These gentlemen came into the house when my master was out."

Did Mr. Francis say anything of what would happen in case Mr. Grand came home while he was there?—When he wanted to go I refused to let him go; I said, "My master will hang me if I let you go." Mr. Francis said, "Sooner than he shall kill you, *I* will die."

*Witness continues.*—Mr. Keble then came near the wall. Whether there was a heap of dirt or a chair on the wall I don't know; Mr. Keble was standing on the outside talking to Mr.

Ducarel. Mr. Keble said, "Give me that gentleman" (meaning Mr. Ducarel). The bearer and syce refused to comply with Mr. Keble's demands. I was at a little distance from Mr. Ducarel with Mr. Shee; Mr. Ducarel was in the hands of the bearer and syce. I said to Mr. Keble, "If you desire it, take Mr. Ducarel away." I did not know at first whether it was Mr. Ducarel or not; afterwards I found it was him. Mr. Ducarel had already given his hand to Mr. Keble; the bearers prevented him. When I saw it was Mr. Ducarel I put my hand and helped him up; afterwards Mr. Keble again desired me to give up Mr. Shee, and said, "I shall be answerable for him." I refused; I said I would not. Four or five times Mr. Keble desired me to deliver Mr. Shee, and that he would be answerable. I refused.

After this Mr. Grand and Mr. Palmer came in. I desired the bearers to open the door. Mr. Grand came and told me to let Mr. Shee go. I did so.

Did you get any money?—Yes, three gold mohurs from Mr. Shee. He gave them that I might let him go, and he promised to give me more.

What hat is that you have in your hand?—I found it in the house. I don't know to whom it belonged.

You say Mrs. Grand desired you to let Mr. Francis go. Previous to that, had you seen Mrs. Grand?—No, I had not.

From the time you first surveyed the ladder to the time you seized Mr. Francis, what time elapsed?—It might be less than one ghurry, or half a ghurry.

About what time of night was it that you first saw Mr. Francis come out?—It was about 11 o'clock. I did not hear the clock strike.

*Cross-examined.*—You say you seized Mr. Francis by the hand. Did you hold his hand from the time you first saw him till he got out of the chair?—No. It was after he offered me gold mohurs that I laid hold of his hand.

Then you had him not by the hand before he offered the mohurs?—No.

You say Mrs. Grand desired you to let Mr. Francis go. What language did she speak?—She spoke Hindustani. She said, "Jemadar, choredo, choredo."

This was a dark night, was it not?—The moon was coming out; it was not quite up.

How can you tell what money the gentleman offered you?—By the jingling I knew them to be gold mohurs.

Tell me the difference between the jingling of gold mohurs and rupees?—Undoubtedly there is a difference.

What difference?—Gold mohurs have a light sound, rupees a dull sound.

*By the Chief Justice.*—Was the whistling before or after Meerun went to call his master?—After Meerun was gone.

Was there any conversation between Mr. Shee and Mr. Francis while you had hold of Mr. Francis?—No.

Was there between Mr. Ducarel and Mr. Francis?—No; there was only running about. I did not hear any conversation while I was there, and when I got up Mr. Francis was gone away. I heard no conversation.

*By Mr. Justice Hyde.*—Where was the hat found?—In the hall below, where I had the fall.

*Anna Lagoorda examined.*—About half an hour past nine o'clock Mr. Grand left Mrs. Grand at home, and went abroad. I desired my mistress to undress, to which she replied, "Mr. Grand will return home about eleven o'clock; until that time I will sit up." She then desired me to sit by her. I then asked leave to go and fetch some betel-nut; as I was going to fetch it, Mrs. Grand ran after me saying, "Nana-jee, fetch a whole candle." I was then upstairs going to another room.

Was you going to or in that room?—I was *in* the room when Mrs. Grand came running to me; I accordingly went down to bring a candle. When I returned with it I found the door of the room from whence I went out locked.

What room was that that was locked?—It was the room where I was cutting betel-nut.

At the time you went for the candle where did you leave Mrs. Grand?—I left her in the same room where I was cutting betel-nut.

Describe how these three rooms are situated.—There are three rooms in one row, the rooms open into one another.

When you returned with the candle did you see Mrs. Grand?—No, she was in the room; the door was locked.

Did you make any and what attempt to get into that room with the candle?—I attempted to open it, but could not. I imagined Mrs. Grand was angry with me.

(*Here several questions were put as to the intercommunication between the rooms and a hall into which two of these rooms opened.*)

For what purpose were these rooms used?—The middle room was the bed-chamber; on each side there was a room.

For what use was that room where you went to eat the betel-nut? —I lived in the room into which I went to eat my betel.

To what use was the third room applied on the other side of the bed-chamber?—It was Mrs. Grand's dressing-room; in the dressing room there was a cot and likewise a couch; in the bed-chamber there were only Mrs. Grand's cot and a few chairs. Besides the hall there was a small verandah on each side.

How long were you in getting the candle?—About a quarter of an hour.

When you returned with the candle and could not get in, what did you do?—I came below stairs; I sat in the jemadar's house, imagining she was angry with me.

When you found you could not open the door did you make any noise?—I did call, "Madam, Madam," two or three times.

Did you receive no answer?—I imagined she was in the dressing-room, and therefore could not hear.

Upon your going down did you see any of the plaintiff's servants? —No, nobody was there.

Did you in the yard give information to any person of what passed upstairs?—Yes. Mr. Grand's servant, Meerun, asked me if my mistress was gone to sleep. I said, "No;" I imagined she was either angry with me or was afraid. I went below to get a candle, and when I returned I found the door locked. Meerun went out into the compound and walked about, and he saw a ladder

Did you see any person seized?—Yes, I saw a gentleman there in the possession of Mr. Grand's servants at a distance. I ran up and called Mrs. Grand, and acquainted her of a gentleman having been taken up by the servants.

Who opened the door?—On my calling Mrs. Grand the door was opened (*sic*).

On your giving information to your mistress, what did she do?—Mrs. Grand went out into the verandah and looked downwards. I went downstairs, and did not go up again.

Did you at that time hear any conversation between that gentleman and your mistress when she came into the verandah?—No, I did not.

Did you after that night see your mistress downstairs?—No, I did not; after the troubles were over I came and found Mrs. Grand upstairs.

Mr. Grand went out every Tuesday night. When he was gone from home did your mistress read, or in what manner did she dispose of herself?—Sometimes she read, sometimes she played with me, and went to bed at eleven o'clock.

The night preceding these troubles had your mistress been out?—Yes, she went to a ball.

Do you know at what time Mrs. Grand came home from the ball?—About four in the morning on the Tuesday.

*By the Chief Justice.*—After you found the door locked and went down again, where did you stay when you heard the gentleman seized in the compound?—There is a horse stable, where three or four women lived; I was with them.

*Mr. Gerard Gustavus Ducarel* examined.*—Was at Mr. Grand's house on the 8th December.

On what occasion did you go there?—I was called by Mr. Shee; I was asleep in my bed; Mr. Shee came to my bedside, awaked me, and desired me to get up immediately, as Mr. Francis was likely to be murdered; that there was no time to lose: upon which I got out of bed immediately, and without putting on any clothes more than I lay in, went out into my own hall, where he asked me if there was anybody else in the house—if there was, to call him. I answered, Mr. Shore was, and knocked at his door and desired him to get up. Mr. Shee asked me if I could get at any sword or weapon; I don't recollect making him any answer. Mr. Shee told me that Mr. Francis was seized in Mr. Grand's house: we both pushed at the gate to

* Ducarel apparently was not the style of auxiliary (physically speaking) whom a judicious man would select to stand by him in an expected "encounter" against superior numbers. According to Francis he cannot have been far removed from a dwarf. He accompanied Francis on a visit to Paris in 1784, and is thus alluded to in a letter to Mrs. Francis: "Ducarel has found his uncle and aunt, or rather they have found him. He was forced to get on a chair to put his arm round his uncle's neck; and he has worn my blue box to rags to keep his feet from dangling in the chaise. And so, 'Ma chère moitié' je vous embrasse." His name occurs several times in Francis's letters from England to India. In one to Shee, he says, "Ducarel lives a hundred miles off in perfect obscurity."

Blackwood for 1868 is responsible for this anecdote about him. Francis received a letter from him from Bath, expressing doubts as to the soundness of the views that both had held as to the immortality or otherwise of the soul of man, and desiring to know whether Francis still retained his former opinions.

The following is said to be Francis's unceremonious answer: "You d——d old fool. Have not you and I exhausted every argument that could be used over and over again in India on the subject referred to in your letter? and were we not invariably and logically led to the same conclusion? Now, however, I do entertain some doubts in regard to the soundness of our conclusion, and I will tell you why.

"I went yesterday to see Mother Bainbrigg hanged. She died without a struggle. I said to myself, as I beheld her swing, 'You monster, there must be something more than this in store for you.' Possibly, therefore, we may be wrong after all; the soul may be immortal."

endeavour to get in, but found we could not open. Mr. Shee then went a little way from the gate to a long ditch without the wall, crossed the ditch, got up on the wall, and called to me to follow him, which I did, and got upon the wall likewise; after which we jumped down into the compound and went in at a door leading into the lower hall. As soon as I got into the lower hall, I saw a person sitting in a chair either at the further end of the hall or in the little passage that leads out of it on the opposite side; some other person was standing near him. Almost at the same instant that I entered the hall he started up from his chair and ran towards the door that I had come in at; in his way he struck against something with a good deal of violence; after that I saw no more of him, for almost immediately some of the servants came up and seized me, telling me I had caused the person to run away, and that they were determined to seize me. I struggled with them a little, but found it to no purpose, except that of getting from the hall to the outer door, where I saw that Mr. Shee was likewise seized. I expostulated with the people to let me go, but to no manner of purpose, until Mr. Keble called out from the verandah of his house adjoining to know what was the reason of the disturbance.

You say when you came in at the door leading to the house, you saw a person sitting in a chair, and some other people; could you distinguish who it was?—I could not.

*George Shee examined.*—In answer to questions states that, fearing evil consequences and failing to dissuade Mr. Francis (who told him of his intention) from going to Mr. Grand's house, he determined to prevent any evil that might ensue: that he followed Francis towards plaintiff's house, and walked about in the street and sometimes to a distance, going to and fro: saw a man come out and heard whistling; saw Mrs. Grand in the verandah above stairs, and discovered from her that there was a disturbance in the hall; she mentioned no name. Tried to get in by himself, first by persuading the jemadar to open the compound gate; then endeavoured by himself to force the gate, but failed; then it occurred to him to go over to Mr. Ducarel's house. Having ultimately got in, he (Mr. Shee) rushed upon the jemadar and "threw him on the ground;" after being exhausted by his tussle with the jemadar, he was himself in turn seized and thrown down by a peon.

"I think it necessary here," he adds, "to declare in contradiction to what has been said, that neither the plaintiff nor Captain Palmer ever used abusive language to me personally." There were several gentlemen present all the time plaintiff was there—Mr. Shore, Mr.

Ducarel, Captain Palmer and Mr. Keble. Nothing material passed in the house afterwards that he can recollect. He first heard of Francis's intention to go to Mr. Grand's house in conversation with defendant the day before, and again at six o'clock on the particular day.

For what purpose did defendant mention he was going?—To see Mrs. Grand.

Was any name mentioned? was Mrs. Grand's name mentioned? —It was.

If you can challenge your memory, will you acquaint the Court what was mentioned, what more than Mrs. Grand's name?—I believe it was that he (defendant) would go and see Mrs. Grand on Tuesday.

Did you understand from defendant that Mrs. Grand had any knowledge of his intention?—No, I did not.

Do you know why Tuesday night was fixed on?—I believe it was because plaintiff was going to the club.

Do you say this from anything defendant said?—It was derived from the tenor of his conversation.

If you say, sir, you derive your knowledge from Mr. Francis's conversation, what was it?—It was from defendant's saying that he meant to go to plaintiff's house while plaintiff was at the club.

Do you know at what time the members of that club meet?—I know nothing of the club.

At what time did defendant come to your house?—About ten o'clock.

Who was with defendant when he came?—Nobody.

How did he come?—He walked.

Was his usual sowary * with him?—No.

For what purpose did defendant come to your house?—To change his dress.

In what dress did he come?—His usual dress.

What did he put on?—Black clothes.

Do you mean a complete suit of black clothes?—I cannot exactly tell; he put a black coat on.

Do you know whose clothes they were?—Defendant's.

* *I.e.* retinue, or the customary attendants; in this sense it would imply even palanquin bearers. A lady who has given an account of Calcutta social life at this period says with reference to this subject "palanquins are indeed such state appendages that if a gentleman at Calcutta, which is frequently the case, chooses to walk when on a visiting party, his palanquin must follow him in the same form in every particular as if he himself was within, a departure therefrom being deemed a solecism in polite etiquette." ("Hartly House.")

How came they to be in your house?—He sent them there.

About what time?—I do not recollect.

Was it usual for him to keep any suits of clothes at your house?—No, sir.

Can you say how many days these clothes were at your house before this?—Several days before.

Did defendant tell you why he did so?—The purpose for sending the clothes was, I understand, for defendant to wear them when he went to see Mrs. Grand.

Do you know why defendant put on black clothes that night?—I believe it was because a man in black clothes is less exposed to view at night, less liable to be seen.

You dissuaded defendant from going; you then knew the purpose for which he was going?—I thought defendant was going at an unseasonable hour, and therefore I dissuaded him.

Do you know for what purpose defendant went?—Defendant did not tell me for what purpose he was going.

If defendant did not tell you directly, was anything said by him to lead you to form a judgment?—Defendant told me he was going to Mrs. Grand's. I formed my own conclusion.

From what was the danger to arise from defendant going to plaintiff's house?—I thought should plaintiff return at that unseason-hour and find defendant in his house, very dangerous consequences might ensue.

Merely from a civil visit did you suppose that danger would ensue?—I did not say a civil visit.

It was from your own conclusion that you supposed the danger?—It was.

When defendant quitted your house to go to Mrs. Grand's, who went with him?—Nobody.

How soon did you follow him?—Shortly after; I suppose in a very few minutes.

And when did you next see defendant?—I set out on foot and walked towards plaintiff's house, and I went to the house, where I saw a man in black who I supposed to be defendant; I then went up a little lane, and when I returned again defendant was not there.

From the corner of the wall did you see where defendant was?—I walked up the lane; when I returned defendant was not there.

There was a small ladder produced in court here. Have you seen that before?—I have, sir.

When did you last see it before to-day?—I saw it at plaintiff's house. I believe I saw it.

When did you first see it? I saw it first in the hands of a black carpenter several days before.

Do you know that carpenter?—No, I do not.

Where was that black carpenter at the time?—I saw it in the yard where the carpenter was working.

Where was that?—In my yard. Defendant told me that he would take it as a particular favour if I would get a ladder made for him. He did not tell me the use of it, nor did I care what use he put it to.

After the ladder was made what became of it?—It remained in my compound.

By whom was it taken away?—By defendant.

When?—At that night; defendant carried it that night to plaintiff's house, I suppose, as I saw it there afterwards in plaintiff's hands.

From the time you left defendant at the corner of the wall to the time when you saw him in plaintiff's house, what time do you think elapsed?—I believe it must have been upwards of an hour.

Did you by any means know when plaintiff went to the club? —No.

When you first saw defendant in the house where was he?—He was sitting in a chair.

Was any violence offered to him?—A man was holding him in the chair.

Did you apprehend his life was in danger? Not from those people, but if plaintiff came in.

It has been in evidence that when you were seized you offered the jemadar money to release you?—Yes, I did, sir. Finding myself pressed, I offered, amongst other expedients, three gold mohurs.

Were you present in the room in your own house when defendant changed his clothes?—I was.

Had defendant any money in his pocket?—He had silver rupees. I did not see any gold mohurs.

What quantity do you suppose there were?—About fifteen or twenty rupees.

Is it very usual for gentlemen in general to carry money about them in this country?—I don't know that it is, sir.

Do you yourself, sir?—Very often.

Have you any now, sir, about you?—I have not, sir.

Do you know Mrs. Grand?—Very well, sir.

Do you know about the time she came to the Settlement, after her marriage?—About a year or two ago.

Do you know where she now is?—I was told she is at Chandernagore.

Did you see her on your way down?—I did not.

Does Mrs. Grand speak English?—Not generally, perhaps one word.

Does defendant talk French?—He does, sir, fluently.

Witness visited at her house and saw her often at balls, etc., knew that for ten or twelve months back defendant took particular notice of her; has known him hand her to table even when ladies were present whose husbands were of higher rank.

In the month of November last defendant gave a ball at which plaintiff and Mrs. Grand were present?—Yes, sir.

You of course were present; were there any ladies of higher rank than Mrs. Grand there?—There were many.

Do you recollect any particular marks of attention paid by defendant to Mrs. Grand?—He danced a country dance with her.

Did he dance with any other ladies?—I don't recollect.

Did you not sit at either of the tables where defendant sat or where Mrs. Grand sat?—I do not believe I did.

Did defendant get up during supper-time to go from her table?—I was engaged attending another lady, and did not observe.

Are you appointed to any place out of Calcutta?—I am appointed to Chandernagore.

Soon after the transaction which is the cause of this action, search was made after you. Were you then at Chandernagore?—I was not.

Had defendant a knowledge of your absence from Chandernagore?—He did not know it.

When did you quit Calcutta after the transaction at plaintiff's house?—I quitted Calcutta the last of December.

Will you say what induced you to quit Calcutta?—My friends advised it.

Was defendant one of those friends?—He was.

Did defendant know the place where you were going?—He did.

Where did you go?—I went to Purnea.

At whose desire did you return?—At defendant's desire.

In what manner did you receive the wish of defendant?—By a line from him.

At what time did you receive the letter?—I received it about the 27th of last month.

Previous to your departure had you any knowledge of this action being brought?—I heard there was an action to be brought.

From whom had you this knowledge?—I heard from defendant that it was to be brought.

*By the Chief Justice.*—I hear you were a good deal about defendant. Did you, sir, from your living with Mr. Francis, observe any particular attention paid by defendant to Mrs. Grand?—A very great partiality.

Who gave directions to make the ladder?—I gave directions.

You were apprehensive from defendant's going to Mrs. Grand's house; do you not think that it would have been better avoided by not letting him shift at your house?—I could not prevent him.

Why did you give the assistance for the ladder?—Mr. Francis requested me, and I could not refuse him any request that I did not think dishonourable.

When a person is going to the house of a man's wife in his absence, to see his wife at that hour of the night, and you apprehend that if he (the husband) comes home, dangerous consequences would happen, do you think it honourable to give that person assistance?—I did not think it lending assistance; it has been propagated in Calcutta that I have sent messages from defendant to Mrs. Grand. I now take this opportunity of declaring upon my oath that I never, directly or indirectly, carried any message, verbal or written, from defendant to Mrs. Grand or Mrs. Grand to defendant.

I shall ask no more questions, as I see we shall not agree upon the point of honour, for I confined honour to morality.

*Simeon Droze examined.*—Do you remember about the time when plaintiff was married did you hold any office there?—My name was made use of as one of the guardians. I was not present at the marriage.

Do you know Mrs. Grand's age?—I really do not know.

About what age was she when she came to the Settlement?—I have heard about sixteen, and from her appearance I supposed so.

Witness further deposed to the marriage—knew them to be a happy couple—frequently saw Mrs. Grand at public places and at the Harmonic.

*By the Chief Justice.*—Has plaintiff had any children?—No, not that I hear of.

*Robert Sanderson examined.*—Has known the plaintiff and his wife since their marriage; they lived in his house with him for ten months.

You have then, sir, had occasion to observe how they lived together, whether in a happy state or otherwise?—As much as I ever knew a married couple, during the time they were in my house. They went to Chandernagore, and afterwards an event* happened in my family which prevented my visiting anybody.

Are you acquainted with Mr. Grand's rank in life?—I know he is a Company's servant, and has an office in the Board of Trade.

You have heard what has been given in evidence in this action. Have you since that seen Mr. Grand?—I have.

In what condition was he?—As miserable as a man could be.

Of what period of time are you now speaking?—Of the first time that I saw him after this cruel affair.

Do you know what has occasioned their separation?—This affair, which has been given in evidence.

You say you saw Mr. Grand after this transaction happened; to what do you impute his miserable state?—From the behaviour of Mr. Francis on this occasion.

*Cross-examined.*—You say you apprehend Mr. Grand's miserable state to be owing to Mr. Francis's behaviour to Mr. Grand's wife; explain, do you mean any that passed under your own eye or his supposed behaviour?—From his supposed behaviour.

Having gone through the sworn testimony of the eye-witnesses to this night's work, the readers, who wish to see a wonderful instance of woman's credulity, should turn to the account which Lady Francis has given as her version of the story; much of it has been reproduced in a condensed and somewhat paraphrased form in the second volume of Francis's "Memoirs," to which I must refer the curious. For the benefit of those not within reach of the book, I may briefly mention a few of the circumstances that they will be surprised to hear, viz. that poor Mrs. Grand was married to a worthless old Frenchman who treated her very badly, and who looked out for some means of paying off his heavy card losses by blackmailing some rich man whose visits were encouraged. That Francis's sorrow for this ill-matched beauty melted into love, which was fanned into such passionate despair by the steady rejection of his overtures, that he fell into a fever, which lasted exactly six months. Pity now so moved the lady that she consented to one stolen interview. Where (like Antonio in Massinger's play, it may be supposed, "In the best language his true tongue could tell him, and all the broken sighs his sick heart lend him,") Francis was in vain pleading his suit when he was rudely set upon by a band of armed "ruffians" (purposely placed

* He refers to the death of his daughter, Mrs. Barwell.

ready by Grand, who had got wind of the intended meeting), who, having first cunningly got possession of the lover's sword (fortunately for themselves), held him down in a chair, while the outraged husband called for a weapon to take the prisoner's life. Meantime the hapless lady, from the window of the room into which they had locked her, called out in fluent English, "For God's sake, come! they are murdering him." The *Deus ex machina*, who obeyed this summons, was the faithful little Ducarel, who "very resolutely rushed into the house" and sword in hand fell upon "the gang." Francis, on seeing his friend, "threw off those about him, who were glad to take refuge in flight, and the two adventurers made an orderly retreat."

*O sancta simplicitas!* The admiring and devoted wife who left this pyramid of sentimental fiction on record professed to have got the materials from Francis himself. Truly there *is* a charity that believeth all things and thinketh no evil.

Francis was not much given to recording his defeats. Yet he did make a note of this one in his diary, viz. "March 6: Judgment against me in the Supreme Court."

Turning again to the notes of the industriously accurate Justice Hyde, we find what amount the judgment was for, viz.—

"In the 2nd Term, 1779, on Saturday, March 6: Judgment was pronounced for the plaintiff. Damages, fifty thousand sicca rupees."

Then his Lordship adds, probably with some satisfaction, "50,000 sicca rupees are equal to five thousand one hundred and nine pounds, two shillings and eleven pence sterling, reckoning according to the weight and fineness of the silver."

"Mr. Justice Chambers was of opinion it was not proved the defendant had committed adultery; and therefore there ought to be judgment for the defendant."

Unfortunately, we are not able to give *verbatim* the judgment of the majority of the Court, as the volume in which Justice Hyde says that he has recorded this and the evidence and arguments is not now forthcoming;* but a copy of the dissenting Judge's opinion is in existence, having been printed by Hicky, in his newspaper, two months after Francis left India, and apparently with the object of making light of the charge, as the damages are airily mentioned as a "moderate sum," in comparison, we presume, with what might have been, if Francis's persecutors had had their way, viz.—

* In the short memoir of Sir R. Chambers by his widow, an extract from his will is given, from which it appears that some note-books (about twelve in number) were bequeathed to him by his Brother Hyde. These ought to contain valuable and curious information, if still in existence.

"*Sir Robert Chambers's opinion or protest in the cause of Grand* versus *Francis.*

"I am fully of opinion that the charge in the plaint is not proved:

"1st.—Because it appears to me that there is no proof, either positive or circumstantial, that Mrs. Grand knew of, or previously consented to, his (Mr. Francis's) coming for any purpose, much less for the purpose of adultery.

"2nd.—Because there is no proof, either direct or founded on violent presumption, that they were actually together, much less was there any proof that they committed any crime together.

"3rd.—Because the evidence appears to me to fall short of what is ordinarily considered as proof of any fact, and especially of any crime.

"4th.—Because it falls exceedingly short of what our Common Law considers as proof of adultery.

"And lastly, because I have never read or heard of any action for *crim. con.* in which a verdict has been given for the plaintiff on such presumptions of guilt." *

To this opinion Mr. Hicky subjoins the following *nota bene*:—

"Sir Robert Chambers held the distinguished post of Vinerian Professor at Oxford, when he was appointed a Judge at the Supreme Court; and Sir Elijah Impey was Council (*sic*) on the side of His Royal Highness the Duke of Cumberland and Lady Grosvenor in that memorable *crim. con.* affair.† Hudibras observes—

"'What shall we say when Doctors disagree,
And soundest Casuists doubt like you and me!'"

He then adds, with glib familiarity—

"In legislation, Heliogabalus, though a sad dog, instituted one very favourable and just law, which was the establishing a female jurisdiction to sit in judgment upon all trials relative to the sex."

* Sir James Stephen ("Nuncomar and Impey," vol. ii. p. 112), judging of course only from the evidence brought forward in my account of the trial, thinks Impey (and Hyde) wrong; and that the damages awarded were exorbitant for a mere trespass with intent to seduce.

† Tried before Lord Mansfield, July, 1770. Junius attacked the charge to the jury. Lord Campbell says that the bad law of the judge was soon forgotten amid the ridicule excited by the correspondence of the lovers. Horace Walpole wrote that, except a few oaths in the lady's, the letters of the R.H. were quite inferior in grammar, spelling, and style, being those of a cabin boy. One of them began, "Here I am all by myself at see."

In the face of the above very decided opinion of Justice Chambers, and of Justice Hyde's note, there seems very little foundation for the story (repeated by Kaye) that he weakly named thirty thousand rupees as a compromise between the one hundred thousand suggested by Hyde and the fifty thousand by Impey.

Nor does there seem to be any foundation for the other time-honoured story (also repeated by Kaye) in connection with this judgment, viz. the alleged interruption of the Chief Justice, while he was delivering judgment, by Mr. Justice Hyde * with the eager suggestion or reminder of "siccas, siccas, Brother Impey," with the view of making the damages as high at the awarded figure as possible. Mr. Merivale says that he could find no confirmation of the old joke; it was probably invented to point the moral as to the reputed virtuous indignation of Hyde against all "gallantry in the chamber." The story seems to have been first promulgated in a book of "Personal Recollections," by John Nicholls, M.P., published in 1822. The author was in the House of Commons with Francis, and had known Impey and Hyde before they went to India. He mentions the Francis-Grand episode, giving such an inaccurate account of it that it is clear he is merely retailing hearsay gossip; for instance, he speaks of Mrs. *Le* Grand being admired for her beauty, for the sweetness of her temper, and for her fascinating accomplishments; and of Mr. Francis descending from the lady's apartment "by a rope ladder *after* an alarm had been raised," etc., etc. The evidence derived from such a source is very questionable; but the story is not supportable from any point of view. Without attaching too much importance to the improbability of a Puisne Judge on such an occasion addressing the Chief Justice as "Brother," instead of "My Lord," we have but to see that the damages were laid in the plaint in siccas, and were presumably, as a matter of course, awarded in the same coin.†

* My friend Mr. James S. Cotton told me that he had seen in the possession of a friend some papers which had belonged to Sir R. Chambers, amongst which was a lengthy memorandum discussing the damages in this case; the writer (no doubt Hyde, J.) proposed to assess them at a lac of rupees (as stated above from tradition) justifying this heavy amount as being Francis's official yearly salary, and in conformity with the Court's practice in the cases of less-exalted culprits.

† Indeed, it would seem that even though "siccas" were not specified in the plaint, the judgment would have contemplated them in the word "rupees." This would appear to be the inference from the following case reported in Hyde's own notes, viz.: "An action for assault and imprisonment. An assault was proved, but no very great injury; therefore the Court thought three hundred rupees sufficient damages.

"In the plaint the damages were alleged 'eighty thousand rupees'" (how

Francis was also mulcted in the plaintiff's costs of the suit amounting to sicca rupees 947-8.

Mr. Grand omits to say in his "Narrative" that, having secured Francis's rupees,* he next proceeded to settle accounts with Shee, whose friendly offices "to save his *noble* patron" on two occasions Mr. Grand was evidently not disposed either to forget or forgive.

The law was the weapon which he again had recourse to. To see what the nature of the action was, we must for the last time rely on the quaint fidelity of Justice Hyde's notes—

"*3rd Term.*

"Thursday, June 24, 1779.

"*Present:*

"SIR E. IMPEY, MR. JUSTICE CHAMBERS, and MR. JUSTICE HYDE.

"[Hyde came first; Impey second; the Court sat at 9.42; Chambers came about 10.15.]

"*G. F. Grand* versus *George Shee.*

"An action of trespass, for breaking and entering the house of the plaintiff on the eighth day of December, 1778. The plaint states first breaking and entering the house."

Mr. Grand did not make much by this, as the verdict was "one rupee damages and one rupee costs."

In Francis's diary there is the briefest allusion to this wind-up of the legal proceedings arising out of his evil-doing, and, with the proverbial feeling of the transgressor to the man he has injured, he adds this comment: "A la fin ce scélérat est écrasé."

This may be the most fitting opportunity for briefly endeavouring to trace the personal feelings of Francis towards the Judges who tried this case, with the object of seeing what ground there may be for the

unconscionable litigants seem to have been in appraising their damages in the last century), "without saying what sort of rupees. Impey said, if this is so wholly uncertain as to have no meaning at all because it is not said current, Arcot sonaut, sicca, or some other particular sort of rupees, then defendant may take advantage of it in arrest of judgment. Hyde: I incline to think 'rupees' named without any distinction must mean sicca rupees, because those are the proper coin of this country. I proposed to let the Advocate for the plaintiff choose what kind of rupees we should name for the damages, as he judged would be best for his client if a motion in arrest of judgment should be made, and Impey assented to it. The advocate named sicca rupees, and we gave judgment accordingly."

* Filed with the other papers in this suit is one duly witnessed and signed by Grand, in which he acknowledges himself to be "fully satisfied, contented, and paid."

charge that he afterwards allowed influences, presumably arising out of the verdict, to actuate not only his private, but his public conduct in regard to those men.

Towards Hyde he was peculiarly hostile. A few months after the trial he writes in his Journal (December, 1779): "Again I urge H. to push the Supreme Court as common cause, and on grounds which equally interest us both. I tell him plainly that the only way is to attack, and that we ought in own defence to solicit the Court of Directors to address the King to remove Hyde. Hastings seems to relish all this perfectly, and promises he will act properly. By what he says I suspect Impey and Chambers are very well disposed to leave Mr. Justice Hyde to his own reflections."

As regards Chambers, the defendant in the late suit would have been less than human, if he had not ever afterwards thought of him as a "wise and upright Judge, an excellent young man."

Without in the smallest degree insinuating that Chambers's dissent from the verdict was influenced by considerations independent of those springing from an honest weighing of the evidence, it may be pointed out that long before (as well as after) the trial, he and Francis were the closest official allies, if indeed not something more.

So far back as November, 1777, we find Francis noting as follows in his Journal: "Show Chambers my recommendation of him to Lord North. He pledges himself to me in return."

A month later, when the overtures for a coalition between Hastings and Francis (immediately on the arrival of Wheler) fail, owing to the latter's flat refusal to the plan of accommodation proposed through Elliot, he puts an "N.B." in his diary: "Justice Chambers entirely approves my resolution." On another occasion when, during a private visit to Hastings, the latter "professes the warmest resentment against the Supreme Court," Francis communicates this to Chambers.

In the November following the trial he chronicles that he stands godfather to Chambers's son, and dines at his house with Impey and Hyde. This and other similar entries suggest that Francis maintained (outwardly at all events) friendly social relations with all his late judges, and with Hastings, viz. December 9. "Talk with Sir E. Impey last night at the Harmonic." December 26. "This night Hastings and Impey supped at my house." In the month previous, November 2, he records, "Last night an invitation was sent to me from Mr. and Mrs. Hastings to dine with them to-morrow."

Francis has been described as a good hater, but he could also be a good friend, ever active and aggressive in behalf of his friendship as well as of his enmity. This is abundantly shown in his letters to India after his return to England, where his intrigues to supplant Impey by Chambers were incessant; and the inference from those letters is strong, that Francis's action in this respect was dictated by no public spirit, but by a desire to gratify private feelings. He had been barely at home a month, when in a letter to Sir John Day he says, "Nundcomar is returned, and, like Cæsar's ghost with Ate by his side, is now raging for revenge." A month later, when writing for the second time to Chambers (whom henceforth he habitually addresses as "dear friend"), he encourages him thus—

"Notwithstanding anything Impey may tell you to the contrary, be assured from *me* that, except Mr. Dunning, the Supreme Court have not a friend or approver even in Westminster Hall. The Chancellor will either give up or certainly not defend Impey. He is a condemned man. There is no power that either can, or is inclined to, save him from public disgrace at the best. The friends of Hastings have tried every artifice to make it be believed that you were implicated by accepting a post of profit in the Police; but I have cleared you completely up to the end of last year, and it stands rather better than if you had (*sic*, had not?) been so charged.* . . . With respect to *your* interests, you may rest assured that I will be alert in my attention to them. But you must be aiding and assisting them yourself. Hyde is despised in the same way in which Impey is execrated. *You* must stand clear and wide of both."

Again, soon after Impey's return to England, Francis writes to Sir R. Chambers, after reminding him that "I have always confided in your friendship." "As soon as Mr. Hastings is disposed of one way or another, I have season to believe that the impeachment of the other (Impey) will be attempted, and with some better prospect of success." He then gleefully adds: "To the best of my judgment he will be hard run, and I hear he is very uneasy about it. . . . Let the event of the prosecution be ever so favourable to him, a minute and public inquiry into all his conduct cannot but be very afflicting to him."

To his *fidus Achates* Shee, he writes about the same time (December, 1786) in a similar strain—

"The prosecution of your friend, Mr. Hastings, will be revived

* Mr. Impey, in the Memoir of his father, says that soon after the recall of Sir Elijah had been carried, motion was given in the House of Commons for a censure on Sir R. Chambers for having accepted the office of Company's Chief Justice at Chinsurah, but that it was postponed and dropped finally, owing to the interposition of Francis with his friend General Smith, who had given the notice, and who was also chairman of the Committees of the House.

CARICATURE OF FRANCIS.

See p. 265.

with a renewal of vigour as soon as Parliament meets. He has had a pleasant summer of it.

"An attempt will also be made to impeach Sir Elijah Impey, in whose fate I know you are interested." And to Mackenzie he writes out at the same time, "Mr. Hastings, I am well informed, is sunk into the lowest state of misery and dejection. Major Scott, with infinite effort, maintains a continued ghastly smile upon his face," etc., etc.

And lastly, when Sir Robert Chambers is at length confirmed as Chief Justice,* Francis writes out to congratulate him on an advancement: "So long and so dearly earned, and so well-deserved;" and after thanking God that he has got it, he finally assures him: "I look back to old times, and remember old friends with a tender, affectionate interest, considering them as objects in which I have long had a property."

After this disgression we go back to the sequence of events.

That the nocturnal expedition, at whose finale so many members of society assisted, soon became public property—goes without saying; and that it made a great noise in Calcutta may be gathered from these two entries in Francis's Journal—

"*December* 12, 1778.—Handsome behaviour of Wheler against the clamours of this cursed place."

"*December* 13.—H. and B. (Hastings and Barwell) mean enough to send that business home to the Court of Directors."

Francis in his private letters, too, at this time expresses his annoyance at the Governor-General's frequently bringing the scandal before the Council; he felt, and probably with some reason, that this sudden censoriousness came badly from the husband of Mrs. Imhoff and from the "gallant" of her fellow-voyager, Sarah Bonner, who had himself shocked even Calcutta in quite recent memory. As usual, he took care that Lord North should get early intimation of the affair from himself. Hicky, ever on the alert to vilify Hastings, and indirectly palliate the conduct of Francis, has the following "anecdote" with reference to the above in his *Gazette* for 1781.

"An intimate friend of Mr. B—w-ll's expressing to him one day his surprise that he should second Mr. H—— in that extraordinary and illiberal censure which appeared on the proceedings of the C—t

* Though Impey arrived in England in June, 1784, no motion about complaining of his conduct was made in the Commons till December, 1787.

In the previous month he resigned his office which (with its salary ?) he held for four years after leaving India. Chambers was not gazetted Chief Justice in his place till January 22, 1791, and sworn in on September 3 in the same year. The *Calcutta Chronicle* says that a salute was fired from the ramparts of Fort William on the occasion.

on the conduct of Mr. F——s respecting Mrs. G——, replied with great ironical honour: 'By G—d, I did not wish it, but I could not help it. I envy F—— beyond measure, but I must go along with H—— in these matters.' The latter part of the confession may be of some little apology for Mr. B—— on the score of necessity, but what possible excuse can be found for his colleague in offering so warmly to censure a vice which his whole life had uniformly passed in the practice of, unless, indeed, we suppose it to be the second act of his penitence, as we may reckon the first the honourable alliance he had previously entered into.

"When this gentleman * was proposed some years ago in Leadenhall Street to be sent out high in his office, his abilities, among other qualifications, were mentioned. 'Abilities,' replied Lord Clive, with a mixture of contempt and indignation, 'I knew him some time in India, and never heard of any abilities he possessed, except for seducing the wives of his friends.'"

It was not apparently for about three months after the trial that Mrs. Grand consented to pass into the "protection" of Francis. It is not improbable that he went to Chandernagore to seek her, and that the following entries point to the renewal of their intimacy, with its result—

"*June* 26, 1779.—At Chandernagore: *ut vidi, ut perii.*"

"*June* 27, 1779.—At Chandernagore: curious explanation with La Merlière, *à ce qui me parâit on ne demande pas mieux, etc.*"

Francis seems to have deferred to respect for appearances so far as not to have received the lady into his house in Calcutta. In this he acted in accordance with a rule he laid down on first arriving in India. Among his papers his biographer found the following, entitled, "Hints for my own conduct." It contains seventeen sagacious maxims which he proposed to act up to. The twelfth of these begins, "If *certain connections* should be formed, to keep at a distance." The two words underlined by Francis most probably refer to a possible entanglement such as we find him walking into now. It is interesting, too, to note that his action now is consistent

* It is not very clear to which gentleman Hicky wishes to refer here. I am inclined to think to Barwell; though it is quite possible that the anecdote composer may not have known that Clive was *not* in the habit of expressing himself disparagingly of Hastings' abilities. It was Clive who got Hastings sent in Council to Madras; and when Hastings was promoted to Governor of Bengal, Clive wrote to him, "I am convinced that you have not only abilities but personal resolution, etc." "I am sure that you are not wanting in abilities."—The notoriety of Barwell's infatuation about the enchantress who posed as a married woman, though not really so, may have reached Clive. (See Appendix.)

not only with the above maxim, but with the particular in the code of ethics, the violation of which he had some years before denounced as especially disgraceful.

When Francis, as Junius and Philo-Junius, is scathing the Duke of Grafton, he writes (referring to the notoriety of the Prime Minister's liaison with Miss Nancy Parsons), "But if vice itself could be excused, there is yet a certain display of it, a certain outrage to decency and violation of public decorum, which, for the benefit of society, should never be forgiven. It is not that he kept a mistress at home, but that he constantly attended her abroad. It is not the private indulgence, but the public insult of which I complain. The name of Miss Parsons would hardly have been known if the First Lord of the Treasury had not led her in triumph through the Opera House, even in the presence of the Queen." In another letter to the same personage he says, "For the sake of your mistress the lover shall be spared. I will not lead her into public as you have done. . . . Her sex, which alone made her amiable in your eyes, makes her respectable in mine."

There is little doubt that Francis established Mrs. Grand at Hooghly. It should be mentioned to his credit that he seems to have arranged that his companion should not be isolated, or quite socially ostracised in her new position, but be visited by friends. He is able to record that Chambers and his wife come to sup with us; also that Chambers and Wheler came to visit us. The fact of Lady Chambers still keeping up friendly relations suggests that there were extenuating circumstances, giving the sinned-against young wife some claim to countenance and sympathy.

However this may be, Francis made frequent trips up the river during the last half of the year 1779, while his thoughts were much occupied on matters amatory, viz.—

"*September* 9.—Go up to Hughely, where I propose to stay till we hear decisively from England. If it be possible to avoid it, I will never meet these villains in Council again."

"*September* 17.—*O! Cara Phillide, rendi mi il cor.*"

"*September* 29.—*Quæ spiravit amores.*"

"*October* 12.—In the evening returned to Hughely."

"*October* 16.—At Hughely."

"*October* 17, *Sunday.*—Ditto: *Ridet hoc, inquam, Venus ipsa, rident simplices nymphæ.*"

"*November* 2.—At Hughely, where I propose to stay as long as I can, and visit Calcutta as seldom as I can. Last night an invitation was sent to me from Mr. and Mrs. Hastings to dine with them to-morrow. Considering the terms on which we parted yesterday, and that I never received such an invitation before, it is an odd unaccountable circumstance, and subject to infinite speculation."

The next entry is November 4.—*Abiit, evasit, erupit*, but there is no clue as to the place or person meant.

"*November* 6.—At Hughely."

"*November* 7.—Go to Council in the evening."

"*November* 8.—Council. Return at night to Hughely."

"*November* 15.—Return at night to Hughely. *Quoquo vestigia tendit, componit furtim subsequiturque decor.*"

"*November* 20.—Hughely. *Pulchrior multo, juvenumque prodis publica cura.*"

"*November* 21.—Ditto, all these days at Hughely, busily employed in writing letters home. Return at night to Calcutta."

"*November* 24.—Return at night to Hughely; *ferus et Cupido semper ardentes acuens sagittas.*"

This is the last entry in his Journal that refers to the Hooghly attraction; there is no further allusion to Mrs. Grand (at least in the extracts which his biographer gives from his Indian diary), unless the asterisks in the following stand for her name.

"*February* 17, 1780.—This day Mr. Barwell sends to desire leave to pay his respects to * * * *; offers of a passage to England, etc."

The whole entry of February 17 shows that the writer was at the time in Calcutta. Could Barwell's proposed visit refer to the house in Calcutta? If so the lady (conjecturally) veiled by the asterisks may have after all come there, and this may account for no further record of visits to Hughely. In *Hicky's Gazette*, in January, 1780, is advertised "an elegant modern built house at Hughely, lately inhabited by Major Baggs." So that cousin Baggs was domiciled at Hooghly in 1779, while Francis was so frequently there to and fro, and may have contributed to the sociability of the latter's menage, and officiated as Cerberus over the shrine, during the councillor's reluctant absences at Calcutta. The world perhaps could not have provided a more efficient one. Could he have been the Cataline referred to in the entry of November 4? Major Baggs was ordered out of India by the Court of Directors, and started on January 3, 1780—then Francis may have brought his unprotected friend to Calcutta—all this of course is mere speculation.

Barwell sailed from Calcutta in the *Swallow* on March 3, 1780, having two days previously gone to Francis's house, as the diary records, "to take leave with a fine palavering speech."

If the entry of the 17th refers to a proposal of Barwell's that Mrs. Grand should be a passenger in the *Swallow* under his auspices,

Francis, holding the ideas of Barwell which he did, regarded it probably with as much composure as he would a proposal to pen a wolf and a lamb into the same fold. In any case, the presumption is strong that Mrs. Grand did not leave India for several months later; it is very probable I think that the following paragraph from Hicky's *Bengal Gazette*, December 2, 1780, refers to her: "Samuel Tolfrey, Esq." * (whose name we have seen as that of one of Francis's attorneys in the trial) "has embarked for Europe with a fortune of three lakhs of rupees: he intends proceeding from Celon (*sic*) or Coringa in the Dutch ship that carries home Mrs. G——d—."

Now, Francis himself, according to a letter of Warren Hastings, left India on December 3, 1780, having first "engaged a passage in a Dutch ship, which he has left for one in the *Fox*," and this is explained by the very last entry in the Indian diary so often alluded to: "*November* 7.—Discover at last that it is impossible to go in the Dutch ship, so resolve to take my passage in the *Fox*, Captain Blackburn." His cousin Tilghman was amongst the few fellow-passengers in the *Fox*.†

Some writers have more than hinted that even *in India* Francis was not the only "protector" into whose hands Mrs. Grand fell.

Lord Mahon, for instance, in his "History" (vol. vii.) goes so far as to name the other gentleman with whom Mrs. Grand was said to have "returned to Europe as the companion" when "forsaken" by Francis, viz. a Mr. William Macintosh. He refers to an unpublished biography of Mr. Charles Macintosh (a quotation only, from which he had seen in the *Quarterly Review*, vol. lxxxiv.) as his authority.

The biography alluded to by Lord Mahon is a very inconsiderable brochure by the son of the Macintosh who invented the waterproof preparation which bears his name. An appendix of a few pages professes to give some account of the writer's uncle, William Macintosh, which is rather rambling, and certainly does not savour of authenticity—indeed a good deal of it is simple rubbish. The foundation of the story in the *Quarterly Review* which Lord Mahon

* In the same issue occurs "An original epistle written by S— T—f—y, Esq., Attorney-at-law to a young lady lately married who rejected his suit—"Oh, listen, my fair, to your poor distressed client," etc., etc. It is somewhat doubtful, however, whether the attorney did embark in a Dutch ship after all, as *a* Mr. Tolfrey is amongst the passengers of the *Prime*, Captain James Dundas, mustered at St. Helena on October 15, 1781.

† His fellow-passengers in *Fox* were Mr. Harwood, Mr. Tilman (*sic* in Hicky), Mr. and Mrs. Lacam, Mrs. Evans.

thought worth referring to, is probably this sentence: "What gives some additional colour to the probability of such having been the case, is the circumstance of the intimacy which at one time subsisted between Mr. William Macintosh and Madame Grand, afterwards Princess Talleyrand. This lady was a native of Scotland, had been the widow of a British officer, and married as her second husband a French gentleman, who afterwards obtained a divorce from her in India; the defendant in the action being the celebrated Mr. (afterwards Sir Philip) Francis. Madame Grand returned with Mr. William Macintosh to Europe in 1781."

This William Macintosh was the author of a very trumpery book of travels in Europe, Asia, etc., published in 1782. He was for a few months in India in 1779. He left Calcutta in the *Ganges* on February 6, 1780, and joined the convoy which left Madras in the April following.

As said before, there is strong presumption that Mrs. Grand was still with Francis on February 17. There is abundant internal evidence in the travels (which are written in the form of letters to friends describing the progress of his journey) which convinces me that Madame Grand was not a fellow-passenger in the ship with Macintosh, nor one of the two ladies (with their four children) whom he eventually landed with and took care of in Ireland, in January, 1781. To justify my conviction on this point, which is supported by certain facts in "Price's Observations" on Macintosh's travels, would take up more time than could reasonably be given to it here.

M. Pichot says, while noticing the "Memoirs of Francis," "Aussi Francis, condamné voulut-il en avoir pour son argent, et il vécut pendant une année avec Mme. Grand, jusqu à ce qu'elle se laissa enlever par un autre protecteur qui l'emmena en Europe."

Here are two writers in different quarters stating that Mrs. Grand went from India to Europe with a "companion" when the Francis liaison came to a close. An old proverb assures us that there is never smoke without fire. I long vainly sought for this fire, little thinking that a clue to it was so near as in the "Dictionary of National Biography." About a couple of years ago a little volume of short memoirs of some "Famous Women," etc., came to my notice; it was written by Mr. John Fyvie, and had been quite recently published. It was there stated in the brief article on Mrs. Grote, that her father had travelled in the same Europe-bound ship as Mrs. Grand, Mr. Fyvie naming Pondicherry as the port of departure. On consulting the article on Mrs. Grote in the "Dictionary of National Biography," I found the same companionship alleged, and from the same French port in India, the authority quoted in each case being mainly that of Lady Eastlake who published a memoir of her friend in 1880. On referring to the latter, entitled a "Sketch of Mrs. Grote," it was there found that the authoress, on information supplied by Mrs. Grote herself, says that in the "East Indiaman" which conveyed the latter's father to Europe (1781) "Madame Grand, subsequently wife of Talleyrand, then leaving India on account of 'irregularities' which had caused Mr. Grand to divorce her, was also a passenger." This led to an intimacy—and all the rest of it. Mrs. Grote's father was a member of the Indian Civil Service; his official career was so eventful and distinguished that it may as well be briefly recalled (as traced in the old records of the India House) before dealing with the episode referred to above, or with any details connected with it.

The gentleman in question was Mr. Thos. Lewin, who was appointed a writer on the Madras establishment in 1770, when about eighteen years old. Amongst other appointments he served in the military department at Fort St. George, and there acquitted himself so well "with much propriety and attention" that he and another secretary (in the Civil Department) were specially recommended to the favour of the Court of Directors in a letter, March, 1778. Later he seems to have become private secretary to the Governor. In October, 1780, the President and Council of Fort St. George deputed him to England with despatches for the Honourable Company "relative to the war in the Carnatic, and to give information respecting such particulars as were not contained in those advices" (India Office Records). An official letter which Mr. Lewin wrote to the Court of Directors soon after his arrival in England gives some particulars as to what befell him in the discharge of this duty. His instructions, dated, his letter says, October 2, were to embark on board H.M. sloop of war *Nymph* for the Cape of Good Hope,* and thence to convey his despatches to Europe on a neutral ship. He re-embarked at the Cape. "But in my passage from thence on board a Dutch ship, the destination

* His brother, Mr. Richard Lewin, also a Madras official, was despatched in the *Nymph* by the Government of Madras with the appointment of "Resident" at the Cape, "for the purpose of giving intelligence respecting the motions and designs of our enemies, and to procure such assistance as may be wanted by any of H.M. or Honourable Company's ships putting in at the Cape." The simultaneous deputation of the two brothers on duties calling for discretion, tact, and resolution shows in what estimation their capacity was held by the official authorities under whom they served.

of the vessel being unexpectedly changed from the Texel to Cadiz on account of war which had newly broken out between England and Holland I thought it my duty to destroy the despatches under my care." "Being lately arrived from Spain on my parole to the States of Holland I beg to request that on obtaining my release from that Court I may be permitted to return to my duty at Fort St. George," etc., etc.

This letter is dated September 4, 1781, London.

The *Nymph* * got to the Cape in the middle of December, but it is not recorded on what date the despatch-bearer changed into the Dutch vessel—then no doubt considered "neutral"—nor when she sailed from the Cape, but it must have been before March 31, 1781, as only then did official intelligence arrive there that Great Britain had declared war against the United Provinces in the previous December. England was thus at war with a coalition of all the maritime powers in Europe, while in a deadly grapple with her provoked and revolted colonies in North America and with Haidar Ali in India. Mr. Lewin, though he applied for permission to return to India without prejudice to his rank, did not however do so for over two years, having in the mean time got into hot water with a no less august institution than the House of Commons, which happened in this wise. Mr. John Whitehill (temporary governor of Madras during a portion of 1777–1778, and again in 1780, when he held the reins on the departure of Sir Thos. Rumbold) had fallen under the reproof of Warren Hastings and his Council, who suspended him (end of October, 1780) for action, or perhaps inaction, in his government, not necessary to be detailed. On the report of the Governor-General reaching the Court of Directors, they dismissed the Governor of Madras, and the whole matter was brought to the notice and inquiry of Parliament afterwards. Mr. Whitehill had been a warm friend and official patron of Mr. Lewin who had been much in his confidence.

In May, 1782, the Chairman of the Committee of Secrecy appointed to inquire into the causes of the war in the Carnatic (Right Honourable H. Dundas) reported to the House of Commons

* The *Nymph*, Captain Stevens, was the vessel which brought from Madras to Calcutta the disastrous news of Haidar's irruption and of Sir Hector Monro's defeat, etc. She arrived in the Hooghly on September 22, 1780. She probably went back to Madras at once to announce Hastings' answer to the urgent appeal for help, and the active war measures for relief which his fertile mind immediately set on foot. Mr. Lewin's voyage began on October 18 (Family Records), but he does not state in the official letter quoted above where he actually embarked, but the context indicates Madras.

"that Mr. Lewin, late secretary to the Council at Madras at the time Mr. Whitehill was governor, had disobeyed the repeated orders of the Committee for attending them," for which he was declared guilty of breach of privilege of the House, and ordered to be taken into the custody of the sergeant-at-arms. "Having withdrawn himself from the kingdom, the House of Commons on May 8 resolved that he had absconded in order to avoid being examined, and addressed his Majesty to issue his proclamation for apprehending him." The reason apparently why Mr. Lewin did not answer the Committee's summons was that he did not feel himself at liberty to disclose certain official or other actions which confidentially came to his knowledge without being authorised to do so, by his late official chief, who had probably not yet returned to England. This difficulty was before long got over, and in January, 1783, he, by the advice of Mr. Whitehill, surrendered himself, and was taken into the custody of the sergeant-at-arms. He duly asked forgiveness, and was brought to the Bar of the House, and reprimanded by Mr. Speaker, and ordered "to be discharged on paying the customary fees" (a euphemism no doubt for a substantial fine).

This little interlude does not appear to have interfered with his official prospects at all. He returned to Madras and ascended the ladder of preferment, holding some important posts. He was always tenacious of what he considered his rights, and did not hesitate to urge them on the authorities and dispensers of official patronage abroad, or to appeal over their heads to those at home. He took two more long furloughs (as formerly allowed, until reduced to a maximum of two years). In 1800 he sought permission to return to duty, but it was denied him for having overstayed his leave, and he then retired from the Service.

Now to return to the Madame Grand episode. We have already shown ground for belief that she sailed from the Hooghly in a Dutch vessel in December, 1780. But the alleging that she sailed for Europe in an "East Indiaman," and from "Pondicherry" (on the Madras coast), made it desirable to clear up this point if possible, especially as Lady Eastlake, the authority chiefly quoted, did not produce her interesting sketch of Mrs. Grote until she was at an age so advanced that her memory may have been occasionally at fault. The likeliest way to find Madame Grand's ship was to seek Mr. Lewin's, if the story was true that they were fellow-voyagers. To discover, therefore, the unnamed Dutch ship into which Mr. Lewin changed at the Cape (at a date when she was practically a neutral) and a list of her passengers was the needed solution. I regret to say that my searchings for these at home or abroad have been quite unsuccessful. This is the more provoking as I was assisted in my quest by the courteous archive keepers at the Cape and at the Hague, and at Cadiz, where the British consul exhaustively aided my inquiries, being moved to do so through the great kindness of his Excellency the present British ambassador at Madrid. I also consulted Dr. G. McCall Theal, the learned historian of South Africa and formerly archivist at Cape Town, who most kindly told me that in all his searching of records either there or at the Hague, or elsewhere, he had never come across a passenger list of the year in question containing the names I was looking for, one of which (that of the lady) he would have at once recognised.

In this difficulty it occurred to me to go to what might prove to be the fountain head, and to crave the assistance of the present representative of Mr. Lewin's family. I had formerly had the pleasure of knowing in India Colonel Lewin, now of Parkhurst in Surrey, so I had the less hesitation in asking him to tell me, if there were no objection, whether family tradition or possibly records were in existence which could throw any light on the alleged episode in his grandfather's young days (which had found its way into print), and on the voyaging which led to the acquaintance with Mrs. Grand—and its consequences. Colonel Lewin knew of old that I had written a little about Madame Grand, and therefore why I was interested. My friend, in the most cordial and generous manner, at once acceded to my request, and allowed me access to some well-kept family papers. Amongst these were notes by Mrs. Grote, and by another lady relative, of reminiscences of Mr. Lewin, and of familiar conversations with him in the family circle, wisely committed to writing for the information of his descendants. I shall extract a little presently from these rich drafts on the memory so pleasantly recorded, enough to afford a further insight into the variegated life in his young days of this favoured Anglo-Indian of the old school. But the question that led to my being allowed to see these filial reminiscences may as well be disposed of at once. There is no room to doubt, from the evidence of these family papers, that the future Princesse Talleyrand was a fellow-passenger in the oft-referred to Dutchman which bore Mr. Lewin and his despatches to Europe. Whether the ship was the same one in which, according to the Calcutta newspaper announcement, the lady took her passage from the Hooghly (as it presumably was), or whether she changed ship at the Cape for another of the same nationality, there is nothing to show. In the family papers the putting into Cadiz is somewhat amplified; it is there stated that

THOS. LEWIN, ESQ.
MADRAS CIVIL SERVICE.
(When young.)

THOS. LEWIN, ESQ.
MADRAS CIVIL SERVICE.
(In advanced age.)

*See p.* 275.

the Dutchman was waylaid by two French warships which drove or "carried her" into the Spanish port, Mr. Lewin hastily tearing up his despatches and throwing the fragments out of his cabin window. At all events it is certain that he and Madame Grand were together on this adventurous voyage from the Cape; also that he had so ingratiated himself with his fair companion, and had so beguiled her of her loneliness, that she accompanied him from Cadiz to Lisbon, and thence in a Portuguese vessel to England, where she yielded to his solicitations and threw in her lot with him temporarily. They stayed some time in London, at a house in Russell Place, Fitzroy Square, and went thence to Paris, where they separated (after no long association apparently), he settling an annuity on her which, according to Mrs. Grote's recorded belief, she continued to draw for her life. Before we feel inclined to morally exalt ourselves and give thanks that we are not as other men are, or were, let us bear in mind that at this period the gentleman, good looking, amiable, and winning, was about eight and twenty, and that the lady, one of the most physically attractive women of her time, was only eighteen. Also how tempting any distraction, let alone love-making, must have been to a young couple to mitigate ennui amidst the appalling dulness of a tedious voyage—and that in a Dutch ship.

There is abundant evidence in Lady Eastlake's sketch and in those family reminiscences, especially those of Mrs. Grote, that her father was a man of no ordinary ability. Her early teaching was in his hands, and "she inherited from him her own brilliant powers and intelligence" as she did her devotion to, and skill in, music. The gifts born with him he must have assiduously improved by cultivation from his youth upwards, as he became a fine musician, playing well on the violin and violoncello; a chess player far above the average; familiar with some modern languages and with French literature. He was a member, too, of the famous Beefsteak Club. In youth he is represened as slight and neatly built and of middle stature, of graceful presence, and of winning, courteous ways. We need not wonder to hear that the fair sex made much of such a fine gentleman, who repaid them with a courtesy at once devoted and grateful. His excursions into the fashionable and venal gallantries of the day were, it would seem, not few, and were attended with quiet respect for those he favoured, and with princely liberality. Though only ten or eleven years in India, at this time he had shaken the pagoda tree so successfully, and guarded the fruit of it so carefully, that he must have returned with a considerable fortune, which he proceeded to lavish on his tastes and on his weaknesses, in that most enjoyable of all times to the exiled Anglo-Indian, if he be young and healthy, *i.e.* when he comes back to the land of his home on his first long furlough. Those were the halcyon days when money was easily acquired in India, when Mr. Barwell had just left Bengal and Sir Thos. Rumbold Madras with prodigious fortunes. The latter (who had preceded Mr. Whitehill) had, as alleged in Parliament, remitted home £160,000 in three years' government of Madras on a moderate official salary! *

Mr. Lewin betook himself mainly to Paris with introductions to aristocratic French circles—from friends met in Pondicherry (?) it is said. At all events, he joined the gay spendthrift crowd who fiddled and danced almost on the brink of the Revolution. He was wont to join the Royal hunt at Marly, and "to drive four-in-hand," and to ruffle it with the best of the young bloods of the period.

He used to tell his family circle that he had seen Marie Antoinette dance a minuet with the Comte d'Artois. One anecdote which evidently touched Mrs. Grote's delightful sense of humour may be recalled here. Her father engaged the great automaton chess player in Paris one day, and managed to get the better of his antagonist, and was in a fair way to win the game when "the figure" raised its arm and (accident or design?) swept the pieces off the board! This automaton was also credited with oracular gifts, and it was the allowed fashion to put a question to it under certain conditions. Mr. Lewin, prompted by his ruling weakness, put this poser to the oracle, "Will there be any women in Paradise?" The figure had, I suspect, an Irish interior, because, *more Hibernico*, it answered the question by asking another, which must have appealed forcibly to the sympathy of the questioner—"Would it be Paradise without them?"

So this versatile Anglo-Indian, more or less typical of an age long passed away, evidently quaffed nectar, steadily through his first furlough, entitling him to say with the preacher, All things have I seen in the days of my vanity. But though he occasionally flew to the bowers "where Pleasure lies carelessly smiling," and though his pre-nuptial failings did not always lean to virtue's side, still the open way in which they are alluded to by his friendly recording relatives, goes far to suggest that it might truly be said of them in extenuation what Burke said of vice, "that it lost half its evil by losing all its grossness." Nor did he roam long in quest of fleeting pleasure. He

* Rumbold, however, during his career as an Indian Civil Servant, had longer opportunity of acquiring money than in his tenure of the Madras Governorship. Once in his early career he exchanged the pen for the sword, and, with his patron Clive, fought at Plassey. His name appears amongst those voting at the historic Council of War; like his chief (at first) he voted against immediate action.

early came to the old conclusion that to "hold it for life we must find it at home."

He found it in marrying a young lady scarcely sixteen—a Miss Hale, the attractive daughter of a beautiful mother, Miss Chaloner, who married General Hale, a distinguished soldier who had served at the taking of Quebec and seen the last moments of Wolfe. Mr. Lewin and his very young bride went to India early in 1784. They had a numerous family; their learned and witty daughter Harriet, Mrs. Grote, was born in 1792.

On his retirement, they settled at the Hollies, near Bexley, which he had inherited with a substantial income from his father. He died in 1843, aged ninety. One pathetic little incident, which Mrs. Grote records, connected with our main subject, may fittingly close this sketch. This entry is in her father's diary under date December 15, 1835, "Heard that the Princesse Talleyrand was dead." She had died three days before in Paris. Who can divine what thoughts were aroused in making this brief entry, what going back to the buried treasures of the long ago! at the sad and lonely age, too, when

> "We hurry to the river we must cross,
> And swifter downward every footstep wends;
> Happy who reach it ere they count the loss
> Of half their faculties and half their friends."

## II

The story having thus taken Mrs. Grand out of India, we had now better return to the "Narrative," to get a general idea of Mr. Grand's after-doings as a Bengal civilian in the last quarter of the eighteenth century. Immediately after the trial, viz. in April, 1779, his "health being sensibly affected," he "was advised by those friends who deeply felt for him, to change the air;" and a berth was secured for him in Patna, by an exchange of appointments with Mr. J. H. Taylor, Head Commercial Assistant to the Factory there.

In 1781 he appears to have been in Benares during Hastings' visit there, and to have joined in the night escape to Chunar after the tumult, as he gives the names of several of those who comprised Hastings' suite on the night of August 21. Amongst whom was his own brother, Lieutenant John E. Grand, who was killed soon after in a fight against some rebellious zemindars.

The following extract seems to show that Francis's sicca rupees went eventually towards founding an enterprise in Tirhoot, which has since grown into a magnificent "industry."

"In 1782 I was transferred by Mr. Hastings from Head Assistant to a commercial factory (in which the duty consisted of prizing (*sic*) cloths, seeing saltpetre weighed and loaded, attending to the accounts, etc.) to the government of two considerable provinces, involving the settlement and collection of revenues and maintenance of justice; the provinces were Tirhoot and Hajeepoore.

"I took possession of a country yielding a revenue of above seven laacks of rupees, but which had suffered from the depredation committed by those who were compelled to abandon the charge to me, and had besides been in revolt owing to the intrigues of the Rajah of Benares, Cheyt Sing, whose baneful influence had spread so far, and would have spread further, had he not been checked in time by Mr. Hastings' wise and spirited measures.

"I recovered a large balance due from the farmers to Government, quieted and appeased without bloodshed every disturbance, brought back the disobedient to a just sense of their errors, augmented the revenue, *introduced the manufacturing of indigo after the European manner*,* encouraged the establishment of indigo works and plantations, erected three at my own expense, and thus possessed at that moment a fortune of £15,000 sterling, looked forward to a proportionate augmentation by continuing in my station and extending my manufactories, which, with my houses, lands, furniture, tent equipage, horses, boats, stood then upon a valuation of £10,000 more."

In the *Bengal Gazette*, February, 1782, Hicky records this transfer of Grand to Tirhoot in his usual delicate style. "Mr. G——, who has lately been much employed in reading and digesting Milton on divorce, will, we hear, in a few days, be appointed collector of Turott (*sic*) in the Behar province."

While Grand was holding this Tirhoot appointment, he wrote a letter to the Chief Justice, which is in original amongst the Impey manuscripts. It shows that the writer was not only quarrelsome and self-important, but a sneaking sort of man also. His object was to bespeak the Chief Justice's influence while forwarding the following copy of a Government letter which seemed to give him much dissatisfaction. He signs his rather grovelling letter to Impey, "your obliged and most devoted friend and servant."

* The passage I have italicised is confirmed by some remarks made in a suit in Equity in 1794 about an indigo concern in which Grand was defendant. The *Calcutta Chronicle*, in reporting his legal proceedings, says, "Mr. Grand, by very extensive works having laid the foundation of that valuable manufacture in Behar." Mr. John Prinsep is generally believed to have introduced indigo making into Bengal.

"The Honourable the Governor-General and Council having passed a decision on the charges preferred by you against the Judge of the Adawlut at Derbungah, have directed us to inform you that the charges appear to be grounded entirely on the misrepresentation of your servants, and desire you will be more cautious in future. They have also expressed their satisfaction at the conduct of the judge throughout the whole matter laid before them." "May 8, 1783."

Lord Cornwallis arrived in September, 1786, and Mr. Grand went to Calcutta to pay his respects to his new chief, and to make reports and suggestions, "as," he unaffectedly observes, "one of the ablest revenue servants and one of the most intelligent regarding the customs and usages prevailing in the provinces of Behar."

A measure soon followed, which seems to have taken Mr. Grand quite by surprise, and to have been inexplicable to him, though to us, perhaps, the reason is plain enough, seeing that it was ordered by the Governor-General, who first established purity and justice as the pillars of our rule in India, and who put a stop to the unsalutary combination of executive authority with commercial pursuits.

He thus pathetically refers to the hard fate that overtook him—

"On August 26, 1787, I was in full possession of my appointment, and my fortune was in that progressive state as described in 1785. I was in the enjoyment of every comfort, elegance, and luxury of life. I was beloved and respected by those living with me; my assistants, Messrs. David van der Heyden (since M.P. for Westloe), Mr. Henry Colebrooke (since Member, Supreme Council), together with Mr. Steel, my surgeon, and Mr. Purvis, my private secretary (since retired to England with a considerable fortune derived from the indigo manufactories); * and I will say, because I challenged the contrary to be proved, almost venerated by the natives of every description under my government, whose tears on hearing of my removal accompanied me from the place of my residence to the bank of the Ganges, where the limits of the district ceased—a distance of twenty-five miles. On August 27, 1787, by one stroke of his Lordship's pen, was Mr. Robert Bathurst nominated Collector of Tirhoot and Hajeepore, and thus every hope and fair-built prospect existing on the preceding day completely blasted. Thus the blow was struck, and from that date I fell perhaps never more to rise. View the portrait and feel ! ! !"

* Even accepting Mr. Grand's own account of himself, we can fancy what a short shrift such a district official, thus complacently serving two masters, had to expect at the hands of the writer of the following noble letter, regarding another member of the Civil Service :—

To ———, Esqr.

SIR,

My personal esteem for you and my sincere regard for my friend the Duke of Grafton, made me feel the deepest concern at being under the necessity

In 1788, without solicitation on his part, he was appointed Judge and Magistrate of Patna, an office which he describes "as a gold chain honourable but burthensome and totally bereft of every emolument." He was shortly afterwards directed to give up and dispose of his indigo concerns in Tirhoot; against this he remonstrated, and finally proving contumacious, and charges as to his conduct as Judge of Patna having been laid, he seems to have been removed from the Service.

He did not, however, leave India then, but remained there a few years longer, trying, apparently, to get reinstated. His name turns up occasionally in old Calcutta newspapers. Thus in December, 1793, he is found serving on the Grand Jury. In June, 1794, he is the officer employed to despatch the Mail Packet for Europe from Diamond Harbour. In November of the same year he is one of the commissioners for a scheme of a general lottery. Finally he sailed for Europe in February, 1799, in a vessel carrying neutral colours. He changed into a small brig at the Cape, where he stayed for a short time, and eventually got to Dover in March, 1800.

The first stage of Grand's voyage affords a good instance of the dangers and miseries encountered by poor Anglo-Indians who had then to go down to the sea in ships searching for health. They were first of all detained over three weeks in the river at Kedgeree in a stifling, badly found ship through fear of the celebrated French frigate *La Forte*, which was playing havoc at the Sandheads with English shipping. Finally, to their intense joy and relief, they saw her towed up the river by her English capturer, *La Sybille*, which was commanded by Captain Edward Cook, son of the great navigator. An account of this famous sea-fight is given in "The Adventures of a Master Mariner," by Captain R. W. Eastwick (1891), whose ship had just been taken by the *La Forte*, he himself being a prisoner on board her with several other Englishmen. The action

of removing your son from his collectorship of ——. From his general good character and from other circumstances I do not attribute his behaviour to corrupt motives; yet his official misconduct was of such a nature that I could not save him without marking a partiality which must have destroyed all respect for my Government. But although unfortunately mine is the duty of the rigid judge, an affectionate father has another part to act. It is for you to believe your son innocent of all moral wrong; and when you lament that the error into which he has fallen must materially affect his fortune, do not aggravate the calamity, which, God knows, is severe enough, by the addition of your unkindness.

I am, etc., etc.,
CORNWALLIS.

occurredon the last night of February, 1799, during brilliant moonlight, in or near Balasore Roads. The *Forte* was a fine large frigate of fifty guns and three hundred men; the *Sybille* of forty-four. The latter stole in on the Frenchman with all her lights covered up, and was at first mistaken for a merchantman. The *Forte* was too high to bring all her guns to bear on her antagonist, who raked her and dismasted her in fifty-five minutes. She lost over fifty killed and eighty-five wounded; amongst the former were the fine old Admiral De Sercé (a pupil of Suffrein's), the captain and first, second, and third lieutenants. The second captain, who was thus left in command, was a mere lad, and asked Eastwick, with tears in his voice, to hail the British frigate that the *Forte* had struck. The *Sybille* lost only fifteen or twenty in killed and wounded, but amongst the latter was her gallant young captain, who was badly hit in both arms. He lingered for over three months, and died miserably in Calcutta in the following May, aged 27. He was given a public funeral, and was buried in North Park Street Cemetery. The East India Company put up a monument to him in Westminster Abbey. Fifteen sloops, each with a guard of soldiers, were sent down for the conveyance of the prisoners to Calcutta on the day after the action. It must have been a proud day for the city when the *Forte* was seen being towed up the river by the *Sybille.* This, apparently, did not occur until April 2.

Amongst his fellow-passengers was a Mahomedan of distinction, Mirza Aboo Taleb Khan, who afterwards wrote an account of his travels, and in this we get a personal glance at the husband of Mrs. Grand, viz.—

"A Mr. Grand was in the next cabin, a very passionate and delicate gentleman." In May a terrible storm overtook them. . . . "During this scene Mr. Grand, who was of an enormous size, and whose cabin was separated from mine only by a canvas partition, fell with all his might upon my breast and hurt me excessively; what rendered this circumstance more provoking was that if by any accident the smallest noise was made in my apartment he would call out with all that overbearing insolence which characterises the vulgar part of the English in their conduct to Orientals, 'What are you about? You won't let me get a wink of sleep,' and such other rude expressions."

From the Court of Directors, too, he failed to get the redress which he had so calculated on that he had accepted pecuniary advances from friends, to reimburse whom he was obliged to sell all that he had, and to transfer his annuity for their benefit. As I shall have occasion later on to refer to the agency by which Mr. Grand was extricated from his difficulties, I had better give *verbatim* what he has chosen to tell us on this subject himself—

"After suffering privations and hardships which fell heavy at my time of life, I was relieved by the generosity of a friend, who had a lively remembrance of attachment, and obligation for the conduct which I had observed during prosperity. With what was left me out of this sum, being two-fifths of its amount, I departed for the Continent, my tried friends in England approving of the same, and repeating their assurance they would not be unmindful to bring forward my claims and a reconsideration of my case, when they saw a proper opportunity to exert themselves in behalf of their injured friend.

"By this same liberal friend was I offered a handsome pension to live at ease and to enjoy for the remainder of my days where the local (*sic*) was most agreeable; and even I was enjoined by the warmest friends of my youth and career in life, through whom this bounty was tendered, viz. Sir Elijah Impey and Mr. Wombwell, to accept of it, and quit the paths of ambition and the future trouble which might again arise and befall me from public situations.

"I rejected this munificence intended, not from pride, but from a consideration I had other ties which demanded I should not sink into perfect repose whilst active faculties permitted (me) to discharge with credit stations to which I might be elevated. With these sentiments I assented readily to the proposition subsequently made to me from the Batavian Government to repair to the Cape of Good Hope in a high station, with the promise of a higher, and the eventual assurance of those friends to whose interest in my behalf I felt sincerely grateful, that both rank and fortune were once more within my reach, and that nothing would be spared to throw me into the state during my sojournment abroad of the truly pleasing one—*otium cum dignitate;* with these prospects and the fullest reliance of performance did I embark, vested with my new honours after the treaty of Amiens, in a time of profound peace, and with the strongest hope of its continuance, for my destination. The unfortunate war which soon burst out after my arrival, has deprived me of those advantages to which I looked with fond delight, not so much for what concerned me personally, but for the gratification of others, and which, from the honesty of those on whose promises I implicitly trusted, I am persuaded I should otherwise have reaped. Accustomed to vicissitudes, nay, seemingly born to experience such, I behold this last with philosophic contemplation, *flecti non frangi.*

The occupation of the Batavian Republic having gone (on the Cape becoming a British Colony), Mr. Grand was appointed by the new Commander, Lieutenant-General Sir David Baird, to be "Inspector of H.M.'s Woods and Lands;" but he seems soon to have lost this employment also, and then probably subsided into private life. The only other references to him personally that I have seen are in Sir James Mackintosh's "Memoirs," who, on his way home from Bombay (his ship having put in at the Cape), records in his diary: "*January* 16, 1812.—At the African Club, where I went to read Newspapers and Reviews, I met Mr. Grandt (*sic*), the first husband of Madame Talleyrand; he is rather a gentleman-like old man, a native of Lausanne, sent here with an office during the peace."

And in a book published anonymously in 1816, entitled "Sketches of India, etc., together with Notes on the Cape of Good Hope, etc., written at those places in 1815," the author says, "In Cape Town I met with Mr. Grand, a gentleman whose life appears to have been an uninterrupted series of vicissitudes and misfortunes." Grand must have poured his woes with dramatic effusiveness into this gentleman's ears until he bewildered him, for the tragic version of them which the sympathetic listener retails is this.

"When Lord Cornwallis assumed the reins of Government in Bengal, he was expelled to make room for some of his Lordship's partisan's; infamous attacks made on his character—his integrity called in question, and this without any defence being allowed: to use his own words, he was prejudged and proscribed. His domestic misfortunes commenced with the seduction of his wife (the present Madame Talleyrand), by Sir Philip Francis, on the day of marriage (*sic!*), and terminated, if I may use the word, by his being deprived almost of bread by the British Government at the Cape. I found him the gentleman and much esteemed."

It is much to be regretted that, from the time of Mrs. Grand's arrival in France, there is a wide gap in her history, for the filling up of which, so far as the present writer has found, no materials of any authentic value have yet come to light. One would like to know how sixteen years in the very bloom of this beautiful woman's life were passed. Seductive influences, no doubt, beset her, as she was "blest with as great a beauty as Nature durst bestow without undoing." To such a dangerous gift much should be forgiven, its possessor should not be judged by too rigid a standard. Her yieldings to temptation in the very blossom of her youth we may know something of, but of her resistings then or afterwards we know nothing. This makes more sad the reflection that she did not escape the lot which one, who had much experience of woman's heart and woman's frailty, says overtakes those who have been similarly betrayed into early folly.

"For the first step in error none e'er can recall,
And the woman once fallen for ever must fall,
Pursue to the last the career she's begun,
And be false unto many, as faithless to one." *

We certainly have what Lady Francis says on the early part of this hiatus, and she professed to have open to her a source of information which probably could be most valuable; but unfortunately what this lady committed to paper concerning the Grand affair, turns out to be such a compound of superficial truth and solid error, in those particulars which can be submitted to proof, that we are bound to regard the whole of it with caution, and with the suspicion that much of what Francis in his old age chose to tell his second wife on this subject was intended to amuse or to mislead.

Still, there is nothing very improbable in her account, which is briefly this, that, on Francis's arrival in England from India,† Mrs. Grand went to reside in France, where she put herself into the charge of two respectable ladies, and though largely (if not mainly) dependent on the slender support which they could give her, she refused any assistance from Francis. That he frequently went to see her in Paris and Spa, but that she, though acknowledging her affection for him and her attachment for no one else, "resisted the temptation of renewing the improper part of her intercourse with him." That he met her suddenly one day in England at the commencement of the French Revolution, and that she tried to avoid him; having been driven from France with other emigrants, she had determined, while in England, to remain concealed from him. And that, on the whole, she conducted herself with such decorum as finally "to secure a most brilliant establishment in marriage and the protection of the respectable Josephine." I may add, as in some degree confirmatory of the above, that a foot-note in Vol. II. of the "Memoirs" quotes a passage in a letter from Francis soon after his return to England to an intimate friend in India, which very probably refers to Mrs. Grand, viz. "You will be glad to hear that —— is established at Paris, creditably in the society of Madame Vanlée." I suspect that the 'n' in this last word is a misreading or a misprint for 'r'; and remembering that Varlé is given in the Calcutta Marriage Register as the spelling of the maiden name of Mrs. Grand, it seems not unreasonable to infer that

* From some unpublished verses by Lord Byron (1814), in private possession.

† Francis arrived in England (October 19, 1781) some considerable time (how long is uncertain) after Mrs. Grand; he may have never learned of the Dutch ship consequences—or never told his second wife of them if he had.

the blank stands for her, and that she was living with some relative on the father's side.

On the other hand, to show what sort of stories circulated in France relative to the years between Madame Grand's arrival there and her second marriage, one may be quoted, not because I believe it to be in the least more susceptible of proof than many others, but because it professes to be so circumstantial as to names, places, dates, etc., etc.

A work in four volumes published in London in 1834 (four years before his death), entitled "Life of Prince Talleyrand," is without the author's name, but is evidently a translation of a work published in French in Paris in the same year, the name of the author being given in the catalogue at the British Museum as C. M. de Villemarest. This book says correctly enough that Madame Grant (*sic*) was born at Tranquebar, and it produces what purposes to be a summary of an account given by a British Naval Officer, Lieutenant Nath. Belchier; namely, that Madame Grant succeeded in the month of August, 1792, in escaping from France, having witnessed under her very windows (in Rue de Mirabeau, afterwards called Rue de Montblanc) the massacre of the porter * of the house in which she resided. In her hurry she left behind everything she possessed, and landed at Dover with her maid, and with about twelve louis in her pocket.

There Belchier made her acquaintance, and learned that her property had been sequestered in France. The lady had been married in India to an English gentleman, the union did not prove happy, and she left India before her divorce from her husband was pronounced. This circumstance turned out most favourably, as she was thus still a British subject, and had the right to claim her property from the Government. A gentleman named O'Dryer set off with Belchier for Paris, with full powers to act for Madame Grant in the recovery of what was left there. In this they eventually succeeded; leaving Paris again on November 19, carrying with them her property, part of which was gold, and much money and bank bills, diamonds, pearls, and other jewels, etc. Having overcome innumerable difficulties, they delivered her fortune back to Madame Grant, and both refused any pecuniary recompense. The

* It will be remembered that it was on August 10, 1792, that the massacre of the Swiss guard occurred. So infuriated were the brutal mob at the heroic devotion shown by the guard at the Tuileries that almost all their country-men, the Swiss porters in the hotels, etc., of the city, were butchered by bands of savages, who rioted through the streets after the sacking of the palace.

account concludes by recording that Mr. Belchier calls God to witness (why is not apparent) that his only object was to thus succour a Royalist lady then very ill, and, in spite of her sufferings, of remarkable beauty. Though this work seems to have appeared in Madame Grand's lifetime, the translator in the English copy adds, in the form of a foot-note, that the greater portion of the plate and objects of value thus preserved did not belong to Madame Grand, but to a French nobleman, who was thought to have preceded the Bishop of Autun in her affections, and who, during many years of distress in England, was often heard to deplore that she had despoiled him of all the valuables he had left. The nobleman's name is given as Viscount de Lambertye, who is said to have returned some years after to France, and being in want, was advised to apply to the then Madame de Talleyrand. His demands were stated to be granted, he thought, at the suggestion of Talleyrand. Instead of four hundred thousand francs, he consented to accept, without any written deed, nine francs daily, which were paid from 1808 till his death in 1813.

It is curiously suggestive that another work, published in London many years before the one just quoted from, alludes in an indirect way to the story attributed to Belchier. This book is in two volumes (London, 1805), written in a spirit most hostile to Talleyrand, and says, amongst other things, that, in a petition to the Directory in 1797, Madame Grand proved herself to have been a Danish subject, and that the Minister of Police allowed her, as such, to return to France with a Danish pass. In a foot-note in this book, reference is made to another, "Les intrigues de C. M. Talleyrand," which is alleged to say that when Mr. Grand heard of his wife's flight to England, not knowing her circumstances, *i.e.* the wealth recovered for her by Belchier, forgot that he had been injured, and sent her "an unlimited credence from Switzerland." We know, of course, that Mr. Grand was in India in 1797; but I quote the statement for what it is worth, lest if, by any chance true, I should be omitting a circumstance which redounds highly to his credit. It will be remembered that in his "Narrative" he alludes mysteriously to "a friend" who was substantially grateful for conduct of his when in prosperity.

Many pages would be occupied were an attempt made to give even a summary of the fables written by French authors as to the first acquaintance of Madame Grand with Talleyrand. Their number seems to suggest how little was really known on a subject, in regard to which information, one must suppose, from the many stories that were current, was eagerly sought.

In July, 1797, Talleyrand became Foreign Minister, through the influence, it is said, of Madame de Staël with Barras the Director. Some authors say, that it was very soon after this that Madame Grand came under his notice; one of them, indeed, declares that he had from the Prince himself, whose secretary he was, the circumstances of their first meeting which, in one form or another, are given by several writers, namely: that Madame Grand naïvely presented herself to the Minister of External Relations, in alarm at the report which she had heard from the best authority, that Bonaparte was about to invade England, and had promised to give the Bank of England up to pillage; her visit was with the object of begging Talleyrand to get a guarantee that her property, which was all locked up there, should be saved for her. That her friends, amongst whom was M. de Montrond, had advised her to hasten to him for this purpose. The story goes that the Foreign Minister saw the joke that had been played upon her, but being too polite to tell her so, quieted her with a document guaranteeing the safe delivery of her plate, jewels, etc., to any person she may name, as soon as ever Bonaparte's army had entered London! The one point worth noting in this story is, that it keeps up the idea of the lady being in possession of considerable property in the days of the Directory.

A work which passed through several editions, published in London, before and about up to 1808, is entitled "The Female Revolutionary Plutarch." It professes to give an outline of the histories of many ladies, and of Madame de Talleyrand amongst them. The retailing of scandal seems to be its sole object. The author's name is not given, but is acknowledged to be that of "The Revolutionary Plutarch," another defamatory production generally attributed to M. Lewis Goldsmith, father of Lady Lyndhurst. In this book the details of the money and valuables recovered by Belchier (who was then only twenty-one) are given: the amount was over twenty-five thousand pounds. Before her emigration it states, "the train of life she led at Paris was exceedingly extravagant; she was surrounded by depraved gallants." Talleyrand had been in her company at Paris before her arrival in England; but if among her admirers, he was never supposed to have gone farther. "In courting her in London he was at first more in love with her fortune than with her person, or rather by enjoying the one, he hoped to be enabled to dispose of the other." This work also says that after passing four years in England, Madame Grand returned to Paris under a fictitious name inserted in a neutral pass, and that she continued to reside with Talleyrand, incognito, till 1797. He then presented a petition to the Directory in her name, in which she proved herself to have been born a Danish subject, though married to an Englishman. This petition was approved by the Minister of Police, but from prudence she remained under the protection of the Danish Minister, Chevalier Dreyer. Her general Calcutta antecedents are also told in this book, with tolerable accuracy.

Other accounts say that about 1797 Madame Grand arrived in Paris from London, almost without resources, being charged by some *émigrés* with certain negotiations which got her watched by the Police, and for protection from whom she sought an interview with Talleyrand, who was immediately captivated by her.

Even that most respectable authority, Madame de Rémusat, in her published "Memoirs," allows a theatrical element in their first meeting. Her version is this, "Under the Directory Madame Grand wished to go to England, where her husband resided (*sic*), and she applied to M. de Talleyrand for a passport. Her beauty and her visit produced apparently such an effect upon him, that either the passport was not given, or it remained unused. Madame Grand remained in Paris; and shortly afterwards she was observed to frequent the Hotel of External Relations, and after a short time she took up her abode there."

However, as pointed out by M. Pichot, the accounts which assign 1797 as the date of the acquaintanceship are contradicted by a letter which M. Michaud (Junior) says that he himself saw, and which Talleyrand must have written early in 1796.

Whether Talleyrand met Madame Grand in England, where he was early in the Revolution, or in New York, as some allege, or elsewhere, it is circumstantially mentioned in the "Biographie Universelle" by Michaud, that she came to Paris with him from Hamburg in the first days of 1796; that Talleyrand had very little money then, and went into a modest furnished lodging. He soon had the vexation to see arrested and sent to prison his travelling companion, on suspicion of her having had intimate relations with some emigrants at Hamburg. To obtain her release, Talleyrand himself was obliged to write to Barras, the Director. The characteristic letter, for the authenticity of which M. Michaud vouches, is probably known to many readers, but for those who may not have seen it, I here give it—

"CITOYEN DIRECTEUR,

"On vient d'arreter Mme. Grand comme conspiratrice. C'est la personne d'Europe la plus eloignée et la plus incapable de se mêler d'aucune affaire. C'est une Indienne, bien belle, bien paresseuse, la plus désoccupée de toutes les femmes que j'aie jamais rencontrées. Je vous demande intérêt pour elle. Je suis sûr qu'on ne lui trouvera pas l'ombre de pretexte pour ne pas terminer cette petite affaire à laquelle je serais bien faché qu'on mit de l'eclat. Je l'aime—et je vous atteste à vous, d'homme à homme, qui de sa vie elle ne s'est mêlée et n'est en état de se mêler d'aucune affaire. C'est une véritable Indienne, et vous savez à quel degré cette espéce de femme est loin de toute intrigue.

"Salut et attachment,

"CH. M. TALLEYRAND."

Readers in India will, perhaps, conclude from the above, that the astute Talleyrand had something to learn about the dove-like proclivities of veritable "Indiennes."

M. Capefique, who in a later edition of the "Biographe Universelle" calls Madame Grand "rare et nonchalante beauté indienne," says, in allusion to the above letter—

"De Talleyrand au temps du Directoire avait réclaimé pour elle la protection de Barras et l'avait publiquement sollicité de lui rendre la liberté. On inserra dans les journaux un petit billet de Talleyrand écrit à Barras ; on en a dupuis nie l'authenticité, il est impossible pourtant que personne ait imité ce ton, cette désinvolture du grand seigneur le vieil ami de Lauzun, ecrivant à un gentilhome roué, à Barras sur une affaire galante."*

To conclude about this hiatus in Madame Grand's life which is so difficult to fill in, I may mention here that as a last resource I had an application made for information on this subject to the National Archives at Paris. Everything concerning the Foreign Minister's mistress and wife must have been thoroughly known to the French Police, more especially as her name seemed to have been often before them. It occurred to me that possibly something would be on record, which after so long a lapse of time might, without indiscretion, be made available for literary or historical purpose.

The answer which was sent to me from Mr. Alfred Maury, the Director-General, was as follows :—

"On a trouvé plusieurs dossiers au nom de Grand ; mais aucun ne se rapporte à la future Princesse de Benevent. Il est à supposer que s'il existait un dossier à son nom, il a été detruit comme bien d'autres pendant le ministere de Talleyrand et de Fouché."

This will be a good opportunity for seeing what French chroniclers of this time say of the beauty of Madame Grand, which soon became

* This letter is given in the "Memoirs of Barras" as published in 1896. He exerted the influence asked for, but seems to have had some difficulty with his colleagues.

the theme of Paris society. M. Colmache was the author of a small volume, translated into English also, called "Revelations of the Life of Prince Talleyrand." In his position as secretary, he seems to have been admitted to the intimacy of the statesman, whose last moments also he witnessed and wrote an account of. He tells some interesting anecdotes about Talleyrand, and disposes of some venerable ones which had long passed current as genuine. He knew Madame Grand before her second marriage, but it is curious that he lays down rather authoritatively that her maiden name was Dayrl, her father a Breton, and that she was born at L'Orient, but taken in early infancy to India. However, as touching her personal attractiveness, his testimony, as that of an eye-witness, should not be open to cavil. "Madame Grand," he says, at the time of her reappearance with Talleyrand, "had the kind of beauty which is the rarest and the most admired in Europe. She was tall and slight, with that languor in her carriage peculiar to creole ladies; her eyes were well open and affectionate (caressants), her features delicate, her golden hair playing in numberless curls, set off a forehead white as a lily. She had, moreover, preserved a child-like grace in her expression and throughout her whole person; it was this which distinguished her from those Parisian ladies who might, perhaps, rival her in beauty, and made her resemble rather Madame Récamier than Mme. Tallien or Mme. de Beauharnais." "The Female Revolutionary Plutarch," in describing her, remarks, "With manners naturally easy, with passions naturally warm, and with principles light, she unites something pleasing, something seemingly unaffected, unstudied and simple." Madame de Rémusat, says on the same subject: "She was tall, and her figure had all the suppleness and grace so common to women born in the East.* Her complexion was dazzling, her eyes of the brightest blue; and her slightly turned-up nose gave her, singularly enough, a look of Talleyrand himself. Her fair golden hair was of proverbial beauty."

* Nineteen years before Madame Grand saw the light, Southern India (Anjengo in Travancore) had given birth to another beauty, also, who was destined to bewitch two historical characters of high literary renown, viz. Eliza Draper (wife of a Bombay civilian) beloved by Sterne and by the Abbé Raynal. Some of her captivating graces are, as in the case of Madame Grand above, attributed to her Oriental birth. Raynal wrote that Eliza's name would for all time rescue the insignificant Anjengo from oblivion, and adds, "Anjenga c'est à l'influence de ton heureux climat qu'elle devait sans doute cet accord, presque incompatible, de volupté et de decence qui accompagnait toute sa personne. Le statuaire qui aurait en à representer la Volupté l'aurait prise pour modèl. Elle en aurait également servi à celui qui aurait eu à peindre la Pudeur."

On Madame Grand's return to Paris, one writer says that she resided at Montmorency, where Talleyrand visited her, and where high play was indulged in by those frequenting their society. He adds that, "she was an inoffensive pleasing companion at table and beautiful as Venus herself, which was all that he (Talleyrand) looked for."

If we are to believe what some French authors say on the subject, the marriage of Madame Grand with Talleyrand was brought about as dramatically as their first meeting.

Up to 1801 Talleyrand was under the ban of excommunication pronounced against him in 1790 by Pius the Sixth, and the liaison of the ex-Prelate, though a public scandal, might have been tolerated were it not that his demi-official receptions as Foreign Minister were held by Madame Grand. One account relates that Fouché brought to the notice of the First Consul a scurrilous article in an English newspaper upon him, whereon Bonaparte in a rage sent for Talleyrand: "No wonder," said he, "that we are villified in England when we expose ourselves to it by the conduct of our public Ministers; the Envoys and Ambassadors for Foreign Courts are, I understand, compelled to wait upon your mistress: this must not continue."

"Neither shall it," retorted Talleyrand, "they shall henceforth wait on my wife." It is stated in the memoirs of Baron Meneval, private secretary to Napoleon, that Talleyrand asked permission to marry, but Napoleon for some time discountenanced it as indecorous in one so recently secularised.

Madame de Rémusat gives a somewhat similar explanation of the marriage, but with the important exception that it was by no means a proposition of Talleyrand's. This lady, from her position at the French Court, had the best opportunities for learning the actual facts, and her version is, in all probability, the true one.

From this we learn that Madame Grand did the honours of Talleyrand's table and salon, and "with a good grace;" but that difficulties arose with the ambassadresses, some of whom would not consent to be received at the Foreign Office by the lady presiding there, whereupon the latter complained, and the protests of both sides came to the ears of the First Consul, who at once sent for Talleyrand and told him that Madame Grand must leave the house. This was not so easy to accomplish. Madame Grand, with admirable promptitude, went to Josephine and supplicated her to procure her an interview with Bonaparte.

Baron Meneval says that he saw Josephine one day in Napoleon's cabinet to which she had ascended by the private staircase, and that she induced him to come down to her rooms and hear Madame Grand. Contemporary evidence tells us that at this time she was, though not in the hey-day, still in the rich maturity of her charms; she was nine-and-thirty. But what of that? A woman is never any older than she looks; and Napoleon, when afterwards disparagingly alluding to her at this epoch, acknowledged that "elle etait très-belle femme."

At the interview with the First Consul she fell on her knees—and very probably it was the old story—woman's best weapons, tears and cajoling, triumphed once again, for the softened Bonaparte (who was wont to say that "there are two things becoming to women—rouge and tears") dismissed her saying, "I see only one way of managing this—let Talleyrand marry you, and all will be arranged. You must bear his name, or you cannot appear in his house." Chancellor Pasquier in his memoirs tells that this interview occurred at Malmaison, and that when it was over Napoleon said, "That woman had just shown him how far the wish to satisfy a passionate desire could give eloquence even to the most foolish."

Once bent on making a marriage Bonaparte lost no time, but at once conveyed his decision to Talleyrand, and gave him but twenty-four hours to think about it.

These hours were so well employed by the lady herself, that Talleyrand reluctantly assented, influenced, as Madame de Rémusat conjectures, by "the remains of love, the power of habit, and also perhaps by the fear of irritating a woman whom it is impossible to suppose he had not admitted to his confidence."

Josephine, too, is said to have been a warm advocate for the furtherance of Madame Grand's wishes, an interference which some say Talleyrand did not forget when a few years later he supported Napoleon's scheme for a divorce.

The marriage took place on September 10, 1802, before the Mayor of the 10th arrondissement of Paris, and in the presence of several important and official personages, enumerated in A. Jal's "Dictionary of Biography" (French), many of whom signed the register. Talleyrand's age is given as 48. The bride is described as the daughter of Pierre Worlee and of Laurence Allamay,* his wife, and as the divorced wife of G. F. Grand; she signed the register as C. N. Worlee. To this civil marriage it seems that the Curé of Epinay was induced to give his benediction in his little church next

* Mr. Julian Cotton told me that he found among the archives of the Ministère des colonies a copy of the "Acte de Mariage of Pierre Verlee and Lawrence *Alleigne*."

MADAME DE TALLEYRAND.

FROM A SMALL PORTRAIT BY GÉRARD IN HIS MUSÉE AT VERSAILLES.

*See p.* 292.

day, as Lady Blennerhasset records; otherwise there was no religious ceremony in connection with it.

In the preceding year Talleyrand had obtained from Pius the Seventh a revocation of the excommunication passed on him by the previous Pope, and a sanction for his return to secular life.* Though he himself acted as if he believed this to be authorisation enough for annulling priestly celibacy and for his entry into the marriage state as a layman, the Pope did not, and highly resented the step, and, it is said, made it a condition, when he afterwards came to the French Court, that no one should present to him "cette dame."† The London *Times*, June 29, 1804, when speaking of the splendid preparations for the Coronation of the French Emperor and Empress adds, "Talleyrand will remain excluded, on account of his marriage, from the place which he coveted. He is said to be very much dissatisfied, and Madame de Talleyrand does not conceal her spleen on the occasion." Talleyrand's own relations also were said to be much outraged, so much so, that his mother declined any longer to accept the allowance which her distinguished son made her. Madame de Staël wrote from Paris (June, 1802), to her "beautiful Juliette," Madame Récamier, then in London, "Madame Grand, they say, is to be married to M. de Talleyrand. Bonaparte would like every one to marry bishops, cardinals, etc. I wish it were allowed for all the priests to marry; there would be no more fear of them then."

The First Consul, however, looked askance at the lady whose marriage he had promoted; whether he did so to wound Talleyrand, whom he really never liked, but whom he could not do without, or from personal objection to herself, is not very clear. At any rate according to Madame de Rémusat:

"He treated her coldly, even rudely; never admitted her to the distinctions of the rank to which she was raised without making a difficulty about it; and did not disguise the repugnance with which she inspired him, even while Talleyrand possessed his confidence. Talleyrand bore all this, never allowed the slightest complaint to escape him, and arranged so that his wife should appear but seldom at Court. She received all distinguished foreigners on certain days, and on certain other days the Government officials; she made no visits, none were exacted from her. Provided each person bowed to her on entering and

* The words in the Papal brief are, "ouvrant donc à votre égard les entrailles de notre charité paternelle, nous vous dégageons par la plenitude de notre puissance du lien de toutes les excommunications. Nous vous accordons le'pouvoir de porter l'habit séculier, et de gerer toutes les affaires civiles."

† Pie VII. n'appela jamais Madame de Talleyrand que *cette dame—questa donna.*—("Biog. Univ.")

leaving his salon, Talleyrand asked no more; he always seemed to bear with perfectly resigned courage the fatal *tu l'as voulu* of Molière's comedy."

In no aspect of the case, therefore, could Talleyrand be congratulated; bullied in the first place by Bonaparte because he was not married, and then in disgrace with the Pope because he was.

The First Consul was remarkable for the want of even the ordinary courtesy of a gentleman to ladies, but so pronounced did his cold demeanour to this attractive woman appear to Court society that the wits of the day felt bound to seek some cause for it, not lying on the surface; and accordingly this was one of the anecdotes accounting for his resentment, which went around.

When Madame de Talleyrand appeared first at Court after her marriage, Bonaparte, with patronising impertinence, expressed a hope to her, that the future good conduct of the citizeness Talleyrand would cause to be forgotten the indiscretions (légèretés) of Madame Grand; to which the bride naïvely rejoined, that in this respect, perhaps, she could not do better than follow the example of the Citizeness Bonaparte! *

Napoleon himself has given a very sufficient reason for his action regarding Madame Talleyrand, if he is to be believed. When speaking to O'Meara at St. Helena in a tone of very moral elevation (the austerity of which will perhaps sound strange to modern readers who know his own multitudinous liaisons and moral obliquities), he said: "The triumph of Talleyrand was the triumph of immorality; a priest married to the wife of another, and who had given a large sum to her husband for permission to retain his wife; a man who had sold everything and played the traitor to every side and every one. I forbad Madame T. to come to my Court, chiefly because her

* Madame Junot gives a characteristic instance of the manner in which Napoleon went out of his way sometimes to distress ladies by his insolence. At a ball given at Neuilly by his sister Caroline, the wife of Murat, the Emperor, out of humour, was going the tour of the circle, and stopped opposite Madame Regnault, a beauty of eight and twenty with an exquisite figure. While examining her dress, the simplicity of which made her even more charming and graceful than usual, he remarked bitterly, in a solemn bass voice loud enough for all to hear, "Do you know, madame, that you are looking much older?" The lady had the philosophy to answer firmly, with a smile, "What your Majesty has done me the honour to observe might have been painful to hear had I reached an age when truth is regretted." "With women," says Madame Junot, "the Emperor never joked, or if he did the joke was a thunderbolt." She then adds naïvely, "The strange mania that possessed him of telling wives of the infidelities of their husbands was never agreeable, and sometimes gave rise to very painful feelings."

reputation was run-down (decriée), and because I discovered that some Genoese merchants had paid her 400,000 francs in the hope of obtaining some commercial favours through the intervention of her husband." If true, not a bad stroke of business, it has been remarked, for one reputed to be a fool.

Napoleon had spoken of the Talleyrands even more disdainfully than this at Elba in a conversation with which he favoured Lord Ebrington, who, in the course of it, asked him if Talleyrand was a clever man. The Emperor answered: "certainly, mais que voulez-vous d'un h'omme depourvu de toute principe de toute honte, enfin d'un prêtre defroqué, d'un éveque marié, et marié avec une putain."

It was at Neuilly that the Talleyrands lived after the marriage; Madame de Rémusat writes to her husband at Mayence from Paris, September, 1804: "I called on Madame de Talleyrand yesterday morning; she was very civil, and said she'd tell her husband to tell you she had seen me. She asserted so strenuously and so often that her husband was delighted, happy, and on the best terms with the Emperor, that I was half tempted to doubt it." There also Sir Elijah Impey visited them immediately after the peace of Amiens; and, if there be any foundation for the sentimental scandal of Lady Francis, even the mature bosom of the ex-Chief Justice was not invulnerable to the witcheries of his hostess. But as an extraordinary statement, made in connection with this renewal of acquaintanceship between old Calcutta friends, will compel me again to refer to Mr. Grand's "Narrative," I must be particular in quoting it exactly, more especially as it seems to have been accepted as true by the English and French writers who have reproduced it. In the life of Sir E. Impey, by his son, page 386, we find the following:—

"Among the persons whom we met in the very mixed society of Paris, was the ci-devant Mrs. Le Grand (*sic*), who had lately been married to M. de Talleyrand, then Minister for Foreign Affairs.

"My father renewed his old acquaintance with her; and through the lady he became sufficiently intimate with the extraordinary diplomatist, her husband, to be one of the Englishmen most frequently invited to his table. The *soirées* and *petits-soupers* of Madame de Talleyrand at her charming Villa of Neuilly were at this period about the most select in France, being rivalled only by those of the Consuless Josephine, the literary Madame de Staël, and the fashionable and fascinating Madame Récamier. They invited not only the *Corps-diplomatique*, but all such as were distinguished by their station or talents.

"At one of these assemblies, myself being present, this remarkable *rencontre* took place of persons not likely even to have met beneath the same roof under any circumstances less fortuitous. These persons were

Mr. and Mrs. Fox, Sir Elijah and Lady Impey, M. and Madame de Talleyrand, Sir Philip Francis, and Mr. Le Grand!"

Mr. Impey writes as an eye-witness. In the first place it may be observed that on his own showing he was only in Paris during the visit he alludes to, for a portion of December, 1801, and of January, 1802. Now, as we have seen already, there was no Madame de Talleyrand till September, 1802, and Francis was not Sir Philip till 1806. But allowing for some little confusion in dates, it would be safer to assume some strange betrayal of memory, or mixing up of circumstances, on Mr. Impey's part, than to believe that such an unfortunate meeting of conflicting elements would not have been guarded against by one, of whom Talleyrand's secretary testifies,—"she was unrivalled in the tact and *convenance* with which she received company." Philip Francis as a septuagenarian had nothing to gain or lose by not being frank on this particular point with his second wife, who distinctly says, that he told her that he as well as Sir E. Impey was in Paris after the peace, and that he received a message from Madame Grand telling him of her prospects, and asking him not to attempt to see her, lest M. Talleyrand might take offence; and so much did she deprecate even an accidental meeting at that critical time, that, to avoid all chance of it, she expressed her intention of making a little excursion into the country. To carry out her wishes, Francis says that he hastened his own departure from Paris, and that he never set eyes on her again, "that the only intercourse which took place was a few elegant books which she sent him with a short note, merely to tell him that she had not forgotten him." He also said that Talleyrand, whom he did meet then and at other times, was always ungracious to him in manner, and gave no encouragement to an acquaintanceship. There is quite enough probability in all this to shake our faith in evidence to the contrary, coming even from a truthful witness who may have got confused about his reminiscences.

But Mr. Impey's story was not new; he published his father's life in 1846, and over thirty years before that, the alleged coming together of incongruities at Neuilly had been in print, and found its way to the Cape of Good Hope, possibly to the African Club there, where it came under the observation, and aroused the indignation, of poor old Mr. Grand, and inspired this postscript to his "Narrative," dated April 30, 1814, viz.—

"A miserable author, denominating himself the Modern Plutarch,*

* The anecdote is not in the "Modern Plutarch," which is a poor collection

has had the impudence to assert 'that at a dinner given by M. de Talleyrand in 1802, then the Minister of France for Foreign Affairs, there sat down to table the former Mrs. Grand with her former husband, Sir Elijah Impey, who had presided on the Bench in the action-at-law brought by him before his tribunal, and Sir P. Francis, who had committed the injury.' I treated the remark at the juncture, when I saw the publication, with the contempt so unfounded an assertion merited, and it had accordingly escaped my memory when I was finishing the narrative of my life which I have given. . . . I feel myself compelled to animadvert thereon, and, out of justice to both parties implicated in this illiberal and false observation, to refute this calumny in all its points.

"I do, therefore, call God to witness that to my knowledge I never saw the first Mrs. Grand, *Neither in India nor in Europe* from that melancholy Sunday, viz. December 13, 1778—the sensation of which day I have described, and which fixed our eternal separation. We remained from that moment like those who, having lived for a time in the height of happiness, have witnessed that happiness suddenly and unexpectedly interrupted by one being cut off never in this world to meet again. Persons of this stamp never can forget the ties which had existed. We knew the delicacy of each other's sentiments, and never once thought of infringing that line of conduct which such a sense of feeling naturally prescribed. Those whose minds are congenial will credit my assertion; they will be reckoned in the number of my English readers, for with most of the French such an idea would be condemned as preposterous in the extreme. I have known some of this nation very amiable men, yet assuming the liberty which an Englishman would, however intimate, refrain from, that of entering into your domestic concerns, express themselves to the following effect on this subject: '*faites divorce aujourdhui, mon cher, mais remariez vous demain; c'est la plus belle femme qui existe.*' Such was the only sacrifice which the uncommon charms of her beauty had created with such men. They deemed it alone requisite for *l'etiquette ou l'usage du monde* to be observed in the manner which I have related. Such is the difference of sentiment existing between two nations only separated from each other by a branch of the sea; nevertheless, each thinking that honour guides their respective nations.

"I certainly went to Paris in 1802, and with the exception of the friend of my youth, Mr. Wombwell, and my lamented friend Sir Elijah Impey, saw during my sojournment in that capital none of the other persons mentioned. I lodged at the Hôtel du Cercle, Rue de Richelieu, an hotel for the accommodation alone of male strangers. Madame de Talleyrand was, as I understood, inhabiting Neuilly, a residence in the environs of Paris appertaining to M. de Talleyrand. It was in the

of brief biographies published at Berwick in 1811; but in the "Female Revolutionary Plutarch," which must be the book that Grand referred to. But even in this book it is not apparently told for the first time, but is merely quoted; the ancedote ends with the remark, "It is difficult to carry connubial toleration and revolutionary politeness farther."

height of summer, and few people of rank frequented the city. I gratified my curiosity in seeing the public buildings, etc., and after an abode of a very few days departed for Switzerland, etc., etc."

There we may leave the dramatic *rencontre* at "the charming Villa of Neuilly." But Mr. Grand's postscript suggests some considerations on another matter. His solemn statement in this, while perhaps literally true, conveys an impression the reverse of true; it certainly does so, if, when he parades their mutual delicacy and the absence of all thought of infringing what it prescribed, he wishes it to be believed that he not only did not actually see his former wife, but had no communication, direct or indirect, with her. No one reading this disingenuous postscript would suspect, for instance, that a very prominent object in this visit to Paris (which was spent in "seeing public buildings") was the negotiating with the Talleyrands for an appointment which would provide him with a livelihood, and which, above all, would get him out of Europe. Mirza Abu Taleb Khan, whose book of travels before referred to was not translated from the Persian until some years later, visited Paris, he says, in *May*, 1802, and saw Sir E. and Lady Impey there with "their beautiful daughter." Impey, he understood, was trying to recover a large sum of money which in the early part of the Revolution he had placed in the French funds. He goes on, "I was much surprised to meet here my shipmate Mr. G——d. He had come to Paris to improve his fortune through the interest of Madame Talleyrand, to whom he once had the honour of being husband. I understand she has since procured for him an appointment under the Dutch Government at the Cape of Good Hope."

This oriental gentleman does not seem to have much doubt as to the object of Grand's visit to Paris.

From his former allusion to the offer of a handsome pension from a certain "liberal friend" tendered through Sir E. Impey, and his acknowledging that he did see the latter during this Paris visit, it may fairly be inferred who the friend in need was, and that the go-between in the final negotiations was the wily old Chief Justice. From another source, too, we find that Sir Elijah was in Paris in 1802. His son, in a letter from Newick, April, 1802, says that his father was refused a passport for getting out of France, though Talleyrand applied for one for him to Berthier, Minister at War. For a knowledge of the circumstances attending on Mr. Grand's deportation from Europe to the Cape, I have again to express my indebtedness to an interesting little volume of "Recollections of Talleyrand," brought together by M. Amédée Pichot. Before quoting him, it may be well to premise that in the Act de Mariage between Talleyrand and Madame Grand (September 10, 1802), she is described as the divorced wife of G. F. Grand, by an Act pronounced in Paris in April, 1798 (le 18 germinal, an. vi.) —*i.e.* just two years before Grand arrived from India. How the divorce (presumably obtained under the law of republican France) was brought about, or whether money facilitated it, I have come across no evidence which will show. However, the fact of its having been got nearly four and a half years before his marriage, contradicts this statement of Madame de Rémusat, with reference to the alleged necessity for hush-money, viz. "It appears that Mr. Grand, who lived in England, although little desirous of receiving a wife from whom he had long been separated, contrived to get himself largely paid for withholding the protest against the marriage, with which he repeatedly menaced the newly wedded couple."

M. Pichot also has it, that the divorce was only obtained just before the marriage, and was not consented to till a large sum was paid.

We have already seen what Mr. Grand has told us himself about his going to the Cape consequent on a "proposition made to me from the Batavian Government;" he also gives a translation of the order defining the appointment, with its emoluments, to which he was nominated—

"Extract from the Consultation of an Assembly of the States governing the Batavian Republic—

"In this Assembly it was this day proposed, and after mature deliberation resolved, to nominate Mr. G. F. Grand to the station of Privy Councillor of the Government at the Cape of Good Hope. He is accordingly appointed and established in the above situation with a salary annexed thereto of 2000 Caroli guilders annually.

"And further it was resolved to transmit copies of his nomination to the Secretary of State for Foreign Affairs, to the Directors of the East India Company, and to Mr. G. F. Grand, in order to serve for their respective guidance.

"S. DASSAVAEL,
"*Secretary.*"

This is dated ten days after the marriage of the Talleyrands, *i.e.* September 20, 1802; and some light is thrown on the spirit which guided the Assembly's "mature deliberations" by the following autograph letter sent a month later by Madame de Talleyrand herself to M. Van der Goes, the Minister for Foreign Affairs of the Batavian Republic:—

"MONSIEUR,

"Je ne veux pas tarder davantage à vous remercier de votre obligeance, et de tout ce que vous avez bien voulu faire pour M. Grand à ma demande.

"L'empressement et la grâce que vous y avez mis, me prouvent, Monsieur, que l'on ne compte pas en vain sur votre amitié, et cela m'autorise à vous demander un nouveau service. C'est celui de faire enjoindre à M. Grand de s'embarquer sans délai, étant tout â fait inconvenant qu'il prolonge son séjour à Amsterdam, où il est déjà depuis un mois,* *fort mal à propos.*

"Je vous serai donc tres-obligé de vouloir bien lui faire parvenir le plus tôt possible (chez M. M. R. et Th. de Smeth, à Amsterdam) l'ordre pour son embarquement, vous priant, Monsieur, de recevoir d'advance tous mes remercîments à cet égard et d'agreer l'assurance de ma plus parfaite consideration.

"TALLEYRAND-PERIGORD, NEE WORLEE."

She was evidently very proud of her new name, because only twelve days after her marriage (1 vendemiaire, an. xi.), in writing to the same correspondent, she says: "You will see, sir, by the name which my union with M. de Talleyrand gives me the right to bear, how the tender and sincere affection of that amiable friend has made me the happiest of women."

As M. Pichot remarks, it was a stroke of high diplomacy as well as national economy on Talleyrand's part to get the Batavian Republic (which could refuse nothing to France since 1795) to provide for Mr. Grand. That Talleyrand himself was the suggester of an application to his Netherlands' colleague is evident from a passage in a letter from Madame Grand to M. Van der Goes in the month preceding the marriage (3 fructidor, an. x. = August 20, 1802) "M. de Talleyrand m'autorise à vous mander qu'il vous aura une obligation particulière de ce que vous ferez pour moi à cette occasion." And again, when the Batavian Minister announces to her the embarkation of Grand, in the fulness of her gratitude she writes: "M. de Talleyrand is as sensible as I am of your kind offices, and charges me to repeat to you all that I have already conveyed to you of his recognition, and his desire to give you proofs of his attachment and consideration (January 2, 1803)."

* It so happened that this delay saved Grand's life. The ship which he ought to have embarked his distinguished person in (the *De Vrede*) was wrecked off Dungeness, and all the passengers were lost.

But the putting to sea of Mr. Grand was not destined to quite bring to an end the bride's apprehensions about him; it was not for nothing that she wished to hasten his departure; probably no one knew better than M. de Talleyrand how long the Peace of Amiens was going to last. The rupture came (May 16, 1803); but the only concern which the renewal of war had for poor Madame de Talleyrand was in connection with Grand's voyage. What if it were not over? What if some dreadful British cruiser were to capture the ship transporting him, and land himself back again in Europe? Here would be a sorry trick for fate to play her, after matters had been arranged so nicely, too; this would be "*fort mal à propos*" with a vengeance! To whom could she more suitably confide her new anxieties than to her tried ally, Van der Goes? That sympathising friend was equal to the occasion, and with a gallantry that never failed, he again came to her relief, with the intelligence which calmed her fears, that Councillor Grand had arrived at the Cape.

Readers are referred by M. Pichot for the proofs of the authenticity of this curious correspondence, to a history of the "Diplomatic Relations of the Batavian Republic," published at the Hague, only in 1864, by Professor Wraede, of the University of Utrecht, to whom the autograph letters were communicated by Baron Van der Goes, son of Talleyrand's friend. In Dr. G. McCall Theal's "History of South Africa, vol. iii. (1891),* we find a little more about this appointment of Mr. Grand, viz. "There are strong indications in the official documents that both M. De Mist (Commissioner-General at the Cape, 1803-4) and General Jansen (Commander-in-Chief) were not unfavourably disposed towards the Orange party, though they served the Batavian Republic faithfully. . . . Another instance of jealousy of French influence occurred in the treatment of a man named George F. Grand, who arrived in South Africa in April, 1803, and claimed the position of Privy Councillor and the second place in the Government. De Mist knew nothing whatever of the man or the office, and he was not as much as named in any despatches received from Holland. His pretensions, therefore, were disregarded, though he was treated with courtesy. He was by birth a Swiss, but had been for many years in the service of the English East India Co. until, for some unexplained cause, he was dismissed. He could not speak a word of Dutch. At length particulars concerning him were received from Holland, where, it appeared, he had been appointed

* My friend Sir David Barbour, who had occasion to study South African questions, was thoughtful enough to kindly bring Dr. Theal's valuable work to my knowledge for information about Grand's position at the Cape.

consulting Councillor, with a salary of £166 13*s.* 4*d.* a year. He had been for some time separated, but not legally divorced from his wife, owing to her seduction by the celebrated Philip Francis, and she was then married to a French Minister of State of the highest rank. This being the secret of Grand's appointment, M. De Mist did not pay much regard to the importunate requests for a seat at the Council, if not the second place in the Government. He was informed that he would be consulted in matters relating to the Indian trade, of which he was supposed to have special knowledge. To this vague position he was at length obliged to submit." In other words, the honest, stolid Dutchman politely compromised the matter by giving Mr. Grand his pay and no work. It will be seen that the Cape records were not accurate as to the point of Grand not being at the time "legally divorced."

As we shall have no further occasion to refer to Mr. Grand, it is only fair, before dismissing him, to notice another incomprehensible statement disparaging to him and to Madame de Talleyrand, which appears in a footnote in Mr. Impey's Life of his father, and which has been reproduced, with acceptance seemingly, in the "Memoirs of Francis"—

> "Part of the sequel of Le Grand's history I can supply: After the Peace of Paris, in 1815, he came to London; so did Madame la Princesse de Benevento. His object was to publish the particulars of the lady's life at Calcutta in revenge for his disappointment at Batavia—hers to seek redress for the publication. I saw it; it was a paltry book, printed at the Cape. They both applied to me. I advised the author to suppress his work, and the Princess not to go to law. This advice, of course, was very unpalatable to both: the lady took a legal opinion, and the gentleman took himself off. What became of him since, I know not; but the libel shortly disappeared, and the matter seems to have ended as amicably as before."

All I can say about this is that, if Mr. Impey read the book, which he says he saw, he would not thus have hashed up an old blunder of MacFarlane's (in "Our Indian Empire") and called the narrative a libel. Those who have gone through the numerous extracts which have been given from it, will have seen that Mr. Grand never imputed even blame to his wife, frail though she was, and that he alludes to her with gentleness and with kindness; to those who can read between the lines, it will be probable, too, that he writes under a sense of obligation for favour conferred. Where, then, is the libel for which redress was to be sought? He tells us himself of the philosophical way in which he took his disappointment about the official post found for him, and his words do not breathe much of the spirit of revenge—against a woman, too, who did her utmost for him, for her own sake as well as for his. The man, moreover, even whose correct name Mr. Impey does not know, never went to Batavia, but to the Cape of Good Hope, which, it is violently improbable, he ever left again, as, with the proverbial triumph of hope over experience, he dared a second marriage, and this time successfully, as we may gather from two or three contented passages in his "Narrative," viz.—

"I feel blessed in my second domestic attachment, and I thank Heaven daily that what I have been denied in consequence, say worldly honours and riches, it has pleased the Almighty to compensate me in unimpaired faculties and an uncommon share of health and activity far surpassing what might be expected in my years (February 1, 1808)."

"Sir Elijah Impey congratulated me (in reference to his escape from shipwreck), observing that he trusted this Almighty miraculous deliverance portended at once that I am reserved for happier days * than those which I had recently experienced. I thanked him, and must gratefully repeat his prediction has been accomplished, in the enjoyment of the blessings of health, of a composed mind, and of an amiable partner, and a continued cheerful residence with her worthy family."

The last sentence in the dedicatory letter (introducing his "Narrative") written in 1814, when he was at least sixty-six, and evidently at peace with the world, and disposed to stay where he was so, is, "You know the sequel—happy in my second choice of a partner, I upbraided not the worldly opportunity lost. My happiness centred alone in domestic concerns. May you be blessed in the like manner, should it ever be your lot to deplore, as I did, the cruel separation which forced me from the first." I must leave to others the task of reconciling, if they can, these passages with Mr. Impey's footnote; I cannot fancy a more difficult one.

Whatever may have been the indiscretions chargeable to Madame Grand, her conduct after her acquaintanceship with Talleyrand began seems to have been without reproach. In only one instance afterwards was the whisper of scandal heard about her. When

* Those happier days might have been bitterly marred; poor Mr. Grand just escaped having had occasion to cry, like Ahab of old: "Hast thou found me, oh mine enemy?" for about 1806 the offer of the Governorship of the Cape, with the Order of the Bath and the rank of Privy Councillor, was offered to Francis, but declined. This appears from a statement of claims submitted by him to the Prince Regent, in which he refers to it, and to his having been unfairly passed over for the Governor-Generalship of India.

Napoleon was attacking Spain he got into his power (1808) the Spanish princes, *i.e.* Ferdinand, the eldest son of the King, his brother (Don Carlos), and his uncle (Don Antonio). These he sent with their suite to the Chateau of Valencay, the country seat of Talleyrand, who was then Grand Chamberlain, and ordered him to have them there kept in easy, cheerful confinement, and to do all in his power to amuse them. This was all the harder on Talleyrand, as he is understood to have disapproved of Napoleon's dealings with the Spanish princes, who had thrown themselves into his arms. In the letter in which the Emperor conveyed his orders to Talleyrand he said, "There would be no harm in sending for some comedians if you have a theatre at Valencay. Madame de Talleyrand and four or five ladies might also remain at the Chateau. There will be no inconvenience should the Prince of Asturias (Ferdinand) fall in love with a pretty woman, especially if she can be depended on. It is of the greatest importance that the Prince of Asturias should not commit any blunder. . . . I have determined to send him to a country seat, and to surround him with pleasures and supervision." * Mr. McCabe, in his volume on Talleyrand (1906), says that after Napoleon had enticed the princes to Bayonne, and forced Ferdinand to abdicate the throne on which he had succeeded Charles IV. after the Spanish Revolution (1808), he wrote to Talleyrand on May 1, "King Charles is a frank, good-looking fellow. Ferdinand is a brute, very malicious, and very hostile to France." A few days later he wrote again, about receiving and guarding the princes at the mansion he had just bought, adding sarcastically (?), "Your mission is an honourable one: to receive and entertain three illustrious personages is quite in keeping with the character of the nation and with your rank." Talleyrand received 75,000 francs a year for maintenance of the princes, which he drew after he ceased to be Grand Chamberlain. The spiteful tongues of "all Paris" said at the time that Madame de Talleyrand played her part in the arrangements for amusement in a manner much more calculated to please the Emperor than her husband. This little scandal, however, may have only had its rise, when, some few years later, Peninsular affairs going badly for the French, Napoleon desired to treat with Ferdinand for his restoration, to whose overtures the latter made a dutiful reply, adding,

* The Prince of Asturias was at this time twenty-four years old, and a widower, having been married at so early an age that (as Hookham Frere, the British Minister at Madrid, wrote to Lord Liverpool), "His innocence and simplicity were so great as to have produced a very ludicrous embarrassment." *Vide* "Life of Lord Liverpool," vol. i. p. 90.

*Copyrighted by*] [*Fishel, Adler, and Schwartz, New York.*

PRINCESSE TALLEYRAND.

FROM A PORTRAIT BY MADAME VIGÉE LE BRUN.

*See p.* 305.

"I have spent five years and a half very pleasantly, and would willingly pass the remainder of my life at Valencay." * The supplement to this story is that, when rumour brought to the Emperor's ears the secret of Ferdinand's being enabled to enjoy his enforced idleness without ennui, he was mean enough to introduce the matter in conversation to the Chamberlain, to which Talleyrand calmly observed, "It is true, sire, that it would have been better, both for the honour of your Majesty and for mine, that there never had been anything to do with these Spanish princes." This anecdote is given also in the memoirs attributed to Fóuché, who says that it occurred at a *levée* in the midst of courtiers, and adds, "Never did Napoleon display so much confusion as after receiving this severe lesson, given in a manner which showed such a high sense of good breeding." McCabe (*op. cit.*) says that it was Don Carlos who repaid his host by becoming the lover of Princess Talleyrand; Madame de Rémusat affirms it was only platonic. This discrepancy suggests the small foundation for the rumour. The same author gives a slightly different version of the Emperor's interview (with Talleyrand) when in a rage, and discussing public affairs with his staff. "To Napoleon's brutal observation, 'You did not tell me that the Duke of San Carlos was your wife's lover,' Talleyrand quietly retorted, 'I did not think it redounded either to your Majesty's honour or mine.' The only remark that Talleyrand made to the Court dignitaries present when the Emperor had flounced out of the room was 'What a pity that such a great man had not a better education.'"

It is said that Madame de Talleyrand's great elevation gave her but short-lived happiness, and that, like most *parvenus*, she went but indifferently through the trials of prosperity. Stories are told of her affectation of royal state, in having maids of honour, pages, etc., which possibly have some truth in them, as an anecdote relates that when courtiers came to congratulate Talleyrand on his advancement by Napoleon in 1806 to the rank of Prince of Benevento, he stopped them with, "Eh! Mon Dieu, vous vous trompez; ce n'est pas ici—c'est à Mme. de Talleyrand qu'il faut faire vos compliments, les femmes sont toujour bien aises d'être princesses."

A couple of those stories are thus told in an article on "Talleyrand at the Congress at Vienna," in *Temple Bar* for April, 1883.

"Talleyrand had been accompanied to Vienna by Madame de Talleyrand, whose eccentricities were hardly compatible with perfect soundness of mind. . . . We shall content ourselves with citing two

* See the "Marriages of the Bonapartes," by the Hon. D. A Bingham.

anecdotes on the faith of a most trustworthy eye-witness. The Princess had two young nieces (*sic*) in her suite who had not yet entered their teens. Her practice was on the evenings of her receptions, when a sufficient company had assembled, to direct a pair of folding doors to be thrown open, through which the two young ladies made their *entrée* into the salon with their arms encircling each other, and proceeded to execute a series of *pirouettes* round the room, ending at last with a graceful curtsey before Madame de Talleyrand.

"This was comparatively an innocent oddity on her part, although it bored her guests. Her second oddity was more mischievous, and caused great offence. She would frequently, during the evening receptions, ring the bell, and order her groom of the chamber to say that she was not at home, and after the lapse of a quarter of an hour or twenty minutes she would ring the bell again and give a counter order. The consequence was that husbands who called for their wives had to go home without them, and wives who came in search of their husbands could find no admittance; and all that Talleyrand could say when a diplomatist of the highest rank remonstrated with him was, 'Mais, mon cher, que voulez-vous que je fasse. Ma femme est si bête.'"

Talleyrand was too much of an aristocrat himself, and had too keen an appreciation of the ludicrous not to feel humiliated at Madame's pretensions; and this, added to his irritation caused by her jealousy of his relations, and their cordial detestation of her, was, perhaps, a factor rendering separate establishments desirable. Possibly, too, he wished for separation on other grounds. Raikes, in his Journal, says that this occurred in 1815, and that long before that time he had been the favoured lover of another lady, whose daughter, a fascinating beauty (designated as the Duchess of D———), eventually presided over Talleyrand's house. Against such a formidable conjunction of adverse influences, Madame la Princesse had now but little to oppose, because at this epoch, as we learn from a contemporary, Time was making his inevitable mark. and "the elegance of her figure was injured by her becoming stout," and (alas! that it should be to tell) "this afterwards increased, and by degrees her features lost their delicacy, and her complexion became very red." Whatever may have led to the separation, or whether it occurred under the Empire or the Restoration, one of the conditions of it was that Madame was to reside in England on the allowance of sixty thousand francs a year, and not to return to France without Talleyrand's consent. The Duke of Wellington told Lord Stanhope that he was applied to by the Princess in 1815 to mediate a reconciliation between her and Talleyrand. Whether the sojourn in England was long or short we know not, but that she returned to France is vouched for in the well-remembered answer of Talleyrand to the king, who slyly asked with affected interest if it was true that Madame de Tallyrand was in France. "Rien n'est plus vrai, Sire, il fallait bien que j'eusse aussi mon vingt Mars." *

The establishment which Madame Talleyrand maintained after the separation from her husband was at Auteuil, and there she entertained society and regulated her household in strict imitation, it is said, of that of Talleyrand's. All the domestic details being so conducted, and all the surroundings so arranged, as to keep in active life a memory that was very dear to her. M. Colmache says that in those days he was often the bearer of kind messages to her from Talleyrand, if it ever became known to him that she was in the least out of health. In M. Pichot's collection of souvenirs, there is one relating to the Princess's life at Auteuil, which may be quoted, as the author vouches that he had it direct from the proprietor of the Villa Beauséjour there, which she rented. It appears that there was attached to her as companion a countess of the old *régime*, one of whose duties was to follow her at a respectful distance when she went out on foot: if the countess happened to come a little too near, the Princess turned and said severely, "Comtesse, vous perdez le respect." There are (to use a homely phrase) "many ups and downs in life," but we doubt that there is often seen a stranger contrast than the one which this anecdote suggests—namely, between the position of this "Princesse" censuring a gentlewoman of high birth for coming too close to her nobility, and that of the trembling young wife of some years back, whom we saw at midnight appealing in vain to a native servant in India, to release her captured lover and so to save her reputation.

In spite of the high position that Madame Grand made for herself, there is no observation more common about her than that she was a very stupid woman; so widely has this been disseminated that its belief has been established, and, perhaps, the most prominent characteristic now recalled of this half-forgotten celebrity is her proverbial silliness. Most reigning beauties, it may be observed, are credited with dulness; the impression seems to have been always general that a pretty face and a comely figure are incompatible with any other endowment. One has not to be long in the world to learn that "Mrs. So-and-So is certainly very handsome, but insipid to a painful degree, nothing whatever in her;" indeed, there would appear

* On March 20, 1815, Napoleon re-entered the Tuileries on his escape from Elba, Louis XVIII. having quitted them at midnight on the 19th.

to be something rather soothing than otherwise in the reflection that our neighbour's beauty is counterpoised by stupidity, and that "Fortune will never come with both hands full."

It is not improbable that something of this too hasty generalisation, coupled with a little envy, helped to propagate the belief that has so long outlived Madame Grand. It may be worth while, if only as a matter of curiosity, to see how far a few circumstances in general acceptance regarding her career justify this belief.

I have already glanced at the stories connecting her prominently with negotiations on behalf of émigrés; she is also mentioned as having at one time been brought to Paris by a Mr. Bellamy—"Pour la meler à des intrigues financieres." * Several writers on Talleyrand (Lady Blennerhasset amongst them) aver that as Foreign Minister he accepted large "considerations" from various European Courts for his countenance to their interests in the treaties with France, and that Madame Grand gave him valuable assistance in smoothing little difficulties with ambassadors, by reminding those who did not offer sufficiently liberal terms, how handsomely other negotiators had acquitted themselves. All this may possibly have been untrue, but it would never have been said of a woman who was a fool, whatever else she might have been. Again, it is inconceivable that so shrewd a man as Talleyrand would have allowed her during the four or five years prior to their marriage, to conduct his receptions if, as Madame de Rémusat records, "She was so intolerably stupid that she never said the right thing;" and this at a period when Bonaparte's victories and treaties had filled Paris with ambassadors and foreigners of distinction.

Yet the same authority says rather inconsistently in another place, "I have heard it said she was one of the most charming women of her time," which seems to suggest that Madame de Rémusat had but little personal acquaintance with her. M. Colmache, speaking from his own knowledge of Madame Grand's demeanour at the Foreign Minister's receptions, says, "She dispensed politeness to each and all alike, contenting every one." Mental shallowness and social tact are not necessarily incompatible. He allows that she evinced a certain *inexperience* in the social traditions of the world in which Talleyrand placed her, which amused the wits who frequented her society. Talleyrand fell a victim † to her after

* "Biog. Universelle."

† M. Colmache was constantly at Valencay with Talleyrand, and in his recollections of the Prince's table-talk, which he was in the habit of noting down, he relates that the latter thus once unbosomed himself to him, showing that under

he had escaped the beauty of Madame Récamier and others, and the fascinations of Madame de Staël: his secretary accounts for this "by the *naïveté* which gave so strong a tinge of originality to all which Madame Grand said or did, so unlike the slavery to forms and etiquette which must ever influence professed women of the world such as those by whom he was surrounded."

One of the most hostile, and probably most untruthful, of the contemporary writers who have sketched her, remarks (in the "Female Plutarch," where there is scarcely a good word said of any one) "That Madame de Talleyrand has no pretensions to genius everybody who has frequented her society knows; and she avows with *naïveté* itself that she is a *belle bête*. But a long habit, perhaps from her infancy, has naturalised to her an art to impose, a cunning to deceive, and an hypocrisy to delude, etc., etc. . . . She certainly does not want that social capacity, that good sense and more light accomplishments which good breeding and good company always confer."

A much safer authority, M. Michaud, writes thus of Madame de Talleyrand: "Nous avons eu l'avantage de l'entendre plusieurs fois, notamment à l'epoque de 31 Mars, 1814 (capitulation of Paris), et nous pouvons affirmer que sa conversation sur ce grand evénement n'etait point celle d'une sotte." Philip Francis said of her, that "her understanding was much better than the world allowed." We, who know the circumstances of her premature embarkation on life, can understand how her education, in the ordinary sense, must have been neglected, and this disadvantage must have weighted her heavily ever after; but she was educated in the school of events, and that she profited by such schooling is evident by her rising, in spite of the terrible drawbacks connected with her early years. If not learned herself, she at least affected the society of the learned, even long after living apart from Talleyrand, as may be gathered from many sources. Readers of Moore's Diary will remember his

certain circumstances a woman's very foibles can be delusive and charming: "My passion for Madame de Talleyrand was soon extinguished, because she was merely possessed of beauty. The influence of personal charms is limited; curiosity forms the great ingredient of this kind of love; but add the fascination of intellect to those attractions which habit and possession diminish each day, you will find them multiplied tenfold; and if besides intellect and beauty you discover in your mistress caprice, singularity, and irregularity of temper, close your eyes and seek no further—you are in love for life." That experienced and amusing libertine, Casanova, lays down a similar maxim, "La femme qui parvient à inspirer de la curiosite à un homme, a fait les trois quarts du chemin necessaire pour le rendre amoureux."

recording that he went in Paris (in 1822) to the Princesse Talleyrand's to hear Viennet, a distinguished author, read his tragedy of *Achille*, and may recall the amusing incident, "heard two acts declaimed by him with true French gesticulation; the ludicrous effect of his missing one of the *feuillets* in the middle of a fine speech, and exclaiming in the same tragic tone, 'Grand Dieu ! qu'est ce que c'est que çá ! !'"

Moore also tells how, in the previous year, he had sat next her at a dinner party, and that "she talked much of 'Lalla Rookh,' which she had read in French prose," and "praised Bessy's beauty to me." Surely even Madame de Rémusat would acknowledge that, under the circumstances, these were "the right things" to say?

There are probably very few who have not heard or read the funny mistake about Robinson Crusoe attributed to Madame de Talleyrand; the anecdote has been the round of every newspaper in Europe and America, and will perhaps ever be quoted when her name is mentioned. It is more than likely that this anecdote is mainly responsible for the popular impression about her want of sense. If this piece of "evidence" be broken down, there is really little else to support the allegation of stupidity. Though the story has been worn threadbare, it must be given here again, to show one of the high authorities who have vouched for its truth, and to let the reader see how the narration is tinged with a spite which weakens it as evidence. Napoleon thus told it to O'Meara at St. Helena in 1817:—

"I sometimes asked Denon (whose work * I suppose you have read) to breakfast with me, as I took a pleasure in his conversation, and spoke very freely with him. Now all the intriguers and speculators paid their court to Denon with a view of inducing him to mention their projects or themselves in the course of his conversation with me, thinking that being mentioned by such a man as Denon, for whom I had a great esteem might materially serve them. Talleyrand, who was a great speculator, invited Denon to dinner. When he went home to his wife, he said—'My dear, I have invited Denon to dine; he is a great traveller, and you must say something handsome to him about his travels, as he may be useful to us with the Emperor.'

"His wife, being extremely ignorant and probably never having read any other book of travels than that of Robinson Crusoe, concluded that Denon could be nobody else. Wishing to be very civil to him, she, before a large company, asked him divers questions about his man Friday. Denon, astonished, did not known what to think at first, but at

* "Voyage dans la basse et la haute Egypte pendant les campagnes du Général Bonaparte, par Vivant Denon."

length discovered by her questions that she really imagined him to be Robinson Crusoe. His astonishment and that of the company cannot be described, nor the peals of laughter which it excited in Paris as the story flew like wild-fire through the City, and *even* Talleyrand himself was ashamed of it."

The Emperor was evidently but an indifferent *raconteur*, or his story loses by translation from the Italian in which he conversed with O'Meara. An apology is due to the reader for reproducing so poor a version of this well-known anecdote; as an *amende* I give here the original and best one for the benefit of those who may not have seen it. It appears in "L'Album Perdu," and is attributed to M. Henri Delatouche. It is probably an interesting instance of the gradual improvement for stage purposes of old stories—

Peu de temps après le retour de l'armée d'Egypte et des savants qui avaient été témoins de cette glorieuse expédition, M. de Talleyrand, invita à dîner M. Denon. "C'est, dit M. de Talleyrand à sa femme, un homme très-aimable, un auteur, et les auteurs aiment beaucoup qu'on leur parle de leurs ouvrages; je vous enverrai la relation de son voyage, et vous la lirez afin de pouvoir lui en parler." An effet M. de Talleyrand fit porter dans la chambre de Mme. de Talleyrand le volume promis, et celle-ci l'ayant lu se trouva en mesure de féliciter l'auteur placé à table à côté d'elle. "Ah! monsieur, lui dit-elle, je ne saurais vous exprimer tout le plaisir que j'ai éprouvé à la lecture de vos aventures.—Madame, vous êtes beaucoup trop indulgente.—Non, je vous assure; mon Dieu, que vous avez dû vous ennuyer, tout seul, dans une île déserte! Cela m'a bien intéressée.—Mais il me semble madame, que...—Vous deviez avoir une drôle de figure avec votre grand bonnet pointu?—En vérité, madame, je ne comprends pas...—An! moi je comprends bien toutes vos tribulations. Avez-vous assez souffert après votre naufrage!—Mais, madam je ne sais...—Vous avez dû être bien content le jour où vous avez trouve Vendredi! M. de Talleyrand avait donné à lire à sa femme, peu *liseuse* comme disait la maréchale, Lefebvre, les *Aventures de Robinson Crusoé*."

The tenacity with which the public cling to a time-honoured story, and the reluctance with which they see any attempt at the deposition of an old favourite, was curiously illustrated some years ago, when the *Times* opened its columns to a spirited correspondence as to the authenticity of this anecdote. The occasion was a Review in the *Times* of Sir H. Bulwer's "Historical Characters," where the author introduces this anecdote, naming not Denon, but a Sir George Robinson, as the hero of it (others assign this position to Humboldt). M. Pichot, a staunch sceptic as to the conclusiveness of the evidence which attributes stupidity to Madame de Talleyrand, led the way in an admirable letter, humorous and logical, showing that the old story has not even the merit of originality. He was immediately attacked by one who challenged his dates and authority, and threw out doubts as to the year when a translation of Robinson Crusoe appeared in France: and who also quoted Moore's version as he had given it in his Paris diary of 1821, as though he seemed to imply that this should be regarded as evidence. Mr. Dominic Colnaghi (the eminent engraver, etc., etc., of Pall Mall, who died in 1879) also took part in the correspondence; his argument as to the anecdote's being authentic amounted to this, that his father had heard it in Paris in 1806 from a Miss Dickinson, then said to be the *demoiselle de compagnie* of Madame de Talleyrand. A story, too good to be doubted, is often repeated at the time and place of its origin, till it comes to be believed in, even by contemporaries, but this does not prove that it may not be *ben trovato* nevertheless. The source which M. Pichot suggests for the anecdote in the following passage in his letter leaves little doubt in my mind that he was right in suspecting that Madame de Talleyrand's mistake was the "invention of some English wit or a French *bel-esprit*"—

"Extraordinary again—is it not?—that hitherto English readers have overlooked this passage of a letter of Horace Walpole to Sir H. Mann, dated October 22, 1741.—'The whole town is to be to-morrow night at Sir Thos. Robinson's Ball, which he gives to a little girl of the Duke of Richmond, etc.'

"In a note (Pichot refers to the American Edition of 1812, Lord Dover being the Commentator) to this letter we are told that Sir Thos. Robinson of Rokeby Park, commonly called Long Sir Thomas, is elsewhere styled the new Robinson Crusoe by Walpole, who says, when speaking of him, 'He was a tall uncouth man, and his stature was often rendered still more remarkable by his hunting-dress, a postilion's cap, a tight green jacket, and buckskin breeches. He was liable to sudden whims, and once set off in his hunting suit to visit his sister, who was married and settled at Paris. He arrived while there was a large company at dinner, the servant announced Mr. Robinson, and he came in to the great amazement of the guests. Among others a French Abbé thrice lifted his fork to his mouth and thrice laid it down with an eager stare of surprise. Unable to restrain his curiosity any longer, he burst out with, 'Excuse me, Sir, are you the famous Robinson Crusoe so remarkable in history?'"

At all events a mistake made by a French Abbé may fairly be excused in a lady. M. Colmache says that many of the blunders laid to the charge of Talleyrand's wife bear the unmistakable stamp of the firm of Montrond & Co. As I have referred to this gentleman as an authority on the subject, I may mention that his questioning

Talleyrand as to the truth of the popular anecdote led to his being told one much more likely and nearly as amusing. The Robinson Crusoe incident did not actually happen, said Talleyrand, "but it was guessed at and that was enough; the blunder was ascribed to her without compunction;" and then he added—

"I certainly remember a *naïveté* which she once uttered in the midst of a circle of savans and literati at Neuilly, which would be considered quite as good and become just as popular were it as generally known. Lemercier had volunteered after dinner to read us one of his unplayed and unplayable pieces. The company had gathered round him in a circle; his *cahier* lay already unfolded on his knees, and, clearing his voice, he began in a high, shrill tone, which made us all start from our incipient slumber. '*La Scène est à Lyon.*' 'There now, M. de Talleyrand,' exclaimed the princess, jumping from her chair, and advancing towards me with a gesture of triumph, 'Now I knew that you were wrong; you would have it that it was the *Saône!*' To describe the embarrassment and consternation of the company would be impossible. I myself was perplexed for an instant, but soon remembered the difference of opinion to which she had alluded. As our carriage was crossing the bridge at Lyons, a little time before, she had asked me the name of the river that flowed beneath. I had told her it was 'Saône'; to which she replied, with a truly philosophical reflection, 'Ah, how strange this difference of pronunciation; we call it the *Seine* in Paris!' I had been much amused at the time, but had not thought it worth while to correct the self-confident error, and thus had arisen this extraordinary confusion in the troubled brain of the poor princess. Of course we all laughed heartily at her unexpected sally; but we were grateful nevertheless, for it saved us the reading of the dreaded drama, as no one that evening could be expected to *retrouver son sérieux* sufficiently to listen with becoming attention to all the terrible events which Lemercier had to unfold."

"The keenest shafts of ridicule," continues M. Colmache, "must have fallen pointless against one who joined with such hearty good will in the mirth which was thus raised, without at all agreeing with those who deemed that it was excited at his own expense." Silence respecting his private troubles, an appearance of complete indifference,—politeness, patience, and dexterity in taking his revenge were the weapons, according to Madame de Rémusat, with which Talleyrand met the general condemnation of his marriage. Chancelier Pasquier ("Memoires," published 1893), referring to the marriage, writes: "Ce qu'il y'a de certain, cependant, c'est que s'il existe une circonstance de sa vie sur laquelle M. de T. ne se soit depuis ouvert á personne, sur laquelle il ne se soit laisse pénétrer par aucun de ses amis, c'est celle-la."

Madame de Talleyrand lived to 1835, dying on December 10 in

that year. Curious to relate, even the very close of her extraordinary career was marked by a dramatic incident, which is thus noted by the English papers, though the Paris papers, the *Constitutionel* and the *Journal des Debats*, merely notice her death, the latter paper adding, "La Princesse était d'origine Danoise." The *Morning Herald* of December 17, 1835, says—

"A very curious scene is said to have taken place in the Chamber of the Princess de Talleyrand after she had expired. She had given in her dying moments a casket containing papers to the Archbishop of Paris who attended her, with the injunction to hand them to the Comtesse D'Estignac; that lady having come, the Archbishop proceeded to fulfil the directions of the defunct, when a personage representing the interests of the prince interfered, and said the papers should not be given up. Madame D'Estignac had also a friend who interfered on her behalf of her right to the casket, and violence threatened to terminate the dispute, when a *juge de paix* hastily summoned came in and declared that he would keep the object of dispute in his possession until the right to it was legally decided."

The *Times*, referring to the same occurrence, adds—

"Report says that the casket contained the Princess's jewels and diamonds, value about £40,000. The Comtesse D'Estignac is the daughter of Prince de Talleyrand's second brother, but rumour says that the Duchess de Dino wishes to have them for herself by having them awarded to the Prince de Talleyrand."

Thos. Raikes, who was in Paris at the time, gives in his Journal a somewhat fuller account of this strange incident, and says that it made a great noise, as the dying woman had, when the last religious ceremonies were over, asked faintly for the casket and delivered it with much earnestness to the Bishop as her valid gift and last testimonial of her affection for Madame D'Estignac. Raikes tells that the affair was finally compromised for the sum of 200,000 francs on Talleyrand proving to a mutual friend, by the deeds of his marriage-settlement, that legal right was on his side. The contents were said not to have been divulged. Whether Raikes is an authority to be much depended on is somewhat doubtful. He describes the deceased as having been a Creole, born at Martinique. From his Journal we learn that the declaration of her death was thus inscribed in the Register of the Church of St. Thomas D'Aquin: "On December 12, 1835, there was presented at this Church the body of Catherine, widow of George François Grand, *connue civilement comme Princesse de Talleyrand*," aged 74 years, deceased the night before last, fortified with the sacraments of the Church, at No. 80, Rue de Lisle (query, Lille?). Her obsequies were performed in the presence of Mathew Pierre de Goussot and of Charles Demon (agent of the Prince), friends of the deceased, who have signed with us."

Raikes comments on this sententiously: "It is rather curious that, after all the satanic allusions to Monsieur de T——— in the public journals, his principal agent should be named Demon." * The curious phraseology in the declaration of his wife's death shows, as Raikes points out in another entry, that Talleyrand in his latter days seemed little inclined to perpetuate the recollection of his marriage. With this view he gave directions, the same contemporary journalist alleges, that the inscription on her tombstone should indicate the fact as slightly as possible, and that she should be there described as the widow of Mr. Grand, afterwards civily married to M. de Talleyrand. "Here," says Raikes, "his dominant foible comes out; he hopes that by treating the ceremony as a civil contract at that period of the Revolution, he may now palliate that stigma in the eyes of the clergy which is irremissibly attached to the position of a *prêtre marié*."

In the "Biographie Universelle" we are told that Madame de Talleyrand is buried in the Cemetery of Mont Parnasse, "where one can still see her tomb with a modest inscription surrounded by a simple iron railing."

* * * * * *

Having read some few years ago the above quoted passages from Raike's Journal and Michaud's biographical article on Talleyrand, I felt curious as to the tombstone inscription which the great diplomatist had finally devised or permitted in memory of his wife. To settle the point in the only way likely to be conclusive, I proposed to see the grave for myself—a visit to which I hoped to make an opportunity for, while passing through Paris on my return to India.

At the last moment, however, another route had to be taken; in these circumstances it occurred to me to trespass on the good nature of a friend, an English lady then resident in Paris, and to beg her, if convenient, to go to the grave and to copy for me the epitaph.

My correspondent, with a kindness for which I cannot sufficiently thank her, most readily acceded to my request, and made a pilgrimage to the tomb at Mont Parnasse; as her interesting letter supplies the information which it was thought desirable to have, the liberty of quoting an extract from it is taken—

". . . Regarding the last resting-place of Mme. de Talleyrand, I went over to Mont Parnasse, and, with the aid of an official, succeeded in

* The agent's name was, I believe, "Dem*i*on."

finding the tomb. As you will see by the enclosed extract from the Register kept at the Cemetery,* no mistake was possible in identifying the grave, but it corresponds with the description in one particular only—*i.e.* it is enclosed by a simple iron railing, but as to the 'modest inscription,' if it ever existed, of which there is not the faintest trace, its extreme modesty caused it long since to retire from the public gaze. The tomb was in as miserable a state of neglect as could possibly be imagined, thickly overgrown with rank grass, weeds, and nettles; in keeping with the utterly desolate forsaken look of those few feet of earth (all the more remarkable among so many carefully tended resting-places), a wreath of *immortelles* hung over a corner of the railing, put there, I suppose, by some good Catholic's hand in pity for that melancholy nameless grave. One of the gardeners, a civil young Frenchman, at my request, brought a spade and thoroughly cleared away the accumulated earth and rubbish, with which the stone slab, which is quite level with the ground, was covered to the depth of some five or six inches. Among the *débris* we found, very opportunely, an old scrubbing brush (whatever brought it there?), which served to clean the stone, and effectually convince us that any inscription it may originally have borne must have been a readily effaceable one; certainly not deeply graven, as not the slightest indication of previous word or letter now remains." †

Now we are able to see how thoroughly Talleyrand gave effect, so far as his poor wife's grave is concerned, to what Raikes describes as his disinclination "to perpetuate the recollection of his marriage."

Here I conclude this attempt at collecting and winnowing the scattered records of one whose captivations were celebrated from the Ganges to the Seine; whose beauty—not when at its zenith, but when approaching its decline—was pre-eminent in a brilliant society remarkable for attractive women; and whose name was closely connected with those of actors conspicuous on the world's stage, and was familiar to some of the great historic personages of a memorable epoch.

* The inclosure was a printed tabular form filled in at the time of the visit; it indicated the grave sought for by a division, line, and number; the corresponding entry in the Register described the grave as that of "Talleyrand (Princess de) née Worlée (Cathérine Noël)."

† I saw this grave myself, for the first time, in June, 1886, and found it just as my correspondent described it, even to the wreath, which is of thin metal (at a much later visit the wreath had gone). The railings are very low (about 24 inches). The top of the grave is quite covered with nettles. It is between the tomb of the family "Parisot" and that of one which bears the names "Halbout" and "De Cusse" on it. But should any visitor to Paris care to see it, the locality will be at once indicated by the officials in charge of the accurately kept registry.

As such, Calcutta may fairly claim her as not the least prominent of its passed-away notorieties.*

## POSTSCRIPT.

A work which I wished to consult relating to the period in which the Talleyrand marriage occurred, has reached me only when these pages are ready for the press. I therefore shall merely summarise here, as briefly as the subject admits, what I find regarding Madame Grand. Under the consulate the Bourbons kept themselves privately acquainted with political and social events in Paris. With this object they employed secret and confidential agents, who, under great precautions, sent their frequent reports. Some seem to consist of the ordinary unsifted social gossip of the hour, others are of more serious import. These reports ceased suddenly in December, 1803, probably owing to the more stringent watchings of the hitherto baffled police.

The book is titled "Relations Secrètes des Agents de Louis XVIII. A Paris Sous Le Consulat, 1802–1803." "Publies par Le Comte Rebacle, 1899." Thiers apparently had access to a copy of these reports, and made some use of them in his history. Modern historians seem to attach value to them, and quote from them often.

The first allusion to the lady with whom we are concerned is in a report dated August 2, 1802; viz. "One knows that Talleyrand lives with a lady of little known origin—Danish according to some, English to others, is named Grant (*sic*). This adventuress, beautiful still after her youth, succeeded in making conquest of Talleyrand. The worthy bishop is so taken with her late-lasting beauty that he wishes to marry her. Speaking of Madame Grant, no one asked how she got her name, no one imagined that there was a Mr. Grant in the world. What, therefore, was the surprise of those interested when Mr. Grant, the legitimate husband of the mistress of the minister, descended on Paris—hôtel du Cercle—Rue de Richelieu!†

"However, it was not on a journey of curiosity he came, but on a more serious errand. He came to Paris *pour les beaux yeux de sa femme*, or, rather, for the cash-box of the bishop. He signified to him that, having become aware of his projects regarding Madame Grant, he had come to oppose them. Married, he said, according to the English laws, the divorce obtained by his wife

* See Appendix, "Princesse Talleyrand."

† See extract from Grand's narrative.

during 'the Terror' was absolutely void, and that he valued his marital rights at, say, 80,000 francs. Monseigneur found this proposition *malhonnête*, and wished to evade it, but Grant held on and menaced him with further demands, reflecting in his speculative mind that he ought not to abandon so cheaply (*à si bon marché*) the ownership of his wife now become so precious." *

It is added that Talleyrand paid the money? Strange to say there is not a word about the Cape appointment for Grand as the reward for his complacency. If the foregoing may be credited, no wonder that poor Madame de Talleyrand gushed in gratitude, as we have seen, to Van der Goes for coming to her aid, or that she did her best to hustle out of the country the odious and importunate man who appraised her value so highly. A footnote to this report gives her right name Worlee, and that she was of Indian origin; that Talleyrand made her acquaintance at Hombourg in 1795, and brought her to Paris in the following year. In the report of August 27 is this: "We know now beyond doubt that Mr. Grant has come to Paris; and, as if Heaven took pleasure in bringing together here all the personages who have had relations with his wife, we have had a Mr. Francis, whom Mr. Grant surprised in adultery with her, and the judge, whose name has escaped me, who then condemned Mr. Francis at the suit of Mr. Grant, to pay the latter an "amende" of five thousand pounds sterling. I am assured that this judge is often at the house of the Foreign Minister, and that he is much welcomed there. One cannot say as much in the case of Mr. Francis.† It appears that all the time Mr. Grant has known how to turn his wife to very good account (*tirer très bon parti*)."

In the report just quoted from it is added that the negotiation between the Pope and *l'honnête évèque d'Autun* regarding the latter's secularisation is the subject of conversation on all sides. The report of October 3 devotes much of its space to the Talleyrand affairs, viz. "Whether we had been badly informed about the intentions of Mr. Grant in his trip to Paris, or whether Talleyrand by the force of money has made him consent to the divorce, it is certain that the secularised bishop has just married Mme. Grant in the face of the State and of the Church. It must be agreed, however, that he has not sought to give too much *eclat* to the ceremony. This is what they recount of all that has passed.

* We have seen, *ante*, the version of Madame de Rémusat and of M. Pichot as to alleged payments to Grand. Also what Napoleon is alleged to have told O'Meara at St. Helena.

† This partly agrees with what Francis told his wife long afterwards, about his being in Paris at the same time as Impey.

"On the evening before Mme. Grant wrote to Sainte-Foi to come and see her early. He came at ten o'clock, and found her alone with Admiral Bruix (confidential and official friends apparently of Talleyrand). She did not say a word of their intentions, and spoke with a sort of nonchalance of going for an airing. The hour was singularly chosen. 'Where shall we go?' she said. Sainte-Foi, who was up to matters, answered, 'We cannot do better than go to Mousseaux; we shall find there the Mayor, Duquesnoy, with whom we can deal.' The conversation ended there. Mme. Grant got into the carriage with Bruix and Sainte-Foi, and simply said to the coachman—à Mousseaux. On the way no confidences. On arrival we found Talleyrand comfortably recumbent in an easy-chair, and not having any more business air than Mme. Grant. Roderer and Bournonville, the other two witnesses, were with him. No question of anything yet. At length the Mayor, Duquesnoy, appeared with his registers. We shall now finish our arrangement, said the bishop. As a matter of fact the principals and the mayor and witnesses signed one after the other. They get again into the carriage, and set out for Saint-Gratien, where Admiral Bruix has a country house. The curé of Epinay, who was forewarned, did not delay, and contributed in his turn, in the name of the Church, to seal this lovely union."

"After the ceremony Talleyrand begged Bruix to lend him his house *pour achever la noce.* He there passed the night with his new spouse; on the morrow they returned to Paris. Certainly for a Minister of State one could not have shown less etiquette."

"There remained still another embarrassment: how to announce the marriage. The method of gazettes or even of letters seemed too pompous to the modest bishop. Sainte-Foi came to his relief, and said, 'Invite to dinner a numerous society. I shall arrange to come. I shall not arrive until you are all at table, and then in a manner to cause some derangement. I shall then advance towards Madame with a very confused and very embarrassed air, and I shall say, in a manner that every one can hear it, Madame Talleyrand, I am in despair—*Et voila votre mariage annoncé.*' This expedient was pronounced admirable, and they made use of it. The account ends, 'Who can have induced Talleyrand to this marriage is a thing not easy to divine.' It will be seen how much this gossipy account of the marriage differs from that already given, supported by the sober account found in the 'Dict. Biograph.' of A. Jal, where the ceremony is described as being much more formal. At the end of the Agent's report of December 17, 1802, instances are given of the credit and influence of Talleyrand weakening with Bonaparte, and of the latter's not troubling himself to hide his dislike and almost contempt in the discourteous way in which he treated Talleyrand as compared with other ministers bringing their portfolios to him. Then it adds that Mme. Grant, become Madame Talleyrand, shares in the disfavour of her illustrious husband. We have already seen that Napoleon told O'Meara at St. Helena that he forbade Madame Talleyrand to come to his Court. The truculent and public way in which this affront was put upon the wife of one of his chief ministers is thus recounted in this report.

"It appears that, after pressing and reiterated solicitations, the Minister had obtained for her the honour of being presented to Mme. Bonaparte. Persuaded that after that the gates of Saint-Cloud would be always open to her, she did not fail to return the following week without soliciting a fresh permission. As soon as Bonaparte happened to see her, he called out to one of the prefects of the palace before her, 'Qu'est-ce que cette femme vient faire-ici?' Because I have consented to her appearing once before before Madame Bonaparte, does she imagine that I have admitted her in my society? And he ordered the prefet du palais not to let her enter henceforth without express authority."

One of the characteristic anecdotes told of or for Madame Talleyrand appears in a report dated May 3, 1803, which we may as well conclude with. Some time ago, when that same lady saw the Duchess of Dorset (*i.e.* wife of Lord Whitworth, then our ambassador at Paris) decked with a rather handsome necklace of diamonds, she admired it, and exclaimed on its richness. "It is tolerably handsome," said Mme. de Dorset (*sic*), "but nothing extraordinary." Mme. de T. spoke of the price it must have cost. "The price," answered the Duchess, "is not exorbitant, moreover it is not such that M. de Talleyrand could not very well, and without inconveniencing himself, make you a similar present." "Ah! mon Dieu, Madame, comme vous vous trompez s'écria Mme. Grant (*sic*) croyes-vous donc que j'aie épousé le Pape?" "Cette naïveté paraitra sans doute un peu forte, mais la bêtise de Mme. est si bien connue q'on ne risque rien de la lui attribuer."

# ADDENDUM RELATING TO MADAME GRAND

The following anecdote regarding Madame Grand did not come under my notice in time to be quoted in the chapter devoted to her. It is taken from the "Memoirs of the Comtesse de Boigne," (the first part, 1781–1814,) published only last year (1907).

Talleyrand, disgusted with all the rebuffs which were showered upon him at the château (*i.e.* the Tuileries), wanted to go away, and he proposed himself for the Vienna Congress, the importance of the negotiations and the presence of the Sovereigns justifying that of the Minister of Foreign Affairs. His *salon* (she presumably means at Vienna?) was very amusing. The door did not open till after midnight, but all Europe crowded there, and in spite of the strict etiquette of the reception and the impossibility of moving one of the heavy seats occupied by the women, one could always find a way of spending a few moments there which were amusing, or interesting at any rate, for a spectator. Mme. de Talleyrand, seated at the end of the two rows of armchairs, tranquilly did the honours. The remains of her great beauty adorned her stupidity with a fair amount of dignity.

I cannot refrain from telling a somewhat indecorous story characteristic of this courtesan, then such a *grande dame.* My uncle, Edouard Dillon, who in his youth was known as "Handsome Dillon," had had all the successes that such a nickname suggests. Mme. de Talleyrand, then Mme. Grant (*sic*), had been attracted by him, but as his time was occupied elsewhere, he did not pay much attention to her. The rupture of a *liaison*, which greatly affected him, made him decide to leave Paris and undertake a journey to the East. This was an event in those days, and the mere fame of it added an interest of curiosity to his other fascinations. Mme. Grant (*sic*) redoubled her attentions, and finally, the evening before his departure Edouard consented to return home with her to supper after the opera. He found a very charming flat, the table laid for two persons, and all the studied refinements which belonged to Mme. Grant's profession. She had the most beautiful hair imaginable, and Edouard admired it. She told him that he did not yet know what it was like, and after retiring into her dressing-room, she came back with her hair loose and covering her like a veil. She was a second Eve before any dress material had been invented, and with less innocence than her ancestress, *naked and not ashamed.* The supper was finished in this primitive costume. Edouard started for Egypt the following day. This took place in 1787. In 1814 this same Edouard on his return from exile was driving with me to call on the Princesse de Talleyrand, to whom I was to introduce him. "The contrast," he said to me, "is so amusing between this visit, and the one I paid formerly to Mme. de Talleyrand, that I cannot resist telling you of my last and only interview with her." He then related me the preceding story. We were both much amused and curious as to what her attitude would be towards him. She received him wonderfully well and in a very simple way. But after a few minutes she spoke of my head-gear, admired my hair, wondered how long it was, and then, suddenly turning to my uncle, who was just behind my chair, she said : "Monsieur Dillon, you like nice hair, do you not?" Fortunately our eyes did not meet, as it would have been impossible for us to have kept serious.*

* This story is told so circumstantially, and is so respectably vouched for, that one is almost bound not to disregard it in a summary of Mme. Grand's strange career. Still when one looks at it with a microscopic eye, there is seen a difficulty in accepting it. If we get over the surprise at such a story being told by an uncle to his niece, we are confronted by the *militavi non sine gloria* which peeps out here and there in it, which suggests that the old beau delighted to recall for his handsome, attractive companion what a fascinating young fellow her mother's brother had been. Such exploits must be received with the caution, acted on as a well-recognised maxim, to put out of court as a trustworthy witness the vainglorious ingrate who kisses and tells. Nor does the Comtesse de Boigne seem to have been an unbelieving or reluctant recipient of this naughty confidence about the dramatic supper and the tragic nudity of the fair hostess. From a feline pat or two which she gives in the narration, she shows herself not shocked, or sorry to afford it credence. She certainly manifests none of that kindly charity which tells us—

> "To still believe that story wrong,
> Which *ought* not to be true."

Mme. Grand has sins enough to answer for without this of unwomanly indecency being added. It is only fair to say this much for her, that M. Colmache's description of her *chevelure* recalls, as we have seen, "her golden hair playing in numberless curls, set off a forehead white as a lily." Gérard's small portrait of her in our illustrations rather confirms the idea that her beautiful hair, however richly abundant, was rather short and curly than long, and so not well adapted for the Lady Godiva-like use which she made it serve at the supper table according to the story. Incidentally this anecdote suggests that the easy *aplomb* with which the Princess smoothed over a rather delicate situation by her *naïve* question to Mr. Dillon at his interview many years after, shows the belief on the part of some of her acquaintances that she had more wit and readiness and social tact than is traditionally held about her.

MRS. HASTINGS.

FROM A PAINTING BY OZIAS HUMPHREY.

*See p.* 321.

WARREN HASTINGS.

FROM A PAINTING BY ABBOTT.

*See p.* 321.

# CHAPTER X

## LETTERS FROM WARREN HASTINGS TO HIS WIFE

EXTRACTS from some letters of Warren Hastings to his wife, to which have been added a few letters written by Mrs. Hastings (hitherto unpublished).

### PREFATORY NOTE

The fact of a large number of unpublished letters from Warren Hastings to his wife being in existence and available to the public, was first made known to readers in India by Mr. Beveridge, in 1877, in his valuable articles on Warren Hastings in the *Calcutta Review.* These letters, with a vast amount of other papers relating to Hastings which have yet to be explored and utilised by the historian, were acquired by purchase by the British Museum only in 1872. It is with the letters to Mrs. Hastings only that it is proposed to deal at present; these are considered so worthy of special care that they are not shown to the applicant for them in the large general reading-room, but in a smaller one in connection with that containing selected manuscripts.

They are bound in a thin quarto volume, and an attempt has been made to arrange them in chronological order, which has not been very successful, owing to many of the earlier letters being dated with the day of the week only.

In the extracts given from them I have endeavoured to rectify this defect.

The letters may be divided into three series: the first comprises those written from Calcutta in 1780, and are endorsed "Letters from my excellent Husband when I was at Hughly and Chinsura"; during this absence of Mrs. Hastings the duel with Francis occurred. The second series of letters are not in original, but are thus endorsed in very faint ink—"This paper contains a faithful copy of the letters conveyed in quills to Mrs. Hastings while Mr. Hastings was at Chunar: the originals are in Mrs. Hastings' possession, together with the quills in which they are enveloped." The third relate to Mrs. Hastings' voyage to England, and her husband's own doings afterwards until he prepared to follow her.

It may be useful to explain how these letters in all probability got separated from those, not superior in interest, which were long ago printed and published. We may learn this from what Mr. Gleig says in his preface to the Memoirs of the Life of Hastings. Warren Hastings died in 1818; soon after that the whole of the family papers were put into the hands of Mr. Southey, with the proposal that he should become the biographer of the late Governor-General of Bengal. Having kept the papers a good while, Mr. Southey returned them with the avowal that he could not undertake so complicated a task. After a long interval a similar proposal was made to Mr. Impey, and to him the papers were sent. He kept them and laboured at them for six years, but when he died not a word of the Memoir had been written. Again the voluminous and deterrent documents found their way back to Daylesford, where they lay in absolute confusion until 1835, when Mr. Gleig got them and was occupied with them for six years. With all these moves and changes it would be strange if some of the family papers did not get lost or separated. The disadvantage at which the compiler of the Memoir was thus placed, finds expression in this passage in his introduction :—"The letters entrusted to me are not always consecutive, and it has unfortunately happened that precisely at points where most of all it was essential that I should find materials for my biography in the handwriting of the subject of it, such materials are wanting."

Accordingly, in the letters from Hastings to his wife which Gleig gives as being "full of interest," there are many allusions which are scarcely intelligible from want of letters that must have preceded them, and whose absence must have greatly perplexed the biographer.

The letters of Hastings to his wife, remarks Macaulay, who had seen only the few given by Gleig, "are exceedingly characteristic. They are tender and full of indication of esteem and confidence, but at the same time a little more ceremonious than is usual in so intimate a relation." A more extended acquaintance with Hastings' domestic letters will, perhaps, show that this qualification was not altogether justified. He evidently was an inexhaustible correspondent. The letters to his wife were written in the most ungrudging frequency, and although he was thus under no obligation to recompense rarity by length, the length to which most of his letters to her did go was something miraculous in the case of such an Atlas who had such a world on his shoulders. The burden of nearly every one of them is the same—the assurance of his unceasing love—of the aching void her absence has created—his morbid apprehensions and repinings, and his passionate yearning to regain her. All indicate what a lonely man Warren Hastings really was. No one can doubt the earnestness or the depth of sincerity and truth from which these fond outpourings flowed.

"He seems to have loved her with that love which is peculiar to men of strong minds, to men whose affection is not easily won or widely diffused" (Macaulay).

In the excerpta that follow, I have, as a general rule, given the shorter notes of the first series in full; from the rest I have only attempted to extract such portions as may have a local interest and significance for Indian readers especially, and which may tend to elucidate personal character and feeling, and help to afford a nearer view of the inner life of one who belongs to history. "The business of the biographer," says the prince of biographers—quoting the *Rambler*—"is often to pass slightly over those performances and incidents which produce vulgar greatness; to lead the thoughts into domestic privacies, and display the minute details of daily life."

*Calcutta, Sunday morning* (*July* 16, 1780).

"MY DEAREST MARIAN,

"I write this purposely to tell you that I have resolved to meet you to-morrow unless you arrive before the time which I have fixed for my embarkation.

"My plan is to set off in my Feelchehra at 2 o.'c. in the afternoon which will be about the beginning of the flood tide, and of course the time that you will be at anchor.—I shall carry my dinner with me, and feel great pleasure in the project. I hope you will not disappoint me, for I shall not choose to land at Chinchura for many reasons. I will not quarrel with Mrs. Motte, but I will certainly turn her out of her place.

"Adieu, my beloved,

"W. H.

"Compliments to Mrs. Ross, Mrs. Motte, and Mrs. Vernet. I will write to Mr. Ross. Remember me particularly to Mrs. Vernet."

"*Monday evening.**

"I intend to make a second trial of the Manège for the cure of my joints, which continue shamefully stiff and cramped.

"I find that Naylor's distemper is that for which Japan rise is a specific. I shall be obliged to you, therefore, if you will either send me a little, or tell me where I can get it. I have seen nobody and heard nothing. But I have a letter from Madras, which mentions the arrival of the Company's ships *York*, *London*, *Portland* and *Bridgwater*. The only news of consequence is, that it is determined that I am to remain as long as I choose, but with the some associate.† My compliments to Mrs. Ross and Bibby Motte."

(In due sequence, the three letters referring to the duel, given elsewhere, would come in here.)

"*Calcutta, August* 19, *Saturday evening.*

"MY DEAR MARIAN,

"I have nothing new to write to you but what you will find in the enclosed letter. I now wish your return. Indeed I have all along wished it, though for reasons which I have mentioned, and for others

* *i.e.* August 14th. † *ie.* Francis (*see duel*).

which I have not, I opposed my own inclinations. Sir John Day is arrived. I desire you to make my compliment to Mr. Ross, and express to him my concern to hear that he is ill. Adieu my beloved. I now grow impatient to see you.

"Yours most affectionate,

"W. H.

"*P.S.*—Gull is come. I have quartered him with your Taylors (*sic*)."

"*Wednesday evening.*

(He complains of having been out of spirits and health, but tells her he is now better.)

"My sickness is no more than a cold, but it is teazing, and is much to me who am not accustomed to severe complaints, and hate to have any. Yours alone, my Marian, are too much for me to bear.

"Scott certainly goes and with special dispatches from me, which will oblige me to make the most of my time to prepare them. For this purpose I think of locking myself up for two or three days next week at Allipoor."

"*Calcutta, Thursday evening.*

"MY DEAREST MARIAN,

"I wrote an answer to your letter this morning and said in it too rashly that I would make you another visit on Saturday; but waiting to answer Mr. Motte's I have had time to recollect that I cannot go. I have, therefore, destroyed my letter. I have no boat; I hate to borrow. I have a thousand things to do, and I am sadly out of spirits, having been all day tormented with a headache. I am glad that you resolve to accept no more invitations. Mrs. Ross is too good not to approve your reasons, and if you visit nobody, nobody will be displeased . . . I will bespeak your two coffrees."

"*Thursday night.*

"MY MARIAN,

"You are really angry, almost cross, but I forgive you because you give me news of the amendment of your health, too good to allow me to be angry too, and because I am too much pleased with the thoughts of seeing you to-morrow to allow me to be angry with anyone.

(Here comes in directions for posting horses, etc.)

"My plan is this: I go from Council into my chariot at two. I shall be at Barinagur before three. There my pinnace waits for me. Sir John accompanies me. What time I shall reach the carriage I cannot tell; perhaps at six, perhaps at twelve. But be it at what hour it will I must go on, and I beg of you to contrive that I may not disturb the family when I enter Mr. Motte's house. How that is to be managed God and you best know. I am sure I shall break your rest more by not coming at all than by coming late. My Marian, I saw an alligator yesterday with a mouth as large as a budgerow, and was told that it was of a sort which is very common, but not so large. I shall never consent to your going again to Beercool. Adieu my beloved; a sound and sweet sleep be your portion for this night. I will be your nurse to-morrow night.

"W. H."

"*Calcutta, Friday night.*

"MY DEAREST MARIAN,

"I have received your angry letter, but thank you for it notwithstanding; a pity indeed! I wrote to you last night, and I sent away your Beauty* to you this morning. Poor fellow! it will be a kindness to him as well as to yourself, and to me too, if you will be content to walk him till you are both a little stronger. To-morrow I will send you your gun. I am just returned from a visit to Mrs. Scott. Scott is arrived also, and their daughter, a beautiful child. Mr. Irwin breakfasted with me, and appeared in such spirits that I ventured to make enquiry about his wife, which I told him was on your account, and I believe you will rejoice to hear that she has been three days visibly mending, and, by his account, out of danger. I have migrated to my own house; but the Lyon roars so noisily, that, suspecting that he might disturb my rest, I am returned to *our* bed for the night. *Noisily* is not the proper term. The sound is like the scraping of fifty great kettles. I am well. As I am persuaded that your health depends on yourself, I do beseech you to be well too. Adieu.

"Yours ever,
"W. H."

"*Calcutta, December* 17, *Sunday.*

"MY MARIAN,

"I have received your second letter. Have you had mine? I now send you the gun which I promised. I think you will be pleased with it, because it is fine. As to its intrinsic qualities I know nothing of them. If you use it, let me beg of you to let somebody charge it who understands it, and *not to go into the sun.* I repeat these as my earnest requests.

. . . "I saw Mr. Wheler and Miss D. married† last night. How it agreed with them I know not, but it has given me a cold and sore throat. God bless you. Would it not be kind, civil at least, if you were to write a short letter to her, expressing your satisfaction, &c., and regret that you were not present? I did this for you, and she said it was a pity.

* Her horse.

† Mr. Wheler, then Senior Member of Council, married, as his second wife, Miss Charlotte Durnford, daughter of an official in the Supreme Court, whom he left a widow in October, 1784.

"I have sent you the first volume of Coleman's 'Terence,' and recommend it to you for an equally entertaining and improving study.

"Will you give me as much of your white fur as will decorate a dressed suit for New Year's Day, and will you tell me where I shall get it? I desire you to aquaint Mrs. Motte that I intend to make a figure—and no inconsiderable one—in the waistcoat which she did me the honour to give me."

"*Calcutta, December* 22, *Friday evening.*

"MY BELOVED MARIAN,

"I never received a letter that gave me so much pleasure. I have not a word to say in answer but that I am happy, even in the expectation of seeing you in four days hence, and that if you disappoint me, I will not add the consequence.

"I ought to bid you stay till after the first of January; but if I do, I will be shot. I have something to write, but I have forgot it. Adieu my beloved. Compliments to Mrs. Palmer, Mrs. Sands, Mrs. Samson, and dear Mrs. Motte. How I envy her. Adieu.

"Yours ever ever, more than can be written,

"W. H.

"*P.S.*—Tell when you set off, and perhaps I may meet you if I have a chance of it."

"*Saturday evening.*

"I rode this morning to Gheretty, where I arrived a little after eight; and am just returned. Lady Coote made many enquiries after you, and said she hoped you would stop at Gheretty. The morning was pleasant, and though I rode near two miles beyond Pulta, and accomplished the journey in two hours, I walked as many at Gheretty and felt no more fatigue than if it had been but an airing. Are not you glad of this?"

"*Wednesday evening* (ends thus).

"May God bless you and restore you safe and in health to me, and as glad—or but half as glad—to see your husband as he will be to regain the possession of his Marian. . . . My horse is come, but I have not half the impatience to see him as I feel for your arrival. There's a lover! I wish Motte had as much of the warmth of one, but he is in the right a little.

"I have written much nonsense, but it shall go to puzzle you. I believe people are most apt to be foolish when they are pleased."

"*Thursday night.*

". . . I own I am not pleased with your venturing on the water at this season in a small boat, and I make it my request that you will not repeat it. I have made enquiries for a pinnace, but hitherto without success. I will certainly get one for you, and a good one I hope, in a few days. You may then *trive* * about the river as much as you please and neither of us be a loser by it. I had something else to say to you but forget it. I send you a paper of news. I have slept monstrously since I left you, which is a shame.

"*P.S.*—Evans has been puzzling me with a puzzling message from Motte, whom you have puzzled by telling him that you should come away on Monday next, I having before told him that you would send for your pots, pans, spits, and gridirons, and take possession of his house. He had fixed on Thursday for his departure, and now does not know whether to go or stay till you go. I have referred him to you, saying (which is not always true) that nobody knows a lady's mind so well as herself, but that I supposed if you did come to Calcutta on Monday you would again return to Hughly some days after."

"*Friday evening.*

". . . I received your note this morning and thank God that you are well; I do not care for your being sullen. I had rather you should be so —a little—on such occasions. I rode this morning in the manége and have felt the fatigue of it all day, so that I intend to repeat it to-morrow for my cure. I have no news but that I love you dearly, and that is none—as good a one as yours. Adieu, I will see you, or fancy that I do, in two hours, for it is almost ten.

"Yours ever and ever,

"W. H."

* *Trive* (*i.e.*, drive) underlined in the original, intended probably as a playful allusion to Mrs. Hastings' foreign pronunciation of English.

## PREFATORY NOTE

THE second series of letters were written under the following circumstances, which some readers may have forgotten.

Cheyte Sing, the Rajah, or reigning Prince of Benares, having for some time failed to comply with the increasing demands for extraordinary tribute, made on him by the Company's Government to help in defraying their war expenses, his offences were thought to be such as to need early punishment. As his reputed wealth was great, and the Company's exigencies pressing, it was thought a measure of policy and justice to exact from him a large pecuniary mulct of some forty or fifty lakhs. Hastings having determined to take this matter in hand personally, proceeded to Benares. He was accompanied by a suite of about thirty, and by Mrs. Hastings, whom he left either at Monghyr or Patna. At the latter city she was joined by the Impeys, with whom she moved to Baughulpore.

When Hastings got to Benares (August 14, 1781) he caused the Rajah to be put in arrest in his own house, which was on the river, two miles from the suburb in which the Governor-General took up his temporary residence. Large bodies of armed men crossed the river from Ramnugger on the day of the Rajah's arrest, and proceeded to his house. The guard placed over the prisoner consisted of two companies of sepoys, stationed in an enclosed courtyard which contained the apartment where the Rajah was. These sepoys, strange to say, had no ammunition. Major Popham sent another company with ammunition to support them ; but when this reinforcement arrived they found the Rajah's house surrounded, and all the avenues blocked by a multitude of armed men who fired on the helpless Sepoys and their officers within the square. Eighty-two were thus massacred and ninety-two wounded.

In the midst of the confusion the Rajah escaped across the river, and fled with his zenana and effects to Lutteefpoor, a strong fort some thirty miles off.

Hastings sent orders for the nearest military detachment to come to Benares. Meantime a rash attempt, against orders, to carry Ramnugger by sudden assault (August 20) failed most disastrously with heavy loss, which would have been greater but for the skilful withdrawal to Chunar of the remnant of the Company's troops by Captain Blair.

Soon intelligence came that an assault on the Governor-General's position at Benares was in immediate contemplation, and Hastings, with the acquiescence of Major Popham, determined to leave quietly for the fortress of Chunar, about twenty miles away. This move he and his party and his very small force accomplished successfully on the night of August 21.

After the disturbances which ensued in the surrounding districts had been put down, Hastings returned to Benares (September 28).

In Macaulay's essay this precautionary move of Hastings to Chunar is not mentioned, though he does allude to the stratagem by which the Governor-General got his letters summoning assistance conveyed, *i.e.* in quills concealed on the native messengers. He leaves it to be inferred also that only one was sent in this manner to Mrs. Hastings, but as we now see there were several.

"*Chunar, August* 26.

"I am at Chunar, and in perfect health. I entreat you to return to Calcutta. Be confident, my beloved, all is now well, and will be better. I have no fears but for you.

"W. H."

"*August* 27.

"I am here in perfect health and safety; my only present fear is for you. I desire to have no fears. I beg you will return to Baughulpore, and as you shall be advised, to Calcutta. Sulivan* eats, drinks, and is merry. My whole party is well. Be confident, no harm will befall me. My danger was great, but it is all past. May God bless and support you, my most beloved. I feel, and have felt much for you, and am yet unhappy till I know where you are.

"Your ever most faithful and affectionate,

"W. H."

"*September* 8.

"MY MOST BELOVED MARIAN,

"I thank God that my first letter from here reached you, and that I this morning received yours of the 28th in answer to it. It is your first letter, and I shall continue to read it till I get another. It has relieved my fears, but not removed them.

"I hope you have left Patna; but do not stop at Baughulpore, go on to Moorshedabad. It is necessary to my peace of mind, and you may easily return when these troubles and the consequent alarms are past. [He then gives her some details as to the constitution and number and movements of the forces near him and coming to him]. . . I am in perfect health. Sulivan is and has been at all times well and in laughing spirits. Be confident, my Marian, I will return to you triumphant.

"P.S.—I use this blank to tell you that I never loved you as I loved

* Stephen Sulivan, one of his suite acting in the capacity of his private secretary.

you in the midst of my greatest troubles, and have suffered more in my fears for you than I hope I ever shall for myself.

"Yours ever, ever,

"W. H.

"*P.S.*—All my party is well. I am greatly indebted to Colonel Blair for his attention, and to Mrs. White for the clothes now on my back. This is the climate of Paradise. I will remember C. Sulivan."

"*September* 11.

"I was going to write to you when I received yours of the 3rd. You have made me happy, notwithstanding a mixture of pain and apprehension. Do not, my beloved, yield to your fears, or distrust the good influence that guards and supports your husband, that influence which prompted me without apparent reason to leave you, my heart's treasure, in a land of safety. How happy for us both! Tell Sir Elijah that I wrote to him early from Benares two letters, one of great consequence, and I desired Major Eaton lately to write to him. May God bless him for his kindness to you. Tell him I thank him. Read the enclosed and send it to Mr. Wheler. Copy it, show it to our friends. I think you may remain at Baughulpore, but do not if you hear the least alarm. You judged wisely. Exert the fortitude which you possess, and do not suffer any thoughts of me to distress your tranquility or affect your health. I never was better than I am, and have been in all my troubles, and am happy to find by this severe trial that I have a mind which can accommodate itself to every situation, to all but one. I can bear every affliction of which you are not the subject. Sulivan is well and hearty. I deputed him yesterday as my ambassador to the Nabob, who made many enquiries after you. Everyone knows the language which will please me most.

"Adieu, my beloved."

"*September* 15.

"I am in health as usual. Sulivan, if possible, better, and all our party is well. I have one soul wholly engrossed by public affairs, and another that by night and day is ever employed on my dearest Marian. I still hope to see you in another month. Do not be uneasy if you do not receive frequent letters from me, three in four miscarry."

"*September* 20, *Chunar.*

(Marian had "returned" to Baughulpore.)

"You are safe, and I am happy, but do not remain even at Baughulpore, if you hear any alarms go on. You may return to meet me, and the water is your element. I was frightened in reading some of your letters, your wild fancies, and your danger in approaching Patna. I have received a letter from Sir Elijah which has affected me even to a weakness. O that I could see my beloved Marian for one hour. You have been mistaken. I never was surrounded at Chunar, nor in anything like danger, though I have felt all the dangers to which others were exposed

I have lived even luxuriously, and breathed till this last week the air of Paradise." [*Then he gives the military details, which he precedes with,* "Now attend;" *he tells her of Major Popham carrying a fort, Pateeta, by storm, and routing a great rabble which attempted his camp.*] "I saw the firing and progress of the action, which extended four miles. Yet, thank God, our loss in Sepoys was very small and no officer hurt. I cannot rejoice at victories won with blood. . . . . I am glad that Mrs. Sulivan is not with you, and that Sir Elijah is. May God bless and protect you. I was ever happy in my Marian, I am now proud of her. This trial has shown the world that worth of which I only before knew the degree. Tell Mrs. Motte I love and esteem her. I wrote to Sir Elijah.

"P.S.—The Nabob * has behaved honourably, and seems rejoiced at our success, which I carried to him with a congratulation for the Eed or Festival, a point of importance to a superstitious mind. All my party is well, none better than I am."

On September 23 he gives her more details, and adds:—

"On August 21 I fled with four hundred men, and many thousands prepared to attack me from Benares. Armies spontaneously hastened to my aid, and on the 21st of the following month completely retrieved all that we before had lost. Read this to Sir Elijah and Lady Impey, and our friends, with my compliments.

"Adieu, my love."

"*September* 24.

"Major Blair describes Lutteefpoor as a place of great strength. Our plan has proved an excellent one; its effect beyond hope, and equal to one of your best moves at chess. I must yet recur to my fears for your safety. You are not absolutely safe at Baughulpore. I dread a surprise, the last effort of the Rajah's despair. Pray leave it; go anywhere on the river, on the other side of the river, or even on yours below Baughulpore. Consult Sir Elijah on this.

"Adieu, my beloved, my most amiable, my best Marian." †

* One who was attached to the Governor-General's party, Mr. Grand, records in his Narrative:—"During our confinement in Chunar the Nawab Vizier, Azoph ul Dowlah, visited Mr. Hastings. Mr. H. paid him the first visit, and trusted him, though conjured from various quarters not to do so."

† This is the last of the letters from Chunar; several of them seem to have been sent in duplicate.

# PREFATORY NOTE TO THIRD SERIES OF LETTERS.

MRS. HASTINGS sailed for England in the *Atlas* * in January, 1784. Macaulay tells how busy rumour was, as to the money lavished by the Governor-General in providing comforts and luxuries for his wife's voyage. The essayist probably derived his information from this passage by the authoress of "Hartley House," who was living in Calcutta at the time, viz., "The whole place is engaged in adieux, and Mrs. H—— will be accompanied to England (for the Governor sails in a different ship) by a Mrs. M——, who has been presented with five hundred gold mohrs (a thousand pounds) in return for her complaisance in making the voyage with her. Two black girls and a steward are Mrs. H.'s attendants, and the state cabin and round house will be entirely devoted to her use."

In addition to Mrs. Motte † there were among the passengers a Captain Power, and Mr. Clevland, whose memory is still honoured at Bhaugulpore, who died before the pilot left the *Atlas*. A Mr. Doveton, possibly the official despatching the mail letters, was deputed to attend the ship to the Sand Heads, and bring back personal tidings of Mrs. Hastings so far. It seems highly probable too that a Captain Phipps was sent as a fellow-voyager as far as St. Helena with a similar object, for in one of the letters given by Gleig, dated "Benares, October 1, 1784," Hastings says to her, "Last night about nine o'clock Major Sands

* The ships of the East India Company were each commanded by a captain, and had from four to eight officers, all in uniform. The duties were carried on as strictly as in the Royal Navy. The captain, besides his pay, had a free amount of freight, etc. A voyage was worth to him, on an average, £5000. He ranked as Member of Council in India, and received a salute of thirteen guns on landing from a voyage. So writes Captain Eastlake in the "Life of a Master Mariner," 1891.

† Mrs. Motte declined to return to India. There are several pathetic letters from Mr. Motte, who writes of himself as "deprived of the comforts of domestic happiness, and despised by a woman who never behaved with impropriety except to me." She appears to have had as income the rent of Mr. Justice Hyde's house which belonged to her, and which the forlorn husband fears is not enough to enable her "to live genteely in England." ("Letters of Hastings," Grier.) In 1813 we find her at a dinner-party given to the Duke of Gloucester by Mr. and Mrs. Hastings.

Lady D. is still here. On her Depar=
=ture I shall bid Farewell to Allipoor, & count the
Days of my Life as lost to my Existence till the
blessed Moments that shall restore my Marian to
me, & never while I live shall she be again sepa=
=rated from me. Adieu my beloved. Y: ever ever affectionate
I will write to Mrs M. & M. Davy. WHastings

Adieu, my Heart's Beloved. O ever love me, for no
Man ever merited by Love a larger Return of it than I do. — May
the God of infinite Goodness bless & support & protect you! Amen! Amen! Amen! WHastings. —

— My Marian, I love you far

more than my Life, for that is only valuable

as you make it so, nor have I one Gratifica

=tion which cd. tempt me to retain the Burthen

of it, but for the Hope of being again united to you.

May God grant it, & bless & support you!

I am ever my dearest & most beloved of

all Women your most faithful & most affectionate Husband

Warren Hastings.

See p. 333.

brought me the news of Phipps' arrival at Calcutta. May God bless them both for it. Captain Phipps writes that he had your orders to deliver your packet to me with his own hand, and he is coming with it. I have written to accelerate his coming by relays of bearers from two or three stages beyond Patna."

The time and incidents embraced by this series of letters will be best shown by this extract from one written at this period, and given by Gleig, which testifies to the regularity and minuteness with which Hastings kept his wife informed of his movements and doings, viz., "I have now carried forward the history of my life from the 10th January to this time (September 24), comprising the following parts or divisions.

1st. My residence in Calcutta to February 17.
2nd. My journey to Lucknow, ending March 27.
3rd. My residence at Lucknow, a long chapter, closed August 27.
4th. My journey to Benares.
Lastly remain to follow,
5th. My residence at Benares.
6th. My return to Calcutta.
7th. Preparation for my voyage.
8th. The voyage.

When Mr. Gleig published his Memoir most of the letters thus enumerated were not forthcoming, the absent ones that would fit in with the few given by him having (with one exception) since come to light in the British Museum collection.

A strong instance of the incompleteness which Mr. Gleig's work almost of necessity laboured under may be touched on here. In two of the letters to Mrs. Hastings given in the Memoirs, expressions occur the import of which can only be guessed at by the reader, but which the letters of the same period now available fully explain as being referable to what may be alluded to as a domestic incident in the life of Warren Hastings. There were no children born to Mrs. Hastings' second marriage, but she left India with hope of offspring.* Much of her husband's anxiety about her voyage, and of his eagerness to hear from her, proceeded from this cause. His letters, after the receipt of hers from St. Helena, are largely taken up with this topic. I have not thought it fair to extract for publication more on this point than was necessary to convey the fact in explanation of the writer's elation, his hopes and fears, acting up in this respect, I trust, to the spirit of his own feelings, when he says, "I must not expose to writing the fond secrets of my breast, which should be sacredly reserved for yours alone." At the date of this third series of letters the respective ages of Hastings and his wife were fifty-one and thirty-seven.

* Had her condition been known before sailing, the inconvenience and possible danger would probably have been avoided by deferring her voyage. There are no letters, I believe, extant (or available) which communicated Mrs. Hastings' hope to her husband. Many private and family letters were presumably destroyed. The communication seems to have been made from St. Helena on May 15, 1784.

India has been often called the land of separation and regrets; it more deserves to be called so now, perhaps, than in the days of Warren Hastings; and the goings and comings, the partings and meetings again, which form the too frequent domestic experience of European families in India, introduce, now more than ever, an element of pathos into (what is called) Anglo-Indian life, which none but an Anglo-Indian community can sympathise with, or realise to the full. It is but a trite observation that many a husband or parent in eastern exile to-day revolves, like Warren Hastings a hundred years ago, temporary expedients to try and stave off the long voyage and the longer separation, and when the inevitable comes, and he is returning solitary from "the borders of the ocean," like Hastings, too, he writes in his first sad letter westwards, "I followed your ship with my eyes till I could no longer see it, and I passed a most wretched day with a heart swollen with affliction." These old faded letters of a Governor-General should bring home to those who aspire to an Indian career that there is a reverse side to the medal—that there is a common harrow of domestic trial and pain, submission to which will, sooner or later, be the lot of most, for exemption can be purchased no more by the exalted than by the lowly.

"*Culpee, Sunday evening, January* 11, 1784.

"MY BELOVED WIFE,

"I trust to the chance of Mrs. Sands reaching the Cape before you leave it for the safe delivery of this letter; but I have little to write, and scarce a motive for writing, but to gratify my own feelings. I left you yesterday morning. I followed your ship with my eyes till I could no longer see it, and I passed a most wretched day with a heart swol'n with affliction, and a head raging with pain. I have been three tides making this place, where I met my budgerow, and in it a severe renewal of my sorrow. The instant sight of the cabbin (*sic*), every object in it, and beyond it, brought my dear Marian to my imagination, with the deadly reflexion that she was then more than 200 miles removed from me, and still receding to a distance which seems, in my estimation, infinite and irretrievable. In the heavy interval which I have passed, I have had but too much leisure to contemplate the wretchedness of my situation, and to regret (forgive me, my dearest Marian, I cannot help it) that I ever consented to your leaving me. It appears to me like a precipitate act of the grossest folly; for what have I to look forward to but an age of separation, and if ever we are to meet again, to carry home to you a burthen of infirmities, and a mind soured perhaps with long, long and unabated, vexation. Nor is it for myself alone I feel, though I have been possibly more occupied than I ought to have been by the contemplation and sensation of my own suffering. Yours have been, and I am sure are at this time greater than my own, and I fear for their effects on your health. I shall dread the sight of Mr. Doveton. Yet, oh God of heaven! grant me good tidings by him. Indeed, my Marian, I think that we have ill-judged. The reflexion has often for an instant occurred to me that we were wrong, but I constantly repressed it. I urged everything that could fix the resolution beyond the power of recall, and felt a conscious pride in the sacrifice I was preparing to make. It is now past.

"I said that I should trust to the chance of Mrs. Sands delivering this letter to you at the Cape. She is now in the Danish ship, once the *Fortitude*, lying at this place, and expects to leave the river on Thursday next; possibly she may be later. I will send another letter to her from town. I shall sail again with this night's tide, and if I find myself within reach of Calcutta in the next, I intend to finish my voyage to-morrow in the feelchehra.* Possibly my apprehensions may be less gloomy when I have quitted this weary scene; but of one thing I am certain, that no time nor habits will remove the pressure of your image from my heart, nor from my spirits, nor would I remove it if I could, though it prove a perpetual torment to me. Yesterday, as I lay upon my bed, and but half asleep, I felt a sensation like the fingers of your hand gently moving over my face and neck, and could have sworn that I heard your voice. O that I could be sure of such an illusion as often as I lay down! And the reality seems to me an illusion. Yesterday morning I held in my arms all that my heart holds dear, and now she is separated from me as if she had no longer existence. O my Marian! I am wretched; and I shall make you so when you read this. Yet I know not why, I must let it go; nor can I add anything to alleviate which I have written; but that I love you more by far than life, for I would not live but in the hope of being once more united to you. O God grant it! and grant my deserving my blessed Marian fortitude to bear what I myself bear so ill, conduct her in health and safety to the termination of her voyage, and once more restore her to me with everything that can render our meeting completely happy. Amen, amen, amen.

"Yours ever, ever affectionate,

"W. HASTINGS."

(The next is written from Calcutta on the day after he reached it (January 12). In it occur these passages.)

"I am not yet reconciled to our separation, and it seems to me the greatest of all follies that I should have taken so much trouble to make myself miserable and you unhappy, who were the object of it. I can now conceive many expedients by which the purpose of your voyage might have been as effectually answered, and what may you not have suffered even in your health from this. But I will complain no more. Since my return I have had so much employment for my mind that it has been much relieved: yet the instant that I am left to myself, and my ivory cot affords me no comfort, all my distresses rush back upon my thoughts, and present everything in the most gloomy prospect. . . .

* A large native boat; so called from the prow being commonly decorated with the figure of an elephant's head.

"I talk to you, but I receive no answer; nor can you hear me till I shall have forgotten what I have written. I miss the sweet music of your voice which none but myself have ever heard, and the looks of heaven which I am sure have never been cast but on me alone. I strive by the violence of imagination to see and hear you; but I cannot yet effect it. Yet you are not a moment from my remembrance, nor would I for the world that you should lose your place there, though you are a torment to me. I do not expect Doveton back these ten days, and with what terror shall I meet him, yet how impatiently do I wait to see him; may he bring me good tidings of you, and I will be comforted for all the past. From the state in which he leaves you I shall form my judgment, and with confidence of the remainder of your voyage. Remainder, good God; what a length is yet to come, and how much more before I can begin mine, that is to convey me to you! But enough, enough."

"*January* 15.

"Mr. Doveton arrived last night and brought me letters from Mrs. Motte, C. Cowper, and Mr. Phipps. These and particularly the first ought to have satisfied me, but they renewed the painfulness of my situation and my fears for your health, for I well knew the acuteness of your feelings and the inability of your frame to support them. I shall now wait with the most anxious impatience for the return of the pilot who, Doveton tells me, may be back in sixteen or seventeen days. . . . I have begun to set my house in order, and intend to give everything to the principal charge of Francis.* I have ordered an advertisement to be made for the sale of Allipoor and Rishera, and shall clear myself as speedily as I can of other incumbrances. I shall go to Allipoor to-morrow (Friday) and pass the remainder of the week there, because it will be agreeable to Lady D'Oyly. When she leaves me I believe I shall quit it for ever.

"I am in hourly expectation of the determination of the Board on a point of very great consequence to my credit in the close of the public service. I have made an offer of going to Lucknow for the purpose of making an arrangement of our concerns in that Government, the state of which you knew when you were with me. If I go I shall have a world of difficulties to encounter, and hazard to my reputation, but I know that if anything can relieve the affairs of that country, my presence will (I can say this to you, and you will not think it presumption); possibly I may close this by telling you that I do not go at all. I have done all that I could to gain this point, but shall be glad in my heart if I am defeated in it; for I wish it only on public grounds, every consideration of private interest strongly opposing it. I daily expect letters overland written after the receipt of mine by the *Surprize* packet in which I declared my resolution of resigning my office, and desired that my successor might be nominated; what may be the event of this declaration I cannot foresee;

* Dr. Francis, his own medical attendant.

but whatever it may be, my resolution is fixed and unalterable, and it will be so concluded when it is known that you are gone before me.

"I have fulfilled every obligation which I owed to the service, and done almost more than any other man, against such inducements as I have had to restrain me, would have done. But, my Marian, do not entertain hopes of improvement in our fortune. If your love for me is, as I am sure it is, superior to every other wish, you must be content to receive your husband again without other expectations—poor in cash, but rich in credit (at least he hopes so), and in affection unexampled. He is infinitely more concerned about his constitution than his wealth, trusting to the justice of his country for at least a competency, and to the good sense of his Marian for a sufficiency in whatever they may have for a subsistence.

"Since I wrote the preceding part of this letter, I have seen Mr. Wheler; he has promised his assent to my proposed visit to Lucknow, having declared the same in terms in a written minute to the Board, so that I have considered it as done past recall. Scott will have the copies of what has passed in Council upon the occasion if you wish to see them. There is nothing in them, but their conclusion, in which you can be interested."

"*January* 21, *Calcutta.*

"I have written three letters to you by Mrs. Sands in the hope of her overtaking you at the Cape. I scarce wish you to receive them, for they are written under the influence of sorrow, discontent and desponding, and something like the consciousness of infinite and incomparable folly in the recollection of the abundant pains which I had been taking to effect my own wretchedness.

"May the event prove the reverse. The resolution and its execution were very sudden, and I look back for the grounds of both and scarce can trace them—none that satisfy me. I only recollect that my enthusiasm to sacrifice every consideration that regarded myself to the preservation of your health I thought only on the sacrifice, nor inquired of myself, till it was too late, whether it might have been attained by easier means and nearer our reach, or whether those which were chosen were not as likely to increase as to remedy the evil.

"But I have already torn up one sheet because I had half filled it with gloomy complaints. I will not afflict you more, and it is unmanly."

(He then recapitulates some of his doings since their separation, and again alludes to the selling of his property.) * And he adds—

* Viz.: "I have actually advised the sale of it (Alipoor) in three lots, the old house and garden forming one, the new house and outhouses the second, and the paddock the third. I have parted with all my mares except four which have colts." The same property as part of the Estate of W. Hastings was again advertised for sale in April, 1785. The "old house" was presumably Belvedere, though not named in the advertisement. The "new house" that still known as "Hastings

"Other schemes of retrenchments and economy I am forming, and they afford me a pleasure in the prospect which is connected with them. . . . Let but a few months pass and I will begin to count the time which shall yet remain and please myself with its diminution. Continue, my sweet Marian, to love me, for in that hope and belief alone I live."

[January 26, 1784. Is endorsed—"Received July 29."]

(Speaks of his intended journey to Lucknow, by boat to Patna, and to the Banks of the Soan, and thence (by land) and with a military escort.)

"I am not greatly afraid of what my friends in the Council may do in my absence, because I think they have not the courage to recall or thwart me and render themselves answerable for the consequence. . . . But be it (his health) good or bad, I will live to see you in England, and no consideration that the kings or Parliaments of the earth can offer me shall prevail upon me to exceed the time which I have allotted to the period of service; and how, my Marian, will you receive a healthless and pennyless husband? Will your heart reproach him with precipitancy and improvidence, or will it lay both to the account of an affection which could disregard wealth and every blessing upon earth if they could only be obtained by a separation from the object of it? I have already yielded too much, too much to the opinions of others in consenting to, aye, and in urging your departure, too much to the public, which will not thank me, nor know the value of the sacrifice in remaining without you. . . .

"I am ever, my dearest and most beloved of all women, your most faithful and most affectionate husband,

"WARREN HASTINGS."

"*January* 31; *closed February* 6.

(Acknowledges the anxiously expected letter from her by the pilot. He sorrows for the death of Clevland, and bemoans the afflictions which the voyage must have brought her.)

house," built about 1776. Mackrabie writes in February of that year, "Col. Monson dined with us in the country: after dinner we walked over to the Governor's new-built house. 'Tis a pretty toy but very small tho' airy and lofty. Those milk-white buildings with smooth shiny surface utterly blind one." This description inclines me now to think that the "bijou" house where Mrs. Fay visited Mrs. Hastings in May, 1780, and which she calls Belvedere, was really the smaller and newer house further south. Mrs. Fay made her visit when only just arrived in Calcutta, and could easily have confused the names. Hastings gave a concert party "at Belvedere his Garden" in February, 1776, to which Mackrabie was invited. Possibly after his marriage he may have retained Belvedere for his large social receptions only, and lived in the smaller building as his country house, or he may have sublet Belvedere. The question is one of local interest only—being to this day often discussed in Calcutta.

". . . Your motive for sending back the sloop * was consistent with the generous and unequalled sensibility of my dear Marian. This is her peculiar virtue, and too often her misery, and as often mine. Yet I wish that the vessel could have attended you three days further, for Mr. Doveton tells me that in that run you would fall in with lighter breezes."

(He hugs his grief, and endeavours to analyse what his sensations were at their recent parting.)

"Oh God, what a change was effected in the state of my existence within the compass of a few minutes, and what were my reflexions while I passed from the ship to my pinnace. My imagination presented you before me as I held you in my arms but a few moments past gazing with fondness and with despair on all the wealth that my soul ever thought to amass. I still felt the moisture of your sweet lips and the warm pressure of your last embrace, and my heart told me that I had lost you for ever. I taxed myself with indifference to your happiness and my own, and was stupified with astonishment at the labour which I had with so persevering an industry taken to destroy both. I had bestowed a large portion of my time on the means of arranging it. I had used contrivances to overcome some difficulties which oppose it, and I had parted with a large portion of my fortune to accomplish it; and having conducted you to the borders of the ocean and seen you irrevocably departed, I was returning with the contemplation of the complete success which had attended so many exertions, and with a heart full of execration which had no object but myself for having made them. . . .

"I return to my dear Marian, and shall borrow many an abrupt and solitary interval to indulge myself in this semblance of conversation with her; but how faint the resemblance. I experience indeed a momentary illusion, but it instantly disappears and shows me through the void, all the delights of that entertainment whose image I seek and which my fancy cannot recover; the beloved face,† the animated and varied expression of

* The pilot sloop which attended the *Atlas* (with instructions presumably to accompany her farther than was usual) brought back the body of Mr. Clevland preserved in spirit. He was interred on January 30 in South Park Street Cemetery, where his tomb may still be seen. The slab of white marble on its front bears a long inscription (now barely legible) enumerating his eminent public services, and his amiable personal qualities. This valuable civil servant died at the early age of twenty-nine.

† The passionate affection of Warren Hastings for his wife never outgrew its spring; neither time or fruition seemed to lessen the fascination which even her physical attractions had for him. As their honeymoon lengthened and lingered, we find him, though in wintry age, a willing captive still, happy with the same wound, and thus harping on the same string—"your good and amiable mother" (he writes to her son in 1803), "who continues even in beauty to exceed every woman who comes within my observation," etc.

In this same letter Hastings tells his stepson how he loves him and his wife, "as the children of my adoption and of my heart's election."

features, the look of benevolence unspeakable, the sweet music of her tongue, and a thousand imperceptible graces that embellished her words and gave them the power of impression exceeding the strongest effects of the understanding. Your letter presents none of these attractions, yet it contains your words and conveys your thoughts, and I had rather brood over the melancholy passions excited by it, than be a sharer in the most pleasing entertainments that nature or art could afford me. . . .

"I go (to Oude) on a bold adventure, from a divided and hostile Council, to a scene of difficulties unsurmountable but by very powerful exertions, to a country wasted by famine and threatened with an invading enemy; to a Government loosened by a twelve months' distraction, its wealth exhausted, and its revenue dissipated. I go without a fixed idea of the instruments which I am to employ or the material on which I am to act; with great expectation entertained by others, but very moderate of my own; and my superiors at home labouring to thwart, and if they can, determined to remove me, and all this as well known to the Indian world as to our own. Add to all the foregoing a mind unequal to its former strength, and a constitution very much impaired. Yet I go with confidence, and should go with a cheerful heart, but for a strange sensation of removing still further from my Marian, though it is the time, not distance of place, that I ought to measure.

"Mr. Wheler said that he would agree to it whenever the Nabob's invitation arrived, and Mr. Stables in his coarse manner objected, because he said he doubted whether the Governor could be lawfully absent, and he expected me to be shortly dismissed from my office. These were not his words, but the sense was implied in them. New arrangements were shortly expected, he said, from England, and let them come, most joyfully should I receive and submit to them. . . .

"Richard Johnson is appointed our Public Minister at Hyderabad, Mr. Holland's former station. Mr. Thomson, who is too sick to accompany me, is nominated to be the Company's advocate in the room of Mr. Lawrence, who is dead.

"I have still Sir Charles Blunt and Major Conran dead weights on my hands, and Mrs. Ramus * teazing me for her stupid husband. I know you are interested in these points, and therefore I write them.

* If we may credit the cynical Francis, poor Mrs. Ramus had some ground for hoping for a slice of patronage pie, seeing that it was Marian who provided the "stupid husband" for her. In November, 1779, Francis notes, "Sir J. Day appears to be excessively hurt at the marriage of Ramus with Miss Vernet; he says that it has been hurried on in a most extraordinary manner by Mrs. Hastings. This lady, since she married poor Hastings, has taken a strange turn to matchmaking. She now knows what it is to be married." Ramus, moreover, had influential friends in England, and the judicious Hastings was careful to promote the wishes of such in the exercise of his patronage. It was in behalf of this same gentleman that the following tolerably broad hint was conveyed to Francis by the Private Secretary of the Prime Minister:—"April, 1776. I have received a letter this morning from Mr. Nicholas Ramus, First Page to his Majesty, in which he

"Thompson tells me that you carried with you copies of Munny Begum's letter, and of mine to the Court of Directors written in her behalf, and Davy says you have the letters from the king and his minister with your titles; I therefore do not send them.

"Tiretta's * lottery drawn, and the prize has fallen to himself. In the enumeration of articles of news I must not forget to inform you, my good Marian, that the Church scheme which you had so much at heart goes on most prosperously, and I expect the foundation to be laid in less than two months. The body will be a square of 70 feet, and will be decorated with a handsome steeple.†

acquaints me that a letter has come to his hand from his son, Mr. Henry Ramus, dated August 5, in which he expresses great mortification that he had not then been so fortunate as to obtain any mark of the favour and protection of the Governor and Council of Bengal." No wonder that when these views of the duties expected of him in Bengal were frequently urged, this sarcastic Councillor should write, "My friends in England are very good to me, they give me as many opportunities as I can desire, and more than I can avail myself of, of serving persons of merit in this country; and they leave me the credit of it, clear of any return in England."

* Tiretta was, I believe, an architect and land surveyor, and also I think registrar of leases in Calcutta; he was wealthy. His name is still preserved in that of a bazaar in Calcutta. There is a quaint letter from him to Hastings, introducing a young lady who came to England from Calcutta. "Miss Josephin de Carrion, sister of that unfortunate and lovely consort which for the space of three years has made my happiness, and which six months ago I had the misfortune of losing for ever, leaving me a little babe as a pledge of her friendship." His wife died in 1796, and was buried in the Portuguese burying-ground, but nearly two years afterwards, "owing to circumstances too painful to relate," the widower had the remains exhumed and transferred to a grave in a cemetery which he bought for the purpose, and where her tomb is still standing. Tiretta presented the new cemetery called after him (in Park Street) to "all the Catholic Europeans or their immediate descendants dying in this Settlement." On the tomb she is described as "Uxor Edwardi Tiretta, *Tarvisini.*" It may be worth noting that 'le jeune Comte Tiretta de Trevise" is the name of one of the many boon companions whose unsavoury exploits in the service of Venus, Casanova tells of in his extraordinary Memoirs. Casanova made his acquaintance early in 1757; he was then twenty-five, of a good appearance, with a noble and jovial air. He had fled to Paris from Venice to escape the consequence of a breach of trust there, and arrived destitute. Casanova set him up, and put him in the way of making a rather discreditable living. He witnessed in disreputable company the horrible execution of Damiens the would-be regicide, and was much given to gambling, fighting, and love-making. After the loss of a favourite mistress "par suite d'une douloureuse maladie," he told his patron that he wished to try his fortune in India, and Casanova gave him a letter to a friend in Amsterdam, whence he was sent to Batavia. There he got into trouble, being apparently a thorough scamp. He made his way to Bengal, where he prospered mightily, as one of his relations told Casanova that he was there in 1788—rich, but unable to realise his fortune and return to his country.

† The present St. John's, whose centenary was commemorated in 1887. The first stone was laid in April, 1784. It was opened for service on Sunday, June

"My heart is filled with sentiments and emotions which I cannot write, but nothing new which you may not infer from those of your own. I never cease to think of you and with a tenderness which no words can describe. I too severely feel that you form a part of my existence. I remember when the cares and fatigues of the day made no impression on my spirits, because I looked on the comforts which were to follow the close of them and which never failed to efface them. Do you, my sweet Marian, recollect with what pleasure I always returned to you after a morning of fatigue—how peevishly I have sometimes resented your absence if you disappointed me of your company at dinner—how often during the course of it I have quitted my company to enjoy a momentary interval of your delightful conversation. And can I now lose you for eighteen long months without impatience, without anguish? Indeed I cruelly feel it. I miss you in every instant and incident of my life, and everything seems to wear a dead stillness around me; I come home as to a solitude; I see a crowd in my house and at my table, but not the look of welcome which used to make my home a delight to me; no Marian to infuse into my heart the fulness of content, and make me pleased with everybody and with everything about me. Even in my dreams I have lost you. This is not all, but I must not expose to writing the fond secrets of my breast, which should be most sacredly reserved for yours alone. I am unhappy, and shall be so, nor do I wish to be otherwise till I am again in possession of you."

The letter in which the following extract occurs is endorsed: "Received on the evening of my arrival in London, which was the 28th July."

"*Calcutta, February* 7.

"The *Neptune*, which will carry this with public dispatches to Bussora, will wait there for a returning packet and possibly for the reply to this. . . . Write only by land conveyance, none by sea will reach me. I am fixed in my resolution to follow you by the end of December. Nothing but death or bodily restraint shall have the power to detain me. Indeed, I have stayed too long, had I not the calls which I have to depart, for my constitution is not capable of those exertions which I have been accustomed to make, nor likely to bear more than the term of service which I have prescribed to it. I have no more to write that I can trust to so doubtful a conveyance but that I live only in my love for you and in my hopes of being reunited to you never to part again.

"Adieu."

24, 1787. I have a note from an old newspaper that the collection made that day amounted to over 3000 sicca rupees. The Rev. W. Johnson preached the sermon, and took for his text Psalm xciii. 5 ("Holiness becometh thine house for ever"). Zoffany presented the altar piece. Tradition says that all the figures are likenesses of Calcutta notorieties of the day: Judas being represented by Tulloh the auctioneer, who thought, poor man, that he was sitting for St. John.

* * * * * * *

"*Calcutta, February* 11.

(Tells her of an illness he has had, lest she should hear an exaggerated account of it from other sources.)

"My greatest suffering arose from the contemplation of the picture before me as I lay in my bed, and the reflection of the vast distance which separated me from my Marian.

"She knew not whether I was sick or well, nor if my complaint increased could her fortitude be put to another severe trial, or I awake to the sight of her spirit sent to relieve me.

"In these reflections I more than once turned my face towards the spot where the beautiful apparition formerly stood before me when I was in a state which, but for so powerful an aid might, and I believe would, have proved fatal to me. But my eyes met not their desire, and my imagination but faintly represented it. . . . Did I tell you in my last that the Board had agreed to erect a monument* at Baughulpore in honour of poor Clevland's memory? I enclose what I propose for his epitaph, if approved by my colleagues, to whom I have not yet shown it.

"I send you a scrap of Persian poetry written by a living friend of Sir Wm. Jones: it will be a good lesson for you and Mrs. Motte; it has a few touches of good poetry, but not one of nature. I have received many of your letters, my Marian, but never mistook one of them for a bottle of rose-water, nor the cossid who brought it for a Fawn of Khoten."

*February* 19.

("Off Nya Serai." Says that he left for Lucknow on the evening of the February 17. Dr. Balfour went with him; Dr. Francis did not.)

"I am now on my way to Sooksagur,† which I expect to reach by

* Bishop Heber says in his Journal (1824):—"Mr. Clevland's monument is in the shape of a Hindo Mut, in a pretty situation on a green hill, and the natives still meet once a year in considerable numbers, and have a handsome poojah in honour of his memory."

Thackeray in his "Four Georges" (the lecture on George IV.) refers to the affection of the natives for Clevland's memory, as mentioned by Heber.

† Sooksagur was in the district of Nuddea, about forty miles from Calcutta, on the left bank of the Hooghly. Mr. C. Grant, in his sketches of rural life in Bengal, says, "The original house was built by Warren Hastings as a country residence for himself and three other civilians, and for the purpose of their having an English farm where experiments in the growth of coffee and other productions of that character could be tried. It was indeed the first property connected with the soil of Bengal out of the 24 Pergunnah's possessed under sanction of Government by Europeans. Bholnath Chunder, in "The Travels of a Hindoo," records his journey up the river in 1845, and says, "Fifty years ago there were many houses in Sooksagur. The Marquis Cornwallis often came here to spend the summer months. The Revenue Board was also established here on its removal from Moorshedabad. The river encroached upon and washed away the greater part of Sooksagur, leaving not a vestige of its numerous buildings. In the great inundation of 1823 a good-sized pinnace sailed through the Sooksagur Bazaar.

noon. . . . Poor Croftes, with the gout in the head and in defiance of it and of my intreaties, hurrying after me to make my reception at his house most welcome and salutary. . . . The night before last you appeared before me; and it is strange, for the first time, in my sleep; you had returned to me from sea, and looked pale and dejected with sickness. I feel, my Marian, a degree of pain in the thought that I am now moving daily from you ; and what a length of time ; how filled with events that will add to the measure of it, is yet to pass before I can even begin to count off the days which remain of our separation. Oh God ! preserve us both in life and health till the close of that period arrives, and give us years of happiness in compensation for those which we have suffered in absence from each other.

"You left the wrong copy of your will, which was endorsed 'to be taken with you.' I have given it to Croftes, and my own I have left with Larkins."

"*Nuddea, February* 23.

"I have found out a method to see and converse with you whenever I sleep; and I have had your company every night for these four nights past, but you do not always wear the looks of kindness which I am sure you always will wear if ever again I see you in substance."

"*February* 24."

(Describes the progress of his journey.)

"While I was preparing to land at Baughulpore, I received a parcel of letters which I took with me into my palankeen, and the first subject of amusement which they presented to me was a private letter from Mr. Wheler and Stables communicating the enclosed intelligence. This was a fine encouragement on the commencement of my journey to prosecute it to the length of 800 miles. It occupied my thoughts during the greatest part of the night, but (thank God) without spoiling my appetite for breakfast.

"On a full examination of it I do believe it to be a forgery, and if it is one, it was aimed at my present commission, though I know not how such a design could have originated, as this certainly did, at Madras. It is not possible for the Parliament to have passed such unpopular and important Acts so early in September, for they were not in effect assembled. Neither is it possible for the news of it to have passed from England to Bombay making a zigzag to St. Helena in three months and a half, as impossible is it that they should have got it at Tranquebar from Bombay in twenty-two days. Besides, what budget have I given to Major Scott, I believe it to have been fabricated in the shop of Lord M———y.

* * * * * * *

"I should give one-half of my life for the certainty of beginning the other half with you to-morrow. But I would not wish for the immediate possession even of such a blessing, at the purchase of such a mortification as to be thrust out of my seat by such fellows as Ld. M———y, Mr. Francis, and General Richard Smith.

* * * * * * *

"Your god-daughter is a very fine laughing girl."

"*February* 28, *Baughulpore.*

"I forgot to tell you that Munny Begum* expressed her regret of your departure in terms which seemed too natural to have proceeded from mere civility. I was pleased to hear her say that she grieved on my account as much as for her own loss in your departure and the necessity which occasioned it."

"*March* 1, *Patna.*

Recapitulates, in case of accident, a good deal that was contained in previous letters. When alluding to the starting on the present journey says:—

"I went on board my pinnace very low, but happy to be relieved from the tumult and importunity of Calcutta, for no one had mercy on me, and my gates though shut let people through like a sieve. . . .

"Having been my own servant so long it is a great comfort to find my own people again about me, and Turner† who has joined me here from Thibet has brought me with other presents from the Lama, a labadda, a furred cap and a pair of boots which would keep me warm in Siberia; among other things a box of genuine musk in powder, which I shall send by the post to Dr. Francis to be sent to you. Oh, my sweet Marian, what would I give to be able to convey to you all that has passed in my mind during my long journey. You occupied every step of it and filled my heart with an affection which others may have felt but which never warmed the breast of any man living in a degree exceeding the warmth of mine. Many a severe pang too have I suffered in the gloominess which sometimes seized my imagination, often has my throat swelled and the tears have filled my eyes while your image floated in the vision of my fancy; and yet though my hours have been hours of affliction, I know not how to account for it, but they have yielded a sensation so like to happiness that I would not part with my reflections for all the blessings which the world could yield without you. This is an inconsistency which your heart will understand by the similitude of his own feelings—at least I believe so—; much more I

* This lady, who was on such friendly terms with Hastings, was the widow of Meer Jaffir Khan; in 1772 Hastings had appointed her to be guardian to the young Nawab of Moorshedabad. It will be remembered that one of the charges brought against Hastings by Nuncomar was of having received a large bribe from the Begum for the appointment. The Begum denied the allegations of Nuncomar, and Hastings pronounced the letter from her, which Nuncomar produced, to be a forgery. The majority in the Council deposed Munny Begum.

† Lieutenant Turner. In another letter he refers to him as "a young kinsman of mine."

could say but cannot trust sentiments so sacred to the uncertain conveyance of a letter. I live only in the hope of regaining the possession of my adored Marian; I would not live if that hope had entirely forsaken me, and yet how many chances are against me, but I will not think of them.

"I have the pleasure to send you with this a part of the occupation of my journey. It was begun while I lay on my bed sick in Calcutta, but the greater part was composed between Calcutta and Baughulpore. I do not believe that the wealth of the world could have bribed my genius to produce such a composition had you not formed the principal subject of it, and my imagination not been assisted by the hope of its becoming a future source of entertainment to you. If your own feelings meet and acknowledge those which I have described give it a place in the collection of the former effects of your inspiration. But if you read it with a composed mind, and admire it only as a production of mere poetical merit (for so much I am sure of from the partiality of your judgment), burn it, for it is good for nothing. My hopes are more sanguine. I expect to see it written in the book and in the fair *scrawl* of my dear Marian's own hand, and if it should prove the last of your volume, it will complete an assemblage of which there are few examples of so many poetical attempts, God knows whether good or bad, produced from the strength of a mind heated by love alone, without the least inspiration of natural genius, and without a sentiment in the whole collection that exceeded the truth, and few that equalled the feelings that gave birth to them.

"Find out means to let me know that you have received this, for I would not have it fall into other hands for the world, and should be grieved that you missed it."

The next is from Buxar, March 8. It ends—

"Compliments to Bibby Motte. I have always a little love for her; it would be called a great one were not yours too near it to lessen it by the comparison."

"*Lucknow, August* 13."

(Endorsed "Received April 18, 1785.")

". . . Scott writes that the minister would write to me in His Majesty's name to put off my departure for another year. My whole life has been a sacrifice of my private ease and interests to my public duty, and to more, to public opinion, and this requisition may come to me in such a form as to have the force of an obligation. In that event I shall bid everlasting farewell to all my hopes, for the period which nature has fixed for the duration of my service is already past, and the attempt to prolong it to another season must end me, or which would be worse, send me home laden with infirmities, besides other hazards. . . . I am not pleased with Scott's going into Parliament,* and less with his annexing

* Major John Scott, the energetic but ill-selected agent of Hastings in England, was M.P. for West-Looe from May, 1784, to 1790, and then for

to it the plan of securing his seat for myself. I reserve to myself the privilege of chusing my own mode of life, and shall certainly not prefer one which shall exact from me the sacrifice of my ease and health and at the same time place me in a condition unsuited to my talents. Another year in India will disqualify me to leave it, by the want of means to pay my passage.

"Among the many causes of uneasiness which I suffer in my present situation, there are two which I can only mention to you, because to others I might expose myself to the ridicule of giving myself too much consequence.

"It is possible that the mistaken zeal of my friends may prompt them to solicit for me the grant of honours or a pension which I may be compelled to reject. You are already pretty well acquainted with my sentiments upon both these points. I should be sorry to be reduced to the necessity of doing what may be deemed by others presumption; but as I am content to remain in the humble sphere in which I was born, I have a right to refuse whatever shall place me in an improper comparison with others, to whom I do not allow an equality with me. These reflexions have been thus renewed by an extract sent me, I forget by whom, of a newspaper paragraph which I will enclose in this.

"My friends may proclaim my moderation, but they mistake in asserting that I shall think my *services rewarded by the settlement of a fifth or a sixth part* of the sum of Lord Clive's jagheer for life, or by *any* settlement that shall terminate with my life. If any such provision shall be made for me, or any title given me that shall place me on a level with his Lordship of Madras, even your influence, my Marian, shall not prevail upon me to accept of either."

(In the letter the newspaper cutting is enclosed.)

"This jagheer," it says, "is £30,000 a year—a sum so enormous that it never did or could enter in the head of any friend of Mr. Hastings to bring forward so extravagant or so barefaced a proposition to the con-

Stockbridge, whence he was turned out on petition in 1793, and ordered to be prosecuted for bribery. He took the additional name of Waring on acquiring an estate in Cheshire. I find from a note by the Editor of the Cornwallis Correspondence, that Scott had been married three times, the last being to Mrs. Esten, the actress, who it is there alleged had been long notorious for her gallantries, hence the allusion in the following, which appeared on the occasion of the third marriage.

"Still she is young and still she's fair,
Our cheers and plaudits sharing,
And though well known for ages past,
She's not the worse for *wearing*."

Scott would seem to have been a much greater success in Parliament than Macaulay's allusions to him imply. His interest for the present and future generations, however, is due to his being the grandfather of the dramatist and novelist, Charles Reade.

sideration of a general court; but the fact is that, in conversations, and conversations only, some very respectable and independent proprietors have observed that the falling in of (the late) Lord Clive's jagheer this year might give the East India Company a favourable opportunity of rewarding the services of Mr. Hastings by settling upon him, when he quits India, a fifth or a sixth part of the amount of it annually for his life, supposing it should appear, as it is generally understood, that his fortune is very inadequate to his station."

* * * * * * *

"How often have you heard me declare in the most resolute terms that I never would be seen by you under the disgusting circumstances of a state of sickness; yet the last sixteen months that we passed together were a period of continued illness or of a habit laboring under the effects of illness. In all that long interval you were never from me, and where was my resolution? *

"Major Toone has often told me how much he was shocked at my appearance when he first saw me after his return to Bengal, and yet I was then thought, and thought myself, to be well recovered.

"You had been the close and hourly spectator of all the changes which I had passed through, my bosom associate at a time in which you ought to have been removed to a distance from me, and what was worse, in daily consultation with my physicians.

"It is true that I am indebted to my first illness for such a proof of your affection as is almost without example, nor in the whole course, or during the consequences of it, have I ever perceived any alteration in that tenderness which I before experienced, and which constituted the great and only blessing of my life. Yet I almost regret that you did not leave me earlier, and in the many solitary moments in which my thoughts dwell on the remembrance of those which I have passed with you without the mixture of other subjects (for you are never absent from my recollection), I cannot conquer the apprehension that having seen me so long under circumstances so unfavourable, and these too the last and of course such as must ever accompany your remembrance of me, the delicacy of your affection may suffer, if it have not already suffered, some diminution. Were I present with you, my constant attentions and the evidences which my love would produce every hour and every instant of its reality, would prevent that effect on a heart so generous as yours. But what have I now to support my interests in it during so long a separation? You will remember many instances of unguarded levity, petulancy, and that kind of indolence which wears the appearance of indifference: and I much fear that these will be more ready to obtrude themselves on your recollections

* Mrs. Hastings was present with others at her husband's bedside during his last illness. Gleig tells how, "not without a visible effort," Hastings drew a cambric handkerchief which was at his pillow over his face. Those who were weeping near him, finding that he suffered it to remain for some time, gently removed it, and saw that he was dead.

* * * * * * *

than those instances of my behaviour which might excite your kinder remembrance of me. I could run over a long catalogue of offences with which my conscience has often reproached me, and every trivial incident which could bear that construction, and which escaped my notice at the time in which it happened, now appears with a black dye before me. It is not so in my remembrance of your behaviour which I look back upon with love, respect and admiration, and wonder how I could suffer whole hours (but never days, there I must do myself justice) to pass without seeing you when you were but a few steps removed from me. Yet, my sweet Marian, remember with what delight you have known me frequently quit the scene of business and run up to your apartment for the sake of deriving a few moments of relief from the looks, the smiles, and the sweet voice of my beloved.

"I have resolved to carry Sands home with me, and David Anderson, whom I prevented from returning to England at the time that I undertook my present commission. These are my two great agents. Sands manages all my expenses, and with such care and economy that I shall be a gainer, instead of losing, as I did by my last expedition, above a lac and a half of rupees.

"I have been privately told that the friends of Richard Johnson are amongst my worst enemies in England. He is a sad fellow if this be true. Be on your guard both with him and Middleton.*

* In this passage, which is very suggestive of the secrecy and caution which were characteristic of Hastings, he mentions two well-known protéges of his, whose names occur frequently in the proceedings relating to the Court of Oude, where Middleton had been Resident, and Johnson Assistant-Resident. They got into bad odour with the Governor-General for a time, owing apparently to a want of vigour in the measures necessary for replenishing the Honourable Company's treasure-chest. Among the Impey manuscripts one folio volume is filled with letters from these two officials to the Chief Justice during the year 1782, keeping him informed of all that was going on at Lucknow, and asking for his intercession in their behalf with Hastings. Johnson especially deprecates the Governor-General's displeasure. These letters testify to Impey's being largely in Hastings' confidence about matters at Lucknow, and to his being willing to incur trouble about State affairs not connected with his own official duties. Nathaniel Middleton at a later period was called "Memory Middleton," and after his death "Middleton of Unhappy Memory," in allusion to his evidence at Hastings' trial. Johnson went by the nickname of "Rupee Johnson." Hastings was under a delicate obligation to Johnson, if we may believe the following authorities, viz. :—Francis writes (October, 1777), "Army contract given to Johnson for three years, brother of the worthy gentleman who negotiated Mrs. Imhoff's divorce;" a week later:—"Job for Johnson; Hastings sometimes has qualms—Barwell never." Hicky puts the matter more coarsely:—"June, 1781. A correspondent observes that Dick Squib will unquestionably succeed Mr. Bristow as Resident at the Court of Oude, for two very good reasons, first because he was instrumental in effecting a certain *sham* divorce; and secondly for fear he should betray some secret transactions of the *Great Mogul* and Nat Chucklehead, into which he has wormed himself with his wonted cunning. Can any man possess greater merits?"

"My Marian, I am miserable. Though I know it to have been impossible that you should have written to me, yet my disappointment has tortured me with sensations (for I cannot call them reflections of the mind) similar to those which could arise from the worst suggestions of evil. It seems as if I had totally lost you, or (God forgive me) that you had totally forgotten me. I see you nightly, but such is the sickliness of my imagination that you constantly appear to turn from me with indifference, nor can my reason overcome the gloom which these phantoms leave on my mind, for it is the effect of bodily distemper, independent of the understanding. How hard! My dreams vex me with unreal evils, and the real happiness of my past life appears as a dream, as a dream past long since, and the traces almost effaced.

"P.S.—I will send you the impression of a most beautiful seal which I have had cut with your titles."

Note.—Here there is a wide hiatus in the British Museum letters, *i.e.* between August 13 from Lucknow, and November 20 from Calcutta. Only two of the letters that intervened are in Gleig, viz. one from Benares, dated September 24, closed October 11, and one from Calcutta, dated November 14. In a postscript to the former, dated October 8, he says:—"Phipps arrived yesterday morning and delivered me your letter (viz. from St. Helena). I am the happiest man living, but it is not in a P.S. that I can answer it or say what my feelings have been and are from the perusal of it. I will not believe that I have been raised in my hopes above the heights of mortality to be dashed to the earth with a severe fall. . . . Your permission, my Marian, was unnecessary; all mankind knew it as soon as I did, and some before, and in truth I think all the world is mad with joy for it." It is strange that in the two following letters, that of November 14 and 20, he does not refer to this "it." Not till the letter of December 5 does he profess to answer the St. Helena dispatch. This may be explained either by the fact of the later letter being conveyed by a channel which he expected would outstrip the two previous ones, or from these latter being intended for other eyes besides those of his wife. We gather that he sometimes confined himself to general topics, even in his letters to her, owing to the reasons given in this passage from the Benares letter referred to above. "What a letter have I written, and who that read it without the direction would suspect it to be written by a fond husband to his beloved wife? Perhaps my other letters, if intercepted, would appear to bear too much

Richard Johnson was one of the eighteen Europeans on the Jury panel challenged by Nuncomar. He was one of the suite of Hastings in the night escape to Chunar. He was for a short time British Resident at Hyderabad. He was elected Chairman of the General Bank, Calcutta, in 1788, and when he retired from the service he seems to have joined a banking firm in London, with whom Hastings kept his account. He was on the most friendly terms with Mr. and Mrs. Hastings in England; both wrote to him frequently, the former always signing his letters "yours affectionately."

of the real character of the writer, and atone more than they ought for contrary deficiency of this. But the subject and occasion required it. The first part was intended for a duplicate by another hand, and all that follows to this page for communication."

"*Calcutta, November* 20, 1784.

(Tells of his return journey down.)

. . . "But from the evening of my arrival in Calcutta to this day I have not enjoyed a moment of bodily ease, but have had all the devils of languor, dejection of spirits (a thing unknown at Lucknow), nightly oppression, feverish heat and headaches, which I had for my companions this last year at this season of it. For these reasons I eat no supper, go to bed at ten, abstain wholly from wine and every other liquid but tea and water. I ride every morning and gently, and use the cold bath as often as I ride, and will oftener if I am prevented from riding; if this will not do I will diet myself on pish-pash, or bread and water, or live like Cornaro on the daily subsistence of an egg, but I will have health in some way, though I may forego all the blessings of it. Blessings? What blessings can it yield me? Let me have but existence and freedom from pain, with the full exercise of my mental faculties. I desire no more till I see the last of Saugor Island.

"My friend Wilkins has lately made me a present of a most wonderful work of antiquity, and I am going to present it to the public. Among many precepts of fine morality I am particularly delighted with the following, because it has been the invariable rule of my latter life, and often applied to the earlier state of it before I had myself reduced it to the form of a maxim in writing. It is this: '*Let the motive be in the deed and not in the event.* Be not one whose motive for action is the hope of reward. Let not thy life be sport of inaction. Depend upon application' (that is, as it is afterwards explained, the application of the rule of moral right to its consonant practice without care for the event, as it may respect ourselves). 'Perform thy duty, abandon all thought of the consequence, and make the event equal, whether it terminate in good or evil, for such an equality is called application.'

"To this good rule I will adhere, careless of every event but *one*, and that shall console me, though the voices of all mankind shall cry out against me. And what is that one? Oh God grant me the blessing of a satisfied conscience, and my Marian to reward it. . . . I will send with it by this conveyance the firman confirming your high titles, and the translation. The former is a beautiful sheet of paper, and that is all it's worth, for though your virtues merit honours greater than kings can bestow, yet these will not raise your station in life an inch—no, not the breadth of a hair—above that of Mrs. Hastings in your own country (I mean England, for that is your own). Nor were they given to your worth, even in this, for had you been destitute of every quality and accomplishment which you possess, you might have been the Queen of Sheba, the Goddess of Fortune, or whatever excellence you had chosen for your own appellation. So don't be proud of your titles; let the Queen of Sheba, if she knows it, boast that her name is united to yours. Your husband, too, is the adopted son of a king, and sworn brother of an heir-apparent, yet the height of his present ambition is speedily to become a private gentleman, and in that character all the royalty that now runs in his veins will be lost, and even his great father will forget that he gave it him. Remember these reflections when you look at your firman, and be sure not to forget them when you show it. I know you will, for my Marian has her foibles, and, God forgive me, but I have known my own vanity accompanying her, and have gazed on her with full eyes of love and delight when she gave her pride, her graceful pride, its full career. This is meant as a lesson against pride—don't mistake it for encouragement. . . .

"I have given your shawls which Johnson provided for you to Captain Joe Price, who has undertaken to convey them safe to your hands. He will not tell me how, and you may depend upon receiving them. . . .

"I am now writing at Alipore; for it has been put up to sale and bought in again. I have sold Rishera for double the sum that was paid for it. This is a riddle, and I leave it to your sagacity to unravel it.

"Adieu, my heart's beloved. O ever love me, for no man ever merited by love a larger return of it than I do."

Alipore, Sunday, December 5, 1784. Closed the 8th, at night.

Is in answer to Marian's budget from St. Helena, and begins, "I am now again reading your most delightful though painful letter."

He dwells on his delight at learning from this letter that when she left St. Helena on May 15 it was "in perfect health and in the full assurance of being in a state which might in its event make me most truly the happiest of all mankind." His thoughts revert to this subject every now and then, and any topic seems to furnish an occasion for introducing it.

"I too, my Marian, have often reproached myself, and sometimes ungenerously murmured at you, for our separation. It was, I own, *my* act. But do not give me credit for it, I was provoked and intimidated to it. I was told by everyone that it was absolutely necessary; somebody, I forget who, I believe it was Sir Elijah, put the dreadful case to me that should you stay and fall a sacrifice to my weakness, how would I reproach myself as the cause of your death. You too once said, feelingly, speaking of some lady who died, 'Ah! she staid a year too long.' These reflexions stung me and fastened on my resolution. Yet am I now glad that it was so. [I now persuade myself that it has been the cause of saving your life. . . . Perhaps, too, it has been the preservation of my own, for I am not sure that I should have left

Calcutta had you staid in it.] The words thus [ ] marked were written by impulse and without reflecting that the event to which it relates is now past the course of fate. It has happened or is impossible. But I will let the words stand for a happy omen. Am I not superstitious?

"I thank you for your care of yourself. Your mode of living was also very like my own; I was always in bed by ten and dressed before sunrise. I am compelled to exceed in Calcutta, but not very much. I have found that when I can adhere to my early hours and morning rides I get tolerable health. I have also made trial of total abstinence from wine, of which I have already experienced the benefit, and will continue it.

"Yes, my beloved, we will have many walks together, and infinitely more delightful than those of Alipore. Many an excursion too from home. I have a variety of schemes of pleasure playing in my imagination which will all derive their relish from your society and your participation of them. Let me but follow and be once more in possession of my heart's treasure, I care not for what may happen without doors if I have but what I wish within.

"I thank you for your kindness to my little horse, and the mango plants, not that I care three cowries for the latter, and, when I think of you, as little do I care for the former; but they are indications of affection, and therefore I am delighted to be told of them. Apropos, poor Sulliman begins to grow old and wants the vigour which he had, though he retains his spirit. I have resolved to leave him as you did Beauty, under charge of Mr. Thompson, who will be kind (to him) for your sake and mine as long as he lives. . . ."

He alludes to his having been ill and to her nursing him on a former occasion, and adds (referring to an illness he had after Marian's departure)—

"I knew that if it were possible for me to be blessed with your presence, I should find you as anxiously watchful for my safety, and feel the same effect of your kindness that I had done. I regretted the want of it, and at the same time blamed the indiscretion that had ever allowed you, in breach of my resolution and established maxim of years, to approach me in the hour of sickness. For this I a thousand times reproach myself, and I think I know how to prevent the like weakness hereafter. Yet would I give the world to attend you, had you the same occasion, for even sickness has not the power of making you unlovely, and I am sure it has ever heightened my love with the sight of your suffering, and the dread of worse. . . .

"I am mightily pleased, and if anybody should read this but yourself he would say, 'and mightily foolish!'—and let them say it. All the wise men that have ever written about love have agreed to call it a folly, and so pronounce him only truly wise and truly happy who can confine his search of happiness to himself alone, and is totally exempt from all impressions of external accidents. In this sense I am far gone in folly indeed, so far that I had rather be miserable with my present feelings than cured with apathy.

"I am vexed that nobody will talk of you to me. It was the case even when you were with me. No one ever mentioned your name to me, except in the common form of civility. I must except Mrs. Samson; she would praise you to me for an hour together, and had she been fond of talking, it was the sure way to engross all the conversation to herself, for I never interrupted her but to encourage her to lengthen the subject.

* * * * * * *

"How sweetly playful, how bewitching my Marian is when she is in spirits, and how perfectly in her expression and manner different from all the rest of womankind; you cannot conceive how perfectly your image starts up before me as I read some passages which are most characteristical of you.

"My mind is naturally gloomy and yours sprightliness itself, which has some time changed the quality of mine. As an ancient poet, speaking of his Marian, says:

> 'And sprightliness whose influence none can feel,
> But catch the infection, and enliven'd grow.'

* * * * * * *

"What might not have been the consequence of so many complicated assaults on my poor Marian's tender frame, especially the last; how fatal to our hopes, and even to our existence, for I am convinced that mine is bound to yours, and I hope it is. But I ought not to complain, since it has proved the strength of your constitution in that particular about which I am now most anxious.

* * * * * * *

"But the event is passed conjecture, hopes, and wishes. I will arm myself for the worst, I will let the best operate as it may, that I shall be most unphilosophically elated with.

. . . "A third gale! Indeed your trials have been very severe. Few men confined to their cabins under such circumstances would have maintained so equal a mind,* or thought with fondness on their absent wives or mistresses, with all the elements threatening them with instant dissolution. You may say what you please. I affirm that you have a truer principle of courage than any woman that I know; a strong sense of danger, with a spirit collected and conscious of its obligations, and (as Francis says) I will bring witnesses to prove it.

"You conjure me not to set my heart on it. Indeed but I do, and so peremptorily, that it will be almost broken if I am disappointed; but I ought not to say so, considering what may have happened when you are reading this.†

* "*Mentem servare æquam rebus in arduis,*" his own motto.

† That these hopes were doomed to disappointment may be seen from the opening sentences of one of the letters in Gleig, dated December 26, 1784,

"Oh my Marian! what a surprise of pleasure is it to me to read my own maxim in the following quotation of one of yours—'Besides' (I must quote the whole because I am proud of it), 'besides you have that self-satisfaction, and it has always been your characteristic that you on all occasions have acted as a man of virtue and honour ought to do, whatever consequences may ensue. Surely that is a bliss, &c.' If I add the context, my eyes will overflow; they do almost, and I shall not see to write it correctly. . . . I may not know it before the proper time of my departure, as the event cannot have much exceeded the end of August. To reason upon probabilities on such a subject may be useful to myself, but must be totally uninteresting to you; you know what has passed and may in one event (which God forbid, for yet something is left even in the happiest state for a reverse) renew your afflictions. I am not happy, my Marian, while my heart swells with the hope of supreme happiness; I hope too much to be easy. . . .

"I have this morning (the 8th) received a letter from the Prince addressed to you, with a present of a *rezy* and a shawl handkerchief. These I will send you by the *Surprise*. They are according to the etiquette; so accept them as they are intended, and don't examine them by their qualities, for they are of ordinary fineness. I am pleased with this mark of his delicacy and attention, for I am sure it proceeded from himself. I am not a little pleased that you should receive this evidence of the notoriety of the Governor-General's affection for his Marian. Had you been merely his wife, the Prince would no more have thought of paying this compliment to you than of writing to the Queen of Sheba.

"And the letter will please you; Scott* is translating it. I will enclose the translation with it in this letter.

"I have yet an hour's work to put all that I have written to you in three long letters into their proper packages with their enclosures, which are many. This will only enclose the two letters from the Prince and Munny Begum, with a little one from Capt. Scott accompanying them. I could not refuse him, and what he writes is, I am sure, the tribute of a good heart."

*Calcutta, December* 29, 1784.

(In this letter, the last of this series in the British Museum collection, he writes his determination to sail for England in the *Berrington* in the following month).

Calcutta—"I have received your letter of 3 August informing me of your safe arrival in England. I received it on my return from the play. I could not go to bed, but sat reading it till past two, and afterwards lay long after counting three without being able to close my eyes. Whether I was happy or unhappy in reading it I cannot tell you. I fear my disappointment on one subject equalled my joy for your safety—the close of your perils and the promise that you soon would be as well as you ever had been at any period of your life. I have since thought only on the good; and I thank God for it."

* Captain Jonathan Scott.

"Mr. Pitt's bill,* and the injurious reflections which he has cast upon me, are the grounds of this resolution; not as they excite my resentment, for I have not suffered a thought of myself to influence me, but as they are certain indications of his acquiescence in my return according to the terms which I have constantly stated as those which should determine it. One obstacle yet remains, and that I shall immediately put to the trial. You know the promise which I have made to the Nabob Vizier. That I must fulfil, and you will probably know the result before you receive this. I have said nothing to Scott about Mr. Pitt's bill, because I should hurt his feelings, and I know that he was not aware of its malignity; yet I must say to you, but to you only, that his support of it astonishes me, for an act more injurious to his fellow-servants, to my character and authority, to the Company, to the proprietors, especially who alone have a right to my services on the principle of gratitude, and to the national honour, could not have been devised, though fifty Burkes, Foxes, and Francises had clubbed to invent one. I am well, but keep myself so by attention which would be misery to another. But what care I for Society. My days pass in incessant writing, reading, hearing, and talking, and even close with weariness, and little headaches which sometimes grow to great ones. If I am doomed to remain another year, and survive it, I must carry witnesses of my identity, or return, like Ulysses, an old man and beggar to my/his (*sic*) Penelope, and with only one scar, which can not be seen, to convince you that I am your husband. Don't practise Mrs. Blair's advice to Mr. Cooke upon me.

"Adieu, my most beloved,

"W. H."

## NOTE.

The foregoing selection and extracts from the private letters of Warren Hastings appeared, for the first time, in the earliest edition of this book so far back as 1882, and again in the second and third editions. They have not been added to, being considered as specimens on a scale sufficiently ample to exemplify the nature and character of the whole. Typographical and other errors that had got into the text from hasty transcribing originally have been, it is hoped, corrected. It is but candid to allow that during the long interim, I have heard many, and read not a few comments (both in India and at home) on these letters, which suggested a doubt whether the memory of Hastings was well served by their publication—whether

* Pitt's India Bill became law on August 13, 1784. Its object was to deprive the East India Company of political power, which was thereby vested in a new ministerial department called the Board of Control. The double Government system, the foundation of which it laid, continued down to November 1, 1858.

even the pursuit of history justified intrusion into ground so sacred. Little or nothing was brought out in these letters, it was alleged, to add to our knowledge of the public acts, or to increase the fame of one of the greatest of Englishmen. They were so trustingly written for one reader alone, was it fair, it was asked, to make manifest, even as a tribute to his heart, the confessed weakness of a most devoted husband and lover, racked through his boundless affection by a solicitude for an absent wife, which urged him to seek willing refuge in morbid fancies and wailings, in what he himself calls broodings over "the melancholy passions" her letters aroused?

These questions can, no doubt, be looked at from various standpoints; they can only await the judgment of individual opinion. This can be better formed perhaps by those who read the whole of the letters as written in full. An opportunity for this is now available, as "the Letters of Warren Hastings to his Wife" have been re-introduced and published (1905), *in extenso* for the first time, by the learned authoress who writes as Sydney C. Grier. Any one studying this lady's work, as a careful transcriber, editor, and annotator, can not but feel admiration for the wonderful and conscientious industry displayed in every page of her excellent book. And those who know something about British-India and its history must be struck with the accurate and varied knowledge she has acquired of the period concerned in the later years of Hastings' government. The letters, as by this authoress presented, are accompanied by much introductory and explanatory detail, historical, biographical, and (wisely or not) controversial. It all teems with information, welcome probably to the appreciative few rather than to the many. In these fast-living days it is not easy to find in England general readers evincing the interest that might be expected, even in such great men as Clive and Warren Hastings and many others who gave their labour and their lives to India. It can hardly be hoped, therefore, that there will be many caring to hear about the men and women whose only claim to notice is that they were, for a brief moment comparatively, brought into friendly or official association with a great Governor-General. Hence it is to be feared that Miss Grier's assiduous labours in compiling her biographical sketches may not meet with the attention they deserve. Indeed, she seems to have provided for this by having the letters printed in a larger type, which admits of their being more easily picked out and read consecutively. The present writer gladly acknowledges the pleasure and profit which he has derived from Miss Sydney Grier's book.

# SPECIMENS OF LETTERS WRITTEN BY MRS. HASTINGS

THOSE who may have now read so many letters written to Mrs. Hastings, may perhaps be curious to see what sort of letters were written by her. Widely scattered through the Hastings and the Impey manuscripts in the British Museum are several of Mrs. Hastings' letters; very few of these were written in India, or to her husband. Those subjoined seem to be worth reproducing either as touching on matters of interest, or as being fairly illustrative of her style. One of them is thus indorsed by Mr. Impey; "Though a German, she wrote and spoke English correctly and elegantly—though with a foreign accent." Several of her letters suggest that she had more individuality and strength of mind than one might be inclined to infer from the letters addressed to her by her husband-lover. Readers must draw their own conclusions as to the indication of character suggested by the first of the few letters which follow. I have come across no earlier letters from Mrs. Hastings.

This was written to the Chief Justice at Calcutta when Mr. and Mrs. Hastings were at Patna on their way down to the Presidency. It is long, and I have omitted some passages here and there which were devoid of interest. Readers will not fail to remember Macaulay's burning words in connection with the surroundings of the incident referred to by Mrs. Hastings.

*From Mrs. Hastings to Sir Elijah Impey.*

"MY DEAR SIR,

"I am flattered by the anxiety which you express concerning my health. I have the satisfaction to tell that I am better, but I mend—piano, piano. I doubt not it will give you pleasure that we are so far on our way to Calcutta; we were at Buxar on the 14th. . . . You are become very wicked since you left us, I laught (*sic*) very heartily about the leg, but admire the *goodness* of the lady, the *true spirit* of *religion* works in her.

"I have heard from Mr. Middleton, but not to my satisfaction; it was as much as I can recollect of it to the folowing (*sic*) purpose:—'The Nabob had intended to send you a present of horses, elephants, palanqueens, &c., &c., but I told him that they would be of no use to you, that he had better send something which you might be able to wear, to which he agreed; but as he had then nothing by him that was worth your acceptance he requested you to please yourself at Benares, and that he would pay for it; the sum which he alowed (*sic*) was one lakh of rupees;' but I rejected it, as it appeared mean to me to accept a present in that mercenary form.

"I dare say you know that Mr. Middleton and His Excellency (*she means the Nawab Vizier*) had left Lucknow on the 2nd of this month to go to Fayzabad and quell the diabolical spirits of the old Begum and the Bhow Begum, which was accomplished on the 13th. The Nabob's party were put in possession of the Kella without effusion of blood. The two eunuchs, Baber and Jawar Ally Cawn, delivering themselves into the Nabob's custody. Had His Excellency's troops come only the enemy were resolved to attack him; they were between three and four thousand well-armed, and furnished with a large store of ammunition.

"I hope that this late step will settle matters to the satisfaction of Mr. Hastings and advantage to the Company."

Then the letter proceeds to inquire after her god-child—dear Marian—and ends—

"Mr. Hastings desires me to give his best compliments to you and Lady Impey, and I request that you will believe

"Me your sincere humble servant,

"M. HASTINGS.*

"*January* 20, 1782."

* It would be instructive to know what sympathy the writer of this letter obtained from her correspondent, touching the want of "satisfaction" in the communication from the Lucknow Resident. The predatory instincts which are historically attributed to Elijah Impey must have received a severe shock, on learning the scruples which Mrs. Hastings so naïvely explains actuated her when she "rejected" the Nabob's "present." When the wife of the Governor-General penned these lines, little did she foresee what a noise the "late step," which she so artlessly hoped would "settle matters," was destined to make in the world. Little did she dream when writing complacently of the move to "quell the diabolical spirits of the old Begums," that before seven years went by, fifty guineas would be paid for a single seat in Westminster Hall to hear a British statesman—the most brilliant and effective Parliamentary orator of that or of any later time—giving *his* version of that expedition to Fyzabad while denouncing the "oppression, rapacity and perfidy" employed against the plundered Princesses of Oude. Sheridan described the alleged rebellion in Oude as "plotted by two feeble old women, headed by two eunuchs and suppressed by an affidavit."

It will be noted too that this highly placed lady did not think it "mean" to accept a present from a Native. She only objected to the mercenary form of that proposed. Ten thousand pounds' worth of jewels would have been more to her

(To the same—written about March or April, 1783.)

"MY DEAR SIR,

"I flatter myself that Lady Impey is perfectly recovered, but I am not easy yet till I hear it from yourself; so pray inform me by a line, and tell me if I may come to see her. My affectionate compliments attend her. How do you bear this hot weather? and how dose (*sic*) it agree with your sweet children?

"I am, my dear Sir Elija (*sic*),

"Your sincere humble servant,

"M. HASTINGS."

"*Allypoor*, Monday morning."

In March, 1797, Hastings, writing from Daylesford to Richard Johnson, Esq., at Stratford Bank, Stratford Place, London, on business matters, says:—

"I have written to Lord Roseberry requesting that he will be pleased to pay, or caused to be paid, to Messrs. Edwards, Templer and Co., the remaining sums when they shall become due for the price of my late house in Park Lane."

On the same day Mrs. Hastings also writes to this gentleman, and thanks him "for all the trouble you have taken about my house in Park Lane," and is glad to learn "that all the money matters regarding it are amicably settled," and then goes on—

"What trouble his Lordship has given us! By the Lord! I would not sell an other (*sic*) house to him if I had one to dispose of, and he wish to be the purchaser.

taste; they would have been portable and convertible. Her love for jewels and for the display of them is curiously exemplified in an anecdote which Mr. Foster at the India Office kindly drew my notice to. It is to be found in Mr. W. Hoey's "Memoirs of Delhi and Faisabad" (vol. ii.) translated from the original Persian, viz.: An emissary from the Lucknow Court, one Bahar Ali Khan, visited Calcutta in 1780 for the purpose of interviewing the Governor. He took a few curios as presents with him, which, however, he came to think were not adequate to the Governor's rank.

When he came into the Governor's presence, "Mrs. Hastings was playing with some kittens near him. She had placed pearls worth many thousand rupees in a large bowl, and she was throwing the kittens in upon them. They could not climb out, for when they tried to stand up the pearls slipped under their feet. She was a long time at this sport. In her ears were ear-drops each worth fifty thousand rupees." In the face of what he saw, Ali Khan hesitated to produce his own presents. But he presented a costly saddle which Nawab Salar Jang had sent, and some precious stones which the Bahaw Begum had given from her own treasury, also some phials of "itr" (ottar). The account of the interview goes on that Hastings took the matter in hand himself, and would accept nothing but the ottar, for certain politic reasons which he gave there and then.

"You are good in thinking of my son Charles, and I am sure he would feel himself obliged was he to know what a warm advocate he has in you; yet in the present instance you are wrong, Charles has not given up £10,000, as you state it, nor has he lost anything by his late arrangement, as my gift to him was £30,000 including the £10,000 for his wife's settlement.

"But some months ago I promised my Charles that I would make up another £10,000 for him, and in consequence of that promise I gave him £4000 in India stocks, and told him that when I had disposed of my house that I would make up the sum which I had promised him. I request you to carry the £2000 which Mr. Walford owes me to Charles accounts (*sic*), and when Lord Roseberry makes his first payment to me to take £4000 for my son, which will make up the sum of £10,000; that is £4000 in the stocks, £2000 from Mr. W., and £4000 from the sail (*sic*) of my house in town. Then he will be master of £40,000, which will bring him in yearly £2000. This sum will enable him to *live very comfortable* with his beloved Charlotte, and my mind will be easy respecting my beloved children. Whatever my fate may be let me see my children happy and comfortable. The deposit money I request you to keep for my use or rather for my beloved Hastings! * as he may want cash. Has the bond been paid by Mr. Townsend's executors? How much has Mr. Hastings overdrawn at your bank? Pray let me know a little about it. My enquiry (you know) does not proceed from curiosity, but from a wish to save my dear husband anxiety of mind.

"I am, my Dear Sir,
"Yours sincerely,
"M. HASTINGS."

"*Daylesford, April* 3, 1797.

"To Richard Johnson, Esq.
"MY DEAR SIR,—

"I request you will have the goodness to send the enclosed letter to the post. Have you received an answer from Stuttgard that the £200 † have been received; I have not. You will be so good to place £1000 of the deposit money, which will be paid on the 9th of this month by Lord Roseberry, to Mr. H.'s account and the remainder to mine. Walford's answer to Mr. H. was such as I had expected, 'that he could not pay at present, that he had an account to settle with the Governor of nine years' standing;' little of course will come of the £2000 to dear

* The note of exclamation is so placed in the original.

† This money was for her mother, whose address is thus written in a clerkly hand on the back of the original of this letter, viz.,

A Madame Madame,
Baroness de Chapusetin,
Veuvè de Baron Chapuset,
Née St. Valentin,
à Stutgard.

good Mr. Hastings ; what a grievous thing it is that my husband will not settle all his affairs! how easy would his mind be if he was to know *exactly what he owes, and what was due to him.* I intreate him oftened (*sic*) on this subject, and pray him to settle his affairs, he promisès, but does not like to look into the state of his affairs. This negligence may arise from knowing that he cannot extricate himself from his troubles. How cruel it is that a man who has served his country so long and so faithfully should at last be obliged to harrass his days and nights with the gloomy thoughts—how he is to live! Indeed it is a shame on the Court of Directors to let such an old servant as he is bestow a thought how he is to live. I do firmly believe that if it was requested of them that they would relinquish the £50,000 and let him have the pension, £4000 annually. How comfortable could we then live! * If there should be a change of ministers I think it will be done. Pray are you acquainted with D. Scott, the present Chairman? I think he is an excellent channel to canvas, besides he is a good man, and *feels*, I am sure, for the Governor.

"Adieu, my Dear Sir,

"Believe me, yours sincerely,

"MARIAN HASTINGS."

"P.S.—I hope your dear children are well and all those you love." †

(Mrs. Hastings had gone to London to see her daughter-in-law, while Colonel Imhoff was with Hastings at Daylesford.)

"*March* 19, 1804.

"I am grieved to hear, my beloved husband, that you have still a cold, and that your deafness is worse. What heart-breaking intelligence to your poor Marian. I will hope that this will find you still at Daylesford, though you tell me in your letter of yesterday that you purpose leaving Daylesford to-morrow. I would advise you, my love, not to risk your valuable person to a visit at General G., as it will again expose you to a change of bed, which I think is exceedingly dangerous with a cold upon you. I would advise you to leave Daylesford on Wednesday very early, and be in Portugal Street at night, where you will meet with a most affectionate welcome, and be sure of a well-aired bed and a good fire.

* I believe that this or some similar arrangement was ultimately carried out. At all events the last twelve or fourteen years of Hastings' life were free from financial embarrassment through the liberality of the Honble. E. I. Compy.

† In another letter about this time to the same gentleman, Mrs. Hastings gives this specimen of her practical turn of mind when referring to a box, the question of whose safety had given her some temporary anxiety, viz. "Give me leave, my good Sir, to mention to you that I think your clerks are not so regular in their pranch (*sic*) of the business as they ought to be." And she then proceeds to detail, in a business-like way, what steps should have been taken to secure the due custody and recognition of a box given in charge to the Bank.

"My cold is better to Day (*sic*), though I *feasted* at dinner at Mrs. Grindall with dear Charlotte. I shall not go out to-night. I think it will be best to sell the fat cow; you will get good price for it, and if we want any part of her we can have it.

"I am truly concerned to hear that my beloved Charles' cough still continues to torment him; I had flattered myself that the fine pure air would cure his cough, and make you quite stout; pray give my love to the dear Coll. (*sic*).

"Sir Isaac Heart (?) just called with the accounts that Lord Keith had sent the accounts of B.'s arrival at Boulong with a great force. Well, our Government is much alarmed at this intelligence. The weather does not seem favourable for the invasion; it rained all day yesterday, and to-day it snows and wets and is a most gloomy day. I prayed for you and dear Charles at Church yesterday. Adieu, my best and dearest husband; may the Almighty restore you to health, and give you all you desire and deserve.

"Ever your affectionate wife,
"M. H."

Warren Hastings' life was prolonged far beyond his own expectations, viz. to the age of eighty-six (nearly). Ten years before his death he wrote to his stepson, Imhoff—

"If my life can be of benefit to those whose affections, and mine for them, attach me to it, I think I can securely reckon upon the chances of its holding out one year more at least, after the proof which my perfect recovery in so few days from a disorder which if not dangerous was attended during some hours with as much pain as I can remember to have ever suffered.

"I am sure it was the same disorder that your dear mother endured on the first night of our visit to Stoneleigh Abbey, and I think I understand it so scientifically, that if your dear lady wishes to catch it, for an experiment, I can (but the Devil take me if I do) put her in the same way of obtaining it in a given time."

Hastings died on August 22nd, 1818. Almost his last act was to dictate a letter to the Court of Directors asking their consideration for his wife when deprived of his income. She survived him for nineteen years. Amongst the British Museum MSS. is a long letter from Mrs. Hastings to her godson, Sir C. D'Oyley, in India, expressing her gratitude and joy on hearing that at a public meeting in Calcutta its inhabitants had voted a statue to be erected, as she says, "to the memory of that great and blessed spirit." The statue alluded to is that now in the Town Hall, Calcutta, a memento of the respect and love which the English in India ever had for Hastings.

All through his career he had their confidence and sympathy.

He felt he could rely on their support under all circumstances, and the consciousness of this must have been no inconsiderable factor in enabling him to come triumphantly through the long struggle with hostile colleagues who sought to thwart his measures and subvert his Government. Nor was this generous and kindly feeling destined to wither when his presence was withdrawn. Warren Hastings is perhaps the solitary instance of a European whose life having been devoted to India, could not, with reference to his countrymen in the East, say with David: "I am forgotten as a dead man out of mind. I am like a broken vessel." The active and enduring love and veneration of Calcutta for his name and memory are wonderful for the singular rarity of such a manifestation.

## POSTSCRIPT.

As bearing on the manifestation of Calcutta's affection for Hastings, I find an old Calcutta newspaper thus bringing before its readers an honourable tribute which gratitude and respect had unostentatiously paid to him long after any material recognition of it was possible on his part, viz.: "One very curious anecdote is through this letter" (*i.e.* that of one from Hastings to the Court of Directors which had been quoted from) "for the first time disclosed to the public. It appears that, pending Mr. Hastings' trial, a subscription was actually made in India to enable him to pay the expenses, and, in fact, seventeen gentlemen subscribed and paid the sum of £1000 each. On this subject Mr. Hastings thus expresses himself": I am indebted for those remittances to the generosity of individuals; they were granted for the express purpose of relieving my wants. They were received in the years 1790, 1791, most seasonably at times, in which but for them I should have been reduced to great distress. I do not mention this as an excuse for my accepting them; I mention it only to show that while I was an object of envy to some, and of jealousy to others, under the imputation of possessing inordinate wealth, and when, in addition to the charge of extravagance, I was publicly accused of the most corrupt disposal of it, I was actually on the verge of penury, and of wanting the means of acquiring the common necessaries of life, but in the degrading resource of private credit, to which I have since been actually compelled to submit." He also wrote as follows to the chairman of the Court of Directors when invited by the latter to declare the true state of his affairs after the expenses of the impeachment. "With respect to Mrs. Hastings the sum of one lakh of sicca rupees was assigned to trustees for her use as a marriage settlement in 1777. At that time all my fortune was lent upon mortgages, and the bill was returned. When it was ultimately paid the sum with interest amounted to £22,234. This by the sale of jewels grew to £40,000, from which £10,000 were deducted for the purchase of a house and furniture in Park Lane, lately made over as a security for that sum assigned by the marriage settlement of Mrs. Imhoff, the wife of her son. I declare upon my honour, and even by all that is more sacred, that I have never added to her fortune since the day of my marriage."

The fact seems to be that Hastings was a man quite devoid of thrift, who did not know the value of money, and who, in consequence, spent more than he could afford really. He did not know what he had, or, as his wife wrote, what he owed or what was due to him. He wrote as follows to Richard Johnson (April, 1797), in reference to the sale of his pictures by Christie, and also the contemplated sale of his horses. "As to better times, are you my friend the comforter that bid me look for them? You certainly know that bad as they are they must of inevitable necessity be worse."

He also refers to the heavy war taxes, and ends "yours affectionately."

In allusion to Mrs. Hastings having wealth unknown to her husband, Wraxall says this: "Nor did any censure ever attach to her conduct, unless we consider as such the accusations which her own and her husband's enemies raised against her, of amassing wealth by presents received from native princes and princesses, usually conveyed in the shape of diamonds or other gems. It was asserted that though Hastings might be poor, yet his wife was rich and rapacious." Wraxhall's latest editor, Mr. Wheatley, adds in a note to this that Mrs. Hastings lost large sums by the failure of a house in the city" (he gives no particulars, no authority).

Perhaps Macaulay's is the most kind and charitable conclusion to come to; he says he is inclined to give credit to the story that she accepted presents with great alacrity, and that she thus formed, "without the connivance of her husband, a private hoard amounting to several lacs of rupees." But he commends her moderation, too. "The influence of Mrs. Hastings over her husband was indeed such that she might easily have obtained much larger sums than she was ever accused of receiving."

## CHAPTER XI

### AN OLD CALCUTTA GRAVE

"Calcutta is one great graveyard of memories"

I HAD some intention of letting this book end with a chapter under the heading of "Calcutta Under Ground," or some similar title. In it I proposed to invite the reader to accompany me in a hasty ramble through the cemeteries longest in existence, and while pointing out a grave here and there, to briefly tell what little I may have picked up regarding its tenant, and to recall what claim he or she may have had to be remembered in such a retrospect. It occurred to me, too, that such an excursion would give an opportunity of urging the reasons why some of the tombs at least should be saved from the ruin to which so many have gone, and all are hastening.

But so much space has been given to those who lived in Calcutta in the last century, that none is left for those who died and were there buried. My sepulchral gossip, therefore, must be suppressed. Perhaps it is as well. I fear it must be recognised that English people, either at home or abroad, are animated by no strong sentiment regarding what may be called the sacred relics of the past. If they were, there would scarcely be room for a Society which is at work even in England at this moment, having for its object the preservation of the memorials of the dead in the churches and churchyards of Great Britain. This Society has a heavy task in trying to secure the sympathy and support of a mere fraction of an apathetic public. Its proceedings show that the almost incredible neglect and desecration of such memorials, even countenanced by parochial authorities, are as much in operation to-day as they were some centuries earlier. The uphill work which it has set its kindly hand to, may be judged of from a single instance. At a certain English vicarage a late incumbent paved his coach-house with tombstones from the churchyard, and replied, when remonstrated with, that "the families had gone from the parish, or had died out"! Well, if these things are done in a green tree, what surprise need be expressed at the passive neglect which meets one at every step through the Christian cemeteries of Calcutta; neglect which finds its cause and excuse in this reverend person's logic—the families have gone from the parish.

Even putting aside the financial difficulty which circumstances in India render very formidable, it must be sorrowfully confessed that the obstacle confronts one on the threshold, of the hopelessness of arousing the necessary amount of general sympathy for doing anything towards rescuing for identification, even the tombstones of those who died in exile, in a country where the European from his very arrival, looks and pines for the day when he may be favoured enough and fortunate enough to be able to leave it again, and then —let the dead bury their dead—and look after their own monuments too.

In fact it comes to this, that, unless in the case of direct kindred not very remote, the memorials of the dead of a previous generation have but little chance of being looked after by those succeeding, if some national title to preservation, or circumstances amounting to such, cannot be set up. This can be done for many tombs in Calcutta. Its very oldest cemetery offers several claimants, so many testimonies to the price that England has always paid for her footing in India. Let me instance the tomb of Admiral Watson, whose services and achievements were gratefully recognized by the monument to him in Westminster Abbey. He, with Clive, was the re-founder of the city of which Job Charnock, who lies near him, was the founder. When the ground was being prepared for the building of St. John's Cathedral, amongst the very few old graves that were spared, but which now receive no due conserving care, were those of the Admiral and of the little shipmate for whom he sorrowed, Billy Speke, the midshipman of the *Kent*, who got his death wound at the capture of Chandernagore in the struggle for the re-establishing of British power in Bengal.

I hope that some one with local influence will plead for the preservation of this heroic young sailor's tomb, before the ominous words "too late" have to be recorded, and will recall for modern Calcutta his sad and tender story as told by the good surgeon, Dr. Ives, who attended him. He was a brave man's son, and his death is a striking instance of the truth of an observation made by Sir W. Hunter in writing of the Calcutta cemeteries, and noting the high proportion of the graves of the young, that to the early fathers of Calcutta the curse on the re-builder of Jericho came bitterly home, "He shall lay the foundation thereof in his first-born, and in his youngest son shall he set up the gates of it."

From amongst the many graves that I had marked for prospective notice, I shall, however, here bring forward one. I make an exception in this one's favour, partly because its claim to kindly recognition seems to me to be little short of national, and partly because it has found no other advocate.* The tomb for which I crave consideration is not that of a first-born or of a youngest son, but of a younger daughter. One who shows a high title to the tender enshrining of her memory, and to all possible manifestations of respect for it, on the part of English people, inasmuch as she inspired some of the most exquisite poetry in our language.

In South Park Street Cemetery there is a monument over a grave which bears this inscription on a black marble slab :—

"In Memory of

The Honourable

*Rose Whitworth Aylmer,*

Who departed this life March 2nd, A.D. 1800.

Aged 20 years.

What was her fate? Long, long before her hour
Death called her tender soul by break of bliss,
From the first blossoms to the buds of joy,
Those few our noxious fate unblasted leaves
In this inclement clime of human life."

It may not be superfluous to recall for some in the present generation, the circumstances which associate this old Calcutta tomb with the name of a man who "is among the most striking figures in the history of English literature, striking alike by his character and his powers;" † a great master in verse; a prose writer of the highest rank—Walter Savage Landor. Not long after leaving Oxford (1797) when about twenty-one years of age, Landor was staying at a then secluded spot on the Welsh coast, where he met and was on friendly terms with Lord Aylmer's family. One of the young ladies of this family became his especial favourite. Miss Aylmer was at this time some four years younger than Landor, and they seem to have been

* This was the case when this sketch was first published; since then Rose Aylmer and her tomb have been noticed by various writers.

† See "Landor" by Professor Sidney Colvin (1884). The few circumstances recalled in the text are taken from this gentleman's writings about Landor, and from Forster's biography.

MONUMENT OVER ROSE AYLMER'S GRAVE IN CALCUTTA.

*See p.* 368.

thrown much together, in the excursions and similar amusements which their quiet life afforded opportunity for. The tender and lasting impression which his young friend made on Landor is seen in the sad and gentle allusions to her in some of his poetry written many years after the time to which it refers. Thus one little poem which relates to his young companion of old days, and to two of her mother's latest descendants, entitled, "The Three Roses," begins:—

> "When the buds began to burst
> Long ago with Rose the first,
> I was walking, joyous then,
> Far above all other men,
> Till before us up there stood
> Britonferry's oaken wood,
> Whispering, 'happy as thou art,
> Happiness and thou must part,'" etc.

In another called "Abertawy" (the Celtic name for Swansea), he lovingly goes back to one of their rambles on the seashore, and tells, how to provide a seat for the weary maid and himself, he had to pluck up from a moss-grown bank some "tiniest thorniest" rose bushes.

> "At last I did it—eight or ten—
> We both were snugly seated then;
> But then she saw a half-round bead,
> And cried—'Good gracious! how you bleed!'
> Gently she wiped it off, and bound
> With timorous touch that dreadful wound.
>
> To lift it from its nurse's knee
> I feared, and quite as much feared she,
> For might it not increase the pain,
> And make the wound burst out again?
> She coaxed it to lie quiet there,
> With a low tune I bent to hear;
> How close I bent I quite forget,
> I only know I hear it yet."

It is curious to note that Landor's introduction to fame was indirectly or accidentally associated with Miss Aylmer. She happened to lend him a book from the Swansea circulating library, a poor romance by Clara Reeve. At the end of this he found the sketch of a so-called Arabian tale, which arrested his fancy and led to his constructing his first important work, "Gebir." This, we are told, was the delight of Southey and afterwards of Shelley. The former reviewed it, and wrote to a friend, "I would go a hundred miles to see the anonymous author"; to another he wrote, "There is a poem called 'Gebir,' written by God knows who, sold for a shilling; it has miraculous beauties." *

Lady Aylmer, the widow of Henry, the fourth baron, married secondly Mr. Howell Price. Possibly it was in consequence of this re-marriage that her daughter Rose went to Calcutta to her aunt, Lady Russell, wife of Sir Henry Russell, then one of the puisne judges, who was afterwards made Chief Justice, and eventually a baronet. He and Lord Aylmer had married sisters, the daughters of Sir Charles Whitworth, and sisters of the Earl of Whitworth. An expression in one of the "gravely tender" lines from the poem "Abertawy" already referred to, seems to indicate that Miss Aylmer's going to India was not her own choice :—

> "Where is she now? Called far away,
> By one she dared not disobey,
> To those proud halls, for youth unfit,
> Where Princes stand and Judges sit.
> Where Ganges rolls his widest wave
> She dropped her blossom in the grave;
> Her noble name she never changed
> Nor was her nobler heart estranged."

The *Calcutta Gazette* in the first week of March, 1800, thus records the sad event here referred to: "On Sunday last at the house of her uncle, Sir Henry Russell, in the bloom of youth and possession of every accomplishment that could gladden or embellish life, deplored by her relatives and regretted by a society of which she was the brightest ornament, the Honble. Miss Aylmer."

When the news of her death reached Landor, his thoughts, we are told, were "for days and nights entirely possessed" by it. "During his vigils," says Professor Colvin, "he wrote the first draft

* Landor's biographer allows that 'Gebir' is unknown to the present reading generation. The poem illustrates the manner in which the genius of Landor affected his contemporaries, not by influencing the many, but by exercising mastery over the few who ultimately rule the many.

Perhaps the only quotation ever heard from it now is from the sea nymph's description of the "sinuous shells of pearly hue," the concluding lines of which are :—

> "Shake one, and it awakens; then apply
> Its polish'd lips to your attentive ear,
> And it remembers its august abodes,
> And murmurs as the ocean murmurs there."

of the little elegy, 'carved as it were in ivory or in gems,' which in its later form became famous."

> 'Ah, what avails the sceptred race?
> Ah, what the form divine?
> What every virtue, every grace?
> Rose Aylmer, all were thine.
> Rose Aylmer, whom these wakeful eyes
> May weep, but never see,
> A night of memories and of sighs
> I consecrate to thee."

"Just, natural, simple, severely and at the same time hauntingly melodious," these, adds Professor Colvin, "are the lines which made afterwards so deep an impression upon Charles Lamb." "Many things I had to say to you, which there are not time for," wrote the latter to Landor. "*One*, why should I forget? 'Tis for Rose Aylmer, which has a charm I cannot explain. I lived upon it for weeks." "I have just seen Charles and Mary Lamb living in absolute solitude at Enfield. I found your poems lying open before Lamb. . . . He is ever muttering Rose Aylmer"—is the testimony of Crabbe Robinson.

It is noteworthy that the effect obtained by the iteration of the young girl's two beautiful names at the beginning of the fourth and fifth lines is an afterthought.

All who read the little elegy to-day will, I think, realize its indefinable charm, and agree with Mr. Forster that "its deep and tender pathos could hardly be surpassed; in delicacy and sweetness of expression it is perfect."

A more recent literary authority (Professor George Saintsbury) is thus moved by it:—"You may read Rose Aylmer for the hundredth time with the certain effect of that 'divine despair,' which inspires and is inspired by only the greatest poetry." And Mrs. Meynell has well said:—"Never was a human name more exquisitely sung than in these perfect stanzas."

There is an incident touching the close of Landor's life told by his biographer, which, as it is gratifying to read, I add here, though it has no immediate connection with the present subject.

He died in his eighty-ninth year in Florence, and his remains were laid in the English burying-ground there.

One of the last letters he received in Italy was from his old friend Lord Houghton (better known as Monckton Milnes); it introduced to him a young English poet, who had recorded that he came "the youngest to the oldest singer that England bore," prompted by the sole desire to see him and to bear to him the gratitude and thankfulness of many others of his countrymen who might never hope to see him. "It was but natural that this should give pleasure to the old man, in the sense of fame it brought so closely home to him." And when he passed away in that same year (1864), he who had visited him so lately—this Algernon Swinburne—paid worthy homage to his memory in a little poem, the concluding stanzas of which may perhaps be quoted in a page, the aim of which is to lead to the preservation in another city of a tomb so intimately associated with Landor's name, and around which so many interesting memories cluster:

"And thou, his Florence, to thy trust
Receive and keep,
Keep safe his dedicated dust
His sacred sleep.
So shall thy lovers, come from far,
Mix with thy name,
As morning-star with evening-star
His faultless fame."

## SUPPLEMENT.

Soon after the appearance of the above in the second edition of this book, I had the pleasure to learn that a kind and sympathetic hand had executed the repairs needed to arrest the destructive agencies which, as pointed out, were getting into vigorous operation on this tomb.

Should any resident or visitor of Calcutta feel disposed to go and see Rose Aylmer's grave it will be found at the edge of the central main walk (from the entrance gate), on the left-hand side, at the further corner of the second pathway leading eastward. The monument over it may easily escape notice, and is best looked for as being next beyond one with gilt lettering on its tablet, which, being conspicuous, is a land-mark with the undertaking fraternity, and is referred to by them as "The Juno Monument."

Strange to say, this grave also, like that of Rose Aylmer next it, has a claim on the interest and sympathy of all our people, and for a similar reason, viz., as that of one associated with a name illustrious in English literature, a poet greater than Landor—Lord Byron. The tomb is that of a young sailor, Captain William Mackay, who died in 1804, and the inscription over it recalls his "manly fortitude," which "his interesting narrative of the shipwreck of the *Juno* will testify to future times." Such indulgent forecasts by sorrowing friends are not often realized, but this one came nearer to being so than most, owing to the little narrative having fallen into the hands of Byron, with whom, as a schoolboy, it was favourite reading, and the deep impression which it made on him was shown when he came to write the shipwreck in Don Juan.

As I find myself gossiping after all about another Calcutta grave, it may be well before going further to give a particular or two of this shipwreck in the Indian seas, which was destined to become so notable.

The *Juno*, an old and badly-found ship of 450 tons, left Rangoon for Madras in the end of May, 1795. She was heavily laden with timber, and had a mixed crew of Lascars and Malays, with a few Europeans, including the captain and first and second mates (Wade and Mackay). The captain's wife and her ayah were also on board; there were seventy-two souls in all. The ship took the ground when leaving Rangoon and strained herself badly. She then, in a leaky condition, which from the start demanded constant pumping, encountered a succession of heavy gales. By June 20 the water in the hold had gained so much as to be nearly up to the lower deck. The main-mast was cut away that night, but part of it falling on board, the ship broached to suddenly, and the sea broke over her so that in two minutes she filled and settled down, scarcely giving time to her people to escape into the rigging.

Being timber-laden, she did not quite sink, but was submerged. Next morning they found that the whole of the upper deck was washed away. In this condition the wreck was driven for over 250 miles along the Pegu coast. Nearly every creature on board was clinging in the mizzen-rigging, a few in the fore-rigging, a sea-washed chasm yawning between them. They were utterly without food or shelter, and were alternately baked and drenched. Daily and hourly their number decreased as through death or exhaustion they dropped into the sea. Mackay gives a curious experience quite opposed to the belief almost universally held, viz. the relief afforded by drinking salt water. His thirst on the third day was so intolerable that to assuage it he drank about two quarts of sea water, preferring to die from that than from thirst. To his amazement it revived his strength and spirits and gave him a sound sleep. He continued this treatment and found the intestinal torment that it caused was easier to bear than burning thirst. Eventually the wreck drifted to land near a jungle on the coast of Arracan, and on July 13 some fourteen survivors were got on shore; of these nine finally reached Rammoo. The list of the survivors adds another instance to the many, of the battle not being always to the strong, for amongst those who lived through those twenty-three days and nights of such awful suffering were Mrs. Bremner, the captain's wife, her ayah, three old men, a lad, and Mackay. The first account of this wreck was sent to India by the magistrate of Chittagong and appeared in the Calcutta newspapers. Two years afterwards William Mackay wrote the detailed narrative of it in the form of a letter to his father, which was published. It was this publication which Byron read when he was at Dr. Glennie's school at Dulwich.

Several other names more or less eminent in English literature are also indirectly called up by reference to this narrative. Thus, Dr. Charles Mackay (the "people's poet," author of "Cheer Boys, Cheer," etc., etc., who died on Christmas Eve, 1889), tells in a book of literary recollections entitled, "Through the Long Day" (1887), how when breakfasting with Sam Rogers, the poet, his host in speaking of Byron remarked that Tom Moore had told him that the chief incidents following the shipwreck in Don Juan were taken from a little book called the "Wreck of the Juno." *That*, said Dr. Mackay, was written by my grand-uncle; he then lent the book to Rogers, who on returning it wrote that he now quite agreed with Moore's opinion, that the simple grandeur of the young sailor's prose was far superior to Byron's poetry. Byron, no doubt, had recourse to various accounts of shipwrecks when preparing himself to depict that in Don Juan, but certainly the most pitiful situation is taken from the "Wreck of the Juno."

As this long-forgotten narrative is now a very scarce book, I copy here, from page 20 of the original, the incident to which Lord Byron's memory was so indebted.

"Mr. Wade's boy, a stout and healthy lad died early and almost without a groan; while another of the same age, but of less promising appearance, held out much longer. The fate of these unfortunate boys differed also in another respect highly deserving of notice. Their fathers were both in the foretop when the boys were taken ill; the father of Mr. Wade's hearing of his son's illness answered with indifference 'that he could do nothing for him,' and left him to his fate. The other, when the account reached him, hurried down, and, watching for a favourable moment, crawled on all fours along the weather gunwale to his son who was in the mizzen-rigging. By that time only three or four planks of the quarter-deck remained just over the weather quarter gallery, and to this spot the unhappy man led his son, making him fast to the rail to prevent his being washed away. Whenever the boy was seized with a fit of retching, the father lifted him up and wiped away the foam from his lips, and if a shower came he made him open his mouth to receive the drops, or gently squeezed them into it from a rag. In this affecting situation both remained four or five days, till the boy expired. The unfortunate parent, as if unwilling to believe the fact, raised the body, gazed wistfully at it, and when he could no longer entertain any doubt, watched it in silence till it was carried off by the sea. Then, wrapping himself in a piece of canvas, sunk down and rose no more, though he must have lived two days longer, as we judged from the quivering of his limbs when a wave broke over him." If the reader will now turn to the second canto of Don Juan, and read the verses beginning—

> "There were two fathers in this ghastly crew,
> And with them their two sons," etc.

(v. 87 to 90), he will see with what fulness and closeness of detail Byron gives the above incident. A late most kindly and cheery writer, James Payn, whose pleasant and healthy novels help to beguile the tedium of many an Anglo-Indian bungalow, says "In Perils and Privation," when referring to the page in the narrative extracted above, "In all the annals of shipwreck I know no more pathetic picture than this." Here, then, is another grave appealing to us through the memories associated with it for its preservation. May it not appeal in vain.

## POSTSCRIPT.

The following extracts from an article on the wreck of the *Juno*, in a Scotch journal, published in August, 1897, and signed A. Polson, will, I hope, lend further interest in the preservation of this gallant sailor's tomb—

In the old churchyard at Lairg, in Sutherlandshire, there stands a square monument with the name of a Mackay on each of the four sides, and the inscription:—"Their bodies lie in the opposite quarters of the globe, but their monument is erected here where their memory is dearest, near the remains of their pious fathers, and amidst many loving friends, whose gratitude will attest that fraternal affection has not overcharged this record of their virtues." One side tells of Rev. John Mackay, a descendant of the many fighting Mackays of Scourie, on the West Coast. He, after being educated at Edinburgh and Utrecht, was settled in Lairg in 1714, and the "strong minister," or "John the Baptist," as he was nicknamed, had to gain the respect of the people by showing that he could fight as well as pray. On another side is the name of the "strong minister's" son, Thomas, who succeeded him, and many strange stories were told as to how they inspired terror to evil-doers and managed their congregations. Hugh Mackay, this second minister's son, had the old fighting taint so strong in him that he declined to study for the ministry, left the manse, and enlisted in the East India Company's service. There under Wellington he soon rose, and before the great battle of Assaye had charge of the commissariat department. At the battle, Wellington's army consisted of only 4500 men, to whom were opposed no less than 50,000. Mackay asked to be allowed to leave his post and join in the attack, but got a flat denial. Again he asked, but again was refused; but from such a fight as he loved he was not to be debarred, and as Colonel Welsh in his reminiscences says:—"By a noble act of disobedience Mackay joined his own corps; and, leading the charge of his own regiment in a line with the leading squadron of the noble veterans of the 19th Dragoons, Mackay rode up to the enemy's guns and fell, man and horse, at their very muzzles at the very moment of victory." On that field only one monument was raised, and it was to the memory of Captain Hugh Mackay.

The name on the fourth side of the monument is that of William Mackay, the narrative of whose sufferings in the ill-starred *Juno* first directed Lord Byron's attention to shipwrecks, and whose additional adventures on the African coast, where he did much for British soldiers, surely entitle him to be taken out of the long list of Scotland's forgotten heroes, and to have, as Ossian puts it, "his fame sung." In his early youth nothing delighted young Mackay more than boating on Loch Shin, and he early went to sea, so that at twenty-four years of age he became at Rangoon second mate of the *Juno*, a ship of 450 tons burden, very much out of repair and in all respects badly provided for sea, and which was at that time taking in a cargo of teak for Madras.

* * * * * * *

As soon as Mackay recovered from his illness he went to sea again as chief mate of the *Anna*, chartered by the East India Company for carrying rice to England, and in August, 1796, with his vessel converted into a troopship, he proceeded against the French and Spanish West Indian Islands. When this unpleasant work was finished he again went to India, and in 1801 took charge of the brig *Perseverance*, which had been fitted out by a spirited individual at Calcutta on his own account. On opening his sealed orders in the Bay of Bengal he found he had to go to Mocha on the Red Sea to furnish supplies for General Baird's army, which was to co-operate with Sir Ralph Abercromby in Egypt. Not far from Cape Guardafui he saved a detachment of the 80th Regiment when their transport, the *Fidelissimo*, got on the rocks, and themselves were perishing with thirst on the Abyssinian shore. At Mocha he found that Baird's army had proceeded to Egypt, and he followed it to Suez. He says:—"On

MONUMENT OVER GRAVE OF CAPTAIN WILLIAM MACKAY IN CALCUTTA.

*See p.* 377.

the 18th December I arrived at Suez—exactly nine months from the day I left the pilot. It is mortifying to have been so unfortunate in making my first voyage as a commander; but it is some consolation to think that I have conducted the vessel in safety, and without the loss of a man, though a very difficult navigation in a season of the year in which the voyage was never attempted before; and the loss of fourteen ships of the expedition in different parts of the Red Sea affords me additional reason of thankfulness to Providence for His guidance and protection, without which no skill or exertion of mine would have been sufficient." Having reason to doubt the fidelity of the person who was intrusted with the cargo across the desert he accompanied it himself in three trips to Cairo, and in the last was attacked by Bedouin Arabs. He returned to Calcutta in 1802, and after another short voyage he quitted the sea and died at Calcutta in 1804, when only thirty-three years of age, after having hardships crowded into his life which make it astonishing that he should have lived so long. In his simple short story he has suggested means of palliating distress, of averting danger, and showed patience under calamities the most intolerable, and hope and courage in situations which to us seem the most desperate.

The full inscription on this Tomb in Calcutta is as follows:—

Sacred
To the Memory of
CAPTAIN WILLIAM MACKAY
Who died 27th March, 1804,
Aged 32 years.

---

This marble would express
The affection of Relations
And Esteem of Friends
For him whose Characteristics
Were unaffected worth and Manly Fortitude.
In how eminent a Degree
He possessed the latter Quality
His interesting Narrative of
The Ship-wreck of the *Juno*
Will testify to future Times.

# APPENDICES

## I

## THE HAMILTON TRADITION

A STORY in connection with this embassy has been handed down, and so often repeated that it would probably be impossible to shake general belief in it now—at all events in Calcutta where it is very dear.

It is worth while, however, to consider whether some facts, which are indisputable, are consistent with this story, or whether much of it is only tradition, vague and unsubstantiated.

The Envoys to Delhi were accompanied by Mr. Wm. Hamilton in the capacity of surgeon. He opportunely cured the Emperor Farukhsyar of a disease, as to the nature of which unofficial writers are not quite agreed. It is alleged that on being asked by his grateful patient what reward he desired, the surgeon unselfishly and patriotically asked that the Bengal petition should be granted. His request was acceded to, and the Royal command was given for the necessary Firman. The Envoys regularly transmitted to the Bengal Government a minute account of their proceedings at the Mogul Court; a copy of these curious records may be seen amongst the Orme MSS., and, in less detail, in Mr. Talboys Wheeler's "Early Records of British India." The main facts gathered therefrom would seem to be these—

The Embassy arrived in Delhi in July, 1715. In the October following, the Emperor, who was about to be married, was surgically treated by Mr. Hamilton for a glandular swelling in the groin, and was publicly announced as cured on November 23. Referring to this in their report, the Envoys tell their Government that, on November 30, "As a reward for Mr. Hamilton's care and success, the King was pleased to give him in public" certain (enumerated) presents. "We have esteemed this as a particular happiness, and hope it will prove ominous to the success of our affairs." Further presents were given afterwards to the surgeon as well as to the Envoys. On December 7 the Emperor was married. For some months after this the Bengal petition did not even reach the King through the formal channels. At length, in March, 1716, the chief go-between, when implored as to its fate, asked, with true Oriental stolidity,

"What petition? Have I not done all your business?" Still later the Envoys write this, "We were in hopes that we should have got those petitions granted us by means of Khan Douran, and that afterwards the Vizier would not gainsay it, as at least by a little bribery it might have passed." Again, "We shall be obliged to make a new address to the Vizier, which will not only protract the negotiation, but must lay us open to a denial, and at the best be very expensive." All this does not say much for the substantial or thoughtful gratitude of the monarch; nor is there any reference whatever to the alleged request of Hamilton, or to any promise of Farukhsyar. These delays went on till June, 1717 (*i.e.* to two years), by which time Hamilton had not seen his august patient for a twelvemonth. The probability is that the Viceroy in Bengal was frustrating the Embassy's object by bribing the Court Officials a little higher than the Envoys could. Suddenly, however, the Embassy's requests were granted in full, but only apparently because the news had reached Delhi that the English at Surat had withdrawn to Bombay to escape the oppression of the Nawab at Surat, and the Emperor was alarmed lest the English should again make war on the Mogul trading and pilgrim vessels on the western coast. The concessions were seemingly wrung by fear, not given in gratitude. When the Envoys were publicly taking leave of the Mogul Court, a very unexpected and determined effort was made by the Emperor to detain Mr. Hamilton as a gilded prisoner, lest his professional services should be again needed. This was only obviated by the strongest remonstrance and intercession, and by the Embassy's "writing a very pathetic address to His Majesty." The story in its popularly accepted form is told by Colonel Tod in his history of Western Rajputana, published in 1829. He, however, qualifies his narrative with the words, "If history has correctly preserved the transaction." There is a good deal of virtue in this "if." As in his version he says that the Embassy came from Surat, he probably mixed up Hamilton with Dr. Boughton, of whom a similar story (also unsupported, according to Sir H. Yule) is told as occurring about 1644. Tod traces the story of Hamilton's magnanimity and the King's gratitude, to Scott's history of the successors of Aurungzebe (1786). The author was Captain Jonathan Scott, Persian Secretary to Warren Hastings, to whom he dedicated this translation. In a footnote he gives a very sensational account of the circumstances attending the "operation" performed by the surgeon. He adds, "Mr. Hamilton, soon after his return to Bengal, died of a putrid fever, and the Emperor, not satisfied with the account of the event, sent an officer of rank to Calcutta to examine the truth from the natives, whose solemn testimony and that of the Europeans were taken to Delhi. I had this anecdote from Mr. Hastings, who tells me that at his first arrival in India there were living witnesses of the circumstances of it; and Mr. Hamilton's monument was to be seen in the burial-ground of Calcutta upon which the account of them was engraved." It may be added with reference to this, that both the English and the Persian inscriptions, still to be seen on Hamilton's tombstone, are silent as to any Imperial concessions being made as a reward to him. It may also be remarked that Warren Hastings did not arrive in India until thirty-three years after Hamilton's death. Could the circumstance, animadverted on in the following extract from a letter of the Court of Directors (February, 1756), have helped to obscure the evidence touching the Emperor's alleged reward to Hamilton? viz. "An original letter from the chief, and others at Patna, *and a leaf torn out of the original diary of Mr. Surman's Embassy to the great Mogul* were picked up in a public necessary house which the writers make use of, and are now in our hands, where (? *sic*) we are informed many fragments of papers of great importance have likewise been seen. (Selections from Records of Government, p. 71.) No wonder if writers on early Indian history have difficulty occasionally in getting at the facts.*

* "The most earnest oral tradition will in a little while lose its distinctness, undergo essential though insensible modifications. Apart from all desire to vitiate the committed word, yet little by little the subjective condition of those to whom it is entrusted will infallibly make itself felt: in such treacherous keeping is all which remains merely in the memories of men," etc.—Archbishop Trench (Hulsean Lectures).

# II

## INSCRIPTIONS ON THE NEW HOLWELL MONUMENT

### Written by Lord Curzon

These lists not only show more fully the names of those who actually perished in the Black Hole, as given by Holwell, but largely supplement them. They also most deservedly include and commemorate the names of several other Europeans who died during the siege.

The inscriptions as now seen were all written by Lord Curzon himself.

I.

This monument
Has been erected by
Lord Curzon, Viceroy and Governor-General of India,
In the year 1902
Upon the site
And in reproduction of the design
Of the original monument
To the memory of the 123 persons
Who perished in the Black Hole Prison
Of old Fort William
On the night of the 20th of June, 1756.
The former memorial was raised by
Their surviving fellow-sufferer
J. Z. Holwell, Governor of Fort William,
On the spot where the bodies of the dead
Had been thrown into the ditch of the ravelin.
It was removed in 1821.

II.

To the Memory of
Edward Eyre, William Baillie,
Revd. Jervas Bellamy, John Jenks,
Roger Reveley, John Carse, John Law,
Thomas Coles, James Valicourt,
John Jebb, Richard Toriano,
Edward Page, Stephen Page,
William Grub, John Street,
Aylmer Harrod, Patrick Johnstone,
George Ballard, Nathan Drake,
William Knapton, Francis Gosling,
Robert Byng, John Dodd,
Stair Dalrymple, David Clayton,
John Buchanan, and Lawrence Witherington,
Who perished in the Black Hole prison.

III.

The names inscribed on the tablet
On the reverse side to this
Are the names of those persons
Who are known to have been killed
Or to have died of their wounds
During the Siege of Calcutta
In June, 1756,
And who either did not survive
To enter the Black Hole prison
Or afterwards succumbed to its effects.

IV.

The names of those who perished
In the Black Hole prison,
Inscribed upon the reverse side
Of this monument,
Are in excess of the list
Recorded by Governor Holwell
Upon the original monument.
The additional names, and
The Christian names of the remainder,
Have been recovered from oblivion
By reference to contemporary documents.

V.

To the memory of
Peter Smith, Thomas Blagg,
John Francis Pickard, John Pickering,
Michael Collings, Thomas Best,
Ralph Thoresby, Charles Smith,
Robert Wilkinson, Henry Stopford,
William Stopford, Thomas Purnell,
Robert Talbot, William Tidecomb,
Daniel Macpherson, John Johnson, and
Messrs. Whitby, Surman, Bruce,
Montrong, and Janniko, who perished
During the Siege of Calcutta.

VI.

To the Memory of
Richard Bishop, Francis Hayes,
Colin Simson, John Bellamy,
William Scott, Henry Hastings,
Charles Wedderburn, William Dumbleton,
Bernard Abraham, William Cartwright,

Jacob Bleau, Henry Hunt,
Michael Osborne, Peter Carey,
Thomas Leach, Francis Stevenson,
James Guy, James Porter,
William Parker, Eleanor Weston, and
Messrs. Cocker, Bendall, Atkinson, Jennings.
Reid, Barnet, Frere, Wilson,
Burton, Lyon, Hillier, Tilley, and Alsop,
Who perished in the Black Hole prison.

Several surgeons seem to have been amongst those who obeyed the call of duty to the last. Captain Mills supplied Orme with the information that "At the time the fort was taken there was escaped" (*i.e.* presumably in the confusion at the moment of the enemy's entrance) two Doctors Noxes (*sic*), and Doctors Gray, Taylor, English, and Lewis. Orme gives the names as Knox and Inglis. Dr. Fullerton also escaped at the same opportunity, to become later the sole survivor of the Patna massacre. He behaved at that dreadful time (and on many other occasions) with high courage and nobility. It so happens that medical officers have played a conspicuous part in many of the great tragedies in British Indian history. From the days of Holwell and Fullerton down to our own ; down to Dr. Brydon of Afghan fame, the solitary European remnant of a slaughtered army, staggering into Jelalabad from Jagdallak, and whom the writer can well remember chatting with in Sir Colin Campbell's camp in 1857, soon after this man, with a charmed life, came out with the survivors of the famous garrison of the Lucknow Residency, where also he was fated to bear his part, getting a bullet through the body early in the siege.*

* Brydon was twice wounded during his escape from Cabul—a sword cut on the head the first day, and another on the wrist just before reaching Jelalabad. He owed his life to the nobility of a poor commissariat follower, who, when mortally wounded after struggling through the blocked pass, insisted on Brydon taking his pony. This officer wrote from Jelalabad, in 1842, these lines (quoted by Peel in the House of Commons) : "My life has been saved in a most wonderful manner, and I am the only European who has escaped from the Cabul army. Two natives only have reached this place, making, with myself, three persons out of an army of 13,000." Dr. Brydon died in England in, I think, 1873.

## III

# NOTE ON THE SITE OF THE BLACK HOLE

I NEVER had the good fortune to make the personal acquaintance of the late Mr. C. R. Wilson. We had corresponded, and he had been good enough to send me from time to time his contributions to the Asiatic Society and to the public Press, regarding the excavations in old Fort William and its precincts, in connection with which he had so industrious and conspicuous a part. I had long looked forward with great interest to discussing these matters with him, but the opportunity, to my great regret, never came, and his too early death was the final frustration of my hope.

The duty which Mr. Wilson imposed on himself was to verify and interpret very extensive excavations made in 1891–92, by the light of a plan of the first Fort William, made in 1753, by a professional expert, Lieutenant Wells, who had been recommended by Colonel Scott, Chief Engineer. The plan, showing the fort in outline and in considerable detail (scale 100 feet to the inch), had come to light since the date (1883) of the previous underground investigation of a portion of the old fortress by Mr. R. Bayne, a professional engineer in the employ of the East India Railway. Fortunately, at the later date (1891–92), the investigator was able to devote much time and intelligence, aided by enthusiasm, to his undertaking. The plan he pronounced as "showing every mark of care and accuracy, and agreeing fairly well with what Mr. Bayne discovered in 1883." Still Mr. Wilson had not worked very far at his task before he saw reason to be somewhat disappointed with his guide, which he considered faulty, or, at least, unsatisfactory in places; the fault, apparently, being determined from an inability to reconcile the gradually unfolded underground facts with the details outlined in the plan.*

* It is not clear to me whether some of his difficulty in reconciling the gradually uncovered facts with the plan, may not have arisen from structural alterations and additions, or demolitions, between January, 1757 (recovery of Calcutta) and the period when "the new works are in some forwardness," as Captain Brohier writes in August, 1757, when urging the "keeping of the present fort in repair." We find Clive from Muxadavad bustling the Council "to commence the fortifications." In January, 1758, they report "our works are now carried on with great vigour and despatch, many thousand people being at work." In the

Before going further, it may be well to note what exceptional difficulties Mr. Wilson found confronting him when he came to try and interpret by his plan what he found underground in the south-eastern limits of the buried fort. He writes, "I have now to call attention to another serious inaccuracy in Wells's plan." This appears to be a mistake of twelve (12) feet in the length of the curtain wall between the main (E.) gate and S.E. bastion, *i.e.* the difference between 150 feet and the 162 feet, which Wells should, it seems, have shown, "and so vitiates its whole representation of this corner of the fort." This rather considerable error Mr. Wilson accounts for as follows: "Whoever drew the plan, he did not discover the mistake till he came to put in the details of the rooms along the E. curtain, south of the gate, then, finding that there was not sufficient room to put those details in properly, he crowded them together." "This, I think, is clearly the case with the cross walls." "Evidently this side of the fort was subject to a good deal of alteration, and for this reason, or it may be from a desire to make the fort appear more symmetrical than it really was, Wells's plan comes far short of its usual accuracy." It will be readily allowed how handicapped the investigator must have been, who had to fix on the site of a room in this actual locality by the aid of a guide which he saw such reason to discredit. How desirable it became to get all the collateral support, if any, for the conclusion arrived at. It speaks well for Mr. Wilson's perseverance and the overcoming of discrepancies generally, when he is able to write, "but my doubts have all yielded to patient excavation."

It is by no means my object, in this note on the site of the Black Hole, to take exception to or to challenge Mr. Wilson's conclusions regarding it. I give all consideration to the fortunate and favourable nature of his opportunities, and the care and unwearied diligence with which he availed himself of them, and to my own want of technical knowledge.

following month, the Board of Works complaining of the difficulty of getting "artificers and labourers," orders were issued "that no artificers shall be employed by private persons after February 1." The reason for all this feverish activity was the expected presence of the French in the river. It is only fair, however, to assume that Mr. Wilson had the probable results of all this labour, going on for months, in view. In a footnote he doubts that anything came of it, save the digging of a huge ditch (Clive reported this "finished" early in 1757; 30 feet wide and 12 feet deep, it went all round the fort, presumably that which was filled up in 1766), and the converting of the old factory into barracks for the military, "till proper barracks are built within the new works." Whether his surmise was correct or not, it is useless to speculate now, in the absence of any trustworthy records or details on the subject that I know of. However, I have no means, or occasion, to deal with the general subject, so I confine my attention to Mr. Wilson's excavations at the south-eastern end of the old fort, and to his conclusions regarding the historical site there of most interest to modern readers.

It must not be forgotten that the greater part of the large Volume II. of Mr. Wilson's "Old Fort William" did not receive the inestimable advantage of his own revision. His account of the excavations and his topographical deductions, etc., appear at the end of this volume, just as he had written them in a long and admirable contribution to the Asiatic Society's journal some years before. His meritorious labours, as detailed in the volumes referred to, have recently been included in the Indian Record Series—Old Fort William, under the ægis, and endorsement of the Government of India. Therefore it seems to me desirable to take this the first suitable opportunity that has offered since the publication of this Government record, to notice a misapprehension into which the author has fallen—no doubt unconsciously, from incompleteness of information, or possibly forgetfulness—viz. when briefly summing up the difference between his own views and those of Mr. Bayne, regarding the site of the Black Hole, Mr. Wilson writes (vol. ii. p. 246): "Fortunately for Mr. Bayne the errors of his two premises contradicted each other, and thus when he made an excavation in the passage, north of the General Post Office, where he expected to find the Black Hole, he actually did come across one of its walls. But, like words, walls cannot be interpreted apart from their context." This statement errs on the side of insufficiency, as Mr. Bayne, on the occasion referred to, came across a good deal more than a wall, which Mr. Wilson concedes was one of those belonging to the prison cell. I do not think Mr. Bayne could ever have seen Mr. Wilson's Asiatic Society's contribution (1893), or he would probably have remarked on it, possibly demurred to it, and so rendered this note superfluous. I venture to do so now (for I am quite ignorant of Mr. Bayne's fate) in fairness to a gentleman whose accuracy and care in dealing with excavations, not in the old fort only, I can well testify to. Before alluding further to the excavation in question, I hope I may be forgiven for recalling a personal detail or two. I was on a long absence in England when Mr. Bayne began his building work in the precincts of the old fort, and I never made his acquaintance until immediately after he had read his valuable paper to the Asiatic Society early in 1883. During that year I had many opportunities of discussing topographical matters and details with him relating chiefly to the fort and its neighbourhood. He was full of information as to demolitions in Calcutta generally. His modesty and earnestness as an explorer, which were very noticeable in his manner, appear, I think, in his contribution about the fort. Most of his work of that kind was done in the little time snatched from his very onerous professional duties. I lost sight of him, I think, in the following year. In his *conjectural* plan of the south-east corner of the fort—a plan sketched long before he had had any opportunity of testing its accuracy by excavation—he was wrong as to the shape of the cell, which he made a square, for reasons which his paper show; and in assuming that the stairs to the bastion would be in the corresponding position to that in which he found it in the case of the north-east bastion, which was built *later* than the south-east one, *i.e.* he conjectured that the bastion was led up to from the south, and that the stairs would be against the south curtain. If Wells's plan be right, symmetry was not followed, as he shows the stairs against the east curtain. Mr. Bayne may have been in error in other conjectures also, but I am unable to form an opinion about this. But to come to the excavations that we are now concerned with. When the time was ripe for it (October, 1883) Mr. Bayne sought official permission to open up the ground in the immediate neighbourhood of the General Post Office, where his measuring and plotting signified to him the buried cell ought to be. The necessary sanction being obtained, he told me one evening that early next morning he would break ground in the place indicated, and asked me to meet him there. I drove down from the United Service Club, where I was then living, between 9 and 10 a.m., and found my friend standing on the edge of a wide excavation, and he explained to me the remains and structures showing in it, so far as his local knowledge, experience, and reasoning led him to interpret them. As Mr. Bayne was under orders to go up country on railway duty, and as the excavation could not remain open long without inconvenience to traffic, and was very likely to arouse much interest and questioning, it was arranged that I should write a brief explanatory account of it to the *Englishman* for general information. This I took an early opportunity of doing. An extract from that letter will perhaps best convey what the structures were which Mr. Bayne brought to light, and which were not limited to *one* wall. Let me premise that the excavation looked more like a trench than anything else, owing to the curtain wall being the only one exposed to any depth, the other structures, west of it, being only exposed sufficiently to show their surfaces, and also owing to the length from north to south being greater (more than the roughly guessed eighteen or twenty feet of some of the chroniclers) than was generally held. In fact, when looked down on, the chamber seemed more an oblong than a square.* The letter explains,

* It is worth noting perhaps that the visitor (Asiaticus) who, I say in the text, visited the actual Black Hole in 1812, makes a similar remark that the chamber was "long and narrow," and dark, of course. This suggests to me here a consideration which often occurred to me, viz. that in any of the gossipy letters and accounts from and of Calcutta, written, say, twenty to twenty-five years after the recovery, there is little or nothing said about the tragedy of 1756. Mackrabie, for instance, never recalls it, though he writes of the old Fort chapel and the Custom House there. Grandpré, writing of his visit to Calcutta thirty-four years after "the troubles," gives such an inaccurate account, that one must conclude that he is retailing what he picked up as the current belief in the Calcutta of his time, viz. "The conqueror, when he got possession of the fort at Calcutta, had the prisoners which he took there thrust one upon another into a hole outside the fort, from which those only were fortunate enough to come out alive who happened to be uppermost in the heap; the rest were suffocated. In remembrance of so flagrant an act of barbarity the English, who were conquerors in their turn, erected a monument between the old fort and the right wing of the building occupied by the civil officers of the company, on the very spot where the deed

that the first thing to be seen is a portion of a plastered wall not quite three feet eight inches thick (this plaster, by-the-by, which was smooth and white, was quickly made away with by relic hunters). "This (No. 1) is part of the eastern outside wall or curtain, it was originally eighteen feet high. About (exactness is not aimed at now) fourteen feet and a half further from the spectator (west) is another wall (No. 2) nearly level with the ground, and beyond that again, *i.e.* about twelve feet further west another similar wall (No. 4), and with it a portion of a round pillar, which was one of a row that with wall (No. 4) carried the low sloping roof of a verandah. Standing with his back to the east he will see on his right hand a low cutcha-looking wall (No. 3). The soil has been hollowed out to the right of it at the end nearest to him to show its thickness, viz. only about eighteen inches. It is carried back from wall No. 1 to wall No. 2, both of which it met. Thus three sides of a chamber are seen, that to the east is wall No. 1, that to the west is wall No. 2, that to the north is wall No. 3 (this wall, it was contended by Mr. Bayne, carried the door). The fourth (southern) side is not disclosed, being under a portion of the northern end of the Post Office building." This could only be a conjecture. I added there were two concrete floors uncovered; the lower one seemed to have been liable to inundation, as Mr. Bayne's previous experience at the northern laying bare of old fort floors led him to consider that what was found on it was river silt—a circumstance which perhaps led to its having been raised at some time by several inches. The above account, or the material substance of it, appeared afterwards in the Second Edition of my book, but not in the Third Edition, so it may have escaped Mr. Wilson. It was also given in a memorandum on the subject written for the information of Lord Dufferin at his request. This I find has been reprinted with several other demi-official papers in vol. ii. of Mr. Wilson's book (by, I presume, the hand that finally revised it), and may also well have never come under his notice. It will be seen from the above description of Mr. Bayne's "excavation in the passage north of the General Post Office" that there was more found in it than Mr. Wilson would seem to have realized. The parallel walls inside the curtain thus brought into view were running north and south, were thick and solid, and, with the uncovered floor, presented features familiar to the excavator's eye.

Mr. Wilson gives the area of the cell as eighteen feet by fourteen feet ten inches, and says: "South of the Black Hole there were no more rooms, the remaining space being taken up by a straight staircase fifty feet long, built against the east curtain wall leading to the S.E. bastion."

was committed." Asiaticus seems to have been moved to see and enter the cell merely because the fort was doomed in 1812 to the demolition which did not come to it for some time later. Did the interest or sentiment (call it what we may) about the Black Hole remain dormant for many years? The Indian Record Series, etc., did not come before they were wanted to guard against the forgetting or perverting history.

He thus makes the stairs almost the strongest point in favour of the site contended for.

Before dealing with this very important point, let us consider whether Mr. Bayne's opinion receives any little extraneous support from descriptive expressions historically used regarding this prison cell.

By any one fairly familiar with the accounts of those who at the time wrote about the Calcutta siege and tragedy, and the general "troubles," it will be, I think, allowed that Holwell, as a writer of English, was head and shoulders over any of them. His keen trenchant criticism, and his vigorous straightforward narratives were not to their taste, and they did their best to disparage him by spiteful recrimination, as they sickened and scribbled and wrangled at Fulta. Nevertheless, as Holwell has come down to us, in the capacity of a descriptive writer, he is second only to his great contemporary Orme, the historian; he is as full and lucid in his explanations, and as accurate in his details; he is also comparatively free from Orme's blemish, tediousness. Being a good scholar and a clear-headed man, he is careful and discriminating in the choice of his words, he does not use them at haphazard. When on his voyage home, in restored health and at his leisure, he thus describes the Black Hole prison: ". . . One hundred and forty-six wretches thus crammed together in a cube of about eighteen feet, shut up to the eastward and southward by dead walls and by a wall and door to the north, open only to the westward by two windows strongly barred with iron." Here he clearly means to differentiate between a wall and a *dead* wall. How far south the latter was we cannot tell—possibly it was a portion of the bastion. If this writer meant to describe a chamber, such as is shown in Wells's plan and marked by Mr. Wilson as No. 16 (see Wells's plan attached), would he not have said it was between two *walls* (partition or cross-walls), and backed by a *dead* wall—the eastern curtain? Again, Holwell, in describing the torrent-like rush by which they were thrust into the prison cell, adds: "Few amongst us—the soldiers excepted—having the least idea of the dimensions or nature of a place they had never seen." Any surviving soldier who had ever had the misfortune of being confined in it, or presumably any of the military officers, would have known the limited dimensions, and that the chamber was a cul-de-sac with no opening at the further (southern) end; but why should those ordinarily frequenting the fort have been altogether ignorant of the nature of a room which was quite open to observation from the south, round, or by, which was a free passage (Mr. Wilson says there was a space of eight feet between the south cross wall and the stairs) from the west verandah to the east curtain, and which no one could help seeing who had occasion to go up on the south-east bastion by the staircase shown? (see again Wells's plan). The chamber would have been less familiar if it had terminated in, or abutted on, a *dead* wall.

Lastly, to come to the stairs, Mr. Wilson mentions it thus: "As regards the staircase to the south-east bastion, I have, unfortunately, very little to say. This staircase is mentioned by Holwell, and is shown by Wells in his plan. It is a long staircase. Its head (*sic*) is put by

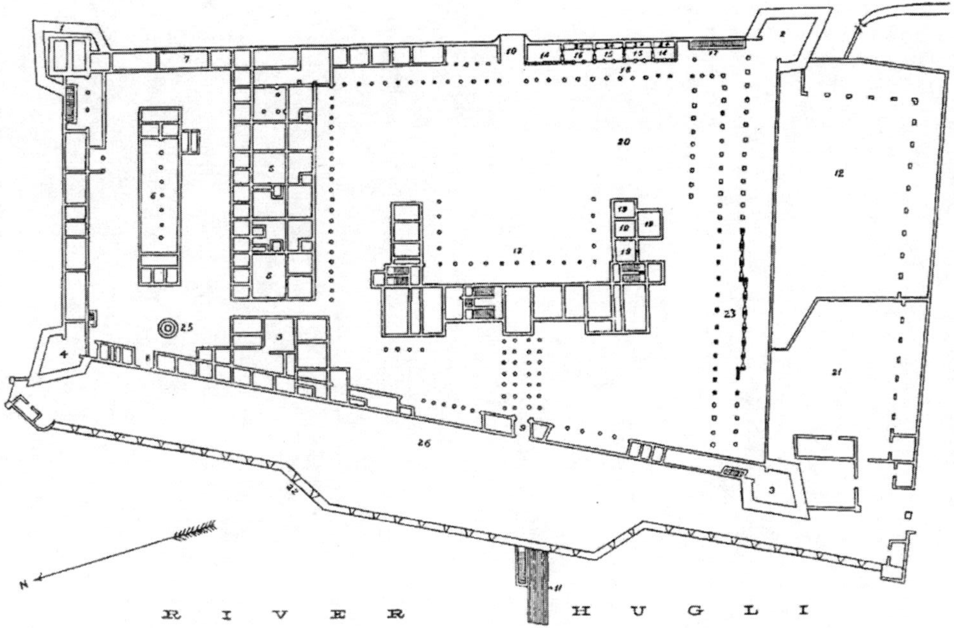


**REFERENCES.**

1 N.E. Bastion
2 S.E. Bastion
3 S.W. Bastion
4 N.W. Bastion
5 Writers' Buildings
6 Armoury
7 Laboratory
8 North River Gate
9 South River Gate
10 East Gate
11 Landing Stage Stairs and Crane
12 Export and Import Warehouses
13 Governor's House
14 Court of Guard
15 Barracks
16 Black Hole
17 Stairs to S.E. Bastion
18 Verandah
19 Governor's Apartments
20 Parade
21 Carpenter's Yard
22 River Wall
23 Arcades still standing
24 Wooden Platform
25 Flagstaff
26 Wharf

FORT WILLIAM, 1756.

LIEUT. WELLS' PLAN OF OLD FORT WILLIAM IN 1753 (SIC) (REDUCED).

See p. 390.

Wells at about eight feet from the south face of the southernmost cross-wall, and its foot at a distance of about fifty feet. I have not been able to find any trace of it by excavation, but I see no reason for doubting its position to be correctly marked by Wells."

Is it quite safe to assume that what was there in 1753 was still in the same place and state in 1756? The stairs, we are told, took up fifty feet of (sorely-needed) room, and the years between 1753 and June, 1756, were years of active setting the house in order, active, at least, for the slow-going, expense-fearing, conscript fathers of Calcutta,* who, if averse from military improvements, were surely able to see the business advantage of making more space, especially if this could be done economically. Here, for instance, is an entry (February, 1754), bearing on the suggestion just made: "The import warehouse-keeper acquainting the Board that there are places in the Factory which might be easily converted into go-downs, proper for keeping the Company's broad cloth, he desires the Board will please direct it to be done, that the Company may not only be saved the expense of renting go-downs, but be at a greater security by keeping their woolen (*sic*) goods in their own Factory. Ordered the Buxey do set about it immediately."

It may well have occurred to those economical factors to gain some room by shortening or shifting or altering the south-east stairs: there is, however, no evidence of this. That *some* change was effected there is suggested by the fact of Holwell writing of *two* south-east bastions co-existing, *i.e.* the old and the *New*. What this latter was or to what date "new" refers (presumably later than the date of Wells's plan?) I have never seen an explanation that satisfied me. "This (Wells's) staircase is mentioned by Holwell," writes Mr. Wilson. Holwell, it is true, mentions *a* stairs; but the words in which he introduces this detail do not quite support the idea that it was that shown by Wells, viz. The prisoners were sitting down quietly in the piazza or verandah west of the barracks and of the Black Hole Prison, which were thus at their backs. "Besides the guard over us another was placed at the foot of the stairs at the south end of this verandah leading up to the south-east bastion to prevent any of us escaping that way." This accurate writer does not say that the stairs was lying alongside the east curtain behind, (the distance from which to the wall which carried the second line of arches (*i.e.* western) is given by Mr. Wilson as "31 feet 3 inches from inside to inside" (vol. ii. p. 240)), but Holwell does say the stairs was at the south end of *this verandah*, *i.e.* that in which they were then sitting. It would be easy to err in attaching undue weight to these suggested verbal niceties or distinctions in Holwell's narrative, when considering a question dependent of necessity for its solution on the material evidence of ascertained structure.

* Spies, we are told, were carefully excluded from Calcutta early in 1756 and before, lest they should report to the native powers what defensive preparations were in hand.

In any case, what has been here put forward in treating of an old-time discussion must be regarded now as possessing but little general interest.

Not having had the indispensable advantage of seeing, and, with assistance, following the relation of, the carefully conducted excavations of 1891–92, I do not presume to be in a position to offer any opinion regarding the results gathered from them, much less to say that the investigator's conclusions are not fully justified. The difference between Mr. Bayne's conjectural, or contended for, site, and that fixed on by Mr. Wilson is but a few feet at the most.

As already seen, befitting honour was given to this historic site by order of, and under active intervention of, a Governor-General, whose manifested deep respect for the past, its relics and its deserving dead, India has good reason never to forget.

# IV

## HASTINGS AND IMPEY IN RELATION TO THE TRIAL OF NUNCOMAR

IN two former editions (first and third) of these collected sketches, it was thought best to keep clear of the controversial topics in which the trial of Nuncomar has proved so fruitful. Their introduction would have interrupted the narrative and would have been unnecessary, and indeed unsuited, for the simple object which I had before me, when recalling and re-telling for modern Calcutta some of the most noted episodes of its early days.

A writer in an Indian periodical, who did me the honour of noticing my small volume, took me to task, in a friendly way, for this omission, and urged that it was a duty, not to be put aside, of any one who raked up the embers of this old trial, to express an opinion for the general reader, as to how far the obloquy attaching to the memories of Hastings and Impey in connection with the name of Nuncomar was merited.

One difficulty in fulfilling this suggested duty, arises from the necessity of first arriving at the opinion—of making up one's mind in short, whether to adopt the popularly accepted belief as to the unscrupulous iniquity of Hastings, and the judicial turpitude of Impey, or to resignedly take a place amongst the unbelieving "idiots and biographers" scoffed at by Macaulay.

It is very evident that there is room for a wide diversity of opinion on the subject, when we see that the two authors who have most recently taken it up, and treated it with a breadth and closeness of scrutiny, and an amplitude of detail never before attempted, have each come to conclusions diametrically opposed to those of the other.

It would be presumptuous, as well as superfluous, on my part to offer any opinion as to the way in which the author of "Nuncomar and Impey" * has acquitted himself of the task that he took upon him. It may be allowable, however, to say this much, that the work of Sir James Stephen gives evidence that he entered on the minute inquiry which it necessitated, in a liberal spirit, and conducted it with conspicuous impartiality, and with a desire to find out and to tell the whole truth.

* "The Story of Nuncomar and the Impeachment of Sir Elijah Impey," by the late Sir James Fitzjames Stephen, K.C.S.I.

A very inadequate idea would be formed of the scope of "The Trial of Nunda Kumar"* from its title, for its author has enriched its elaborate detail with an amount of historical information (some bearing on, some collateral to the main subject), which shows surprising research, and a successful diligence in tracing out the antecedents and surroundings of many of the actors in the drama, quite extraordinary. In addition to the qualification of a mind trained to habits of patient investigation, Mr. Beveridge has also brought to bear on a labour, which he has thrown himself into with great earnestness, an acquaintance with Bengal, its languages and its people, derived from many years' residence amongst them, and a long experience of practical judicial work.

I have been under obligation to both these works in compiling the trial narrative. They must be studied attentively by any one desiring to know the full details of an event closely connected with the first workings of the Regulating Act, and Supreme Court Charter of 1773, which mark the creation of *British* India.

As this book may, perhaps, meet with readers who have not had access to, or leisure for, the exhaustive works just referred to, it may be permissible for me, in the interest of such, to say what was the impression, when I laid these books down, left on my mind as to the reasonableness of the conclusions to which each examiner of the facts invited his readers.

Mr. Beveridge has avowedly written chiefly for lawyers and students of history: by these he wishes to be judged.

As a layman, writing in a discursive unmethodical way, for only lay readers, I must for obvious reasons avoid the technical matters in controversy, and confine my remarks to the few main points which are of general interest.

And first, as to the question which has still the most import and interest for us. Had Nuncomar a fair trial? Mr. Beveridge falls far short of adopting the extravagant language in which the charge under this head was set forth in the motion for impeachment, where it is alleged that throughout the trial Impey manifested an ardent wish and determined purpose to effect the prisoner's ruin and death, and with this in view summed up the evidence "with gross and scandalous partiality." But he goes a good way in the same direction when he says that the trial was unfairly conducted, that the *desire* of the judges was to break down Nuncomar's witnesses, that in particular the Chief Justice's manner was bad throughout, and that the summing-up was unfavourable. Sir James Stephen's answer to this article of the Parliamentary charge is, that the trial was scrupulously fair, and that the summing-up was perfectly impartial and gave every possible advantage to the prisoner; that Impey's conduct in the trial was not only just, but favourable and indulgent to Nuncomar. He thinks there was ample evidence to support the verdict, adding, however, these significant words, "I may, however, say that if no evidence at all had been called for the prisoner, and the case rested solely

* "The Trial of Nunda Kumar," by H. Beveridge, Bengal Civil Service.

on the evidence for the prosecution, I should not have convicted Nuncomar." Here this eminent lawyer differs widely from the committing magistrates, who, having heard only one side, had "no doubt" of the guilt of the accused, and having thus prejudged him were anomalously allowed to take part (a very active part) in the capital trial afterwards. Surely, this fact alone was enough to prejudice the jury.

Mr. Beveridge has a good deal to say, and does so with much force, on a vulnerable point in the charge—I mean the passage (quoted in the narrative) beginning, "The nature of the defence is such that if it is not believed, it must prove fatal to the party," etc. Sir James Stephen allows that here the Chief Justice went too far (as regards an Indian trial, as I understand his footnote), and Mr. Beveridge shows that prisoners are now never convicted (in Indian courts) because they set up false defences.*

Mr. Beveridge believes that Nuncomar was innocent, and so did the "majority" before him, and he certainly strikes on suggestions favourable to him which were not so put to the jury, and brings forward much, if I may venture the opinion, which seems to render it probable that the jewels-bond was genuine, and that some of the evidence for the prisoner was more worthy of credence than it was held to be. He considers that the Chief Justice "was not patient enough, or had not enough knowledge of the circumstances to say whether Nuncomar was guilty or not," and that the jury were "prejudiced and incompetent." He distinctly repudiates any insinuation that the jury or Impey *knowingly* condemned an innocent man. Very probably, Impey and his brethren *would* have been better fitted to conduct the trial, if they reckoned their judicial experience in India by years instead of by months; and as for the very probable prejudice of the jury, that is a consideration which, as Sir James Stephen says, does not affect the value of the evidence, but it does affect the value of the verdict apart from the evidence. It is too late in the day, however, to speculate now on a point which no one is ever likely to determine, viz. whether there was a mistake or not in the verdict. Neither this question nor that of the machinery of the Court have anything to do with the *animus* imputed to the Chief Justice. Regarding this, I think the inference is fully warranted, which Sir James Stephen has drawn from a study of Impey's general behaviour during the trial, namely, that so far from showing a desire to secure a conviction, he would have been pleased if the jury had relieved him of further responsibility by acquitting the prisoner.†

* Nuncomar's conviction seems to have been mainly due to the effect produced on the jury, by what was considered to be the perjury of his witnesses.

† Any inference deducible from native tradition, which is necessarily vague, must of course be of little value; but as in some remote degree bearing on the actual conviction of Nuncomar, I may mention that I often spoke on the subject with respectable native gentlemen in and near Calcutta, to ascertain what impression they had on the subject, handed down by tradition or otherwise. When any answer was forthcoming, it was nearly always to the same purport, viz. that

The most grievous charge that Impey had to answer, was that which may be noticed next, viz. that when Nuncomar had been convicted and sentenced to death, he corruptly refused to respite him pending the submission of his case for the consideration of the Sovereign. Mr. Beveridge speaks with no uncertain voice here: "The execution was iniquitous, even on the supposition of Nunda Kumar's guilt, and was the result of a plot to stifle inquiry into bribery and corruption." His view is more definitely put in the following vigorous words which are meant to apply perhaps as much to the sentence as to the refusal to respite: "What I and every honest man who knows the facts blame Impey for is, that he allowed himself to be prejudiced by his partiality for Hastings, and his hatred of the majority, and that he hanged Nunda Kumar in order that peculators in general, and his friend and patron Hastings in particular, might be safe." Sir James Stephen's answer to this charge is: that Impey had no power to respite*; that the whole of the Court was responsible for the course taken; that they were vested with discretionary power, and that they exercised it in good faith to the best of their judgment, and on reasonable grounds, thus fulfilling their only obligation in the matter.

To a Member of Parliament (George Johnstone, Governor of West Florida), who seems to have referred about the execution to Impey, the latter gave the chief motives which he said actuated him in deciding not to grant a respite—they are motives which would, and most probably did, equally influence the other judges. Their substance is thus briefly given: "That the crime was aggravated by perjury and forgery, and that the Executive Government had by their conduct made it impossible for the Court to respite Nuncomar without incurring the loss of their own inde-

Nuncomar came to grief from having imprudently quarrelled with the Lord Sahib of the day, which quarrel was taken up by the "Sahib log" (European gentry) of Calcutta, who, as jurors, paid him out for it; and that what the verdict would be, was a foregone conclusion from the fidelity of the jury to Hastings, not from the partiality of the judges, whom tradition seemed to hold quite blameless in the matter. That Nuncomar was apprehensive of the hostility of the jury is evidenced by the extensive challenge which he resorted to in such a small European community. And that native litigants regarded the jury, not the judges, as the arbiters of their fate, for good or for evil, may be inferred from this passage in a petition to Government from one Ramnat Das (Calcutta, 1767): "I have heard much of the justice of the English law." . . . "I am very desirous of laying my case before the *juries* at the next sessions." (Selections from "Unpublished Records of Government.")

* No doubt, as Sir James Stephen allows, if Impey had successfully used his influence with any one of the judges in favour of a respite, that, with his casting vote, would have been decisive; but this does not make him personally chargeable with a refusal to respite. In his own defence before the House of Commons he said: "Though called to answer as for acts done by me singly, those acts not only were not, but *would not* have been done by me individually." The words I have put in italics are not suggestive of Impey's having had great influence over his colleagues.

pendence and the suspicion of having been either bribed or intimidated." Sir James Stephen says that the motives alleged by Impey deserved to be attentively considered, and might have honestly convinced rational men that Nuncomar ought not to be respited—regarding the question as one of discretion. He does not say that they fully justified the decision of the judges not to respite. "I think," he concludes, "that this proceeding was not unjust, though I do not affirm that it was not mistaken. Lastly, I do not believe that Impey or any of his colleagues acted as they did in order to serve a political purpose."

I see no reason whatever to doubt that the motives stated by Impey were not the predominant and true ones. He was not over stating the consequences, I think, when he wrote: "No explanation could have made the natives understand that the escape from justice, if the sentence had not been carried into execution, had not been occasioned by the artifice of the prisoner, unless indeed it had been attributed to corruption or timidity in the judges, or a controlling power in the Governor-General or Council." Whether or not they ought to have been above or regardless of consequences is another question. No doubt very perfect people would have been, but judges, like other men, can only act according to their lights. One is naturally perhaps disposed at this distance of time to think that the deciding not to respite the prisoner was a blunder, because—to mention no other reason—it put such a weapon into the hands of the majority; and to ask whether the authority of the Court, new though it was, could not have been vindicated by some measure far short of summary execution. But no one is now in a position to estimate the significance which the interferences of the Council wore to the judges, or to appreciate all the local circumstances which urged them to the course which they adopted in defence, as they believed, of the trust committed to them. We probably have no conception of the jealousy with which the new Councillors on the one hand, and the new Supreme Court on the other, guarded against encroachment on their exclusive privileges. This very power of reprieving was a sore point with the new Government; it was a prerogative not only conferred by Charter on the judges, but taken away from the Executive power; so that Francis when discussing the Regulating Act, etc. (Appendix Vol. I. Memoirs), complains "we are not trusted with the exercise of mercy possessed by our predecessors. We can neither stop a prosecution, nor pardon after conviction. Even the office of recommending to the Royal mercy is reserved to the Court of Judicature." The assertion of their power and position, and the resenting of all interference with their functions, would seem to have been a ruling passion with the new judges. It is conceivable that men, thus bristling with the importance of their office, may not always have been in the frame of mind best adapted for dispassionate judgment. Two years before Impey's letter to Governor Johnstone, he wrote this to Thurlow (1776)—

"The hauteur, insolence, and superior air of authority which the new members of the Council use to the Court may be partly discernible in the style of their minutes, but on the spot they maintain no colour of decency. My conduct to them has been absolutely the reverse, and I believe they are the more angry with me for it."

And this two years later—

"Every dispatch from England brings accounts of actual or intended addresses to Parliament or H.M.'s Ministers levelled against the Court. At present one, said to be presented by the Company to Lord Weymouth, is in the possession of Mr. Francis, which has been circulated about the settlement with intimation that by the next advice intelligence will arrive that 'the wings of the Court have been clipt.'"

To Dunning, in the same year (1778), he wrote—

"It was extremely painful to me to inflict the punishment of imprisonment on him (the Company's attorney), but the only possible means of supporting the least credit and authority in the Court, is to show that though the Governor-General and Council may not be punishable personally for outrages committed against the Court, yet it is out of their power to protect their agents." *

Mr. Beveridge specifies the corrupt motives which he maintains were rightly attributed to Impey, thus "there are many kinds of corruption, and in this case, I do not suspect Impey of killing Nunda Kumar for a money reward. But if he strained the law in order to convict him, and if he, in Macaulay's words, 'sitting as a judge,' put a man unjustly to death in order to serve a political purpose, he acted corruptly." The kind of corruption alleged does not lie at his door, if the facts marshalled by Sir J. Stephen establish, as they seem to me to do, that he was tried and convicted according to the ordinary course of law; and that the stay of execution was decided against by the judges in the due exercise of their discretion, as the occasion did not appear to them a proper one for mercy. The decision may have been a deplorable mistake, but, right or wrong, it was come to in good faith.

Was Hastings the real mover in the business? as Macaulay puts it. This is the point which Mr. Beveridge thinks the most interesting of all, and he has elucidated his consideration of it with a curious knowledge of local and general contemporaneous historical matter. He maintains that there is strong circumstantial evidence that Hastings was the real prosecutor. Sir James Stephen thinks "that Mohun Persaud was the real substantial prosecutor of Nuncomar, and that Hastings had nothing to do with the prosecution; and that there was no sort of conspiracy or understanding between Hastings and Impey in relation to Nuncomar, or in relation to his trial or execution." † The arguments in support of these very different conclusions should be read in full.

* All these extracts are from the Impey MSS., Br. M.

† Sir James Stephen, relying mainly on evidence of Farrer, shows that the criminal proceedings grew naturally out of a previous civil suit. Mr. Beveridge gives reasons for questioning Farrer's memory, and contends that there had been no attempt at a prosecution before May, 1775. But supposing, for argument's sake, a "mover in the business" to be necessary, why should not this be

Mr. Beveridge's contention has enabled me to go only as far as allowing that he suggests further grounds for *suspicion* that Hastings was connected with the prosecution. It is but just to Mr. Beveridge, however, to mention prominently the one point in his argument which has made a strong impression on me. It will be remembered that the foreman of the jury complained to the Chief Justice about Farrer in connection with a proposed petition for respite, and that Impey in open court censured Farrer—with, I think, some display of truculence. Permission for Robinson to make his complaint had been solicited by a Mr. Belli, who forwarded certain correspondence to the Chief Justice. Mr. Beveridge states positively that at the time Mr. Belli was private secretary to Hastings, and a member of his houshold. His note to Impey did not say that he was authorised by the Governor-General to act as the go-between, and he may have so acted on his own motion; but it is not unreasonable to suspect, that if the foreman of the jury could not approach the Chief Justice without an introduction, the introduction with which he would provide himself would be from some one more important than Mr. Belli in his *private* capacity. In any case it shows great indiscretion, to say the least of it, on the part of Impey (considering the rumours that must have been then going about) to be holding communication with any one in Government House at such a time. But though the Belli incident, as known to us, may be very difficult to get over, it must, I fancy, have admitted of an explanation which would absolve Hastings of complicity with it. It appeared on the Parliamentary record as an item, I presume, of the proceedings. Did it give rise to comment?

Francis was prompting the impeachment, and must have known all the circumstances of Belli's position in Calcutta. His ingenuity, if anybody's could, would have brought into full significance an incident so suggestive of more than suspicion at a *primâ facie* glance; yet there is no evidence, that I know of, that this was attempted. Does not, as Macaulay argues, the failure of severe malevolent scrutiny entitle one to be considered free of those blemishes which it has not brought to light?

But all arguments as to Hastings being the prosecutor, etc., are unnecessary if, as Mr. Beveridge maintains in one of his chapters, that he practically admitted "having employed Impey to hang Nuncomar." This is adopting Macaulay's view of the significance of the words, "My

Durham, the Company's lawyer? Captain Price says that he *was* the man who set the ball rolling (apparently towards the end of April). Price says that he did so to squeeze money out of the Rajah, "on the idea that he should be able to quash the evidence." But Durham is known to have been a friend of Hastings; is it violently improbable that on finding a good opportunity of discrediting Hastings' accuser, he made use of it—with a vengeance? A lawyer would have known the full value of carrying the war into the enemy's country, and how to do it at the right time; and he would take good care to work in such a manner that even the Governor-General should not know who the *Deus ex Machina* was.

fortune, honour, and reputation,"* for which Hastings wrote he was once indebted to the support of Impey. Sir J. Stephen considers that the passage in which those words occur obviously refers to the support given by Impey and the other judges to Hastings when he submitted his resignation question to them.

Mr. Beveridge brings forward much to show the inapplicability of the words to the resignation support. He argues that if Impey had been against Hastings, then the decision of the rest of the judges in his favour would have served his purpose; that, as a fact, Hastings was only half-pleased with the support of the judges on that occasion, and told his friend Sulivan so, and expressed gratitude for only Barwell's support at that critical time.

As Sir James Stephen shows, in the same year in which Hastings wrote the above words in reference to Impey, the latter wrote in a similar strain to Dunning about Hastings, viz. "The power which is exerted against me would not have existed in the hands in which it is if I had not helped to keep it there."

It is clear that Impey attached much merit to the action of the judges in the resignation dispute from this passage in another letter of his to Governor Johnstone.

> "I think it impossible for any impartial persons (and such the Directors ought to be) not to see that the Judges have had, in all their judgment and proceedings, attention to the interests of the nation and Company. Why else interfere to quiet the disturbances at Madras? Why mediate between Mr. Hastings and Sir John Clavering, when each claimed and actually possessed the seat of the Governor-General in different departments. If the Judges, at the risk of censure if they were wrong, had not interposed, to what must they have appealed? Did anything remain but the *ratio ultima regum?* It was expected, and all the bazaars were shut up."

There can be little doubt, I think, that Impey and Hastings referred to the same occasion for support, in their respective letters. To hold that they referred to the hanging of Nuncomar, involves the assumption not only that they had conspired to iniquity, but that each had the folly and transcendental meanness to peach on himself and on his fellow-conspirator; Hastings to one of the Court of Directors, and Impey to the head of the Bar in England! The whole controversy might be perilled on the answer to this single question. Did any two men, subject to the

* These words, or words of exactly similar import, seem to have been in fashionable use at this time. Mr. Beveridge shows that Hastings used phrases like these in correspondence in April and May, 1775, with reference, too, to Nuncomar's accusations. Again, in 1783, he wrote "my name and fortune would be blasted." In one of the addresses to Impey occurs the phrase, "our reputations, our fortunes, and, perhaps, our lives;" and in Impey's letter to Johnstone, he speaks of "my fortune and character." In fact, the phrase was more or less of a formula used in no very definite sense.

ordinary impulses of human nature, ever act in such violation of its instincts?*

Mr. Beveridge is too shrewd a writer (as many pages in his book show) not to feel conscious that some excuse is necessary to account for Hastings' unnatural and compromising "confession" of the desperate remedy to which he had been driven once, so he is conjectured to have been off his guard when writing to Sulivan. "If Impey did hang Nunda Kumar in order to serve Hastings, we can not doubt that the latter would feel grateful to him, and an expression of his feelings might easily slip out in an unguarded moment." "For these reasons I hold that Macaulay's intuition was right, that Hastings was referring to the Nunda Kumar case, and that he accidentally and virtually confessed that Impey had hanged Nunda Kumar in order to support him." Warren Hastings had few "unguarded moments" in his life—probably never—when he had his pen in his hand. Here is what he wrote of himself in March, 1775, in the midst of all the concerted attacks of the new Councillors:—"I thank God I have hitherto possessed both my judgment and understanding undisturbed." And this is what Francis, no mean judge of character, wrote of him in 1776, after a close personal study:—"His reserve, whether natural or acquired, is so excessive, that I firmly believe he never reposed an entire confidence in any man." "The effect of his singular equanimity," says Macaulay, "was that he always had the full command of all the resources of one of the most fertile minds that ever existed: accordingly no complication of perils and embarrassments could perplex him."

Mr. Beveridge, however, has the satisfaction—and it is no small one—of feeling that his study of the Nuncomar episode has justified him in adopting the conclusion of the great honest statesmen who believed in the guilt of Hastings and of Impey. He has ranged himself on the winning side. And no one seems to know this better than Sir James Stephen. "I am sorry for him," he says (speaking of Impey). "I believe him to have been quite innocent: but this book will be read by hardly any one, and Macaulay's paragraph will be read with delighted conviction by several generations."

When Macaulay was but proposing to the *Edinburgh Review* the article on Warren Hastings, which has fastened such a stain upon its subject, he wrote to the editor, "I hardly know a story so interesting, and of such various interest. And the central figure is in the highest degree striking and majestic. I think Hastings, though far from faultless, one of the greatest men that England ever produced. He had pre-

* There are innumerable letters in the Hastings and in the Impey MSS. which passed between these two men: some in original, some in rough draft. They are on all sorts of official and domestic subjects. Hastings often consulted Impey on certain questions, and Impey not unfrequently asked favours of Hastings on behalf of his friends, but always in a becoming, delicate manner; everything was straightforward and open. Certainly if there was a "bond of infamy" between them, no sign of presuming on it crept out in their private correspondence.

eminent talents for government, and great literary talents too; fine taste, a princely spirit, and heroic equanimity in the midst of adversity and danger. He was a man for whom Nature had done much of what the stoic philosophy pretended to do for its disciples. 'Mens æqua in arduis' is the inscription under his picture in the Government House at Calcutta, and never was there a more appropriate motto."

With what hesitation must he have brought himself to conclude that such a man once connived at another's death to shield himself from the charge of corruption. The earnestness and reluctance of his belief in Hastings' fellowship with the alleged crime, are indicated by the sophistry with which he attempts to half condone it, and by the fiercer light into which he drags, as if to relieve his conscience, the criminality of him who was but a subservient instrument.

The Nuncomar story which Macaulay told, with such consummate skill that it has petrified into polished marble, was but the revival of that of which Francis laid the foundation in Calcutta, and perfected in England. With it the ex-Councillor went to Burke and Fox and Gilbert Elliot,

> 'And in the porches of their ears did pour the leprous distilment'

with such gratifying effect, that he was soon able to write to one of a band in Calcutta whom Hastings called "the lees of Mr. Francis," "Impey will certainly be demolished, and, I think, with public disgrace. . . . You will be delighted to read my examination before the Select Committee, and still more that of Mr. Shakspeare; between us Impey and Barwell are fairly made as black as the devil. . . . But for the demolition of the Supreme Court of Judicature we should have no consolation in this transitory life."

When he saw that the impeachment was a-ripening, he wrote with prophetic exultation to another kindred spirit in Calcutta, "Let the event to their persons be what it may, the charges will gibbet their characters to all eternity." A strong prejudice must have existed against Impey—fomented no doubt by Francis and other enemies abroad and at home and aided, perhaps, by the personal equation of objectionable bearing and manners. Wraxhall knew him personally and was prejudiced in his disfavour—a feeling which neither the expression of his countenance, nor his manners tended to dispel. Honest Lord Cornwallis, in a familiar letter to a friend, says, "I am very sorry that things have gone so much against poor Hastings, for he certainly had many amiable qualities. If you are in the hanging mood you may tuck up Sir Elijah Impey without giving any one the smallest concern."

The name of Impey may with truth be substituted for that of the Duke of Grafton in the following passage,* and with peculiar appropriateness, as the artist was in each case the same. It was Junius who etched the popular portrait of the Duke of Grafton; it was Junius, too—with the

* "Early History of C. J. Fox," by G. O. Trevelyan.

mask laid aside—who did the same for the first Chief Justice in India. "The portrait, which has been bitten into the national memory by the acid of Junius, has never been obliterated. A popular conception which has lasted for a generation is likely to last for a century, and when it has outlived a century it may die, but cannot be corrected. Doing penance, Grafton (Impey) will continue to stand in his white sheet beneath the very centre of the dome in the Temple of History."

# V

## HASTINGS AND THE IMHOFFS

IN a former edition of this book, I said that it was perhaps questionable whether Hastings' love was in this case "patient of delay." On reflection I now think I was not justified in saying so much. It is due to the character of Hastings, and of Mrs. Hastings, to hold them free (as Sir C. Lawson in his "Private life of Hastings" most fairly argues) from any reproach which even the gossiping society of Calcutta never, so far as we know, visited them with. But, circumspect as he may have been, say from even no higher motive than that of policy (knowing that even the "chaste as ice cannot escape calumny"), the position of Mrs. Imhoff in relation to him, in the absence of her husband, cannot but have seemed to society of that period to be an equivocal one. And this in spite of all his prudence and jealous care. The accomplished lady who has published in extenso and edited the Hastings' letters, there refers more than once to a previous work, "The Great Proconsul," where she devotes some pages to the history of Mrs. Hastings preceding her second marriage. The authoress there pronounces those to be guilty of "attempting to defame a dead woman" who point to a disrespectful reference to Mrs. Imhoff in a letter from Hastings' "false friend Macpherson as showing her position was an equivocal one." Whether Mr. Macpherson's letter (alluding to the "fair female friend") does show this, or does lend any strength to the contention founded on it, will not alter the fact of the position. But as I, for one, have resorted to the argument by the quotation in the text, it becomes only fair to notice what Miss Grier considers the refutation of it. She says, 'they' (the defamers) "have not observed that it is evident from a later letter that Hastings called Macpherson sharply to account for the phrase; or that later still, the unabashed Macpherson, pretending not to understand the rebuke, speaks of Mrs. Hastings in exactly the same terms when Hastings and she had been married for two years." We are not given the reference for Hastings' rebuke, which can only be inferred from Macpherson's subsequent letters, as those of Hastings to him are not forthcoming. The letter quoted from in the text is dated Madras, July 11, 1775; several letters passed between these two old colleagues after that, but it is not until seven months later that one is found from Macpherson which could be referred to as "pretending not to understand," viz. on

February 9, 1776, he writes: "I have been on the rack to guess the circumstance you hint at that displeased you in one of my letters; I write you with an open soul, and often with a careless hand, yet no man living respects you more; judge, then, of my uneasiness till I know the circumstance you had in view." It will be remarked here that it is not the use of a "phrase" or "expression" that Macpherson desires to learn about, but of a "circumstance," twice referred to. I think therefore that Miss Sydney Grier is mistaken in supposing that the later letter had any reference to the former one. In any case, if Hastings was offended by a phrase, he either lacked gall, or the wound was not very deep; as in November, 1777, we find him, a few months after his marriage, writing thus to Macpherson in England, "my last letter was dated July 26, with it I sent a letter to Mr. Woodman (*i.e.* Hastings' brother-in-law) containing my request that he would show all my despatches to you, my confidential friend; and I introduced him at the same time to you by the same title;" this is signed, "most affectionately and truly yours." In 1782 he writes to Lord Shelburne, rather effusively of Macpherson and his other colleague, Stables, as "men of unexampled benevolence and equality of temper, warmed with a cordial affection to each other, and a confidence in mine to them."

Wraxall ("Historical and Posthumous Memoirs" as republished 1884, edited by Mr. Wheatley), in speaking of Macpherson from personal knowledge, praises his amiable character and his independent loyalty to Hastings and his Government. He adds this also, "He achieved even a more difficult task, that of acquiring Mrs. Hastings' regard, though he opposed her wishes or views on more than one occasion." Before going further, it may be noted that Wraxall, in giving (vol. iv.) his version of the Hastings-Imhoff marriage "and all the circumstances which produced that union," permits himself to use significant expressions (all the more disparaging because offence is apparently not intended) in comparison with which the words "equivocal position" are mild and colourless. Yet I have seen no exception taken to Wraxall—

*Dat veniam corvis, vexat censura columbas.*

The whole story connected with the second marriage of Warren Hastings remains still in much obscurity. Some few details not known to the original purveyors of information on the subject have since turned up here and there, without throwing much additional light on it. (Amongst these may be mentioned the letters written in 1772-1773, by Dr. Tysoe Hancock, originally quoted by me in my first edition—and a German book published only in 1889). Shortly summarised, the bare facts not in dispute are these: Baron Carl Von Imhoff, with his wife (aged twenty-two) and child, embarked for Madras early in 1769 on board the *Duke of Grafton*. The Baron was skilled in miniature painting, and had exhibited a specimen of this when he and his wife appeared in London in 1768. It was as a commissioned officer, provided with a cadet-ship in the Madras Army, that he was proceeding to

India (Dr. Hancock's letters and India Office records). Among the many passengers on board the Indiaman, was Warren Hastings, then returning, after a four years' absence, to India, owing to straitened circumstances. He had got an appointment as Member of Council at Madras. He was at this time a widower, and somewhat over thirty-six years of age. The opportunities of the voyage gave rise to an intimacy between the Imhoffs and Hastings; one ostensible result of which was much hospitality shown them in Madras by the new Member of Council. Imhoff lived with his wife in Madras from the end of 1769 to the end of 1770. He resigned his military commission in September, 1770, giving as his reason in an official letter to the Madras authorities that "his pay was insufficient to support himself and family," adding that, "he had with the approval of the late Governor (Mr. Dupré) practised a liberal art for a livelihood." He got permission to go to Bengal, where no doubt there was a wider field for his now adopted profession. When he then went to Calcutta, Baroness Imhoff remained behind at Madras, "and lived in Mr. Hastings' house on the Mount chiefly, I believe" (wrote Dr. Hancock). But she followed her husband within a year, arriving in Calcutta in October, 1771. The Imhoffs lived in Calcutta together, he working at his profession until February, 1773, when the Baron went to England by himself—and never returned. Hastings arrived in Calcutta as Governor of Bengal a year previously, *i.e.* in February, 1772, some four months after Mrs. Imhoff.

The additions (with the inferences, embellishments, and conclusions) woven round the above rigid facts, are mainly, that Hastings fell in love with the Baroness on board ship, a result that was precipitated by the accident of her devoted care and nursing of him through a severe illness. Macaulay, in his summing up of the situation, which is so familiar to us, is rather apologetic than censorious about it, and to justify this attitude is very severe on the Baron. Imhoff, he bluntly says, was called into Council by his wife and his wife's lover. It was arranged that the Baroness should institute a suit for a divorce in the Courts of Franconia, that the Baron should afford every facility, and that during the years which might elapse before the divorce, they should continue to live together. Further, it was agreed that Hastings should "bestow" some very substantial marks of gratitude on the complaisant husband, and in due time marry the lady and adopt the children whom she had "already" borne to Imhoff.* Gleig says cautiously, "the divorce was obtained in Franconia Courts after much delay; the

* This adoption clause suggests a later bringing in (*ex eventu*) when the fact was known. Sir C. Lawson (*op. cit.*) writes: "There was a son, Ernest, who did not long survive;" he also refers to a daughter, but he is wrong in this, at all events in her name. There were Charles and Julius we know, but the matter is very obscure. The German authoress says that two sons were born in Madras. This is almost certainly a mistake arising from confusion of facts and dates. But the statement prompts the question what was "agreed" as to the very possible contingency of other children coming "during the years which might elapse, etc."?

Baroness became Mrs. Hastings, and the Baron returned to his native country a richer man than he ever could have hoped to become by the mere exercise of his skill as a painter." Macaulay adopts this, but in more decided language. "About this time" (middle of 1777) "arrived the news that, after a suit which had lasted several years, the Franconian Courts had decreed a divorce between Imhoff and his wife. The Baron left Calcutta carrying with him the means of buying an estate in Saxony. The lady became Mrs. Hastings." One may infer from the turn of the words used by Gleig and his reviewer that both were under the impression that the Baron had not left India, until the news arrived which enabled Hastings to fulfil the compact, alleged to have been made in 1769 on board ship. Wraxall, with a lofty disregard for dates, says, in his account: "About the time when Hastings was appointed to the Government of Bengal, January, 1772, a termination of her marriage with Imhoff took place, which union, as having been originally celebrated in Germany, was asserted to be capable of dissolution by mutual consent." "This amicable divorce was not, however, effected without the aid of money;" then, greatly daring, he adds, with a circumstantiality that is not uninteresting, "Hastings having, in fact, paid to Imhoff a sum considerably exceeding £10,000, with which acquisition the fortunate painter quitted India, and returning to his native country, there bought an estate out of the produce of his wife's attractions. Mrs. Imhoff followed her lover to Calcutta, and as soon as her husband had transmitted authentic intelligence that the divorce was obtained, the new Governor-General of India"—here he indulges in a round-about objectionable expression for which "married her" will better serve. Wraxall is the only "authority" that I happen to have seen who ventures to put into figures the price said to have been paid. The historians here quoted from were not a little indebted evidently to a footnote about Baron Imhoff by the nondescript translator of the *Syur ul Mutaquerin*, who called himself Hadji Mustapha, viz. "The story reported of this lady is singular enough. Born at Archangel in the very north of that very northern country, Russia, she married a gentleman officer who was reformed (*sic*) and who, finding that matters went ill with him, repaired to England to seek a livelihood, and from thence to India, where he lived by pencilling miniatures, for which he had some small talent. But the governor having put it in his power to purchase an estate in Saxony, he divorced his wife, which was espoused by the former."

Who was Baron Imhoff? A German lady, Henriette von Bissing, published in 1889 a life of Amalie, his eldest child by his second marriage (she became celebrated as a poetess, and married a Colonel von Helwig). The authoress is very inaccurate as to dates and facts regarding the Indian career of her subject's father; as to why he went to the East, or why he left it, etc. But she seems to have had plenty of material for showing what he was by birth, and what his career was after his return from India. Baron Carl von Imhoff was well born, and descended from an old Nürnberg family, and, we are told, that he was endowed with all the advantages that the descent from such a house, naturally talented, can bring. He entered the Wurtemberg Military Service, where he attained the rank of Captain before he resigned it. He married a lady said to be of noble French extraction, whose family (named Chapuset), this authoress says, he had known as emigrants settled in Stuttgart. She was then in her early youth and very attractive. Why or when he and his wife came to England is not recorded. Having private influence at the English Court, through the keeper of the robes to Queen Charlotte, it is believed, he possibly thought he could profitably employ his gift of miniature painting there. From England he turned his professional (?) aspirations to India. At all events his Court interest (presumably) obtained for him a cadet-ship from the East India Company on the Madras military establishment. After his return from Bengal he married Louise von Schardt in 1775. She was then a lady of the Court of Gotha; she was the youngest of three sisters, the eldest of whom was Frau von Stein (of Goethe's correspondence). From this German work, and some stray expressions in it, one does not gather the idea that Imhoff brought much money with him from India, viz. "with the remainder of his fortune he bought the paternal estate from his brothers." "By reason of his limited circumstances he had undertaken the management of the estate, Morlach, in 1775."

Many letters which passed between him and his wife are given, and show that the Baron was a most kind, considerate, and fond husband and father. He often tells her, when away from him with her own people, of the progress of his miniature painting—an art which he never ceased to cultivate. When the eldest daughter was born she was named Amalie after her godmother the Duchess. He was an occasional guest at the Coburg Court, and was on friendly terms with the King of Wurtemberg. The establishment which he and his wife maintained at Morlach (near Nürnberg) was necessarily a modest one for his position, but his letters show that he was intimate with the chief families around. The daughter Amalie became her father's special care and favourite pupil. She was welcomed in his studio. At eleven years of age she spoke French and English fluently, the latter being the favourite and most practised language of her father. Eventually Baron Imhoff became asthmatic, and had to break up his paternal home, and travel in search of health. He moved his family to Weimar, and was overtaken by death at Munich at the age of fifty-four, "defamed by uncommon fate" Frau von Bissing obscurely adds. He does not seem to have left his family well off. Sir C. Imhoff made the acquaintance of Amalie and the rest of her kindred "at the request of his dying father," so Mrs. Hastings writes. One of the daughters, Marian, seems to have often applied to her step-brother for assistance. Mrs. Hastings became godmother to one of the children of her first husband's second marriage at his request. She sent £500 to the one named Marian. These highly creditable and suggestive facts I learn from Miss Sydney Grier's books.

It would be a poor compliment to the ladies whom Carl von Imhoff married (one well born and well descended, and of many attractions, the other a member of a highly intellectual family in good position) to deny that he had some of the winning qualifications commendable in women's eyes. If we look to his own family and his influential connections, his meritorious reasons for going to India, and his honestly working there for a livelihood, which his pay as an Ensign could not yield. If we consider the well-vouched-for purity of his life and associations after his return home, it is hard to believe that as a young officer he became *repente turpissimus*, and made the sordid bargain about his wife and children which, in its related form, so smirches his character, and, let us bear in mind, not *his* character alone. One writer has closely followed another in giving details which could have been known only to the principals who had the strongest reasons for silence. The two who, without quoting any authority, are mainly responsible for the generally accepted Hastings-Imhoff story (Wraxall and Macaulay) were ignorant of much we know now, as has been shown. It would be idle to contend that the circumstances of Imhoff's departure from Calcutta, his never returning, and his remarrying in about two years do not stand in need of explanation. All that we know, and can deduce from, is that Hastings did marry his divorced wife (four and a half years after Imhoff's departure) and did adopt her children. But have we really any evidence that he paid the husband to connive at affording the opportunity for this?—the gravamen of the charge is this. It is assumed that Imhoff could have made little or no money by his adopted profession in India ; yet it is one that has always commanded high remuneration for Europeans practising it there. Wealthy natives especially would seek the services of such an artist, and all the more because he was ostensibly on friendly terms at Government House. Imhoff devoted nearly three years to it in Madras and Bengal. Why he should have remained so long in India and not gone home at once to seek a divorce (if there was an "agreement"), it is difficult to guess. Frau von Bissing says that she saw amongst the papers of the Imhoff family what she calls a "confession" from Marian Imhoff, "which caused a divorce." What she may have seen perhaps was a copy of the pleading or other legal explanation, as to why a divorce was sought ; some such document under her own hand would presumably be necessary for the satisfaction of the court that could grant divorce, for incompatibility of temper or some such cause. Local Calcutta gossip alleged that Richard Johnson (of Lucknow fame) was the negotiator of it on the Hastings side. However, this may be, much sympathy has been given to Mrs. Imhoff: Mr. Beveridge is the only writer that I know of who has said a word on the husband's side in arrest of judgment. Some authority can I suppose be alleged for most stories, however extravagant : and assertion if positive enough and frequent enough, gradually comes to be mistaken for proof occasionally. It was Thackeray, I think, who remarked that the popular version of any story which survives will probably be the least authentic. The difficulty of coming to a just conclusion about this particular story may be inferred from the incompleteness of the information that has been afforded us ; so perplexingly deficient is it as almost to suggest intentional suppression.

Here are a few instances.

1. Where was Marian Chapuset born? We do not know.

2. Where or when was she married to Baron Imhoff? We do not know.

3. How many children were born to her by him? We do not know.

4. In what particular court was her divorce from him obtained; how, or when? We do not know.

5. Baron Imhoff was free to remarry in 1775, and did so; Mrs. Imhoff was not free until two years later; why this long delay? We do not know.

6. This mother of a family was remarried at Calcutta, August 1777, in her maiden name, as Miss Anna Maria Appolonia Chapusettin. Why this apparent ignoring of her first marriage? We do not know.

The late Sir James Fitzjames Stephen, in his veneration for Hastings, for his splendid services to his country, and his wondrous talent for administration in the face of enormous difficulties, regarded him as the ablest Englishman of the eighteenth century. But he considered "his connection with Mrs. Imhoff not creditable to his memory."

Whether this able and kindly man would have modified this latter judgment, if he had known more of the facts than those alleged in Macaulay's Essay, I cannot say.

But in any case, matters will not be mended by regarding everything said in disparagement of Baron Imhoff as unassailable. Where so much is in the dark, it is fairer, and more prudent to suspend judgment, and stand in the ways—and wait for light.

## VI

## THE INTRIGUES OF A NABOB

WHOEVER has occasion to get a comprehensive view of the picture-gallery of morals and manners of Old Calcutta, to see its society in its shadows as well as in its lights, cannot afford to ignore some unwholesome contemporary literature. A volume entitled as above made no little noise in Calcutta at one time, as it arraigned one who had quite recently been a very prominent member of the community, for "friendship violated and the sacred laws of hospitality disregarded," and for several other crimes and misdemeanours. Mr. Barwell was the alleged culprit. The book was dedicated to the Honourable Court of Directors, and the story which it purported to tell was more or less typical of that, which was vaguely believed in England about many, if not most, Anglo-Indian "nabobs." An outline of it may therefore be given, especially as it introduces two or three names which we have already met in better company. The subject warns us that the contents must be very lightly skimmed for readers of an age a hundred years later than the publication.

The author was a Mr. Henry F. Thompson, who apparently held an appointment in the marine service of the East India Company. This gentleman, on returning to England from a voyage to the East, met in low society, and became enamoured of, a young person named Sarah Bonner, who, though at the time but sixteen years old, had already passed through some unfortunate vicissitudes which made the kindness and generosity that Thompson lavished upon her very acceptable. When the time came for the sailor's return to India, he discovered that he could not contemplate a long separation from one whom he had for some months protected; accordingly, as a means of avoiding this, and of providing an answer to inconvenient questions, he informed his friends that he had just married a wife, and then arranged that she and his own sister should be sent out together to Calcutta in a short time after him.

Of the sister no further mention is made.

When afterwards trying to account for his infatuation, Mr. Thompson describes his enslaver as one "whose charms were of the bewitching kind; they infused a soporiferous poison into the mind, benumbed and stupefied the reasoning powers, and left her sole mistress of the head and heart of her lovers."

Thompson returned to Bengal armed with letters to Governor Verelst, Mr. Becher, and other influential officials; but all they could do for him was to get him appointed second officer of a ship then setting out on a voyage. When he got back to Calcutta from this voyage he found that the lady, who ever afterwards passed as "Mrs. Thompson" in Calcutta society, had arrived, and had been in Bengal since October, 1769. Thompson immediately proceeded to make his nominal wife as comfortable as he could, and provided her with a house, which was "genteely furnished, and soon honoured with the visits of persons of the first distinction of both sexes." Amongst the distinguished visitors was Mr. Richard Barwell, then holding an appointment in Calcutta. This benevolent man placed his suburban house at the disposal of the young couple, and shortly after obtained an appointment for Thompson, that of Deputy-Paymaster at Berhampore, with 7000 rupees a year. To Berhampore, however, Mrs. Thompson declined to go, avowing a preference for Calcutta, coupled with Mr. Barwell's country house.

Thompson had not long taken up his appointment when certain changes in the official world at Calcutta got Barwell himself sent to Mootigeal, seven miles from Berhampore. His patron soon proposed that the Deputy-Paymaster should live with him. The latter agreed, and professed himself "as happy as could be, wanting nothing but the society of the woman he held most dear." Possibly it was with the object of breaking up an association, which it was foreseen would lead to a grave public scandal, that Thompson soon found himself suddenly and peremptorily recalled to Calcutta. In vain Barwell exerted his influence to get the order countermanded, but the Government were inexorable, and Thompson went to the Presidency to wait for other employment. In the mean time he resumed his tenancy of Barwell's garden-house. The first shock which his feelings received on his arrival at Calcutta was from the coolness of the reception extended to him by his fair ensnarer; the next from his discovering after a little time, that she was often surreptitiously receiving letters from Mootigeal, sent under cover to a Mr. Cator, who was also occupying apartments in the garden-house. On contriving to see a little of this correspondence, the unwelcome fact became known to him that shortly after "Mrs. Thompson's" arrival in Calcutta, while awaiting the sailor's return from the voyage previously mentioned, "the sapper and miner was at work," as Sergeant Buzfuz puts it, Mr. Barwell made her acquaintance, and had proceeded some lengths towards ingratiating himself. Any illusion he may have been under as to the disinterestedness of their patron's friendship, must have been cruelly dispelled, when he read that in Mr. Barwell's opinion, he (Thompson) was "a most uncouth semblance of humanity," "a downright man machine," whom the fair one was entreated to have no familiarities with of any kind. This was a point on which the absent admirer seemed to be nervously sensitive and exacting, for in one letter he expressed his apprehensions regarding the attentions of a Mr. Robert Sanderson, who "wishes to startle you or coax you to drop your connection with me, for the greater enjoyment his age and discretion are capable of affording you." Coquetry must have been an effective weapon in the armoury of this Delilah, as the following passage was one which met Thompson's prying eye :—"You do my affections great wrong, and your own beauties great injustice ; look in your glass, it will convince you you have charms capable of warming old age ; can a young man be indifferent to them ? I have exerted all my endeavours to effect the wish of my heart, and have drawn upon myself, in the attempt to keep your husband here, all that malevolence could invent to prejudice me in the estimation of my friends." Unhappy Mr. Thompson was further doomed to find this somewhat rueful but candid sentiment : "I love you, I wish you was with me and your husband at a distance." The writer of the book leaves it to be inferred that he considered from passages in the discovered correspondence (such as this, "No, my dear Madame, I will never ask any sacrifice to my peace that shall sink your name in the opinion of the world") it was not too late to save the woman, for whom he still retained affection, from taking any extreme step. He therefore said nothing of his discovery to Barwell, but told her that he would forgive everything if she would leave the country, and so withdraw herself from further temptation. To this she had all but consented, when the tide of events proved too strong for her. A sudden death in the upper ranks of the Civil Service gave promotion to Barwell, and again brought him to Calcutta. This accident opened up a prospect which the enterprising young lady was only too ready to make the most of. Very soon matters between her and Mr. Barwell were in such train that she felt in a position to tell her first benefactor that "his presence was eminently disagreeable," and to offer him, on the part of her new paramour, an annuity, if he would betake himself out of India. She further stimulated his acceptance of her terms by threatening that, in case of refusal, she would make known her true position, and thus free herself from restraint. Even the ordinary capacity of Thompson realized what this alleged threat conveyed, viz. that, if it came to a question of cold-blooded purchase much more might be squeezed out of Dives if he was allowed to remain under the impression that he was dealing with an injured *husband* instead of merely with a deserted lover. Thompson accordingly continued to dissemble ; a bargain was struck, and a deed of trust was executed by Warren Hastings and Robert Sanderson, under which Barwell was to pay £5000 for the benefit of Sarah Thompson and her two children, and an annuity of £300 to Thompson, who was bound not to molest or trouble Mr. Barwell on account of Mrs. Thompson." This occurred in March, 1772. It must not be forgotten that we have only got Thompson's side of this story.

To throw dust into the eyes of society it was next arranged that the ex-paymaster should go to China first, giving out that it was his intention to return to Calcutta. Eventually he made his way to Europe. He had not been there long when he received a letter from Mr. Barwell telling him that "it had become necessary to your own character, and the peace of your family, that you should make one more voyage to India, although you should immediately return to England with Mrs. Thompson and the little ones." In those days of slow voyages, much time must have elapsed before he again reached Calcutta in compliance with the above request. He arrived but to find that the frail one had sailed for England in the *Anson* in September, 1775. Public opinion, he says, had become too strong for Barwell; he had received official intimation that the scandal (intensified by the general impropriety of his companion) must no longer continue. Whether the very tolerant society of those days brought any pressure to bear on a member of Council, may perhaps be open to question. It is just as likely that for Barwell the tempting fruit had turned to ashes. Indeed, we know from other sources that in this very year 1775 he was proposing to himself to "purge and live cleanly as a nobleman should"—to sow his wild oats and marry. At all events Thompson was informed that there was nothing for him to do but to go back again. This he agreed to do on condition of a fund being established for the sure payment of his annuity. No steps were taken towards this till he was on board ship, when Barwell provided him with a letter of instructions to his brother in London, and got him to "sign a paper."

When after a tedious voyage he produced the "instructions" in London, he was told by Captain Barwell (also a sailor) that they gave him nothing whatever, and that the paper which he had signed before leaving India cancelled the deed formerly drawn. The latter part of the narrative is very obscure; the writer makes heavy drafts on the credulity of his readers regarding his own guileless and simple nature. The inference is perhaps legitimate that Barwell came to learn what the conspiring couple had concealed, and had availed himself of some proviso made in case of Thompson's failing to keep his side of the compact. In revenge Thompson told the story of his multitudinous sorrows for the edification of the British public. His book came out in 1780, the year in which his wronger left India. He gave it the alternative title of "Or Bengal, the Fittest Soil for Lust," and stuffed it full of letters said to have been written by Barwell during his brief madness to the charmer, who seems to have employed her "soporiferous poison" to some purpose, as the victim's letters and poetry testify to the truth of the observation, "amare et sapere vix deo conceditur."

There is a coincidence or two suggested in these letters, and by some dates which come out in the narrative, that are worth recalling. In one Barwell says, "I will write to Mr. Imhoff about the picture, an allusion which goes to show that Imhoff was at this time in the *bonâ fide* practice of his profession. The Imhoffs and Mrs. Thompson were old acquaintances, as they had been fellow-voyagers to India in the *Duke of Grafton* in 1769, which ship, it may be remembered, also carried, on the same voyage, Warren Hastings and his fortunes. It was possibly, in consequence of this acquaintanceship, that Hastings became one of the executors of the deed of trust aforesaid, in a week or two after his taking over the Governorship of Bengal. He must have had misgivings as to complications of a delicate nature, arising out of the presence of Mrs. Thompson in a community to which her fellow-passenger, Marian Imhoff, had been already translated from Madras. Mr. Barwell's relations with Hastings' fellow-signatory Sanderson, were of a curiously complicated nature. He began by being jealous of this gentleman, then made him trustee in his mistress's behalf, and concluded by marrying his daughter.

# VII

## PRINCESSE TALLEYRAND

WHILE preparing the second edition of this book, I had the gratification of making the personal acquaintance of the widow of the Monsieur Colmache, the Secretary of Talleyrand, whose souvenirs I have expressed myself in the text as so much indebted to.

Madame Colmache is an English lady resident in London. She lived for many years in Paris, during five of which she was domiciled in the household of Prince Talleyrand. If this lady should ever see fit to bring together and publish her reminiscences of remarkable people and times, for the observation of which she had most favourable opportunities, her work ought to be not only historically interesting, but very agreeable reading, judging, if I may take the liberty of saying so, from the pleasant freshness with which in conversation she goes back to old times.

The personal recollection in which she was kind enough to especially interest me, related of course to Princesse Talleyrand. Madame Colmache, however, knew nothing trustworthy of her pre-Talleyrand days, and could only speak of what she was in advanced life, as she had never seen her until the Princesse had been long separated from Talleyrand. It was to the latter's credit that he always wished that the members of his household should pay the respect and courtesy of a duty call on his wife, on certain annual *fête* days, even after they came to live apart. Madame Colmache has a vivid recollection of paying such a call at the house in the Rue de Lille on a new year's day. She recalls the hauteur which the old lady affected, as she received her visitors seated on a high-backed chair on which the Talleyrand arms and motto appeared; these were displayed on several articles of furniture about the room, such as the stool on which her feet rested, the parrot's cage close by, etc. On another chair next her was her snuff-box, as she freely indulged in the fashion of snuff-taking.

Her once luxuriant hair, which now bore evidence of the heavy hand of winter, was dressed with a sort of muslin coiffure, from which descended bands or white ribbons (which might be described as chin stays) which partly covered the cheek and neck, and caused the face to look dwindled, but which were not otherwise unbecoming, as they served to conceal some of the unwelcome encroachments of Time, who had so long proved debonair and gentle to the fair old dame. On the particular occasion referred to, the visitors were received in a room where the light was carefully subdued—almost excluded; and my informant remembers being struck by the fact that the Princesse was so sitting, that through a slit in the partially closed shutters, a ray of bright sunlight played on the top of her head, and lit up a solitary straying tress which still retained a tinge of its golden beauty—a veritable "rose in the wilderness left on its stem to show where the garden had been." It was, therefore, but the near tradition of Princesse Talleyrand's beauty that Madame Colmache could personally testify to, and that this especially lay in her wonderful complexion and hair. So proud was the owner of these that she was acustomed to appear abroad attended by a negress, with the object, it was said, of giving effect by contrast to her most dazzling attractions.

On Madame Colmache being shown a photograph of the painting of Madame Grand, supposed to be in India, she said that the pose of the head and neck, and the large eyes, were very characteristic of the Princesse. But, more strange to say, she was much struck with an indefinable likeness in the photograph to something in Talleyrand's face, thus independently confirming in a great degree the remark made by Madame de Rémusat about the facial similarity between Talleyrand and his wife. Madame Colmache is inclined to give credence to the few anecdotes given in the text regarding Princesse Talleyrand, and to others which testify to her often behaving after the manner of a bad type of parvenu. One of these is given in M. Colmache's recollections as follows:—

"I myself once witnessed a curious instance of that total forgetfulness of the '*jadis*,' which seems to be the peculiar failing of persons who have risen from obscurity to rank and fortune. I was one day descending from the *perron* of the hotel in the Rue St. Florentine, when a hackney coach entered the courtyard and drove up to the vestibule. I was greatly surprised to behold alighting from it, fine as Court-robes and towering plumes could make her, the Princesse de Benevento herself. I of course hastened down the steps to offer her my arm on alighting. 'My carriage struck against the lamp post at the entrance of the Tuileries,' said she, in answer to my inquiring look, 'and the wheel came off. I was forced to return home in this absurd-looking vehicle.' Then, turning to the wondering lacqueys, she added, in a tone of disgust and scorn which no language can describe, as she pointed to the coachman, 'Qu'on paie ce malheureux!'" Madame Colmache also believes in the answer attributed to Talleyrand when he said, either in seriousness or in fun, to one (Madame C. thinks to M. d'Aligre) who ventured to express astonishment that the Prince should have entrusted his happiness to such a *bête* as Madame Grand, "Voyez-vous une femme d'esprit compromet toujours son mari—une femme bête ne peut compromettre qu'elle meme."

It appears that at the time of the Princesse's last illness there was great excitement in the household of Talleyrand, who was also very ill himself at the time, as it was known that some inconvenient pecuniary complications might arise if Talleyrand were to die first. Messages therefore were incessant, Madame Colmache says, to the Rue de Lille, and when the Princesse's death was announced, it was felt to be a relief and a solution of a difficulty.

Madame Colmache remembers seeing a portrait of the Princesse in the possession of Talleyrand; it was in pastel, and the subject was represented in youthful loveliness. The portrait of her by Gérard to which I have referred in the text is a very small full-length, taken probably about the time of her marriage with Talleyrand, or a little later, though in it she looks much younger than her years were then. The little portrait well brings out the rich beauty of her hair and complexion, to which no photograph could do justice. It was described for me as follows by the correspondent who wrote to me about her grave. A more recent visit of my own to the Musée at Versailles enables me to endorse the faithfulness of the description.

"I had an opportunity of visiting Versailles and inspecting the picture of Madame de Talleyrand, and with some difficulty succeeded in finding the poor forgotten Beauty, for, whatever her mental and moral endowments may have been, that she was a woman singularly attractive in outward form, Gérard's 'counterfeit presentment,' of her leaves no room to doubt. The portrait is that of a lovely highbred-looking young woman; tall and graceful, with exquisitely fair complexion, delicate colouring, wavy hair of the rare shade called *blonde cendrée*, dressed rather high on the head and curling over the temples; large blue eyes, small Greek nose, and little mouth with full red lips. She is attired in a low-necked and short-waisted dress, which appears to be of some soft filmy white material, probably Indian muslin, displaying a finely-moulded bust and arms, and tiny feet in white satin slippers.

"On neck, arms, and in her ears are pearl ornaments, and one hand, the right, holds an open letter, while the other hangs by her side. She is leaning against an open projecting French stove, on which are two brown Etruscan vases. Behind her are a drapery of green silk and a large cushioned sofa covered with the same material. . . .

"The picture hangs in the small ante-room of the second etage, attique du midi; it is between the portraits of Madame Récamier and Prince Talleyrand, and is numbered 4867."

## POSTSCRIPT.

This obituary notice appeared in the *Times*, January 26, 1904.

The death was announced last week of Madame Georgina Alicia Colmache, in her 93rd year, at the house of her daughter, Earl's Cour Road, London. Born of English parents in 1811, the year in which her personal friend Wm. M. Thackeray was born, she was educated at Chantilly at the once famous school of Madame Vertfeuille, and married in 1834 M. Edouard Maurice Colmache, of the French Embassy, Private Secretary to Prince Talleyrand. Left a widow at the age of 34, she brought up and educated her four children by the aid of her journalistic pen, contributing to many well-known papers and journals, including the Paris *Figaro*, Milan *Perseveranza*, *Morning Star* (and others) for over 40 years. Her ready wit and singularly happy manner made her society much esteemed, and she numbered among her personal friends Georges Sand, Rossini, Chopin, Rosina, Lady Lytton, Thackeray, Dickens, Cobden, Helen Faucit, and many others.

## VIII

## THE MOVE TO CHUNAR

THE impression seems to be very general that the night escape to Chunar by which Hastings and his party gave the slip to those who were preparing to attack his position at Benares, gave rise to the Hindostanee couplet so familiar to subalterns and others in India, viz.—

> "Ghore păr howdah, hathi păr zeen,
> Jeldi bhag gya, Warren Hasteen." *

The circumstances of the move to Chunar leave no ground for the applicability of those lines to it. Hastings occupied some detached buildings known as Mahadur Dass Garden House in the suburbs of Benares; his wounded were a mile from there, and could not be protected—his whole position was untenable. He suddenly resolved to leave it, and to gain the open country before the enemy at Ramnugger, having any notice of his design, could cross and attack him in narrow streets and broken ground. Orders were issued only between seven and eight p.m., and by eight the line was in motion. "Having been retarded," Hastings writes in his official report of this matter, "and impeded by an incredible tumult of servants, palkis, and baggage of all kinds which for a time threatened total destruction to our march. Fortunately this enormous mass took the wrong road, which left the right one with a free and undisturbed passage for the Sepoys. On the way we past Captain MacDougal's battalion about nine o'clock; we sent him timely notice of our movement; he turned and joined us. Early next morning we arrived at Chunar." Hastings' party, besides his suite, consisted of four hundred Sepoys. He committed the wounded to the charge of Nawab Saadut Ally Khan, "who faithfully and liberally" took care of them till Hastings returned to Benares. The move was no doubt a hasty one, and entailed the temporary loss of or separation from the baggage. No account of it alludes to the presence of elephants amongst the party. There were two 6-pounder guns, dragged presumably by bullocks. One of his suite (G. F. Grand), who refers in a narrative to this night march, speaks of the Governor-General "trudging on foot through the narrow streets of Benares on one of the closest nights in that climate." Hodges,

* "Saddle on elephant, howdah on steed,
Quickly he ran away, Warren Hasteen."

the artist, who was also of the party, alludes only to palanqueens as a means of conveyance. Young Colebrooke, who was Persian interpreter, says *some* of the gentlemen (himself included) were on horseback.*

No contemporary account makes any reference to the presence of a hostile rabble, who, as the story goes, jubilantly improved the occasion by shouting the above distich or some similar words. Those who refer the rhyme to a later occurrence and a much less important person are far more supported by probabilities, viz. In the Maharatta campaign of 1804, Holkar with a large force compelled to a precipitate retreat a very much smaller one sent to watch him by Lord Lake. The latter force was commanded by Colonel Monson, and had enough to do in making its way to the shelter of Agra, hotly pursued by the Maharatta cavalry. Then the distich is said to have come into existence, the urgency and hurry of the retreat being signified by the saddles being thrown on the elephants and the howdahs on the horses. Some accounts that I have met with, while acknowledging that the lines were applied to Monson's force (Kulnel Munseen being substituted as the final words), insist that they were only a travesty on those first applied to Warren Hastings. As I have said, I am unable to trace any reasonable ground for the latter tradition, which certainly exists. The suspicion may without much violence to probability be hazarded, that the oft-quoted couplet, in its present garb, owes its origin to no more classical parentage than might have been forthcoming at some mess-table in a British camp. As a matter of fact, the couplet owes any interest attaching to it, to its having been quoted, and its application misunderstood, by Bishop Heber in his Journal (1824). "Of the sultan-like and splendid character of Warren Hastings, many traits are preserved, and a nursery rhyme which is often sung by children, seems to show how much they were pleased with the Oriental (not European) pomp, which he knew how to employ on occasion, etc., etc." Readers need not be reminded that Macaulay fell into the same mistake, and adopted Heber's misapplication of the "jingling ballad" when painting Hastings as being "fond of state," and sometimes dazzling the natives with "more than regal splendour." The very reverse of all this would be nearer the truth. "I am averse to parade myself and have never used it"—is the expression of Hastings' own sentiments on the point. His customary disregard of state is strangely testified to by one who accompanied him on the very expedition to Benares of which the sojourn in Chunar was an incident. Mr. Hodges, R.A., in his "Travels in India," writes: "When the Governor-General went on shore" (*i.e.* at Patna, on his way up) "it was scarcely possible to proceed from the multitude which pressed on every side to salute him. When he had passed them, all appeared struck with the simplicity of his appearance and his ready and constant attention to prevent any injury to the meanest individual from the irascibility of his chubdars or other servants who endeavoured to keep them from pressing in. They could not but contrast this appearance and conduct with that of their Nabobs, whom they had never seen

* See *Asiatic Quarterly Journal*, October, 1887.

except mounted on lofty elephants and glittering in splendour with their train, followed by the soldiery to keep off the multitude from offending their arrogance and pride."

A note also in Elphinstone's "British Power in India," gives the quaint translation of a passage in the Native Historian, contrasting the dignified simplicity of Hastings' usual appearance in public, with the impressive and dazzling State maintained by M. de Bussy (1750–5), who to his French magnificence added all the parade and pageant of native manners and customs. "Governor Hastings always wore a plain coat, and never anything like lace or embroidery. His whole retinue a dozen of horse-guards; his throne a plain chair of mahogany."

# INDEX

THE END

PRINTED BY WILLIAM CLOWES AND SONS, LIMITED, LONDON AND BECCLES.

# SELECTIONS FROM REVIEWS

## OF PREVIOUS EDITIONS

"When I came out to India in this very month four years ago, one of the companions of my voyage was that delightful book 'Echoes from Old Calcutta,' by Mr. Busteed, formerly well known as an officer in the Calcutta Mint and now living in retirement at home. There I read the full account of the tragic circumstances under which old Fort William, which stood between the site where I am now speaking and the river, was besieged and taken by Siraj-ud-Dowlah, in 1756. . . . It was Mr. Busteed's writings accordingly that first called my attention to this spot and induced me to make a careful study of the site and surroundings of old Fort William . . ."—Extract from Speech by H.E. Lord Curzon of Kedleston, Viceroy and Governor-General of India.

"As we turn over the delightful pages of 'Echoes from Old Calcutta,' responsive to Mr. Busteed's gentle summons, the dead rise for an hour from their slumber."—SIR AUCKLAND COLVIN in "Memoirs of his Father."

"Mr. Busteed's very interesting and amusing book."—SIR JOHN STRACHEY in "Hastings' and the Rohilla War."

"See a most amusing and careful book 'Echoes from Old Calcutta,' by H. E. Busteed."—SIR FITZ JAMES STEPHEN in "The Story of Nuncomar."

"Mr. Busteed's valuable and entertaining 'Echoes from Old Calcutta,' revised, enlarged, and illustrated with portraits and other plates rare or quaint. It is a pleasure to reiterate the warm commendation of this instructive and lively volume which its appearance called forth some years since."—*Saturday Review.*

"There is always a pleasant attraction about old colonial history, especially when the social habits of the founders of Greater Britain are treated with spirit and accuracy. Accordingly, when the first edition of Dr. Busteed's work on Old Calcutta appeared, it was welcomed by the *Academy;* and for the like reason we take advantage of the appearance of a second edition to renew to our readers the recommendation which we then offered. There is also an appendix of important documents. In spite of Dr. Busteed's modest disclaimers, the book has more than an antiquarian value, being written in a very attractive though unambitious style."—*Academy.*

"Dr. Busteed has done very well to prepare a second edition of his highly interesting papers on Old Calcutta. He has thoroughly revised the chapters, some of which are practically rewritten, and has been enabled to give an ampler selection of the letters of Warren Hastings to his wife."—*Army and Navy Gazette.*

"It is not surprising to find that a new edition of Dr. Busteed's 'Echoes of Old Calcutta' has been called for. Although written especially for Calcutta readers, the book deals in an entertaining way with some of the most important episodes in the history of our Indian Empire. The chapters on the Black Hole and Madam Grand, and the letters of Warren Hastings, are especially interesting, but the whole book is readable. The new edition is enlarged and illustrated."—*Sunday Times.*

"We are glad to see a new edition, 'considerably enlarged,' of this interesting book. Dr. Busteed takes us back to a period, not very distant in point of time, but yet very curiously unlike our own. His first chapter is on the 'Black Hole.' What a world of difference there is between the Calcutta of 1756 and the Calcutta of to-day? And yet we sometimes doubt whether we are much more at home now in India than the Company was in the days of Siraj-ud-Dowlah. Anyhow, it is as profitable as it is interesting to be taken back and given a glimpse of the day of small things, when, as was the case in 1756, the garrison of the Fort 'consisted of about one hundred and eighty men, only a third of whom were Europeans.' After 'The Black Hole' comes a chapter on 'Philip Francis,' and, of course, a discussion on 'Francis' as 'Junius.' Dr. Busteed is a determined Franciscan. 'Nuncomar' is the next subject treated of. The 'Duel between Hastings and Francis' follows. 'Home and Social Life' is full of curious details, among them being the fact that Francis won so much money at whist that he was enabled to leave India long before he had expected. It was a wild life indeed that Anglo-Indians used to live in those days. We have an account of the life and death of the first Indian newspaper; and a history, which is at least as long as the subject deserves, of Madam Grand, the lady who plays so prominent a part in the life of Philip Francis. Finally, we have letters of Hastings to his wife."—*Spectator*.

"Being chiefly Reminiscences of the Days of Warren Hastings, Francis, and Impey. By H. E. Busteed, M.D., C.I.E. The additions made to Mr. Busteed's most interesting volume make it of considerably increased value. Unpublished letters of Warren Hastings and of his wife, an extra chapter and an appendix are among the new features of the present issue. Besides these, we have the curious and historically important illustrations of the notorious 'Black Hole' (as it appeared in the memorable June of 1756) from clever conjectural 'restorations' by the author, with the assistance of Mr. De Wilde as draughtsman. There is also a portrait of Mr. Holwell, the most eminent of the survivors of the tragedy, supplied by one of his existing descendants. The book centres mainly round three principal figures, Hastings, Impey, and Sir Philip Francis. The duel of the latter with Hastings, his liaison with Madam Grand, and the trial which it entailed are, of course, among the "Echoes" which Mr. Busteed has preserved for us. The Nuncomar incident brings Sir E. Impey once more into publicity, and the correspondence between Hastings and his wife shows us the former in his domestic and more pleasing character. Added to this, are reminiscences of Calcutta society a hundred years or more ago, when the voyage from England was an affair of six months or more, and when there was no Simla or no sea-going steamers to break the monotony or avert the fatal influences of the Indian climate. The book is altogether a very entertaining one, and likely to meet with as cordial a reception in England as it has experienced on the banks of the Hooghly."—*Bookseller*.

"The second edition of Dr. Busteed's 'Echoes from Old Calcutta' has been enlarged and in great part rewritten. Though 'Old Calcutta' is not much more than a century old, its history has required a great deal of research, and its deep interest deserves it. For full and detailed information about the 'Black Hole,' about the times and doings of Hastings and Francis, and other celebrities and incidents of Calcutta in the eighteenth century, this book is one of the most convenient and trustworthy sources of information. The edition is enriched by a number of useful illustrations."—*Scotsman*.

"'Echoes from Old Calcutta'—being chiefly reminiscences of the days of Warren Hastings, Francis, and Impey, by H. E. Busteed, C.I.E., is now in its third edition, and the get-up and printing, together with the many illustrations, reflect credit on the publishers, Messrs. Thacker, Spink & Co. of Calcutta. The book itself is an extremely interesting one. Mr. Busteed has a great many details to fill in, and not a few corrections to offer, on the well-known essays of Macaulay; and indeed to some extent he enters on new ground altogether, giving a vivid picture of Calcutta Life one hundred to one hundred and fifty years ago, such as can be found nowhere else in a readily available form. There are in all some three hundred and forty pages, and there is not one of them which can be called dry or uninteresting."—*Ceylon Observer.*

"Dr. Busteed's 'Echoes from Old Calcutta' is a work so widely known that we confess to a feeling of surprise on learning that it has only now reached its third edition. The author has recast a large part of the work, and has introduced much fresh material. 'It has been well said,' he remarks, 'that the merit of a book rests fully as much on what is left out as on what is put in; with this truth in view, a good deal of matter which might be deemed lacking in interest for the general reader has been withdrawn. Under this head falls the well-worn controversy connected with the trial of Nuncomar, which may now be permitted to rest where the late Sir James Stephen left it.' But while the controversy is withdrawn, the account of the trial, which remains one of the most interesting chapters in the book, is preserved intact. The special feature of the present edition is a remarkable series of illustrations, which give vitality and a sense of personal touch to the narrative. They include two sketches of the Black Hole, a view of Fort William in 1736, from a print in the India Office, a street scene in Calcutta, 1786, showing Writers' Buildings and the old Mayor's Court, another of the same year showing the ramparts of the old Fort and Holwell's Monument. Among the portraits we find Mrs. Mills, of Black Hole fame, J. Z. Holwell, Sir Philip Francis, Sir Elijah Impey, Mr. Justice Hyde, Mr. Justice Chambers, Mr. Richard Barwell, Miss Benedetta Ramus, Madam Grand, Mr. and Mrs. Hastings, and Madam de Talleyrand." —*The Englishman.*

PRINTED BY WILLIAM CLOWES AND SONS, LIMITED, LONDON AND BECCLES

## ERRATA

Page 58, line 33. For "Junius identified, etc.," read "Discovery of the Author of Junius." The allusion to "the book" in Lord Erskine's letter as quoted suggests a possible misprint in the date originally, *i.e.* if he was referring to either of Taylor's books.

Page 142, footnote. A coincidence of historical interest referring to the first celebrated ball in Government House described by Lord Valentia should not have been omitted, viz. that one of the successors of the Governor-General of 1803 also gave a great commemorative ball in the same building on the exact centenary (January 6, 1903), where the guests appeared in the costumes of a hundred years before, the Viceroy (Lord Curzon) wearing the uniform of Lord Wellesley.

Page 208. The words following (identifying) "Thane" should have been in a footnote.

Pages 305, 306. The extract from an old *Temple Bar* article quoted in the previous edition should have been corrected or omitted. The anecdotes there retailed, though "on the faith of a most trustworthy eye-witness," were probably instances of the many curious ones in circulation about Madame de Talleyrand. Whether true or not, the scene of the eccentricities could not have been at Vienna. The facts would seem to be that Talleyrand was not only *not* "accompanied to Vienna by Madame de Talleyrand," but that her discovering that this distinction was reserved for another lady was the proximate cause of bringing about the separation which her husband had probably for some time decided on. It was his intellectual and fascinating niece, wife of his nephew, Count Edmond de Périgord, and daughter of his intimate friend the Duchesse de Courlande, who did the social honours in Talleyrand's salon during the famous Vienna Congress. This lady afterwards became the Duchesse de Dino. It is said that in the circumstances ushering in the breach or estrangement between Talleyrand and his wife, there was not overmuch consideration shown to the latter. It was on Napoleon's reappearance from Elba that she went to England, and there Talleyrand evidently wished her to stay; her early return to Paris would, perhaps, have been embarrassing to him—for various reasons. However, negotiations must have led to terms and compromise and her amicable acceptance of the situation, as she returned to the Continent and (eventually) settled in Paris.

Page 320*a*, line 9, for "Vienna?" read "Paris." Line 26, for "fame" read "idea."

Page 367, line 27. The old graves "which now receive no due conserving care." Happily these words do not apply any longer. The cemetery of St. John's Church came in for the marked attention of the late Viceroy, who had the churchyard cleared and renovated, the graves restored, the turf relaid, etc. Further, it was satisfactorily arranged through Lord Curzon, with a view to its future care, that this graveyard, so closely and pathetically associated with our earliest Calcutta history, should be taken over as a public trust by the Bengal Government.